FAMOUS BOMBERS
of the Second World War

FAMOUS BOMBERS
of the Second World War

William Green

SECOND EDITION REVISED

Illustrated by G. W. Heumann and
Peter Endsleigh Castle, A.R.Ae.S.

MACDONALD AND JANE'S · LONDON

First published in 1975 by
Macdonald and Jane's Publishers Limited
Paulton House, 8 Shepherdess Walk
London N1 7LW

Reprinted 1976

ISBN 0 356 08333 0

Printed in Great Britain by
Redwood Burn Limited, Trowbridge & Esher
and bound by Dorstel Press, Harlow

CONTENTS

INTRODUCTION

What *was* the most famous bomber of the Second World War? Was it the superlative Superfortress which literally delivered the *coup de grace* to Japan, the Liberator or the aesthetically more appealing Fortress? Many British readers will insist that the honour should go to the Lancaster, which spearheaded RAF Bomber Command's night offensive against Germany from mid 'forty-two, or to the ballerina-like little Mosquito, the wartime exploits of which were to become legendary, while German readers will almost certainly select the supremely versatile and ubiquitous Junkers Ju 88.

It is, of course, all very much a matter of opinion. Fame—the condition of being much talked about—was not entirely conditional upon success. Indeed, many an aircraft was to owe its claim to fame, at least in part, to propaganda rather than exploit, its intrinsic qualities and attainments being grossly exaggerated in the interests of public morale, but the twenty-five aircraft whose development and careers are described on the following pages were all to some degree *famous*. All suffered their vicissitudes and all were subjected to adverse criticism at some time during their careers; they endeared themselves to some crews and were abused and vilified by others, but they all achieved a measure of fame and several of them were truly great.

The Wellington, the mainstay of RAF Bomber Command during the most desperate period of the war in so far as the Allies were concerned, repeatedly proving its ability to absorb a fantastic amount of battle damage as it built up a brilliant record, achieved the dubious distinction early in its operational career of disproving the belief that large bombers could individually and in small formations attack heavily defended targets in daylight without fighter escort. The Marauder, during the early stages of its service life, was labelled the "Widow Maker" along with less printable epithets, yet by 1944 it was suffering a lower rate of loss in the European theatre of operations than any USAAF aircraft. In Northern Europe, the Liberator was found to be alarmingly prone to catching fire as a result of superficial combat damage yet in the Pacific it reigned supreme; the Fortress certainly failed to live up to its popular name during the early phases of the war, yet it finally emerged as perhaps the outstanding heavy day bomber.

Successful or otherwise, however, the bombers whose stories are told in this book all made an important contribution to aerial warfare and all wrote their names indelibly on the pages of military aviation history. They reveal clearly the amazing metamorphosis in bomber design that took place during the dramatic years of World War II, as they range from warplanes that were mature when war began, through those that achieved maturity during the conflict, to those which, evolved during the war itself, saw action during its closing stages. The radical nature of the transformation in design that they portray can be perceived by comparing the maximum speed of 266 mph at 11,800 feet of the Blenheim with the more than 460 mph attainable at two-and-a-half times the altitude by the Arado Blitz; by comparing the RAF's heaviest bomber at the beginning of the conflict, the Whitley with a normal gross weight of 28,200 lb and defensive armament of five rifle-calibre machine guns, with, say, the Superfortress, which, normally weighing in at 120,000 lb and carrying a dozen half-inch guns plus a 20-mm cannon, had a short-range bomb load of no less than two-thirds the earlier 'heavy' bomber's loaded weight!

The score and five bombers of five different nationalities described varied widely in appearance and operational efficiency, but they had one thing in common: they all possessed some claim to fame.

WILLIAM GREEN

(*Above*) *The Heinkel He* 111*P-6, powered by Daimler-Benz DB* 601*N engines, was the last production sub-type of the P-series bomber which equipped the major proportion of the eighteen He* 111 *Kampfgruppen with which the Luftwaffe entered the war. (Right) The progenitor of all He* 111 *bombers, the He* 111*V*1, *which was flown for the first time at Marienehe at the beginning of* 1935 *by Gerhard Nitschke.*

THE HEINKEL HE 111

Few were the inhabitants of England's capital and southern counties to whom, in the dramatic months of 1940, the distinctive and disagreeable note of the Heinkel He 111's engines was unfamiliar, for this machine, the first modern medium bomber to be acquired by the Luftwaffe, bore the major burden of the German bombing offensive against the British Isles during the main phase of the "Battle of Britain". Despite its shortcomings, which became more marked as the war progressed and which were in no small part due to the continual process of modification and extemporisation to which the bomber was subjected, it retained its place as a standard Luftwaffe combat aircraft throughout the war. Produced in infinitely greater quantities than its compatriot and contemporary, the Dornier Do 17 and its derivatives, the He 111 was twice taken out of mass production but returned to the assembly lines when the new types with which it was to be replaced failed to materialize.

During the opening phases of the war the Heinkel He 111 was undoubtedly a formidable offensive weapon. An elegant, well-built, well-planned aircraft with good flying characteristics, the He 111 was certainly a thoroughbred, inheriting its shapely contours from its single-engined predecessor, the He 70 Blitz, which, at the time of its appearance, had been

justifiably acclaimed as the most aerodynamically efficient aeroplane to have flown. Like so many other German warplanes of its era, the He 111 was first revealed to the world in civil guise. The machine publicly displayed for the first time on January 10, 1936 at Tempelhof Airport, Berlin, was ostensibly a ten-passenger commercial transport, but its sleek, beautifully streamlined fuselage and low-drag elliptical wing were obviously designed for maximum performance at the expense of passenger comfort. Indeed, passenger accommodation was extremely cramped, a forward compartment between the wing spars providing seating for four passengers, a further compartment aft of the rear spar accommodating six passengers. The aircraft's more lethal intent was patently obvious, and what was *not* publicly revealed on that January morning in 1936, when the headlines of German newspapers were proclaiming the existence of "The Fastest Machine in Civil Aviation", were the facts that the first prototype, which had flown nearly a year earlier, had been built as a bomber, and that the first pre-production models of the bomber variant had already left the assembly lines at the Rostock factory of the Ernst Heinkel Flugzeugwerke!

It was to be claimed that the conception of the Heinkel He 111 had been inspired by a specification

7

issued by the German airline, Deutsche Lufthansa, for an airliner suitable for high-speed passenger and mail services, but the Günther brothers, Walter and Siegfried, who were responsible for the design of the new aircraft, were well aware that any order for such a machine placed by D.L.H. would be extremely limited, and that the development of a machine suited only for the commercial role would not be an attractive commercial proposition. Accordingly, they designed a dual-purpose aircraft; one that would also be suitable for use in the bomber role by the Luftwaffe, the existence of which was shortly to be revealed to the world. In fact, so much more suitable for a militant role than for civil purposes was the design that they evolved that it is surprising that Germany made any attempt to disguise its true function beneath civil markings.

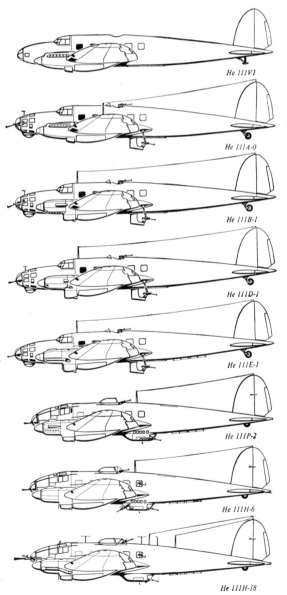

He 111V1

He 111A-0

He 111B-1

He 111D-1

He 111E-1

He 111P-2

He 111H-6

He 111H-18

Development of the He 111 design was commenced early in 1934, only one year after the appearance of the internationally successful He 70, and the first prototype, designated He 111a, was completed during the following winter. Powered by two BMW VI twelve-cylinder Vee liquid-cooled engines of 660 h.p., the He 111a, or He 111V1 as it was subsequently to be known, was flown for the first time early in 1935 from the partially completed runway at Ernst Heinkel's new Marienehe factory by the company's chief test pilot, Gerhard Nitschke. The initial flight test programme revealed that the flying characteristics of the new machine were far superior to those of the He 70, which had left much to be desired, and a speed of 214 m.p.h. —closely comparable with that of any of the world's standard fighters at the time—was attained at an early stage in the testing. Structurally, the He 111V1 was an orthodox cantilever low-wing monoplane of metal stressed-skin construction in which excrescences had been kept to a minimum. The long, slim nose terminated in a transparent cone for the bombardier, and provision was made for the installation of a single 7.9-mm. machine gun in this cone, mounted in a traversing slot. It was proposed to take care of attacks from behind and below by a gun position in a re-tractable "dustbin" ventral turret and a dorsal position protected by a small windscreen, each of these positions housing one 7.9-mm. MG 15 machine gun. Offensive armament was to comprise a 2,200-lb. bomb load, the bombs being housed vertically in what was to be the "smoking" compartment of the civil variant. Empty and loaded weights were 12,764 lb. and 16,755 lb. respectively, range was 930 miles and service ceiling was 17,720 ft.

The second prototype, the He 111V2 (D-ALIX *Rostock*), and the first prototype of the commercial version, followed closely on the heels of the bomber prototype, and differed from its predecessor primarily in providing accommodation for ten passengers with a mail compartment in the nose. Minor changes included the provision of fillets at the wing trailing edge roots and the replacement of the tail skid by a wheel. The third prototype, the He 111V3 (D-ALES), flown in the spring of 1935, was again a bomber and intended to serve as a prototype for the initial production He 111A, while the He 111V4 (D-AHAO *Dresden*) was the second commercial prototype and the aircraft publicly revealed at Tempelhof in January 1936.

By mid-1935 the bomber variant had entered production at Rostock, and by the end of 1936 the first pre-production He 111A-0 bombers were being evaluated at the Luftwaffe's Research Establishment at Rechlin. The service test pilots' reports on the bomber were not entirely favourable as they considered that, with its two BMW VI 6.0Z engines it was seriously underpowered. In fact, the pre-production model could hardly attain 190 m.p.h. with the ventral gun "dustbin" *retracted*! It was decided that the bomber would be re-evaluated when re-engined with either the Daimler-Benz DB 600A or the Junkers Jumo 210Ga. By the time this decision had been reached the Heinkel

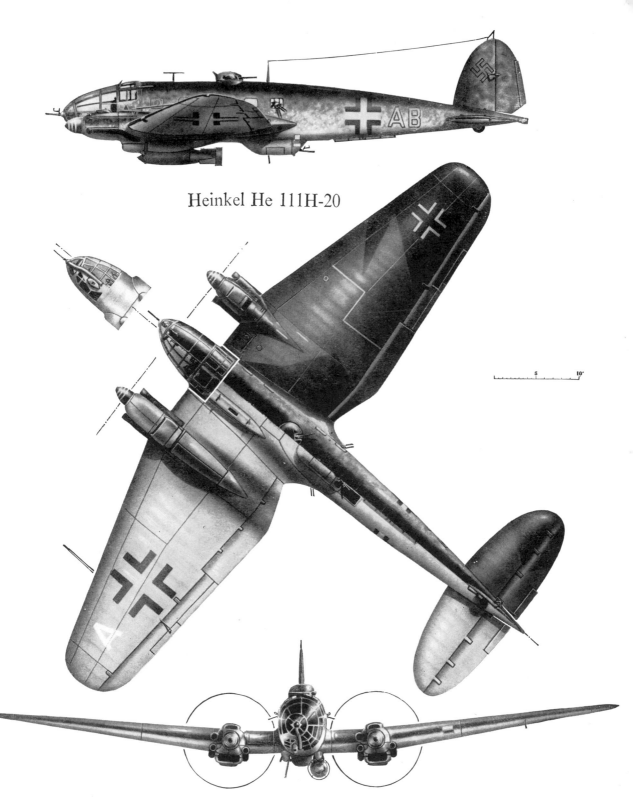

Heinkel He 111H-20

FINISH AND INSIGNIA: *The He 111H-20 illustrated employed pale blue under surfaces, the blue being dappled with sea grey on the fuselage sides and merging with forest green fuselage upper decking. The upper surfaces of the wings and horizontal tail surfaces employed a "splinter" camouflage pattern of dark forest green and olive green. The national insignia appearing on the fuselage sides and wing under surfaces consisted merely of a broad black outline, and that on the wing upper surfaces took the form of a standard black cross with white edging. The letters "AB" aft of the fuselage insignia were stencilled on in black outline (as was also the swastika on the vertical fin), and the letter "A" appeared in white outboard of the national insignia under the port wing, and the "B" appeared under the starboard wing.*

One of the ten He 111A-1 bombers purchased by the Chinese government with members of the Chinese purchasing mission.

concern was well advanced with the completion of a batch of He 111A-1 bombers, and as a result of the Luftwaffe's refusal to accept them Ernst Heinkel sought permission to export these aircraft. As Germany was short of foreign currency, permission was granted and, stripped of the standard Luftwaffe bomb sight, radio equipment and self-destroying charge, ten of the He 111A-1s were sold to the Chinese government. Simultaneously, one of the pre-production He 111A-0 bombers was re-engined with two of the then new Daimler-Benz DB 600A twelve-cylinder inverted-Vee water-cooled engines rated at 1,000 h.p. for take-off, and re-designated He 111V5 (D-APYS); this aircraft attained a maximum speed of 255 m.p.h.

In the meantime the He 111V1 had been converted as a transport, and two further civil transport machines had been built (D-AQYF *Leipzig* and D-AXAV *Köln*) under the designation He 111C, but D.L.H. displayed little interest in the potentialities of these aircraft, claiming that they were underpowered and too expensive to be commercially practicable. In fact, despite the general belief that D.L.H. did employ these machines—a belief fostered by the appearance of numerous photographs of the type bearing D.L.H. insignia and the numerous "route-proving" flights purported to have been carried out by this airline with the He 111C—no machine of this type was accepted for commercial operations, both airliner prototypes and the two He 111Cs having been transferred to a special and highly secret Luftwaffe unit which, led by Oberst Rowehl and based at Staaken, undertook long-distance reconnaissance flights over Britain, France and the Soviet Union under the guise of commercial route-proving flights. One of Rowehl's "civil" He 111s actually crashed during one of its photo-reconnaissance flights over foreign territory, but its secret was never revealed.

The remarkable success of the He 111V5 with DB 600A engines was immediately rewarded by substantial quantity production orders for the fledgeling Luftwaffe, and in the years that followed this one aircraft type was to do much to place Germany in the vanguard of international bomber design. It may even be said that until the commencement of the Second World War the He 111 was probably supreme among medium bombers. The first pre-production He 111B-0 and production B-1 bombers were delivered to the Luftwaffe during the closing months of 1936, and after extensive testing the pre-production aircraft were returned to Heinkel to serve as test-beds for new equipment and as prototypes for later variants. The

He 111B-1, which offered a notable advance in striking power over the Dornier Do 23G and Junkers Ju 52/3Mg 3e which it supplanted, was generally similar to the He 111A-1, apart from its power plants, but it soon gave place on the production lines to the He 111B-2 which featured improved DB 600C engines and a new hemispherical nose gun mounting. This, in turn, was supplanted in 1937 by the pre-production He 111D-0 and production D-1 with the 1,050 h.p. DB 600Ga engines with enlarged ventral radiators in place of the earlier wing surface radiators. The drag-producing exhaust stubs were carefully faired over, and the maximum speed was increased to 254 m.p.h., representing a 24 m.p.h. increase over the B-2 variant. In battle condition, with the ventral "dustbin" extended, maximum speed was reduced to 230 m.p.h.

Despite the military success of the He 111 and the failure of the He 111C to arouse the interest of D.L.H., Ernst Heinkel still entertained hopes of selling a civil variant and, accordingly, the He 111G was evolved. The elliptical wing which characterised all early variants of the He 111, although attractive from the aesthetic viewpoint and also aerodynamically efficient, left much to be desired from the production viewpoint, and the Günther brothers had designed a new wing of simplified construction and straight taper which was eventually to be adopted for the bomber. In the summer of 1936 this new wing was fitted to the He 111V7 for flight testing, and was also adopted for the He 111G, the first two examples of which (D-AEQU *Halle* and D-AYKI *Magdeburg*) retained the BMW VI engines of the He 111C. The third G-series aircraft (D-ACBS *Augsburg*), which was under test at Rechlin during the summer of 1936, was powered by 800 h.p BMW 132A radials, while the fourth and fifth machines received DB 600Ga engines. D.L.H. still refused to accept the type, despite the very much improved performance of the last two machines, and the aircraft were eventually taken over by the Luftwaffe (the fourth machine, the He 111V16 D-ASAR, was eventually used as a personal transport by Erhard Milch), one being sold to the Turkish government. With the completion of the five He 111Gs, the civil career of the design came to an end; and although the full circle was to turn towards the end of the He 111's production life when it was produced once again as a transport, its subsequent career was to be almost entirely of a more lethal nature.

On May 4, 1936, work had commenced on a new factory at Oranienburg. This plant was intended specifically for the production of the He 111 bomber and was to have a capacity of one hundred machines per month. A year to the day after the first work on the factory had commenced, the first bomber rolled off its assembly line. The year 1937 also saw the abandoning of any further attempt to disguise the true purpose of the He 111, for squadrons equipped with

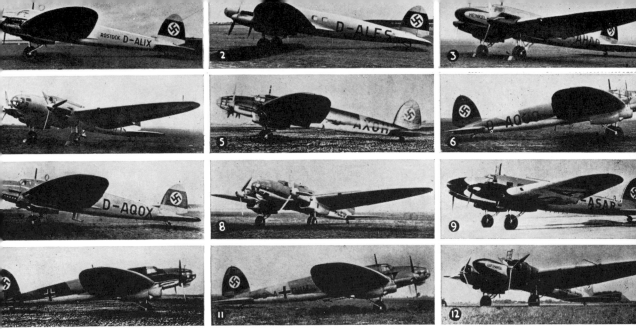

(1) *The He 111V2, first commercial transport prototype.* (2) *The He 111V3, second bomber prototype and prototype for the A-series.* (3) *The He 111V4, second airliner prototype publicly revealed on January 10, 1936.* (4) *The He 111V5, prototype for B-series converted from He 111A-0.* (5) *The He 111V6, first prototype for the E-series.* (6) *The He 111V8, test-bed for the nose section subsequently employed by the P- and H-series.* (7) *The He 111V9, first prototype of the D-series converted from an He 111B-0.* (8) *The He 111V10, second prototype for D-series.* (9) *The He 111V16, the fourth aircraft of the G-series, used as a personal transport by Erhard Milch.* (10) *The He 111V17, a converted He 111D airframe for engine tests.* (11) *The He 111V18, a converted He 111D-0 for testing bombing equipment.* (12) *The third G-series aircraft and the only He 111 to be fitted with radial engines.*

this type were demonstrated in public at Nuremberg on the Reichsparteitag of that year; He 111B-1s were sent to Spain to re-equip the bomber element of the Condor Legion, and on November 22, 1937, an He 111 was reputedly flown by Flugkapitan Gerhard Nitschke and Flugzeugführer Hans Dieterle over 621 miles with a 2,200-lb. load at the remarkable average speed of 313 m.p.h. The aircraft performing this flight was, however, a prototype of the radically different He 119.

The inability of the Daimler-Benz A.G. to produce sufficient DB 600 engines to keep abreast of He 111D airframe production resulted in the adoption of another power plant of generally similar power, the 1,050 h.p. Junkers Jumo 211A, and with these engines the bomber was designated He 111E. A pre-production He 111B-0 had been converted to take two Junkers Jumo 210Ga engines under the designation He 111V6 (D-AXOH) and served as a prototype for the He 111E, later being transferred to Junkers, by which concern it was employed as a test-bed for variable-speed airscrews. It is of interest to note at this juncture that the He 111V9 (D-AQOX) and V10 (D-ALEQ), although bearing later prototype numbers, were actually prototypes for the D-series bombers. The He 111E-0 was powered by the Jumo 211A-1 and the production E-1 was similarly powered. In order to reduce drag, semi-retractable radiators were adopted, the oil coolant radiator was relocated on the upper part of the engine cowling, and the He 111E-1 had a maximum speed of 267 m.p.h., a cruising speed of 202 m.p.h., a service ceiling of 22,950 ft., and a loaded weight of 23,370 lb. The He 111F differed from the E-series in having the straight tapered wing of the He 111V7 and He 111G,

first leaving the assembly lines in the autumn of 1937. The He 111F-0 retained the Jumo 211A-1 engines, but the F-1 had the improved Jumo 211A-3.

The use of the He 111 in Spain was to have a marked and, for Germany, unfortunate effect on the shaping of future German air strategy. The bomber element of the Condor Legion, K/88, which had been sent to the aid of General Francisco Franco Bahamonde, the principal leader of the insurgents, initially operated with Junkers Ju 52/3Mg aircraft. These were supplanted by He 111B-2, D-1, E-1 and F-1 bombers which were fast enough to evade most of the fighter aircraft employed by the Republicans, and Kampfgruppe 88 evolved the technique of unescorted daylight attacks. The first operational sortie made by the He 111B bombers of K/88 took place on March 9, 1937, when they bombed the airfields of Alcalá and Barajas. The comparatively light opposition encountered by the bomber squadrons inclined the German High Command to the belief that they could continue to operate fast medium bombers with but light fighter protection. In fact, they even believed that it would be possible for the fast medium bomber to lay waste any country without opposing fighter defences having an opportunity to interfere. It was also believed that the relatively light defensive armament of three 7.9-mm. machine guns carried by the He 111 had proved to be adequate in view of the negligible losses suffered by the bombers over Spain. What serious misconceptions these beliefs in fact were was to be revealed over Britain in 1940. The Turkish Air Force had previously ordered thirty He 111F-1 bombers and, as a tailpiece to this export order, during the war years

Heinkel HE IIIH-3
Cutaway Key

1 Starboard navigation light
2 Starboard aileron
3 Wing ribs
4 Forward spar
5 Rear spar
6 Aileron tab
7 Starboard flap
8 Fuel tank access panel
9 Wing centre section/outer
   panel break line
10 Inboard fuel tank (154 Imp
   gal/700 l capacity)
   position between
   nacelle and fuselage
11 Oil tank cooling louvres
12 Oil cooler air intake
13 Supercharger air intake
14 Three-blade VDM airscrew
15 Airscrew pitch-change
   mechanism
16 Junkers Jumo 211D-1
   12-cylinder inverted-vee
   liquid-cooled engine
17 Exhaust manifold
18 Nose-mounted 7,9-mm
   MG 15 machine gun

19 Ikaria ball-and-socket gun
   mounting (offset to
   starboard)
20 Bomb sight housing
   (offset to starboard)
21 Starboard mainwheel
22 Rudder pedals
23 Bomb aimer's horizontal
   pad
24 Additional 7,9-mm MG 15
   machine gun (fitted by
   forward maintenance
   units)
25 Repeater compass
26 Bomb aimer's folding seat
27 Control column
28 Throttles
29 Pilot's seat
30 Retractable auxiliary
   windscreen (for use
   when pilot's seat in
   elevated position)
31 Sliding entry panel
32 Forward fuselage bulkhead
33 Double-frame station
34 Port ESAC bomb bay
   (vertical stowage)
35 Fuselage windows
   (blanked)

36 Central gangway between
   bomb bays
37 Double-frame station
38 Direction Finder
39 Dorsal gunner's (forward)
   sliding canopy
40 Dorsal 7,9-mm MG 15
   machine gun
41 Dorsal gunner's cradle seat
42 FuG 10 radio equipment
43 Fuselage window
44 Armoured bulkhead
   (8-mm)
45 Aerial mast
46 Bomb flares
47 Unarmoured bulkhead
48 Rear fuselage access cut-
   out
49 Port 7,9-mm beam MG 15
   machine gun
50 Dinghy stowage
51 Fuselage frames
52 Stringers
53 Starboard tailplane
54 Aerial
55 Starboard elevator
56 Tailfin forward spar
57 Tailfin structure
58 Rudder balance

59 Tailfin rear spar/rudder
   post
60 Rudder construction
61 Rudder tab
62 Tab actuator (starboard
   surface)
63 Remotely-controlled 7,9-
   mm MG 17 machine gun
   in tail cone (fitted to
   some aircraft only)
64 Rear navigation light
65 Elevator tab
66 Elevator structure
67 Elevator hinge line
68 Tailplane front spar
69 Semi-retractable tailwheel
70 Tailwheel shock-absorber
71 Tail surface control linkage
72 Fuselage/tailfin frame
73 Control pulley
74 Push-pull control rods
75 Master compass
76 Observation window
   fairing
77 Glazed observation
   window in floor
78 Ventral aft-firing 7,9-mm
   MG 15 machine gun in
   tail of "*Sterbebett*"
   ("Death-bed") bath

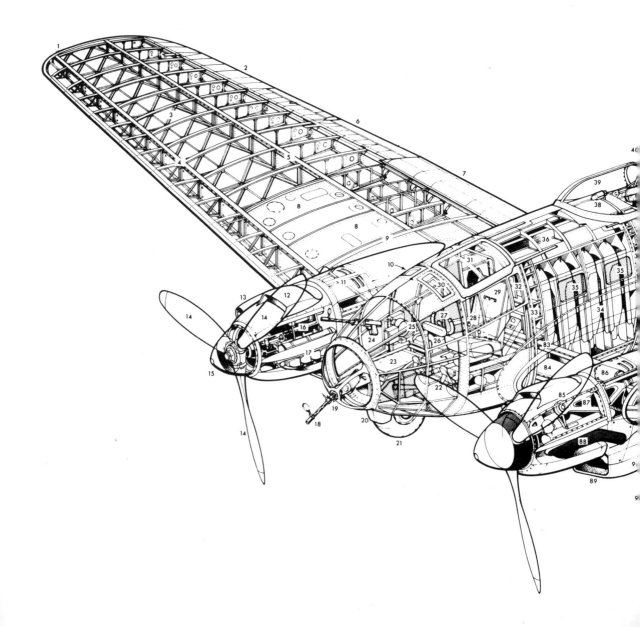

79 Ventral bath entry hatch
80 Ventral gunner's horizontal
   pad
81 Forward-firing 20-mm
   (Oerlikon) MG FF
   cannon (for anti-
   shipping operations)
82 Rear spar carry-through
83 Forward spar carry-
   through
84 Oil cooler
85 Anti-vibration engine
   mount
86 Oil tank
87 Engine bearer
88 Exhaust flame-damper
   shroud
89 Radiator air intake
90 Radiator bath
91 Port mainwheel
92 Mainwheel leg
93 Retraction mechanism
94 Mainwheel door (outer)
95 Multi-screw wing
   attachment
96 Trailing-aerial tube (to
   starboard of ventral
   bath)
97 Rear spar attachment

98 Port outboard fuel tank
   (220 Imp gal/1000 l
   capacity)
99 Flap control rod
100 Landing light
101 Pitot head
102 Pitot head heater/wing
    leading-edge de-icer
103 Flap and aileron coupling
104 Flap structure
105 Aileron tab
106 Tab actuator
107 Rear spar
108 Forward spar
109 Port aileron
110 Port navigation light

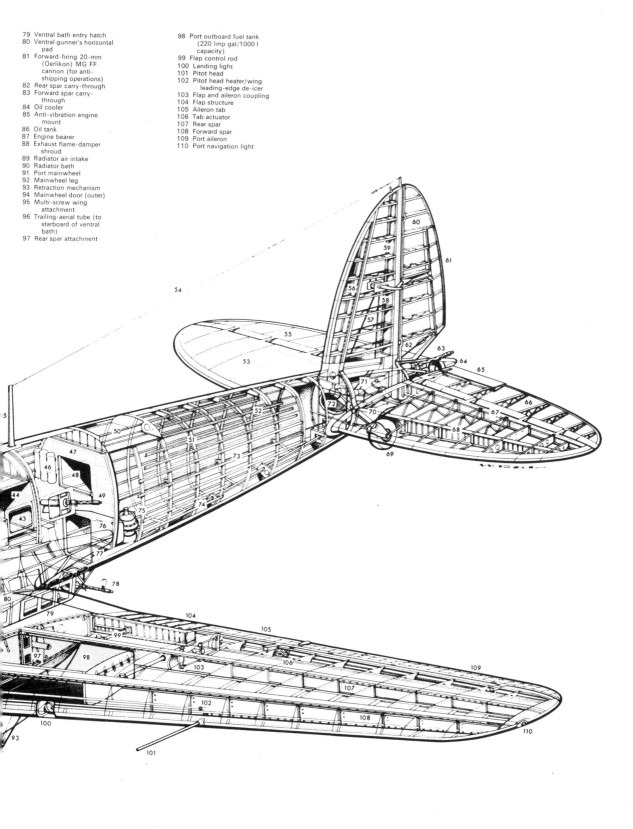

when Turkey could no longer obtain spares for her bombers from Germany, Britain was able to meet most of the Turkish government's requirements with spares and components salvaged from the substantial number of He 111 bombers brought down over the British Isles at a time when the Luftwaffe still laid store by its experiences over Spain.

At one time it was proposed to place in production the He 111J which employed the airframe of the He 111F married to a pair of Daimler-Benz DB 601As engines, but these proposals were abandoned in favour of the more radically modified He 111P. The fore-runners of the P-series were the He 111V7 and V8, respectively conversions of an E-0 and a B-0. The He 111V8 (D-AQUO), which flew some time before the V7, was powered by two DB 600A engines and retained the elliptical wing. The most noteworthy departure from previous models was the new shortened and broadened oval nose section. Whereas the pilot's windscreen had previously broken the upper fuselage contour in the conventional manner, this was now contained entirely within the contour of the fuselage, resulting in lines unbroken by any projection. The

pilot was seated in the port side of the nose which was fully glazed, and this, the glazed roof and side windows provided the necessary vision. The instrument panel was attached to the roof, and in order to provide the pilot with the maximum possible forward view the universal mounting for the nose gun was offset to starboard, thereby giving the peculiar unsymmetrical effect which was to characterise all wartime He 111s. For landing in poor visibility the pilot could elevate his seat so that his head projected through a sliding panel, in which position it was protected by a small retractable windscreen. The new nose section offered the crew magnificent visibility, although when the sun was behind the aircraft the curved transparent panels tended to emulate mirrors, seriously inconveniencing the pilot. The He 111V7, which followed the V8, employed a somewhat modified nose, was fitted with the straight-tapered wing, and featured a permanent, well-faired ventral gun position in which the gunner lay prone. This cupola, which replaced the earlier "dustbin", offered a 90° cone of fire for the protection of the tail.

Embodying these modifications, the He 111P entered quantity production for the Luftwaffe, the first pre-production He 111P-0 bombers leaving the assembly line late in 1938, and the first quantity deliveries of the He 111P-1 commencing in the spring of 1939, this type rapidly replacing the obsolescent He 111Bs, Ds and Es, although a number of He 111Fs remained in service at the beginning of the war. The He 111P-1 was powered by two 1,150 h.p. Daimler-Benz DB 601Aa liquid-cooled engines, with which it attained a maximum speed of 264 m.p.h. at 12,300 feet. Cruising speed at sixty-one per cent power was 230

14

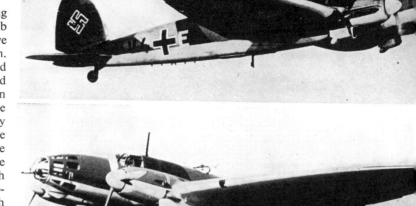

(*Above, top*) *The He 111E-1, externally similar to the earlier B-series but powered by Junkers Jumo 211A-3 engines.* (*Immediately above*) *The He 111D-1 which replaced the B-series in 1937. This was powered by DB 600Ga engines and lacked the wing surface radiators of the He 111B.*

m.p.h. at 13,120 feet, service ceiling was 24,100 feet, and initial climb rate was 890 ft./min. Defensive armament remained three 7.9-mm. MG 15 machine guns, one mounted on a universal joint in the nose and operated by the bombardier, one on top of the fuselage and fired by the radio-operator who was protected by a sliding transparent hood, and the third in a ventral cupola below the wing trailing edge. Possessing none of the power-operated turrets which characterised British medium bombers, this defensive armament, which had remained unaltered from the very first prototype, was soon to be found pathetically inadequate, and the greatest shortcoming in what was otherwise an efficient and formidable bomber. The centre section bomb bay had a maximum capacity of 4,410 lb., and the largest bomb normally carried was a 550-pounder, eight of these being stowed nose-up in individual cells, four on each side of a gangway.

Numerous sub-types of the He 111P were introduced onto the production lines, including the P-2 with different radio, the P-3 dual-control trainer, the P-4 with provision for carrying a single bomb externally, and the P-6 with 1,200 h.p. DB 601N engines. The principal reason for the relatively limited production of the P-series was the appearance of the more effective He 111H which, employing Junkers Jumo 211A engines, did not make inroads on the supply of DB 601 power plants which were required for Messerschmitt Bf 109 and Bf 110 fighters. The prototype of the H-series bomber, the He 111V19 (D-AUKY, Werke Nr. 1808), was essentially similar to the He 111P-1, apart from its engines, and the pre-production He 111H-0 and production H-1 bombers, powered by the 1,000 h.p. Jumo 211A-1, began to leave the assembly lines in the summer months of 1939. However, when on September 1, 1939, German forces invaded Poland, a considerable proportion of the eighteen Kampfgruppen equipped with He 111 bombers and forming the backbone of the Luftwaffe's striking force had P-series bombers, and the bulk of the remainder of their aircraft (which totalled 780 machines) were obsolescent F-series machines, very few He 111H bombers having reached the squadrons.

The Heinkel He 111H was destined to become by far the most important variant of this bomber and to appear in a variety of sub-types. At the outbreak of war nearly 1,000 He 111 bombers had been produced, and the total production for 1939 itself was 452 machines. With the tapering-off of production of the P-series in 1940 production was concentrated on the He 111H and rose rapidly—756 machines being com-pleted in 1940; 950 in 1941; 1,337 in 1942; 1,405 in 1943, and 756 in 1944.

The first He 111H-1 to be brought down over the British Isles was destroyed by fighters near Edinburgh on October 28, 1939, and subsequently H-series bombers began to appear in increasing numbers as the Kampfgruppen flying obsolescent He 111F bombers re-equipped. During the opening months of the war the Luftwaffe began to realise that the He 111H possessed inadequate defensive armament with which to oppose determined fighter attack. The He 111H-2 (Jumo 211A-3 engines) displayed the first results of this re-assessment of the bomber's defensive ability, two additional 7.9-mm. machine guns being mounted to fire through the side windows to provide additional protection from beam attacks. Another machine gun was fitted in the ventral gondola of some machines, firing forward. The He 111H-3 was powered by 1,200 h.p. Jumo 211D-1 engines, and some aircraft of this type were fitted with a single 20-mm. MG FF cannon in the nose. The traverse of this gun was limited, however, and it was employed principally for low-level attacks on shipping.

Despite the knowledge that the Luftwaffe now possessed of the fighting qualities of the Spitfire and Hurricane, when the air assault on Britain commenced on August 13, 1940, which date was given the somewhat dramatic code-name of "Adler Tag", it was still believed that the speed of the He 111 could be relied upon in part to offset any possible inadequacy in the strength of the escorting fighter formations. This belief proved to be a costly one for the He 111-equipped Kampfgruppen whose formations suffered disastrously from the depredations of R.A.F. fighters. Desperate measures were subsequently adopted to add

15

(Above) An He 111 *P-6. (Below) An initial production*
He 111*P-1.*

guns and armour, and after the Battle of Britain the He 111 was largely withdrawn from the day bombing role and transferred to night bombing.

The Heinkel He 111H-3 might be considered typical of all H-series variants, and was of orthodox light alloy stressed-skin construction. The fuselage consisted of transverse frames and longitudinal stringers to which the smooth skin was flush-riveted, and the wing was of two-spar, open-girder type design, the main plane being attached to the centre section just outboard of the Jumo 211D-1 engine. Tankage was provided in the wings for 760 Imp. galls. of fuel, but a fuselage tank could be added to bring the total capacity up to 945 Imp. galls. The crew varied from five to six members, comprising the pilot, bombardier, radio-operator and two or three gunners. The weights varied

according to the equipment installed, but one He 111H-3 which was brought down virtually intact over the British Isles in 1940 (Werk Nr. 6353—built at Oranienburg and originally delivered to the Luftwaffe on August 22, 1939) had an empty weight of 14,400 lb., a normal loaded weight of 25,000 lb., and a maximum permissible overload weight of 27,400 lb. The He 111H was generally popular with its crews and possessed pleasant handling qualities with good control characteristics and excellent stability and manoeuvrability. The He 111H-4 differed from the H-3 in having two Jumo 211F-2 engines of 1,340 h.p. In addition, a metal strengthening plate was added beneath the fuselage to permit the external carriage of a single bomb of 2,200-3,970 lb. weight, the internal bomb-bay being replaced by a protected fuel tank with a capacity of 184 Imp. gal. The H-5 reverted to the Jumo 211D-1 engines but could lift a maximum external bomb load of 5,510 lb.

From the earliest days of the war, Kampfgeschwader 26 equipped with the He 111H had been selected to undertake shipping attack, and a parallel development was the use of the He 111 for minelaying around Britain's coastline, principally, after the fall of France, by Kampfgeschwader 4. The He 111H was not entirely successful in the anti-shipping role, and suffered heavy losses owing to its limited armour protection. After exhaustive trials at the bombing school at Grossenbrode, however, the aircraft was proved to be highly suitable for torpedo attack. Subsequent trials at Grosseto, in which all types of German bombers were tested in the torpedo-dropping role, confirmed the suitability of the He 111H which could carry two torpedoes externally, and the He 111H-6 appeared. The first unit to undergo conversion was I/KG.26, and by the end of April 1942 the first

This He 111*H-1 displays increased radio equipment for search and anti-shipping duties. The anti-shipping role was first undertaken by the Kampfgeschwader* 26 *equipped with this type.*

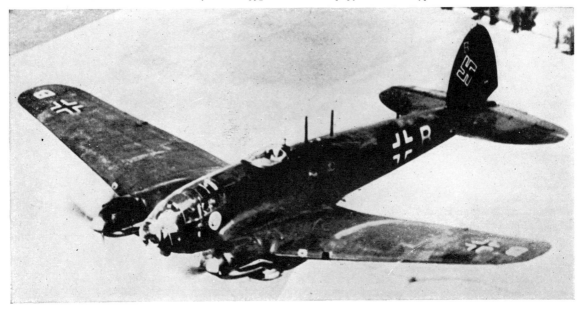

crews were ready for operations and were based at the newly constructed airfields of Banak and Bardufoss in northern Norway. By June the whole Gruppe, with a strength of forty-two He 111H-6 torpedo-bombers, was ready for operations, and the strength of the torpedo force grew rapidly, the whole of this being deployed against the Anglo-American convoys taking supplies to the northern Russian ports by September. The He 111H-6 proved to be an effective and important weapon, and was produced in substantial quantities, both for bombing and torpedo attack, appearing on all the fronts on which the Luftwaffe was engaged. The H-6 was powered by Jumo 211F-2 engines, and some machines were fitted with a remotely-controlled machine gun (7.9-mm. MG 17) in the extreme tail cone of the fuselage. Some machines were experimentally fitted with a grenade tube in the tail from which explosives could be ejected hopefully, but with little assurance of success, in the path of pursuing fighters, but this proved to be of greater danger to the bomber than to enemy interceptors. Another protective device was a combined balloon-cable fender and cutter, an immense framework extending from a point some little distance ahead of the fuselage nose to both wingtips, and weighing some 550 lb.; this equipment was fitted to a number of He 111H-3 and H-5 aircraft which were re-designated He 111H-8.

During 1942 it had been proposed to allow production of the He 111H

(Above, top) An He 111H-6, one of the most widely-used versions during the early war years. (Above, centre) An He 111H-16. The forward-firing 20-mm. MG FF cannon in the ventral gondola can be clearly discerned. (Immediately above) An He 111H-16 with external bomb load.

to run down as it was anticipated that production of the He 177A heavy bomber and Ju 288 medium bomber would have attained a suitable stage to permit service introduction. The failure of both types necessitated the expedient of once again stepping up the output of the He 111H, despite its obsolescence, for the factories were already tooled-up for this type, it was easily turned out, easily maintained, and relatively economical in man-hours and material. It could be used satisfactorily on the Russian front for tactical bombing because of the less formidable nature of the Soviet defences, although it lacked the range required for the strategic bombing of Russian industry.

The next sub-type to be manufactured in quantity was the He 111H-10, which appeared in service in 1943. Although basically similar to the H-6, the H-10 had a modified mid-upper gun position which was protected by screens of armour-glass and which housed either one 13-mm. MG 131 machine gun or an MG

81Z installation (comprising two 7.9-mm. MG 81 machine guns). The 4,410-lb. bomb load was housed completely internally, a single 20-mm. MG FF cannon was mounted in the nose, and the remotely-controlled tail-mounted MG 17 machine gun was retained. The He 111H-11 was a conversion of the H-6 for long-range attack, an additional fuselage fuel tank raising the total fuel capacity from 942 Imp. galls. to 1,166 Imp. galls., and five external bomb racks under the fuselage each carrying one 550-lb. bomb. Relatively few examples of the He 111H-11 entered Luftwaffe service, and the H-12 was a modified version for launching the Henschel Hs 293 bomb. The He 111H-14 was an improved H-10 with special radio equipment for shipping attack. Radio equipment included the standard FuG 16 and, in addition, FuG "Samos" with PeilG V and APZ5, and FuG 351 "Korfu", and aircraft of the H-14 type were used by the Sonderkommando Rastedter, of the Kampfgeschwader 40 based at Bordeaux-Merignac in

Loading Italian practice torpedoes on an He 111H-6 torpedo-bomber at Grossenbrode airfield in 1941.

1944. Without the special radio equipment the He 111H-14 was used as a medium bomber in Russia, primarily in areas where it was unlikely to come into conflict with the latest land-based enemy fighters. The He 111H-16, like the H-10, -11 and -14, was powered by two Jumo 211F-2 engines, and this variant differed from its predecessors in having rearranged flight instruments, extended transparent panels to improve forward view, and anti-dazzle screens. This sub-type was delivered to the Luftwaffe in substantial numbers. The He 111H-18 was merely an H-10 with large flame

dampers over the exhaust pipes to increase its suitability for night attack.

By the spring of 1944, Russian progress on the ground had forced an evacuation westwards of Luftwaffe ground organisations, carrying many important targets outside the range of the He 111H-equipped units. The re-equipment of these units with the He 177A had been envisaged, but this had been held up by continual technical difficulties with the newer bomber, necessitating the continued quantity production of the He 111H. Disregarding the brief appearance of the He 177A's of Fern-Kampfgeschwader 2 at Stalingrad at the end of 1942, the first He 177A aircraft did not appear on the Russian front until the summer of 1944, and in the meantime a more powerful version of the He 111H with improved defensive armament was produced to fill the gap resulting from the failure of the larger He 177A.

The new variant, destined to be one of the last of the sub-types of this bomber, was the He 111H-20 which began to leave the assembly lines in 1944. Initial production models were powered by a pair of Junkers Jumo 213A-1 engines developing 1,776 h.p. for take-off and 1,600 h.p. at 18,000 feet. Later production

The He 111H-8 fitted with a combined balloon-cable fender and cutter.

machines were powered by the Jumo 213E-1 fitted with a three-speed two-stage supercharger and induction cooler, and developing 1,750 h.p. for take-off and 1,320 h.p. at 32,000 feet. With the latter engines, the He 111H-20 attained a maximum speed of 295 m.p.h. and possessed a service ceiling of 32,800 feet. Defensive armament was radically changed, and comprised a single 13-mm. MG 131 hand-operated machine gun in the nose, an electrically-operated free-blown EDL 131 dorsal turret containing one MG 131 machine gun, another MG 131 machine gun in a heavily-armoured ventral gondola, and twin 7.9-mm. MG 81 machine guns in each of two beam positions. Maximum loaded weight was 35,270 lb. The He 111H-21, the last bomber production variant, was intended for the night bombing role exclusively, and differed from the H-20 merely in having large flame dampers over the exhaust pipes of the Jumo 213E-1 engines.

Experiments undertaken at Peenemünde with launching FZG-76 flying-bombs from aircraft had revealed that the He 111H was the most suitable available aircraft for this purpose. The FZG-76 was slung on a carrier placed under the starboard wing between the engine and fuselage, and by a simple release gear the missile could be successfully launched from a height of 1,500 feet and, aimed in the direction of a large city, its chances of landing in a built-up area were considerable. Early in September 1944, after a short launching course, aircrew withdrawn from semi-defunct bomber units were posted to a reconstituted Kampfgeschwader 53 in north-western Germany and, under conditions of extreme secrecy, this unit commenced operations from Venlo on the German-Dutch border. The FZG-76 missiles were launched at night over the North Sea against London, and 865 missiles were launched between the commencement of operations and December 13, 1944, but losses resulting from R.A.F. action and accidents were heavy, and the advance of the Allied armies soon brought these operations to a halt.

The final production H-series aeroplane, the He

A modified Heinkel He 111H-1.

The He 111V19 (D-AUKY), prototype for H-series.

A pre-production He 111H-0.

111H-23, represented the turning of the full circle, and marked a not inappropriate ending to the production life of an aircraft which, although intended from the beginning principally for the bombing role, had ostensibly commenced its existence as a transport. Intended as a fast paratroop transport with accommodation for eight fully-equipped paratroops, the H-23 possessed the nose of the H-16 variant, the EDL 131 turret first introduced on the H-20, and Jumo 213A-1 engines. The ventral gondola carried no armament and was specially modified to provide a dropping hatch for the paratroops.

The story of the He 111 would not be complete, however, without reference to the fantastic Zwilling, or

The He 111Z-1 "Zwilling" five-engined glider-tug. A production batch of ten He 111Z-1s was completed in 1942.

The He 111H-16 was evolved from the H-6 and H-10, and was built in substantial numbers. The flight instrument layout was improved and the nose was more extensively glazed.

Twin He 111, which was evolved in 1941 as a tug for large troop- and freight-carrying gliders, such as the Me 321 Gigant. Designated He 111Z, this monstrosity was basically two He 111H-6 airframes, each less one outer wing, and joined together outboard of a port and starboard engine by a length of wing which carried a fifth Jumo 211F-2 engine. The result was a five-engined aircraft with two separate fuselages and tailplanes, the pilot sitting in the port fuselage. The overall dimensions included a span of 115 ft. 6 in. and a length of 54 ft. 5½ in., take-off weight was 63,050 lb., and the performance included a maximum speed of 270 m.p.h. at 19,290 feet. Two prototypes were built in 1941, and these were followed in 1942 by a batch of ten He 111Z-1 glider tugs. Various proposals were made for bomber and reconnaissance variants of the Zwilling, including the He 111Z-2 long-range bomber which was to have carried four Henschel Hs 293 radio-controlled glider bombs for anti-shipping duties, and the Z-3 long-range reconnaissance version which, with four 66 Imp. gal. drop tanks, would have attained a range of 2,670 miles. However, neither bomber nor reconnaissance version was built.

Intended from the birth of the Luftwaffe as one of the principal weapons of the future Blitzkrieg, the He 111 had placed Germany in the forefront of world medium bomber development. It was forced, however, to soldier on long past its allotted span owing to the inability of the German aircraft industry to produce a suitable replacement, and was already approaching obsolescence when called upon to carry the major burden of the Luftwaffe's bombing offensive against the British Isles. Despite continual improvements, it could not keep pace with the rapidly changing requirements of air warfare, and during the last years of the war was no longer the formidable weapon with which the Luftwaffe had attacked Poland.

Heinkel He 111H-6

Dimensions :	Span, 74 ft. 1½ in. ; length, 54 ft. 5½ in. ; height, 13 ft. 9 in. ; wing area, 942,917 sq. ft.
Armament :	One flexible 7.9-mm. machine gun in extreme nose ; two 7.9-mm. MG 15 machine guns firing laterally through side windows ; one forward-firing 20-mm. MG FF cannon in ventral cupola ; one flexible rearward-firing 7.9-mm. MG 15 machine gun in ventral cupola ; one flexible 7.9-mm. MG 15 machine gun in dorsal position, and one fixed remotely-controlled 7.9-mm. MG 17 machine gun in extreme rear of fuselage. External bomb load carried underneath the fuselage up to a maximum of 5,510 lb., or two LT 950 or standard Navy torpedoes.
Power Plants :	Two Junkers Jumo 211F-2 twelve-cylinder inverted-Vee liquid-cooled engines rated at 1,340 h.p. at 2,600 r.p.m. for take-off and emergency, and 1,060 h.p. at 2,400 r.p.m. at 17,000 ft.
Weights :	Empty, 14,400 lb. ; disposable load, 10,600 lb. ; normal loaded weight, 25,000 lb. ; maximum permissible loaded weight, 27,400 lb.
Performance :	Maximum speed, 258 m.p.h. at 16,400 ft. ; cruising speed (61% power), 224 m.p.h. at 16,400 ft. ; stalling speed, 74 m.p.h. ; climb to 13,120 ft., 16.8 mins. ; service ceiling, 25,500 ft. ; range (with maximum bomb load), 760 miles ; maximum range, 1,740 miles.

The first operational model of the Mitchell, the B-25A, was delivered to the 17th Bombardment Group in mid-1941.

THE NORTH AMERICAN MITCHELL

Named after William Mitchell, the far-sighted, crusading American colonel of the 'twenties who was court-martialled for his outspoken views on air power, and posthumously raised to the rank of brigadier-general, the North American B-25 was possibly the best all-round light-medium bomber of the Second World War. Operationally efficient, this docile, adaptable machine had an excellent all-round performance, with particularly good handling characteristics, and it was one of the most popular of combat aircraft among all Allied aircrews. Had the Mitchell never attacked another objective, it would have ranked among the truly historic aircraft of the war for its fantastic attack against Tokyo in 1942, when it operated from the flight deck of the U.S.S. *Hornet*. It was manufactured in larger quantities than any other American twin-engined bomber, no less than 9,816 Mitchells being accepted by the U.S.A.A.F., although many of these were destined to find their way to the British, Soviet and other Allied air forces. The peak number of Mitchells in the U.S.A.A.F. service thus never exceeded 2,656 aircraft, but this exceptionally fine bomber made its mark on every far-flung front of the Second World War.

The B-25 Mitchell had its origins in an Army Air Corps circular proposal of 1938 for a twin-engine medium bomber. This circular proposal resulted in a number of projects from several manufacturers, and North American Aviation—which company's experience in bomber design was limited to the abortive XB-21—conceived in February 1938 an advanced project to U.S. Army Specification

G

98-102, which was followed by the construction of a prototype designated NA-40 by the company. This was a shoulder-wing monoplane with two radial engines in underslung nacelles, twin fins and rudders, and the nosewheel undercarriage then becoming fashionable in the United States.

The NA-40 was of clean, if somewhat angular, design, with a long and narrow cockpit "greenhouse", and a

(Immediately below) An early production B-25 with horizontal outboard wing panels, and (bottom) one of the first nine production B-25s with unbroken dihedral from root to tip of the wing.

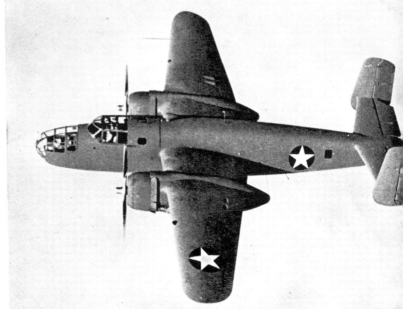

THE NORTH AMERICAN MITCHELL

(Above) Predecessor of the Mitchell, the NA-40-1, and (below) the first production NA-62, or B-25, with constant wing dihedral.

rather bulbous transparent nose for the navigator/bombardier, including a flexible mounting for a hand-held 0.3-in. M-2 machine gun, with 500 rounds. Additional proposed armament included three fixed 0.3-in. guns in the wings, with 500 r.p.g., and a further gun of similar calibre in each of the mid-upper and rear lower hand-held positions, with another 500 r.p.g. The normal crew comprised three members, and the maximum bomb load was 1,200 lb.

As the NA-40-1 Attack Bomber, the prototype was completed at the beginning of 1939 with two 1,100 h.p. Pratt and Whitney R-1830-S6C3-G fourteen-cylinder radial engines, and was flown for the first time in January by Paul Balfour. It had a normal gross weight of about 19,500 lb., a wing span of 66 ft., and a maximum speed of 265 m.p.h. In mid-February 1939, the engines were changed to Wright Cyclone

GR-2600-A71 radials, developing 1,350 h.p. for take-off, and as the NA-40-2, or NA-40B, the prototype was flown from Los Angeles to Wright Field in March for Air Corps evaluation. With the more powerful engines, the NA-40-2 had a maximum speed of 285 m.p.h., and gross weight had been increased to 21,000 lb. After two weeks of flight testing, the NA-40-2 was taken up by Major Younger Pitts, who was on assignment from Barksdale Field, Louisiana, for the attack bomber test programme owing to the shortage of regular Wright Field test pilots. During an attempt to turn into the Wright Field approach, Major Pitts lost control of the aircraft which crashed and was destroyed by fire. Fortunately, the crew escaped without injury, and the mishap was judged by the Air Corps to be no reflection on the design or construction of the NA-40-2.

Export versions up to NA-40-7 had been planned by North American, and the meagre reports from the brief flight test programme suggested that the bomber was capable of an outstanding performance. The Air Corps, however, suggested numerous design changes, and North American Aviation, therefore, undertook an extensive redesign programme, under the leadership of J. L. Atwood and R. H. Rice, to meet revised specifications, the developed model receiving the company designation NA-62. At 2,400 lb., the bomb load demanded by the revised specifications was double that of the NA-40, and increased stowage space was obtained by replacing the raised cockpit with one conforming to the top line of the fuselage, simultaneously rearranging the internal bomb stowage arrangements. This also made for improved aero-dynamic design, and lowering the wing attachment point several feet gave a better mainspar location in the fuselage, in addition to altering the general aspect of the aeroplane. The nacelles for the Wright Cyclones

(Left) The eighth RB-25A (42-196), originally designated B-25A, and, in the background, the thirteenth RB-25A (42-201). (Below) A B-25A of the 17th Bombardment Group.

were extended aft of the wing, and improved in profile, while the addition of a hand-held 0.5-in. gun in a new, bulbous tail cone position, plus the modification of the transparent nose, was accompanied by an increase in the crew accommodation from three to five.

Army approval of the redesign was obtained on September 10, 1939, a few days after the commencement of the Second World War, and ten days later North American were awarded a contract for the construction of 184 medium bombers to this design, under the designation B-25. As the type was ordered "off the drawing board", there was no XB-25 as such, and the first of the twenty-four B-25s which were to be delivered in that year was flown for the first time on August 19, 1940, after the delivery of a static test airframe on July 4th to Wright Field. The design of the B-25 required 195,000 engineering manhours in the production of 8,500 original drawings. It was powered by two 1,700 h.p. Wright Cyclone R-2600-9 engines, providing a maximum speed of 322 m.p.h. for a gross weight of 27,310 lb. As the fuselage of the NA-62 had been widened compared with the original NA-40 in order to accommodate an additional pilot, the wing span was increased to 67 ft. 6 in., but after the first nine B-25s had left the production line, the wing geometry was changed to give the Mitchell its characteristic "gull" configuration.

During tests with the first B-25 at Wright Field, it had been found that directional stability in the bombing run was not entirely satisfactory, and excessive dihedral on the mainplanes was suspected. To remedy this, the original unbroken dihedral from root to tip was reduced by re-rigging the outer wing panels to an absolute horizontal setting. This was to remain unchanged on all subsequent production models. Armament of the first B-25s comprised three 0.3-in. hand-held machine guns, mounted one in the nose and two in midship positions, plus the single 0.5-in. Browning in the tail. Maximum offensive overload was 3,600 lb. of bombs.

In 1941, as a result of air combat reports from Europe, modifications were introduced into the North American production line at Inglewood, California, to improve the operational status of the B-25. Self-sealing fuel tanks and armour protection for the pilots were incorporated and, as the B-25A, forty aircraft so modified followed the initial series of twenty-four production machines, which, at about this time, were officially christened Mitchells. The first combat formation to receive the Mitchell was the 17th Bombardment Group (Medium), which, in mid-1941, re-equipped from Douglas B-18s at McChord Field, near Tacoma, and spent several months on operational trials with the new aircraft. After Pearl Harbour, the 34th, 37th, and 95th Squadrons, which comprised the 17th Bombardment Group, were diverted to anti-submarine patrols over the Pacific, and on December 24th one of their Mitchells became the first American twin-engined bomber to sink a Japanese submarine.

By that time the first B-25Bs had entered service, 119 being built by North American in 1941. The B-25B featured extensively revised defensive armament. The beam and tunnel guns were replaced by dorsal and ventral electrically-operated Bendix turrets, each mounting two 0.5-in. machine guns, the ventral turret being fully retractable, with the guns fitting into slots in the fuselage, and incorporating a periscope for its sighting by the gunner who kneeled above it. The transparent tail cone was greatly reduced in size, and became a prone observation post, while a separate

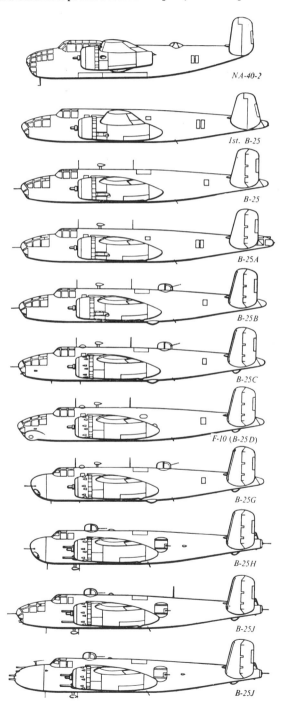

NA-40-2

1st. B-25

B-25

B-25A

B-25B

B-25C

F-10 (B-25D)

B-25G

B-25H

B-25J

B-25J

(Above) A B-25B Mitchell and (below) the first of twenty-three B-25Bs (FK161) supplied to the R.A.F. as the Mitchell I.

photographic station was located between the mid-upper turret and the tail.

The B-25B Mitchell was the type used for one of the most famous and spectacular operations of the whole war—the attack against Tokyo in April 1942. The conception of this bold scheme necessitated the availability of aircraft with an overall range of 2,400 miles carrying a 2,000-lb. bomb load, and capable of taking-off from the deck of an aircraft carrier steaming as near as possible to the Japanese coastline. Although twin-engined aircraft had not previously operated from carriers, the requirements for this operation narrowed the A.A.F. choice to the B-25 or the B-26, and the Mitchell was eventually selected on the basis of its superior take-off performance.

Volunteer crews were selected from the squadrons

of the 17th Bombardment Group, and also from the 89th Reconnaissance Squadron. The B-25Bs were modified for the operation by the removal of the lower gun turret, thereby saving 600 lb., and installing fuel tanks in its place which, with the 41.6 Imp. gal. (50 U.S. gal.), brought the total internal fuel capacity to 950 Imp. gal. (1,141 U.S. gal.). The B-25B normally carried 578 Imp. gal. (694 U.S. gal.), and the maximum gross weight was raised to 31,000 lb. Despite this high take-off weight, under the tuition of naval experts, the B-25 pilots found that they were able to take off in a run of 700–750 ft. during training. A special low-level bomb sight was installed instead of the secret Norden sight, both for operational and security reasons, the proposed bombing altitude being only fifteen hundred feet, and to discourage Japanese fighters from making stern attacks, two *wooden* "0.5-in. guns" were placed in the extreme rear fuselage.

Sixteen B-25B Mitchells eventually sailed on the U.S.S. *Hornet*, lashed down on the flight deck since they were too large to be stowed below, and 800 miles from the Japanese capital they made their precarious take-offs, led by Lt. Col. James H. Doolittle. This was further out than had been planned, because of an unfortunate encounter with a Japanese patrol boat, and although the Mitchells successfully bombed targets in Kobe, Yokohama and Nagoya, as well as in Tokyo, all sixteen were subsequently lost through bad weather and shortage of fuel when attempting to find their designated terminal bases in China. Fortunately, most of the crews were saved, and although the damage inflicted by their attacks was inconsiderable, the courageous mission came as an incalculable boost to American morale after the reverses at Pearl Harbour and elsewhere in the Pacific. It also served to demonstrate Japan's vulnerability to aerial attack, resulting in the retention in the home islands of four first-line fighter groups then urgently needed in the Solomons.

One of the Mitchells from "Shangri-La", as the

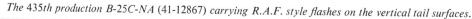

The 435th production B-25C-NA (41-12867) carrying R.A.F. style flashes on the vertical tail surfaces.

(Above, left) A hybrid B-25D supplied to the R.A.F. as the Mitchell II (FW212). This was basically similar to the U.S. Navy's PBJ-1D, featuring beam gun positions similar to the B-25H, and a single 0.5-in. tail gun. (Above, right) An all-black stripped B-25C employed as a courier aircraft between India and China. (Below, left) A B-25D-10-NC, and (below, right) a B-25C-20-NA of the Nationalist Chinese Air Force.

then anonymous *Hornet* was christened by President Roosevelt, was put down near Vladivostock, where its crew was interned and the aircraft confiscated by the Russians. The Mitchell was no novelty to the Soviet Union, however, Russian pilots and ground crews having been sent to the United States late in 1941 to convert to the type, which was subsequently to be supplied in considerable quantities under Lend-Lease. The delivery of a first batch of seventy-two Mitchells to the Russians began in March 1942, when Pan American Airlines ferry crews flew them to Africa, via Miami, and then up to Habbaniya, in Iraq, and Teheran, Iran, where they were collected by Russian pilots. By the end of 1942, 102 Mitchells had been flight-delivered to the Russians, with whom, as with everybody who flew them, they were extremely popular, and the grand total of 870 B-25s was eventually diverted to the Soviet Union, of which 862 arrived at their destination. All but five of these, which were shipped to northern Russian ports by water, were flight delivered, 128 being flown over the South Atlantic Ferry Route to Abadan, and the remainder over the Alaskan-Siberian Ferry Route, Soviet pilots taking the aircraft over at Fairbanks.

Other Lend-Lease B-25Bs were supplied to the Royal Air Force, which received twenty-three (FK161 to FK183) as the Mitchell I, but these were used only for familiarisation and training, and did not reach operational status. The Dutch air forces in the Netherlands East Indies had been promised some Mitchells in late 1941, but so desperate was the situation in the South Pacific after that time, that the aircraft were taken over by the 13th and 19th squadrons of the 3rd Bombardment Group, U.S.A.A.F., in Australia. In April 1942, ten Mitchells equipped with auxiliary fuel tanks accompanied three B-17 Fortresses from Darwin to the Philippines, where, for several days, the bombers raided Japanese-held docks, air and harbour facilities from concealed air strips without suffering any combat losses. The Mitchells of the 3rd Bombardment Group also began operations against targets in New Guinea early in April, and from that time onwards, the Mitchell played an increasingly important role in the air warfare over the Pacific.

Additional combat equipment, following the widespread use of the Mitchell in different theatres of war, resulted in the production of the B-25C by North American at Inglewood, where 1,619 were constructed

The PBJ-1D was basically a B-25D airframe but differed in having a tail turret with a single 0.5-in. gun, and beam positions similar to those of the later B-25H. This particular aircraft had nose-mounted radar, and the normal offensive load consisted of depth charges and bombs.

(Above) A B-25G-10-NA (42-65128) with a 75-mm. M-4 cannon, and (below) a PBJ-1H (basically a B-25H-51-1NA) with wingtip radome.

weight of 41,800 lb. In addition to four main wing tanks with a total of 558 Imp gal. (670 U.S. gal.), these models had a bomb-bay tank of 487 Imp. gal. (585 U.S. gal.), bringing the maximum fuel load to 1,143 Imp. gal. (1,255 U.S. gal.).

Armament remained a single hand-held nose gun, with 600 rounds, plus twin 0.5-in. guns in the upper turret, with 400 r.p.g., and similar weapons in the retractable ventral turret, with a total of 700 rounds. For offensive purposes, alternative loads of one 2,000-lb., two 1,000-lb., six 500-lb., eight 250-lb. or twelve 100-lb. bombs could be accommodated in the bomb-bay, except when the additional fuel tank was installed for ferrying purposes. Extra fuel was also carried by the unarmed photographic-reconnaissance version of the Mitchell, ten of which were converted from B-25Ds in 1943 under the designation F-10. These were used for photographic-reconnaissance training, cameras being mounted in a tri-metrogen arrangement in a "chin" fairing, and also in the aft fuselage. The R-2600-13 engines were replaced by -29s, and the combat weight was restricted to a reduced figure for increased speed.

On the main production variants of these aircraft, the B-25C-1 to -25-NA, and the B-25D-1 to -35-NC, distinguishable by the introduction of individual exhaust stacks attached to each cylinder with special exit fairings incorporated into the cowl skirt sections, an additional 253 Imp. gal. (304 U.S. gal.) of fuel was provided in six auxiliary wing tanks, plus a further 104 Imp. gal. (125 U.S. gal.) in a waist tank, bringing the maximum fuel capacity for ferry purposes to 1,402 Imp. gal. (1,684 U.S. gal.), and the combat weight to 33,500 lb. The armament was also increased by the addition of another machine gun fixed in the nose (with 300 rounds), which, in the flexible gun, was increased to 0.5-in. calibre. In some of the early production B-25Cs and Ds the lower turret was not fitted, but most of the production batches had provision for increased bomb stowage.

during 1941. The principal change concerned the introduction of an autopilot, which had first been fitted to the B-25Bs employed on the Tokyo raid, while another modification was the installation of R-2600-13 engines. North American began another Mitchell production line at Kansas City, manufacturing an essentially similar model designated B-25D-NC, 2,290 being produced. The basic versions of the B-25C and D had a normal combat weight of 29,500 lb., with a more rarely used maximum permissible take-off

It became possible to carry two 1,600-lb. armour-piercing bombs in the bomb-bay, or three 1,000-pounders, in addition to the previous combinations, maximum offensive load for short-range operations being raised to 5,200 lb. by the addition of eight

This B-25H-1-NA (43-4134), the thirtieth production machine, differed from the G-model in having a lighter T13E1 type 75-mm. cannon, the dorsal turret moved forward, and other modifications.

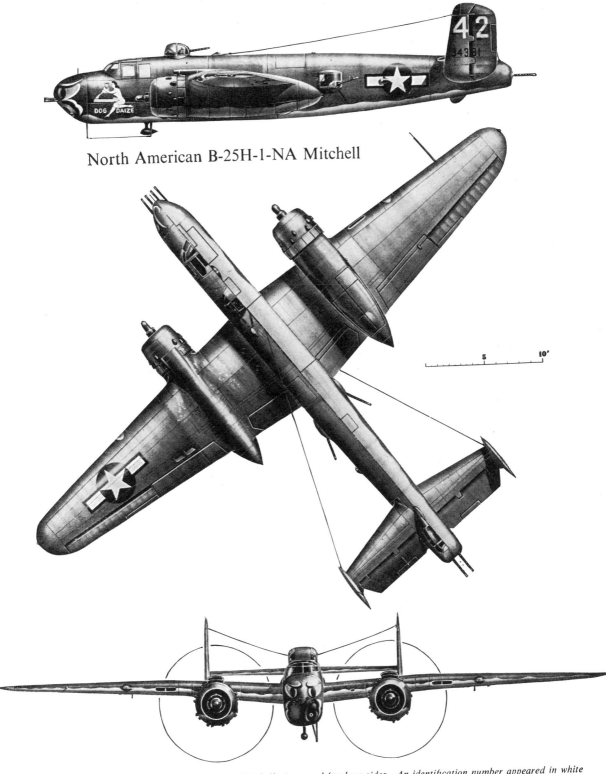

North American B-25H-1-NA Mitchell

5 10'

FINISH AND INSIGNIA: *Most B-25H-1-NA Mitchells in the Pacific Theatre had olive drab upper surfaces and neutral grey under surfaces. The blue-and-white national insignia appeared on the upper port and lower starboard wing surfaces and fuselage sides. An identification number appeared in white on the vertical tail surfaces, together with the serial number in black (i.e., 34381). Late production B-25H Mitchells were operated with an overall natural metal finish.*

27

The B-25J was produced in larger numbers than any other version of the Mitchell. The photograph depicts a B-25J-15-NC (44-28844) with natural metal finish.

250-lb. bombs on external racks. The external racks made their début on the Mitchell in the B-25C-1 and B-25D-1 series, and these permitted the carriage of a single short 22.4-in. torpedo weighing 2,000 lb. beneath the fuselage. The Mitchell was employed in only limited numbers as a torpedo plane against Japanese shipping, but more extensive use was made of the external wing racks for carrying six to eight bombs of 100–325 lb. weight.

Substantial quantities of the B-25C (NA-82) and B-25D (NA-87) were supplied to the R.A.F. as the Mitchell II, respective batches including fifty-five (FL164–FL218), thirty-nine (FL671–FL709), twenty-three (FR362–FR384), five (FR393–FR397), forty (FV900–FR939), sixty-seven (FR141–FR207), two

(Above) A U.S. Navy PBJ-1J, equivalent to the B-25J.

(Immediately below) A B-25J-1-NC (43-4004), and (bottom) a B-25J-25-NA (44-30052) supplied to the Soviet Air Forces.

hundred and thirty-one (FV940–FW280), forty-four (HD302–HD345) and twenty-nine (KL133–KL161). These aircraft were initially used to equip Nos. 98 and 180 Squadrons in No. 2 Group—then in Bomber Command—in October 1942, and completed their first operation on January 22, 1943, with a raid on oil refineries in Belgium. They subsequently continued to attack tactical targets, and were joined by Nos. 226, 305, 320 and 342 Squadrons in the 2nd Tactical Air Force. No. 320 Squadron was manned entirely by Dutch personnel, and became operational in July 1943. Shortly before, the remnants of the Royal Netherlands Indies Army Air Corps, which had reached Australia, had formed No. 18 R.A.A.F. Squadron, also equipped with Mitchells, and the Netherlands government eventually received no fewer than 249 Mitchells under the Lend-Lease programme. Four B-25C Mitchell IIs were supplied to the R.C.A.F. on a cash reimbursement basis, and twenty-nine were sent under Lend-Lease to the Brazilian Air Force, while the U.S. Navy operated Mitchells in considerable numbers as the PBJ-1C and -1D on anti-submarine duties. The naval Mitchells were equipped with radar, and their normal offensive load comprised depth charges, but they were used as torpedo-bombers on occasions.

Two examples of the B-25C were converted by North American to incorporate thermal de-icing systems for the wings and tail surfaces, and with minor differences these became the XB-25E and the XB-25F —the first of the Mitchell series to bear an experimental or prototype designation. Neither aircraft was developed, but the modification of another B-25C, which became the XB-25G, had far-reaching consequences. The Mitchell had been achieving considerable success in the South Pacific in attacking ground or ship targets with its fixed forward-firing armament. The latter had been greatly augmented in the field in 1942–43 by the installation of batteries of eight 0.5-in. machine guns in the noses of some of the B-25Cs of the 90th Squadron of the 3rd Bombardment Group, but an almost unprecedented additional "punch" was now proposed. Following successful experiments in the United States with a Douglas B-18A Bolo, it had been found practicable to perform air-to-ground

Three hundred and fourteen B-25Js were delivered to the R.A.F. as the Mitchell III, being used principally with the 2nd T.A.F. The photograph depicts one of the first batch to be delivered (HD378).

firing with a standard Army 75-mm. field gun, and this was destined to become the primary armament of the B-25G.

The 75-mm. M-4 cannon, which was 9 ft. 6 in. long and weighed about 900 lb., was mounted in a cradle extending beneath the pilot's seat, and accommodated in a shortened armoured nose fairing. A hydro-spring mechanism formed part of the gun mounting to take up the 21-in. recoil each time the weapon fired its 3-in. 15-lb. shells, of which twenty-one were carried and loaded by the navigator/cannoneer. Two 0.5-in. Browning guns were also mounted in the nose, and aimed and fired at the same time as the cannon as anti-flak and sighter weapons. These had 400 r.p.g., as did those in the upper turret, while the lower turret —which was not always fitted to the G-model because hydraulic fluid and dust frequently obscured its sighting system, rendering it so much dead weight—had 350 r.p.g.

With a crew of four, the B-25G retained the same power plants as its immediate predecessors, and 405 examples were built at Inglewood (Blocks -1 to -10) during 1942. The new nose reduced the overall length to 51 ft., and the maximum speed fell to 278 m.p.h. The 75-mm. cannon of the B-25G Mitchell was the second largest gun fitted to any aircraft, being exceeded in size only by the 105-mm. weapon installed in the experimental Piaggio P.108A, and was used against ship and ground targets by A.A.F. squadrons in the Pacific and the Mediterranean from late 1943 onwards. Two B-25Gs (FR208 and FR209) were supplied to the R.A.F. for evaluation purposes, but did not reach operational service. The U.S. Navy received a few as PBJ-1Gs.

The 75-mm. cannon installation was not entirely successful. Lieut. Gen. George Kenney, commanding the U.S. Far East Air Forces, had agreed to accept sixty-three B-25Gs, and when the first arrived, in July 1943, it was tested against Japanese targets by Lieut. Col. Paul I. Gunn. He found the cannon to be accurate, but it proved impossible to fire off more than about four shells in each attack, during which the Mitchell was extremely vulnerable to ground fire as no evasive action could be taken. To increase the offensive firepower, Colonel Gunn recommended the installation of four 0.5-in. machine guns in individual external "packages" below the cockpit area of the B-25G, but after field modifications to provide these weapons, the blast during their firing caused considerable skin fractures in the adjacent structure. The latter was, therefore, strengthened at the Townsville Field Modification Centre in Australia, where, by September 1943, some 175 B-25Cs and Ds had earlier been converted for ground strafing. Although the B-25Gs used their heavy cannon against flak positions, shipping and other targets, particularly when softening-up New Britain, where 1,253 rounds of 75-mm. ammunition was expended by the Mitchells in thirty-six days, and in the Marshalls campaign of early 1944, worthwhile targets became increasingly scarce, and the big weapons were, in most cases, therefore removed. In their place were installed two additional 0.5-in. machine guns in each aircraft.

The B-25G was succeeded on the Inglewood line in 1943 by the B-25H-1 to -10, of which 1,000 were built. Although this version retained the 75-mm. nose cannon—of the later and less weighty T13E1 type— the remaining armament was extensively revised, and considerably augmented by additional weapons. The fixed 0.5-in. guns in the nose were doubled in number to a total of four, with 400 r.p.g., except in a few early B-25H-1s, and the forward-firing armament was further augmented by the standardised installation of two more "packaged" 0.5-in. guns on each side of the armoured nose. The dorsal turret was moved to a new location just aft of the cockpit, and the lower turret was deleted in favour of a completely new arrangement of rearward-firing armament. Waist hatches provided mountings for a 0.5-in. gun, with 200 rounds, on each side of the fuselage, which terminated in a revised position for a tail gunner, with twin "fifties" in a power-operated mounting, and 600 r.p.g.

The B-25H, therefore, carried the extraordinarily potent armament of fourteen 0.5-in. guns plus a 75-mm. cannon, and could also carry up to 3,200 lb. of bombs, or a 2,000-lb. torpedo. Its crew of five comprised pilot, navigator/radio-operator/cannoneer,

A U.S. Far East Air Force B-25J-27-NC (44-30865) modified in the field with a "solid" nose containing eight 0.5-in. guns.

flight engineer/dorsal gunner, midships gunner/camera operator, and tail gunner. Overall length of the B-25H (PBJ-1H in the U.S. Navy) was 51 ft. 3¾ in., and it was fitted with either R-2600-13 or -29 engines, still of 1,700 h.p. for take-off. The first B-25H arrived in the F.E.A.F. in February 1944, entering service with the 498th Squadron, but the heavy cannon conferred the same disadvantages as the B-25G, and it was abandoned in the South-West Pacific by August 1944. By that time, the 509 Mitchells in the F.E.A.F. outnumbered all other types in the Command.

Most widely produced version of the Mitchell was the B-25J built at the Kansas plant of North American where 4,318 were turned out between 1943 and 1945. In this variant, the Mitchell returned to its primary function of bombing, the "solid" nose of the B-25H being replaced by the transparent fairing and bombardier's accommodation found in earlier Mitchells. With the exception of this extra crew member, and the glazed nose containing only two fixed and one movable 0.5-in. machine guns, each with 300 rounds, the B-25J was similar to the B-25H, with the same armament layout and powerplants. For very short range operations, the maximum bomb load of the B-25J was 4,000 lb., but a more normal offensive load comprised six 500-lb. weapons, or three 1,000-pounders. The 2,000-lb. bomb station was deleted on the 151st B-25J-1 and subsequent variants.

The B-25J-NC was built (Blocks -1 to -35) with minor differences in radio and other equipment, and was supplied to the U.S. Navy as the PBJ-1J. The R.A.F. received 314 B-25Js (HD346–HD400, KJ561–KJ800, and KP308–KP328) which were operated as Mitchell IIIs, again principally with 2nd T.A.F. Field modifications to some of the A.A.F. B-25J Mitchells resulted in their reversion to the ground attack role, with "solid" noses containing eight 0.5-in. guns, and in terms of firepower, the resultant B-25J-27 or -32 aircraft, to enumerate two examples, were the most heavily armed of the Mitchells, with no fewer than eighteen heavy machine guns. These variants were used principally in the Pacific theatre, where under-wing stubs were also fitted for carrying four 5-in. rocket projectiles outboard of each engine nacelle. Some of the U.S. Navy PBJ-1Js also had additional offensive capability, together with wingtip radomes for sea search.

The first B-25J Mitchells had arrived in the South-West Pacific area in the spring of 1944, but they soon proved unsuited to conditions in that combat theatre, where medium bombers were used almost exclusively at low altitudes. The Mitchell had by then generally

replaced the B-26 Marauder as the standard medium bomber in the Pacific, but as the low-altitude techniques did not call for the services of a bombardier, the U.S. Far East Air Forces replaced the transparent noses of their B-25Js with the eight-gun installation previously mentioned. These field modifications resulted in the inter-block numbers in the later B-25Js, which were adapted from nose "kits" supplied from the United States, but from September 1944, aircraft equipped with "attack" armament instead of the bomber-type nose arrived in the S.W.P.A. direct from U.S. production lines. Even these, however, were locally adapted by the F.E.A.F., principally by the addition of a 125 Imp. gal. (150 U.S. gal.) fuel tank in the radio compartment.

In its many forms, the Mitchell continued active operations right up to the end of World War II, by which time it was in service with the Chinese Air Force—the 1st Bombardment Group (Medium) of the Chinese-American Composite Wing had been formed in Karachi in October 1943—which air arm received 131 Mitchells under Lend-Lease. It was also performing a valuable non-operational task in the form of aircrew training, which had been initiated with some of the earlier variants of the B-25. As these became obsolescent, they were stripped of some operational equipment, and as AT-24s, were used for advanced training. The AT-24A, B, C, and D were training variants respectively of the B-25D, G, C and J, but were subsequently redesignated TB-25s, following the cancellation of the AT classification.

One of the select band of Allied aircraft that could claim to have been engaged on every major battlefront of the Second World War, the Mitchell built up an unrivalled tradition of service, and there can be few more dramatic examples of the constant development of a basic design under the exigencies of war than that offered by this remarkable aircraft, which was destined to linger on in the service of many of the world's air arms far into the postwar era.

North American B-25J Mitchell

Dimensions : Span, 67 ft. 7 in. ; length, 52 ft. 11 in. ; height, 15 ft. 9 in. ; wing area, 610 sq. ft.

Armament : Thirteen 0.5-in. Colt-Browning machine guns in nose, package, waist, upper turret and tail, with a total of 5,000 rounds. Ground attack version with five additional 0.5-in. nose guns. Maximum short-range bomb load, 4,000 lb. ; normal offensive load, 3,000 lb.

Power Plants : Two Wright Cyclone R-2600-29 fourteen-cylinder air-cooled radial engines with two-speed mechanical superchargers, each developing 1,850 h.p. as a war emergency rating for take-off, and 1,700 h.p. at normal sea level rating. Military rating at 13,000 ft., 1,450 h.p.

Weights : Empty, 21,100 lb. ; combat, 33,500 lb. ; maximum permissible, 41,800 lb.

Performance : Maximum speed, 275 m.p.h. at 15,000 ft. ; normal operating speed, 200 m.p.h. ; initial climb rate, 1,110 ft./min. ; service ceiling, 25,000 ft. ; range and endurance (with 3,200-lb. bomb load and 811 Imp. gal. of fuel at maximum cruise power), 1,275 miles in 5.4 hours.

(*Above*) *The first Blenheim off the assembly line* (*K7033*) *and* (*right*) *the original Type 142 "Britain First".*

THE BRISTOL BLENHEIM

When, in the summer of 1936, the Bristol Blenheim made its début, it was immediately hailed as a major step forward in combat aircraft design which placed the British aircraft industry in the forefront of fast day-bomber development. It was the first modern all-metal cantilever monoplane of stressed-skin construction to be placed in production for the Royal Air Force and, as such, it denoted the beginning of a new era in the equipment of that air arm. For several years acute uneasiness had existed concerning the obsolescence of the R.A.F.'s operational equipment; uneasiness accentuated by developments abroad. The emergence of the Blenheim, representing such a tremendous technical advance over the aircraft which it superseded, did much to still this disquiet. More than any other aeroplane it sounded the death knell

of the fighting biplane; it set a pattern in light-bomber design which other nations were not slow to follow, yet the Blenheim was fated never to fulfil the very high hopes that were placed in it.

One of the key types selected by the Air Ministry for the re-equipment of the rapidly expanding R.A.F. of the late 'thirties, the Blenheim, at the time of its service introduction, was possessed of a performance which enabled it to outpace most contemporary service fighters. Yet, such was the pace of combat aircraft evolution during those last two years of peace in Europe that when the R.A.F. went to war, in September 1939, it soon discovered that the Blenheim was not the redoubtable weapon that it had supposed. Its shortcomings soon manifested themselves in the hard school of aerial combat; it was to prove

The first Type 142M Blenheim (*below*) *made its initial flight on June 25, 1936, and, together with the second machine off the assembly line, served as a test and trials aircraft. It flew initially with Mercury VI-S.2 engines.*

The fifth Blenheim I off the production line, K7037 (above) was issued to No. 114 Squadron which, by March 1937, had become the first unit to be equipped with the new bomber. K7037 was the first Blenheim produced to full production standards.

woefully vulnerable to fighter attack; it was to be found deficient in both defensive armament and armour. Nevertheless, it was to bear the brunt of much of the fighting on every front to which the R.A.F. was committed for the first three years of the Second World War, and, despite its limitations, it was to serve valorously. A parallel might be drawn between the Blenheim and the Curtiss P-40. Like the American fighter, it was praised and abused, lauded and vilified, but it was all that was available, and however divergent were views of the effectiveness of the Blenheim as a weapon, it was one of the truly historic aircraft of the war.

In the years immediately preceding the war, the Blenheim had been more in the news, it had been more widely discussed and, in foreign aviation circles, it had aroused greater controversy than any other British bomber, and to the Blenheim was to go the distinction of being the first British warplane to cross the enemy's frontier after Britain's declaration of war on Germany, on September 3, 1939. At 12.01 hours on that day, one minute after the declaration took effect, a Blenheim IV (N6215) of No. 139 Squadron took-off from Wyton on a reconnaissance sortie. Its task was to photograph the German fleet at Kiel and, on a flight lasting 4 hr. 49 min., it took seventy-five photographs from an altitude of 24,000 ft.

On the following day, ten Blenheim IVs drawn from Nos. 107 and 110 Squadrons based at Wattisham undertook R.A.F. Bomber Command's first bombing sortie of the war by attacking German warships in the Schillig Roads. Blenheims were subsequently active with the Advanced Air Striking Force and the Air Component of the British Expeditionary Force in France until the time of that country's capitulation; they made many low-level daylight raids over Occupied Europe until late in 1941; they fought against appalling odds in the defence of Burma and Malaya; they served conspicuously in the Western Desert; they were active against enemy shipping from Norway to the Bay of Biscay; they were among the very few types to serve with *all* R.A.F. Commands—Bomber, Fighter, Coastal, Training and Army Co-operation, and they served with many foreign air forces, both Allied *and* enemy! Indeed, one of the Blenheim's chief claims to fame was its ubiquity.

The Blenheim's progenitor, the original Type 142, had been instrumental in disrupting Air Ministry

The export of Blenheim Is began in 1937, and the photograph below depicts one of two machines supplied to Yugoslavia in the spring of 1938. The Blenheim I was manufactured under licence by the Ikarus factory at Zemun, the first licence-built machine flying in March 1939, fifty-nine being in service with the Royal Yugoslav Air Force at the time of the German attack.

Turkey received twelve Blenheim Is between October 1937 and July 1938, and a further eighteen were purchased before the end of 1938. Later, the Turkish Air Force received small quantities of Blenheim Vs.

complacency with what was, for its time, a phenomenal performance. This performance, which revolutionized official thinking, bested by a handsome 40 m.p.h. the highest speeds attained by fighters then in service with the R.A.F. In some respects, the Blenheim may be compared, therefore, with the Mosquito which came after. There was, however, one vital difference between the development backgrounds of the two aircraft: Whereas the Mosquito was born of a conviction that the high-speed, unarmed bomber had a future as a military machine, the Blenheim was born casually—almost accidentally—from some work on high-speed commercial aircraft. The first of these, and, therefore, the *real* forefather of the Blenheim and the Bristol twins which followed it, was, oddly enough, never built. This was the Bristol Type 135, a small, low-wing cabin monoplane designed to carry six to eight passengers at a cruising speed of 180 m.p.h.

As no suitable engines were available for the Type 135 with the required power of about 350 h.p., Bristol developed the sleeve-valve Aquila nine-cylinder single-row air-cooled radial specifically for their projected aircraft. Among the advanced features embodied by the

Type 135 was all-metal, stressed-skin construction, and a good deal of favourable comment was aroused when a mock-up fuselage of the project was displayed at the *Salon International de l'Aéronautique* in Paris in 1934. The project was the work of Bristol's chief designer, Captain Frank Barnwell, who had been responsible for the majority of Bristol designs since the First World War. Among those interested in the project was the newspaper proprietor, Lord Rothermere, who informed the Bristol Aeroplane Company that he would be prepared to purchase an aeroplane of about this size and performance, capable of making non-stop flights between the principal cities of Europe. The Type 135 lacked the range to fulfil this task, and so Captain Barnwell laid out a new aeroplane—the Type 142—which, based on the earlier design, was specifically intended to fulfil Lord Rothermere's requirements.

The aircraft was designed around two 640 h.p. Bristol Mercury VI nine-cylinder air-cooled radial engines, and the original project drawings were dated April 27, 1934. At that time, the aircraft, with eight passengers, was expected to offer a maximum speed of

The Blenheim I (L1348) illustrated below was used for early photographic reconnaissance experiments at Heston. With boosted engines, reduced wing span, a special "camotint" finish, and the dorsal turret removed, this Blenheim achieved a speed of 296 m.p.h. at 8,000 ft. The lower glazed nose panels were removed, and cameras were installed in small bulges in the fuselage belly.

the order of 250 m.p.h. Simultaneously, a parallel scheme was drawn up for a less advanced and less expensive aircraft to succeed the original Type 135 project, and this was allocated the Type number 143. Lord Rothermere ordered a prototype of the Type 142 in mid-1934, and the Bristol company themselves financed construction of the Type 143.

Carrying the identification "R-12" on its fuselage sides—the registration G-ADCZ was later allocated to the aircraft—the Type 142 made its first flight at Filton on April 12, 1935, piloted by Captain Cyril Uwins, the company's chief test pilot. Retaining the basic wing design of the Type 135 project, the Type 142 featured a fuselage of reduced cross section which resulted in an exceptionally slim, all-metal monocoque structure accommodating six passengers, a "bay window" in the nose providing the pilot with an excellent field of vision. The main undercarriage members retracted into the engine nacelles, and the two 640 h.p. Mercury VI radials drove fixed-pitch, four-blade wooden airscrews. These airscrews were replaced by Hamilton Standard controllable-pitch, three-blade metal units for the Certificate of Airworthiness trials at Martlesham Heath, and the performance of the prototype exceeded the most sanguine expectations.

The official report of the trials conducted with the Type 142 at Martlesham Heath, in June 1935, indicated that the aircraft achieved 285 m.p.h. when flying at maximum loaded weight. This was 30 m.p.h. faster than the maximum speed of the fighter which, but a short time previously, had won the protracted contest for the F.7/30 specification—the Gloster Gladiator—and which was about to be ordered into production for the R.A.F. It was hardly surprising, therefore, that the Air Ministry should approach Lord Rothermere for permission to make further tests. He went one better, and presented his aeroplane to the Air Council, naming it the "Britain First".

Trials with the Type 142—now bearing R.A.F. insignia and the serial number K7557—continued while Barnwell turned his thoughts to ways and means of translating the basic design into a useful military aeroplane. As it happened, military roles had already been considered for the parallel Type 143. There had been, for instance, a proposal in December 1934 to use a variant of this type for coastal and general reconnaissance duties, and in January 1935 had come the Type 143F project—a fighter-bomber for the Finnish Air Force with Mercury VI engines replacing the Aquila IIIs, a 20-mm. Madsen cannon in the nose, and a dorsal gunner's position. Although neither of these projects materialized, and the Type 143 itself was not to fly until January 20, 1936, they were links in the chain which led, in the summer of 1935, to a proposal for the Type 142M, a bomber based on the design of the "Britain First".

Initially, the Type 142M project envisaged a crew of two with a pair of Aquila or Mercury engines. A 1,000-lb. warload was to be carried over a range of 1,000 miles. A major difference from the "Britain First" was the raising of the wing on the fuselage by sixteen inches in order to provide space in the fuselage below the main wing spars for a bomb-bay capable of housing four 250-lb. or two 500-lb. bombs. The design retained the curiously short nose of the "Britain First", but an incidental disadvantage resulting from the raising of the wing from low to mid position was the restriction placed on the pilot's view to the side by the high-placed engine nacelles. The tailplane was increased in span and raised on the

Although few Blenheim Is remained in service with home-based bomber squadrons at the outbreak of World War II, a night-fighting version, the Blenheim IF (above) saw fairly extensive service. The machine illustrated belonged to No. 614 (County of Glamorgan) Squadron.

fuselage; the adjustable incidence gear was removed, resulting in an increase in elevator chord and the introduction of trim tabs; the tailwheel was made retractable—linked to the main undercarriage members by cable to avoid hydraulics at the rear end of the fuselage; structural strength was increased; a 0.303-in. Browning machine gun and a bomb-aiming station were provided in the fuselage nose, and provision made for a semi-retractable gun turret in the dorsal position.

On July 9, 1935, the first design conference on the project was held between the Bristol design team and Air Cdre. Verney, Director of Technical Development at the Air Ministry. In view of the fact that the results of trials with the "Britain First" were indisputable, it was to be expected that the Air Ministry would move swiftly, and by August specification B.28/35 had been drawn up to cover detail design of the Type 142M proposal, a contract had been placed for 150 machines "off the drawing board", and the name "Blenheim" had been bestowed upon the type. With this order in hand, the Bristol company had no need to bother with prototypes—in any case, the "Britain First" had furnished a pretty good idea of the characteristics to be expected in the bomber—and, therefore, the first two Blenheims off the assembly line at Filton served as test and trials aircraft. The first of these (K7033) made its initial flight on June 25, 1936, but before this milestone had been attained, the Bristol design office had already commenced the study of a variety of projects based upon the Blenheim.

During 1935, while detail design of the Blenheim was the principal activity, Bristol prepared at least three designs based on or developed from the Type 142M. These designs included a 37,500-lb. four-engined bomber which, submitted in December 1935 and possessing no Type number, employed a standard Blenheim cockpit married to a new, slim fuselage, a 96-ft. span wing, and four Mercury IX engines. Three years later this project was to be revived to form the

basis of the Bristol tender to the B.1/39 specification for a medium-heavy bomber which, in the event, was not proceeded with. The Type 149 was a slightly modified Blenheim intended for the general-purpose role to specification G.24/35, two Aquila AE-3M engines stretching the range, and the Type 150 was a torpedo-bomber with internal stowage for one torpedo, and two Bristol Perseus VI engines to specification M.15/35. In April 1935 a further Blenheim variant was evolved, the Type 152. This combined in one machine the requirements of both G.24/35 and M.15/35 with the only exception that the torpedo could not be housed wholly within the bomb-bay. This development was later to see production as the Beaufort. Meanwhile the Type 149 project had been revised to incorporate a forward navigation table, as in the Type 152, and in this form the aircraft was also adopted by the Air Ministry which ordered 150 in November 1936. The type was named Bolingbroke, and production was covered by specification 11/36. Interest in this type was expressed by the air forces of both Canada and Australia.

By this time, however, as already noted, the Blenheim was already in the air, and in December 1936 the Bristol company had been instructed to proceed with production with all possible speed—a year later, twenty-four Blenheims were being delivered from the Filton factory each month, and Rootes Securities and A. V. Roe factories were being brought into the production programme. The initial production model was the Blenheim I powered by two 840 h.p. Mercury VIII engines, although the first example (K7033) was initially flown with Mercury VI-S.2s. At the Martlesham trials, this aircraft achieved 281 m.p.h. at 12,000 ft., despite its loaded weight of 11,000 lb. compared with the 9,000 lb. of the "Britain First". A few small changes were made on later aircraft. For instance, the landing lamp in the starboard wing was deleted; the shape of the side cockpit windows was modified, and controllable gills were

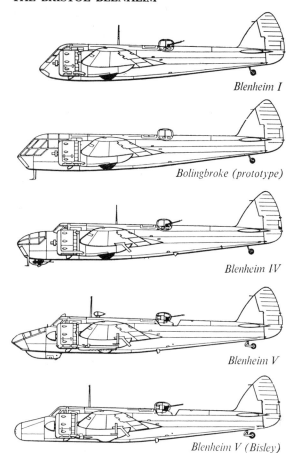

Blenheim I

Bolingbroke (prototype)

Blenheim IV

Blenheim V

Blenheim V (Bisley)

added to the engine cowlings. A little later, airscrew spinners were abandoned, together with the retractable tailwheel, as unnecessary luxuries.

In service form the Blenheim I carried a crew of three, comprising a pilot, navigator-bombardier, and wireless-operator-gunner, and armament comprised one forward-firing 0.303-in. Browning machine gun in the port wing, and one Vickers "K" gun in a Bristol hydraulically-operated dorsal turret. A 1,000-lb. bomb load was carried internally. The fuselage, which was built in three sections, was a light alloy monocoque built up of formers and open-section stringers, with Alclad skin riveted to the flanges of the formers and stringers. The wings, which were also built in three sections, comprised spars built up of two heavy high-tensile steel flanges with a light, single-plate Alclad web, reinforced with vertical stringers, between them. The ribs were made from Alclad sheet, the whole being covered by an Alclad stressed-skin. Bristol-Frise mass-balanced ailerons and split trailing-edge flaps were carried, and small trim tabs in the

ailerons were adjustable on the ground. The construction of the tail assembly was similar to that of the wings. A servo-tab was fitted in the rudder, and rudder and elevators were aerodynamically and statically balanced. All moveable control surfaces were fabric covered.

Fully equipped, the loaded weight of the Blenheim I rose to 12,500 lb., but a maximum speed of 285 m.p.h. was attained at 15,000 ft., speeds at 10,000 and 20,000 ft. being 269 and 277 m.p.h. respectively. Range, fully loaded at 220 m.p.h., was 1,250 miles, endurance was 5.65 hrs., initial climb rate was 1,540 ft./min., and service ceiling was 27,280 ft.

The first aircraft to go to a squadron, the third machine off the line (K7035), arrived at Wyton early in 1937, and by March of that year No. 114 Squadron had become the first Blenheim-equipped unit. The appearance of the Blenheim at the Hendon Display of that year caused a considerable stir, and the type was soon equipping R.A.F. squadrons in Iraq and India. In service it was giving an excellent account of itself, and some exceptionally fast flights, both by single machines and formations, were recorded. A Blenheim squadron flew from Dhibban to Aboukir, a distance of 811 miles, in 3.25 hours, the average speed being 250 m.p.h., while one machine flew from Abbotsinch to Upavon against a head wind and in poor visibility yet covered the 335 miles in seventy minutes, giving an average speed of 280 m.p.h.

Production of the Blenheim I by Bristol, A. V. Roe and Rootes Securities totalled 1,552 machines, and these served with the following home and overseas bomber squadrons of the R.A.F. from March 1937 onwards: Nos. 8, 11, 21, 30, 34, 39, 44, 45, 55, 57, 60, 61, 67, 82, 84, 90, 101, 104, 107, 108, 110, 113, 114, 139, 144 and 211. Few Blenheim Is remained in service with home-based bomber squadrons by the outbreak of war, having been superseded by the later Mk.IV, although a few Blenheim Is saw operational service in the bombing role during the early stages of the fighting in the Western Desert. As the Blenheim IF, however, the type did see fairly extensive operational service in the night-fighting role, some two hundred being converted from bombers by the attachment of a pack housing four 0.303-in. Brownings under the forward fuselage. Blenheims of this type undertook the first night-intruder sorties of the war, on December 21-22, 1939, and largely pioneered airborne interception radar, scoring their first success with this revolutionary development on July 22, 1940.

One Blenheim I (L1348) was the subject of an interesting experiment in the early days of photographic reconnaissance activities at Heston. This aircraft had its wing span reduced by 3 ft., the dorsal turret re-

FINISH AND INSIGNIA: *The Bristol Blenheim IV illustrated belonged to No. 18 (Burma) Squadron and featured dark earth and dark green camouflage on the upper surfaces of the wings, fuselage and tailplane, and sides of the fuselage and vertical tail surfaces, and so-called Sky Type "S" (light blue-green duck egg) under surfaces. The national insignia comprised "C" type blue-white-red roundels on the* *fuselage sides, outlined in yellow, with corresponding tail flash, and "B" type red-and-blue roundels on the upper surfaces of the wings. The serial number "V6083" appeared in black on the aft fuselage. The letter "A" identifying the individual aircraft and the letters "FV" identifying the squadron were painted in pale grey.*

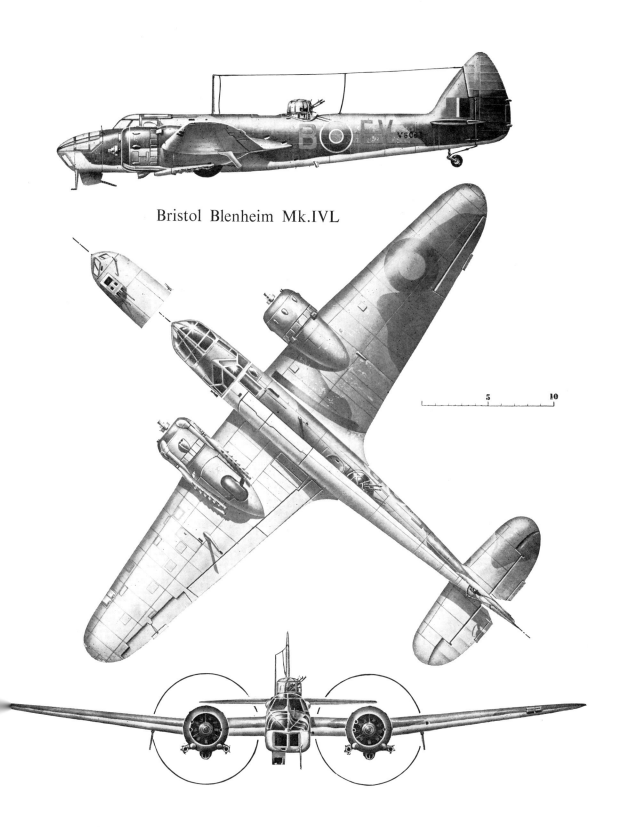

Bristol Blenheim Mk.IVL

(Above and left) This early production Blenheim I (K7072) was set aside in 1937 as the prototype Bolingbroke. Initially, the whole windscreen was moved forward by three feet, but before the aircraft flew the forward panelling was lowered below the pilot's line of vision. This was later "scalloped" on the port side (as seen lower left), and the aircraft shipped to Canada. This aircraft was not designated Blenheim III, an error first perpetrated during the war years which has persisted until now.

moved, the engines boosted, a special "camotint" finish applied, the lower nose panels filled-in, and cameras installed in small bulges in the fuselage belly. The refinements served to increase the speed of this aircraft at 8,000 ft. from 274 m.p.h. to 296 m.p.h.

It was to be expected that the performance of the Blenheim, with all its attendant publicity, would not escape unnoticed abroad, and several batches of the Mk.I version were exported, while manufacturing licences for the type were acquired by Finland and Yugoslavia. Twelve Blenheim Is were delivered to the Turkish Air Force between October 1937 and July 1938, followed by a further eighteen before the end of 1938. Two were purchased by the Yugoslav government, and licence manufacture was initiated by the Ikarus factory at Zemun, Belgrade, the first Ikarus-built Blenheim flying in March 1939. An additional twenty-two Blenheim Is were diverted from the R.A.F. to Yugoslavia as part of the British government's policy of strengthening the Balkan *Entente* against possible attack by Germany. At the same time fourteen were delivered to Rumania. When Germany attacked Yugoslavia on April 6, 1941, the Royal Yugoslav Air Force possessed fifty-nine Blenheims (twenty-three with each of the 1st and 8th Bomber Regiments, and thirteen with the 11th Independent Group). Blenheims of the 1st Bomber Regiment made extremely valorous low-level

The Fairchild-built Bolingbroke IVW (below) was fitted with 1,200 h.p. Pratt and Whitney Wasp R-1830 fourteen-cylinder radials, and fifteen aircraft of this type were delivered.

The first eighteen aircraft built by Fairchild were essentially replicas of the Bolingbroke prototype (K7072) and were known as Bolingbroke Is, but the standard Canadian production model was the Mercury XV-powered Bolingbroke VI, one of which (9048) is illustrated above. The Bolingbroke IV was redesigned extensively to U.S. standards and for U.S. and Canadian equipment. One machine completed with 990 h.p. Wright Cyclone R-1820-G3B radial engines (right) was designated Bolingbroke IVC. This aircraft bore the serial number 9074.

attacks on German armoured columns invading Yugoslavia from Bulgaria, during which the Regimental Commander was killed by fragments from his own bombs, and those of the 8th Regiment were employed against targets in Hungary and Austria, and made attacks on Graz and Vienna. Many Yugoslav Blenheims were destroyed on the ground, and those that survived the onslaught were incorporated in the Croat Air Force.

Another country to order the Blenheim I was Fin-land, who received eighteen between July 1937 and June 1938. Finland also acquired a manufacturing licence for the bomber, which was placed in production at the Government Aircraft Factory at Tampere, the Mercury engines being produced at the Tampella Machine Works. The Finnish Blenheim Is had an enlarged bomb-bay capable of accommodating both Swedish and American bombs, and sometimes operated with fixed skis in place of the normal wheel

One Bolingbroke I (717) was fitted with twin Edo floats and redesignated Bolingbroke III (below). Although the possibility of having interchangeable wheel, ski or float undercarriages was considered, only one machine was tested with floats.

The first sixty-eight Blenheim IVs produced were actually Mk.I airframes, and to distinguish true production aircraft from these hybrids later machines were designated Blenheim IVL. A late production Blenheim IVL (V5382) is illustrated above.

undercarriage. The first batch of fifteen Blenheim Is was delivered by the Tampere factory in 1941, and production continued until 1944, a further forty machines being built. In addition to the Blenheim Is, the Finnish Air Force received twenty-four Blenheim IVs from the United Kingdom prior to the second Russian assault.

An early production Blenheim I (K7072) was set aside, in 1937, for conversion as a prototype for the Bolingbroke, the Type 149, of which 150 had been ordered. The unusually short nose which had characterized the Blenheim gave place to a lengthened structure which, in the first place, retained the contours of the Blenheim I, the whole windscreen and bombardier's window assembly being moved forward bodily by about 3 ft. Before the aircraft had flown it was realised that the pilot's view—the position of his seat being unchanged—was inadequate, to say the least! The windscreen was, therefore, moved back to its original position, with the forward transparent hooding lowered below the pilot's line of vision. In this form, K7072 flew for the first time on September 24, 1937, but the view for landing still left something to be desired. The forward hooding on the port side was, therefore, "scalloped" to produce what was later to become the characteristic nose of the Blenheim IV.

In this form the Bolingbroke was now adopted by the Royal Canadian Air Force, and negotiations commenced with a view to producing the bomber in Canada. Plans for producing the Bolingbroke for the R.A.F. at Filton, Bristol, were cancelled, however, in favour of maintaining the supply of Blenheims to re-equip R.A.F. squadrons overseas. The prototype Bolingbroke, K7072, was shipped to Canada in due course to assist in the production of Bolingbrokes by Fairchild Aircraft Limited at Longueuil. The first batch of eighteen Bolingbrokes were built to Bristol drawings, and were essentially replicas of K7072, with Mercury VIII engines. These were designated Bolingbroke Is. The standard Canadian version, redesigned extensively to U.S. standards and for U.S. and Canadian equipment, was the Bolingbroke IV with Mercury XV engines, and 125 examples of this model were built. The Bolingbroke II was a Mk.I rebuilt to Mk.IV standards after a crash, and the Bolingbroke III was another Mk.I completed as a float-plane with twin Edo floats and Mercury XV engines. One Bolingbroke IV completed with 990 h.p. Wright Cyclone R1820-G3B nine-cylinder air-cooled radials was designated Mk.IVC, and fifteen delivered with 1,200 h.p. Pratt and Whitney Twin Wasp R-1830 fourteen-cylinder two-row air-cooled radials were designated Mk.IVW. Finally, following production of the Bolingbroke IVs, a batch of IVT trainers were built, equipped for bombing and gunnery training, flying training, and drogue target towing, etc.

In 1938—the year in which Frank Barnwell was killed when making the second flight in a light monoplane that he had built privately—Air Ministry interest in the Bolingbroke revived, and it was decided to put a generally similar aircraft in production at Filton until the Type 152 Beaufort became available. The Type number 149 was retained, but the aircraft was designated Blenheim IV, and this variant differed from the preceding production version of the Blenheim in only two major respects—a new forward fuselage with the lengthened nose, a stepped windscreen introduced on the Bolingbroke, and long-range tanks in the wings. The first sixty-eight Blenheim IVs were actually Mk.I airframes, and did not have the long-range wing, and to distinguish the true production aircraft from these hybrids, the later machines were usually designated Blenheim IVL, or, when carrying the gun tray beneath the fuselage (which, containing four 0.303-in. Brownings with 500 r.p.g., was similar to that carried by the Blenheim IF), as the Blenheim IVF.

There was no prototype of the Blenheim IV, and production had begun to switch from the Mk.I to the later type before the end of 1938. The Blenheim II and III did not reach fruition, and it is no longer certain which variants were covered by these designations. Some documents suggest that the Blenheim II was intended to be the Blenheim I with a long-range wing, and the Blenheim III was basically the Blenheim IV with a short-range wing. This cannot now be confirmed, but it *is* certain that the prototype Bolingbroke, K7072, was *not* designated Blenheim III, an error first perpetrated during the war years which has persisted until now.

All Blenheim IVs had Mercury XV engines rated at 920 h.p. for take-off—similar engines were installed retroactively in some Blenheim Is—and the initial loaded weight was increased progressively from 12,500 lb. to 13,800 lb. and, eventually, to 14,500 lb. Initially, the Blenheim IV had a single Vickers "K" gun in a Bristol B.I.Mk.III dorsal turret, and a single, forward-firing 0.303-in. Browning, but the need to increase defensive armament in order to stave off fighter attacks was rendered patently obvious at an early stage in the fighting. Various unorthodox modifications were made by squadrons in the field, and among these was one machine with two fixed guns, one in each engine nacelle, firing rearwards, while another had a fixed, rearward-firing gun in the fuselage tail. A standard modification was subsequently incorporated which comprised a single free-mounted Vickers "K" gun on a gimbal mounting in the nose and a rearward-firing Browning in a blister attached to the emergency hatch in the floor of the fuselage nose. A B.I.Mk.IIIA dorsal turret housing two Vickers "K" guns was introduced and, later, this gave place to a B.I.Mk.IV turret with twin Brownings. Later still, a Frazer-Nash controllable mounting with two rearward-firing Brownings was fitted under the nose.

At the outbreak of war, R.A.F. Bomber Command had six squadrons of Blenheim IVs forming No. 2 Group. Two of these squadrons were immediately flown to France as part of the Advanced Air Striking Force, while the Air Component of the British Expeditionary Force included a further four squadrons equipped with Blenheim IVs. Prior to the outbreak of war, twelve Blenheim IVs had been ordered by and delivered to the Royal Hellenic Air Force, although an order for eighteen aircraft of this type for the Royal Swedish Air Force was refused. As previously recounted, twenty-four Blenheim IVs were supplied to the Finnish Air Force and, early in 1940, a quantity was delivered to the Turkish Air Force to supplement the Blenheim Is previously supplied.

Within a few days of the commencement of the main German offensive, on May 10, 1940, the Blenheim squadrons attached to the A.A.S.F. had been decimated, having proved particularly vulnerable to fighter attack. Nevertheless, after the collapse of France, the Blenheim IVs of No. 2 Group continued to operate by daylight over the Continent, frequently without fighter escort, although attrition was high. The daylight activities of Bomber Command's Blenheims included many noteworthy sorties, such as the daring attack on Bremen, on July 4, 1941, for which Wing Commander H. I. Edwards was awarded the Victoria Cross, and a memorable attack on Cologne in the following month. An equally important task for the Blenheim squadrons during the early war years was strikes against enemy shipping in the Channel and the Bay of Biscay. These strikes were invariably made at altitudes of the order of 50 ft., and the aircraft suffered severely from the intense anti-aircraft fire of escorting warships, but on occasions

During the war years, the Portuguese Air Force received a number of Blenheim IVs and Vs, some having made forced landings in Portugal and others being supplied direct from the United Kingdom. The photograph below depicts Portuguese Blenheim IVs.

The prototype Blenheim V (AD657) was fitted with a ground-attack nose, but the type was never produced in this form. The name "Bisley" had been allocated to this model but supplanted by that of Blenheim V before the prototype flew.

the Blenheim manifested a remarkable ability to absorb damage and remain in the air. This quality could hardly be better illustrated than by the Blenheim which, weaving violently to avoid intense fire from an enemy destroyer, actually struck the water. The impact was so violent that one of the engines was wrenched completely out of its mounting, and the tips of the airscrew of the other engine were badly bent, yet the Blenheim's pilot succeeded in nursing the crippled aircraft back to a coastal airfield! Blenheims were based on besieged Malta in 1941, accounting for a remarkable amount of enemy shipping in the Mediterranean; others played an important role in the fighting in the Western Desert, but in the Far East, Blenheims defending Singapore suffered sorely at the hands of Japanese fighters. Blenheim IVs last operated with Bomber Command on August 18, 1942, giving place to Douglas Bostons and de Havilland Mosquitoes, but overseas these aircraft fought on with the R.A.F., the S.A.A.F., and the Free French Air Force.

Like the Blenheim I, the Blenheim IV was built by A. V. Roe and Rootes Securities, in addition to the parent company, and a total of 1,930 was produced, eventually operating with the following bomber squadrons at home and overseas: Nos. 8, 11, 13, 14, 15, 18, 21, 34, 35, 39, 40, 45, 52, 55, 57, 67, 87, 88, 90, 101, 104, 107, 108, 110, 113, 114, 139, 142, 150, 162, 203, 218, 223, 226, 244, 326, 327, 342, 454, 500, 608 and 614. The Blenheim IV also flew operationally with Nos. 53 and 59 Squadrons on Army Co-operation and Coastal Command duties and, in its Mk.IVF version, with thirteen fighter squadrons.

One Blenheim was fitted with a fixed nosewheel undercarriage for taxying tests, but did not fly in this form. This was part of an investigation into tricycle undercarriages in connection with the Type 155 design in 1938, to meet specification B.18/38. The Type 155 was not unlike the Beaufort in general design, the essence of the requirement being that it

should employ materials "not in general use" for aircraft construction, and be suitable for large-scale production by sub-contractors outside the aircraft industry. This design eventually formed the basis of the A.W.41 Albemarle later produced by A. W. Hawksley at Gloucester.

In January 1940, the Bristol company suggested, in the light of experience in France, that a specialised variant of the Blenheim could serve as a direct support bomber, having a new front fuselage with a battery of machine guns. The project envisaged alternative roles of interim fighter and dual-control trainer. The Air Staff thinking on this subject was outlined in specification B.6/40, and Bristol's ideas were then consolidated into a new machine, the Type 160, to meet this requirement. Responsibility for detail design of the Type 160 was delegated to Rootes Securities, a large-scale producer of Blenheims, and the name Bisley was selected for the new development. The principal difference from the Blenheim IV was the provision of a new nose section housing four 0.303-in. Browning machine guns with 1,000 r.p.g. An improved, armoured windscreen was provided, the cockpit was armoured, and a Bristol B.X dorsal turret, with two Brownings and a gyro gunsight, was installed. For the low-altitude close-support role, the Bisley was to have had a pair of Mercury XVI engines with cropped impellers and operating on 100 octane fuel.

Before the prototypes of this new design were completed, the specification was revised to include high-altitude bombing as an alternative role. This new demand was met, in the case of the Bisley, by the development of a new, interchangeable front fuselage, the high-altitude version having a bombardier's station with offset aiming panels, and a faired "bath" underneath to serve as a foot-well for the bombardier when navigating, and as a housing for a Frazer-Nash mounting carrying two Browning guns for rearward

The Blenheim V had a very short service life as its performance left much to be desired. It served in the Middle and Far East, but when Blenheim V-equipped units reached Italy losses were such that they were hurriedly re-equipped.

defence. The engines became Mercury XVs or XXVs and the gross weight was raised to 17,000 lb.

Two prototypes were built and the name Blenheim V had supplanted that of Bisley before either of these flew. The first Blenheim V prototype (AD657) with the ground-attack nose flew at Filton on February 24, 1941, and was followed by the second prototype (AD661) with the high-altitude nose. All production of the Blenheim V was undertaken by Rootes Securities Limited at Speke and Stoke-on-Trent, 940 machines being built in all. Deliveries of the Blenheim V three-seat high-altitude bomber with the semi-glazed unsymmetrical nose commenced in the summer of 1942, the two-seat close-support variant having been abandoned, and No. 18 Squadron was the first unit to receive the new equipment. This squadron, together with Nos. 13, 114, 244, 454 and 614, flew Blenheim Vs in the Middle East, and Nos. 11, 42, 113 and 211 employed the type in the Far East. First mention of the Blenheim V on operations was made in November 1942, when the Allied landings were proceeding in North Africa, and Acting Wing Commander H. G. Malcolm was awarded a posthumous Victoria Cross for his gallantry when leading a formation of No. 18 Squadron's Blenheim Vs during the following month. However, the service life of the Blenheim V was destined to be a short one, for the performance of the type left much to be desired, and with a loaded weight of 17,000 lb., the two 830 h.p. Mercury engines left the Blenheim V decidedly underpowered. Losses on operations were such that, on reaching Italy the squadrons equipped with this type were re-equipped with Martin Baltimores and Lockheed Venturas. Production ceased in June 1943, and the Blenheim V remained operational in the Far East until the end of that year.

Many Blenheim Vs were converted for use as dual-control trainers, being among the first R.A.F. aircraft to employ two-stage amber night simulation filters, and these were flown by Fighter Command operational training units. In 1942 a number of Blenheim Vs in the Middle East were transferred to the Turkish Air Force, and a number were received by the Portuguese Air Force which already operated several Blenheim IVs which had made forced landings in Portugal and been "interned".

While the exploits of the Blenheim during wartime operations were overshadowed by those of other types, this aircraft made a significant contribution to the development of the R.A.F. The Blenheim was one of a handful of types on which Bomber Command cut its teeth; with it the R.A.F. learned much of daylight operations over enemy territory which was to prove of inestimable value later in the war. Again, the Bristol company's experience in designing and building the Blenheim found expression in a whole series of successful types, such as the Beaufighter. Thus, the Blenheim, although not the most effective of weapons, is fully deserving of its place among the truly historic aircraft of the Second World War.

Bristol Blenheim IV

Dimensions:	Span, 56 ft. 4 in.; length, 42 ft. 7 in.; height, 9 ft. 10 in.; wing area, 469 sq. ft.
Armament:	One fixed forward-firing 0.303-in. Browning machine gun with 400 rounds; twin 0.303-in. Browning guns with 600 r.p.g. in B.I.Mk.IV dorsal turret, and two remotely-controlled Browning guns on rearward-firing Frazer-Nash mounting under the nose, with 1,000 r.p.g. Normal bomb capacity, 1,000 lb.
Power Plants:	Two Bristol Mercury XV nine-cylinder air-cooled radial engines rated at 905 h.p. at 2,750 r.p.m. for take-off, and (maximum for five minutes) 995 h.p. at 2,750 r.p.m. at 9,250 ft.
Weights:	Empty, 9,790 lb.; normal loaded, 13,500 lb.; maximum loaded, 14,400 lb.; normal service load, 3,710 lb.
Performance:	Maximum speed 266 m.p.h. at 11,800 ft., 259 m.p.h. at 15,000 ft.; initial climb rate, 1,500 ft./min.; time to 5,000 ft., 3.7 min., to 10,000 ft., 7.2 min.; service ceiling, 27,260 ft.; maximum range, 1,460 miles at 169 m.p.h.; normal cruising speed, 198 m.p.h.

The Boeing Model 299, progenitor of all Fortresses, was first flown on July 28, 1935, but destroyed three months later.

THE BOEING FORTRESS

Few other aircraft of the Second World War gained the universal affection of their aircrew over so long an operational period as did the Boeing B-17 Fortress, which formed the spearhead of the American bombing offensive in Europe from beginning to end, as well as serving in every other theatre of war. No single aircraft type contributed more to the defeat of the Luftwaffe, both in the air and on the ground, than the Fortress, which enabled tangible expression to be given to the controversial U.S. policy for the strategic assault of Germany by day in the face of formidable political argument as well as desperate enemy opposition.

A curious feature of the Fortress's history is that its reputation as the leading Allied day bomber was established despite its inferiority in many respects of performance compared with its combat contemporary, the B-24 Liberator, and the bomb load of U.S.A.A.F. Fortresses over Europe was usually no more than that carried by the diminutive de Havilland Mosquito. Far fewer Fortresses than Liberators were built, 12,677 Fortresses being accepted by the U.S.A.A.F. between July 1940 and August 1945, equipping a maximum of thirty-three overseas combat groups by August 1944. The Fortress achieved fame, however, on the strength of several outstanding attributes. Of these, perhaps the most important were an excellent high-altitude capability, and the ability to absorb an amazing amount of battle damage. To these attributes were added, in its later variants, an exceptionally heavy defensive armament, though the true combat potential of the Fortress was achieved only after a long period of gestation.

The Fortress's true beginnings can be traced to the early 'thirties when, in the perennial feud between the Army Air Corps and the Navy, the ascendancy of aircraft over surface vessels for coastal defence was grudgingly conceded. The Material Division of the Army Air Corps enthusiastically issued, in 1934, a requirement for a bomber with a range of 5,000 miles carrying a bombload of 2,000 lbs. at 200 m.p.h., as one of the first results of the new policy. Project "A", as this requirement was dubbed, was intended to produce an aircraft capable of reinforcing Hawaii, Panama, or Alaska without requiring intermediate servicing facilities. A development contract for this project was placed with the Boeing Airplane Company, which, under the leadership of Edward C. Wells, began designing a very large four-engined aircraft, the Model 294. A year later, the Army Air Corps was to order one prototype of this design under the designation XBLR-1 (later XB-15), and this was eventually to fly on October 15, 1937, becoming the largest military aircraft to have flown at that time.

While work was proceeding on the Model 294, in August 1934, the Army Air Corps announced a competition for a multi-engined bomber, and Boeing immediately initiated the design of a smaller, but still large by contemporary standards, bomber also powered by four engines. The majority of the world's air forces were equipped with twin-engined bombers, and other manufacturers entering designs in the Army Air Corps contest were proposing twin-engined machines. Thus, as the design was a purely speculative effort on the part of Boeing with no possibility of compensation in the event of the aircraft failing in the contest, the decision to produce a four-engined machine was a daring gamble. The full facilities of the company were immediately concentrated on the new project, construction of which commenced on August 16, 1934, under the designation Model 299.

Boeing had previously pioneered the forerunner of modern high-speed transport aircraft with retractable undercarriages in the form of the

A Boeing Y1B-17 (35-149), thirteen of which were ordered for service tests.

The Y1B-17 equipped the 2nd Bombardment Group of the G.H.Q. Air Force, the task of this unit being the development of operational techniques.

all-metal Model 247, and the new bomber might have been described as a direct aerodynamic and structural combination of the Model 247 transport and the Model 294 bomber. The same clean airframe formula and structural methods employed by the Model 247 were married to the basic arrangement of the Model 294, and the result was as beautifully proportioned a military aircraft as had been conceived anywhere in the world at that time. The design was based on a large wing spanning 103 ft. 9 in.—which, surprisingly, was only 8 ft. 3 in. greater than that of the twin-engined Douglas DB-1, the Boeing entry's most significant competitor—and featuring a relatively deep section at the root, blending with a clean, circular-section fuselage surmounted by a large, graceful tail assembly.

Powered by four 750 h.p. Pratt and Whitney Hornet R-1690-E nine-cylinder radial air-cooled engines, the B-299, as the prototype was officially known, rolled out of the factory bearing standard Army Air Corps insignia but, being a company-owned aircraft, also bearing the civil registration X-13372. It was imaginatively christened "Flying Fortress", a name which, as a registered trade-mark, was later to be applied to innumerable variants of the basic design. It carried eight crew members, and there were four blister-type defensive machine gun stations, all of which could accommodate a single manually-operated 0.3-in. or 0.5-in. gun, and a station for a fifth machine gun in the nose. Up to eight 600-lb. bombs could be housed internally, and loaded weight was 43,000 lb. The B-299—which was to be subsequently referred to as the "XB-17" although, in fact, it bore no military designation—was flown for the first time on July 28, 1935, at Seattle by L. R. Tower, and from the very beginning demonstrated the superiority of its conception. After a short period of factory testing, on August 20th it was flown to Wright Field for Army Air Corps evaluation, flying the 2,100 miles non-stop at an average speed of 232 m.p.h. It immediately began to prove itself capable of the specified performance of a maximum speed of 200–250 m.p.h. at 10,000 feet; an operating speed of 170–200 m.p.h. at the same altitude; a service ceiling of 20,000–25,000 feet, and an endurance

of 6–10 hours. Unfortunately, the full military potential of the B-299 had not been investigated when tests were tragically interrupted. On October 30, 1935, with Major P. P. Hill and Boeing's test pilot, Leslie R. Tower, at the controls, the aircraft stalled into the ground after a take-off with the controls inadvertently locked, and burned out.

Although the aircraft was officially found blameless for this accident, the Army Air Corps' plans to order sixty-five examples of the new bomber during 1936, instead of 185 other aircraft, were abandoned, and only the thirteen Y1B-17s ordered for evaluation on January 17, 1936, were proceeded with, together with an additional airframe ordered for static test purposes. Thus began a long struggle in which the future of the Fortress was often to be in the balance while the few proponents of strategic air power in the Army Air Corps sought to convince their tactically-minded compatriots and the U.S. naval staff of their far-sighted wisdom.

The evaluation batch of Y1B-17s (originally ordered as YB-17s but changed to Y1B-17s on November 20, 1936, to indicate that they were procured from "F-1" funds) were given the manufacturer's designation Model 299B, and were basically similar to the original B-299, apart from the installation of the 930 h.p. Wright Cyclone GR-1820-39 (G2) engine, a station for an additional crew member, and minor changes to the armament and undercarriage. The first Y1B-17 was flown on December 2, 1936, but the Army Air Corps' battle for strategic air power was not assisted when, five days later, the brakes of this aircraft fused on landing, and the Y1B-17 nosed over. Damage was not severe, but a Congressional enquiry was ordered. Nevertheless, the first Y1B-17 was delivered to the

The Y1B-17A (37-369) differed from the Y1B-17 in having turbo-superchargers.

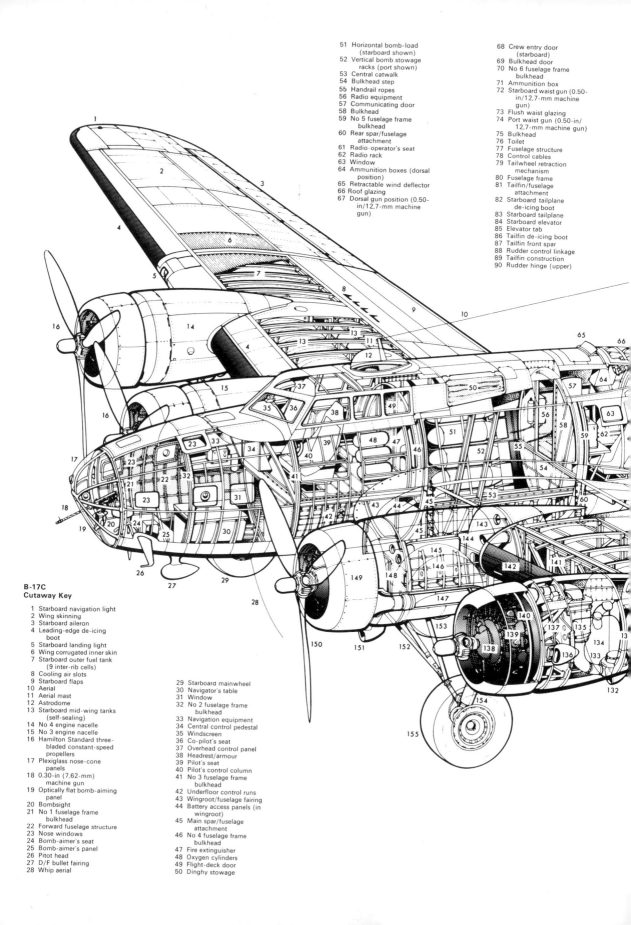

51 Horizontal bomb-load
(starboard shown)
52 Vertical bomb stowage
racks (port shown)
53 Central catwalk
54 Bulkhead step
55 Handrail ropes
56 Radio equipment
57 Communicating door
58 Bulkhead
59 No 5 fuselage frame/
bulkhead
60 Rear spar/fuselage
attachment
61 Radio-operator's seat
62 Radio rack
63 Window
64 Ammunition boxes (dorsal
position)
65 Retractable wind deflector
66 Roof glazing
67 Dorsal gun position (0.50-
in/12,7-mm machine
gun)

68 Crew entry door
(starboard)
69 Bulkhead door
70 No 6 fuselage frame
bulkhead
71 Ammunition box
72 Starboard waist gun (0.50-
in/12,7-mm machine
gun)
73 Flush waist glazing
74 Port waist gun (0.50-in/
12,7-mm machine gun)
75 Bulkhead
76 Toilet
77 Fuselage structure
78 Control cables
79 Tailwheel retraction
mechanism
80 Fuselage frame
81 Tailfin/fuselage
attachment
82 Starboard tailplane
de-icing boot
83 Starboard tailplane
84 Starboard elevator
85 Elevator tab
86 Tailfin de-icing boot
87 Tailfin front spar
88 Rudder control linkage
89 Tailfin construction
90 Rudder hinge (upper)

B-17C
Cutaway Key

1 Starboard navigation light
2 Wing skinning
3 Starboard aileron
4 Leading-edge de-icing
boot
5 Starboard landing light
6 Wing corrugated inner skin
7 Starboard outer fuel tank
(9 inter-rib cells)
8 Cooling air slots
9 Starboard flaps
10 Aerial
11 Aerial mast
12 Astrodome
13 Starboard mid-wing tanks
(self-sealing)
14 No 4 engine nacelle
15 No 3 engine nacelle
16 Hamilton Standard three-
bladed constant-speed
propellers
17 Plexiglass nose-cone
panels
18 0.30-in (7,62-mm)
machine gun
19 Optically flat bomb-aiming
panel
20 Bombsight
21 No 1 fuselage frame
bulkhead
22 Forward fuselage structure
23 Nose windows
24 Bomb-aimer's seat
25 Bomb-aimer's panel
26 Pitot head
27 D/F bullet fairing
28 Whip aerial

29 Starboard mainwheel
30 Navigator's table
31 Window
32 No 2 fuselage frame
bulkhead
33 Navigation equipment
34 Central control pedestal
35 Windscreen
36 Co-pilot's seat
37 Overhead control panel
38 Headrest/armour
39 Pilot's seat
40 Pilot's control column
41 No 3 fuselage frame
bulkhead
42 Underfloor control runs
43 Wingroot/fuselage fairing
44 Battery access panels (in
wingroot)
45 Main spar/fuselage
attachment
46 No 4 fuselage frame
bulkhead
47 Fire extinguisher
48 Oxygen cylinders
49 Flight-deck door
50 Dinghy stowage

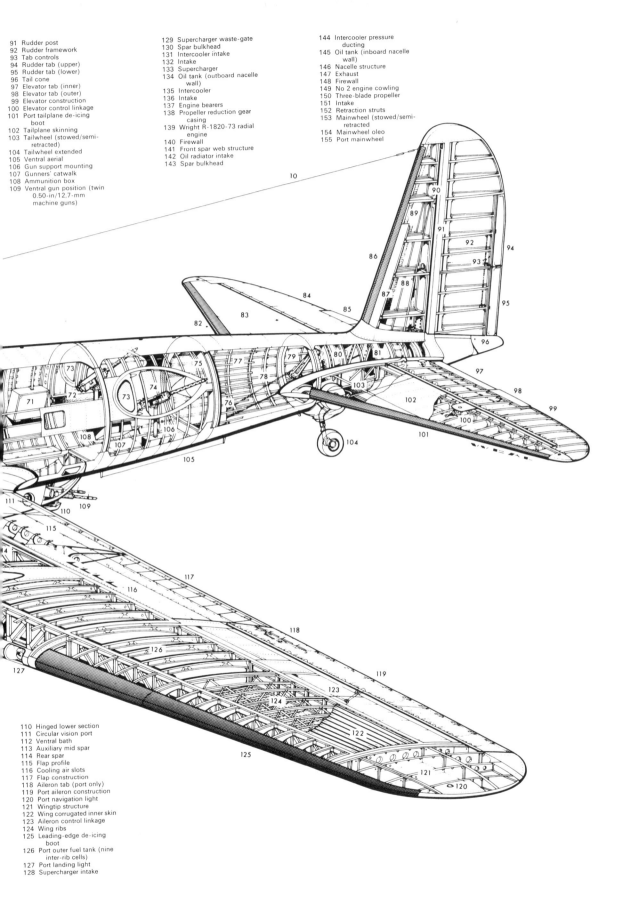

91 Rudder post
92 Rudder framework
93 Tab controls
94 Rudder tab (upper)
95 Rudder tab (lower)
96 Tail cone
97 Elevator tab (inner)
98 Elevator tab (outer)
99 Elevator construction
100 Elevator control linkage
101 Port tailplane de-icing boot
102 Tailplane skinning
103 Tailwheel (stowed/semi-retracted)
104 Tailwheel extended
105 Ventral aerial
106 Gun support mounting
107 Gunners' catwalk
108 Ammunition box
109 Ventral gun position (twin 0.50-in/12.7-mm machine guns)

129 Supercharger waste-gate
130 Spar bulkhead
131 Intercooler intake
132 Intake
133 Supercharger
134 Oil tank (outboard nacelle wall)
135 Intercooler
136 Intake
137 Engine bearers
138 Propeller reduction gear casing
139 Wright R-1820-73 radial engine
140 Firewall
141 Front spar web structure
142 Oil radiator intake
143 Spar bulkhead

144 Intercooler pressure ducting
145 Oil tank (inboard nacelle wall)
146 Nacelle structure
147 Exhaust
148 Firewall
149 No 2 engine cowling
150 Three-blade propeller
151 Intake
152 Retraction struts
153 Mainwheel (stowed/semi-retracted)
154 Mainwheel oleo
155 Port mainwheel

110 Hinged lower section
111 Circular vision port
112 Ventral bath
113 Auxiliary mid spar
114 Rear spar
115 Flap profile
116 Cooling air slots
117 Flap construction
118 Aileron tab (port only)
119 Port aileron construction
120 Port navigation light
121 Wingtip structure
122 Wing corrugated inner skin
123 Aileron control linkage
124 Wing ribs
125 Leading-edge de-icing boot
126 Port outer fuel tank (nine inter-rib cells)
127 Port landing light
128 Supercharger intake

The initial production model of the Fortress, the B-17B, was the first model to equip an operational unit of the U.S.A.A.C.

Army Air Corps at Langley Field, Virginia, on March 1, 1937, followed by a further eleven to equip the 2nd Bombardment Group of the G.H.Q. Air Force, under Lt. Col. Robert Olds. The equipping of this Group was completed by August 5, 1937, while the remaining Y1B-17 was sent to Wright Field for development testing.

The task of the Group was to develop operational techniques for long-range bombing missions, starting virtually from scratch, and simultaneously prove the weapon upon which many of the Army Air Corps' hopes for the future were pinned. The Fortresses operated over the entire United States in fulfilling this task, under all weather conditions, and in February 1938, six aircraft from the 2nd Bombardment Group left Miami, Florida, on a remarkable goodwill flight to Buenos Aires for the inauguration of the Argentine President. This provided an excellent opportunity to practise long-range navigation and flight procedures, and the Y1B-17s made only one stop, at Lima, Peru, on the 5,000-mile outward leg. Many other records, including an east-west flight across the United States in twelve hours fifty minutes, and a west-east crossing in ten hours forty-six minutes, were established by the 2nd Bombardment Group with its Y1B-17s.

The nucleus of strategic air power in the Army Air Corps was the G.H.Q. Air Force, and in 1936 it had been planned to have at least two B-17 groups, one on each of the east and west coasts, within this organisation. As a follow-up, a further fifty B-17s were to be procured for 1938, together with eleven Project "A" aircraft for development purposes. The U.S. Navy had disputed the need for these aircraft as duplicating their carrier-borne forces, and the Army considered that its tactical needs would be best served by large

numbers of the twin-engined Douglas B-18 bombers. General Andrews, the commander of the G.H.Q. Air Force, recommended in 1937, however, that his bombardment groups should be entirely equipped with four-engined bombers such as the B-17, but a further setback was suffered by the protagonists of strategic air power following the interception of the Italian liner *Rex* by three Y1B-17s of the 2nd Bombardment Group when the vessel was 725 miles east of New York. Such was the indignant reaction of the U.S. Navy, that the Army Chief of Staff verbally agreed to restrict all Army Air Corps coastal defence missions to within one hundred miles of the American seaboard. As an additional blow to the strategic school, in 1938, the Secretary of War directed the Army Air Corps in its plans for 1940 to procure only light, medium and attack bombers!

The Munich crisis provided the turning point in the fortunes of the Fortress, and while plans were hurriedly drafted to provide an overall increase in the striking power of the Army Air Corps, development of the Fortress was accelerated, although large-scale production was destined not to get under way until just before the United States' entry into World War II. The twelve Y1B-17s of the 2nd Bombardment Group had flown 9,293 hours, or some 1,800,000 miles, without serious accident, and provided a vast amount of invaluable information. Because of their success, and the fact that one of them had successfully survived an inadvertent spin, the Y1B-17 airframe originally ordered as a non-flying article for static tests was assigned instead to special flight trials under the designation Y1B-17A, or Model 299F. Flown for the first time on April 29, 1938, the Y1B-17A was fitted with Moss/General Electric turbo-superchargers to its Cyclone GR-1820-51 (G5) engines.

The B-17C Fortress had an increased gross weight and more powerful engines.

These were initially mounted flat on top of each engine but subsequently located beneath the engine nacelles, and the aircraft, which was delivered to the Army Air Corps on January 31, 1939, raised the operational ceiling of the Fortress well above 30,000 ft. Its maximum speed was 311 m.p.h. (as compared with 256 m.p.h. for the Y1B-17), and the Y1B-17A established a load-carrying record by carrying 11,000 lb. over a distance of 620 miles at an average speed of 238 m.p.h. Normally, the bomb load was

Twenty B-17Cs were delivered to the R.A.F. as the Fortress I, being operated by No. 90 Sqdn. The photo depicts the ninth Fortress I (AN526).

restricted to a very much smaller figure in order that sufficient fuel could be carried for long operating ranges. Representative figures were an overall range of 1,500 miles carrying a 2,400-lb. bomb load.

The Y1B-17s were redesignated as B-17s after the completion of the service test period, and the Y1B-17A became plain B-17A. In the meantime, orders had been placed for thirty-nine production Fortresses which were originally designated Model 299E by the manufacturer but later redesignated Model 299M. The Army Air Corps designation for this first production model was B-17B, the first aircraft of this type flying on June 27, 1939. Externally, the B-17B differed little from the Y1B-17, apart from the replacement of the original transparent nose cone incorporating a bubble-mounted machine gun by a new Plexiglas fairing; a revised rudder of increased area, and larger flaps. In place of the ventral cut-out below the nose where the bomb-aiming panel of the Y1B-17 had been located, the B-17B had an optical flat in the revised nose fairing over which the famous Norden bombsight was mounted. This piece of equipment, which was a gyro-stabilised sight later linked with the auto-pilot through automatic flight control equipment, was to receive much publicity during the early days of World War II. This was partly due to its alleged ability to place a bomb in a pickle-barrel from 30,000 ft., but primarily because it was installed, carefully covered, in the aircraft only immediately before take-off and removed after landing, always under the supervision of an armed guard.

Major internal changes in the B-17B were the relocation of crew positions and a change from pneumatic to hydraulic brakes, and this was the first version of the Fortress to equip an operational unit of the Army Air Corps, all thirty-nine B-17Bs being delivered between July 29, 1939, and March 30, 1940. As part of the Thirtieth Anniversary Celebrations of the Air Corps, a number of record-breaking flights were made by Fortresses, including a non-stop flight by a B-17B from Burbank, California, to New York in nine hours fourteen minutes at 265 m.p.h., and in November 1939 seven Fortresses flew from Langley Field to Rio de Janiero, Brazil, on a goodwill and training mission.

With an order for a further thirty-eight Fortresses in 1939, production gradually gathered momentum. The new order was for the improved Model 299H, or B-17C, in which the gun blisters were removed from the fuselage sides and the ventral blister was supplanted by an extended "bath". The nose gun was replaced by two guns in side windows, twin 0.5-in. guns were mounted in both dorsal and ventral positions, self-sealing fuel tanks were installed, and armour protection was provided for the crew. Loaded weight was increased to 49,650 lb., and 1,200 h.p. Cyclone GR-1820-65 (G-205A) engines were fitted. The first B-17C flew on July 21, 1940, but prior to this date, a further forty-two Fortresses had been ordered. These were of the B-17D version, which could be distinguished from its immediate predecessor only by its cowling flaps. Some revisions were made to the electrical system, and provision was made for an additional crew member.

When war commenced in Europe in September 1939, the Army Air Corps possessed only twenty-three Fortresses in service, and of all this force's equipment at that time, only the Fortress was to be considered as a first line aircraft after Pearl Harbour. Fifty-three Fortresses were delivered in 1940, and in the spring of 1941 twenty B-17C Fortresses were allocated to Britain under Lease-Lend. Known to the manufacturers as the Model 299T, and dubbed Fortress I by the R.A.F., the B-17Cs equipped No. 90 Squadron at West Raynham in May 1941 and, although the U.S. government understood that they were to be employed for training purposes, the Fortresses began operational sorties on July 8, 1941.

The twenty Fortress Is had all but the single nose gun replaced by 0.5-in. Browning guns, and self-sealing fuel tanks were installed. The R.A.F. intended to utilise the high-altitude capabilities of the B-17C to evade enemy fighters during daylight missions, but the aircraft were destined to be dogged by ill fortune. After the first Fortress I had wiped off its undercarriage when landing in England, a second was lost after returning from an early operational sortie over Brest, disintegrating on touch-down as a result of battle damage. The first Fortress I was cannibalised for spares, and a third was accidentally burned on the ground. An operational sortie was made by three Fortresses against Oslo, Norway, and all three were destroyed by German fighters. A seventh Fortress was lost during a high-altitude test, and an eighth appeared in a vertical dive from cloud and went straight into the ground. The first sortie with Fortress

49

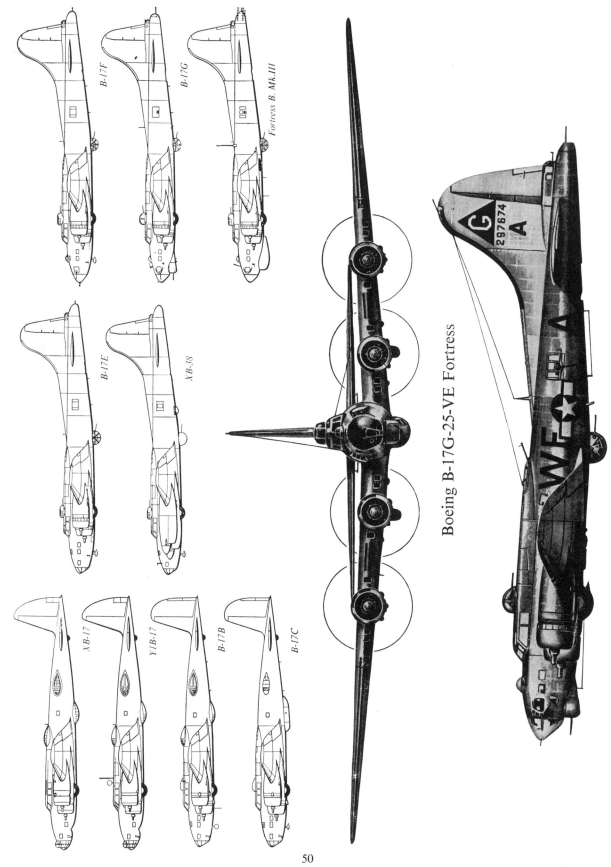

B-17F

B-17G

Fortress B. Mk.III

B-17E

XB-38

XB-17

YIB-17

B-17B

B-17C

Boeing B-17G-25-VE Fortress

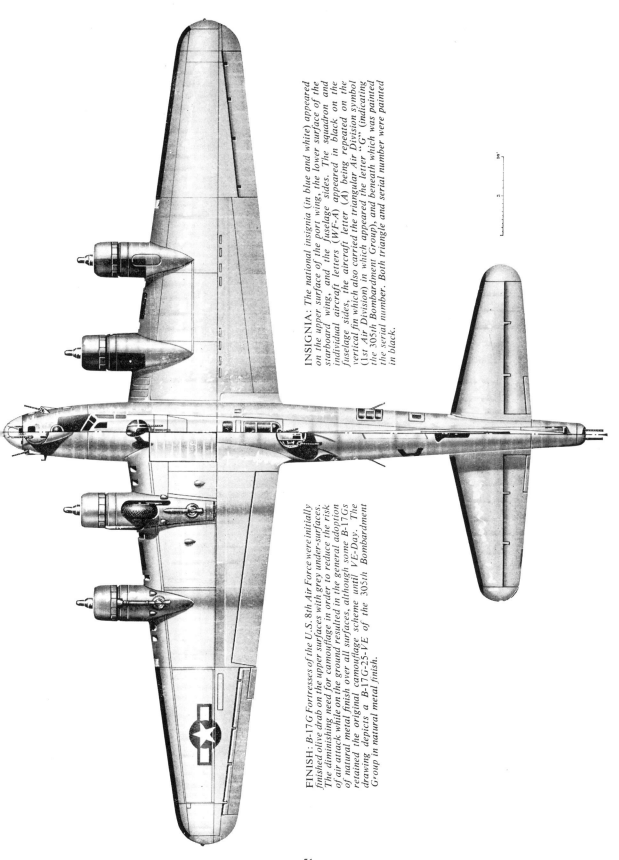

INSIGNIA: The national insignia (in blue and white) appeared on the upper surface of the port wing, the lower surface of the starboard wing, and the fuselage sides. The squadron and individual aircraft letters (WF-A) appeared in black on the fuselage sides, the aircraft letter (A) being repeated on the vertical fin which also carried the triangular Air Division symbol (1st Air Division) in which appeared the letter "G" (indicating the 305th Bombardment Group), and beneath which was painted the serial number. Both triangle and serial number were painted in black.

FINISH: B-17G Fortresses of the U.S. 8th Air Force were initially finished olive drab on the upper surfaces with grey under-surfaces. The diminishing need for camouflage in order to reduce the risk of air attack while on the ground resulted in the general adoption of natural metal finish over all surfaces, although some B-17Gs retained the original camouflage scheme until V-E Day. The drawing depicts a B-17G-25-VE of the 305th Bombardment Group in natural metal finish.

51

(*Above*) *The 207th production B-17E (41-2599), and* (*left*) *the first production B-17E (41-2393).*

Is had been flown from Polebrook on July 8, 1941, against Wilhelmshaven, and by September they had completed twenty-two attacks, including Bremen, Brest, Emden, Kiel, Oslo and Rotterdam, but from the earliest days numerous mechanical failures had been suffered, the guns had a tendency to freeze up at altitude, and the defensive armament was patently inadequate. Thus, European operations were abandoned. Four of the Fortress Is were sent to the Middle East, where, until May 1942, they undertook night attacks against Benghazi and Tobruk. In October 1941, the few remaining Fortress Is in Europe were transferred to R.A.F. Coastal Command, operating with Nos. 206 and 220 squadrons from Benbecula on maritime reconnaissance. One Fortress I, however, found its way to India in July 1942, and was there taken over by the U.S.A.A.F.

In the meantime, the Army Air Corps had converted its B-17Cs to B-17D standards by the revision of the electric system, and the installation of self-sealing tanks, more extensive armour, etc., and most of the B-17Ds went to equip the 19th Bombardment Group in the Philippines. Thirty-five Fortresses were stationed on Clark and Del Monte Fields from May 1941, and more than half of these were destroyed on the ground at the former base during the initial Japanese attack on December 8,1941. The remainder, with spares cannibalized from damaged aircraft, fought a valiant rearguard action, bombing Japanese shipping and other targets from Mindanao, Java, and finally Australia, until the sole survivor, the famous "Swoose" (40-3097), was withdrawn to the U.S.A. early in 1942.

The B-17D Fortress displayed a number of weaknesses when opposed by Japanese Zero-Sen fighters,

as had also the R.A.F.'s Fortress Is when opposed by Luftwaffe fighters some time earlier, and it was soon obvious that insofar as defensive armament was concerned the bomber failed to live up to its popular name. Although it must be admitted that the name was intended to convey the machine's original task of defending American shores as flying "artillery batteries" rather than indicate particularly heavy defensive armament. An extensive redesign programme destined to rectify the bomber's operational failings had already been initiated, however, in conjunction with wide scale plans for mass production, and the result was the radically altered B-17E, or Model 299O. Aesthetically, the B-17E was a retrograde step, but militarily it was to turn a relative failure into a remarkable success.

While structural details and general layout of the B-17E were similar to those of earlier Fortresses, a completely new empennage was fitted, with an extended dorsal fin and wider span tailplane, for greater stability and, therefore, better accuracy in high-altitude bombing. Earlier Fortresses had suffered a notable blind spot at the tail, a shortcoming that had been quickly seized upon by opposing fighters, and the depth of the rear fuselage of the B-17E was substantially increased and a manually-operated turret housing twin 0.5-in. guns placed in the extreme tail. Except in the nose, where two 0.3-in. guns were provided on socket mountings, the smaller calibre guns were supplanted throughout by "point-fives". Two of these were mounted in a Bendix electrically-operated turret positioned immediately aft of the flight deck. Provision was made for two machine guns firing upward from the radio compartment, a single 0.5-in. gun was mounted behind each of two rectangular apertures with removable windows in the waist of the fuselage, and a power-operated turret was mounted ventrally, just aft of the wing. This was remotely-controlled from a periscopic position below the waist hatches, but this soon gave place to the unique Sperry ball turret, the gunner actually aiming the guns from inside the turret. Ball-turret gunners had to be small

52

A B-17F-70-BO (42-29807) of the 305th Bombardment Group, 40th Combat Wing of the U.S. Eighth Air Force.

men for obvious reasons. The net result was a truly formidable array of defensive power. The standard crew was increased from nine to ten members, and at 54,000 lb. all-up weight, the B-17E was seven U.S. tons heavier than the original B-299. It was forty per cent faster than the precursor of all Fortresses, and although powered by the same engines as the B-17D, it was very little slower than its immediate predecessor, with a maximum speed of 317 m.p.h.

The first B-17E flew on September 5, 1941, and a production run of 512 machines had been embarked upon. The U.S. Army Air Force (which had changed its name from U.S. Army Air Corps on June 20, 1941, as part of a new and more autonomous system of organisation) now encouraged the organisation of a manufacturing pool whereby the Boeing, Vega and Douglas companies would all manufacture the B-17E, although, in fact, by the time the plan reached fruition, the later B-17F was ready for production, this becoming the first model to be manufactured jointly by the three companies. The main Boeing facility at Seattle was augmented by another large factory in Wichita, while a new plant of the Douglas company at Long Beach was opened specifically for Fortress production. Fortresses built by Boeing, Douglas and Vega received suffixes to their basic designations in order to identify the actual manufacturer, these being B-17F-BO, B-17F-DL (Douglas-built Fortresses produced at Santa Monica were designated B-17F-DO in order to differentiate them from the Long Beach-built machines), and B-17F-VE respectively. When production of the Fortress terminated in May 1945, of the 12,726 built, 5,745 had been built by Douglas and Vega.

Owing to the exigencies of war, most of the B-17E Fortresses were sent overseas immediately on entering service, some reinforcing the Pacific theatre to which the 7th Bombardment Group had flown in December 1941, and others being flown across the North Atlantic to Britain. Immediately the first six B-17E Fortresses arrived in Java, in January 1942, they were sent on a mission to attack an approaching Japanese invasion fleet which they severely mauled. They also succeeded in inflicting casualties on opposing Zero-Sen fighters which had not previously encountered Fortresses with tail armament and persisted in making stern attacks. The B-17Es experienced some trouble, however, with the periscopic ventral turret which was soon to be replaced by the ball turret.

While the Fortresses fought a retreating war in the Pacific, the foundations of the American daylight offensive in Europe were being laid with the formation of the Eighth Air Force in the United Kingdom. The Fortress was to be its primary equipment, the first arriving at Prestwick on July 1, 1942, but reliance was placed on the formation firepower of unescorted Fortresses flying at high altitude for defence against

(Immediately below) A Fortress IIA (FK185) employed as a test-bed for the Bristol B.16 nose turret mounting a 40-mm. Vickers "S" gun. (Bottom) A B-17F-95-BO (42-30243) with external racks for two 4,000-lb. bombs.

THE BOEING FORTRESS

opposing enemy fighters. In August 1942, plans were agreed between the Eighth Air Force and the R.A.F. for a co-ordinated day and night non-stop bomber offensive, and on the 17th of that month the Americans launched their part of the programme. Twelve B-17Es, including 41-9023 "Yankee Doodle" carrying Brig. Gen. Ira Eaker (founder of the Eighth Air Force), of the 97th Bombardment Group flew to attack the marshalling yards at Rouen-Sotteville in France, while another six flew a diversionary sweep. The formation was escorted by Spitfires and sustained no losses, and only two Fortresses were missing from the next ten operations. Deteriorating weather and mounting opposition had begun to change the picture, however, when the North African campaign diverted a large part of the Eighth Air Force strength, with the result that Fortresses converged on Egypt from the United Kingdom, India and the U.S.A. to assist in the battle against Rommel. Fortress groups continued to operate in the Middle East, and then from Sicily and Italy.

Forty-five Boeing-built B-17Es were supplied to the R.A.F. in mid-1942, and operated by Coastal Command as the Fortress IIA. One of these (FK185) was experimentally adapted to mount a Bristol B.16 nose turret in place of the normal transparent fairing. This turret housed a 40-mm. Vickers "S" gun which was remotely-controlled from a sighting station beneath. The turret had a traverse of 30° in azimuth and 40° in elevation, and was intended for use against surfaced submarines. The Fortress IIA first entered service with No.59 Squadron at Thorney Island in August 1942, and assisted other Coastal Command aircraft in closing the Atlantic Gap. A few Fortress IIAs also served with Bomber Command.

Less well-known variants of the B-17E included the XC-108 (41-2593) which was converted for use by General Douglas MacArthur in 1943 as a special personnel transport. With Cyclone GR-1820-97 engines, the XC-108 was stripped of all armour and armament, except the nose and tail guns, and could carry up to thirty-eight people within its 48,726-lb. gross weight. Extra windows were installed, and the interior was arranged with office and living space. Another B-17E (41-2595) was modified to carry a heavy freight load as the XC-108A, and was intended to test the feasibility of converting obsolescent bombers as freighters. A large cargo door was cut in the port side of the fuselage, and gross weight was increased to 49,000 lb.

One B-17E (41-2401) was experimentally fitted with four Allison V-1710-89 twelve-cylinder liquid-cooled inline engines each rated at 1,425 h.p., the conversion being undertaken by the Vega company as the XB-38. With the new engines installed, this aircraft flew for the first time on May 19, 1943, and the increased power available raised the maximum speed of the XB-38 to 327 m.p.h., while the gross weight was increased to 58,000 lbs. The basic airframe remained the same as that of the B-17E, apart from slight revisions necessitated by the installation of the new power plants. A full comparison of the XB-38 with the standard B-17E could not be made for, as a result of an engine fire which could not be extinguished, the prototype was destroyed on June 16, 1943, and as the Allison engines were in great demand for the P-38 Lightning and P-40 Warhawk fighters, work on two additional XB-38 conversions was cancelled.

In April 1942, the Model 299P, or B-17F, was introduced onto the production lines, and outwardly this variant differed from the B-17E only in having an extended Plexiglas nose which was frameless except for the optically flat bomb-aiming panel, paddle-blade airscrews for maximum operating performance under tropical conditions, and some revision of the engine cowlings to incorporate dust filters and to allow the feathering of the wider airscrew blades. The B-17F did, however, incorporate more than four hundred design modifications to improve its fighting efficiency. Self-sealing oil tanks were introduced, additional electrical power sources were provided, changes were made in control settings, and, in later production batches, the Cyclone GR-1820-97 engine with a "war emergency" rating of 1,380 h.p. at 25,000 ft. was installed, and extra fuel cells, known as "Tokyo Tanks", were fitted in the wings. Improvements were also made in the bomb stowage, brake system, communications equipment and oxygen system. Some models had a single 0.5-in. gun in a cheek mounting on each side of the nose. As the gross weight was

Originally the ninth production B-17E, this aircraft was experimentally fitted with four 1,425 h.p. Allison V-1710-89 liquid-cooled engines in 1943, and redesignated XB-38.

One of the forty-five B-17Es supplied to the R.A.F. as the Fortress IIA. The aircraft illustrated is FK212 of No. 1435 Flight, R.A.F. Coastal Command.

increased by 2,000 lb. over that of the B-17E to a normal maximum of 56,000 lb., the undercarriage was strengthened, and the war overload weight initially became 65,000 lb. This was later increased to a formidable 72,000 lb. Nineteen B-17Fs were supplied to the R.A.F., most of these being operated by Coastal Command as Fortress IIs. These were withdrawn from operations from 1944 onwards and used as crew trainers or for meteorological reconnaissance duties with Nos. 251, 517, 519 and 521 (Met.) squadrons.

Owing to the constant modifications being applied to aircraft on the production lines and the immense scale of production orders, a system of "Block Designations" was instituted, and this system was first applied with Fortress models to the B-17F. Thus, the first Boeing-built B-17F Fortresses became B-17F-1-BO, and all aircraft in this production block were identical insofar as equipment and installations were concerned. Blocks B-17F-5-BO, -10-BO, etc., followed, the intervening numbers being left to indicate subsequent changes made at modification centres. Production of the B-17F continued for fifteen months, during which 2,300 were built by Boeing, 600 by Douglas and 500 by Vega. The B-17Fs produced by the three companies differed slightly in internal details, particularly in armament, but the most commonly used initial arrangement comprised one 0.3-in. gun with 500 rounds in the nose; two 0.5-in. guns with 300 r.p.g. in the waist; two 0.5-in. guns with 400 r.p.g. in the dorsal turret; two 0.5-in. with 500 r.p.g. in the ball turret; and two 0.5-in. guns with 565 r.p.g. in the tail. The maximum bomb load of the first B-17Fs was 9,600 lb. but on typical missions to Germany, Eighth Air Force Fortresses carried 4,000-5,000 lb. over operating ranges averaging 1,400 miles. Beyond these distances, the bomb load fell rapidly, so that the effective combat radius of the B-17F was about a maximum of 800 miles.

Later modifications already referred to increased the fuel capacity of the B-17F from 2,550 to 3,630 U.S. gallons, and later aircraft (B-17F-30 to -130-BO, B-17F-20 to -65-DL, and B-17F-20 to -50-VE) had external racks under the inner wings for the carriage of two 4,000-lb. bombs, bringing the maximum short-range load to 17,600 lb. Under certain conditions, it became possible to carry eight 1,600-lb. armour-piercing bombs internally and two 4,000-lb. bombs externally, raising the total bomb load to 20,800 lb. With this load, all manoeuvres were restricted, and the effective range became extremely small. External bombs were, therefore, very seldom carried, and although all subsequent models had lugs and controls for their attachment, the racks beneath the wings were not installed at the factories.

With the U.S.A.A.F., the B-17F enabled an immense striking force to be built up in the European Theatre of Operations, and after a hard winter gaining experience against short-range targets, the Eighth Air Force began penetrating Germany with an initial mission against Wilhelmshaven on January 27, 1943. The Luftwaffe concentrated an ever-increasing fighter force against the American daylight offensive, and the bombers were repeatedly engaged in vicious air battles. These involved losses which frequently rose above ten per cent, particularly on operations outside the limited radius of A.A.F. and

(*Above and left*) *Originally the second B-17F-1-BO (41-24341), this aircraft was converted by Lockheed-Vega as the XB-40 experimental long-range escort fighter. Twenty B-17F Fortresses were converted as YB-40s for operational evaluation but proved unsuccessful.*

R.A.F. escort fighters. As the majority of the Eighth Air Force's B-24 Liberators were operating in the Middle East, the Fortress constituted nearly all the American formations flying from the United Kingdom. For the maximum defensive power, the Fortresses flew in tight formations known as combat boxes, each of about eighteen aircraft, and two or three such boxes were stacked vertically into a combat wing.

In the Allied Combined Bomber Offensive, the Eighth Air Force was given the initial objectives of the German aircraft, ballbearing, and oil industries, for precision attack in direct contrast with the R.A.F.'s area bombing. One of the most spectacular but costly formation operations performed by Fortresses was an early attack on targets at Regensburg, Wiener Neustadt, and Schweinfurt. The force attacked these targets in succession on August 17, 1943, 146 aircraft making the deep penetration to Regensburg before flying on to bases in Algeria, while three-and-a-half hours later, delayed by bad weather, 230 Fortresses took-off for the other targets. Of the first wave, twenty-four bombers were shot down while thirty-six were lost on the later mission. Although heavy damage was inflicted on the enemy, a week of such operations would have wiped out the Eighth Air Force. On a second Schweinfurt mission, sixty of 291 Fortresses were lost, and Luftwaffe fighters proved the vulnerability of unescorted bomber formations. The German tactics consisted of breaking up the American formations by long-range attacks with heavy rocket projectiles, and then shooting down isolated bombers piecemeal. The Luftwaffe soon discovered that head-on attacks against the B-17F were the most effective, there being the least defence from that quarter, and many modifications or "lash-ups" were made in the field to provide the Fortress with additional nose armament. Later production batches (including the B-17F-70 to 130-BO, the B-17F-35 to 65-DL, and the

B-17F-35 to 50-VE) had additional mountings for hand-held machine guns in "cheek" installations.

Many means of improving the defensive capabilities of the Fortress formations were considered, and a Boeing-built B-17F (41-24341) was converted by Vega as an experimental bomber escort under the designation XB-40. A power-operated turret with two additional 0.5-in. machine guns was installed in the roof aft of the radio compartment from which it was controlled. Additional armour was fitted and, instead of bombs, the bomb bays served as containers for a large quantity of ammunition. Twin 0.5-in. guns replaced the single guns in the waist positions, and a twin-gun "chin" turret, similar to that later standardised for the B-17G, was fitted. The normal ammunition load was increased by more than fifty per cent. Twenty Vega-built B-17Fs were converted as YB-40s to evaluate the escort bomber concept in combat, and these saw brief operational service over Europe in mid-1943. The armament of the YB-40s apparently varied, but it was considerably heavier than that of the XB-40, and several reports indicate the installation in the extreme nose and tail of power-operated turrets each containing four 0.5-in. guns. The total armament was reportedly as high as thirty automatic weapons of various calibres, ranging from 0.5-in. to 20-mm. and even 40-mm. cannon in multiple hand-held installations in the waist, plus additional power-operated turrets above and below the fuselage. The first Eighth Air Force sortie to be accompanied by YB-40s was undertaken in May 1943 against St. Nazaire but on later missions these heavily laden aircraft proved incapable of keeping up with the normal B-17Fs in climb and combat cruise. By August 1943 the YB-40 was recognised as a failure, and the remaining aircraft were reconverted as bombers or employed as gunnery trainers in the U.S.A. The YB-40 weighed 63,500 lb. and achieved 285 m.p.h.

The large-scale arrival of B-17Fs in the United Kingdom enabled the Eighth Air Force to continue a steady expansion towards the end of 1943, and to maintain the tempo of operations in the bad weather of that winter, a number of Fortresses were fitted with H2X radar (also known as "Mickey" or B.T.O.—Bombing-Thru-Overcast) in place of the ball turret. These aircraft acted as pathfinders, indicating bomb release points by visual signals. The daylight bombing offensive was further accelerated on January 1, 1944, by the formation of the U.S. Strategic Air Forces in Europe, combining the operations of the Eighth Air Force from the United Kingdom and the Fifteenth Air Force from Italy.

A slightly unusual operation began in the summer of 1944, with the launching by the Eighth Air Force of Project "Castor", otherwise known as Project "Perilous". Some of the more elderly B-17Es and Fs categorised as "war-weary" were stripped of all but the minimum equipment necessary for flight as radio-controlled bombs and redesignated BQ-7. The aircraft were packed with ten tons of Torpex, a British explosive possessing 50 per cent greater effect than amatol, and provided with a pilot and radio operator whose job after take-off was to set the controls and arm the warload. The crew then had to bale out before crossing the English coast, leaving the crewless BQ-7 under the radio-control of an accompanying Fortress which directed the flying bomb onto a selected target. About twenty-five Fortresses were used by the 3rd Air Division under this project, which declined suddenly in popularity in August 1944 after a crewless BQ-7 Fortress got out of control and crashed in an East Anglian wood. The resultant crater was roughly a hundred feet in diameter, and when another "Perilous" BQ-7 decided to circle a British industrial area for some time on its own initiative before flying out to sea, the project was abandoned as being a little *too* perilous.

One B-17F-40-VE (42-6036) was converted as a V.I.P. transport under the designation YC-108, and when a shortage of transport planes suitable for carrying fuel over the "Hump" from Burma to China arose in 1943, a Boeing-built B-17F (42-30190) was converted as a fuel tanker with a gross weight of 52,000 lb. under the designation XC-108B. One B-17F was transferred to the U.S. Navy, although no naval designation was applied to this aircraft, and sixteen B-17Fs were converted as long-range photo-reconnaissance aircraft under the designation F-9. These had tri-metragon cameras installed in the nose, and other cameras in the bomb bay and aft fuselage. These were converted by the United Air Lines Modification Center at Cheyenne, Ohio, in 1942. The F-9A differed slightly in the type and arrangement of the cameras installed, and they were redesignated F-9B after additional camera changes. Altogether, sixty-one B-17Fs were converted to F-9 standards, but were used to a relatively limited extent.

To improve defence against head-on fighter attacks, another modification was introduced onto the Fortress production lines in July 1943, in the form of a power-operated Bendix "chin" turret mounting two 0.5-in. machine guns and similar to that first used on the XB-40. Together with other modifications, the "chin" turret resulted in the B-17G, the last and most extensively produced version of the Fortress. When production terminated in 1945, a total of 4,035 B-17G Fortresses had been built by Boeing, 2,395 by Douglas and 2,250 by Vega. The B-17Gs built by these companies differed slightly in their internal equipment and in the precise location of the waist guns which were permanently enclosed for the first time in this model, instead of being mounted behind removable hatches.

With the two "cheek" guns sharing 610 rounds of ammunition, and the "chin" turret with 365 rounds, the total armament of the B-17G was thirteen 0.5-in. machine guns, although on the last production batches (B-17G-105 and -110-BO, B-17G-75 to -85-DL, and B-17G-85 to -110-VE), the radio compartment machine gun was not fitted. The number of rounds for the waist guns was doubled from 300 r.p.g., and the later variants also incorporated the so-called "Cheyenne" tail gun mounting modifications. This gave the twin "fifties" an improved field of fire in the B-17G-90-BO, -50-DL, -55-VE and subsequent batches which also had a reflector gunsight instead of the former ring and bead. With this mounting, the later B-17Gs had a length of 74 ft. 4 in., a decrease of 5 in. over earlier models. With other modifications, this mounting was installed in the field, at service bases in the United Kingdom and Italy, where a few B-17Fs were also fitted with the Bendix "chin" turret.

The B-17G Fortress entered service with the Eighth and Fifteenth Air Forces late in 1943, and eighty-five were also received by the R.A.F. as the Fortress III. The first thirty were Boeing-built and the remainder were Vega-built. Some of these were operated by Coastal Command and, in February 1944, the first Fortress IIIs equipped No. 214 Squadron of Bomber Command at Sculthorpe. These Bomber Command Fortress IIIs operated with No. 100 Group on special radio countermeasures missions, fitted with electronic devices to confuse and jam enemy radar. With No. 233 Squadron, the first Fortress III unit of Bomber Command, they later took part in clandestine operations from Tempsford and Oulton until the unit's disbandment in July 1945. Fortress IIIs also operated during R.A.F. Bomber Command's mass night attacks, being employed as decoys to confuse enemy night fighters, and also for dropping "window". The Fortress IIIs operated by R.A.F. Coastal Command usually carried twelve 400-lb. S.C.I. bombs or sixteen 250-lb. depth charges, and had the "cheek" mounted machine guns removed, while radar was fitted in place of the ball turret.

While the R.A.F. used B-17G Fortresses for special duties, it is a little-known fact that a Luftwaffe unit, the notorious I/K.G.200, also operated captured Fortresses for the ferrying, parachuting, and supply by air of secret agents. Wearing German insignia, the Fortresses were used with other Luftwaffe and captured Allied machines, especially for long-range operations. One of the first of these was in the spring of

A B-17G-25-VE Fortress of the 305th Bombardment Group. The B-17G employed the power-operated Bendix "chin" turret and was the last production model.

1944 in the Western Desert, and involved the construction and maintenance of a string of secret airstrips and fuel dumps. A captured Fortress was also used to parachute agents into Jordan in October 1944, and others were used in Europe. In German service, the Fortress was given the cover designation of Dornier Do 200.

Production of the B-17 reached its peak in March 1944, when 578 Fortresses were produced, but thereafter began to decline in favour of the B-29 Superfortress. The maximum number of Fortresses in service with the U.S.A.A.F. at any one time was in August 1944, when a total of 4,574 was on strength.

In the last production models of the B-17G, the former General Electric B-2 turbo-superchargers of the GR-1820-97 engines were replaced by an improved B-22 type raising the operating ceiling from 30,000 to 35,000 ft. Many B-17Gs were converted for other than bombing and were redesignated. Ten were converted for the photo-reconnaissance role under the designation F-9C, and forty B-17G Fortresses were transferred to the U.S. Navy and given the designation PB-1W. Fitted with radar in a massive belly housing, they were used for airborne early warning and anti-submarine duties, and sixteen of these were used by the U.S. Coast Guard as the PB-1G for patrol and search. Towards the end of the war, some 130 B-17Gs were converted to B-17H and TB-17H search-and-rescue aircraft, carrying an air-borne lifeboat under the fuselage for release by parachute.

The Fortress had dropped no less than 640,036 U.S. tons of bombs on European targets during the war years. This compares with 452,508 U.S. tons dropped by B-24 Liberators and 463,544 tons dropped by all other aircraft. According to records compiled by its manufacturers, the Fortress destroyed twenty-three enemy aircraft per thousand sorties as compared to eleven by B-24 Liberators, eleven by U.S. fighters, and three by all U.S. light and medium bombers. It has been established, however, that the very high claims of enemy aircraft "kills" were greatly exaggerated, largely because the same aircraft was often credited to all the gunners in the formation who had fired at it. Nevertheless, while there is no means of arriving at a true assessment of the number of "kills" scored by the Fortress, there can be no doubt that the total was formidable.

By its almost unrivalled period of first-line service, the Fortress proved itself one of the classic bomber designs of all time. Its performance proved a triumphant vindication of the principles of air strategy and bomber design established by a few far-sighted airmen and engineers in the U.S.A. long before World War II.

Boeing B-17G Fortress

Dimensions : Span, 103 ft. 9½ in.; length, 74 ft. 4 in.; height, 19 ft. 1 in.; wing area, 1,420 sq. ft.

Armament : Thirteen 0.5-in. Browning machine guns in chin, nose, dorsal, centre-fuselage, ventral, waist and tail positions, with a total of 5,770 rounds. Maximum short-range bomb load, 17,600 lb.

Power Plants : Four Wright Cyclone GR-1820-97 nine-cylinder air-cooled radial engines with General Electric B-22 exhaust-driven turbo-superchargers each developing 1,200 h.p. for take-off and 1,380 h.p. under war emergency conditions at 26,700 ft.

Weights : Empty, 32,720 lb.; equipped, 38,000 lb.; normal loaded, 55,000 lb.; maximum overload, 72,000 lb.

Performance : Maximum speed, 300 m.p.h. at 30,000 ft.; maximum continuous speed, 263 m.p.h. at 25,000 ft.; initial climb rate, 900 ft./min.; service ceiling, 35,000 ft.; range and endurance with a 4,000-lb. bomb load, 1,850 miles in 8.7 hours at 25,000 ft. (63,500 lb. a.u.w.) on 2,810 U.S. gal. of fuel.

One of the eighty-five B-17Gs supplied to the R.A.F. and operated as the Fortress G.R.III.

(Right) The prototype S.M.79 Sparviero, which appeared in 1935, differed little from the major production model, the S.M.79-II (above). The S.M.79-II was normally powered by three 1,000 h.p. Piaggio P.XI RC 40 engines, whereas the prototype had a trio of 780 h.p. Alfa Romeo 126 RC 34 engines.

THE SAVOIA-MARCHETTI SPARVIERO

The quality of Italian warplanes was subjected to much derision during the Second World War as a result of the propaganda of Italy's antagonists. Despite the numerous international records gained by Italian aircraft prior to the war, it was widely believed that the Regia Aeronautica's combat equipment fell far short of world standards. This belief had little foundation in fact, however, for although the Italian aircraft industry was to prove itself incapable of keeping pace with the Regia Aeronautica's attrition rate, and clung to production and constructional methods long discarded by other major aircraft industries, its designers produced sound military aircraft which, embodying excellent craftsmanship, bore comparison with the best extant.

One such machine was the Savoia-Marchetti S.M.79 Sparviero which, predominant among Italian bombing aircraft, was an extremely efficient machine and perhaps the most successful land-based torpedo-bomber of the war. To the Italian nation, the Sparviero was everything that the Spitfire was to the British and the Zero-Sen was to the Japanese. Many of Italy's most famed wartime pilots, such as Faggioni, Marini, Buscaglia, Di Bella, Cagna, Aramu, Farina, and Cipriani, were associated with the Sparviero, and the exploits of Italy's torpedo-bombing squadrons, equipped with this type, the Aerosiluranti, were almost legendary. Capable of absorbing a remarkable amount of battle damage, the S.M.79 was viewed with affection by its crews, and when the more modern S.M.84 began to appear, the crews were reluctant to transfer from the reliable Sparviero to the later type. The S.M.79 was the backbone of the Regia Aero-

nautica's offensive capability, and was produced in greater numbers than all other Italian multi-engined bombers combined.

Derived from the S.M.81 Pipistrello and designed by Alessandro Marchetti, the S.M.79 made its début late in 1934, ostensibly as an eight-passenger high-speed commercial aircraft. The first prototype, which bore the civil registration I-MAGO, possessed exceptionally sleek contours, despite its designer's sentimental regard for the three-engined arrangement considered out-dated in most other countries, and was powered initially by three 610 h.p. Piaggio Stella engines which, after initial tests, were replaced by a trio of Alfa Romeo 125 RC 35 nine-cylinder air-cooled

The S.M.79P was initially flown with Piaggio Stella engines (above), but these were soon supplanted by Alfa Romeo 125 RC 35s (below).

59

The S.M.79-1 was used operationally by Italy's Aviación Legionaria in the Spanish Civil War. This equipped the 8o and 111mo Stormi Bombardamento Veloce, and is illustrated above in Spanish Nationalist insignia.

4,410-lb. payload over a 1,000-km. closed-circuit at an average speed of 266 m.p.h., but by this time it was patently obvious that the S.M.79 was better suited for military use than to economical commercial operation, and the second prototype, which had emerged in 1935, had been completed as a medium bomber, quantity production of this version having already been initiated for the Regia Aeronautica. Commercial development of the basic design did, however, continue in parallel with the bomber, emerging in 1937 as the S.M.83.

As a bomber, the S.M.79 did not differ greatly structurally from its civil predecessor, but a streamlined fairing was added above the flight deck to house the upper gun, giving the machine a characteristic hump which was to result in the S.M.79 being dubbed the "hunchback" in service, and a ventral gondola was added to accommodate the bombardier. The initial production model for the Regia Aeronautica, the S.M.79-I, was powered by three Alfa Romeo 126 RC 34 nine-cylinder radials each rated at 780 h.p. for take-off and 750 h.p. at 11,150 ft. The capacious fuselage was a welded steel-tube structure with duralumin sheet skinning over the forward section, plywood covering most of the upper fuselage, and fabric covering the sides and bottom. A fireproof bulkhead separated the nose engine from the spacious flight deck which accommodated pilot and co-pilot side by side with dual controls, with the wireless operator to starboard and the flight mechanic to port in separate compartments aft. The fairing above the flight deck accommodated a single fixed forward-firing Breda SAFAT 12.7-mm. machine gun with 350

radial engines each rated at 750 h.p. at 2,300 r.p.m. at 11,480 ft. The S.M.79P, as the commercial prototype was designated, obtained its Certificate of Airworthiness on July 20, 1935, and employed mixed construction. The fuselage comprised a welded chrome molybdenum steel-tube framework with fabric and plywood covering, and the wings were fabric-covered wooden structures. Within a year of its appearance, on September 24, 1935, with Colonel Biseo at the controls, the S.M.79P established 1,000 and 2,000-km. closed-circuit records with a 2,200-lb. payload at average speeds of 242 m.p.h. and 236.7 m.p.h.

During the following year, the S.M.79P, re-engined with Alfa Romeo 126 RC 34 engines offering 780 h.p. for take-off, bettered its previous records by carrying a

Developed in 1936 for export, the S.M.79B (below) was delivered to the air forces of Iraq, Brazil and Rumania with various engines. The S.M.79B illustrated here is powered by two 1,030 h.p. Fiat A.80 RC 41 radials.

rounds, and a similar gun on a flexible mounting with 500 rounds was mounted beneath a sliding panel at the rear of the fairing. The bombs were stowed vertically in the bomb-bay occupying the centre fuselage, and alternative internal loads included two 1,100-lb. bombs, five 550-lb. bombs, or twelve 220-lb. bombs. Aft of the bomb-bay, a ventral cupola housed the Jozza bombsight and the bombardier was provided with a flexible 12.7-mm. Breda SAFAT gun to protect the underside of the bomber. A 7.7.-mm. Lewis gun mounted in the fuselage could be fired through lateral windows.

The cantilever one-piece wing was of three-spar type and entirely of wooden construction, the fuel tanks, containing 5,622 lb. of fuel, were slung between the spars of the wing centre section, and two auxiliary tanks could be fitted in the rear of the engine nacelles. Slotted flaps extended along the wing trailing edge between the ailerons and the outboard engine nacelles, and automatic Handley Page slots were fitted on the wing leading edges outboard of the engines to ensure in low-speed lateral stability. The vertical and horizontal tail surfaces were steel-tube frameworks with fabric covering, and the main undercarriage members retracted into the outboard engine nacelles. The S.M.79-I attained a maximum speed of 267 m.p.h. at 13,120 ft., and 224 m.p.h. at sea level. Cruising speed was 228 m.p.h. at 9,840 ft. and 233 m.p.h. at 19,685 ft., an altitude of 3,280 ft. was attained in 3 min. 28 sec., 16,400 ft. was reached in 19 min. 45 sec., and service ceiling was 21,325 ft. Cruising at 211 m.p.h. at 16,400 ft. with a 2,755-lb. bomb load, the S.M. 79-I had a range of 1,180 miles. Maximum range without bomb load was 2,050 miles.

The three-engined arrangement of the S.M.79-I obviously attracted the Regia Aeronautica on the score of increased safety, and the greater chance that the bomber would have of regaining its base with one engine out. The view was evidently taken that frontal attacks by fighters at the speeds at which the S.M.79 would operate were unlikely and, in any case, would be taken care of by the fixed forward-firing gun. However, most of the world's air arms believed implicitly in the need for nose armament, and the twin-engined formula had been universally accepted for the medium bomber. The S.I.A.I. Savoia-Marchetti had previously developed a twin-engined version of the S.M.81 Pipistrello bomber which, in Regia Aeronautica service, was powered by three engines, and foreseeing that a twin-engined version of the S.M. 79 would have greater export potential than the version produced for the Regia Aeronautica, Marchetti evolved the twin-engined S.M.79B specifically for export.

The S.M.79B differed from the standard S.M.79-I primarily in having an entirely redesigned nose accommodating the bombardier and a flexible 12.7-mm. Breda SAFAT machine gun. The prototype of this version of the Sparviero appeared in 1936 and, powered by two 1,030 h.p. Fiat A.80 RC 41 eighteen-cylinder two-row air-cooled radials, attained a

maximum speed of 255 m.p.h. at 15,100 ft., and 225 m.p.h. at sea level. Cruising speed at 70 per cent power at 18,400 ft. was 224 m.p.h., and at 62.5 per cent power was 215 m.p.h. at the same altitude. At the latter speed, a 2,640-lb. bomb load could be carried over 995 miles and a 1,320-lb. bomb load over 1,400 miles. The S.M.79B was widely demonstrated abroad, being shown to the air arms of Argentina, Belgium, Czechoslovakia, China, Brazil, Finland, Yugoslavia, Iraq, Spain, Turkey, Rumania and Russia. While competing in a contest for a medium bomber organised by the Argentine government in 1937, a question was raised regarding the manoeuvrability of the S.M.79B. The Savoia-Marchetti demonstration pilot promptly took-off and executed four loops! The S.M.79B won the contest but, in the event, the Argentine government decided to purchase thirty-five Martin 139-W bombers owing to the uncertainty of obtaining spares from Europe in the event of war. However, in 1937, the Iraqi government purchased four S.M.79B bombers

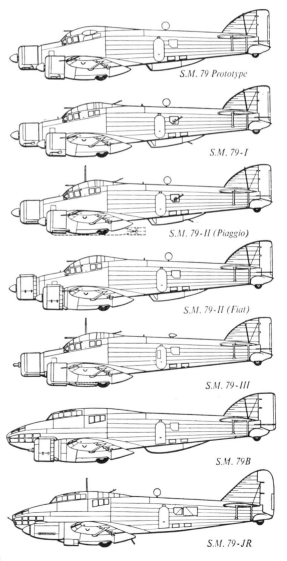

S.M. 79 Prototype

S.M. 79-I

S.M. 79-II (Piaggio)

S.M. 79-II (Fiat)

S.M. 79-III

S.M. 79B

S.M. 79-JR

THE SAVOIA-MARCHETTI SPARVIERO

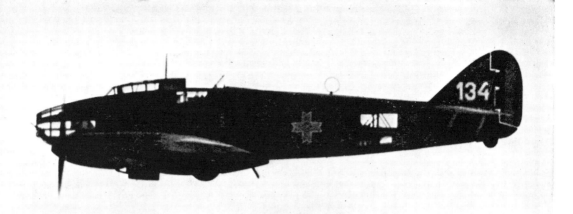

The Rumanian government purchased twenty-four S.M.79B bombers equipped with 1,220 h.p. Junkers Jumo 211Da engines. This version, which was designated S.M.79-JR, was later built under licence by the Industria Aeronautica Romana, and a Rumanian-built machine is illustrated above. Noteworthy changes include the redesign of the vertical tail surfaces and the replacement of the ventral gondola by beam hatches.

(Above) A late production S.M.79-I, and (below) an S.M.79C of the Sorci Verdi Istres-Damascus-Paris team.

powered by Fiat A.80 engines, and the Rumanian government purchased twenty-four with 1,000 h.p Gnôme-Rhône K.14 Mistral-Major engines. Later, three S.M.79B bombers were delivered to Brazil with 930 h.p. Alfa Romeo 128 RC 18 radial engines.

At this juncture, it is of interest to record that the S.M.79B was so successful in Rumania that it was decided to adopt a more powerful version of the aircraft as the standard bomber of the expanding Rumanian Air Force. Accordingly, the initial order was supplemented by an order for a further twenty-four machines powered by the 1,220 h.p. Junkers Jumo 211Da liquid-cooled twelve-cylinder inline engine, and simultaneously a manufacturing licence was acquired for the type which was built by the Bucharest factory of the Industria Aeronautica Romana. Designated S.M.79-JR, the Jumo-engined version attained a maximum speed of 276 m.p.h. at 16,400 ft. and cruised at 19,000 ft. on 70 per cent power at 234 m.p.h. An altitude of 10,000 ft. was attained in 8 min. 40 sec., and service ceiling was 24,260 ft. The SM 79-JR weighed 15,859 lb. empty and 23,788 lb. loaded, and was subsequently employed extensively by Rumanian elements engaged on the Russian front. Another Balkan country to adopt the S.M. 79 was Yugoslavia, the Royal Yugoslav Air Force acquiring forty-five standard S.M.79-I tri-motor bombers, these equipping the 7th Bombing Wing and the 81st Independent Bombing Group at the

One of the most effective land-based torpedo-bombers of the Second World War, the S.M.79-II (below) entered production in October 1939 to equip Italy's torpedo-bombing squadrons, the Aerosiluranti.

Savoia-Marchetti S.M. 79-II Sparviero

NOTES ON FINISH AND INSIGNIA: *The most common finishes applied to S.M.79-II bombers of the Regia Aeronautica comprised mottled sand-yellow and olive green over all upper surfaces, with stone-grey under-surfaces, or dark sea green upper surfaces with duck-egg blue under-surfaces. Some machines did, however, feature an irregular camouflage pattern of terracotta and sand-yellow over the upper surfaces. The national insignia, the Fasces (a bundle of rods bound up with an axe in the middle, its blade projecting), appeared in silhouette form in black, the blades always pointing outwards, on a white disc outlined in black. This appeared on the upper and lower surfaces of the wings. A white cross appeared on the rudder, with a reproduction* of the arms of the House of Savoy superimposed above the horizontal bar. On each side of the cowling of the central engine appeared a single fasces in brown with yellow binding. A broad white band was normally painted around the rear fuselage. The number of the Squadriglia appeared in black on each side of the fuselage, followed by the number of the individual aircraft in a second colour. The numerals were approximately half the depth of the fuselage in size. Examples are: "252-3", indicating the third aircraft of Squadriglia 253 (which was part of the 131º Gruppo Autonomo Aerosiluranti), and "10-7", indicating the seventh aircraft of Squadriglia 10 (of the 28º Gruppo Bombardamento Terrestre).

63

time of Germany's assault on that country. The S.M.79-I was not very popular with the Yugoslav pilots who considered its landing characteristics to be poor.

During 1937, sixteen standard S.M.79 Sparvieri were modified for use in establishing a number of prestige records and for participating in international races. The standard engines were replaced by 1,000 h.p. Piaggio P.XI RC 40 radials, eleven machines (S.M. 79T) were fitted with increased tankage for transatlantic flights, and the other five (S.M.79C) were modified to participate in the International Istres-Damascus-Paris Air Race. Stripped of all armament and with the upper gun fairing and ventral bombardier's gondola removed, these aircraft took first, second and third places in the race, the winning aircraft averaging 217 m.p.h., and attaining an average speed of 263 m.p.h. on the Istres-Damascus leg. In January 1938, a trio of S.M.79s, known as the Sorci Verdi (Green Mice), made a very fast flight between Rome and Rio de Janeiro in two stages, covering the 6,214 miles in 24 hr. 20 min., averaging 255 m.p.h. Throughout 1938 the S.M.79 undertook numerous other record-breaking flights, and the type gained no less than twenty-six international records.

While the S.M.79 was engaged in enhancing Italy's aviation prestige abroad, civil war had been raging in Spain, and the Aviación Legionaria had been sent to the aid of the Nationalist forces. The Spanish Civil War provided the Regia Aeronautica with an admirable opportunity to test its latest warplanes under operational conditions, and as production deliveries of the S.M. 79-I had attained a considerable tempo, the 8° and 111mo Stormi Bombardamento Veloce (the 8th and 111th Fast Bomber Groups) were equipped with the new bomber and sent to Spain where they achieved considerable success. The S.M.79-I proved capable of eluding the majority of the opposing fighters, and rapidly built up a reputation for reliability and efficiency.

The Regia Aeronautica had for long been interested in torpedo bombing and, early in 1937, after conducting tests with the S.M.81 Pipistrello, the Supreme Command of the Regia Aeronautica selected the S.M.79 for further trials. Savoia-Marchetti had undertaken studies as to the most suitable means of launching a torpedo so that it entered the water obliquely, and in March 1937 a special rack to carry a 450-mm. naval torpedo was fitted to a standard S.M. 79-I, together with a special aiming device. The torpedo, which had a 375-lb. warhead, was offset to one side under the fuselage, and trials were conducted at Gorizia in November 1937. The development of air-launched torpedoes had been undertaken in other countries with limited success, largely due to aerodynamic difficulties in launching torpedoes from aircraft and to depth-control and fusing problems. For instance, in Germany trials showed forty-nine per cent failure despite the fact that the Whitehead Fiume patents had been acquired from Italy. However, trials with the S.M.79-I were highly

successful and, in March 1938, it was decided to undertake a further series of trials but with two torpedoes under the aircraft. Savoia-Marchetti developed a twin launching device and, in August 1938, the first tests were made at Gorizia. With two torpedoes slung under the fuselage, the S.M.79-I's flying characteristics became extremely sensitive, and performance was drastically reduced, but after some modifications to the launching racks, the Regia Aeronautica decided to adopt the aircraft for its land-based torpedo-bombing units, the Aerosiluranti.

In order to improve the characteristics of the aircraft when carrying two torpedoes, the 1,000 h.p. Piaggio P.XI RC 40 engine was adopted as standard for the torpedo-bomber and, as the S.M.79-II, the type entered production in October 1939. Previously, a small series of S.M.79-I bombers had been fitted with 1,350 h.p. Alfa Romeo 135 RC 32 eighteen-cylinder air-cooled radial engines, and one series of S.M.79-II aircraft was later fitted with 1,030 h.p. Fiat A.80 RC 41 radials, but virtually all torpedo-bombing machines employed the Piaggio engine. The S.M.79-II carried two types of torpedo; one with a 375-lb. warhead produced by the Silurificio Whitehead di Fiume, and the other with a 352-lb. warhead produced by the Silurificio Italiano di Napoli. Both torpedoes were of 450-mm. calibre and were normally launched from approximately 320 feet altitude at 185 m.p.h. Later, in December 1941, a 440-lb. warhead was adopted as standard, and torpedoes of this type were supplied to the Luftwaffe whose torpedo-bombing techniques owed much to those evolved by the Aerosiluranti, and whose torpedo-bombing school was eventually established at Grosseto, on the West coast of Italy.

When the S.M.79-II entered production in October 1939, licence production being initiated by Aeronautica Macchi and the Officine Meccaniche "Reggiane" S.A., eleven Stormi (Groups), each comprising four Squadriglie (Squadrons), were equipped with a total of 385 S.M.79-Js based in Italy, Albania and the Aegean Isles, and by June 10, 1940, when Italy entered World War II on Germany's side, the number of S.M.79-I and -II aircraft possessed by the Regia Aeronautica had increased to 594 machines of which 403 were ready for immediate offensive operations. The Regia Aeronautica possessed a first-line strength of 975 bombers, and, thus, the Sparviero equipped nearly two-thirds of Italy's bomber forces. Subsequently, the S.M.79 Sparviero was active throughout the Mediterranean, in the Balkans and North Africa, equipping the 8°, 9°, 10°, 11°, 12°, 15°, 30°, 32°, 34°, 36°, 41° and 46° Stormi. Its most successful role was that of torpedo-bombing, and the Aero Siluramento Squadriglie achieved considerable success, sinking the carrier H.M.S. Eagle, the destroyers Jaguar, Legion, Southwall, Husky, Kujavik II, as well as other British naval vessels and numerous cargo ships.

The Sparviero was also used extensively for strategic reconnaissance, level bombing and, during the later stages of the fighting in North Africa, for close-support duties, but perhaps its most unusual role was that of remotely-controlled guided bomb! One S.M.79 was adapted to take a radio-control guidance system developed by General Ferdinando Raffaeli, packed with explosives and launched against the British Fleet lying off the coast of Algeria on August 13, 1942. A pilot took the S.M.79 off the ground, set it on its course, and then left the aircraft. The missile was guided towards the British warships by remote radio control but, due to a fault in the radio circuit, the S.M.79 went off course and crashed in the Klenchela Mountains in Algeria. When, on September 8, 1943, Italy capitulated, thirty-four S.M.79 Sparvieri, mostly from the 41°, 104°, 131° and 132° Gruppi, reached the Allied lines to form a part of the Italian Co-Belligerent Air Force, serving as level bombers, torpedo aircraft and transports.

In the area of Italy still under German domination, a new Italian air arm was formed, the Aviazione della Repubblica Sociale Italiana, and this force also continued to use the Sparviero, introducing an improved version, the S.M.79-III (sometimes referred to as the S.579). The S.M.79-III was built in relatively small numbers in northern Italy, and all S.M.79-II aircraft that still existed in the R.S.I. were brought up to -III standards. The S.M.79-III differed from earlier models in carrying a forward-firing 20-mm. cannon and in being generally "cleaned up". The ventral gondola was deleted, new, lengthened airscrew spinners were fitted, the exhaust pipes were extended, and later radio equipment was installed. The S.M.79-III equipped a Gruppo Aerosiluranti led by Captain Faggioni until his death during an attack on Allied shipping at Nettuno, after which it was led by Major Marini. The Gruppo operated extensively against Allied shipping in the Mediterranean, and even attacked Gibraltar on the night of June 4–5, 1944.

(*Above*) *One of a small series of S.M.79-II fitted with 1,030 h.p. Fiat A.80 RC 41 air-cooled radials.*

Some twelve hundred S.M.79 Sparviero bombers were delivered to the Regia Aeronautica during the aircraft's production life, and the type was undoubtedly one of the most successful warplanes evolved by the Italian aircraft industry. It possessed excellent handling qualities and was favoured over all other bombers by its crews. Despite the derision to which it was unfairly subjected, it was held in respect by its antagonists and was fully deserving of a place among the most famous of the Second World War's combat aircraft.

Savoia-Marchetti S.M.79-II Sparviero

Dimensions :	Span, 69 ft. 6⅝ in. ; length, 53 ft. 1¾ in. ; height, 13 ft. 5½ in. ; wing area, 656.598 sq. ft.
Armament:	One fixed and two flexible 12.7-mm. Breda SAFAT machine guns, and one flexible 7.7-mm. Lewis machine gun. Internal bomb load : two 1,100-lb., five 550-lb., or twelve 220-lb. bombs. As a torpedo-attack aircraft : two 450-mm. torpedoes.
Power Plants :	Three Piaggio P.XI RC 40 fourteen-cylinder air-cooled two-row radial engines each developing 1,000 h.p. at 2,200 r.p.m. at 13,120 ft.
Weights :	Empty, 16,755 lb. ; useful load, 8,157 lb. ; loaded, 24,912 lb.
Performance :	Maximum speed, 270 m.p.h. at 12,000 ft. ; maximum cruising speed, 255 m.p.h. at 9,800 ft. ; range (with 2,755-lb. bomb load), 1,243 miles. ; climb to 13,120 ft., 10 min. 25 sec., to 16,400 ft., 14 min. 30 sec. ; service ceiling, 22,966 ft.

The final development of the Sparviero, the S.M.79-III (below), was introduced into service by the Aviazione della Repubblica Sociale Italiana, but had been developed prior to the Italian Armistice. It embodied a number of refinements to improve its operational performance.

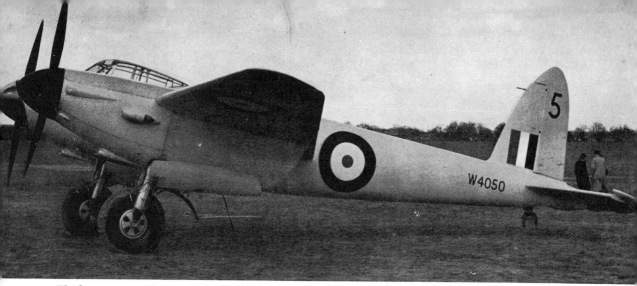

The first prototype Mosquito (W4050) flew for the first time on November 25, 1940, four days short of eleven months from the beginning of detail design.

THE DE HAVILLAND MOSQUITO

Many of the world's greatest combat aircraft have been born not as the result of some officially-inspired specification but because of the unshakeable conviction of one man or a group of individuals in a revolutionary idea. Few if any better examples of this could be cited than that of the de Havilland Mosquito, which diverged so far from official views pertaining at the time of its conception that it came within an ace of being stillborn. Credit for the Mosquito formula— that of a bomber relying for its defence on its ability to outpace any intercepting fighter—went to the de Havilland company alone, and it was their belief in the "rightness" of this formula which, more than any other single factor, gave the Royal Air Force one of the most potent weapons of the Second World War.

The essence of the Mosquito was the combination of two Rolls-Royce Merlin engines, the smallest practicable airframe, extreme aerodynamic cleanliness and a high power-to-weight ratio. The result was a performance which surpassed that of any other operational aircraft available to any of the combatants between September 1941 and the early months of 1944, but the Mosquito's most amazing attribute was its prodigious versatility which, as the war progressed, resulted in its being described as almost "all things to all men"—or Commands of the R.A.F. Its exploits were legendary; it was a constant thorn in the enemy's flesh. Whether it was disrupting gatherings addressed by Germany's war leaders deep in the heart of enemy territory, attacking Gestapo Headquarters at rooftop height, or merely keeping Berliners in their air-raid shelters, the Mosquito's activities were front page news.

Aesthetically, the Mosquito was one of the most appealing combat aircraft designs ever evolved and, like most really beautiful aeroplanes, it possessed delightful flying characteristics. It radically altered bomber concepts and set records for progress from initial drawings to flight tests, and from flight tests

to active operations. Indeed, only twenty-two months elapsed between the first drawing being made and the Mosquito's début over enemy territory, reflecting the greatest credit on the foresight and skill of its design team.

The possibility of developing a fast bomber was first investigated by the de Havilland Aircraft Company in the summer of 1938, by which time the company had been concentrating on the design and development of civil aircraft for some fifteen years. In May of the previous year, the beautifully-proportioned and perfectly streamlined four-engined Albatross had begun its flight trials, and the success achieved with this 32,500-lb. transport, with its cruising speed of 210 m.p.h. at 11,000 ft. on a total of only 1,280 h.p., led to a study of its military potential. As a bomber, the Albatross would have carried a 6,000-lb. bomb load to Berlin at 210 m.p.h. with a fuel consumption of 2.5 miles per gallon. This was a starting point. Further design studies were then made, but throughout the emphasis was placed on speed. Defensive armament was viewed as parasitic, and, in view of the company's extensive experience in wooden construction, it was natural that this material should come into consideration. Before the end of 1938, de Havilland directors had held informal discussions with the Member for Research, Development and Production at the Air Ministry, Sir Wilfred Freeman, who encouraged the company to continue their investigations, although he was unable to sponsor them officially.

In October 1938, the ideas of the team, which was led by Geoffrey de Havilland, and included R. E. Bishop as chief designer and C. C. Walker as chief engineer, had crystallized as a wooden monoplane powered by a pair of Merlins. The retention of wooden construction for an aeroplane which was intended to raise combat aircraft speeds into the 400 m.p.h. category was unusual, but the company was

Flown for the first time on September 8, 1941, the Mosquito B.IV Series I was the first production bomber aircraft in the series. Later machines of this mark had extended engine nacelles.

used to wood and had wood-working equipment available. The D.H.95 Flamingo transport, which employed all-metal stressed-skin construction, was on the verge of flying, but it was obvious to the de Havilland team that the metal industry would have its hands more than full if war broke out. Furthermore, the use of wood would make possible far greater dispersal of production, and simplify repairs. Some variants of the proposal included various forms of rearward armament, and two- and three-seat aeroplanes were considered.

With the outbreak of war, in September 1939, design effort on the project was redoubled, and Air Ministry interest began to harden. After considerable hesitation, the design team's preference for a crew of only two and for an aircraft completely devoid of defensive armament was officially accepted, and a basic requirement for a 1,000-lb. bomb load and a range of 1,500 miles was agreed. The speed was to be "as good as a fighter", and insofar as detail design was concerned, the team was given a virtually free hand. All this was finally agreed on December 29, 1939, and the first official specification prepared in 1940—B.1/40—committed to paper the terms upon which de Havilland's radically different bomber was to be accepted. The official interest at this time—and it was neither over-enthusiastic nor widespread—was only in the unarmed bomber. On its own initiative, however, de Havilland's team designed their aeroplane from the outset with provision for guns or cameras so that it could serve equally well as bomber, fighter or photo-reconnaissance aircraft—another example of farsightedness.

An official order for fifty aircraft to be built in accordance with the B.1/40 specification reached de Havilland on March 1, 1940. The small size of the order was due in part to the luke-warm interest evinced in the project in some quarters, and to the realisation that alternative versions might well be developed which would render the committing of one type to large-scale production from the outset a some-

what short-term policy. For several months after the placing of the contract, the whole programme was in jeopardy. At that period of the war, when Britain's whole future hung in the balance, it was natural that all efforts should be expended on aircraft which were known quantities, and that a machine which seemed, to some officials at least, a mere pipe dream, should find itself at the very bottom of the priority list. In one Ministry of Aircraft Production programme for the aircraft industry compiled soon after the Dunkirk evacuation, de Havilland's bomber was omitted entirely, and its future looked black indeed. So long as the project was not on this official programme, no materials for its construction could be purchased, and it was largely due to the fact that the DH.98, as the type was designated by de Havilland, made so few demands on strategic materials that it was eventually reinstated.

Three aircraft of the initial order for fifty machines were allocated for prototype trials, and construction of these went ahead during those difficult days of 1940, while materials and parts for the production batch were assembled. On October 3, 1940, four bombs dropped by a low-flying Junkers Ju 88A hit the Hatfield plant and destroyed eighty per cent of these materials, but by good fortune no damage was suffered by the first prototype machine. The name "Mosquito" was adopted for the new aircraft, and no more appropriate appellation than that of this gnat-like fly of the genus *Culex*, with its vicious sting, could have been selected in view of its subsequent operational career. On November 25, 1940, four days short of eleven months from the beginning of detail design, the first prototype (W4050) made its maiden flight at Hatfield, with Captain de Havilland at the controls. This prototype Mosquito, finished bright yellow overall, was powered by a pair of Rolls-Royce Merlin 21s, delivering 1,280 h.p. for take-off and 1,480 h.p. at 6,000 ft., and could take four 250-lb. bombs in its belly. Flight trials soon demonstrated the astonishing agility of the Mosquito, and the upward

H*   67

rolls with one airscrew feathered and the fast runs at speeds approaching 400 m.p.h. performed by Geoffrey de Havilland before guests at Hatfield left no doubts in the minds of onlookers as to the potentialities of the design.

By this time, interest in the Mosquito as a bomber had dwindled in favour of a fighter version, the rightness of which was no doubt accentuated in the official mind by the fighter-like characteristics displayed during Geoffrey de Havilland's demonstrations, and the contract was amended to comprise twenty bombers and thirty fighters. De Havilland were able to accommodate four 20-mm. and four 0.303-in. guns in the Mosquito's nose, but the change in the contract caused some delay in production as the wing spar of the Mosquito for the fighter role had to be strengthened, and other components already made for the bomber were no longer useable.

The Mosquito fighter prototype (W4052)[1] was built at Salisbury Hall, London Colney, and flew on May 15, 1941, and the third prototype (W4051), equipped as a photo-reconnaissance aircraft, flew on June 10, 1941. In the meantime, the bomber prototype had completed its factory trials, and had been handed over for official trials on February 19, 1941. Something approaching a year had been saved in construction and prototype trials by the use of wood instead of metal for the Mosquito's structure. By July 1941 confidence in the Mosquito was complete, and the de Havilland company found themselves faced with production programmes out of all proportion to anything they had previously handled. While plans were made to move production of the Airspeed Oxford trainer out of the Hatfield factory to free the assembly lines for Mosquitoes, steps were also taken to establish Mosquito production elsewhere—at de Havilland's Leavesden plant in the first instance, and later at the factories of Standard Motors, Percival Aircraft and Airspeed.

[1] The story of the Mosquito fighter variants is told in detail in *Famous Fighters of the Second World War*, Volume I, a companion work to this.

Meanwhile, further changes in the original batch of fifty Mosquitoes had been made, this now comprising ten Mosquito I photo-reconnaissance aircraft, thirty Mosquito II fighters and ten Mosquito IV bombers. The designation Mosquito III had been reserved for the dual-control training variant which was to be ordered under later contracts, and it is indicative of the lessening of interest in the bomber variant that this, the predecessor of all other versions, should receive the last in the initial series of mark numbers when these were officially confirmed. The original flight trials with W4050 had shown that few modifications of any consequence were required. In fact, the only modification called for which offered any serious difficulties was the need to extend the engine nacelles aft of the wing trailing edges. These terminated short of the flap hinge lines on the prototype, and when lengthened necessitated the division of the flap into two parts. The original short nacelles were retained on the ten Mosquito I photo-reconnaissance aircraft, and the ten Mk.IV bombers on the original contract, and the latter were known as the Mosquito B.IV Series I, the first of these (W4072) flying on September 8, 1941. Later Mk.IVs with lengthened nacelles were designated Series II, but no additional Mk.I reconnaissance machines were built.

The first deliveries of the Mosquito to the R.A.F. were made in mid-1941, and the operational début was marked by a Mk.I (W4055) on September 20, 1941. Operated by the Photographic Development Unit at Benson, the aircraft made a daylight reconnaissance sortie over Brest, La Pallice and Bordeaux. Chased by three Messerschmitt Bf 109s, the Mosquito easily eluded the German fighters at 23,000 ft., and thereafter Mosquito sorties became a daily occurrence, and with only ten aircraft (including the prototype, W4051), the P.D.U. was able to mount as many as ten sorties a day!

The bomber was a little later in attaining service status, as the Mk.IV Series I did not become operational, and the squadrons had to await the delivery of the Series II. The ten Series I aircraft had Merlin

A standard production Mosquito IV Series II (DK290). First deliveries were made to No. 105 Squadron in the spring of 1942.

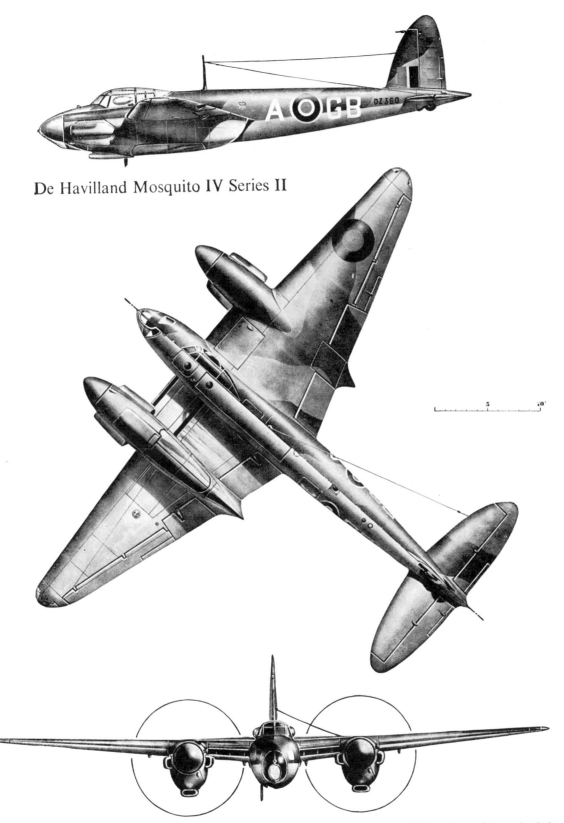

De Havilland Mosquito IV Series II

FINISH AND INSIGNIA: *The de Havilland Mosquito IV Series II illustrated belonged to No. 105 Squadron and featured a dark green and dark earth camouflage pattern over the upper surfaces and fuselage sides and duck-egg under-surfaces. The national insignia comprised "C" type roundels on the fuselage sides with corresponding tail flash, and red-and-blue "B" type roundels on the upper surfaces of the wings. The identification letters on the fuselage sides were pastel green, and the serial number was black.*

A Mosquito IX with underwing smoke canisters.

21 or 23 engines with two-speed single-stage super-chargers and de Havilland Hydromatic constant-speed airscrews, and gross weight was 19,200 lb. In compliance with the original specification, they carried four 250-lb. general-purpose bombs internally. The Mosquito IV Series II with the lengthened engine nacelles and Merlin 21, 23, or 25 engines, was able to carry four 500-lb. bombs with shortened vanes, and after some modifications to increase the size of the bomb-bay, a single 4,000-lb. bomb could be accommodated. Basic weight rose to 20,900 lb., or 22,500 lb. with the 4,000-pounder, and performance included maximum speeds of 300 m.p.h. at sea level and 380 m.p.h. at 17,000 ft., a maximum cruising speed of 340 m.p.h. at 22,000 ft., and an economical cruising speed of 300 m.p.h. at the same altitude. Initial climb rate was 1,700 ft./min., and the service ceiling of 28,800 ft. was attained in 22.5 mins. A total of 263 Mosquito IVs were built, and of these fifty-six were converted to carry the 4,000-lb. bomb, and thirty-two were later modified as P.R.IV photo-reconnaissance aircraft, serving primarily as photo-reconnaissance trainers.

Deliveries of the Mosquito IV Series II to the R.A.F. began in the spring of 1942, and the Blenheims of No. 105 Squadron at Marham had been replaced by the new aircraft by May of that year. The first " Mosquito Bite" was inflicted on the enemy by four aircraft of this Squadron on May 31, 1942, when four Mosquitoes made a lightning daylight attack on Cologne which followed immediately on the heels of the R.A.F.'s first thousand-bomber raid on that city during the previous night. Attacks of this kind were something entirely new to R.A.F. Bomber Command which had to evolve a completely new set of tactics in order to make best use of the Mosquito's potential. This little bomber, it was found, could outpace enemy interceptors and, in consequence, could be sent by day on long flights over enemy territory. Pin-point attacks could be made with an extremely high degree of

accuracy, and a technique was developed to confuse anti-aircraft defences by combining dive-attacks with high-speed low-level passes. Typical of the attacks made by Mosquitoes in these early days of its operational career was that which occasioned the first official mention of this new weapon, and the Mosquito's début on the front pages of the popular press —the daring low-level attack on the Gestapo Headquarters in Oslo, Norway. This spectacular sortie was carried out in September by Mosquitoes of No. 105 Squadron whose aircraft gained the distinction of being the first of their kind to bomb Berlin four months later. This attack, made on January 31, 1943, was carefully planned in order to disrupt a parade addressed by Reichsmarschall Hermann Goering. The fury of Goering at this insult was such that he recalled two experienced fighter leaders from Russia, forming Jagdgruppen 25 and 50 with specially modified interceptors to combat the Mosquito menace. Special tactics were evolved, but the German fighters could only catch up with the de Havilland bomber if they dived on them from a very much greater altitude. As the Mosquitoes frequently operated at considerable altitudes, such manoeuvres were only of value if the British aircraft were discovered by radar well before reaching their target. Such little success was enjoyed against the Mosquito that, in the autumn of 1943, the special Jagdgruppen were disbanded without, so far as is known, scoring one "kill", and the Mosquito continued to roam over Europe unhindered.

Initially, the Mosquito bombers operated mainly as "nuisance" raiders, but as such they became as much a plague to the German populace as were their namesakes in more tropical climes. The mounting daylight offensive by the U.S.A.A.F., flying from bases in the United Kingdom, led, in May 1943, to the withdrawal of Mosquito bombers from daylight operations. In the closing months of 1942, new outlets had been found for the Mosquito's particular attributes in the work of the Pathfinder Force, and in December 1942 Mosquito IVs of No. 109 Squadron, flying from Wyton, had made use of the Oboe radar navigational aid for the first time.

While the Mosquito was gaining its spurs in European skies, production of the type had been initiated in both Canada and Australia. Production was even contemplated in the United States for the U.S.A.A.F. and, although this proposal did not bear fruit, forty Canadian-built Mosquitoes were transferred to the U.S.A.A.F., and employed by that service under the designation F-8 for reconnaissance duties. To initiate production at the de Havilland Aircraft of Canada's Toronto plant, two senior de Havilland engineers flew to Toronto in September 1941. They were followed by jigs, tools, tens of thousands of drawings for the bomber's 24,000 component parts, and certain supplies and parts. The B.Mk.IV was selected as the basic aeroplane for Canadian production, but with Packard-built Merlin 31 engines rated at 1,300 h.p. for take·off supplanting the British-built Merlin 21s. With a 2,000-lb. bomb

(*Above*) *The first Canadian-built Mosquito VII* (*KB*300) *was flown for the first time in September* 1942. *Only twenty-five examples of this variant were built, the principal Canadian-built bomber variant being the Mosquito 25 with Merlin 225s in place of the Merlin 69s* (*right*).

load and a gross weight of 20,677 lb., the first Canadian-built model was designated Mosquito B.VII, and exactly a year from the commencement of the Canadian programme, in September 1942, the first machine (KB300) was flown. Only twenty-five of this variant were built, all being retained in Canada.

Canadian production continued with the Mosquito B.XX which differed from its predecessor primarily in having what was known as the "Standard Wing" and a modified bomb-bay capable of taking four 500-lb. bombs or a single 4,000-lb. "Block Buster". The so-called "Standard Wing" had previously been designed for the Mosquito B.V which did not enter production, and this could take two 40 Imp. gal. or 100 Imp. gal. drop tanks, or two 500-lb. bombs. Powered by Packard-built Merlin 31s or 33s, the Mosquito B.XX had a gross weight of 21,981 lb. The first aircraft of this type for the R.A.F. were delivered by air across the Atlantic in August 1943.

Mosquitoes on routine delivery flights from Gander, Newfoundland, to the United Kingdom, subsequently established many record times for the Atlantic crossing—in October 1944, the 2,200 miles was covered in 6 hr. 44 min. at an average ground speed of 322 m.p.h., and before the end of the war this had been reduced to 5 hr. 30 min., representing a speed of 390 m.p.h. Other Canadian versions included the Mosquito F.B.21 fighter-bomber which corresponded to the British-built Mk.VI and the T.Mk.22 dual-control training model, neither of which was built in quantity. The B.Mk.23 was a proposed high-altitude development of the Mk.XX with Packard-built Merlin 69s, but this was not proceeded with due to the availability of the later Merlin 225 rated at 1,620 h.p. for take-off. The F.B. Mk.24 was a generally similar

The first production Mosquito IX (*LR495*) *which flew for the first time in March* 1943.

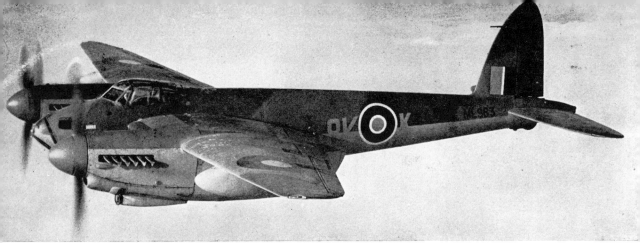

proposal for a high-altitude fighter-bomber variant, but the replacement for the B.Mk.XX was the B.Mk.25 with the improved Merlins 225s. The F.B.26 and T.27 were similarly-powered developments of the F.B.21 and T.22. Several squadrons employed Canadian-built Mosquitoes in Europe and in the Mediterranean, and by August 1945 1,032 Mosquitoes had been produced by the Toronto factory—a notable contribution to the Allied war effort.

In December 1941, de Havilland Aircraft Pty. Ltd. had its proposals for manufacturing the Mosquito accepted by the Australian government, and full plans for the production of the type were formulated during the three months following the attack on Pearl Harbour. Representatives of the Australian company flew to the United Kingdom to acquaint themselves with the methods and materials used in Mosquito construction, and in June 1942 the first drawings arrived in Australia, followed, in November of that year, by a specimen Mosquito II fighter. No production of the pure bomber version of the Mosquito was undertaken in Australia, the first Australian built version, the F.B.Mk.40, being a fighter-bomber based on the F.B.VI but powered by Packard-built Merlin 31s or 33s. The first machine was test flown successfully in July 1943, just thirteen months after the receipt of the initial batch of drawings, and the first deliveries to the R.A.A.F. were made in March of the following year. Apart from active production of the Mosquito, the Australian company assembled and tested a number of imported Mosquito T.Mk.III trainers, replacing the original engines with Merlin 31s so that all R.A.A.F. Mosquitoes would be uniformly powered. These modified trainers were desig-

nated T.Mk.43. An unarmed photo-reconnaissance version of the F.B.Mk.40 was designated P.R.Mk. 40; a version of the F.B.Mk.40 with automatic pilot and two-stage supercharged Merlin 69s was designated F.B.Mk.41, and a similar aircraft without automatic pilot was the F.B.Mk.42. When the Pacific War ended, the Bankstown factory had delivered 108 Mosquitoes, although it was to go on to produce a further 104 machines of this type.

Reverting once again to the Mosquito programme in the United Kingdom, a new bomber variant had been developed to take advantage of the extra power available from the Merlin 70 series of engines with their two-stage superchargers. Two Merlin 72s, rated at 1,290 h.p. for take-off and offering a maximum power of 1,680 h.p., were installed in a Mk.IV (DZ540), and these engines became standard on the Mosquito B.IX, fifty-four of which were built. The Mosquito B.IX was the first high-altitude bomber, and operational ceiling was raised to over 36,000 ft. Overall length was increased from the 40 ft. $9\frac{1}{2}$ in. of the B.Mk.IV to 44 ft. 6 in., and wing area was increased from 435 sq. ft. to 454 sq. ft. The "standard" wing originally developed for the abortive B.Mk.V was fitted, and the standard 2,000-lb. bomb load was carried with which the gross weight was 22,850 lb. In 1944 all B.Mk.IXs were converted to take the 4,000-lb. "Block Buster", with which all-up weight rose to 24,900 lb. Mosquito B.IXs dropped their first 4,000-lb. bombs on Germany during daylight in an attack on Duisberg on November 29, 1944. Previously, B.Mk.IXs fitted with Oboe (which enabled the Mosquito to bomb a target accurately through cloud) had been used in the Pathfinder role by No. 105 Squadron.

The Mosquito B.IX was followed by the B.Mk.XVI which differed from its predecessor in having a pressurized cabin, following the development of this feature on a special prototype (MP469) which had been first flown in 1942. The B.Mk.XVI had the bulged bomb-bay necessitated by the 4,000-lb. bomb (except for the first twelve aircraft off the line) which could be carried as an alternative to the four 500-lb. bombs. The engines were either Merlin 72 (starboard) and 73 (port), or Merlin 76 (starboard) and 77 (port)—the Merlin 73 and 77 incorporated drives for the cabin blower. The Mosquito B.XVI—of which 387 had been built by July 31, 1945—was the principal equipment of the Fast Night Striking Force which had come into being principally to exploit the aircraft's potentialities as a "nuisance" raider. Aircraft of this Force operated from late 1944 until the end of the war in Europe, as many as fifty Mosquitoes at a time making attacks on industrial targets as well as communications, and were responsible among other things for the long series of morale-breaking raids against Berlin, forces of more than 100 Mosquitoes sometimes bombing the German capital in one night. Early in 1945, Mosquitoes began to plant their 4,000-lb. bombs in the mouths of West German railway tunnels in daring low-level attacks, and on the night of May 12–13, 1944, this versatile aircraft made its début as a mine-layer, standard airborne mines being laid in the Kiel Canal by Mosquitoes flying only a few feet above the water, effectively blocking this important and heavily defended waterway for some days.

On March 12, 1945, a new Mosquito bomber variant, the B.Mk.35, made its first flight, and was subsequently placed in production by Percival Aircraft and Airspeed to succeed the B.Mk.XVI. Carrying the same bomb load, the B.Mk.35 had the Merlin 113–114 engines which made it one of the most formidable light bombers developed during the entire war, with maximum speeds of 400 m.p.h. at 17,500 ft. and 422 m.p.h. at 30,000 ft. Its service ceiling was 34,000 ft., and its range with a 4,000-lb. bomb was 1,750 miles at 310 m.p.h. at 30,000 ft., and with a 2,000-lb. bomb load was 2,050 miles at the same speed and altitude. The war ended, however, before this version could reach the squadrons.

Each major development of the Mosquito bomber was paralleled by a photo-reconnaissance variant, having cameras in the bomb-bay together with additional fuel, but being otherwise similar to the bomber. These reconnaissance versions were the P.R.Mk.IX (ninety built), and the P.R.Mk.XVI (321 built to December 1944), and the P.R.34, deliveries of which commenced in November 1944. No fewer than 4,444 Mosquitoes had been built in the United Kingdom up to August 15, 1945—the date of Japan's surrender—divided as follows: de Havilland Hatfield plant, (1941) 21; (1942) 389; (1943) 806; (1944) 1,203; (1945) 635; de Havilland Leavesden plant, (1942) 53; (1943) 379; (1944) 585; (1945) 373. Standard Motors built 916 Mosquitoes, Percival built 198, and Airspeed had built twelve up to V-J Day. Canadian and Australian wartime production brought the grand total to 5,584 aircraft. The following list includes all the R.A.F. squadrons which employed Mosquito bombers up to the end of the Second World War: Nos. 105, 109,

A Mosquito XVI (ML926/G) with a belly-mounted H2S scanner.

128, 139, 142, 162, 163, 192, 571, 578, 608, 613, 614, 627, 680, 692 and 693.

Air Ministry records show that Mosquitoes operating from the United Kingdom up to the end of the war dropped just slightly less than 27,000 tons of bombs, including 15,000 tons dropped by Pathfinder Force aircraft. They suffered fewer losses per thousand sorties than any other Bomber Command aircraft, and an indication of their effectiveness in pinpoint strikes was given in the attacks on V-1 launching sites during 1944. One V-1 site was destroyed for every 39.8 tons of bombs dropped by Mosquitoes. Relative figures for the B-17 Fortress, the B-25 Mitchell and the B-26 Marauder were 165.4 tons, 182 tons and 219 tons respectively. It was singularly fitting that the Mosquito should crown its distinguished operational career by making the final R.A.F. Bomber Command sortie of the war in Europe—an attack against Kiel by Mosquito B.XVIs of No. 608 Squadron on May 2, 1945.

As a bomber of wooden construction the Mosquito was unique; in its multifarious forms it was outstandingly ubiquitous, and it possessed that highly desirable but all too rare ability to make its pilot feel part and parcel of his aircraft. It captured popular imagination from the moment its first daring sorties over Europe became known, and its sensational exploits continued to sustain world-wide interest and enthusiasm to a greater degree than those of any other combat aircraft.

De Havilland Mosquito B.XVI

Dimensions: Span, 54 ft. 2 in.; length, 40 ft. 6 in.; height, 12 ft. 6 in.; wing area, 454 sq. ft.

Power Plants: Two Rolls-Royce Merlin 73 twelve-cylinder 60° Vee liquid-cooled engines rated at 1,290 h.p. at 3,000 r.p.m. for take-off and 1,710 h.p. maximum power.

Armament: One 4,000-lb. bomb internally, or four 500-lb. bombs internally plus two 500-lb. bombs underwing. Maximum bomb load, 4,000 lb.

Weights: Tare, 15,510 lb.; normal loaded, 19,093 lb.; maximum overload, 23,000 lb. Maximum fuel capacity, 788 Imp. gal. internally and two 60 Imp. gal. drop-tanks.

Performance: (At normal gross weight) Maximum speed, 408 m.p.h. at 26,000 ft., 386 m.p.h. at 13,000 ft.; cruising speed, 300 m.p.h.; time to 15,000 ft., 7.75 min.; service ceiling, 37,000 ft.; range (with 4,000-lb. bomb load and 643 Imp. gal.), 1,370 miles at 245 m.p.h., (with 1,000-lb. bomb load and 788 Imp. gal.), 1,870 miles at 245 m.p.h.

The third Seattle-built Boeing XB-29 Superfortress prototype (41-18335) flew for the first time in June 1943, and embodied extensive engine and equipment revision.

THE BOEING SUPERFORTRESS

While the Boeing Superfortress gained for itself undying fame as the first aircraft to drop an atomic weapon, thus bringing about the sudden termination of hostilities in the Pacific, it is also deserving of a place in the history of aerial warfare as one of the principal Allied weapons in the war against Japan. The laborious and costly island-hopping campaign conducted in the Pacific by the Allied forces was undertaken largely to seize bases for Superfortress operations against the Japanese homeland. Once bases had been established, the Superfortresses of the United States 20th Air Force systematically and inexorably erased the industrial cities of Japan one by one with the terrible weapon of fire. The closely packed and lightly constructed Japanese buildings were extremely vulnerable to incendiary attacks, and the destruction wreaked by Superfortresses in some built-up areas amounted to as much as 99.5 per cent.

In addition to these devastating blows against strategic targets, the Superfortresses were simultaneously employed on a highly successful campaign of minelaying in Japanese home waters, thereby applying an economic and logistic stranglehold to the islands of Nippon. The delivery of the two atomic bombs against Hiroshima and Nagasaki was, therefore, in the nature of a *coup de grace*, although essential to shorten the war. The Superfortress was, thus, largely responsible for the final defeat and surrender of Japan without invasion, and the instrument which provided the ultimate vindication of the American visionaries of strategic air power.

After the successful outcome of the struggle by the few proponents of strategic air power to procure the B-17 Fortress—the first U.S.A.A.F. strategic bomber—the way for the introduction of very much larger bombers was appreciably smoother, but the Superfortress was not to be the result of a single specification or design development. It was the product of a continuous series of design studies stemming from the experimental XB-15 of 1937. Such a machine as the Superfortress was first envisaged in the late 'thirties when U.S. military thinking turned to the possibility of an Axis invasion somewhere in the Americas with subsequent enemy air attack against U.S. industrial centres. This concept of "hemisphere defence" called for the production of several types of long-range bombers with operating radii between 1,500 and 4,000 miles, but the 2,000-mile radius bomber specified by the Kilner Board in mid-1939 was perhaps the true starting point for the bomber which was to achieve fame as the Superfortress, although its design origins stretched back even further.

Boeing's design team had included pressurization as an essential in a series of design studies undertaken long before any appropriations were made for a pressurized bomber. The first of these studies, the Model 316, was derived directly from the XB-15, from which it differed primarily in the relocation of the wing from a low to a high position, and the installation of a nosewheel undercarriage—the first to be contemplated for a Boeing design. As the XB-15 had proven seriously under-powered, the Model 316 featured four of the new 2,000 h.p. Wright Duplex-Cyclone R-3350 eighteen-cylinder radials which, it was anticipated, would be more than adequate for the projected bomber's 89,900 lb. gross weight. In March 1938, Boeing had been asked to submit a design study for a pressurized version of the B-17 Fortress with a view to taking maximum advantage of this bomber's high-altitude capabilities. Known as the Model 322, this study resembled the commercial Model 307 Stratoliner in some respects, combining a new, large-diameter circular-section fuselage with standard Fortress wing and tail assemblies. The Model 322 also featured a nosewheel undercarriage and four Pratt and Whitney R-2180 radial engines. Only four gun positions were provided owing to pressurization difficulties, but the bomber had an estimated maximum speed of 307 m.p.h. at 25,000 ft., and a maximum bomb load of 9,928 lb. However, at that time, the Air Corps was receiving insufficient funds for the purchase of adequate quantities of the existing Fortresses, and the project was not taken up officially, although Boeing continued design development as a private venture.

In the next series of studies, Boeing proposed the use of the new liquid-cooled Allison V-1710 engine of 1,150 h.p., and in the Model 333 these engines were installed in tandem pairs. The significance of this project in the subsequent development of the Super-fortress was that, for the first time, it was proposed to utilise two pressurized sections in the fuselage linked by a small-diameter tunnel, and this feature was to be retained in all subsequent design studies up to and including the Superfortress. The Model 333A differed from its predecessor primarily in the reloca-tion of the engines, but because of the low-altitude characteristics of the V-1710 power plant, variations of the project were proposed with the new flat-mounted Wright and Pratt and Whitney radial engines. In February 1939, the Model 333B project was finalised, with four 1,850 h.p. Wright R-1800 engines buried in the thick, 111 ft-span wing, and with a gross weight of 52,180 lb., its maximum speed was estimated at 364 m.p.h. at 20,000 ft.

Because of the restrictions on wing space resulting from the buried engines, the Model 333B would have had a range of only 2,500 miles when carrying a 2,000-lb. bomb load, and this was inadequate for the "hemisphere defence" concept. Thus, a month later, the Model 334 was projected, the wing span being extended to 120 ft. in order to provide sufficient fuel capacity for a range of 4,500 miles. The power plants —this time Pratt and Whitney radials—were still buried in the wing, a twin fin-and-rudder assembly was selected to facilitate the installation of tail arma-ment, and gross weight was increased to 66,000 lb. to permit a maximum bomb load of 7,830 lb. The Superfortress began to take recognisable shape in July 1939, however, with the appearance of the Model 334A project in which both the buried engine in-stallation and the twin fin-and-rudder assembly were rejected in favour of conventionally-mounted Wright R-3350 radials and a single vertical tail surface. The Model 334A featured a high aspect ratio wing of 135 ft. span, and such was the promise of the project that Boeing built a mock-up of the bomber at their own expense in December 1939.

Although these design projects had grown steadily in size, one more step was necessary in order to pro-duce a bomber within the scope of the so-called "Superbomber" specification which was to be issued in January 1940, and this step was taken with the Model 341, design of which was initiated in August 1939. The Boeing Aerodynamics Unit had developed a new high-lift aerofoil for a high aspect-ratio wing of 124 ft. 7 in., and this offered the Model 341 an estimated maximum speed of no less than 405 m.p.h. at 25,000 ft., despite the proposed use of the smaller Pratt and Whitney R-2800 engines of 2,000 h.p. Weighing 85,672 lb., this bomber was expected to have a range of 7,000 miles with one ton of bombs, or a maximum load of 10,000 lb. over shorter distances.

On November 10, 1939, General H. H. Arnold, then Chief of the Air Corps, asked the War Depart-ment for permission to issue a specification for a "Superbomber" to replace the B-17 Fortress and the B-24 Liberator, and the necessary authority was granted on December 2nd. As Data R-40B, the specification was circulated among the Boeing, Lockheed, Douglas and Consolidated companies on January 29, 1940, calling for a bomber with a speed of 400 m.p.h., a range of 5,333 miles, and the ability to deliver a 2,000-lb. load over this range. In the light of early wartime experience in Europe, the original specification was almost immediately modi-fied with regard to defensive armament, and in order to incorporate self-sealing fuel tanks, additional armour, etc.

In order to meet the requirements of the specifica-tion, the Boeing engineers scaled up the overall dimensions of the Model 341 project, replaced the R-2800 engines with the more powerful Wright R-3350s, and came up with the Model 345 which was submitted to Wright Field on May 11, 1940. The Model 345 had a 141 ft. 3 in. wing, and a double-wheeled tricycle undercarriage, the main members of which were designed to retract into the engine nacelles instead of sideways into the wing as in previous projects. The projected bomber possessed a similar range to that of the Model 341, but the maximum bomb load had been increased to 16,000 lb. The estimated speed of 382 m.p.h. at 25,000 feet was slightly lower than that of the smaller project, but the defensive armament had been substantially increased from six manually-operated 0.5-in. guns to ten guns of the same calibre plus one 20-mm. cannon. These were all mounted in Sperry retractable power-operated turrets above and below the fuselage, and in the tail, operated under remote control by gunners looking through periscopes at strategic points.

Evaluation of the preliminary designs submitted by Boeing, Lockheed, Douglas and Consolidated placed them in that order of preference, and con-tracts for preliminary engineering data issued on June 27, 1940, designated the bombers XB-29, XB-30, XB-31, and XB-32 respectively. The Lockheed and Douglas designs were subsequently withdrawn from the competition, but development of the Consoli-dated XB-32 continued as a safeguard against the failure of the favoured Boeing XB-29. On August 24, funds were appropriated for the construction of two XB-29 prototypes, and two XB-32s were also ordered. On December 14, a third XB-29 was ordered, together with a static test airframe.

THE BOEING SUPERFORTRESS

In the event, the rival Consolidated XB-32 was the first of the two bombers to fly—on September 7, 1942—but the teething troubles suffered by this aircraft were such that relatively few had attained service status by the closing months of the war. Backing of the Boeing XB-29 was something of a gamble, since under the normal procurement policy existing in 1940, the bomber could not have been delivered until 1945, and it therefore had to be ordered in quantity before ever the prototype became airborne. Large-scale production was authorised on May 17, 1941, when the U.S.A.A.F. announced that an order would be placed for 250 machines to be built at the Government owned Wichita factory. This contract, which was signed in September, was doubled in January 1942, and in the following month the U.S.A.A.F. announced that the new bomber was also to be built by Bell Aircraft, North American Aviation, and the Fisher Body Division of General Motors. Thus, by the time the first XB-29 made its first flight on September 21, 1942, tooling was well advanced for orders totalling no less than 1,664 machines.

Although each B-29 Superfortress bomber necessitated diverting the material sufficient to build eleven P-51 Mustang fighters, with the corresponding production facilities, the U.S.A.A.F. gamble was based upon the reputation gained by the B-17 Fortress, and the experience of the Boeing company in the construction of large, multi-engined aircraft. These included, of course, the pre-war Model 307 Stratoliner which had been the first pressurized aircraft to enter commercial service, and which gave Boeing a head start with the incorporation of this radical feature in the XB-29. Although strikingly clean in design, the Model 345 was further refined, particular attention being paid to fuselage shape and engine nacelle fairing. The forward fuselage was extended, resulting in an increase in length from 93 ft. to 98 ft. 2 in., and the contours of the streamlined transparent nose were rounded off. The shape of the inner engine nacelles gave cause for particular concern since they each had to house two turbo-superchargers with their intercoolers, plus the twin-wheeled main undercarriage units. The final nacelle shape was one of the cleanest ever produced, although passing more cooling air through than any previous type.

The rear portions of the inner engine nacelles were extended aft of the wing trailing edges which were modified to improve the flap characteristics, and a large dorsal extension was added to the vertical tail surfaces to improve asymmetric handling, but the tailplane and elevators remained exactly the same size and shape as those of the B-17 Fortress, although they were of different section and construction. They were, in fact, flight tested on a B-17 which was also used to develop servo-tabs to lighten the load on all the controls of the Superfortress. Redesign of the bomb bay allowed a large number of small bombs to be carried in addition to the 1,000-lb. and 2,000-lb. bombs originally planned, and at the same time the maximum capacity was increased to 20,000 lb.

Final armament modifications resulted in the Sperry remotely-controlled gun turrets becoming permanently external instead of retractable, but despite this modification, the Superfortress suffered no more drag than the Fortress, although being one-third as large again and, at 114,500 lb., almost twice the weight. Design estimates then indicated a reduced maximum range of 5,333 miles with one ton of bombs which was that originally demanded, and the finalised aircraft met with the complete approval of the U.S.A.A.F., although some service technicians were concerned over the bomber's high wing loading. At one time, some pressure was applied to Boeing to reduce the wing loading by increasing the bomber's wing area, but Boeing engineers succeeded in convincing the critics that any increase in wing area would seriously reduce the machine's performance. Fowler flaps reduced the high wing loading problem during the critical take-off and landing phases of a flight, increasing the lift coefficient of the wing and adding some twenty per cent to the overall area when extended.

A full-scale wooden mock-up of the XB-29 was made available for U.S.A.A.F. inspection from April

The first XB-29 Superfortress prototype (41-002), flown for the first time on September 21, 1942, was completed without the remotely-controlled armament system.

The first Wichita-built Superfortress, B-29-1-BW (42-6242), delivered deficient from the combat-readiness viewpoint and subsequently modified during the "Battle of Kansas".

7, 1941, and a month later the first engineering drawings were released for prototype construction. On June 16, 1941, production engineering began for fourteen YB-29s for service evaluation and 250 B-29s, the first twenty-five machines being required by February 1943. As the Boeing plants were entirely occupied with B-17 Fortress orders, a completely new factory for Superfortress production had to be built at Wichita, and after Pearl Harbour, it was obvious that further facilities would be required. Superfortress production was therefore planned at other plants, including a new Boeing factory at Renton; a factory to be operated by Bell Aircraft and to be built at Georgia, and a Glenn Martin factory at Omaha which was selected to replace the Fisher Body plant at Cleveland originally designated as a Superfortress production source. It was planned that Boeing's Seattle plant would also produce the Superfortress as Fortress production tapered off, and in addition to the airframe assembly plants, the most widespread sub-contracting programme ever planned was established, and such companies as Fisher Body, Chrysler, Hudson, Goodyear, Briggs, Murray and Cessna produced major airframe components.

Powered by four 2,200 h.p. Wright R-3350-13 engines driving three-bladed airscrews, the first XB-29 (No. 41-2) made its first flight from Boeing Field, Seattle, on September 21, 1942, with Edward Allen at the controls. The first airframe was completed without the remotely-controlled armament system in order to accelerate flight testing, but this programme suffered a serious set-back when the second XB-29 (No. 41-3), which had flown for the first time on December 28, 1942, developed an unextinguishable engine fire while making a landing approach on February 18, 1943, plunging into a nearby factory, killing eleven of Boeing's most experienced Superfortress specialists, including test pilot Edward Allen, and a score of workers on the ground.

Some delay was then encountered in the development programme while fire hazards in the XB-29 were reduced, but in June 1943, the third Seattle-built prototype (41-18335) began its flight tests. This third machine embodied extensive engine and equipment revision which resulted from experience gained with its two predecessors, and was soon handed over to the A.A.F. at Wichita for armament and accelerated flight testing. This prototype also crashed, but not before the potential of the design had been indicated. Among the principal changes required for production B-29s were the introduction of four-bladed Hamilton-Standard airscrews, and the replacement of the periscopically-sighted Sperry gun turrets by a completely new system of General Electric turrets controlled from adjacent astrodomes. This change in armament caused considerable delay in the B-29 programme, although the first YB-29 (41-36954), with Wright R-3350-21 engines, left the line at Wichita on April 15, 1943, flying for the first time on June 26, 1943.

By July, seven YB-29s had been delivered to the

The B-29A differed from the B-29 in having a stub wing centre section resulting in a one foot increase in overall wing span. The aircraft illustrated here is a B-29A-5-BN.

A.A.F., and, as representative operational aircraft, they were used to equip new training groups categorised as VHB (Very Heavy Bomber) or VLR (Very Long Range) units. The application of these units had changed considerably from the original conception of hemisphere defence, and eventually differed substantially from the 1940 plan of having twenty-four B-29/B-32 groups to bomb Germany from the United Kingdom and North Africa, plus a possible further two groups operating against Japan from Luzon. It was not until December 1943 that the decision not to use the B-29 against Germany was finally taken, but in the meantime Brig.-Gen. K. B. Wolfe had been given the task of setting up Superfortress combat training units for operations in 1944 against Japanese targets from bases in China. This was done simultaneously with the service testing of the YB-29s, and on June 1, 1943, the first Superfortress unit—the 58th Bombardment Wing (VH)—was activated at Marietta, near Bell's Superfortress plant. One hundred and fifty Superfortresses had been promised for early 1944, enough for four VHB groups, and on September 15, 1943, the Wing Headquarters was re-established at Salina, Kansas, with some of its groups near the Wichita factory. The first Superfortress Wing initially comprised five groups—the 40th, 444th, 462nd, 468th and 472nd Bombardment Groups (VH)—but the last of these was scheduled to remain at Smoky Hill Field, Salina, as an operational training unit. On November 27, 1943, the XX Bomber Command was formed at Salina for overall control of the Superfortress units, and another Very Heavy Wing, the 73rd, was formed with four more groups to absorb the second batch of 150 Superfortresses.

At that time, however, there was only one Superfortress for each twelve crews, since it was not until October 7th that the flight characteristics of the aircraft received A.A.F. approval, and all initial crew training had to be conducted on Martin B-26 Marauders and Boeing B-17 Fortresses. At that time, much of the Superfortress's equipment had not been perfected or, indeed, tested on the prototype or pre-production aircraft, and rather than delay production by stopping the assembly lines to incorporate modifications and equipment, the first production aeroplanes were leaving the lines at Wichita deficient from the combat-readiness viewpoint. The A.A.F. had established modification centres to bring the Superfortresses up to combat standards, but the programme was seriously hampered by the need to work in the open air in inclement weather, delays in acquiring the necessary tools and support equipment, and the A.A.F.'s limited experience with the B-29. Such were the delays that Boeing personnel had to be drafted from the Wichita and Seattle factories to reorganise the programme and assist with the modifications. The period from March 10–April 15, 1944, when the first Superfortresses for combat duty were passing through the modification centres, became known as the "Battle of Kansas".

Towards the end of 1943, the Bell-Marietta and Boeing-Renton plants began turning out production Superfortresses, which, from the former factory, were like the B-29-BW and later B-29-MO aircraft in being powered by R-3350-23, -23A or (when modified) -41 engines, having a war emergency rating of 2,300 h.p. Maximum permissible weight of the first Superfortress series was 138,000 lb., although the normal gross was 133,500 lb. There were slight differences in equipment among the various sub-contracted aircraft, but they all started off with the same armament and fuel capacity. The Superfortress was the first production aircraft to make extensive use of remotely-controlled armament. While manned turrets had been contemplated during early stages of the Superfortress's design, they had been rejected as unsuitable for the altitudes at which the bomber was designed to operate. Four barbettes, each containing two 0.5-in. guns, were, therefore, installed at strategic positions in the fuselage, two on top and two underneath, and controlled remotely from sighting stations in the pressurized areas of the fuselage. These twin-gun barbettes, each with 1,000 r.p.g., could be controlled from a primary or a secondary station, and, in addition, a tail turret under the direct control of a tail gunner, housed two 0.5-in. machine guns and a 20-mm. M-2 Type B cannon with 100 rounds. Fuel was stowed in fourteen outer-wing, eight inner-wing, and four bomb-bay tanks, to give a maximum capacity of 6,801 Imp.gal. (8,168 U.S.gal.), but an early modification added four tanks in the wing centre-section, bringing the total to 7,896 Imp. gal. (9,438 U.S. gal.).

This fuel load gave the Superfortress a maximum range of well over the 5,000 mile figure of the original Project "A", but this was only possible for ferrying purposes, a more normal range being about 3,700 miles with up to 12,000 lb. of bombs. Maximum internal bomb load was 20,000 lb. (for 2,850 miles), with provision for alternatives of four 4,000-lb., eight 2,000-lb., twelve 1,600-lb., twelve 1,000-lb., or forty 500-lb. bombs. Later production versions of the Superfortress had the front upper turret armament increased from two to four 0.5-in. guns, each with 875 rounds, and the last batches (B-29-25 to -65-BA*; B-29-50 to -100-BW, and B-29-20 to

---

* BA = Bell (Atlanta); BW = Boeing (Wichita), and MO = Martin (Omaha). Other manufacturers were BN = Boeing (Renton) and BO = Boeing (Seattle).

-60-MO) lost the 20-mm. cannon from the tail position. Lingering doubts as to the practicability of the remotely-controlled armament system, however, resulted in the completion of one B-29-25-BW (42-2444) with manned turrets. This aircraft featured two power-operated dorsal turrets and two central "ball" turrets each containing two 0.5-in. machine guns, one 0.5-in. gun in each of two beam positions, and two additional 0.5-in. guns in a blister on each side of the fuselage nose.

The Martin-Omaha plant turned out its first B-29 in mid-1944, and completed 536 of the 2,774 Superfortresses of the first series to be built. Effort at the Boeing-Renton factory was devoted entirely to the slightly modified B-29A (production blocks -1 to -75-BN) of which 1,119 were produced. The B-29A differed in having R-3350-57 or -59 engines of the standard 2,200 h.p., and only three centre-wing tanks in all but the first few machines, giving a maximum fuel capacity of 7,734 Imp. gal. (9,288 U.S. gal.). They also lost the single tail cannon (before the four-gun upper turret was introduced), and had a 1 ft. increase in span, to 142 ft. 3 in. as the result of the adoption of a stub wing centre section, the wing of the B-29A being built in seven major pieces as compared with the six pieces of the B-29's wing. Three B-29A-BN Superfortresses were converted by the Pratt and Whitney company to take 3,000 h.p. R-4360-33 engines, and redesignated XB-44, to become test-beds for the later Boeing B-50. This followed an earlier conversion of a YB-29, which was fitted with four 2,600 h.p. Allison V-3420-11 liquid-cooled inline engines for experimental purposes, and became the XB-39. In both cases, the maximum speed was increased to more than 400 m.p.h., despite the increased gross weights of 145,000 and 142,000 lb., and the potentialities of bigger power plants convincingly demonstrated.

One of the biggest drawbacks of the Superfortress was its tendency towards being underpowered at high gross weights, resulting in a certain amount of engine trouble throughout its service life. This was a small price to pay for the truly remarkable rapidity of its

One B-29-25-BW Superfortress (42-2444) was completed with twin manned dorsal turrets and two "ball" turrets, each with two 0.5-in. guns, and a similar gun in each of two beam positions and on each side of the nose.

FINISH AND INSIGNIA: The Boeing B-29-45-MO illustrated is probably the most famous of all Superfortress bombers, being Colonel Tibbets' "Enola Gay", from which the first operational atomic weapon was dropped. This aircraft, which belonged to the 393rd Bombardment Squadron (VH) of the 315th Bombardment Wing, was non-standard insofar as the fore and aft dorsal and ventral gun barbettes were removed, although the manned tail turret was retained. Whereas early production Superfortresses had matt olive drab upper surfaces with grey under surfaces, in common with all aircraft of this type operational with the U.S. Twentieth Air Force in the Far East, "Enola Gay" employed a natural metal finish over all surfaces.

The national insignia, which comprised a white five-pointed star on a dark blue circular field superimposed on a white bar which, in turn, was outlined in dark blue, appeared on the uppe surface o the port wing, the ower surface of the starboard wing, and on each side of the fuselage. When delivered from the factory, the serial number normally appeared on the tail fin in black, but this was invariably deleted in the field to provide space for the group symbol. The Bombardment Group letter "R" appeared in black on the vertical tail surfaces, this being enclosed in a black circle indicating the Air Division. For the atomic strike, the group letter was replaced by a black arrowhead in a circle (this insignia being illustrated by the photograph on page 116). The individual aircraft number "82" appeared in black aft of the national insignia on the fuselage sides, and was repeated above and ahead of the nosewheel housing. The name "Enola Gay" was painted in black below the transparent panels of the flight deck.

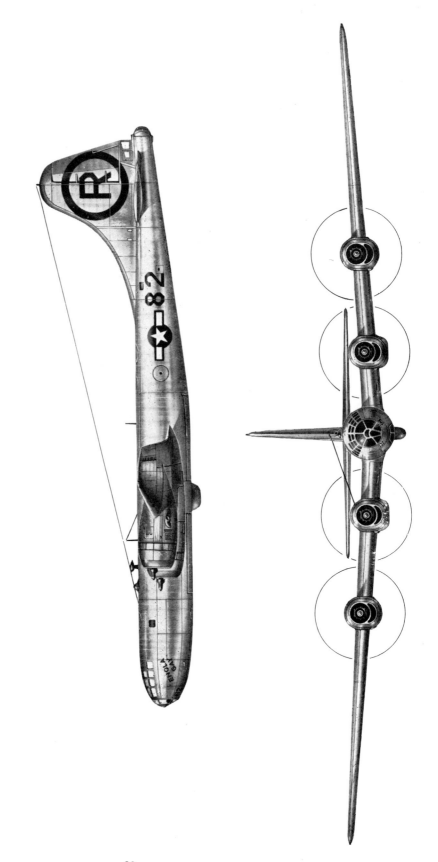

80

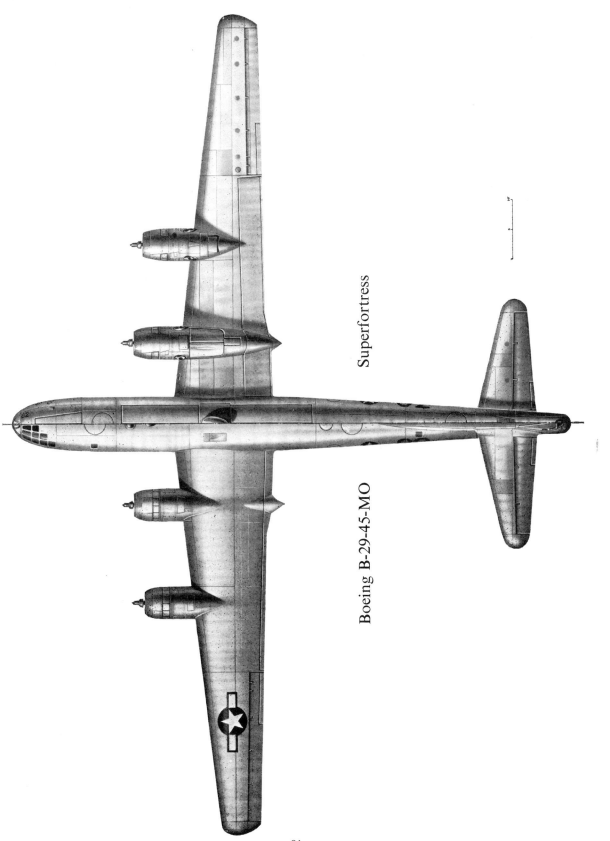

Superfortress

Boeing B-29-45-MO

The B-29-45-MO "Enola Gay" which, piloted by Colonel Tibbets, dropped the atomic bomb on Hiroshima. The aircraft was accompanied on its mission by six other Superfortresses carrying observers and survival equipment.

development, and the Superfortress's operational efficiency far outweighed the inevitable shortcomings. It was little more than eighteen months after the first flight of the XB-29 that the first Superfortress landed in China, on April 24, 1944, at Kwanghan, supported logistically by C-46, C-54, C-87 and C-109 transports, and it is a little known fact that one of the first Superfortresses to go overseas was flown to the United Kingdom in March 1944, to be demonstrated to the 8th Air Force before proceeding to the main Far Eastern Superfortress base at Calcutta. The use of this somewhat devious delivery route was intended to delude the Axis powers into believing that the B-29 was to be used against Germany.

Despite the secrecy with which the Superfortress bases had been prepared, and the various deceptions practised, the Japanese had no difficulty in identifying the Superfortresses as soon as they arrived in the Far East; an arrival delayed by a week due to the aircraft being grounded after several accidents on the ferry route. Five B-29s were lost through engine failures, and four seriously damaged out of the initial batch of 150 sent to India, but when the ferry trips stopped, in March 1945, only three more had been lost out of the overall total of 405 despatched.

Before the Superfortresses began bombing operations from their Chinese bases, they had to assist in airlifting all necessary supplies and fuel over the "Hump". For this task, some were stripped of nearly all combat equipment and, used as flying tankers, each carried seven tons of fuel. This transport role, while vitally necessary, prevented further operational training from being completed, and when the first mission was scheduled—against railway shops at Bangkok, Thailand—most of the 240 crews in XX Bomber Command had an average of less than two hours' B-29 combat training each. A short and intensive training programme was, therefore, instituted, before the combat schedules were planned. Bomb loads were to be 10,000 lb. per aircraft, and with 5,700 Imp.gal. (6,846 U.S.gal.) of fuel, the

aircraft were to weigh 134,000 lb. About one hundred Superfortresses were despatched in daylight from bases in India to attack Bangkok on June 5, 1944, and most of these bombed their targets by radar owing to the bad weather—the latter largely accounting for the five aircraft lost on this initial mission. Somewhat surprisingly, in view of the Japanese awareness of the existence of the Superfortresses in the theatre, Radio Tokyo reported that the Bangkok raid had been made by B-24 Liberators.

All the aircraft of the 58th Bombardment Wing (VH) were Wichita-built B-29-BWs, which were, therefore, the first to bomb enemy targets. From the outset, they made good use of the extensive radar and electronic equipment with which they were provided, which included Loran, BTO, "H2X" (later "Eagle"), "Raven" electronic countermeasures on occasions, and "Ella" IFF. To relieve Japanese pressure in Eastern China, where Brig.-Gen. Claire Chennault's forward airfields were threatened, the next Superfortress mission was scheduled against Japan, where, on June 15th, about fifty B-29s bombed the steel mills at Yawata by night. This operation cost seven Superfortresses, only one due to enemy action, but, like the Bangkok raid, little damage was sustained by the targets.

From thence onwards, the build-up of Superfortress missions was slow and widely scattered until the capture of the Mariana Islands of Saipan, Guam and Tinian in July and August 1944 permitted the construction of five great airfields, each accommodating a wing of 180 Superfortresses and 12,000 men under the newly formed 20th Air Force. These bases enabled the VHB offensive to be concentrated on Japan, after a series of training missions by additional B-29 groups which arrived in the Marianas from October 12th onwards. The first Marianas-based attack against the Japanese homeland took place on November 24th when eighty-eight Superfortresses bombed Tokyo, but the success of this and subsequent daylight attacks was limited.

This B-29-30-BW (42-24473) was the fifty-fourth Wichita-built Superfortress of the second production order (calling for five hundred aircraft) allocated to this plant.

The U.S.A.A.F. was attempting to use the Superfortresses on similar operations to those of the 8th Air Force over Germany (i.e. daylight precision raids in formation at high altitudes). This resulted in poor bombing accuracy, small bomb loads to ensure altitude performance, and considerable engine trouble because of the prolonged climbs required at high gross weights. Maj.-Gen. Curtiss E. LeMay, who had been given the B-29 command in the India-China theatre, took over the Marianas-based Superfortresses in January, 1945, and was immediately keen to try the effects of incendiary attacks against Japanese cities. He also decided, in March, to change the Superfortress's role to that of low-altitude night bomber. This greatly increased the available bomb load of the B-29, and simultaneously decreased its vulnerability over the target since the Japanese possessed little or no night defence organisation.

In the first of these attacks, on March 9th, 334 Superfortresses burned out some sixteen square miles of the heart of Tokyo, killing more than 80,000 people—the greatest destruction of any single raid of the war. Within a few days, four more major cities had been attacked, and thirty-two square miles of destruction added to the score of the Superfortresses. Having met virtually no aerial opposition during their nocturnal attacks, the A.A.F. decided to strip its B-29s of all defensive armament except the two 0.5-in. machine guns in the tail, thus permitting the maximum load of bombs to be carried. In addition to B-29s and B-29As stripped in the field, the Bell-Atlanta plant built 311 Superfortresses with only tail armament and two 0.5-in. guns on special hand-held mountings in the waist positions of the pressurized gunners' cabin, as B-29Bs. With R-3350-51s, or similar series engines to earlier B-29s, these had their maximum speeds increased by 10 m.p.h. to 367 m.p.h. at 30,000 ft. At the same gross weight of 135,000 lb. as earlier B-29s, and carrying a similar fuel load of 5,764 Imp.gal. (6,923 U.S.gal.), the B-29B could carry 16,000 lb. of bombs instead of 12,000 lb. over a range of about 2,600 miles.

As the Pacific War drew towards a conclusion, rapidly accelerated by the depredations of the Superfortresses, about one thousand B-29s were operational in twenty-one combat groups of the 20th Air Force out of a total of forty VHB groups which had by then been formed. In addition to devastating bombing attacks by as many as 600 aircraft in a day, the Pacific-based Superfortresses flew 1,528 mining sorties around Japan in 1945, planting by parachute more than 12,000 mines. These are estimated to have resulted in the sinking of about 800,000 tons of Japanese shipping. Another important task performed by the Superfortresses was photographic-reconnaissance. As no other aircraft had the range to survey B-29 targets for damage reports, a few Superfortresses were modified in the field to carry cameras in mid-1944. The first of these crashed during the initial B-29 mission against Japan in June 1944, but others later photographed Okinawa for airfield sites and as a prelude to the island's invasion.

Meanwhile, technicians at Wright Field were developing an extensively modified Superfortress expressly for photographic-reconnaissance duties, with long-range fuel tanks in the bomb-bay, and numerous K-18 and K-22 cameras to cover oblique, tri-metrogen, and vertical survey. As the F-13A, a number of Superfortresses were converted from B-29-BWs and B-29ABNs, and were sent to the Pacific in November 1944. In the following month, when seven F-13As had arrived in the China-Burma-India theatre, "C" Flight of the 1st Squadron, 311th Photo-Reconnaissance Wing, was established with them, and missions were soon flown to Penang, Bangkok and Saigon. More F-13As later arrived, and these continued to operate on vital photo-reconnaissance sorties until the end of the Pacific War.

The final Superfortress offensive was undertaken mostly at night, but occasionally by day, with P-51D Mustang escort from Iwo Jima, and by May, 1945, Tokyo, Nagoya and Yokohama had been virtually burned out. Bombing techniques employed path-

This B-29A-30-BN (42-94106), like all A-model Superfortresses, differed from the initial production model in having a four-gun forward turret and a stub wing centre section.

finder lead ships, carrying 180 70-lb. M47 Napalm-filled bombs each, followed by the main force with each Superfortress dropping twenty-four 500-lb. clusters of M69 oil incendiaries in a pattern, distributing 8,333 of these bombs per square mile. On some occasions, the attacking Superfortresses suffered heavy losses, not usually through direct combat, and in the Tokyo raid of May 25th, twenty-six B-29s were lost of the 502 despatched. The overall loss rate, nevertheless, at this stage of the offensive, was only 1.9 per cent.

When the B-29-45-MO (44-86292) "Enola Gay" ushered in the atomic age over Hiroshima on August 6, 1945, this was the climax of the most memorable chapter in the development of the Superfortress. From 1943 onwards, when much scientific effort was concentrated on producing an atomic bomb, it was obvious that such a weapon would be very large, and it was realised that the Superfortress would be the only aircraft capable of carrying it. The A.A.F. was made responsible for modifications to the aircraft to render it suitable for ballistic tests on the bomb, and for organising a special operational unit, and work began early in 1944 to produce fifteen Superfortresses capable of carrying the nuclear weapon. The modifications involved were fairly extensive, but the atomic bomb was tailored as closely as possible to fit the B-29.

The unit selected to work up with the new weapon, in mid-1944, was the recently-formed 393rd Bombardment Squadron (VH), within the specialist 509th Composite Group, which was taken over at Wendover Field, Utah, by Colonel Paul W. Tibbets on December 17th. The Squadron's Superfortresses then dropped inert experimental versions of the weapon to test its ballistics, and their training was completed by long-range practice flying from Batista Field, Cuba. In May, the Composite Group, with its parent 315th Bombardment Wing, took its Superfortresses, which were stripped of all turrets and guns except in the tail, to Tinian in the Marianas, where training and conventional bombing sorties over Japan for target familiarization soon began.

Simulated atomic missions were also flown, usually at about 29,000 ft., but dropping T.N.T.-filled, light-cased, 10,000-lb. missiles with similar ballistics to the nuclear bomb. By the end of July, soon after the

first test weapon had been exploded in New Mexico, the Group was ready, and two operational bombs had been ferried to the Pacific by air and sea transport. The first target had eventually been selected as Hiroshima, as the largest un-bombed Japanese city, and seven Superfortresses were designated for the mission. Of these, one was a spare to stand by at Iwo Jima; three were weather reconnaissance aircraft to survey the primary, secondary and tertiary targets, and two were observation aircraft carrying cameras, recording equipment, scientists and technicians to accompany the single strike aircraft, Colonel Tibbet's "Enola Gay". Two F-13As were laid on for subsequent target reconnaissance, and other specially-equipped B-29s, carrying survival equipment, and known as "Superdumbos", were arranged to provide air-sea rescue facilities as in the case of normal Superfortress missions. These "Superdumbos" were, incidentally, the predecessors of later lifeboat-carrying Superfortresses designated SB-29s.

The seven Superfortresses on the first atomic strike had their group insignia and aircraft names painted over for the mission, but wore special so-called "victory" numbers. The crews concerned were given some indication of the power of their special weapon, but not its precise nature. The atomic bomb itself, which had been nicknamed the "Little Boy", was a cylindrical device measuring 129 in. in length by 31.5 in. in diameter. Four antennae bristled from its tail, and, weighing 9,700 lb., it contained 137.3 lb. of Uranium 235. "Enola Gay" took-off from Tinian at 02.45 hours on August 6, 1945, and as the aircraft approached the Japanese coast, the primary target was reported relatively clear for attack. At 09.15 hours, Major T. W. Ferebee released the nuclear bomb at an altitude of 31,600 ft., and a ground speed of 328 m.p.h. At 800 ft. above Hiroshima a powder charge sent one Uranium mass through a hollow shaft into the other mass, and one fifteen-hundredth of a microsecond later fission commenced. With the equivalent force of 20,000 tons of T.N.T., it devastated 4.7 square miles of the city, and killed more than 70,000 people.

Three days later, on August 9th, a second atomic force attacked Nagasaki. Deletion of the aircraft markings resulted in some confusion in official reports of this raid which initially credited one of the observation aircraft, "The Great Artiste" of Major Charles W. Sweeney, with having dropped the second atomic weapon. In fact, this aircraft, which Major Sweeney had flown on observation duties on the Hiroshima strike, was exchanged for another Superfortress, Captain F. Bock's "Bockscar", in order to obviate the necessity of removing the special scientific equipment installed in "The Great Artiste" for the previous strike. Captain Bock took over Major Sweeney's aircraft, and the latter officer released the atomic bomb from "Bockscar". It was only after the war, when it was planned to preserve "The Great Artiste" as a museum piece, that a check of serial numbers in the mission reports revealed the error. In very poor weather conditions, the Nagasaki bomb was dropped largely by radar, but again the results were devastating. When the Japanese surrender followed, on August 14th, no fewer than 828 Superfortresses were airborne on conventional bombing missions. The massive force was then transferred to transport and supply dropping operations, although 462 Superfortresses were mustered to fly over the U.S.S. *Missouri* during the surrender ceremonies on September 2nd.

During the Pacific War, Superfortresses dropped 171,060 tons of conventional bombs on Japanese territory, compared with 6,781 tons for all other aircraft combined. In addition to atomic weapons, some of the Superfortresses were equipped to carry a 22,000-lb. "Grand Slam" or "earthquake" bomb of British design under each inner wing, between the engine nacelle and the fuselage, giving a short-range offensive load of 44,000 lb. These weapons were not used operationally, although after the war some Superfortresses modified to carry a single 22,000-lb. bomb half-buried in the bomb-bay were used in extensive tests against German defences on deserted Baltic islands.

With the termination of the Second World War, development of the B-29C (with improved Wright R-3350 engines) by Boeing-Seattle was cancelled, and the re-engined B-29D-BN, with four 3,000 h.p. Pratt and Whitney R-4360 power plants, was subsequently developed into the newer B-50. When production ceased at Renton on May 28, 1946, V-J Day having resulted in the cancellation of 5,092 Superfortresses still on order in September 1945, although a small number well advanced on the assembly lines were completed, 3,970 Superfortresses had been built, including 2,766 by Boeing at Seattle, Renton and Wichita; 668 by Bell and 536 by Martin. On V-J Day, the U.S.A.A.F. had 2,132 Superfortresses on hand, and many of these were subsequently cocooned for long-term storage.

It makes an interesting tailpiece to the wartime story of the Superfortress to recall the admiration for this splendid bomber evinced by the United States' erstwhile allies, the Russians. In fact, such was their interest in the B-29 that the Russians sequestrated three Superfortresses that, short of fuel after bombing missions against Japan, were forced to land at Vladivostok, the nearest "friendly" territory. The first B-29 to land at Vladivostok was piloted by

The first YB-29 Superfortress (41-36954) was fitted with four Allison V-3420-11 liquid-cooled engines for experimental purposes and redesignated XB-39.

Captain Howard R. Jarrell; the second was the "General Arnold Special", the most famous Superfortress produced by the Boeing-Wichita plant, and the first aircraft over the target on the first B-29 mission of the war, and the third was piloted by 1st Lt. William J. Mickish. The crews were eventually returned to the United States, but their aircraft were retained by the Russians who eventually produced copies of the B-29 under the designation Tupolev Tu-4 as the standard long-range heavy bomber of the Soviet Air Forces. The adoption of this aircraft by the Russians in 1947 was a strange tribute to the soundness of the Superfortress's 1940 conception, but imitation *is* the sincerest form of flattery.

The Superfortress made an immense contribution to subsequent bomber design. It was the Second World War's heaviest production warplane, and the first pressurized aircraft to attain large-scale production. It was also the first to make extensive use of remotely-controlled armament, but perhaps the most remarkable feature of its history was the fact that it was designed, built, tested, and placed in operational service within four years.

Boeing B-29 Superfortress

Dimensions:	Span, 141 ft. 3 in.; length, 99 ft. 0 in.; height, 27 ft. 9 in.; wing area, 1,736 sq. ft.
Armament:	Twelve 0.5-in. machine guns in four remotely-controlled turrets and in the tail, each with 1,000 rounds of ammunition, plus a single rearward-firing 20-mm. M2 Type B cannon with 100 rounds. Maximum internal short-range bomb load, 20,000 lb.
Power Plants:	Four Wright Cyclone R-3350-23 eighteen-cylinder air-cooled radial engines, each with two General Electric turbo-superchargers, rated at 2,200 h.p. at 2,800 r.p.m. for take-off, and with a war emergency rating of 2,300 h.p. at 25,000 ft.
Weights:	Empty, 74,500 lb.; normal useful load, 45,500 lb.; maximum useful load, 60,500 lb.; normal loaded, 120,000 lb.; maximum overload, 135,000 lb.
Performance:	Maximum speed, 357 m.p.h. at 30,000 ft., 306 m.p.h. at sea level; maximum continuous cruising, 342 m.p.h. at 30,000 ft.; economical cruising, 220 m.p.h. at 25,000 ft.; initial climb rate (at combat weight), 900 ft./min.; service ceiling, 33,600 ft.; range and endurance (at 10,000 ft. with 5,585 Imp.gal. of fuel) with 4,000-lb. bomb load, 2,650 mls. in 8.9 hrs., with 10,000-lb. bomb load, 3,250 mls. in 16.4 hrs.

The Vickers Type 271 (K4049), predecessor of the Wellington, which was flown for the first time on June 15, 1936.

THE VICKERS WELLINGTON

Few if any bombers of the Second World War enjoyed a longer or more distinguished operational career than the Vickers Wellington. Blooded in combat at the very outset of hostilities, it carried the lion's share of R.A.F. Bomber Command's night bombing offensive until the operational début of the first four-engined "heavies", and was still first-line equipment when the war ended. Indeed, such was the brilliant battle record of the Wellington that any tribute can be but a pale reflection of the distinctions that this remarkable warplane won for itself. The Wellington's docility combined with a lively performance and its ability to absorb a fantastic amount of battle damage rapidly endeared it to its crews, and its portly, well-fed appearance engendered the nickname "Wimpey" after Popeye's obese friend J. Wellington Wimpey of strip-cartoon fame, an appellation that became as widely known as that with which it was officially christened. More than any other bomber, the Wellington proved the power-operated gun turret to be a formidable defensive weapon, but it disproved the widely-held belief that large bombers could undertake daylight bombing attacks against heavily defended areas without fighter escort.

Like most successful combat aircraft, the Wellington was the result of team work, but it undoubtedly owed its success to the revolutionary geodetic, or "basket weave", system of construction, an ingenious idea the more remarkable for its essential simplicity. When Vickers Limited, through a subsidiary company known as the Airship Guarantee Company, received a contract from H. M. Government to build the airship R.100, they employed an outstanding engineer named Barnes N. Wallis to design the structure. From an airship designed for use on an experimental com-

mercial air service between the United Kingdom and the Commonwealth to a medium bomber built by the thousand in the Second World War may seem a long step indeed, but in the R.100's construction lay the germ of an idea which was to see fruition years later in the Wellington's structure.

The geodetic system of construction—the name being derived from *geodeses*, imaginary geographical lines following the curvature of the earth along a straight path—was designed to carry all loads in the structure along the shortest possible paths. It produced a criss-cross pattern of self-stabilising members by means of which loads in any direction were automatically equalised by forces in the intersecting set of frames. High strength was obtained at low weight. Vickers were not slow to see the advantages which might accrue from this form of construction and Barnes Wallis was teamed up with Rex K. Pierson, then Vickers' chief designer, to produce structural designs. The complex shape of the aeroplane, coupled with the need to cut away some of the multitudinous geodetic members for cockpits, bomb-bays, and gun turrets, presented such difficulties that the originators might well have given up hope of reaping the rewards of their ingenuity. Vickers enjoyed no subsidy to cover the expense of developing the geodetic system, but with faith and perseverance the many hurdles were surmounted, and the company's belief in the soundness of Barnes Wallis's invention was amply vindicated.

The first aeroplane to employ geodetic construction was the Type 246 Wellesley which was built as a private venture to meet the general requirements of specification G.4/31 which called for a general-purpose bombing and torpedo-carrying aircraft. Vickers actually received a prototype contract for a biplane

The first production Wellington I (L4212), which first flew on December 23, 1937, was originally powered by Pegasus X engines.

fulfilling this specification, the Type 253, which was in fact built and flown, but the company had implicit faith in the superiority of their monoplane which, in the event, was adopted for the Royal Air Force. The Wellesley prototype (K7556) did not fly until June 19, 1935, and by that time lessons learned in its design were already being applied to the next, even more ambitious Vickers bomber.

The pattern for this new bomber was set by an official specification, B.9/32, issued in the middle of 1932, for a twin-engined day bomber of appreciably higher performance than any previously envisaged. The promise offered by the forthcoming Bristol Mercury VI S2 supercharged air-cooled radial engines and the Rolls-Royce Goshawk steam-cooled inline engines rendered possible a performance such as that demanded by the specification, and Vickers prepared a design in which these power plants were alternatively applicable. After these preliminary suggestions, submitted in March 1933, had been studied, the Air Ministry revised the specification in September 1933 to give favour to the Goshawk engine, and in the following October Vickers submitted a new design which, employing geodetic construction, was a mid-wing monoplane with a retractable undercarriage and two Goshawk I engines. The mid-wing gave better drag figures at the root junction with the fuselage than a high-mounted wing, and also provided a bomb-bay unobstructed by the main spar of a low-mounted wing.

In December 1933 Vickers were awarded an official contract for the construction of one prototype of their design which, bearing the designation Type 271, was powered by two Goshawks. Six months later, however—by which time construction had already begun—the Air Ministry realised that the Goshawk was not fulfilling its earlier promise, and the specification again had to be changed. As no alternative power plant with a similar power-to-weight ratio as that of the Goshawk presented itself, it was necessary to relax the limit on the bomber's tare weight in order to permit the installation of the heavier and more powerful Bristol Perseus or Pegasus nine-cylinder air-cooled radials. There can be no doubt that this decision saved the design from the early demise which would have resulted if the Goshawk installation, with its complex steam cooling, had been continued.

Vickers eventually elected to use the Bristol Pegasus engine which, in its PE5.SM version, was rated at 850 h.p. for take-off. In production, this engine was designated the Pegasus X, and two of them powered the Vickers Type 271 (K4049) bomber prototype when J. "Mutt" Summers took the aircraft into the air at Brooklands on its maiden flight on June 15, 1936. Although the Type 271 was destined to be completely redesigned before it emerged as the Wellington I, it was itself a major step forward in British bomber design. The fuselage, although portly, was remarkably well streamlined, and the wings were of a higher aspect ratio at 8.83:1 than had previously been attempted in a twin-engined aeroplane, with consequent benefit on performance. The Wellesley-type tail unit initially planned had given place to one of larger area—the single fin and rudder design was borrowed directly from the Supermarine Stranraer flying boat which had twin vertical tail surfaces. The span was 85 ft. 10 in., and the overall length was 60 ft. 6 in., and the Type 271 was designed to be operated by a crew of four, with provision for a fifth crew member when required.

The warload was a maximum of nine 500-lb. bombs, or nine 250-lb. bombs with fuel for maximum range, and defensive armament comprised two Lewis 0.303-in. machine guns, one forward- and one rearward-firing in enclosed, hand-operated cupolas at each end of the fuselage. Provision was made in the design for a hand-operated gun in a retractable dorsal turret, but this was never implemented. At an all-up weight of 21,000 lb., the Type 271 reached 250 m.p.h. at 8,000 ft.

Immediately after making its first flight, the prototype appeared in the new-types park at the R.A.F. Display at Hendon in June 1936, where it created a most favourable impression. This was subsequently confirmed in official trials which followed, and before the end of the year—in August 1936, in fact—a production specification was drawn up around the Type 271 design, and 180 aircraft were ordered to be build to this standard. Hence the Wellington I met the requirements of specification 29/36, and appeared in quite different guise to the basic B.9/32 design.

The prototype Wellington II (L4250) modified to test the 40-mm. Vickers "S" gun in a dorsal turret designed for the Boulton Paul P.92.

THE VICKERS WELLINGTON

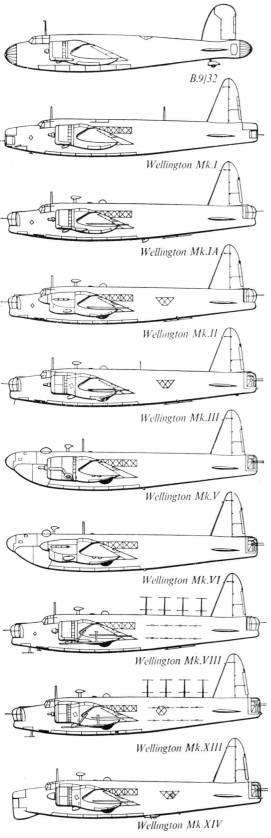

B.9/32

Wellington Mk.I

Wellington Mk.IA

Wellington Mk.II

Wellington Mk.III

Wellington Mk.V

Wellington Mk.VI

Wellington Mk.VIII

Wellington Mk.XIII

Wellington Mk XIV

The original Type 271 prototype was lost in an unfortunate mishap during diving trials. The accident resulted primarily from the unprecedentedly high speeds at which the aircraft could be flown; the horn-balance on the elevator, which was exposed to the airstream at large angular settings of the control surface, produced a control loading too large to be held manually, and the aeroplane flopped onto its back. The pilot was thrown through the cockpit roof by the violence of this manoeuvre, and landed safely by parachute; the other occupant of the aircraft was killed.

At this juncture it is necessary to clarify the design situation regarding the larger and heavier B.1/35 bomber which was eventually to emerge in August 1939 as the Warwick. It has frequently been stated that the Warwick was designed as a replacement for the Wellington, whereas, in fact, it was a parallel project employing the same basic airframe and, as the Type 284, was on the drawing boards a full year before the Type 271 was flown. The Wellington fuselage was geometrically identical to that of the Warwick, with the omission of stations 26-38 amidships, and similarly the geometry of the outer planes was identical for both types. The two variants of the same basic design progressed side by side, the "stretched" version to B.1/35 being intended for Rolls-Royce Vulture, Napier Sabre or Bristol Centaurus high-output engines. None of these power plants was sufficiently advanced at the time to justify placing the Type 284 in production, and the Warwick was destined not to appear in quantity until the summer of 1943, when it was powered by Pratt and Whitney Double Wasp engines owing to a shortage of Centaurus power plants.

Production of the Wellington was initiated at the Weybridge works of Vickers, inside the famous Brooklands motor-racing track, where the company had been building aeroplanes since August 1915. Production plans were being laid even before the official order was received, and the target was set at one Wellington per day, every day! Never before had a British aircraft manufacturer set out to achieve such a high rate of production—measured in airframe weight. A year or so after production started at Weybridge, however, the company was asked to establish a brand-new "shadow factory" at Broughton, near Chester, where it was planned, still more ambitiously, to assemble fifty Wellingtons a month, with all components supplied by sub-contractors. The first production contract placed with the Chester factory was for one hundred machines.

Before the outbreak of war, in September 1939, a third Wellington production line was planned, this time at Squires Gate, Blackpool, and once again Vickers were asked to erect, equip and manage the whole plant. The Blackpool factory was to have a target production rate of no less than one hundred Wellingtons a month, and was to manufacture the complete aircraft rather than rely on sub-contractors. This factory's first contract was for five hundred Wellingtons.

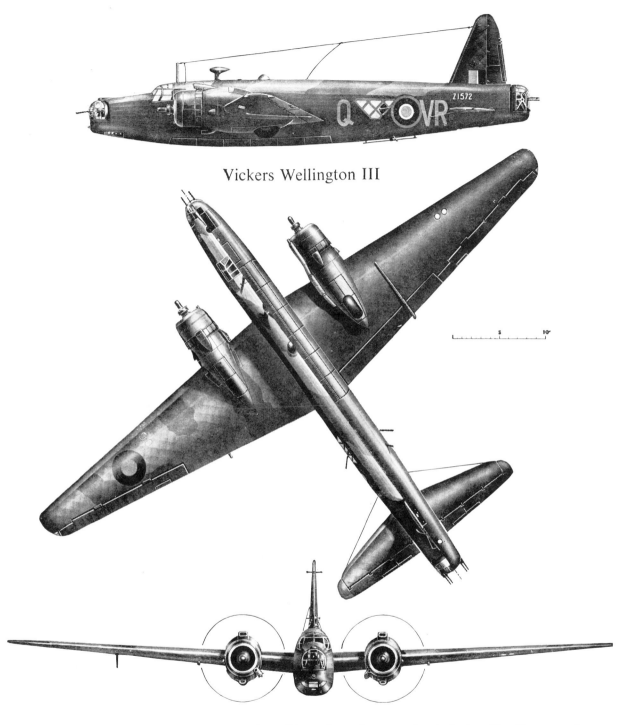

Vickers Wellington III

FINISH AND INSIGNIA: *The Wellington III of No. 419 "Moose" Squadron, R.C.A.F., illustrated was finished in the standard R.A.F. Bomber Command scheme introduced at the end of 1940. This comprised a dark earth and dark green camouflage pattern over the upper surfaces of the wings and tailplane, and the upper fuselage decking, and matt black over all wing, tail and fuselage under-surfaces, extending up the fuselage sides and including the vertical tail surfaces. The "C" type roundels with* *yellow outline appeared on the fuselage sides with corresponding "flashes" on the fin, and "B" type roundels (i.e., red and blue) appeared on the upper surfaces of the wings. The code-letters indicating the squadron (i.e., VR) and the individual aircraft (i.e., Q), and the series number (Z1572) were painted in grey, although on some aircraft the identification letters and serial were painted dull red.*

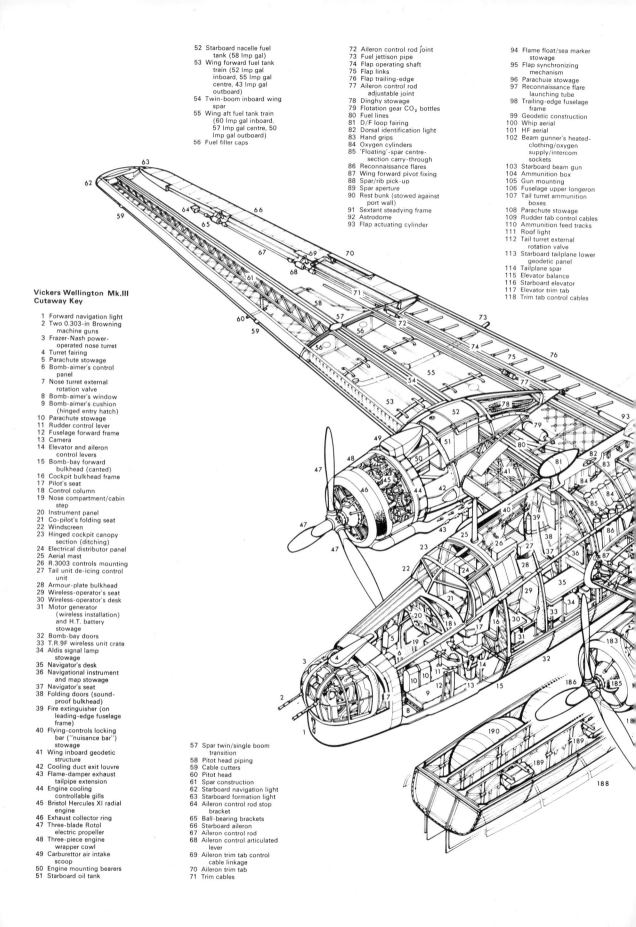

Vickers Wellington Mk.III
Cutaway Key

52 Starboard nacelle fuel tank (58 Imp gal)
53 Wing forward fuel tank train (52 Imp gal inboard, 55 Imp gal centre, 43 Imp gal outboard)
54 Twin-boom inboard wing spar
55 Wing aft fuel tank train (60 Imp gal inboard, 57 Imp gal centre, 50 Imp gal outboard)
56 Fuel filler caps

72 Aileron control rod joint
73 Fuel jettison pipe
74 Flap operating shaft
75 Flap links
76 Flap trailing-edge
77 Aileron control rod adjustable joint
78 Dinghy stowage
79 Flotation gear CO_2 bottles
80 Fuel lines
81 D/F loop fairing
82 Dorsal identification light
83 Hand grips
84 Oxygen cylinders
85 'Floating'-spar centre-section carry-through
86 Reconnaissance flares
87 Wing forward pivot fixing
88 Spar/rib pick-up
89 Spar aperture
90 Rest bunk (stowed against port wall)
91 Sextant steadying frame
92 Astrodome
93 Flap actuating cylinder

94 Flame float/sea marker stowage
95 Flap synchronizing mechanism
96 Parachute stowage
97 Reconnaissance flare launching tube
98 Trailing-edge fuselage frame
99 Geodetic construction
100 Whip aerial
101 HF aerial
102 Beam gunner's heated-clothing/oxygen supply/intercom sockets
103 Starboard beam gun
104 Ammunition box
105 Gun mounting
106 Fuselage upper longeron
107 Tail turret ammunition boxes
108 Parachute stowage
109 Rudder tab control cables
110 Ammunition feed tracks
111 Roof light
112 Tail turret external rotation valve
113 Starboard tailplane lower geodetic panel
114 Tailplane spar
115 Elevator balance
116 Starboard elevator
117 Elevator trim tab
118 Trim tab control cables

1 Forward navigation light
2 Two 0.303-in Browning machine guns
3 Frazer-Nash power-operated nose turret
4 Turret fairing
5 Parachute stowage
6 Bomb-aimer's control panel
7 Nose turret external rotation valve
8 Bomb-aimer's window
9 Bomb-aimer's cushion (hinged entry hatch)
10 Parachute stowage
11 Rudder control lever
12 Fuselage forward frame
13 Camera
14 Elevator and aileron control levers
15 Bomb-bay forward bulkhead (canted)
16 Cockpit bulkhead frame
17 Pilot's seat
18 Control column
19 Nose compartment/cabin step
20 Instrument panel
21 Co-pilot's folding seat
22 Windscreen
23 Hinged cockpit canopy section (ditching)
24 Electrical distributor panel
25 Aerial mast
26 R.3003 controls mounting
27 Tail unit de-icing control unit
28 Armour-plate bulkhead
29 Wireless-operator's seat
30 Wireless-operator's desk
31 Motor generator (wireless installation) and H.T. battery stowage
32 Bomb-bay doors
33 T.R.9F wireless unit crate
34 Aldis signal lamp stowage
35 Navigator's desk
36 Navigational instrument and map stowage
37 Navigator's seat
38 Folding doors (sound-proof bulkhead)
39 Fire extinguisher (on leading-edge fuselage frame)
40 Flying-controls locking bar ("nuisance bar") stowage
41 Wing inboard geodetic structure
42 Cooling duct exit louvre
43 Flame-damper exhaust tailpipe extension
44 Engine cooling controllable gills
45 Bristol Hercules XI radial engine
46 Exhaust collector ring
47 Three-blade Rotol electric propeller
48 Three-piece engine wrapper cowl
49 Carburettor air intake scoop
50 Engine mounting bearers
51 Starboard oil tank

57 Spar twin/single boom transition
58 Pitot head piping
59 Cable cutters
60 Pitot head
61 Spar construction
62 Starboard navigation light
63 Starboard formation light
64 Aileron control rod stop bracket
65 Ball-bearing brackets
66 Starboard aileron
67 Aileron control rod
68 Aileron control articulated lever
69 Aileron trim tab control cable linkage
70 Aileron trim tab
71 Trim cables

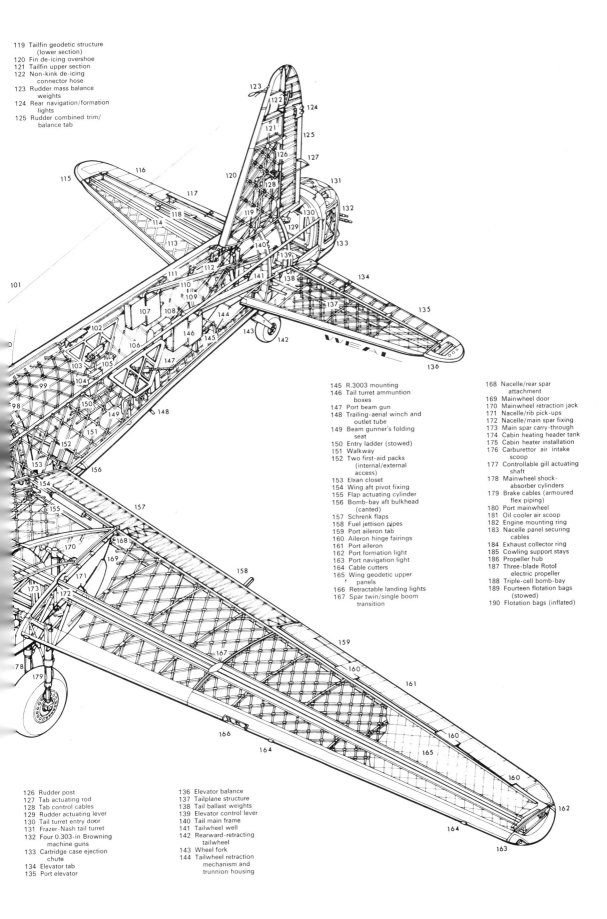

119 Tailfin geodetic structure
 (lower section)
120 Fin de-icing overshoe
121 Tailfin upper section
122 Non-kink de-icing
 connector hose
123 Rudder mass balance
 weights
124 Rear navigation/formation
 lights
125 Rudder combined trim/
 balance tab

145 R.3003 mounting
146 Tail turret ammunition
 boxes
147 Port beam gun
148 Trailing-aerial winch and
 outlet tube
149 Beam gunner's folding
 seat
150 Entry ladder (stowed)
151 Walkway
152 Two first-aid packs
 (internal/external
 access)
153 Elsan closet
154 Wing aft pivot fixing
155 Flap actuating cylinder
156 Bomb-bay aft bulkhead
 (canted)
157 Schrenk flaps
158 Fuel jettison pipes
159 Port aileron tab
160 Aileron hinge fairings
161 Port aileron
162 Port formation light
163 Port navigation light
164 Cable cutters
165 Wing geodetic upper
 panels
166 Retractable landing lights
167 Spar twin/single boom
 transition

168 Nacelle/rear spar
 attachment
169 Mainwheel door
170 Mainwheel retraction jack
171 Nacelle/rib pick-ups
172 Nacelle/main spar fixing
173 Main spar carry-through
174 Cabin heating header tank
175 Cabin heater installation
176 Carburettor air intake
 scoop
177 Controllable gill actuating
 shaft
178 Mainwheel shock-
 absorber cylinders
179 Brake cables (armoured
 flex piping)
180 Port mainwheel
181 Oil cooler air scoop
182 Engine mounting ring
183 Nacelle panel securing
 cables
184 Exhaust collector ring
185 Cowling support stays
186 Propeller hub
187 Three-blade Rotol
 electric propeller
188 Triple-cell bomb-bay
189 Fourteen flotation bags
 (stowed)
190 Flotation bags (inflated)

126 Rudder post
127 Tab actuating rod
128 Tab control cables
129 Rudder actuating lever
130 Tail turret entry door
131 Frazer-Nash tail turret
132 Four 0.303-in Browning
 machine guns
133 Cartridge case ejection
 chute
134 Elevator tab
135 Port elevator

136 Elevator balance
137 Tailplane structure
138 Tail ballast weights
139 Elevator control lever
140 Tail main frame
141 Tailwheel well
142 Rearward-retracting
 tailwheel
143 Wheel fork
144 Tailwheel retraction
 mechanism and
 trunnion housing

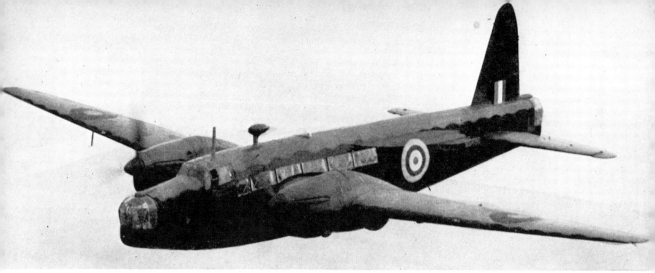

The Wellington II, with 1,145 h.p. Rolls-Royce Merlin X engines, was intended to succeed the Mk.I. The prototype flew on March 3, 1939, and the photo depicts W5480.

A Wellington I with a 48-ft. dia. dural hoop which, energized by an auxiliary motor to produce a magnetic field, was used to explode magnetic mines.

The Wellington IV was similar to the Mk.IC apart from the engines which were Pratt and Whitney R-1830-S3C4-G radials.

In the meantime, on December 23, 1937, the first production Wellington I (L4212) had flown at Brooklands. It was powered, like the Type 271, with Pegasus X engines, and bore the Vickers designation Type 285. As previously mentioned, the production model had been completely redesigned, and the most important change was the redesign of the fuselage in order to accommodate twice the load of bombs. The inclusion of a larger bomb-bay had necessitated a larger fuselage cross-section with a flattened bottom in place of the oval section. The nose and tail armament were amended to incorporate Vickers-designed turrets with Frazer-Nash power-operated controls, and twin guns were mounted in the tail. The proposed dorsal turret was replaced by a ventral gun position, and the Stranraer fin-and-rudder assembly and the

horizontal stabiliser were discarded and new designs introduced. The overall span increased by three inches as a result of the fuselage redesign, and the fuselage was lengthened by six inches.

The production Wellington introduced a retractable tailwheel, and the main undercarriage fairing doors were removed from the wheel legs to be hinged, more conventionally, to the engine nacelles. The crew was increased to five as standard, and long transparent windows were introduced down each side of the fuselage above the wing. Despite the fact that the bomber had been designed primarily for day operations, from the first production Wellington, the aircraft were delivered in night-bomber finish, with dark green and dark earth camouflage on upper surfaces and black undersides. Soon after the initial flight trials had commenced, horn-balances were introduced on the elevators, thus increasing the overall tailplane span slightly.

By the time that the Wellington had achieved production status, further advances had been made in engine development, and the 1,000 h.p. Pegasus XVIII had become available. L4212 first flew with these engines on April 23, 1938, and all subsequent production Wellington Is received these power plants from the outset, and were designated Type 290. By September 1939 the Weybridge factory had reached its target output of a Wellington per day, and the first Chester-built Wellington I (L7770) had just flown. After completing the first contract for 180 Wellington Is, Weybridge progressed to the Mk.IA, and Chester built only three Mk.Is before turning also to the Mk.IA.

The Vickers Type 408 Wellington IA, first flown in 1939, had a further revision of armament, mounting Nash and Thompson hydraulic turrets in nose and tail, and a ventral position, with two 0.303-in. machine guns in each. The crew was increased to six members; some sound-proofing was introduced in the cabin; an astrodome was fitted for the navigator's benefit; a fuel jettison system and discharge pipes were added to the wings, and larger wheels were fitted to cope

This Wellington VI (W5798) was the third of twenty machines originally ordered as Mk. Vs and completed as Mk. VIs. The Wellington VI never reached operational service.

with the gross weight which had risen to 28,500 lb. These larger wheels protruded from their housings when the undercarriage was retracted.

The Type 409 Wellington IB was not produced, but the IA was rapidly succeeded by the IC in which a 24-volt electrical system replaced the 12-volt system employed previously, and the ventral turret was superseded by two Vickers "K" guns mounted to fire from positions in each side of the fuselage and provide protection against beam attacks. The Wellington IA and IC were built in large quantities at Weybridge, where orders exceeded four hundred aircraft by the spring of 1940, and after building the three Mk.Is, followed by seventeen Mk.IAs, Chester went on to build Mk.ICs by the hundred. The Squires Gate factory started with fifty Mk.ICs—the first (X3160) flying in 1940—before proceeding to later marks.

The Wellington I achieved a maximum speed of 267 m.p.h. at 15,500 ft., and with a maximum fuel load of 1,020 Imp. gal. and no bomb load, it could fly 3,200 miles at 180 m.p.h. at 15,000 ft. The ventral turret of the Mk.IA naturally enough reduced performance somewhat, knocking 16 m.p.h. off the maximum speed, and the heavier Mk.IC attained a maximum speed of 250 m.p.h.

Other early variants of the Wellington included the Type 295, the basic aeroplane adapted for use as a W/T and navigational trainer, and the Type 296 troop transport conversion. New Zealand had placed an order for thirty Wellingtons which were to form the islands' first line of defence but, in 1939, despite the need to expand the R.N.Z.A.F. at home, the Wellingtons were handed over to the R.A.F., and eighteen Mk.Is, designated Type 403, were delivered from the Weybridge production line to No. 75 (N.Z.) Sqdn. R.A.F., formed from R.N.Z.A.F. personnel who had been training on Wellingtons and remained in the United Kingdom. The Type 412 was the Wellington IA for the same squadron.

The first Wellington Is reached No. 9 Sqdn. at Stradishall in October 1938, and were flown at the Brussels Exhibition in a formation display. By the

The first prototype Wellington V (R3298) with Hercules III engines.

The Wellington V (R3298) with Hercules XIs and turbo-superchargers.

time the war commenced, six squadrons of R.A.F. Bomber Command were operational on the type, and they were soon in action. Fourteen Wellingtons drawn from Nos. 9 and 149 Squadrons attacked shipping at Brunsbuttel on September 4, 1939, two aircraft being lost on this sortie. Bombing raids and reconnaissance by daylight continued until December 1939, by which time the Wellington had amply proven the fact that its merits were not those of the drawing office alone but of an essentially practical type, and its power-operated gun turrets had given intercepting Messerschmitt Bf 109 and Bf 110 fighters some serious problems. Before the end of the year, however, the Wellington was to achieve one doubtful distinction; it was to teach the R.A.F. the hard lesson that the operation of such large aircraft by daylight at medium altitudes without fighter escort was impracticable. This lesson was driven home forcibly on December 18, 1939, when, of a formation of twenty-four Wellingtons making an armed reconnaissance of the Schillig Roads and Wilhelmshaven, ten aircraft were lost and three were severely damaged. The Wellington was not thereafter used by daylight

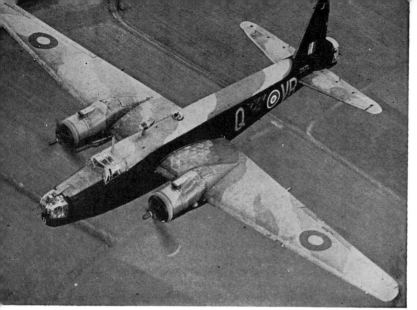

A Wellington III (Z1572) of No. 419 Squadron.

as they became available. Both the Rolls-Royce Merlin X liquid-cooled inline and the Bristol Hercules III air-cooled radial engines were selected for trial installations in Wellington I airframes. With the Merlin engines the aircraft was designated Type 298 Wellington II, and the prototype (L4250) flew for the first time on March 3, 1939. The Hercules-powered variant was the Type 299 Wellington III, the prototype of which (L4251) flew on May 16, 1939.

Production of both these re-engined versions was delayed for some time in order to avoid interruption of the flow of Wellington Is, but both the Mk.II and Mk.III went into large-scale production in 1940 as the Types 406 and 417 respectively, and reached R.A.F. Bomber Command in 1941. In the same year another alternative power plant was introduced in the shape of the Pratt and Whitney R-1830-S3C4-G two-row radial. The first trial installation of these engines was made in a Chester-built Wellington IC (R1220) which was designated Type 410, and this aircraft served as a prototype for the Wellington IV. Another twenty-four Wellington IVs were produced at intervals along the Chester production line of Mk.ICs, followed by a straight production run of 195 Type 424 Wellington IVs before Chester started building Mk.IIIs. The Weybridge factory built the total production quantity of 585 Wellington IIs, and then continued with ICs and IIIs in parallel, while the Squires Gate plant settled into its stride with Mk.IIIs.

The very high rates of production achieved with the Wellington were not reached without difficulty. The build-up to peak production rates came at a time in the war when Britain's industrial resources were at their lowest, and the country was under heavy attack from the Luftwaffe. By September 1940, Vickers'

unescorted, except in Coastal and Transport Commands. In March 1940 the relaxation of a Cabinet decree forbidding R.A.F. Bomber Command to attack land targets permitted the Wellington to take up the role in which it was to find its true métier—that of night bomber. Although designed primarily as a day bomber, the Wellington had been considered suitable for the night role by Vickers from an early stage in its design development, and had, in fact, been entered to meet the requirements of specification B.3/34 which called for a twin-engined night bomber. With its transfer to the night-bombing role, the Wellington operated with conspicuous success, spearheading the R.A.F.'s night offensive against Germany.

While the Wellington was thus getting into its operational stride, important work had been going on in the Vickers design office with the aim of improving the aircraft's performance and efficiency. An early development was that of selecting alternative power plants, partly to provide a second source of engine supply in case Pegasus production should fail, and partly to take advantage of more powerful engines

A Wellington X (X3595) of No. 75 Squadron. It differed from the Mk.III principally in having Hercules XVIIIs in place of XIs.

A number of Wellington Is were converted as Wellington VIIIs for R.A.F. Coastal Command by the installation of A.S.V. Mk.II radar (top), and one of the first Leigh Light installations was made in the nose of Wellington I T2977 (immediately above).

three factories were turning out 134 Wellingtons per month, but in that same month Weybridge was attacked and seriously damaged by a formation of fourteen enemy aircraft. Nevertheless, production continued, and the lowest weekly output recorded was four aircraft. Production was re-established at small factories throughout the district, with Weybridge as the assembly centre, and by May 1941 the peak output had again been reached. The highest monthly output of Wellingtons from each factory was: Weybridge, 70; Blackpool, 102; Chester, 130.

In service the Wellington continued to do well. Notable events were the first R.A.F. Bomber Command attack on Berlin on the night of August 25, 1940, in which seventeen Wellingtons of Nos. 99 and 149 Squadrons participated; the use of Wellingtons in the Middle East from September 1940 onwards, and in the Far East from early 1942; the introduction of Wellingtons of Nos. 109 and 156 Squadrons into the Pathfinder Force in August 1942, and the first operational use of the 4,000-lb. "block-buster" bomb by a Wellington over Emden on April 1, 1941. The Wellington II W5389 was the first aircraft modified to carry this bomb. Another event of 1941 particularly worthy of record was the award of the Victoria Cross to Sgt. J. A. Ward (R.N.Z.A.F.) for his gallantry while serving as second pilot in a Wellington of No. 75 Sqdn. He was the only member of a Wellington crew to receive this award.

The Wellington III was phased into service in 1942, together with the Mks.II and IV, and provided the mainstay of R.A.F. Bomber Command while operational strength of the heavy-bomber units was being built up with four-engined types. A slightly improved version, the Type 448 Wellington X, went into production in 1943, and was destined to be manufactured in larger quantities than any other version of the Wellington, no fewer than 3,500 examples of this mark being built, compared with about 1,500 Mk.IIIs and over 2,500 Mk.ICs. The principal difference between the Mk.X and the Mk.III was the installation of Hercules XVIII engines in place of the Hercules XI. The first six Wellington Xs were DF609, DF686, DF701, DF730, DF740, and HF614, which were produced at intervals on the Mk.III production line at Squires Gate which subsequently shared with Chester the greater part of the Mk.X production. The Mk.X shared with the Mk.III the final Wellington operation with R.A.F. Bomber Command on October 8, 1943. Thereafter, Wellington bombers continued to serve in other commands at home and overseas, and were used extensively by operational training units up to the end of the war.

Another bomber variant, which saw only experimental service, was produced to meet a special specification, B.23/39, which called upon Vickers to develop the Wellington for very high altitude use. An operating altitude of 40,000 ft. was stipulated, with a pressurized cabin for the crew giving an equivalent altitude of 10,000 ft., representing a pressure differential of $7\frac{1}{2}$ p.s.i. This, in 1939, was a very stringent requirement indeed, as little was known about pressure cabins at that time. In some early pressure tests with the prototype cabin, for instance, one of the small windows blew out and the whole assembly became, literally, jet-propelled across the workshop floor—nobody had thought of securing the cabin to the cradle upon which it rested! The first design for a high-altitude Wellington, the Type 407, was based on the use of two Hercules VIII engines, and two prototypes were ordered towards the end of 1939. These were to be produced by converting Weybridge-built Mk.Is. The long, cylindrical pressure cabin was mounted in the forward fuselage, and incorporated a small Perspex dome for the pilot's head. Few other changes were necessary.

As some delays were encountered in producing the Hercules VIII, the first Wellington V, as the type was designated, was fitted with standard Hercules IIIs initially, and flew with these for the first time in September 1940. It bore the serial number R3298 and, with the Hercules III engines, was given the Vickers designation Type 421. Flights up to 30,000 ft. were made, and these were sufficient to bring to light some unexpected problems. With outside temperatures down to –40°C., the main flying controls and trimmer circuits became virtually immovable. This trouble was eventually traced to the solidifying of the grease in the control hinge bearings, and special hydraulic fluid had to be developed to permit operation of the rear

The Wellington G.R.XI with A.S.V.Mk.II radar. Later machines carried the more refined A.S.V.Mk.III in a radome under the nose.

turret and the bomb doors at these extreme temperatures. On one occasion when an oil leak developed in one engine, the oil froze into solid lumps which were thrown off by the airscrew, doing considerable damage to the fuselage.

A constant problem was the icing up of the pilot's dome, windows and main entrance door because of the humidity in the cabin. When this was overcome by drying the air, the crew suffered considerable discomfort. Accumulation of ice on the outside skin made it impossible for the crew to escape in an emergency, and on one occasion when one engine seized and frightening vibration ensued, it took the crew ten minutes to de-pressurize the cabin and open the main door. In fact, the Wellington V was often referred to as the "flying coffin" despite the complete lack of any fatal accidents during this series of trials.

The second Wellington V (R3299) flew in due course with Hercules VIIIs, and the first was later fitted with Hercules XIs and G.E.C. exhaust-driven turbo-superchargers—with these modifications it became the Type 436. On March 1, 1940, a batch of thirty Mk.Vs with Hercules VIIIs was ordered to specification 17/40, but another variant, the Wellington VI with Rolls-Royce Merlin RM6SM two-stage engines, was meanwhile being developed to supersede the Mk. V. The first of the aircraft ordered as a production Mk.V (W5795) was, in fact, completed as the Type 442, or prototype Wellington VI. Only one Type 426 production Mk.V (W5796) was flown, the final nine aircraft of the production batch being cancelled and the remaining nineteen (W5797 to W5815) being completed as Mk.VIs.

With the Merlin 60 engines (the production version of the RM6SM), the Wellington VI attained approximately 38,000 ft., and further troubles manifested themselves. Temperatures down to −65°C. were commonplace (−71°C. was recorded on one occasion), and once again the controls tended to seize, this problem eventually being resolved by diluting the bearing grease with paraffin. The cabin compressor developed a habit of filling the cabin with burned-oil fumes which were thick enough to prevent, on one

occasion, the pilot from seeing his instrument panel! The constant-speed airscrews developed a tendency to run away at these low temperatures, and the work of solving all these problems continued steadily throughout 1941. The subsequent influence of this experimentation on high-altitude flight was considerable. When the time came to modify the Spitfire for high-altitude photographic-reconnaissance duties, the Vickers engineers were called in to give the benefit of their pressure-cabin experience to the Supermarine team.

To reach the target altitude of 40,000 ft., more wing area was soon found to be necessary, and the prototype Wellington VI was later fitted with new outer wing panels which extended the span by 12 ft. With these fitted, the specified altitude was achieved. With the extended wings, the prototype Mk.VI became the Type 443. On August 19, 1941, a production contract for one hundred Wellington VIs was placed, and these were to be in addition to those built on the original Mk.V contract. Of these, fifty-six were later cancelled, and of the others, the first nine were completed as Type 442s, and the remaining production was made up of three Type 431s with special bomb gear, and twenty-four Type 449s fitted with Gee navigational aid. The latter were designated Wellington VIG, and four of these were employed as special radio trainers while the others were made available for operational use. In August 1941 No. 109 Squadron operated some of the original batch of Mk.VIs for trials with Oboe radar, but the altitude performance of interceptor fighters had meanwhile been improved to such a great extent that, with all its teething troubles, there was little point in introducing the Wellington VI into operational service, and in 1943 sixty of the sixty-seven high-altitude Wellington VIs completed were scrapped at a maintenance unit.

Among the many experimental Wellingtons used during the earlier stages of the war, one of the most interesting was the prototype Mk.II (L4250) which was fitted with a very large dorsal turret mounting a 40-mm. Vickers "S" gun, automatic predictor sight, and offset cupola. The turret had originally been designed for use by the Boulton Paul P.92 twin-engined fighter, and its flight trials in the Wellington were a part of the general development of the turret. As first flown in 1941, this aircraft retained the standard single fin-and-rudder assembly, but a twin tail unit was fitted in January 1942 to improve the field of fire. The twin fins and rudders were, in fact, the tips of two standard Wellington fin-and-rudder assemblies, and were mounted inboard on the tailplane and braced to the fuselage by a system of struts. The Vickers type number 416 covered the design of this aircraft which was provisionally known as the Wellington VII.

Another armament experiment was made on Wellington II Z8416 which had a 40-mm. Vickers "S" gun in the nose, controlled by a gunner amidships, sighting through a dorsal blister and having the benefit of coupled range-finder, sight and predictor. This was the Type 439. A Wellington III (BK537), the Type 451, was used for much of the war—and for several years afterwards—as a test-bed for Rotol airscrews, flying with both three- and four-blade units, and a Wellington X (BJ895) was used for some of the first dropping trials with a half-scale model of the Wallis mine which was developed to breach the Mohne and Eder dams. Several Wellingtons were also used for engine development by Bristol and Rolls-Royce, and in November 1942 a Wellington II (W5389/G), the Type 470, began flight testing a Rover W.2B/23 turbojet which was mounted in the extreme rear fuselage. A Wellington II (T2545) operated by Rolls-Royce flew with Merlin 20s and, later, with Merlin 60s driving four-bladed airscrews. The same company had the use of Wellington VI W5797 to develop the Merlin 60 series of engines for the Spitfire and other types. Apart from several Wellingtons used by Bristol with standard Pegasus and Hercules engines, the Mk.X HF616 was flown with Hercules 38s and exhaust-driven turbo-superchargers, and LN718 was used to test the Hercules 100 for the Handley Page Halifax.

In addition to its primary role of night bomber and, later, bomber trainer, the Wellington gave long and valuable service to R.A.F. Coastal Command on maritime reconnaissance duties, and was also employed by R.A.F. Transport Command. The earliest use of Wellingtons in a maritime role was in January 1940, when several Mk.Is were fitted with a 48 ft. diameter dural hoop which was energized by an auxiliary motor in the fuselage to produce a magnetic field. The front turret was deleted and, flying low over the sea, the aircraft was able to explode magnetic mines, enjoying conspicuous success in this role. The first aircraft of the kind had a Ford engine in the fuselage and, known as the Type 418, carried the official designation Wellington D.W.I. Mk.I. Others, with a de Havilland Gipsy engine in the fuselage, were known as the Type 419, or Wellington D.W.IA Mk.I. Plans to produce a similar variant of the Mk.III (Type 428) did not reach fruition.

During 1941 Wellington Is were used on mine-laying duties, and later in the same year, the Welling-ton VIII was developed as a special Coastal Command version of the Mk.IC (Pegasus XVIII). The Mk. VIII existed in two versions, for use as a torpedo-bomber in which role it carried the A.S.V.Mk.II ("Stickleback") radar, or for general reconnaissance with a Leigh Light in a retractable installation in the rear of the bomb-bay, and the nose turret deleted. The Wellington VIII was designated Type 429 by Vickers, and 394 examples were built.

One of the first Leigh Light installations was made in the nose of a Wellington I (T2977) which also carried A.S.V.Mk.II radar. Wellington VIIIs were the first aircraft to use the Leigh Light operationally—on June 3, 1942—and to destroy a U-boat by night with this aid—on July 6, 1942. Out of experience with the Mk.VIII, and to take advantage of powerplant and airframe developments in the Mk.X bomber, came a new series of Wellingtons in 1943. The first of these was the Wellington G.R.XI, intended for use as a torpedo-bomber, and powered by Hercules VI or XVI engines. At first designed to carry the A.S.V.Mk.II radar (Type 454), it was subsequently developed to take the very much more refined A.S.V.Mk.III in a radome under the nose, the front turret being removed. The prototype A.S.V.Mk.III installation was covered by the Vickers type number 458, and production machines were designated Type 459, 180 aircraft of this type being built at Blackpool. The Wellington G.R.XII (Type 455) was a variant of the Mk.XI with A.S.V.Mk.III and a retractable Leigh Light in the bomb-bay. This version could not carry torpedoes. Fifty Wellington XIIs were built at Weybridge, and eight at Chester.

Introduction of the Bristol Hercules XVII engine produced two more marks—the G.R.XIII (Type 466) which had A.S.V.Mk.II and was used as a torpedo-bomber, and the G.R.XIV (Type 467) with A.S.V. Mk.III and a Leigh Light. Production of the G.R.XIII was concentrated at Blackpool, where 843 were built. This factory also built 303 Wellington G.R.XIVs in addition to 538 built at Chester. Development of a Wellington variant for use as an A.S.V. trainer began as early as 1941 when some Mk.Is were converted for this role at Christchurch. The first such conversion was L4244. In 1945 two other variants of the Wellington were designed for use as night fighter crew trainers, equipped with SCR720 airborne interception radar in the nose. These were the T.XVII, converted from Wellington G.R.XIs, and the T.XVIII converted from the G.R.XIII.

The earliest example of a Wellington designed for use as a transport was a Vickers design of 1938, but the first actual use of the type in this role appears to have been in 1940, when the Air Transport Auxiliary at White Waltham converted L4255 for use as an ambulance. In the following year several Wellington Is were converted for use by R.A.F. Transport Command. Designated C.Mk.I, they had the nose and rear turrets removed, the bomb-bay sealed, and seats installed in the fuselage—some carried dummy turrets to camouflage their defencelessness. Later,

A Wellington XIV (MP714) fitted with four rocket projectiles under each wing. A retractable Leigh Light was carried, and A.S.V.Mk.III radar was fitted.

similar conversions of the Wellington IA and IC were made, and were designated C.Mk.XV and C.Mk.XVI respectively. For the airborne forces, one Wellington III (X3479) was modified in 1942 to carry a Smith gun and its team to be dropped by parachute. Another Mk.III (X3286) was the first Wellington to tow a glider—a Horsa—and provision for a glider-towing bridle was made in the production Wellington X. In 1942, also, a Wellington IC (P2522) was converted as a special troop-carrying version (Type 437) and was known as the Wellington IX.

The last Wellington built was a Mk.X (RP561) which was delivered from the Blackpool factory in October 1945. Production from the three factories concerned totalled 11,461 aircraft, and the Wellington served in most of the operational theatres in which the R.A.F. was engaged. It performed in a remarkable diversity of roles, probably unequalled by any other bomber of the Second World War, and its unique geodetic structure, outmoded only because of the inability of its fabric covering to withstand higher air speeds, endowed it with a ruggedness such as was enjoyed by no other twin-engined bomber of its period, and gave the Wellington the reputation of getting its crew back to base despite a fantastic amount of battle damage. The high strength/weight ratio of the geodetic structure made it possible to increase the weight of the bomber from the prototype's 21,000 lb. to no less than 36,500 lb. Geodetics yielded the Wellington, and the Wellington was an aeroplane worthy of the Royal Air Force. It bore with distinction the name of a great British soldier. Other bombers came forward as the war progressed, but none enjoyed a finer reputation.

The Vickers-Armstrong Wellington B.Mk.X

Dimensions : Span, 86 ft. 2 in.; length, 64 ft. 7 in. (guns extended), 61 ft. 0 in. (fuselage); height, 17 ft. 6 in. (tail down), 22 ft. 2 in. (tail up) ; wing area (net) 753 sq. ft. (incl. ailerons).

Power Plants : Two Bristol Hercules VI fourteen-cylinder two-row sleeve-valve radial engines rated at 1,585 h.p. for take-off.

Armament : Two 0.303-in. machine guns in Frazer-Nash power-operated front turret. Four 0.303-in. machine guns in Frazer-Nash power operated rear turret. Maximum bomb load, 6,000 lb.

Weights : Tare weight, 26,325 lb. ; normal loaded, 31,500 lb. ; maximum overload, 36,500 lb. Maximum fuel capacity, 1,236 Imp. gallons.

Performance : (At normal gross weight) maximum speed, 250 m.p.h. at 600 ft., 255 m.p.h. at 14,500 ft. ; cruising speed, 180 m.p.h. ; climb to 15,000 ft., 27.7 minutes ; service ceiling, 24,000 ft. ; range, 1,325 miles at 180 m.p.h. with 900 Imp. gal. fuel and 4,500 lb. bomb load ; range, 1,885 miles at 180 m.p.h. with 1,236 Imp. gal. fuel and 1,500 lb. bomb load.

From a distance this Wellington C.XVI of No. 24 "Commonwealth" Squadron appeared to be fitted with standard nose and tail turrets. In fact, these were painted on in an attempt to camouflage the transport's defencelessness.

THE ARADO Ar 234B BLITZ

Eine Minute nach Zwölf—Too Late! These words summarise Germany's wartime aeronautical research. Germany's leaders gambled on a short war until the autumn of 1940 and the failure of the Luftwaffe's air assault on Britain. The loss of the "Battle of Britain" stressed the fact that the conflict would be of considerably longer duration than that for which they had originally planned, and that combat aircraft of markedly superior performance would be required if the Luftwaffe was to attain the complete air superiority that it had failed to gain with weight of numbers. With these hard facts providing the impetus, German scientists, aerodynamicists and engineers made truly prodigious strides in aeronautical research and development, but their efforts lacked co-ordination and a sound directive from high level, and, inevitably, were too late to have any serious effect on the course of the air war.

An outstanding example on this theme was the Arado Ar 234B Blitz (Lightning) which, although it was to gain the distinction of being the world's first operational jet bomber and thus assure for itself a unique position in aviation history, reached the assembly lines too late to make any really effective contribution to the Luftwaffe's operational strength. Had several groups equipped with this bomber been available to the Luftwaffe even as late as the beginning of 1945, they would have created some very serious problems for the Allies.

The Ar 234 was conceived in the Plans and Construction Bureau of the Arado Flugzeugwerke of

The Ar 234 was designed to employ a jettisonable three-wheel trolley for take-off which was to have been released at an altitude of some two hundred feet, after which it was to be lowered to the ground by means of five automatically-opening parachutes. The trolley was destroyed after the first and second take-offs, and was left on the ground during the third take-off. The photographs above show the second prototype, the Ar 234V2, taking-off on its jettisonable trolley, and below, the fifth prototype, the Ar 234V5, is seen releasing a modified trolley during take-off. The drogue chute can be seen opening.

Brandenburg during the closing months of 1940 as a medium-range reconnaissance aircraft operating at altitudes and speeds providing it with immunity from interception. A team headed by Dipl. Ing. Walter Blume and Dipl. Ing. Rebeski prepared several alternative studies to meet the Reichsluftfahrt-ministerium (R.L.M.) specification which demanded a maximum speed of 435 m.p.h. and a range of

1,242 miles, and that selected was a simple, shapely, shoulder-wing monoplane, with a pair of the new gas turbines underslung on the wing. It was anticipated that the turbojets would have attained production status within eighteen months, and the project was allocated the designation Ar 234.

As originally conceived, the Ar 234 was to employ a jettisonable three-wheel trolley for take-off, and retractable skids under the fuselage and turbojet nacelles for landing. A relatively simple form of construction was employed, the wing being a two-spar stressed-skin structure which rested on a strong, reinforced box-girder section of the fuselage which itself was a stressed skin semi-monocoque. The wing featured dual taper on the leading edge, and its trailing edge carried Frise ailerons of exceptionally narrow chord with mass-balanced gear tabs fitted to the inboard ends adjacent to the large, hydraulically-operated plain hinged two-sectioned flaps. The pilot's cockpit, which was extensively glazed, occupied the nose of the fuselage.

Construction of the first batch of prototype air-frames commenced early in 1941, and progressed rapidly, the first machine, the Ar 234V1, being completed before the end of the war. The development of the Junkers Jumo 109-004 turbojets with which the machine was to be powered had not kept pace with airframe construction, however. It encountered un-expected setbacks despite the fact that bench running had begun in December 1940, and it was obvious to the Arado design team that at least another twelve months would be necessary to bring the engines to a sufficiently reliable stage for installation in the proto-type airframe.

Despite the delays with the Jumo turbojets, work continued on a further seven Versuchs or experi-mental machines, the airframes of which were, for the most part, completed when, in March 1943, the first pair of pre-production Jumo 004A turbojets were delivered to the Arado plant. With these installed, the Ar 234V1 commenced ground trials which extended over some two months because of the somewhat erratic behaviour of the take-off trolley. Finally, on June 15, 1943, the Ar 234V1 was flown for the first time from Rheine airfield, at the controls an Arado test pilot, Flugkapitan Selle. It was planned to jettison the take-off trolley at an altitude of some two hundred feet, the trolley being lowered to the ground by means of five para-chutes. On the first flight this system failed and

Ar 234V1

Ar 234B-2

Ar 234V6

Ar 234V8

Ar 234V13

Ar 234C-1

Ar 234C-3

Ar 234D-1

FINISH AND INSIGNIA: *The Arado Ar 234B-2 illus-trated belonged to Kampfgeschwader 76. The upper surfaces of the wings, fuselage and horizontal tail surfaces employed an irregular "splinter" type camouflage pattern of forest green and olive, and all undersurfaces were sprayed pale blue. The pale blue extended up the sides of the fuselage and vertical tail surfaces and was sprayed in patches with forest green, giving a mottled effect. The national insignia appeared as a black cross outlined in white on the wing undersurfaces and as a white outline on the upper surfaces of the wings and the fuselage sides. A white outline of a swastika appeared on the vertical fin. K.G.76's code desig-nation "F1" appeared in black ahead of the national insignia on the port fuselage side and aft of the insignia on the starboard side. The letters "MT" appeared aft of the national insignia on the port side, the individual aircraft letter (i.e., "M") was painted in a pastel shade (which indicated the Staffel) and was repeated at the tip of the fin. "M" was painted in black outboard of the cross under the starboard wing, and "T" appeared under the port wing. The Werk-Nr. "140173" appeared in black above the swastika on the fin. The external finish was particularly smooth, a heavy coat of plastic filler being spread over all joints and rivets and subsequently polished.*

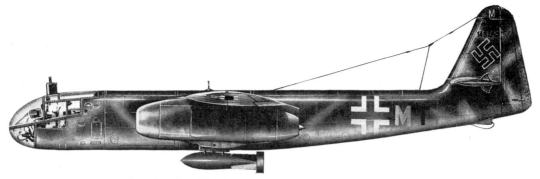

Arado Ar 234B-2/p Blitz

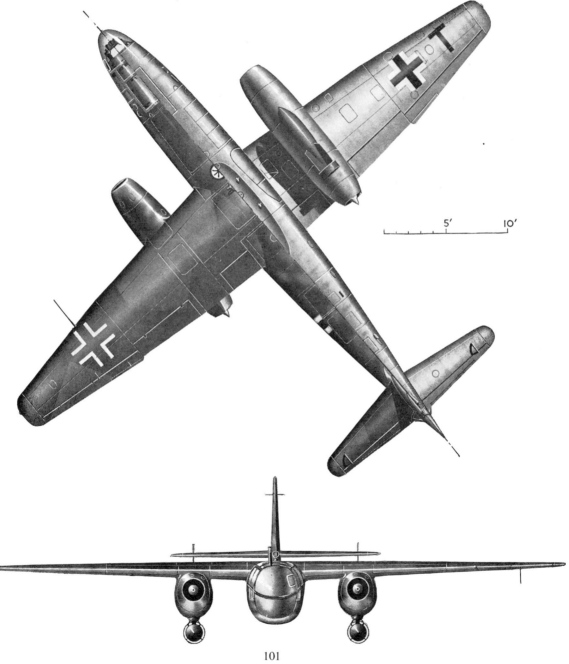

5'   10'

a replacement trolley was hurriedly flown to Rheine in an Ar 232 transport. The second trolley was also destroyed, and for the third flight the trolley was jettisoned at the point of take-off. On subsequent flights the trolley functioned well, although much care was necessary on releasing it to ensure that it did not rebound from the runway and strike the aircraft. To brake the trolley's run after release a drogue chute opened automatically. Flight tests were conducted both with and without the trolley attached, but the landing skids did not prove very successful. Difficulties were encountered with the hydraulic retracting mechanism for the skids which were extended during take-off, and there were several mishaps resulting from an oleo leg gradually subsiding during the landing run until a wingtip was ploughing up the ground. The skids demanded a very long grass runway, particularly in wet weather.

The prototype airframes were completed and tested as rapidly as engines were made available, and the Ar 234V2 followed the first prototype into the air some five weeks later, on July 27th. The first two machines were virtually identical, but the Ar 234V3, which commenced testing on August 25th, differed in several respects. Air was tapped from the compressor of each turbojet to pressurize the cabin, an ejector seat was provided for the pilot, and wing-mounted Rauchgeräte (rocket-assisted take-off) units were fitted to reduce the take-off run. The Ar 234V3 attained a maximum level speed of 466 m.p.h., a ceiling of 41,000 feet, and a range of 746 miles, but

the machine was seriously damaged during an early flight test phase. This accident did not seriously affect the flight test programme, however, as the similar Ar 234V4 had joined the programme on September 15th. This, like its predecessors, was powered by a pair of Jumo 004A turbojets each rated at 1,850 lb.s.t., but the V5 differed in having 1,980 lb.s.t. Jumo 004Bs, commencing its trials on December 20th.

The early prototypes had proved to be relatively pleasant aircraft to fly, demanding few major modifications and exceeding the requirements of the original R.L.M. specification in several respects, but it was obvious to the design team that the airframe could absorb substantially more power and attain very much greater speeds before encountering any serious compressibility effects. As the Jumo 004B was at that time the most powerful single turbojet to have reached test flight status, it was decided to fit each of two further prototypes with four of the smaller and lighter BMW 003A which, running since August 1940, was offering 1,760 lb.s.t. The sixth and eighth airframes, the Ar 234V6 and V8, were selected for the trial installations, and the first of these had the four turbojets mounted in individual underslung nacelles spaced widely on the wing, while the second had the four units paired in two nacelles mounted close to the fuselage.

The Ar 234V8 was the first of the four-engined prototypes to fly, being ready to commence trials on February 1, 1944, but it was found that the aircraft could not be pushed to the maximum speed anticipated as great difficulties arose with airflow and cowling contours. At high speeds, the airflow through the narrow space between the fuselage and turbojet nacelles approached Mach unity, resulting in the formation of severe shock waves. The Ar 234V6, which joined the test programme on April 8, 1944, was more successful, however, and this machine was equipped with two cameras and used experimentally, together with the V8, for reconnaissance sorties during the early summer months of 1944, occasioning much surprise among Allied fighter pilots who found themselves totally incapable of effecting an interception. The V6 had an empty weight of 8,818 lb. and grossed 17,196 lb.

In the meantime, the final prototype of the proposed A-series production model, the Ar 234V7, had been flown by Flugkapitan Selle who lost his life when this prototype was destroyed during an early flight. The aircraft was in the landing circuit when a fire in the port engine burned through the control rods. Selle's place as chief test pilot was taken by Flugkapitan Joachim Carl. The combination of take-off trolley and landing skids employed by the first eight prototypes had not proved particularly practicable. One of its major drawbacks from the operational viewpoint was that, after landing, the aircraft was unable to manœuvre to any extent on its skids and had to be lifted on to its take-off trolley before it could be towed to the dispersal bays for refuelling. This meant that landing areas would be cluttered with aircraft awaiting towing and extremely vulnerable should the airfield be strafed by enemy intruders. Initial trials with the Ar 234V1 in mid-1943 had illustrated the impracticability of the trolley-and-skid arrangement, and work had been initiated immediately on a more advanced variant of the basic design, the Ar 234B. This employed an orthodox retractable nosewheel undercarriage, and the proposed Ar 234A production version was abandoned.

The first prototype for the B-series aircraft, the Ar 234V9, was flown in March 1944. It was powered by

The Ar 234V6 (right), like the Ar 234V8 (below), was powered by four BMW 003A turbojets. The two prototypes differed primarily in the mounting of the engines, those of the V6 being housed in widely spaced, individual nacelles. Both machines were tested at Sorau/Silesia, and were used on experimental reconnaissance sorties.

two Jumo 004B turbojets, and featured an ejection seat and a pressurized cabin. Because of the shoulder position of the wing which would have necessitated an exceptionally tall undercarriage had the wheel wells been placed in the wing, and lack of space in the engine nacelles, the Ar 234V9 featured a narrow-track undercarriage in which the main single-wheel oleo legs were mounted on each side of the central fuselage "box", the main wheels retracting hydraulically forward and inward into fuselage wells. Despite some widening of the fuselage, this narrow track resulted in some lateral instability during taxying. The main-wheel brakes proved inadequate during the landing run, and a tail braking parachute was therefore fitted. Proposed from the beginning of the Ar 234's development, this device was of considerable future significance. The drogue chute decreased the landing run by fifty per cent after deployment as the aircraft touched down, and had no ill effects on controllability. However, when the Ar 234B reached service, the drogue chute was only used in cases of emergency, such as forced landings or landings on small strips.

The Ar 234V10, which flew on April 2, 1944, differed from the ninth machine only in having no provision for cabin pressurization, and was joined by the V11 and V12, which were respectively similar to

The Ar 234V10 was the second prototype for the B-series and was used for tests with rear-firing armament, rocket-assisted take-off units and bombs. The photographs above show the V10 with take-off rockets and, below, with bombs under the engine nacelles and fuselage. Unlike the first B-series prototype, the Ar 234V10 had no provision for cabin pressurization.

the V9 and V10, within a month. Meanwhile, the assembly of twenty pre-production Ar 234B-0 aircraft had reached an advanced stage at Alt Loennewitz, near Falkenberg/Elster in Saxony, and these began to leave the assembly line in June 1944. The first thirteen machines were despatched to the Rechlin Test Centre for intensive evaluation. The Ar 234B-0 differed from the first B-series prototypes only with regard to service equipment, and was one of the very few operational aircraft which progressed from prototype to production virtually unchanged. The Ar 234B-0 had no ejector seat and the cabin was unpressurized. Provision was made for two RB 50/30 or RB 75/30 cameras, or one RB 75/30 or RB 20/30 camera in the rear fuselage, and no armament was fitted. During initial flight tests K-1 Diesel oil fuel was used, but as this was somewhat costly, a cheaper fuel with the same calorific value, J-2, was substituted, and this was carried in two flexible fuselage tanks, the forward tank (between the pilot's cockpit and the leading edges of the mainplane) holding 396 Imp.gal., and the rear tank (immediately

aft of the mainplane centre section) holding 440 Imp.gal. These could be supplemented by two 66 Imp.gal. drop tanks suspended beneath the turbojets.

The pre-production machines were followed by the initial production model, the Ar 234B-1, which, essentially similar, began to appear over the Allied lines in the autumn of 1944. Three Ar 234B-1 reconnaissance aircraft were despatched to the Italian theatre where the Wehrmacht had constantly complained of the inadequacy of reconnaissance reports and the repeated failure of the reconnaissance aircraft available to penetrate into the target areas. The arrival of the trio of Ar 234B-1s radically changed the situation, however, these aircraft flying unarmed at altitudes between 29,000 and 39,000 feet undertaking regular reconnaissances over the Ancona and Leghorn sectors of the front.

A conversion school was established near the assembly plant at Alt Loennewitz where former bomber pilots received several hours' familiarization in a ground trainer before soloing in an Ar 234B-0 or B-1. A high accident rate was suffered because of mismanagement of the throttles resulting in excessive turbine temperatures, particularly with Jumo 004B units fitted with solid blades, and difficulties of asymmetric handling following variations of thrust and surge from the turbojets. Accidents also occurred during landings, the pupils, unfamiliar with such high approach speeds, misjudging the sink rate and distance, or releasing the drogue chute before the aircraft had actually touched down. Power response to throttle movement was much slower than in piston-engined aircraft, and turbojet overheating and nosewheel failures all added to the attrition rate.

Relatively few Ar 234B-1 aircraft had been completed before production switched to the Ar 234B-2. The Blitz had been designed primarily as a reconnaissance aircraft but, at the suggestion of the R.L.M., it had been developed in its Ar 234B-2 variant for the level- and dive-bombing roles. The first Luftwaffe unit to re-equip with the Ar 234B-2 was Kampfgeschwader 76, and mechanics from this unit received training on the type at Alt Loennewitz in the late summer and early autumn of 1944. The Ar 234B-2 was designed to carry a bomb load of 3,300 lb. comprising a 1,100 lb., SC 500 or SD 500 bomb on a fuselage crutch between the wheel wells and a similar bomb under each engine nacelle. Alternatively, a 2,200-lb. SC 1000 or SD 1000 bomb or two 1,100-lb. bombs could be carried by the fuselage crutch when no bombs were carried under the turbojet nacelles. but in service the Ar 234B-2 rarely carried a load greater than 2,200 lb.

A Lotfe 7K tachometric bomb-sight which was located between the pilot's feet for level-bombing enabled a high degree of accuracy to be attained under good conditions. An over-riding control for the automatic pilot (LKS 7D-15) was normally employed with the Lotfe 7K during the bombing run, the pilot disconnecting the control column which then swung clear of the bomb-sight, being reconnected when the bombs had been released. For glide and shallow dive-bombing the BZA 1 computer was provided. An RF2C periscope with a PV1B sighting head was used in conjunction with the BZA 1 computer which fed it with the bombing angle by an electrical remote control system. A switch on the PV1B head enabled it to be used for either forward or rearward vision, the forward field being utilised when bombing with the BZA1 and the rearward field being used as a gun-sight when a pair of rearward-firing 20-mm. MG 151 cannon were installed in the lower aft fuselage. The only protective armour installed comprised a 15.5-mm. plate attached to the rear cockpit wall to protect the pilot's head and shoulders.

The Ar 234B-2 could be fitted with several types of equipment to suit it for alternative roles. For the reconnaissance role with a pair of cameras it was known as the Ar 234B-2/b, and with a Patin PDS three-axes automatic pilot added it became the Ar 234B-2/bp, while with attachment points for two drop-tanks it was designated Ar 234B-2/bpr. When used for pathfinder duties it became the Ar 234B-2/1, similar suffixes to those of the reconnaissance model signifying the installation of Patin PDS and drop tank attachment points.

In the air, the Ar 234B-2 was a relatively pleasant aircraft, although directional stability was poor, a fault common to many other early jet aircraft. Without Rauchgeräte units and with half-full tanks and no bomb load, the Blitz would take-off within 1,100 yards but needed 2,000-2,200 yards fully laden. The shape of the sharp-nosed Frise ailerons had been determined in the Aldershof wind tunnel, although these did not prove entirely satisfactory in service. Unless extreme care was exercised in rigging, and in adjusting hinge shroud distances, etc., the ailerons misbehaved violently at speeds greater than 730 m.p.h., and a common fault was rapid oscillation ("buzz") accompanied by the stick threshing from side to side. Sometimes as many as ten flights were needed for each production aircraft before the

ailerons were adjusted correctly. On production aircraft the fin profile rarely carried on smoothly to the rudder and the result was poor directional stability. On the prototypes where the fin and rudder were hand-made, no bad directional unsteadiness was experienced. Diving speeds were restricted because of jet surge and sensitivity of lateral trim, the latter rendering it difficult for the pilot not well versed in the idiosyncrasies of the aircraft to keep it straight in dives. Normal production testing involved a dive from 10,000 feet up to a true air speed of 530 m.p.h., and no Mach effects were noticeable on longitudinal trim at this speed, but above 560 m.p.h. the aircraft became nose-heavy and the elevators sloppy.

It was not difficult to relight one of the Jumo 004Bs after a flame-out up to an altitude of approximately 10,000 feet, but it was not possible to relight above that altitude. The approach speed (at 13,200 lb.) with 25° flap was 155 m.p.h. and with 45° flap 130 m.p.h. Stalling speed at the latter flap angle was about 110 m.p.h., and the lowering of the undercarriage and flaps had very little effect on trim. A balked landing with flaps and undercarriage down presented no difficulties as the forces could easily be held with one hand whilst retrimming with the other. The Ar 234B-2 was very stable on landing and unaffected by cross-winds, but at least 1,100 yards were required for the landing run with the brakes

Completed in August 1944, the Ar 234V13 (below) was the first four-engined prototype to employ the orthodox under-carriage introduced by the B-series. The four BMW 003A-1 turbojets were mounted in two paired nacelles. These were essentially similar to the nacelles adopted for the C-series (see right).

The Ar 234V14 was generally similar to the pre-production Ar 234B-0, and was used principally for testing equipment to be installed in series aircraft. Of the twenty pre-production Ar 234B-0 aircraft, thirteen were sent to the Rechlin Test Centre.

held on continuously, and the brakes were frequently burned out after two or three landings.

Production tempo of the Blitz began to mount during the autumn of 1944, and approximately one hundred and fifty machines had been delivered by the end of the year. At a meeting held on November 21, 1944, the highest priority was given to the Ar 234B as one of four key production types (the others being the Dornier Do 335, the Heinkel He 162, and the Messerschmitt Me 262), and aircraft were delivered direct to K.G. 76 from the Alt Loennewitz assembly line, but a relatively small proportion of these saw operational use because of the high rate of training accidents, shortages of pilots, and other causes. Nevertheless, the Ar 234B-2 began to appear in increasing numbers over the Allied lines and on at least one occasion reconnoitred over the British Isles.

While production had been gaining momentum, Arado had been busily engaged in the development of more advanced versions of the basic design. The Ar 234V13, which had commenced tests on August 30, 1944, reverted to a similar engine arrangement to that first tested by the Ar 234V8—four BMW 003A-1 units in two paired nacelles. The Ar 234V14 was powered by two Jumo 004B turbojets and was generally similar to the Ar 234B-0 and used for equipment testing; the Ar 234V15 was powered by two BMW 003-A1 engines, and the Ar 234V16 was a particularly interesting experimental model intended for research at high subsonic speeds. It was to have been powered by two BMW 003R composite power plants, each consisting of a BMW 003A-1 turbojet and a BMW 718 bi-fuel rocket motor which augmented thrust by 2,700 lb. for three minutes. Tail surfaces were swept, and four different sets of wings were built for flight testing by this prototype. The first set were of wooden construction and similar planform; the second set

were unswept metal wings of laminar profile; the third set were exceptionally thin swept metal surfaces, and the fourth set were also metal swept surfaces but of laminar profile. Unfortunately, the BMW 303R power plants were not delivered, and, in consequence, the Ar 234V16 was not tested. Neither the Ar 234V17 (two BMW 003A-1 turbojets and pressurized cabin) or V18 (four BMW 003A-1 turbojets and swept wing and tail surfaces) was completed.

The next Versuchs type, the Ar 234V19, was the first real prototype for the more powerful C-series which was entering production during the closing stages of the war. Development of the Ar 234C was seriously hampered by the fact that the experimental assembly plant had to be dispersed to different regions over a period of fifteen months, and shortages of fuel frequently delayed the flight test programme. The Ar 234C was essentially similar to the B-series apart from the fact that it was powered by four BMW 003A-1 turbojets in two paired nacelles. Several detailed modifications were made, including changes in aileron design and skin contours, the nosewheel was enlarged, and air brakes were experimentally fitted. The Ar 234V19 flew for the first time on September 30, 1944, and was intended to serve as a prototype for the proposed Ar 234C-1 production model. This was to have been a high-speed reconnaissance aircraft with a pressure cabin, two cameras in the rear fuselage, and two rearward-firing 20-mm. MG 151 cannon in a pack beneath the fuselage. The estimated performance of the Ar 234C-1 included maximum speeds of 515 m.p.h. at sea level and 542 m.p.h. at 19,700 ft., a range of 920 miles and the ability to climb to 32,800 feet in 11 min. 54 sec.

The Ar 234C-2 was a proposed bomber generally similar to the C-1 capable of carrying one 2,200-lb.

The first production model was the Ar 234B-1 (above) which began to appear over the Allied lines on reconnaissance sorties in the autumn of 1944. It carried no defensive armament or bombs, and was used solely for photo-reconnaissance.

bomb and two 1,100-lb. bombs over a range of 472 miles, or one 1,100-lb. bomb over a range of 995 miles. Maximum speed in clean condition was estimated at 555 m.p.h. at 19,700 feet. Various schemes were proposed for towing a 3,086-lb. bomb or a Fieseler Fi 103 flying bomb, and one project entailed the transportation of a Fi 103 on a cradle on the back of an Ar 234C-2. For launching, the missile was to be raised on the cradle by a series of hydraulically-operated arms to clear the top of the parent aircraft.

The Ar 234C-1 and -2 were abandoned in favour of the multi-purpose Ar 234C-3 for which the Ar 234V20 served as a prototype. It was intended that the Ar 234C-3 be fitted with four BMW 003C turbojets each rated at 1,980 lb.s.t., but the non-availability of these units necessitated the retention of the BMW 003A-1 in the prototype and the initial batch of production machines. The cockpit roof of the Ar 234C-3 was raised to improve visibility, and armament comprised two rearward-firing 20-mm. MG 151 cannon in the fuselage with 250 r.p.g. For the night-fighting role, it was proposed to carry a twin 20-mm. cannon pack beneath the centre fuselage, this being replaced by AB 500 cluster containers of anti-personnel bombs or other weapons for the ground attack role, and the standard range of 550-lb., 1,100-lb., and 2,200-lb. bombs could be carried for level- or dive-bombing attacks. The Ar 234C-3 had empty and maximum loaded weights of 14,400 lb. and 24,250 lb. respectively, maximum speed ranged from 496 m.p.h. at sea level to 532 m.p.h. at 19,700 ft., and range was 765 miles. Only nineteen production Ar 234C-3 aircraft were completed before the end of hostilities, and these were never issued to an operational unit. A reconnaissance aircraft essentially similar to the C-3 was the C-4 which was to have been delivered at a rate of thirty machines per month by June 1944. Like its immediate predecessor, the Ar 234C-4 was to be powered by BMW 003C engines as soon as these became available for installation.

The Ar 234V21 which appeared on November 30, 1944, and the V22, V23, V24, and V25 which were all tested during the following three months, were all prototypes for the Ar 234C-5 single-seat bomber with a pressure cabin and powered by four BMW 003C units, a reconnaissance version being designated Ar 234C-6. The Ar 234V26, completed on March 20, 1945, was built to test laminar-flow aerofoils at high speeds, while the V27 was a test-bed for air brakes.

In view of Germany's concentration on fighter production and development during the closing months of the war, it is hardly surprising that the Ar 234 should be considered for this role, particularly in view of its fine performance. A few weeks before the end of the war in Europe, the Ar 234V28 and V29 appeared, these being prototypes for the two-seat Ar 234C-7 night fighter. Whereas the prototypes were each powered by four BMW 003A turbojets, the proposed production model could be powered by two 2,860 lb.s.t. Heinkel-Hirth HeS 011 or two 2,200 lb.s.t. Jumo 004C turbojets. Armament was to comprise one 20-mm. M.G.151 cannon with 300 rounds in the fuselage and two 30-mm. MK 108 cannon with 100 r.p.g. in a pack beneath the centre fuselage. The Ar 234C-8 was a proposed bomber variant powered by two 2,310 lb.s.t. Jumo turbojets.

Evolved in parallel with the later C-series variants was the Ar 234D, ten prototypes of which were under construction and scheduled for completion by the end of 1945. These were all to have been powered by the Heinkel-Hirth HeS 011, but only two of the prototypes, the V31 and V32, were actually completed before the final collapse. Two D-series variants were proposed, the Ar 234D-1 two-seat reconnaissance aircraft, and the Ar 234D-2 two-seat bomber. A projected night fighter based on the D-series was the Ar 234P, the nose being modified and lengthened to accommodate radar interception equipment, but no prototype had been completed by the end of the war.

The only version of the Blitz to see operational service was the Ar 234B, and only 210 examples of this aircraft had been completed at the time of

The Ar 234C-3 was a multi-purpose aircraft which could be used for close-support, level- and dive-bombing, and night and bad weather fighting. Only nineteen Ar 234C-3s were completed before the end of hostilities.

Germany's final defeat despite the very high priority allocated to the production of this aircraft by the R.L.M. Only a small proportion of these reached K.G. 76, and while they undertook a certain amount of photo-reconnaissance and bombing, their operations being an annoying thorn in the Allies' side, they were too few to seriously affect the issue. The Blitz was thus just another extremely advanced German weapon that arrived too late.

Arado Ar 234B-2 Blitz

Dimensions: Span, 46 ft. 3⅜ in.; length, 41 ft. 5½ in.; height, 14 ft. 1¼ in.; wing area, 284.167 sq. ft.

Armament: Two rearward-firing 20-mm. MG 151 cannon with 200 r.p.g. Maximum bomb load, 3,300 lb. Alternative loads: Three 1,100-lb. SC 500J or SD 500 bombs; one 2,200-lb. SC 1,000 bomb or SD 1000 bomb and two 550-lb. SC 250J bombs; one 3,085-lb. PC 1,400, or three AB 500 or AB 250 anti-personnel bomb clusters.

Power Plants: Two Junkers Jumo 004B turbojets with eight-stage axial-flow compressors and single-stage turbines each rated at 1,980 lb. s.t.

Weights: Empty, 11,464 lb.; loaded (clean), 18,541 lb.; maximum loaded, 20,613 lb.

Performance: Maximum speed, 461 m.p.h. at 19,685 ft., 460 m.p.h. at 26,250 ft., 435 m.p.h. at 32,800 ft.; time to 19,685 ft. (with 1,100-lb. bomb load), 12.8 min., (with 3,300-lb.), 17.5 min., to 26,250 ft. (with 1,100-lb.), 21.6 min., (with 3,300-lb.), 34.1 min.; maximum range (with 1,100-lb. bomb load), 967 mls., (with 3,300-lb.), 683.5 mls.; maximum endurance (at sea level), 1.25 hrs., (at 33,000 ft.), 3.25 hrs.

The Ar 234V21 was the first prototype for the proposed Ar 234C-5 single-seat pressurized bomber powered by four BMW 003C turbojets. The V21 (below) and the similar V22, V23, V24 and V25 were all tested during the last months of the war.

The Stirling I was the first of the R.A.F.'s four-engined "heavies" to see combat, but as the war progressed it was limited by its altitude performance.

THE SHORT STIRLING

The Short Stirling was not merely the first of the Royal Air Force's true "heavies" of the Second World War, it was the *only* British four-engined bomber designed from the outset to take four power plants to see operational service during the conflict, the Lancaster and Halifax having both stemmed from twin-engined designs. Carrying bomb loads far greater than any previously contemplated, the Stirling proved one of the most important landmarks in the history of the R.A.F., for it was the first bomber to be received by that service capable of giving tangible expression to the Air Staff's beliefs in strategic bombing, and delivering, in Winston Churchill's words, "the shattering strokes of retributive justice" with which Germany's industry was to be crippled; the first of the great four-motor bombers which were to play a primary role in the defeat of the Axis powers. Yet the official history of the R.A.F. in the Second World War was to refer to the Stirling as "a disappointment."

This may appear an unfair comment on a warplane which more than fulfilled the requirements of the specification to which it had been designed, but if the Stirling *was* a disappointment, it was also a revealing example of the rapidity with which operational

requirements can change under the exigencies of war. The Stirling's shortcomings could, for the most part, be laid at the doorstep of the short-sighted limitations imposed upon its design by the official specification. This insisted that the wing span should be less than the 100-ft. door opening of standard R.A.F. hangars, and in order to keep the wing loading within reasonable limits, the Stirling's designers were forced to employ a wing of low aspect ratio and high induced drag with, in consequence, an adverse effect on performance. Undoubtedly, had they had a free hand they would have selected a wing of greater span and higher aspect ratio, but in the event the chosen wing, although endowing the Stirling with outstanding manœuvrability for an aircraft of its size, severely restricted the bomber's operational ceiling. This shortcoming increasingly handicapped the Stirling's operations as more effective anti-aircraft defences forced the bomber higher, and proved particularly serious during attacks on Italian targets when its pilots frequently found it necessary to fly *through* the Alps rather than over them! While the hangar door opening dictated the wing span, the size of the fuselage cross section was dictated by the size of

The first prototype Stirling (L7600), above and left, was written off during its first landing when the undercarriage collapsed as a result of the binding of a wheel brake. The undercarriage was extensively modified for the second prototype.

standard packing cases!

Another unfortunate feature of the Stirling was its inability to carry really large bombs. At the time of the bomber's conception, prevalent ideas on strategic bombing demanded the saturation of the target area with large quantities of 500-lb. and 1,000-lb. bombs. The Stirling could carry twenty-four 500-pounders, but its 42 ft. 7 in. bomb-bay, being divided into three longitudinal cells by two girders which gave the fuselage its structural stiffness, could not accommodate the very much larger weapons that became available soon after the Stirling's service introduction, thus imposing strict limitations on the bomber's usefulness.

In view of the restrictive specification, the Stirling was perhaps more of a compromise than most war-

planes. Aerodynamic and operational consideration dictated a mid-mounted wing, but the price paid for the advantages offered by this wing position was an exceptionally tall undercarriage of extraordinary geometry which proved necessary in order to obtain a satisfactory ground angle. This tended to result in a dangerous swing on take-off if the pilot was not adept with the throttles; a problem aggravated by the provision of armour protection and additional armament and equipment which boosted the design gross weight of 52,000 lb. to 70,000 lb., rendering take-offs somewhat marginal operations, especially when being effected from muddy grass fields. The Stirling suffered its full share of take-off accidents and was therefore considered by many to be dangerous.

The Air Staff requirement for a heavy bomber possessing a range and bomb load far in excess of any previously envisaged was formulated in July 1936, and embodied in Air Ministry Specification B.12/36.

The S.31 half-scale flying model of the S.29 Stirling was first flown in 1938 with 90 h.p. Niagara III engines. These were later replaced by 115 h.p. Niagara IVs.

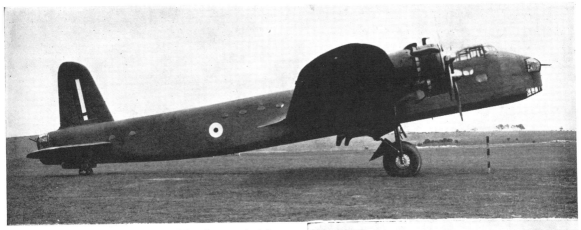

The second prototype Stirling (L7605), above and right, flew shortly after the outbreak of World War II. The undercarriage was modified and spinners were temporarily fitted.

Short and Harland Limited, the Supermarine Aviation Works, and Sir W. G. Armstrong Whitworth Aircraft Limited submitted proposals to meet the demands of the specification, and the two first-mentioned companies were awarded development contracts. Supermarine's contender for the specification—known as the Type 317 with Bristol Hercules engines and as the Type 318 with Rolls-Royce Merlins—was the last design of R. J. Mitchell of Spitfire fame, but the prototypes were destroyed during an attack on the Southampton factory where they were nearing completion, and owing to the company's other commitments, further development of the bomber was abandoned. Meanwhile, Short's contender, then known as the S.29, had been completed and flown.

Because of the relatively advanced nature of the S.29 bomber's design, it was considered advisable to build an aerodynamically similar half-scale flying model to provide information on the flying qualities and handling characteristics to be expected from the full-scale bomber. The wing of the Short Scion Senior, which spanned 50 ft., was essentially similar in planform to that of the proposed bomber, and roughly half size, so modified Scion Senior wing components and engine mounts were employed for the S.31 model when construction of this began in 1937. When first flown in 1938, the S.31 was powered by four 90 h.p. Pobjoy Niagara III seven-cylinder engines, but in the following year these were replaced by 115 h.p. Niagara IVs. The two-seat S.31 was a fairly faithful model of the bomber and weighed 5,700 lb. The engines and their airscrews were roughly half the size of those to be employed by the bomber, representing the slipstream effects to be expected quite well, and bomb doors were fitted so that some idea of the effect of opening and closing the

On the ground one of the most noticeable characteristics of the Stirling was its exceptionally tall undercarriage which is well portrayed by this photograph of an early production Stirling I without dorsal turret.

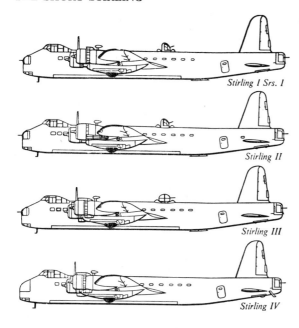

Stirling I Srs. I

Stirling II

Stirling III

Stirling IV

and the Austin Motor Company, had been formed in January 1939. The group had a team of nearly 600 skilled engineers and draughtsmen which was to become one of the most travelled supervisory bodies ever to serve the British aircraft industry. Under its supervision, an organised system of dispersal was established whereby the primary components of the Stirling were built in more than twenty different factories, and a large sub-contracting scheme for smaller components arranged.

Production deliveries of the bomber were disappointingly slow in getting under way, some of the delays being the result of enemy attacks which destroyed a number of early Stirling Is (N3645 and N3647 to N3651) at the Rochester works. Five Stirling Is were also destroyed at the Belfast works, and although the first production Stirling I (N3635) appeared in May 1940, no more than three of these bombers were delivered during the second quarter of that year, with six in each of the third and fourth quarters. Nevertheless, although fewer than half a dozen production Stirling Is were available, the new bomber began to replace the Wellington in No. 7 Squadron, a member of No. 3 Group, during August 1940, this unit thereby gaining the distinction of becoming the first four-engined bomber squadron of the Second World War.

The large, flat-sided fuselage of the Stirling, married to what appeared to be inordinately small wings and an unusually tall undercarriage, gave an impression of lanky ungainliness which was entirely belied by the bomber's manœuvrability. On one occasion, a Short test pilot, demonstrating the Stirling to an R.A.F. crew, pulled up the nose of the large bomber until it stood vertically on its tail and then stalled it in that position. The bomber dropped its nose and returned easily to level flight after a brief dive, but the tail gunner, who had not been warned of this violent manœuvre, had attempted to bale out! Fortunately, he stuck in the escape hatch and succeeded in clambering back into the bomber when it regained its normal attitude. These powers of manœuvre were to prove particularly useful when the Stirling appeared on daylight operations, and the belief that the heavy bomber could "look after itself", current during 1941, was the direct result of a combination of this agility and effective turreted defensive armament.

The structure of the Stirling offered much evidence of its flying boat ancestry, and the wing construction in particular followed closely that of the earlier Short flying boats, and possessed a tapered planform typical of the wings employed by the Empire and Sunderland. The wing was basically a two-spar

full-scale doors of the bomber could be gained. In fact, as the S.31's pilot, Mr. Lankester Parker, said afterwards, he was the only item not to scale.

Flight trials with the S.31 had given the design team a pretty good idea of what they might expect from the S.29 when, in May 1939, the first full-scale prototype (L7600) took-off on its maiden flight. Unfortunately, during its first landing, the prototype's undercarriage collapsed as a result of the binding of a wheel brake, and the machine was a total write-off. This mishap inevitably delayed the flight test programme at a critical period, and the second prototype (L7605), which, like the ill-fated first machine, was powered by four 1,375 h.p. Bristol Hercules II fourteen-cylinder sleeve-valve engines, did not fly until shortly after the outbreak of the war, by which time the Stirling heavy bomber had already entered quantity production.

In October 1938, the Air Ministry had been working to "Programme L" which involved 3,500 heavy bombers to be delivered by April 1942. This quantity was to comprise 1,500 Stirlings, 1,500 Manchesters, and 500 Halifaxes—although, in the event, deliveries were to be about a year behind the target set by this programme—and the scheme led to the concept of so-called "quantity groups". This meant introducing a limited number of new types of aircraft and dividing the total production of each type between several companies. The "Stirling Group", which initially comprised Short Brothers, the Rootes Group,

FINISH AND INSIGNIA: The Stirling B.Mk.III of No. 75 "New Zealand" Squadron illustrated on the opposite page was finished in the standard R.A.F. Bomber Command scheme comprising a dark earth and dark green camouflage pattern over the upper surfaces, and matt black over all wing, tail and fuselage under surfaces, extending up the fuselage sides and including the vertical tail surfaces. The

"C" type roundels with yellow outline appeared on the fuselage sides with corresponding "flashes" on the fin. Blue and red "B" type roundels appeared on the upper wing surfaces, and the code letters indicating the squadron (i.e., AA) and the individual aircraft (i.e., K) were painted dull red as was also the serial number.

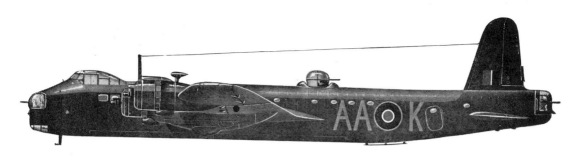

Short Stirling B.III

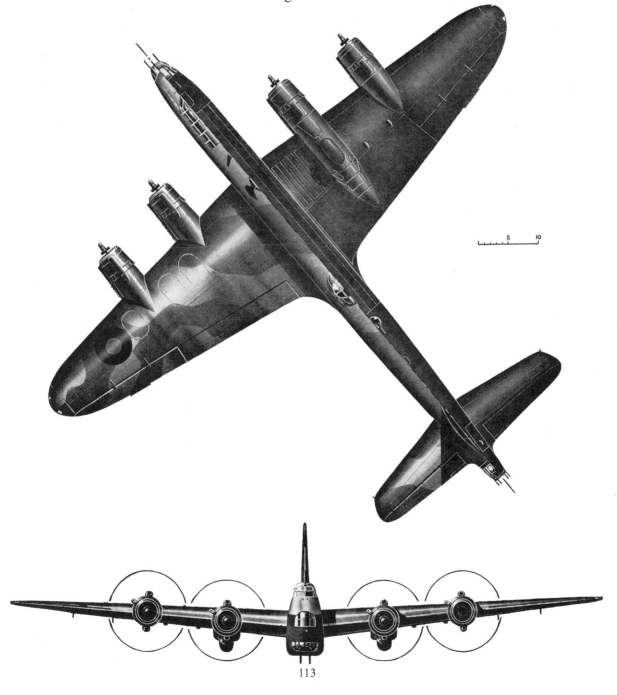

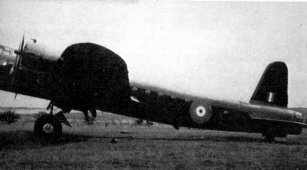

carried in each of the two bays to bring total fuel capacity to 2,692 Imp.gal. Gouge-type trailing edge flaps with a chord equal to forty-eight per cent of the main wing chord were used, these being generally similar to Fowler flaps but having no gaps between them and the main wings, worked solely by the increase in area and angle of incidence.

The fuselage also employed a form of construction similar to that of Short's flying boats, and was of rectangular section with rounded corners built up of transverse frames with aluminium alloy skinning. Two longitudinal beams supported the bombs in a tremendous bay stretching from beneath the flight deck to a point well aft of the wings. The bomb-bay could accommodate seven 2,000-lb. or eighteen 500-lb. bombs, but with the heavier bombs the supplementary wing bomb cells were not used. The defensive armament initially comprised twin 0.303-in. Browning machine guns in a power-operated nose turret, four similar guns in a power-operated tail turret, and two further Brownings in a retractable ventral turret. The last-mentioned turret was only fitted to the prototypes and the first few production aircraft, and this was never employed operationally as it was realised that its extension would reduce speed at a critical moment. Another disadvantage of the ventral turret was its tendency to creep down into the fully-extended position during taxying and take-off, the guns sometimes fouling the ground. After the first few Stirling Is had been delivered, an oddly-shaped Boulton Paul power-operated dorsal turret with twin Brownings was added. The port inner engine was fitted with a twin pump to operate the

structure covered by aluminium alloy sheet flush-riveted to the spars and rib members. The leading edges were armoured and provided with balloon cable cutters, and outboard of the engines most of the space between the spars was occupied by fuel tanks. Seven tanks were installed in each wing with a total capacity of 2,254 Imp.gal., and all but two of the tanks (No. 7 in each wing) were self-sealing, the No. 7 tanks not being used unless maximum range was essential, in which case their contents were used first. Inboard of the engines were bomb cells which, each containing three 500-lb. bombs, supplemented the immense fuselage bay and could also be used to house auxiliary fuel tanks, 219 Imp.gals. being

(Above) The Stirling III (BF509) differed from the Mk.I principally in having its engines installed as "power eggs". Two Stirling Is were converted as prototypes for the Mk.III, one of these (BK649) being illustrated (right), and others were converted to Mk.III standards on the assembly line, such as R9309 (below, right).

nose and dorsal turret, the starboard inner engine having a pump for the tail turret. Later, the turreted defensive armament was augmented in the Stirling I Series II production model by a pair of hand-held 0.303-in. beam guns.

The crew of the Stirling I normally comprised seven members—pilot and co-pilot, navigator/bombardier, radio-operator, engineer/gunner and two gunners—and power was provided by four 1,595 h.p. Hercules XI engines. The outboard engines were mounted centrally on the wing profile, but the inner pair were set lower in order to provide sufficient room for the main undercarriage members to retract into their nacelles. Because of its length and the need to accommodate the wheels between the main wing spars, the design of the undercarriage structure was rather complex, and made use of a system of double-jointed struts.

During the working-up period with No. 7 Squadron many teething troubles were encountered, as was perhaps to be expected with such a radically new aircraft. The characteristics of the Stirling I met with general approval. The controls were good, the ailerons being relatively light for such a large aircraft, although the elevator control had a slightly heavy and sluggish initial movement. The aircraft was extremely stable directionally and laterally, and it was reasonably stable longitudinally, except when fully loaded with the C.G. in the most aft position. With any one engine out of action, the aircraft could maintain height at any weight, although with two

engines out it was difficult to maintain altitude at any weight over 50,000 lb. The maximum permissible take-off weight was 70,000 lb., at which the Stirling I would clear a 50-ft. obstacle within 1,400 yards. The recommended climbing speed from sea level to 10,000 ft. was 150 m.p.h. (I.A.S.) and from 10,000 to 15,000 ft. was 145 m.p.h., this altitude being attained in forty-two minutes.

The production build-up of the Stirling was extremely slow, only fifteen having been delivered by the end of 1940, but the tempo began to increase from the beginning of 1941 with twenty-one machines being delivered in the first quarter of that year. The Stirling was introduced into operational service as rapidly as possible, and on February 10, 1941, three

115

Stirlings of No. 7 Squadron, each carrying sixteen 500-lb. bombs, took-off from Oakington for a night sortie against Rotterdam oil storage tanks, marking the début of "the first of the heavies" over enemy occupied territory. In the following month, No. 7's Stirlings undertook night attacks on the German battle cruisers *Scharnhorst* and *Gneisenau* lying in Brest, but in April some unpleasant tasks fell to the lot of the Stirlings when they commenced daylight sorties. The first of these took place against Emden on April 27th, and no fighter escort was provided, but the Stirlings provided the defending interceptors with a formidable opponent. One of the most famed of their daylight sorties was that made in July 1941 against the *Scharnhorst* which, by this time, was lying in La Pallice. During this month new tactics were evolved, and the Stirling participated in combined "circus" operations, a fighter force accompanying the bomber formation in an attempt to draw the Luftwaffe into battle. During this period of R.A.F. Bomber Command's offensive, the guns of the Stirling accounted for a substantial number of Messerschmitt Bf 109 and Bf 110 fighters, but Luftwaffe fighters had discovered that a burst of fire in the vicinity of the fuselage roundels put the tail turret out of action, and the whole system had to be modified.

Throughout 1941, production deliveries of the Stirling I from Shorts, Rochester, Belfast and Swindon factories, and from the Austin Motor Company at Birmingham, had been steadily increasing, and by the end of the year 153 machines had been produced, and additional squadrons of No. 3 Group had re-equipped with the heavy bomber. By the beginning of 1942, however, the daylight attacks by Stirlings were petering out as German defences were making such sorties extremely hazardous, and the bombers were forced to contain themselves to nocturnal activities, much to the relief of their crews.

Stirlings had previously visited Berlin by night, their first attack on the German capital having taken place on April 17, 1941, and on May 30, 1942, Stirlings participated in the first thousand-bomber raid on Germany. By this time, the Stirling had been joined on operations by the higher-performing Lancaster and Halifax, but although outshone in speed and altitude capability, the Stirling proved time and time again its ability to absorb an immense amount of battle damage and stay in the air. One Stirling of No. 75 Squadron even survived a collision with a Bf 109 fighter, regaining its base less four feet of the starboard wing. Another Stirling from the same squadron succeeded in returning on three engines with the complete rudder shot away, while a No. 218 Squadron Stirling raiding Turin was hit in three of its four engines but succeeded in staying in the air for five hours, eventually landing at Bone, in North Africa. The pilot of this Stirling, Flight Sergeant Arthur Aaron, performed this feat after having his jaw smashed, part of his face torn away, an arm broken and a lung perforated. He was the second Stirling pilot to be awarded a posthumous Victoria Cross, the first being Flight Sergeant Rawdon Middleton of No. 491 Squadron. Despite the fact that a shell splinter had destroyed Flt. Sgt. Middleton's right eye and he had suffered wounds in the body and legs during an attack on Turin, he personally directed the hazardous re-crossing of the Alps and remained at the controls until his Stirling had reached the British coast.

To safeguard against a possible shortage of Hercules engines, in 1941 two Stirlings (N3657 and N3711) were fitted with 1,600 h.p. Wright R-2600-A5B Cyclone 14 engines to serve as prototypes for the Stirling II, but no shortage of the British power plants arose, and only three production Stirling IIs were produced, one by the Rochester factory and two by the Swindon factory. As a result of operational maintenance experience, the next version of the Stirling to reach the assembly lines was the Mk.III. This differed from the Mk.I principally in having 1,635 h.p. Hercules VI or XVI engines which were installed as "power-eggs", considerably easing maintenance. A new twin-Browning dorsal turret was fitted, and various internal changes were made. Maximum speed was increased to 270 m.p.h. at 14,500 feet, but by the early months of 1943 the Stirling was already out-dated. While the Lancasters and Halifaxes were flying at altitudes approaching 20,000 ft., a fully laden Stirling was hard put to reach 12,000 feet. Two Stirling Is (BK648 and 649) served as prototypes for the Mk.III, and another Stirling I (R9254) was used in the development of H2S radar, and was one of the first aircraft to sport the characteristic ventral radome which was to appear on Lancasters and Halifaxes.

As early as 1941, Short's design team had submitted a proposal for an improved version of the basic Stirling in which the wing span was increased to 135 ft. 9 in. and the wing area to 2,145 sq.ft. This, the Short S.34 to specification B.8/41, was to have been powered by four Bristol Centaurus engines and, with an all up weight of 104,000 lb., carry a 10,000-lb. bomb load over 4,000 miles at 300 m.p.h. However, despite the promise of vastly superior characteristics, the S.34 development of the Stirling was not proceeded with.

Peak production of the Stirling was reached in the second quarter of 1943 during which the bomber was being delivered at the rate of eighty machines per month, but by that time the Stirling squadrons were attacking only the less well-defended targets, and the last aircraft of this type to be built for the bombing role were delivered during the third quarter of 1944, when they were retained mainly for use against fringe targets and flying-bomb sites in Northern France. The Stirling had served operationally with Nos. 7, 15, 75, 90, 101, 149, 166, 199, 214, 218, 513, 622, 623 and 624 Squadrons, as well as with Nos. 138 and 161 (Special Duties) Squadrons who operated them from Tempsford during 1942-43 for dropping saboteurs and supplies to partisans in occupied

A Stirling I (R9254), illustrated above, was employed in the development of H2S radar, and was one of the first aircraft to feature the ventral radome later to appear on Halifaxes and Lancasters.

territories. The last sortie undertaken by Bomber Command Stirlings took place on September 8, 1944.

Apart from bombing, the Stirling had also been used for mine-laying and radio-countermeasures, but its primary role from the beginning of 1944 was that of transport, this version being known as the Stirling IV. The prototype Stirling IV (LJ512) was converted from a Mk.III, and flew for the first time in 1943. The nose turret was supplanted by a transparent plastic fairing, the dorsal turret was deleted, and only some machines retained their tail turret. Glider-towing equipment was installed in the rear fuselage, and twelve Stirling IVs were delivered in the last quarter of 1943, transport Stirlings subsequently being delivered at a rate of 30-35 machines per month until mid-1945. Many of the bomber variants were also converted for use as transports in service, and on D-Day, June 6, 1944, Stirling IVs of Nos. 190, 196, 299 and 622 Squadrons towed Airspeed Horsas during their operational début as glider tugs. Stirling IVs also towed gliders during the Arnhem landing, and were subsequently employed to supply fuel to the squadrons of the 2nd Tactical Air Force on the Continent.

The last production variant was also a transport, the Stirling V, which differed from the Mk.IV principally in having a lengthened and redesigned nose, the prototype Mk.V being LJ530. When Stirling production finally terminated in November 1945 with the 160th Mk.V, the grand production total had reached 2,375 machines. Of these, 756 were Mk.Is and 875 were Mk.IIIs, although many were subsequently converted for the transport role.

The Short Stirling possibly was "a disappointment", but this was hardly the fault of the design team or manufacturers, for what other first-line operational bomber was designed to meet the requirements of hangar door openings and packing cases! There can be no doubt that, at the time the Stirling's specification was framed, the operational conditions and requirements that were to exist six years later were not foreseen, and the design of the Stirling was such that it could not be modified to meet the new demands. In consequence, its career as a first-line heavy bomber was relatively brief. Nevertheless, as the R.A.F.'s first four-engined "heavy" of the Second World War, the Stirling occupied a particularly important place in the history of that air arm.

Short Stirling Mk.I Series I

Dimensions: Span, 99 ft. 1 in.; length, 87 ft. 3 in.; height, 22 ft. 9 in.; wing area, 1,460 sq. ft.

Armament: Two 0.303-in. Browning machine guns with 1,000 r.p.g. in nose and dorsal power-operated turrets and four 0.303-in. Browning machine guns with 1,000 r.p.g. in power-operated tail turret. Reserve ammunition 5,750 rds. Maximum bomb loads: Seven 2,000-lb. bombs in fuselage bay (14,000 lb.), or eighteen 500-lb. bombs in fuselage bay and six 500-lb. bombs in wing cells (12,000 lb.).

Power Plants: Four Bristol Hercules XI fourteen-cylinder sleeve-valve double-row radial air-cooled engines each rated at 1,590 h.p. at 2,900 r.p.m. for take-off, 1,460 h.p. at 2,800 r.p.m. at 9,500 ft. maximum power for five minutes, and 1,020 h.p. at 2,500 r.p.m. at 7,500 ft. maximum economical cruising power.

Weights: Tare, 44,000 lb.; empty equipped 46,900 lb.; normal loaded, 59,400 lb.; maximum permissible, 70,000 lb.

Performance: Maximum speed, 245 m.p.h. at sea level, 260 m.p.h. at 10,500 ft.; economical cruising speed, 200 m.p.h. at 15,000 ft.; maximum weak mixture cruising speed, 215 m.p.h. at 15,000 ft.; range (with 980 Imp.gal. and 14,000-lb. bomb load), 740 mls., (with 2,254 Imp.gal. and 5,000-lb. bomb load), 1,930 mls., (with 2,694 Imp.gal. and 1,500-lb. load), 2,330 mls.; time to 15,000 ft. (maximum weight), 42 min.; service ceiling (normal loaded), 20,500 ft., (maximum loaded), 16,500 ft.

The Mitsubishi G4M1 Type 1 Model 11 began its operational career in May 1941 with attacks on Chungking and Chengtu.

THE MITSUBISHI G4M TYPE 1

The time was 12.44 p.m. on August 19, 1945. The place was the small, torrid island of Ie Shima, and the event was possibly the most important Japanese flying mission of the entire Pacific War. At that memorable moment, two rotund Japanese bombers landed on the island airstrip, their arrival presaging the end of hostilities in the Pacific. Painted white overall, and bearing the large green "surrender crosses" on their wings, fuselages, and tails, the pair of emasculated bombers, hastily stripped to carry the Japanese surrender delegation headed by Lieut.-General Torashiro Kawabe, were, appropriately enough, examples of a type that had become all too familiar to the Allies from the first day of the Pacific War.

Dubbed *Betty* by the Allies and known officially to the Japanese Naval Air Force as the Mitsubishi 1-*Rikko*, or Type I Land Attack Aircraft, these bombers had seen action in every Pacific theatre of operations from the Aleutian Islands to Australia; they were the instruments with which Japan gained many of her initial victories, and, for a while, they had numbered among the most feared of Japanese operational aircraft.

The Mitsubishi G4M1 Type 1 Land Attack Aircraft Model 11 was the first new twin-engined bomber to be encountered by the Allies in combat. Both the Army's Mitsubishi Ki.21 and the Navy's G3M2 had been met in numbers over China, and much information on their capabilities was, in consequence, available to Allied aircrews when combat was joined, but even though the 1-*Rikko* had also made its operational début over the Chinese mainland, its appearance in the Pacific came as a complete surprise to the Allies. When these new Mitsubishi bombers were first encountered in the air by American fighters west of the Gilberts early in 1942, far beyond the estimated range of bombers operating from known Japanese bases, they were thought to have been carrier-launched and, as such, examples of a radically new Japanese approach to long-range strategic bombing.

Subsequent encounters at Midway and Guadalcanal and analyses of wrecked 1-*Rikko* bombers found in New Guinea revealed the secret of the bomber's phenomenal range and, thus, this new Mitsubishi product took its proper place as an example of Japanese thinking in the field of land-based strategic bombers. But it was soon to become apparent to both the Japanese Navy and the Allies that within this "thinking" lay the seeds of the bomber's destruction. Japanese insistence on maximum range at the expense of protective armour rendered the 1-*Rikko* supremely vulnerable to air and ground fire. Its immense wing tanks, designed to accommodate more than 1,100 Imp.gal. of fuel, were totally unprotected, and armour protection for the crew was confined to a pancake-sized piece of armour plate located aft of the tail gunner's ammunition storage rack. In fact, the bomber's complete inability to survive enemy fire power and its notorious inflammability rapidly earned for it the term "Type 1 Lighter" from its crews, although the more tolerant dubbed it the *Hamaki*, or "Flying Cigar".

The J.N.A.F. had blundered, for, in developing a versatile heavy bomber for the Pacific War, they had based their design requirements largely on experience gained over the Chinese mainland, and the consequences of this blunder were to be exceeded in seriousness only by the strategical errors of the disastrous Midway and Guadalcanal operations. Conceived as a weapon of offence, the design did not take into account the possibility of aggressive fighter opposition. The result was that, as Allied strength in the Pacific grew, the 1-*Rikko* became totally ineffectual unless enjoying the protection of a strong fighter escort. The limits of the bomber's usefulness were soon clearly drawn, and repeated modifications and revised operational assignments were never able to keep abreast of Allied developments, or instil confidence in the 1-*Rikko*'s crews.

The 1-*Rikko* started life late in 1937 under a cloak of the strictest secrecy in the Central Engineering and Design Department of Mitsubishi Jukogyo KK., located at Oe-machi, Nagoya. Japan had already embarked upon the "China Incident", and there could be little doubt that the world was heading towards general war. An attitude of suspicion and

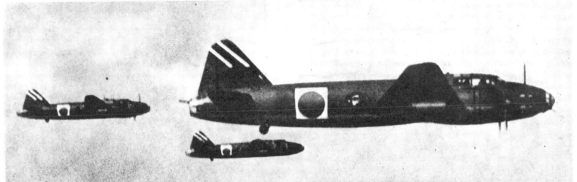

The removal of the bomb doors from some G4M1 aircraft gave the bomber a distinctive "broken-back" profile.

distrust of Japan by the Western Powers led Japanese planners to the conclusion that the days of design dependency upon foreign sources were nearing their end, and that Japan should firmly establish design self-sufficiency within her aircraft industry. An expansion programme for Mitsubishi was proposed in 1937, and actively launched in the following year with a series of secret design projects for both the Army and the Navy, the two most important of which were the 12-*Shi* Carrier Fighter, which was to enter service as the A6M2 *Zero-Sen*, and the 12-*Shi* Land Attack Aircraft, eventually to be accepted as the G4M1.

Secrecy in design and factory expansion was considered to be of the utmost importance in order to avoid alienating foreign sources of materials and tools, the principal of which was the United States. Any suggestion that the J.N.A.F. was actively developing a bomber capable of flying non-stop across the Pacific would, in all probability, have led to a trade boycott of Japan, and an end to vital imports. As long as Japan was still largely dependent on the United States for machine tools, steel billets, and forgings for aircraft and power plant production, the secrecy of the prototype programme had to remain closely guarded.

The Mitsubishi design office at Oe-machi was placed on an overtime basis early in 1938 in order to cope with the new series of indigenous designs for the Army and Navy, and to get the preliminary work on the important 12-*Shi* bomber under way. The J.N.A.F. had issued a design requirement for a heavy land-based bomber possessing a maximum range of 2,990 miles without bomb load, and 2,300 miles with a standard 1,760-lb. torpedo or an equivalent bomb load. The 12-*Shi* bomber was considered as a potential replacement for the Mitsubishi G3M2 Type 96 then entering J.N.A.F. service, and the individual members of the design staff were selected for their known creative abilities and advanced ideas. Headed by Dipl. Eng. Kiro Honjo, chief designer of the earlier Mitsubishi bomber, the team initially considered the development of a large four-engined machine, but this proposal was rejected by the J.N.A.F. which recommended that the 12-*Shi* specification be met with a large twin-engined aircraft. It was agreed that development work on the fuselage of the new bomber should be the responsibility of the 1st Naval Arsenal, the basic design and remaining assemblies continuing to remain the responsibility of Mitsubishi.

Detail design work progressed at a rapid tempo throughout 1938, and by the spring of 1939 various major components were ready for prototype assembly. J.N.A.F. insistence on a twin-engined aircraft necessitated relatively light construction for an aircraft of the 12-*Shi* bomber's size. The wings, which utilised the Mitsubishi 118 aerofoil section as did also the parallel 12-*Shi* fighter, employed a two-spar structure with flush-riveted stressed skinning, and were mid-set on a remarkably bulky, elliptical section, semi-monocoque fuselage. The very size of the fuselage belied the fact that it was intended for a *twin*-engined bomber, a comment made by Heinkel engineers visiting the factory in 1939, and the chosen power plants were a pair of the new Mitsubishi Kasei (Mars) 11 fourteen-cylinder two-row radials. This was the first modern two-row radial evolved in Japan to equal contemporary foreign models in performance, developing 1,530 h.p. at sea level in its initial form. The choice of this engine was fundamental to the performance success of the 1-*Rikko* bombers. Provision was made for seven crew members and, in September 1939, the first 12-*Shi* bomber prototype was completed.

The first flight tests were conducted in October with Mitsubishi test pilot Katsuzo Shima at the controls, and as the results of these initial trials met the design team's most sanguine expectations, it appeared that the way was clear for J.N.A.F. acceptance and quantity production of the bomber.

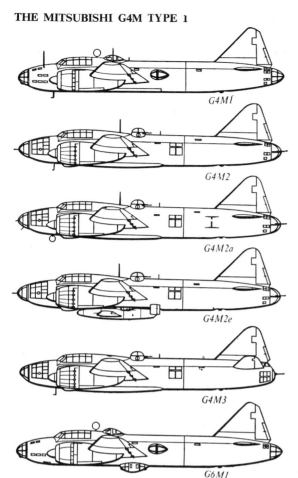

G4M1

G4M2

G4M2a

G4M2e

G4M3

G6M1

at the 3rd Airframe Works at Nagoya on a limited procurement basis. A total of thirty of the immense "fighters" was completed before production was terminated in March 1941. The G6M1 carried ten crew members and an armament of four 20-mm. cannon and a single 7.7-mm. machine gun. It was soon apparent that the "wingtip escort" theory was impracticable as the G6M1 possessed an entirely different performance envelope to that of the G3M2; it was seriously overloaded and therefore unwieldy, and it could not keep formation with the lightly loaded bombers returning from a mission. The whole scheme was, therefore, abandoned, late production models were completed as G6M1-K crew trainers and, ultimately, all remaining aircraft of the type were converted as transports under the designation G6M1-L2, these carrying paratroops in the South-West Pacific.

With the failure of the G6M1, the 12-*Shi* bomber was finally accepted for production as the G4M1 Type 1 Land Attack Aircraft Model 11 in April 1941. From completion of the original bomber prototype in September 1939, followed by a second bomber prototype in December 1940, through an additional thirteen prototypes delivered between January and March 1941, production was stepped up to a rate of twenty-five aircraft a month by November 1941, and somewhat over 180 machines had been delivered to the J.N.A.F. by the time Pearl Harbour was attacked during the following month. The G4M1 was rapidly assigned to operational units, making its first sortie in May 1941 with an attack on Chungking and Chengtu. This raid was undertaken by the veteran Hankow Air Wing, and was the harbinger of things to come, for it also marked the operational début of the A6M2 *Zero-Sen* fighter, then undergoing combat trials in China, in the escort role.

Before launching the Pacific War, the J.N.A.F. had assigned 120 G4M1 bombers to the 11th Air Fleet in preparation for the invasion of the Philippines, the Dutch East Indies and Malaya. The aircraft were ultimately spread in a wide arc aimed at these target areas, with fifty-four aircraft and reserves assigned to the 21st Air Flotilla's Kanoya Air Corps, and an additional fifty-four aircraft and reserves assigned to the 23rd Air Flotilla's Takao Air Corps. With the location and identification of the British battleships *Repulse* and *Prince of Wales* at Singapore in the weeks preceding the War, plans were prepared which were to render British Asiatic sea power impotent in one blow. Twenty-seven of the Kanoya Air Corps' G4M1 bombers were re-assigned to bases

In the event, service approval was to be withheld for more than a year!

The delay was largely due to a proposal made late in 1938 by the Yokosuka Experimental Air Corps. This suggested the development of a heavily-armed escort aircraft which could accompany the slow-flying G3M2 Type 96 bombers operating over China beyond conventional fighter range. A small but insistent group of Naval officers forced the acceptance of the multi-gun escort fighter on the J.N.A.F. who requested that the 12-*Shi* bomber prototype be modified to fulfil this requirement. Despite the protests of the design team, the 12-*Shi* bomber became the 12-*Shi* long-range convoy fighter, and the type was awarded the designation G6M1, thereby bypassing the G4M1 designation assigned to the original bomber project.

Production of the G6M1 began in October 1939

FINISH AND INSIGNIA: *Although early wartime models of the 1-Rikko were finished sea-blue or light green land camouflage, while others employed natural metal finish, late models, such as the G4M2 Type 1 Land Attack Aircraft Model 24 illustrated on the opposite page, were painted to conform to the necessity of overland operations faced by the J.N.A.F. in 1944-45. The machine illustrated belonged to the 763rd Kokutai (Air Corps), all J.N.A.F. medium bomber units being assigned numbers in the 700 series, operating in the Philippines in October 1944. The upper surfaces were painted dark 'ungle green while the* under surfaces employed natural metal finish. The national insignia, the circular red Hinomaru, was outlined in white on the fuselage, and on some machines was also outlined in white on the upper wing surfaces. About ten inches of the wing leading edges to the outboard wing panels were painted yellow on many aircraft—a J.N.A.F. adaptation of the J.A.A.F. "combat stripe" which served as an identification aid. The numerals "763-12" were painted in white across the vertical tail surfaces, denoting the twelfth aircraft of the 763rd Kokutai.*

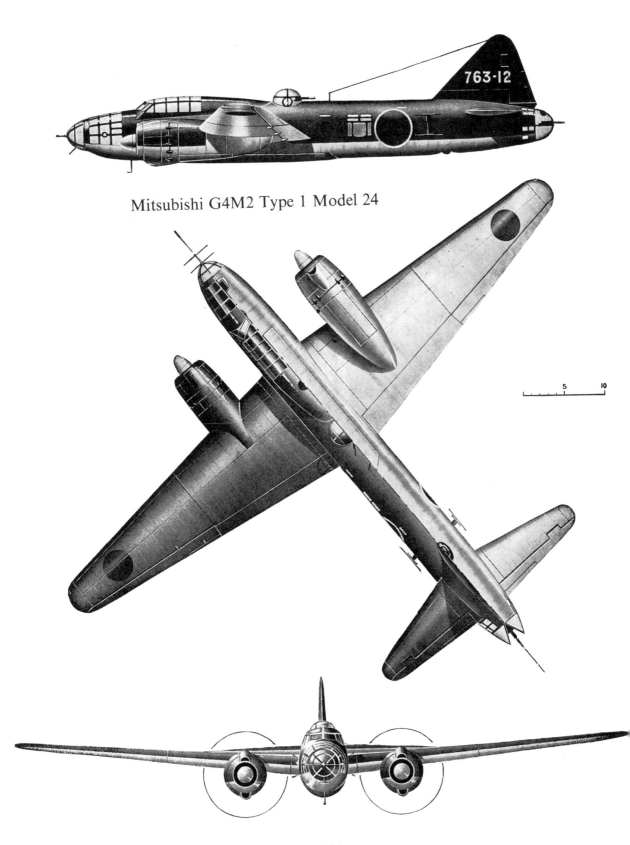

Mitsubishi G4M2 Type 1 Model 24

763-12

5   10

The G4M2 introduced a hydraulically-operated dorsal turret and protected fuel tanks.

in Indo-China which had previously been occupied by Japanese forces, and from these bases they were, subsequently, to attack and destroy the British surface vessels, scoring a tremendous victory which was to have far-reaching effects on military operations in the Pacific.

When, on the morning of December 8, 1941 (Japanese time), war enveloped the entire South-West and Central Pacific, attacks being launched against Pearl Harbour, the Philippines, Malaya, Wake and Guam, fifty-four G4M1 bombers of the 23rd Air Flotilla based on Formosa attacked Clark Field in the Philippines, virtually obliterating the American air formations based there. Two days later, G4M1s, operating from the Indo-Chinese bases to which they had been ordered by Admiral Yamamoto, found the *Repulse* and the *Prince of Wales* cruising off the coast of Malaya, and sank both capital vessels, clearing the way for the Japanese invasion of Malaya and the East Indies. This victory, one of the major Allied reverses of the Pacific War, was accomplished without the participation of a single Japanese surface vessel, and played a major part in establishing the reputation of the 1-*Rikko* as one of Japan's most formidable offensive weapons.

During the weeks and months that followed, the G4M1 appeared ubiquitous. It was encountered in the Marianas, the Marshalls, over New Britain, New Georgia, New Guinea, Peleliu, the Solomons, and the Kuriles. Its record was impressive, and included the sinking of the U.S.S. *Langley*, night attacks in the Gilberts, high-altitude raids on Port Moresby, Australia, and daring daylight attacks against American surface units in the Guadalcanal fighting.

The characteristic "broken-back" profile of the G4M1 which resulted from the removal of the bomb-bay doors was soundly anathematized by Allied forces on the receiving end of the bomber's cargo, but during this period of apparent success, the G4M1 was also displaying its vulnerability.

Attrition was high and, of the initial "available" force of 240 G3M2 and G4M1 bombers possessed by the J.N.A.F. on the day the Pacific War commenced, no fewer than 182 had been lost within three months. The Japanese aircraft industry was hard put to keep pace with this attrition which was considered to be far above the maximum practicable, and many attempts were made to improve the G4M1's performance and defence, resulting in the appearance of the G4M2. In its original service form, the G4M1 carried seven crew members, and defensive armament comprised four 7.7-mm. hand-held machine guns distributed in nose, dorsal and lateral positions, and a 20-mm. cannon in the tail. Early Model 11 aircraft had a full cone tail position, but later production aeroplanes had the tip of the cone cut away in a variety of styles to provide a wider traverse for the cannon.

The performance of the G4M1 included a maximum speed of 266 m.p.h. at 13,780 ft., and normal cruising speed was 196 m.p.h. at 9,840 ft. Service ceiling was 30,250 ft., range was 1,864 miles, and the offensive load comprised a 1,760-lb. torpedo or 2,200 lb. of bombs. Empty weight was 14,860-14,990 lb., and normal loaded and maximum permissible weights were 20,944 lb. and 28,220 lb. Some late production G4M1s had MK4E Kasei 15 engines and were designated Model 12, and others mounted two 7.7-mm. guns in the tail in place of the cannon.

The G4M2, the prototype of which was completed in November 1942, featured a new laminar flow aerofoil and MK4P Kasei 21 radials with methanol-water injection. Provision was made for an additional 330 gallons of fuel in a fuselage tank just aft of the pilot, and some attempt was at last made to protect the fuel tanks. The fuselage tank was protected by layers of rubber sheet and sponge, but the wing tanks were protected from the underside only, rubber sheet being plastered to the inside of the wing skin. In addition to the rubber leak-proofing material, the possibility of fire around the fuel tanks was further reduced by means of a carbon dioxide fire extinguisher system. No provision was made for crew armour, but the defensive armament was extensively revised. The dorsal gun blister of the G4M1 was replaced by a flush, glass-panelled entry hatch, and the first power-operated dorsal gun turret in Japanese practice was provided. This hydraulically-operated turret possessed a 360° traverse and allowed an 80° elevation of the 20-mm. Type 99 Mk.1 (Oerlikon) cannon. The lateral blisters were supplanted by flush panels, and the glazed section of the tail gun position was redesigned, a pie-shaped cut-out permitting lateral and longitudinal traverse of the cannon. The wing and tail surface tips were rounded, the fuselage nose contours were refined and the nose glazing extended, the bomb-bay was redesigned and enlarged, and a fully retractable tailwheel was provided. Variations in armament and equipment, such as the addition of two 7.7-mm. machine guns firing through small ports on either side of the nose section, led to the Models 22a and 22b. The maximum speed of the G4M2 Model 22 was boosted very slightly, but the additional fuel tankage provided a useful increment in range. Empty weight rose to 17,624 lb., and normal loaded and maximum permissible weights became 27,557 lb. and 33,070 lb.

In the meantime, production of the basic G4M1 had continued at the 3rd Airframe Works, 371 machines being delivered in 1942, but with increasing Allied domination of the air, the losses suffered by 1-*Rikko*-equipped units bordered on the disastrous. No. 751 Kokutai, formerly the Kanoya Kokutai or Air Corps, operating from Kavieng, experienced particularly heavy losses. For instance, during an attack on Port Moresby in January 1943, no fewer than ten of No. 751's G4M1 bombers failed to return of the seventeen despatched, and the unit was so weakened that it had to be temporarily withdrawn from operations. With the introduction of the improved G4M2, 660 of which were produced in 1943, the original model was retired from first-line service, subsequently being employed in the maritime reconnaissance, transport and training roles.

In May 1944, the engines of the 1-*Rikko* were again changed, the installation of MK4T Kasei 25 radials offering a useful reduction in fuel consumption and increasing range. The bomb-bay doors were bulged, and the new version entered production in the summer of 1944 as the G4M2a Type 1 Model 24. These bombers entered service rapidly, and were assigned to the 763rd Kokutai of the 2nd Air Fleet defending the Philippines, as well as units based on Formosa, on the Chinese coast and the Japanese home islands. Slight variations were produced as the Models 24a, 24b and 24c.

The basic Model 24 was subjected to numerous experiments. The high-altitude MK4V Kasei 27 engines were installed in one machine which became the G4M2b Model 25, while, with MK4T Kasei 25b engines, it became known as the G4M2c Model 26. The G4M2d was a turbojet test-bed which, in the spring of 1945, was flown with a 1,100 lb.s.t. Yokosuka Ne. 20 mounted beneath its fuselage. One special version of the Model 24, the G4M2e Model 24-J, was built in limited numbers as a parent craft for the Yokosuka MXY8 Ohka Model 11 piloted missile. The bomb-bay doors were removed and special shackles were fitted to carry the Ohka, but, despite a defensive armament of four 20-mm. cannon and one 7.7-mm. machine gun, the G4M2e proved extremely vulnerable to Allied fighter interception owing to the low flying speeds at which the Ohka could be launched. The G4M2e normally approached to within twenty-five miles of the target before launching the Ohka at approximately 175 m.p.h. Prior to the release of the missile, the parent craft was extremely unwieldy. The G4M2e was employed operationally during the American assault on Okinawa but soon withdrawn from service.

The J.N.A.F. insistence on range over protection wavered as Allied fighters took an ever-increasing toll of 1-*Rikko* bombers, and adequate protection for crew and fuel tanks was finally seen to be a necessity. The first result of this change in policy was the G7M1 Taizan (Great Mountain) which, designed to a 16-*Shi* specification, was generally similar to the G4M2 in outline. Designated M-60 by Mitsubishi, the Taizan Land Attack Aircraft was to be powered by two Mitsubishi MK10 Ha.42/11 radials derived from the Kasei series. Design work on the airframe had commenced as early as the summer of 1942, and it was proposed that defensive armament would comprise six 13-mm. machine guns and two 20-mm. cannon, all turret-mounted in pairs. The fuel tanks were protected and adequate provision was made for crew armour. Design delays resulting from a disagreement over the design of the forward fuselage held up the Taizan and, although obviously promising, the aircraft was abandoned late in 1944 in favour of the G4M3 Model 34 which, developed in parallel, embodied certain of the Taizan's features.

The G4M3 Model 34 was a major redesign of the 1-*Rikko*, with emphasis upon fuel tank and crew protection rather than range. Initiated in November 1942, work on the G4M3 Model 34 was delayed by extensive changes to the wing structure. A single-spar structure was eventually selected, this allowing for the installation of large-capacity wing tanks containing 968 Imp.gal. The reduced radius of action offered by the G4M3 was no longer critical as, by the time production deliveries of the new model commenced, Japan was decidedly on the defensive in the Pacific, and her empire had shrunk appreciably. The initial service version was the G4M3a Model 34a, and production was assigned to both the 3rd and 7th Airframe Factories. Minor changes led to the production of the Model 36 with power ultimately changed to an improved model of the Kasei as the G4M3b. Only sixty Model 34 and Model 36 aircraft had been completed when Japan finally surrendered.

The last major development of the 1-*Rikko* series was the G4M3d Model 37 with exhaust-driven turbo-superchargers, work upon which started in August 1944. Owing to teething troubles with the super-chargers, flight trials were delayed until June 1945 and never completed. J.N.A.F. plans for an advanced version, the G4M4, as well as a wooden variant of the 1-*Rikko* were dropped with the decision to concentrate on the newer Ginga class. Thus, development of the 1-*Rikko* came to an end with the remaining aircraft of this type ending the War as short-range bombers, night patrol aircraft, maritime reconnaissance machines, trainers and transports. For maritime reconnaissance, the Model 24 was equipped with a Type 3 MK 6 Model 4 radar set, with Yogi antennae extending from the nose, and flat H-type antennae extending from the fuselage sides. This was a sea-search set calibrated to a range of approximately ninety miles, but in fact at 10,000 feet it was effective against shipping to only some thirty miles.

A total of 2,479 bombers of the 1-*Rikko* type had been produced at the time of Japan's final defeat, and its use as a transport for the surrender delegation was without question the safest mission ever flown by a Japanese crew in an aircraft of this type. The main-stay of the Japanese Navy's long-range bomber formations throughout the Pacific War, the 1-*Rikko* joined combat in a blaze of glory but, owing to a notorious proclivity towards catching fire when hit, a high proportion of all bombers of this type terminated their careers in blazes having unpleasantly final results for their crews.

Mitsubishi G4M2a Type 1 Model 24

Dimensions: Span, 81 ft. 8 in.; length, 64 ft. 4¾ in.; height, 13 ft. 5¾ in.; wing area, 840.929 sq. ft.

Power Plants: Two Mitsubishi MK4T Kasei 25 fourteen-cylinder two-row radial air-cooled engines each rated at 1,850 h.p. at 2,600 r.p.m. for take-off, and having military ratings of 1,680 h.p. at 2,500 r.p.m. at 6,890 ft., and 1,540 h.p. at 2,500 r.p.m. at 18,040 ft.

Armament: One 20-mm. Type 99 (Oerlikon) cannon in hydraulically-operated dorsal turret, one Type 99 cannon in each of two hand-held lateral positions, one Type 99 hand-held cannon in extreme tail, and one 7.7-mm. Type 97 machine gun on ball-and-socket mounting in extreme nose. Maximum bomb load, 2,200 lb. Alternative loads: one 1,764-lb. bomb or torpedo; one 1,100-lb. bomb; four 550-lb. bombs: clusters of twelve 132-lb., 66-lb., or 22-lb. bombs.

Weights: Empty, 18,499 lb.; normal loaded, 27,557 lb.; maximum overload, 33,070 lb.

Performance: Maximum speed, 272 m.p.h. at 15,090 ft., 264 m.p.h. at 6,560 ft.; cruising speed, 196 m.p.h. at 9,840 ft.; time to 9,840 ft. 7 min. 16 sec., to 16,400 ft., 13 min. 21 sec., to 26,250 ft., 30 min. 24 sec.; service ceiling, 29,360 ft.; range (with 968 Imp. gal.), 2,262 mls. at 196 m.p.h. at 9,840 ft.

Torpedoes from G4M1 bombers crippled British naval power in the Far East during the Pacific War's opening stages. Here a torpedo is being loaded aboard a G4M1.

Introduced in 1940, the Junkers Ju 87B-2 illustrated above was one of the most widely employed variants of this dive-bomber.

THE JUNKERS Ju 87

Acclaimed by German propagandists as the scourge of Europe; the aircraft that conquered nations; the supreme weapon, the angularly ugly Junkers Ju 87 dive-bomber attained greater notoriety than any other weapon in the arsenal with which Germany launched the Second World War. It was more widely discussed and aroused greater controversy than many more worthy aircraft; it was one of the most vulnerable of warplanes—slow, unwieldy, and the natural prey of the fighter, yet, within the first nine months of the war, it had acquired an almost legendary reputation.

The German Air Staff itself was divided on the subject of dive-bombing and the employment of the Ju 87, but the Polish campaign appeared to vindicate its protagonists, the Ju 87 knocking out strong points, artillery batteries, and concentrations whenever the Polish forces sought to make a stand. When the German offensive against France and the Low Countries opened in May 1940, the Ju 87 repeated its earlier successes, blasting the Allied armour and defences, paralysing whole armies, playing havoc with communications in vital rear areas, and hounding the streams of refugees. In fact, this Junkers product, which had become synonymous with the abbreviation "Stuka"—from *Sturzkampfflugzeug*, a term descriptive of *all* dive-bombers—was the outstanding success of both Polish and French campaigns. With virtually no aerial opposition, the Ju 87 was fully able to exploit the accuracy of bomb aiming inherent in the steep

dive, as well as the demoralising effect on personnel exposed to this form of attack.

But the use of the Ju 87 presumed control of the air, and the issue was settled in the "Battle of Britain" when, after a few abortive sorties by Ju 87s during which their formations were decimated by opposing Hurricanes and Spitfires, the dive-bombers were withdrawn from the Cherbourg area, and the Ju 87's career had entered the eclipse. The Junkers dive-bomber was still to achieve further successes, in the Balkans, against Crete, and against shipping in the Mediterranean and Allied convoys sailing over the

The first prototype, the Ju 87V1, with Rolls-Royce Kestrel V engine and original deep radiator, replaced after initial flight tests.

The Ju 87V1 with redesigned radiator. Flown for the first time towards the end of 1935, the Ju 87V1 had twin fins and rudders, but tail flutter, which resulted in the destruction of the machine, necessitated a complete redesign of the tail assembly.

(Above) The Ju 87V2, the first prototype to be powered by the Jumo engine, and (below) the Ju 87V3 which embodied some engine cowling and tail redesign.

Arctic Route to North Russian ports, in fact, anywhere where there were no opposing fighters, but the Ju 87 was no longer the decisive weapon that certain factions of the German Air Staff believed would win the war.

German interest in the potentialities of dive-bombing was founded long before the existence of the Luftwaffe was officially proclaimed in March 1935, the month in which the prototype of the new air arm's first true dive-bomber, the Henschel Hs 123, made its début. The Swedish plant of the Junkers Flugzeug und Motorenwerke, the A.-B. Flygindustrie at Malmo, was instrumental in producing an aircraft ideally suited for the dive-bombing role as early as 1928. This aircraft, the K.47, although ostensibly a two-seat interceptor fighter, was the true progenitor of the Ju 87. It received its airworthiness certificate from the Deutsche Versuchsanstalt für Luftfahrt (German Research Institute for Aviation) on March 5, 1929. The K.47 was of extremely rugged construction and possessed excellent stability, and the successful out-

come of the exhaustive testing carried out with this experimental machine encouraged the Junkers concern to initiate work on a more advanced dive-bomber as a private venture. Owing to the necessity for secrecy due to the restrictions placed upon Germany by the Versailles Treaty, progress was initially slow, and detail design of the aircraft, the Junkers Ju 87, did not commence until 1934. The project team was headed by Diploma Engineer Pohlmann, and construction of the first prototypes began early in 1935.

At one time, the abortive testing of the He 50 and He 66 dive-bombers by the embryo Luftwaffe did not augur well for the future of this type of warplane, but Ernst Udet was an ardent supporter of the dive-bomber—it was largely through his influence that the Henschel Hs 123 single-seat dive-bombing biplane was placed in production for the Luftwaffe's first Schlachtgeschwader—and, despite the lack of official support from the Reichsluftfahrtministerium, and preoccupation with the Junkers Ju 52/3M bomber-transport, and other types, prototype construction progressed rapidly, and the Ju 87V1 had been completed and had commenced its flight test programme before the end of 1935.

Powered by a 640 h.p. Rolls-Royce Kestrel V twelve-cylinder water-cooled engine driving a fixed-pitch, two-blade wooden airscrew, the Ju 87V1 was an extremely angular monoplane, the cantilever low wing featuring a unique inverted gull configuration. The main undercarriage members were enclosed by immense "trousers", the tail unit embodied two square fin-and-rudder assemblies, and extremely rugged construction was employed. Special dive brakes had been evolved by Junkers engineers which took the form of slats mounted just aft of the wing leading edges, outboard of the main undercarriage members. It was anticipated that these brakes would reduce diving speeds, enabling the pilot to get closer to his target before pulling out, the bomb thus having a shorter distance to travel and a higher degree of accuracy being attained. Unfortunately, before these brakes could be fitted to the Ju 87V1, the aircraft crashed and was totally destroyed when tail flutter developed during a steep dive.

Although this accident caused a serious delay in the test programme, and necessitated a complete redesign of the tail assembly, the second and third prototypes, the Ju 87V2 and V3, had reached advanced stages of construction. Thus, in March 1936, the new Luftwaffe Research Establishment at Rechlin was already conducting trials with the Ju 87V2. The Ju 87V2 differed appreciably from its predecessor. The twin tail assembly had given place to a large, angular fin and rudder, and a 610 h.p. Junkers Jumo 210Aa twelve-cylinder inverted-Vee liquid-cooled engine driving a Hamilton Standard three-blade controllable-pitch metal airscrew had supplanted the Kestrel with its two-blade wooden airscrew. The overall length of the aircraft had been increased from 33 ft. 1¼ in. to 34 ft. 10¾ in.

Apart from some slight instability, which was corrected in the Ju 87V3 by minor redesign of the vertical tail surfaces, the flight trials of the Ju 87V2 were highly successful, and prior to the dive-bomber trials held at Rechlin in June 1936, the dive brakes had been tested with excellent results. The third prototype, the Ju 87V3, completed shortly after the second machine, bore the civil registration D-UKYQ, and embodied some redesign of the engine cowling to improve the pilot's forward view, an enlarged rudder, and a slight increase in overall length to 35 ft. 2 in.

In the meantime, the advocates of the dive-bomber as a mobile weapon capable of replacing to some extent the use of heavy artillery had increased rapidly, and several other aircraft manufacturers were hastily completing prototypes to compete in the trials to be conducted at Rechlin before Ernst Udet and engineers of the R.L.M. Technical Department. There was still some doubt whether the monoplane or biplane configuration was best suited for dive-bombing, and the Arado Flugzeugwerke, a government-owned concern, had produced a robust, slim two-seat biplane, the Ar 81. The other competitors were, like the Ju 87, monoplanes, these being the Ha 137, a solid single-seater with an inverted gull wing, not unlike that of the Junkers design, developed by Dr. Ing. Richard Vogt of the Hamburger Flugzeugbau, and the beautifully clean two-seat He 118, designed by the Günther brothers of the Ernst Heinkel Flugzeugwerke.

The Ju 87V2 participated in the Rechlin trials, the V3 being held in reserve, and it was soon obvious that the choice rested between this aircraft and the elegant, slender He 118. However, during the final series of dives, the Junkers prototype's performance bested that of its competitor, and the selection of the Ju 87 seemed almost a foregone conclusion. Udet was not entirely satisfied, and decided to flight test the He 118 himself. On June 27th, Udet took off in the He 118 from Marienehe, but his unfamiliarity with the airscrew-pitch control resulted in the aircraft shedding its airscrew and subsequently disintegrating. Udet survived the accident, and the Ju 87 was selected as the Luftwaffe's standard dive-bomber!

The fourth and production prototype, the Ju 87V4

(*Above*) *The Ju 87V4 was the production prototype but still retained the dual taper on the leading edges of the outboard wing panels which characterised all the prototypes. (Below) The initial production model, the Ju 87A-1, was preceded by ten pre-production machines. The photograph depicts the twelfth Ju 87A—the second example of the A-1 variant.*

(D-UBIP), appeared in the late autumn of 1936. This aircraft featured redesigned tail surfaces similar to those adopted for the initial production model; had provision for a single 7.9-mm. MG 17 machine gun in the starboard wing; some modifications to the cockpit canopy, and the centre line of the Jumo 210Aa was lowered by some ten inches in order to improve forward visibility. By this time, work was already progressing on a batch of ten pre-production aircraft, designated Ju 87A-O. Used for extensive tactical trials and experimental flying by company and service test pilots, the Ju 87A-Os were externally similar to the Ju 87V4, but embodied a slightly modified wing planform intended to simplify production. Whereas the leading edge of the wing employed by the prototypes had a slight break in the taper at approximately two-thirds chord, that of the production aircraft was perfectly straight. In order to maintain the wing area at the original figure, the trailing edge taper on the outboard panels was increased.

The initial production model, the Ju 87A-1, was powered by the 635 h.p. Junkers Jumo 210Da engine, and production deliveries commenced in the spring

(*Above and left*) *The Ju 87A-1 entered service early in 1937 with the Sturzkampfgeschwader Immelmann. The Ju 87A-2, illustrated here, was employed principally for dive-bombing training during World War II, although some saw operational service on the Russian Front.*

of 1937, the first Luftwaffe unit to receive the new equipment being the Sturzkampfgeschwader Immelmann—which formation was later to participate in the occupation of Czechoslovakia. The Ju 87A-1 carried a defensive armament of one 7.9-mm. MG 17 machine gun in the starboard wing, and a hand-operated, swivelling 7.9-mm. MG 15 in the rear cockpit. With two crew members, a single 550-lb. bomb was carried by a crutch aft of the radiator housing, swing links lowering and swinging this forward on release in order to ensure that it cleared the airscrew arc. With only one crew member, a 1,100-lb. bomb could be carried by this crutch. The maximum speed of the Ju 87A-1 was 199 m.p.h. at 12,000 ft. without bomb load, and maximum range was 620 miles. Empty and loaded weights were 5,104 lb. and 7,495 lb. respectively, and overall dimensions were:

The Ju 87A was nicknamed "Jolanthe" after a pig which featured in several pre-war German films, and this photo of one of the three Ju 87A-1s sent to Spain in December 1937 for tests with the Condor Legion shows the "Jolanthe" insignia on the port mainwheel "trouser".

span, 45 ft. $3\frac{1}{8}$ in., length 35 ft. $5\frac{1}{8}$ in., height 12 ft. $9\frac{1}{2}$ in., wing area, 343,368 sq. ft.

The two crew members were seated back-to-back under a continuous canopy with hinged sections. The fuselage was an oval structure of light metal construction, built in two halves and joined along the centre line, and the smooth metal skin was riveted to Z-section frames and open-section stringers. The wing was basically a two-spar all-metal structure with

FINISH AND INSIGNIA: *The standard finish applied to Ju 87 dive-bombers consisted of a "splinter" type camouflage pattern of forest green and olive green over the upper surfaces, fuselage sides, and vertical tail surfaces, with pale blue under surfaces. In the Western Desert the upper surfaces were painted sand-brown with irregular dark green patches to blend with the thorn bushes of the desert, and during winter aircraft operating on the Russian Front were temporarily painted white overall. During the Balkans Campaign, Ju 87Bs of the Luftwaffe featured yellow engine cowlings, wingtips and moveable tail surfaces, but normally a broad white band was painted around the rear fuselage. The standard national insignia comprising a black cross with broad white trim which was, in turn, outlined in black, appeared on the upper and lower surfaces of the wings, and fuselage sides, and a black swastika outlined in white appeared on the tail fin. Geschwader, Gruppe and Staffel markings comprised a numeral and three letters (e.g., F5+KE). The first letter and numeral (which was frequently repeated in white on the mainwheel cowlings) indicated the Geschwader, and the last two letters identified the individual aircraft, staffel and gruppe. The numeral was frequently painted in white, yellow, pale blue or pale green to indicate the kette. The combination of letters and numerals appeared on the fuselage sides and, in black, on the wing under surfaces. A red triangle outlined in yellow and usually positioned on the fuselage sides just ahead of the cockpit enclosed the number "87" which indicated 87 octane fuel (B.4), and the production number of the aircraft (e.g., 1427) sometimes appeared in white above the swastika on the fin. The airscrew spinners were painted in a variety of colours.*

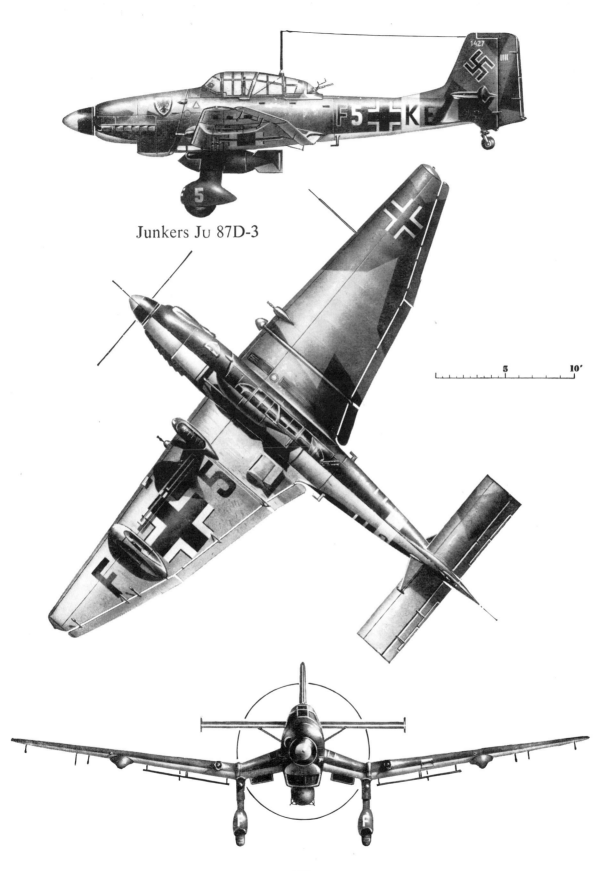

Junkers Ju 87D-3

5   10′

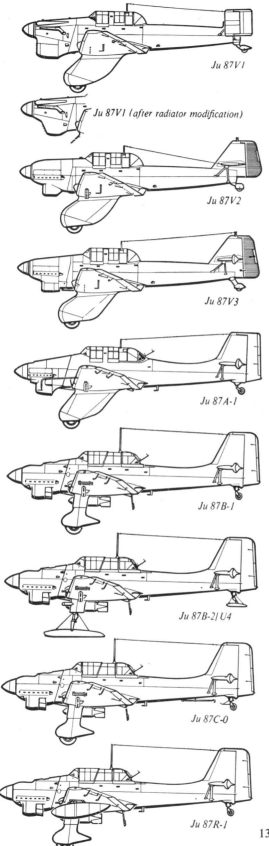

Ju 87V1

Ju 87V1 (after radiator modification)

Ju 87V2

Ju 87V3

Ju 87A-1

Ju 87B-1

Ju 87B-2/U4

Ju 87C-0

Ju 87R-1

closely-spaced ribs and stressed-skin covering, the centre section being built integral with the fuselage and set at a course angle of anhedral and the outer sections being set at course dihedral to give the characteristic inverted gull configuration. The entire wing trailing edge was hinged on the Junkers "double-wing" principle, the outer portions acting as ailerons and the inner portions serving as flaps. The dive brakes, which were lowered hydraulically, consisted of slats which were hinged clear of the wing under surfaces, and turned through ninety degrees in a dive, small red indicators on the top surfaces of the wings indicating the position of the brakes to the pilot. Before commencing his dive, the pilot of the Ju 87A-1 had to throttle back in order to close the cooling gills, switch over to sea level supercharger, and turn the airscrew to coarse pitch. Later production models employed automatic supercharger gear, and a governor which provided automatic constant-speed action by regulating the coarse or the fine pitch of the airscrew. After pulling out and retracting the dive brakes, the pilot had to open the gills immediately in order to avoid overheating the engine. An automatic device was eventually incorporated which, after lowering the brakes, raised the trim tab to make the aircraft nose-heavy. With the release of the bomb, the tab returned to normal position whereby the aircraft became tail-heavy for the pull-out. Aim during dives was attained by a series of red lines of various angles painted on the cabin side panels, the pilot lining these with the horizon.

The Ju 87A-2 was identical to the A-1 apart from the type of airscrew employed, and in order to gain operational experience and perfect their dive-bombing techniques, the Luftwaffe despatched three Ju 87A-1s to Spain in December 1937, to operate with the Condor Legion. Seeing their first action at Teruel, the Ju 87As were subsequently employed in the drive to the Mediterranean coast, the fighting on the Ebro front and the offensive in Catalonia. Although only three Ju 87As were sent to Spain, many different crews flew them in order that the maximum number of personnel would gain experience of actual combat conditions. Such was the success of the Ju 87A that, before the end of 1938, a larger quantity of the later Ju 87B had been despatched to that country, and in the June 1939 issue of the *Junkers Nachrichten*, the house journal of the Junkers company, the operations of these aircraft were described as follows:

"In the Spanish War, the favourite targets of the dive-bombers were road crossings and bridges which played an important part in the system of communications, as well as staff headquarters, harbours and ships. The direct hit of a 1,100-lb. bomb is enough to form a crater which may put even a modern asphalt or concrete road out of commission for days. The effect of well-aimed bombs on bridges and other defence works is still more devastating. As movements of troops in a mountainous country like Spain are very much dependent on roads, even the smallest formation, the dive-bomber 'chain' was a highly efficient means of disrupting the enemy's movements. However, the most successful activities lay in a method of warfare characteristic of the final phase of the Spanish conflict, namely the bombing of ports and ships on the Mediterranean coast. Harbour basins, handling equipment, warehouses, and railway sidings are targets requiring considerable quantities of explosives in consideration of their solid construction. The havoc wrought in the port areas of Valencia, Tarragona, Barcelona, etc., is chiefly due to the activities of the dive-bombers, which also accounted for a large proportion of ships wrecked or sunk."

Relatively few Ju 87A-1 and A-2 dive-bombers had been built before these types were supplanted on the assembly lines by the very much improved and more powerful Ju 87B-1 in the summer of 1938. Incorporating many noticeable external changes, the Ju 87B-1, which followed a batch of ten pre-production machines designated Ju 87B-0, was the first service type to use the Jumo 211Da engine rated at 1,100 h.p. for take-off. The cockpit canopy was entirely redesigned, sliding sections replacing the folding hatches, the vertical tail surfaces were enlarged, the forward-firing armament was increased by the installation of an additional MG 17 machine gun in the port wing, and the "trousered" mainwheel housings gave place to streamlined "spats". The increased power permitted a substantial increase in warload which could comprise a 1,100-lb. bomb under the fuselage, or a 550-lb. bomb in this position and four 110-lb. bombs under the wings, outboard of the dive brakes. Wing span and area remained the same as those for the Ju 87A, but the overall length was increased to 36 ft. 5 in. Empty and loaded weights were increased to 6,085 lb. and 9,370 lb. respectively, and maximum speed rose to 232 m.p.h. at 13,500 ft. Cruising speed was 175 m.p.h. at 15,000 ft., and range with a 1,100-lb. bomb load was 370 miles.

On the eve of Germany's invasion of Poland, the

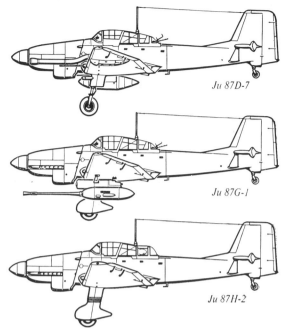

Ju 87D-7

Ju 87G-1

Ju 87H-2

Luftwaffe possessed nine Ju 87-equipped Gruppen, and 335 dive-bombers of this type were on strength, the vast majority of which were of the Ju 87B-1 production version, all examples of the A-model having been withdrawn from the first-line units. Although, on the eve of the European War, the German Air Staff was

(Below) An early production Ju 87B-1 with national insignia, and identification numerals and letters, of the style of 1938, and (right) a Ju 87B-1 over France in 1940.

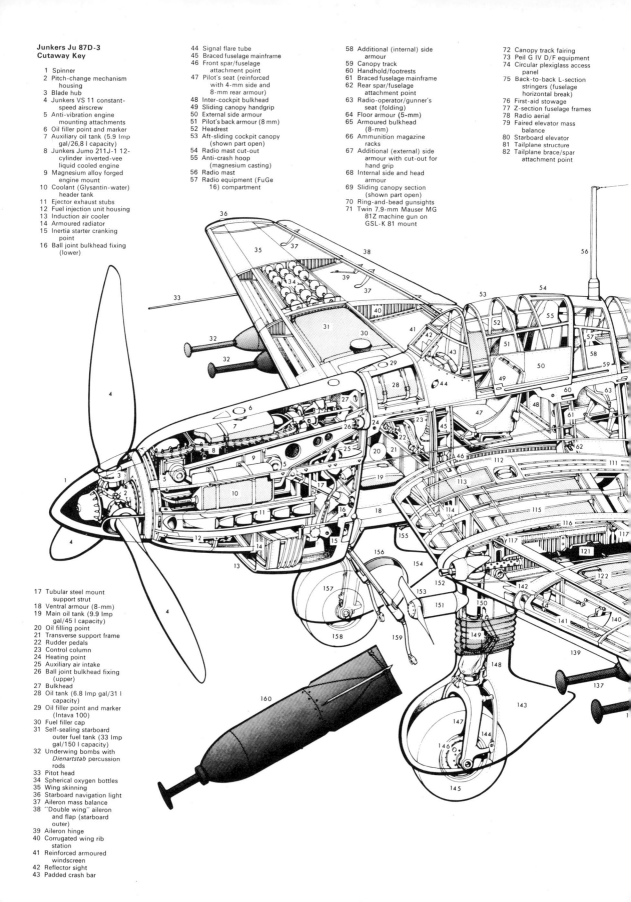

Junkers Ju 87D-3 Cutaway Key

1 Spinner
2 Pitch-change mechanism housing
3 Blade hub
4 Junkers VS 11 constant-speed airscrew
5 Anti-vibration engine mounting attachments
6 Oil filler point and marker
7 Auxiliary oil tank (5.9 Imp gal/26,8 l capacity)
8 Junkers Jumo 211J-1 12-cylinder inverted-vee liquid cooled engine
9 Magnesium alloy forged engine mount
10 Coolant (Glysantin-water) header tank
11 Ejector exhaust stubs
12 Fuel injection unit housing
13 Induction air cooler
14 Armoured radiator
15 Inertia starter cranking point
16 Ball joint bulkhead fixing (lower)

17 Tubular steel mount support strut
18 Ventral armour (8-mm)
19 Main oil tank (9.9 Imp gal/45 l capacity)
20 Oil filling point
21 Transverse support frame
22 Rudder pedals
23 Control column
24 Heating point
25 Auxiliary air intake
26 Ball joint bulkhead fixing (upper)
27 Bulkhead
28 Oil tank (6.8 Imp gal/31 l capacity)
29 Oil filler point and marker (Intava 100)
30 Fuel filler cap
31 Self-sealing starboard outer fuel tank (33 Imp gal/150 l capacity)
32 Underwing bombs with *Dienartstab* percussion rods
33 Pitot head
34 Spherical oxygen bottles
35 Wing skinning
36 Starboard navigation light
37 Aileron mass balance
38 "Double wing" aileron and flap (starboard outer)
39 Aileron hinge
40 Corrugated wing rib station
41 Reinforced armoured windscreen
42 Reflector sight
43 Padded crash bar

44 Signal flare tube
45 Braced fuselage mainframe
46 Front spar/fuselage attachment point
47 Pilot's seat (reinforced with 4-mm side and 8-mm rear armour)
48 Inter-cockpit bulkhead
49 Sliding canopy handgrip
50 External side armour
51 Pilot's back armour (8 mm)
52 Headrest
53 Aft-sliding cockpit canopy (shown part open)
54 Radio mast cut-out
55 Anti-crash hoop (magnesium casting)
56 Radio mast
57 Radio equipment (FuGe 16) compartment

58 Additional (internal) side armour
59 Canopy track
60 Handhold/footrests
61 Braced fuselage mainframe
62 Rear spar/fuselage attachment point
63 Radio-operator/gunner's seat (folding)
64 Floor armour (5-mm)
65 Armoured bulkhead (8-mm)
66 Ammunition magazine racks
67 Additional (external) side armour with cut-out for hand grip
68 Internal side and head armour
69 Sliding canopy section (shown part open)
70 Ring-and-bead gunsights
71 Twin 7,9-mm Mauser MG 81Z machine gun on GSL-K 81 mount

72 Canopy track fairing
73 Peil G IV D/F equipment
74 Circular plexiglass access panel
75 Back-to-back L-section stringers (fuselage horizontal break)
76 First-aid stowage
77 Z-section fuselage frames
78 Radio aerial
79 Faired elevator mass balance
80 Starboard elevator
81 Tailplane structure
82 Tailplane brace/spar attachment point

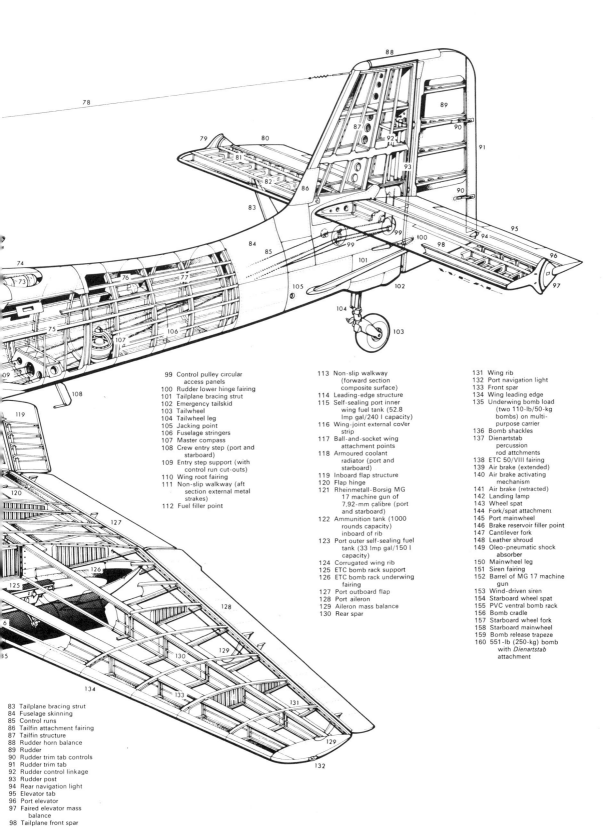

83 Tailplane bracing strut
84 Fuselage skinning
85 Control runs
86 Tailfin attachment fairing
87 Tailfin structure
88 Rudder horn balance
89 Rudder
90 Rudder trim tab controls
91 Rudder trim tab
92 Rudder control linkage
93 Rudder post
94 Rear navigation light
95 Elevator tab
96 Port elevator
97 Faired elevator mass
    balance
98 Tailplane front spar

99 Control pulley circular
    access panels
100 Rudder lower hinge fairing
101 Tailplane bracing strut
102 Emergency tailskid
103 Tailwheel
104 Tailwheel leg
105 Jacking point
106 Fuselage stringers
107 Master compass
108 Crew entry step (port and
    starboard)
109 Entry step support (with
    control run cut-outs)
110 Wing root fairing
111 Non-slip walkway (aft
    section external metal
    strakes)
112 Fuel filler point

113 Non-slip walkway
    (forward section
    composite surface)
114 Leading-edge structure
115 Self-sealing port inner
    wing fuel tank (52.8
    Imp gal/240 I capacity)
116 Wing-joint external cover
    strip
117 Ball-and-socket wing
    attachment points
118 Armoured coolant
    radiator (port and
    starboard)
119 Inboard flap structure
120 Flap hinge
121 Rheinmetall-Borsig MG
    17 machine gun of
    7,92-mm calibre (port
    and starboard)
122 Ammunition tank (1000
    rounds capacity)
    inboard of rib
123 Port outer self-sealing fuel
    tank (33 Imp gal/150 I
    capacity)
124 Corrugated wing rib
125 ETC bomb rack support
126 ETC bomb rack underwing
    fairing
127 Port outboard flap
128 Port aileron
129 Aileron mass balance
130 Rear spar

131 Wing rib
132 Port navigation light
133 Front spar
134 Wing leading edge
135 Underwing bomb load
    (two 110-lb/50-kg
    bombs) on multi-
    purpose carrier
136 Bomb shackles
137 Dienartstab
    percussion
    rod attchments
138 ETC 50/VIII fairing
139 Air brake (extended)
140 Air brake activating
    mechanism
141 Air brake (retracted)
142 Landing lamp
143 Wheel spat
144 Fork/spat attachment
145 Port mainwheel
146 Brake reservoir filler point
147 Cantilever fork
148 Leather shroud
149 Oleo-pneumatic shock
    absorber
150 Mainwheel leg
151 Siren fairing
152 Barrel of MG 17 machine
    gun
153 Wind-driven siren
154 Starboard wheel spat
155 PVC ventral bomb rack
156 Bomb cradle
157 Starboard wheel fork
158 Starboard mainwheel
159 Bomb release trapeze
160 551-lb (250-kg) bomb
    with *Dienartstab*
    attachment

the Luftwaffe maintained air superiority, and the Ju 87 formations were enabled to operate unhindered. To the jubilation of the dive-bomber protagonists, the Ju 87 played a larger part than any other weapon in overwhelming the Polish defences and bringing the campaign to a rapid conclusion. Similar success attended the operations of the Ju 87 in France and the Low Countries, and 280 aircraft of this type were included in the strength of Luftflotten 2 and 3 for the assault on Southern England and the Midlands, 220 of these being possessed by Fliegerkorps VIII. The attacks of the Ju 87Bs against Dover and airfields in Southern England proved a catastrophic failure, and losses were so heavy that, within six days of the so-called Adler Tag, on August 19, 1940, the dive-bomber formations had been

A Ju 87B-1/Trop dive-bomber of the Regia Aeronautica. Several units of the Regia Aeronautica, including the 96mo and 97mo Gruppi Bombardamento Tuffo, and the 208ma and 238ma Squadriglia, employed this aircraft, and at one time it was incorrectly believed that the Ju 87B-1/Trop was being manufactured under licence in Italy.

divided in its opinions as to the employment of the Ju 87, it was generally conceded that it was intended to destroy vital objectives in the heart of enemy industrial centres as well as bridges, ammunition, fuel and food dumps. With the Spanish experience as an example, it was also appreciated that dive-bombing attacks would affect the morale of front-line troops. Tactically, it was to co-operate with the Army, both in supporting its advance and in holding up any counter-attacks of the enemy. In the event, it was to be used much more for softening up the enemy generally, and for attacking communications in rear areas than for directly supporting the Army in the battle area.

From the outset of the German invasion of Poland,

withdrawn from the Cherbourg area to the Pas de Calais from where they could support the Army in the event of an invasion of England.

Production of the Ju 87B increased rapidly at several Junkers-controlled factories, and 603 machines were produced in 1940 as compared with 134 in the previous year. The Ju 87B-1 gave place to the B-2 which differed primarily in having broader airscrew blades, slight revisions of the undercarriage and engine cooling gills, and later internal equipment. Under certain conditions, the bomb load of the Ju 87B-2 could be increased to 2,200-lb, and various modified versions of the basic type were introduced, such as the Ju 87B-2/U1, U2, U3 and U4, the suffix "U" indicating "modification". The modifications

Extensively redesigned and fitted with the more powerful Jumo 211J engine, the Ju 87D-1 (below) appeared in 1940. The letters SE+TX appearing on the fuselage sides and under the wings were the aircraft's radio call sign for factory tests and delivery flight to a maintenance unit, and did not indicate the operational unit.

The Ju 87G-1 first entered service as an anti-tank aircraft in 1942, carrying a 37-mm. BK (Flak 18) cannon slung under each wing. Although possessing extremely poor flying characteristics, the Ju 87G-1 proved to be an effective tank-buster, and saw service in North Africa, Russia, and in limited numbers on the Western Front.

were usually confined to the provision of alternative radio equipment, the addition of extra armour, etc. For instance, the Ju 87B-2/U4 featured additional protection for the rear gunner in the form of a circular armour panel with a square, central armour-glass window, and could be fitted with skis for operation from snow. A conversion of the Ju 87B-1 was designated Ju 87C-0. This variant was intended to operate from the aircraft carrier *Graf Zeppelin* which, in the event, was never completed. The Ju 87C-0 and the few C-1s completed featured electrically-operated upward-folding outboard wing panels. They were stressed for catapulting and featured an arrester hook and a jettisonable undercarriage for emergency "ditching". These were later reconverted as Ju 87Bs.

Another derivative of the B-series was the Ju 87R-1 which was identical to the B-1 apart from provision for the rapid attachment of external fuel tanks under the wings in place of the bombs. The internal fuel cells were also modified, and the J 87R (the "R" suffix indicating Reichweit or Range), had a range of 875 miles. It was employed principally for shipping attack with a single 550-lb. bomb, and the Ju 87R-2, R-3, and R-4 differed only in equipment.

Germany was not slow to furnish her Allies with the Ju 87B, and Italy received substantial quantities of this dive-bomber, several units of the Regia Aero-nautica operating the type from the time of Italy's entry into the war, including the 96mo and 97mo Gruppi Bombardamento Tuffo, and the 208ma and 238ma Squadriglia. It was believed at one time that the Ju 87B was being manufactured in Italy under

licence by the Societa Italiana Ernesto Breda as the Ba 201. In fact, the Ba 201 was an entirely original design, and all Ju 87Bs operated by the Regia Aeronautica were supplied by Germany. Rumania, Hungary and Bulgaria also received quantities of Ju 87B dive-bombers, and the type was evaluated by the Japanese as was also the earlier Ju 87A.

Soon after the outbreak of war, with the production tempo of the B-series dive-bomber rising rapidly, the Junkers team began refining the basic design in order to take full advantage of the Jumo 211J with induction air cooler. The Ju 87D, which appeared in 1940, incorporated extensive modifications, among the most important of which were the improvement in the engine cowling lines gained by removing the oil cooler from its position on top of the cowling and moving it to the position under the cowling previously occupied by the coolant radiator, simultaneously re-positioning the coolant radiator under the wing centre section; the complete redesign of the cockpit canopy, the aft portion of which was faired downwards to give a better streamline form; some improvement in the shape of the landing-gear fairings; improved armour protection for the crew, and increased defensive armament.

Offering 1,400 h.p. for take-off, the Jumo 211J engine enabled the Ju 87D to lift appreciably greater loads, and one 550-lb., 1,100-lb., 2,200-lb., or 3,960-lb. bomb could be carried beneath the fuselage, or four 110-lb., two 550-lb. or two 1,100-lb. bombs under the wings. Defensive armament was increased by the installation of twin 7.9-mm. MG 81 machine guns on a flexible mounting in the rear cockpit, and crew protection was considerably improved, including complete armouring of the pilot's seat with 8-mm. plates at the back and 4-mm. plates at the sides, the provision of an armoured headshield of 10-mm. plate, and 5-mm.

floor, head and side plates for the gunner. Maximum speed of the initial production model, the Ju 87D-1, without bomb load was 255 m.p.h. at 13,500 ft.

Several sub-series of the D-model appeared in quick succession, and these differed from the initial production version to a varying degree. For instance, the Ju 87D-2 merely had a strengthened tailwheel leg carrying a towing hook for cargo gliders, this version being used principally in North Africa, but the Ju 87D-3 was the first specialised ground attack version of the basic design and carried very heavy armour plate to protect the engine and crew from ground fire. Provision was made for two weapon carriers each containing six 7.9-mm. MG 81 machine guns to be mounted under the wings. An alternative gun pack containing two 20-mm. MG FF cannon could be carried under each wing. The Ju 87D-4 was basically similar to the D-3 but provision was made for mounting jettisonable weapon containers. Both the D-3 and D-4 sub-types were extensively employed in the Russian campaign, enjoying considerable success until mid-1942, by which time growing Soviet fighter opposition restricted them to nocturnal operations or areas over which the Luftwaffe still retained air superiority. Rumanian air elements supporting the German attack on the Bessarabian front used Ju 87D-2 and -3 aircraft as did also the Hungarian Air Force contingent attached to Luftflotte IV.

An increase in overall wing span from 45 ft. 3⅓ in. to 50 ft. 0⅜ in. resulted in the Ju 87D-5. Intended primarily for night operations, the Ju 87D-5 featured a jettisonable undercarriage for emergency landings on rough ground, large flame-damper tubes shrouding the exhaust stacks, and special night-flying equipment. The Ju 87D-7, intended for the night ground attack role, was generally similar to the D-1 apart from the installation of two 20-mm. MG 151 cannon in the wings in place of the standard MG 17 machine guns, the deletion of the dive brakes and wing bomb racks, the addition of flame-damper tubes, and the extended wing span, and the Ju 87D-8 was similar to the D-5 apart from the larger wing. Owing to frequent nose-overs on the soft surfaces of Russian airfields, the wheel spats were frequently removed, and a weapon widely used by the Ju 87D in Russia was a wooden container housing ninety-two SC 2 anti-personnel bombs. The container disintegrated soon after release, spreading the small bombs over a wide area.

Production of the Ju 87, which had begun to taper off in 1941, when only 500 were delivered, was boosted considerably in 1942 owing to the non-arrival of anticipated replacement types, 960 being produced in that year. Despite its obsolescence and the proven foolhardiness of operating it in areas where air superiority could not be maintained, the continued usefulness of the Ju 87 in many theatres of war could not be denied, and in 1943 no fewer than 1,672 aircraft of this type were produced. However, in the following year, when the Luftwaffe had lost control of the air in virtually every theatre that it was engaged, production deliveries fell to 1,012 machines, and the Ju 87 finally left the assembly lines. No exact figure for the total

quantity of Ju 87s manufactured is available, but this almost certainly exceeded 5,000 machines.

Among the final models of the basic design was the Ju 87F, an experimental version with oversize tyres which did not attain production status, and the Ju 87G-1 which first entered service in 1942. The Ju 87G-1 was a conversion of the D-5 with two 37-mm. BK (Flak 18) cannon slung under the wings, one outboard of each undercarriage leg, for the tank-busting role. Although extremely unwieldy in the air, the Ju 87G-1 proved highly successful in destroying Russian T-34 tanks, and also saw service in North Africa and in the Western Front. The Ju 87H was a dual-control trainer, and there were versions corresponding to the D-1, D-3, D-5, D-7 and D-8. Converted from operational aircraft, the Ju 87H carried no dive brakes or armament, and the rear section of the cockpit canopy was modified by the addition of transparent side blisters to improve the instructor's view.

Oddly enough, the Junkers Flugzeug und Motorenwerke failed to develop a successor to the Ju 87. Belatedly, after the debacle of the Ju 87 in the "Battle of Britain", the Junkers team initiated work on the Ju 187 which, intended to replace the Ju 87, retained the inverted gull wing configuration of its predecessor, embodied a remotely-controlled gun barbette, a fully-retractable undercarriage, a Jumo 213 engine, and contours which, superficially, resembled those of the Ilyushin Il-2. The project was abandoned, however, when the fighter-bomber proved capable of fulfilling many of the tasks for which the Ju 187 was intended.

The Junkers Ju 87 had greater réclame than any other German aircraft of the Second World War. Its early successes fostered the acceptance of the myth of its invincibility even in the minds of the German Air Staff; its costly failure in the "Battle of Britain" was, thus, a dramatic blow to its advocates. The Ju 87 was aerodynamically an atrocity; it was ugly to the point of absurdity, and it was virtually defenceless against the modern fighter, yet its distinctive shape was, for long, that most feared by Germany's opponents, and this one aircraft type revolutionised the very fundamentals of warfare.

Junkers Ju 87D-1

Dimensions : Span, 45 ft. 3⅓ in. ; length, 37 ft. 8¾ in. ; height, 12 ft. 9⅛ in. ; wing area, 343.368 sq. ft.

Armament : One 7.9-mm. MG 17 machine gun in each wing, and two 7.9-mm. MG 81 machine guns on flexible mounting in rear cockpit. One 550-lb., one 1,100-lb., one 2,200-lb., or (short-range overload condition) one 3,960-lb. bomb under fuselage, or four 110-lb., two 550-lb., or two 1,100-lb. bombs under wings, or two gun packs each containing six 7.9-mm. MG 81 machine guns or two 20-mm. MG 151 cannon under wings plus one 550-lb. or 1,100-lb. bomb under fuselage.

Power Plant : One Junkers Jumo 211J-1 twelve-cylinder 60° inverted Vee liquid-cooled engine with direct fuel injection rated at 1,400 h.p. at 2,600 r.p.m. for take-off and emergency at sea level, and 1,350 h.p. at 2,600 r.p.m. at 820 ft.

Weights : Normal loaded, 12,600 lb. ; maximum permissible, 14,500 lb.

Performance : Maximum speed, 255 m.p.h. at 13,500 ft. ; cruising speed (72 per cent. power), 198 m.p.h. at 16,700 ft. ; climb to 16,400 ft., 19.8 min. ; service ceiling (at mean weight), 23,950 ft. ; range (with 3,960-lb. bomb load), 620 miles, (with maximum fuel), 1,200 miles.

France was the first country to place an order for the Douglas attack bomber, and the photograph above depicts the production prototype, complete with Armée de l' Air markings, five days before its first flight. The initial production model was designated DB-7.

THE DOUGLAS A-20

In some respects, the combat career of the Douglas A-20 was much less spectacular than that of many other bombers employed by the combatants. It was associated with no outstanding operations but remained in first-line service throughout the war; it did not distinguish itself on any particular battle-front, but flew with equal distinction over them all. It did as well in Russia as it did in the Pacific or the Western Desert and withal was one of the most pleasant of all combat aircraft to fly.

If for nothing else, the A-20 deserves to be remembered as a pilot's aeroplane, and its virtues were sworn in a variety of tongues, ranging from Afrikaans to Ukrainian. Its cosmopolitan nature was fundamental in its design, however, for it owed much to the Spanish Civil War and, subsequently, to the urgent need for rearmament by the French. The danger signals of the international situation in 1936 had not been ignored in the United States. Among others, a group of prominent people in American aviation were considering the future requirements of the U.S. Army Air Corps for military aircraft well in advance of the issue of any official specifications. Donald Douglas, Jack Northrop and Ed Heinemann had been concerned together in the development of the A-17 attack bomber at the Northrop Aircraft Corporation, later absorbed by the Douglas Aircraft Company as its El Segundo Division, and they turned their attention towards a possible replacement.

With the co-operation of Wright Field technicians, they drew up a set of performance requirements for an attack bomber project which bore the appellation Model 7A. This project envisaged an operating speed of 250 m.p.h. which, with a load of bombs, three 0.3-in. machine guns and a crew of two, it was calculated, could be achieved with two 450 h.p. engines. No twin-engined attack bomber had previously been accepted for the U.S. Army, so the Model 7A had to break entirely new ground. It was a shoulder-wing monoplane with a conical-shaped fin and rudder assembly, and a semi-retractable dorsal gun turret. Before its design had been finalised, however, details of aerial combat in the Spanish Civil War resulted in its replacement by an attack project of even more advanced conception. The completed portions of the airframe of the Model 7A were scrapped and work commenced on the Model 7B.

With the resignation of Jack Northrop from the Douglas subsidiary on January 1, 1938, design work on the Model 7B was continued under the direction of E. H. Heinemann who had been Chief Engineer for

The predecessor of the DB-7, the Model 7B, is seen here with its "B Type" nose section (immediately below) and with the "A Type" nose, the latter containing four 0.3-in. machine guns.

The DB-7 Boston I (AE458) illustrated (top) was an ex-Belgian contract machine taken over by the R.A.F. for training duties. The DB-7 Boston II (AX910), immediately above, was converted for the night fighting role, under the designation Havoc I, in the winter of 1940–41.

the performance of the Model 7B most impressive, and in February 1939 placed an order for one hundred aircraft, an order destined to be soon increased to 380. Although the prototype was flying in U.S. Army insignia, the French order was the first contract or commitment to be received by Douglas for its vast expenditure of effort. But although the French contract was based on the performance of the Model 7B, so many modifications were demanded to prevent the aircraft becoming tactically obsolete before reaching Europe that the result was virtually a new model! The revised aircraft was designated Model DB-7 ("DB" indicating Douglas Bomber), and this was to serve as a prototype for the A-20 series.

To accommodate up to 1,764 lb. of demolition bombs and the fuel tanks for the requisite range, the fuselage was deepened. Simultaneously, the cross section was narrowed, providing a single cockpit for the pilot with no possibility of position interchange between the navigator-bombardier, who was accommodated in the rounded, transparent nose, and the gunner situated in a cockpit aft of the wings. The wing position was lowered slightly, and the uprated Twin Wasps (1,200 h.p.) were mounted in underslung nacelles. The revised airframe geometry necessitated a longer nosewheel leg, but the semi-cantilever main undercarriage members remained substantially unchanged. Armour was provided for the crew and fuel tanks, and armament comprised four fixed forward-firing French MAC (Manufacture d'Armes de Chatellerault) 7.5-mm. machine guns, and two flexibly-mounted guns of similar calibre with 500 r.p.g. firing above and below the rear fuselage.

The original work force of seventy engineers who had developed the Models 7A and 7B was increased fivefold to speed the drawings of the DB-7 to the tooling and manufacturing groups, and a production line was established before the production prototype made its first flight on August 17, 1939, at El Segundo. Development was complicated by the need to incorporate the many French requirements, including metrically-calibrated instruments and other specialised equipment. Further complications ensued following the crash of the prototype which spun in following an engine failure while carrying Captain Chemedlin of the French Air Mission, the American test pilot being killed when he baled out too low. But despite these delicate international problems, the entire batch of one hundred DB-7s was in the hands of the French by the end of 1939—a truly remarkable achievement!

Unfortunately, the Armée de l'Air was considerably slower in putting these aircraft into service.

more than a year. The Model 7B made its initial flight towards the close of 1938, and its exceptional performance became immediately apparent. Its maximum speed was more than 300 m.p.h., and its manœuvrability was outstanding for a twin-engined aircraft. Powered by two 1,100 h.p. Pratt and Whitney Twin Wasp R-1830 engines, the Model 7B was a handsome aircraft incorporating many novel features. It retained the shoulder-wing configuration and conical vertical tail surfaces of the earlier Model 7A, and had retractable dorsal and ventral turrets mounting 0.3-in. machine guns. Four more 0.3-in. guns were installed in blisters, two on each side of the forward fuselage, and similar installations were to become a common feature of many U.S. attack bombers during the Second World War.

Another design feature to appear initially on the Model 7B which was later to be adopted on a wide, scale was the provision of interchangeable nose sections to suit the aircraft for the alternative roles of bombardment or attack. As completed, the Model 7B prototype had a transparent nose accommodating a navigator and featuring an oblique optical flat panel for bomb-aiming. The entire "B" (Bombardment) nose could be detached from forward of the cockpit and nosewheel and replaced by a "solid" attack or "A" type nose housing four 0.3-in. guns for ground-strafing.

Completion of the Model 7B coincided with the arrival on the Pacific Coast, with President Roosevelt's blessing, of the French Purchasing Commission which was seeking modern aircraft for the re-equipment of the Armée de l'Air. Its members found

The DB-7s were shipped to Casablanca where they were assembled and tested before delivery to conversion units in North Africa and Southern France, but only sixty-four machines had crossed the Atlantic by the time of the German offensive in May 1940. Only *Groupement* 2 became operational in time to play a small part in the Battle for France, twelve DB-7s of this unit joining operations on May 31, 1940, with a low-level attack on German columns near Saint Quentin. Five *Groupes de Bombardement* (GBI/19, II/19, and II/61 at Souk el Arba, and I/32 and II/32 at Mediouna) had a total of twenty-nine DB-7s in North Africa at the time of the French capitulation in June 1940, and these were incorporated temporarily in the Vichy Air Force, although they were later to participate in the attacks on the German strongholds on the French Atlantic Coast before France was finally liberated.

While the original order for DB-7s had been in process of fulfilment, the French government placed a further contract with Douglas for a substantial quantity of a developed version, the DB-7A. To cope with a further

The Douglas A-20 (39-735), illustrated at the top of this page, had turbo-superchargers. This particular machine was modified as the XP-70 for night fighting duties, and no less than fifty-nine of the sixty-three A-20s built were similarly converted. The A-20A (39-725), immediately above, was the first U.S.A.A.C. attack model.

increase in gross weight from 14,000 lb. to 17,319 lb. which resulted from the installation of additional equipment, the DB-7A had 1,600 h.p. Wright Cyclone R-2600 engines in place of the Twin Wasps. The new power plants were accommodated in revised nacelles which had lengthened, more pointed extensions aft of the wing, and "slotted" cowlings with modified cooling gills, redesigned intake and exhaust arrangements. As a corollary to the increased power, the fin and rudder of the DB-7A were substantially increased in area by additional chord towards the tip, resulting in a noticeably less tapered outline. Even the lower-powered DB-7 had exhibited some symptoms of inadequate vertical tail surface in its directional stability and control, and as an experiment the 131st French contract aircraft had been fitted with twin fins and rudders at the tips of the dihedralled tailplane. Serialled U-131, this modified aircraft was known within Douglas as the DB-131, and was flight tested during 1939, but the new arrangement was abandoned in favour of the larger single vertical tail.

It is not generally realised that no fewer than seventy-five Cyclone-powered DB-7As were accepted by the French government before its capitulation from orders totalling 951 aircraft, but few, in fact, reached the Armée de l'Air. The Anglo-French Purchasing Board in Washington hurriedly arranged for Britain to take over the undelivered aircraft a few hours before all French assets in the U.S.A. were frozen. Also transferred at the same time were the DB-7s of a small Belgian order, while other machines

of a similar type found their way into the Royal Air Force via Free French pilots in North Africa and Metropolitan France.

Some confusion arose from the R.A.F. designation system for the various DB-7 variants, and their irregular arrival did not assist matters. About twenty of the original production DB-7s (allocated serial numbers AE457-472 and DK274-277) were the first to arrive, and these were given the designation Boston I, being employed for training and other non-operational duties on which their French instrumentation resulted in some slight complication. On arrival in the United Kingdom, their throttles were found to work backwards (i.e. forward to close) in the then-current French fashion, and these were immediately modified at Speke. In mid-1940, further small batches of ex-French or Belgian contract aircraft arrived, totalling about 150 machines. With R-1830-S3C4G Twin Wasp engines, having two-speed superchargers and Stromberg injection carburettors, in place of the original SC3G single-speed supercharged powerplants, these aircraft had been built as DB-7s, and, on paper at least, were designated Boston IIs by the R.A.F. They carried 270 gallons of fuel in protected wing tanks, and had the usual crew of three. The rear gunner had hatches above and below the fuselage for defensive armament, and as there was no possibility of changing places in the air, his cockpit was fitted with rudimentary flying controls for emergency landings.

Although procured as a bomber, the first application of the DB-7 with the R.A.F. was not directly

The Boston III (W8315), illustrated immediately above, was experimentally fitted with a twin-Browning Bristol turret.

(Above) Most DB-7 aircraft were converted for use by the R.A.F. as Havoc I night fighters. The aircraft illustrated (BD112) was operated on intruder duties from April 1941 by No. 23 Squadron. Some DB-7B Boston IIIs, such as W8325 (left), were converted for intruder operations on the Havoc I pattern.

concerned with such duties. Following the German "blitz" on the United Kingdom, there was a marked shortage of aircraft suitable for night fighting and intruder duties, and capable of carrying the cumbersome early airborne-interception radar. The DB-7 promised to be a useful mount for such equipment, and most of the initial delivery batches were converted as night fighters and intruders, and redesignated Havoc Is. Well over a hundred Boston IIs were modified at the Burtonwood Aircraft Repair Depot, Liverpool, in the winter of 1940, being fitted with armour protection for the three crew members, flame-damping exhausts and much additional equipment.

Originally known as Rangers, about half of the Havoc Is were armed with four forward-firing 0.303-in. Browning machine guns in the under-nose positions originally specified by the French, and a single gas-operated Vickers "K"-type gun of similar calibre in the rear cockpit. Up to 2,400 lb. of bombs could be carried in the bomb-bays for intrusion sorties on which the Havoc I was first engaged in

December 1940. It went into service with Nos. 23, 85 and 93 Squadrons for its initial operational career, and achieved considerable success over the Continent. The Havoc I (Intruder) was known variously as the "Moonfighter" and the "Havoc IV", and there were several other variants of the basic type.

For pure night fighting duties, the Havoc I was fitted with a "solid" nose housing four 0.303-in. machine guns in addition to the normal four forward-firing guns, and carried the A.I. Mk.IV radar. It was also the subject of some unusual experiments. These resulted in the appearance of the Havoc III, later to be known as the Havoc I (Pandora), and the Turbinlite Havoc. The Pandora experiment was conducted by the twenty aircraft of No. 93 Squadron which was charged with the development of a device known as the L.A.M., or Long Aerial Mine. This comprised an explosive charge on two thousand feet of cable which was stowed in the bomb-bay of the Havoc and trailed in the path of hostile bombers.

A slightly greater chance of success was offered by the Turbinlite installation. The noses of some thirty-one Havoc Is were modified to mount the 2,700 million candlepower Helmore/G.E.C. searchlight in conjunction with the early A.I. radar and its "arrowhead" aerials. As the nose was fully occupied with equipment, and the bomb-bay was full of batteries, the Turbinlite Havocs were unarmed, and depended on accompanying Hurricanes to shoot down the enemy aircraft that they were supposed to illuminate. Centimetre radar development eventually made the Turbinlite redundant, but not before a further thirty-nine Havoc IIs had been converted to carry this equipment, and it had served with Nos. 530, 531, 532, 533, 534, 535, 536, 537, 538 and 539 Squadrons during 1942-43.

The Havoc I had a maximum speed of 295 m.p.h.

Owing to inadequate directional stability and control, several experiments were made with the tail surfaces, and the 131st French contract aircraft (above) had twin fins and rudders at the tips of a dihedralled tailplane. Deliveries of the A-20A (right) to the U.S.A.A.C. commenced in 1940.

at 13,000 feet, and a gross weight of 19,040 lb. The ninety-nine Havoc IIs received by the R.A.F. (AH431-529) were some of the DB-7As ordered originally for the Armée de l'Air, and arrived with their original insignia still visible and a certain amount of French equipment installed. They had the revised vertical tail surfaces and extended nacelles housing Double Cyclone GR-2600-A5B engines rated at 1,600 h.p. at 2,400 r.p.m. for take-off. As received by the R.A.F., the Havoc IIs had the transparent nose with its "stepped" side panels which had characterised the earlier DB-7s, but for night fighting duties a heavy forward-firing gun armament was required. Air Chief Marshal Sir William Freeman of the Ministry of Aircraft Production approached Mr. James Martin of Martin-Baker Aircraft to design a multi-gun installation, and the result was a new nose accommodating no fewer than twelve 0.303-in. Browning guns. This remarkable increase in fire power was made possible by the ingenious arrangement of the guns and the use of Martin ammunition boxes. This modified nose was quickly placed in production, and about eighty aircraft were converted at Burtonwood as twelve-gun night fighters.

Although in some respects slightly incidental to the main Douglas Bomber story, these fighter-bomber developments were an essential part of the overall progression of the basic design, and an excellent indication of its adaptability. They also served to emphasize the uncomplaining response of the machine to such inflictions as the absolutely flat nose of the Turbinlite installation, and strongly confirmed the DB-7's remarkably docile handling. The qualities of the design had not been entirely lost on the U.S. Army which, as early as the beginning of 1939, had given a letter of intent to Douglas, and, in July of that year, had signed a formal contract for 123 DB-7s which were to be known as the A-20A.

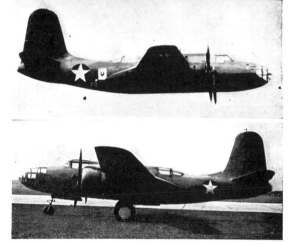

The A-20B (41-267), illustrated above, approximated to the R.A.F.'s DB-7A. It featured rear-firing engine nacelle guns.

British orders had been placed for a further developed model, the DB-7B, which was generally similar to the Havoc II (DB-7A) except for a revised hydraulic system, fuel system, and general instrument layout to R.A.F. instead of Armée de l'Air requirements. The newer model, which the R.A.F. dubbed Boston III, was distinguishable by the modified geometry of its nose transparencies with their oblique contour where they joined the fuselage, an internal tail light in the aft fuselage cone, and a fairing blister over two of the nose guns. During 1940, the U.S. Army Air Corps accepted some three hundred DB-7Bs, but these were destined for the R.A.F. in North Africa, and received the serials W8252-8401 and Z2155-2304. These were not quite the first Boston IIIs, however, since this designation had been applied to a few of the R.A.F.'s DB-7As which had not been converted to Havoc II configuration. As a matter of interest, at least three Boston IIIs were converted as Turbinlite aircraft, while several dozen were converted for intruder operations on the Havoc I pattern. The Boston III

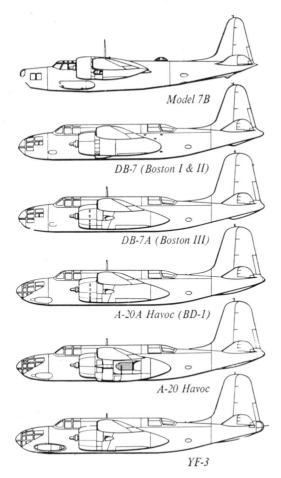

Model 7B

DB-7 (Boston I & II)

DB-7A (Boston III)

A-20A Havoc (BD-1)

A-20 Havoc

YF-3

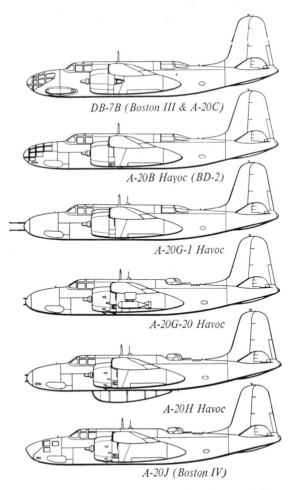

DB-7B (Boston III & A-20C)

A-20B Hayoc (BD-2)

A-20G-1 Havoc

A-20G-20 Havoc

A-20H Havoc

A-20J (Boston IV)

(Intruder) aircraft retained their transparent noses but were painted matt black, equipped with flame-damping exhausts, and fitted with a belly gun pack containing four 20-mm. Hispano cannon. These specially-equipped aircraft operated with some success with Nos. 418 (R.C.A.F.) and 605 Squadrons from mid-1942 onwards.

The Boston III was the first of the DB-7 series to be used by the R.A.F. in its original light day bomber role, and was modified for operational use with No. 2 Group to replace the Blenheim on anti-shipping strikes and short-range tactical sorties. It first entered service towards the end of 1941 with No. 88 Squadron R.A.F. in the United Kingdom, and eventually equipped Nos. 107, 226 and 342 Squadrons, also in the U.K., and in addition Nos. 13, 14, 18, 55 and 114 Squadrons in North Africa where Bostons began to replace the Blenheim early in 1942,

contributing greatly to the slowing down of Rommel's advance on Alexandria. In its day bomber form the Boston's standard armament was four 0.303-in. fixed guns in the nose, plus two Brownings of similar calibre on a high-speed mounting in the rear cockpit and a single gun for ventral defence. Bomb load remained 2,000 lb., but the maximum speed increased to 304 m.p.h. at 13,000 ft., and range with maximum bomb load was 1,030 miles.

As an indication of development growth, the DB-7 had a design weight of 14,500 lb. gross which had increased to 17,319 lb. for the DB-7A. The DB-7B weighed in at 21,500 lb. Although no direct comparison is possible, the first aircraft delivered to the U.S. Army, in 1940, corresponded approximately to the DB-7B in airframe configuration, but their Wright Double Cyclone R-2600-7 engines had turbo-superchargers on the outboard flanks of their nacelles

FINISH AND INSIGNIA: *The A-20G-20-DO of the U.S. Ninth Air Force illustrated had a matt dark earth and olive drab camouflage pattern over the upper surfaces, a second coat of olive drab subsequently being applied over all upper surfaces resulting in light and dark areas of olive overall. All under surfaces were painted a matt neutral grey which met the olive in an irregular wavy line at the extreme base of the fuselage sides. Walkways on the upper wing surfaces* were indicated in yellow, and the national insignia appeared on the upper surface of the port wing, the lower surface of the starboard wing, and the fuselage sides. From September 1943, this comprised a five-pointed white star on a blue disc superimposed upon a white horizontal bar outlined in blue. The number "57" appeared in white on both sides of the fuselage nose and the vertical tail surfaces, and the serial number (286657) appeared in white.

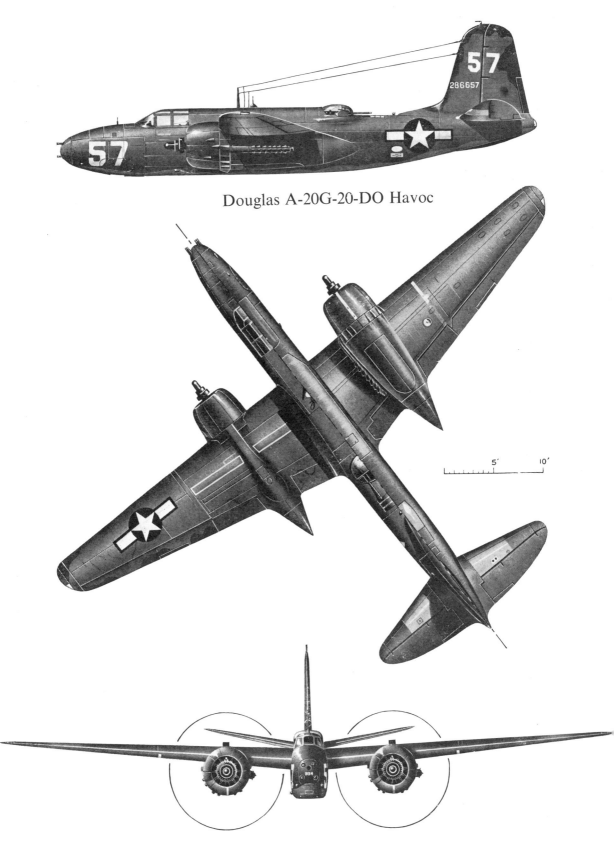

Douglas A-20G-20-DO Havoc

5'   10'

With the A-20C (above) the British and U.S. variants reached standardisation, the R.A.F. designation being Boston III. The DB-2 (left) was a U.S. Navy version of the A-20B, eight of which followed a few BD-1s (A-20As).

and developed a maximum of 1,700 h.p. In all, sixty-three of these machines, known as A-20s, were delivered for Army Air Corps use; none went into service on bomber or attack duties.

Apparently, just before the U.S.A. entered the Second World War, the Air Corps felt the need more for long-range fighters than for attack bombers, being largely on the defensive, and the prototype A-20 (39-735) was, therefore, adapted for night fighting duties. It was re-engined with unsupercharged R-2600-11 engines, fitted with the early British A.I. radar in a "solid" nose, as in the Havoc, and instead of the normal armament of seven 0.3-in. machine guns, four 20-mm. cannon were mounted in a fairing beneath the fuselage. With a crew of two, the XP-70, as this machine was redesignated, served as a prototype for the conversion of a further fifty-nine A-20s as night fighters which were used largely for training in the new art of radar interception. The remaining three A-20s of the initial Air Corps batch were diverted to photo-reconnaissance duties, one of these (39-741) becoming the XF-3, fitted with T-3A cameras in the aft portion of the bomb-bay, and carrying a crew of three. Armament comprised a 0.3-in. Browning gun on each side of the transparent nose; two flexibly mounted Brownings in the rear gunner's position, and a 0.3-in. lower tunnel gun. The other two A-20s which became YF-3s, featured experimental armament installations, including a twin-gun hand-held position in the extreme aft fuselage, as in the B-26 Marauder, and a remotely-controlled Browning gun in the tail of each engine nacelle, firing directly aft.

The first "attack" variant of the DB-7 to be delivered to the Air Corps was, thus, the A-20A, commencing with 39-721 in 1940 from El Segundo. These differed from the A-20 specifications only in having the turbo-superchargers removed and in having 1,600 h.p. R-2600-3 Double Cyclones. The original order was increased by twenty to 143, although seventeen of these were reconverted to a later variant and a few went to the U.S. Navy as the BD-1. In general, the A-20A corresponded to the R.A.F.'s DB-7B Boston III except for its internal equipment and the calibre of its armament. The four forward-firing, two upper and one lower machine guns were all of 0.3-in. calibre, and, as in the YF-3s, there were two more Brownings in the aft engine nacelles. One 1,100-lb. demolition bomb could be carried in the bomb-bay, or a similar load of fragmentation, chemical or smaller G.P. bombs. The maximum speed of the A-20A was a respectable 350 m.p.h. for a gross weight of 18,605 lb.

During 1941, demand for the DB-7 series continued from all sides, and Douglas were hard put to fulfil American and Allied orders. In October, the exiled Dutch government in London ordered forty-eight Boston III-type aircraft, designated DB-7Cs, which called for 45,000 additional hours of work from the Engineering Department. To satisfy British demands for the Boston, Douglas granted Boeing a licence to build 380 DB-7 variants to fulfil lend-lease contracts, and furnished the company with complete detailed designs and master tooling to ensure interchangeability of parts between aircraft built by both organisations.

DB-7 production was also extended at that time to the Long Beach plant of Douglas, where 999 A-20Bs were produced in 1941. The XA-20B was an A-20A fitted purely experimentally in mid-1941 with three power-operated twin-gun turrets above and below the fuselage and in the nose, but production aircraft conformed to previous DB-7 standards. In fact, the A-20B-DL was an earlier version than any of its U.S. Army predecessors, corresponding with the DB-7A

The first R.A.F. squadron to operate the Boston III was No. 88 (Hong Kong) Squadron, one of whose aircraft, BZ377, is illustrated above. One Boston III, W8269/G (right), was experimentally fitted with racks for 60-lb. rockets.

(R.A.F. Havoc II). The A-20B was powered by the 1,690 h.p. R-2600-11 Double Cyclones and had a gross weight of 20,579 lb. This model was the first to mount the 0.5-in. Browning machine gun, having two flanking the transparent nose (which had the older stepped side panels) and a single gun in the rear cockpit. Provision was made for the rearward-firing engine nacelle guns which were remotely controlled by a foot trigger in the rear compartment. Another modification facilitated the installation of temporary auxiliary fuel tanks for ferry flights to the various theatres of war. A few A-20As had been transferred to the U.S. Navy as BD-1s, and eight A-20Bs became BD-2s. Plans were made in 1941 to build no fewer than 1,489 A-20Bs modified for photo-reconnaissance and observation duties under the designation 0-53, but this project was cancelled.

With the beginning of really large-scale production of the DB-7 in 1941 by Douglas at Santa Monica, British and American variants reached standardisation with the A-20C. This was the Air Corps designation for the Boston III with R.A.F.-specified equipment and R-2600-23 engines. The gross weight had increased to 25,600 lb., and the armament was four 0.3-in. nose guns, two similar guns in the upper rear position, and one firing downwards. In all, 808 A-20Cs were built by Douglas at Santa Monica and 140 by Boeing at Seattle. The latter came under lend-lease contracts for delivery to the U.S.A.'s allies which, by that time, included the Soviet Union. By May 1942, 387 Bostons from British allocations had been transferred to Russia. For 1942, 181 A-20Cs were allocated to Britain, so that a good proportion of the 240 Douglas-built Boston IIIs (AL263-502) and 240 Boeing-built machines (AL668-907) were diverted from the R.A.F. to the Soviet Air Force.

Boeing-built aircraft supplied to the R.A.F. under lend-lease were designated Boston IIIA, and differed from the Mk.III only in their electrical systems, in the removal of the "alligator-tail" flame-damping ex-

haust pipes in favour of ventral stubs, and in the extension of the carburettor air intake above the cowling to include tropical filters. Bostons were then making a name for themselves in the Western Desert with the R.A.F., the S.A.A.F., and the U.S.A.A.F. (the Army Air Corps having been redesignated the Army Air Force on June 20, 1940), although the A-20A had been deployed overseas with the A.A.F. before Pearl Harbour. Batches of Boston IIIAs received by the R.A.F. included 157 (BZ196-352), twenty-four (BZ355-378), and nineteen (BZ381-399); they equipped Nos. 88, 107, 226 and 342 Squadrons in the United Kingdom, in addition to Nos. 418 and 605 Squadrons on intruder duties, and Nos. 13, 14, 18, 55 and 114 Squadrons in the Middle East and Italy.

One of the United Kingdom-based squadrons, No. 226, provided the basis for the first operational action by the U.S.A.A.F. in Europe when the personnel of the 15th Bombardment Squadron (Separate) arrived in Britain as the spearhead of the Eighth Air Force in May 1942. The American crews immediately began training on the Boston IIIs of No. 226 Squadron at Swanton Morley, and on the appropriate date of July 4th, six U.S. crews accompanied six from the R.A.F. on a daylight attack at low altitude against four Dutch airfields. The Bostons ran into exceptionally heavy anti-aircraft fire, and two American-manned machines were shot down, but the raid

Production of the Havoc really got into its stride with the A-20G, the first of the series to have a "solid" type nose. The A-20G-10-DO (43-9929) was one of the first machines to have the wider rear fuselage and Martin turret adopted as standard by the A-20G-20-DO production batch.

marked the beginning of American daylight bombing experience which was to prove so decisive in the later offensive.

The Independence Day sortie also provided strong evidence of the Boston's capacity for absorbing punishment. One of the American-manned Bostons lost its starboard airscrew after a flak strike, and suffered severe wing damage as well as an engine fire. It actually struck the ground near its target, but its pilot brought it safely back to Swanton Morley on its remaining engine, and shot up a flak tower with his four front guns *en route*! One or two more sorties were flown with No. 226 Squadron before the American unit received its own A-20Cs in the United Kingdom.

The A-20C was the first variant of the DB-7 series to feature torpedo-carrying capability, with provision for a standard 2,000-lb. naval torpedo carried externally below the bomb-bay. This capacity was not extensively exploited by the R.A.F. or U.S.A.A.F., but the Russian naval air arm made considerable use of the Boston as a torpedo aircraft with not a little success. Other weapon developments were explored by the R.A.F., however, Boston III W8315 being fitted with a twin-Browning Bristol power-operated turret in the mid-upper gun position, and W8269/G having four racks for 60-lb. rocket projectiles beneath each outer wing. The turret modification remained experimental on the Boston III, as did also the rocket projectile installation, but a Martin turret subsequently became standard on later A-20s.

The Martin turret was actually introduced on the next production variant, the A-20G, but before leaving the "C", the conversion of thirteen of the latter for night fighting on an experimental basis must

The XA-20B (below) was an A-20A fitted with three power-operated twin-gun turrets, above and below the fuselage, and in the nose in July 1941. The experiment was not entirely successful and was discontinued.

The R.A.F. received one hundred and sixty-five A-20J Havocs which were known as Boston IVs. The photograph above depicts BZ403, the fourth R.A.F. Boston IV which entered service in August 1944, and operated with the 2nd Tactical Air Force in Europe until the end of the war.

be mentioned. This conversion work was undertaken in 1943, and the resultant P-70A-1-DO was fitted with six 0.5-in. Browning machine guns plus radar in a "solid" nose. Development of the next couple of stages of the A-20 was inconclusive, the A-20D being a cancelled Santa Monica project for an R-2600-7-engined variant without self-sealing fuel tanks, while the A-20E was a revised programme on seventeen A-20As with 1,690 h.p. R-2600-11 engines. Another 1941 experiment was the XA-20F-DE which was an A-20A fitted with a 37-mm. cannon in the nose, and upper and lower General Electric power turrets each mounting two 0.5-in. machine guns.

With the A-20G production had really got into its stride, and 2,850 examples of this variant were produced during 1942 at Santa Monica. Apart from the P-70 conversions, the A-20G was the first of the series to have a "solid" type nose, and the fuselage length

was increased to 48 ft. compared with 47 ft. 4 in. for the A-20C. Having R-2600-23 engines, the A-20G-1-DO had a nose armament of two 0.5-in. machine guns with 350 r.p.g., and four 20-mm. M2 cannon with sixty r.p.g. The cannon projected well forward of the nose, and were supplemented by a 0.3-in. or 0.5-in. tunnel gun with 500 rounds, and a 0.5-in. with a similar amount of ammunition in the rear cockpit. The gunner's position was no longer equipped with emergency flight controls, and provision for photographic equipment was also deleted.

Most of the early A-20Gs were passed on to the Russians, and subsequent models had the nose cannon deleted. Instead four 0.5-in. machine guns with 350 r.p.g. were mounted in the nose to supplement the existing two guns for use against ground targets during low-level attacks. Two 58 Imp.gal. (70 U.S.gal.) fuel tanks were mounted in the bomb-

The A-20H Havoc was generally similar to the G-model apart from the engines and a revised cockpit which offered improved bombing control accessibility. The accompanying photograph depicts an A-20H10-DO (44-308).

The A-20G-40-DO Havoc (*above*) is seen fitted with a 310 Imp.gal. jettisonable fuel tank. The A-20G-1-DO (*left*) had four 20-mm. M2 cannon and two 0.5-in. machine guns in the nose. Most aircraft of this type were passed on to the Russians.

bay to give additional range without affecting bomb capacity which remained at 2,000 lb. This bomb load was doubled from the A-20G-20 onwards which saw the introduction of underwing racks outboard of the engine nacelles and capable of carrying four bombs of up to 500-lb. each. Provision was still made for an external torpedo, although the A-20 series were no longer being used by the A.A.F. for such missions.

The A-20G-20-DO also marked the introduction of a six-inch increase in rear fuselage width to accommodate an electrically-operated Martin turret mounting two 0.5-in. machine guns with 400 r.p.g. The single 0.5-in. tunnel gun was retained for ventral defence. Bomb-bay fuel tankage was increased to a total of 270 Imp.gal. (325 U.S.gal.) which, with a 310 Imp.gal. (374 U.S.gal.) under-fuselage drop tank, gave a total fuel capacity for ferrying purposes of 915 Imp.gal. (1,099 U.S.gal.). This gave an ultimate range of 2,035 miles in 10.5 hours. The A-20G series brought the war maximum weight of the Havoc (which name, incidentally, had been adopted by the A.A.F.) up to 30,000 lb., although critical flight characteristics resulted above 27,000 lb. Combat gross weight of the later A-20Gs was 26,000 lb., which included thicker armour for increased crew protection on ground attack missions, non-ram airscoops,

carburettor anti-icers, and heaters for winterization. Better navigation equipment and Type A-2-bomb-aiming controls were added in the last production A-20Gs which were the -40 to -45-DO batches. These also embodied an improved exhaust ejector system and a modified engine cowling of the "blistered" type as used by the B-25 Mitchell.

The R.A.F. received no A-20Gs, nor any of the A-20H model which followed in 1944. These were generally similar to the A-20G except for the installation of 1,700 h.p. R-2600-29 engines, and a revised cockpit for more accessible bombing controls. Four hundred and twelve were built and, with the A-20Gs, they went into service with the U.S.A.A.F. in the Pacific, the Middle East, and the United Kingdom. The Ninth Air Force made good use of them in tactical sorties over the Continent as a prelude to D-Day, and they proved particularly successful in interdiction attacks, cutting enemy communications and pounding enemy airfields in low-level strikes. The underwing racks were also intended to accommodate chemical tanks which were used for laying smoke screens. This task was undertaken by R.A.F. Boston IIIs on D-Day, the necessary chemicals being carried in bomb-bay tanks and released from four nozzles protruding beneath the fuselage.

In July 1943, the A.A.F. requested that one out of each ten A-20Gs be modified to revert to a bombardier nose with full navigation facilities. This was to conform with the tactics of "bombing on the leader", in which only one aircraft was used to calculate the target position while the remainder of the squadron dropped its bombs at a given signal. These modifications resulted in the A-20J which had a lengthened and frameless transparent nose but was otherwise similar to the A-20G, and the A-20K which was the bombardier version of the A-20H. In all, 450 A-20J Havocs were built in 1943, and 413 A-20Ks had materialised up to the time production of the entire series was halted on September 20, 1944. By that date, 7,385 DB-7s of one sort or another had been manufactured for Britain, Russia and the U.S.A. Of these, 3,125 (including those transferred from R.A.F. deliveries) were allocated to the Soviet Union, 2,917 of these reaching their destination, and 455 were delivered to the R.A.F. under lend-lease. Twenty-eight were supplied to the Netherlands government and thirty-one to Brazil, and the peak inventory for the U.S.A.A.F. was reached in September 1944 when more than 1,700 A-20 Havocs were in service.

The R.A.F. received 169 A-20Js (BZ400-568) which were designated Boston IVs, and entered service in August 1944, and ninety A-20Ks (BZ580-669) which were designated Boston Vs. These aircraft, which had the standard twin 0.5-in. fixed nose armament, continued to operate with the 2nd Tactical Air Force in Europe until the end of the war. Eleven Boston Vs were transferred to the R.C.A.F.

To conclude the DB-7 story, it only remains to mention the odd variants not covered hitherto. An adaptation of the A-20G for night fighting resulted, in 1943, in the P-70A-2-DO. This retained the standard G-model nose armament and twenty-six were so converted, while a single A-20G-10-DO was fitted with a "solid" nose containing radar and radio equipment, and armed with three 0.5-in. machine guns in a large blister on each side of the fuselage. This became the P-70B-1. A project to use other A-20Gs and Js as night fighter trainers (P-70B-2) did not materialise. One unexplained Havoc development was the reconversion of at least one A-20J (43-9929) back to "G" standard, with the "solid" nose and six-gun armament, but this change may have been effected in the field.

A more obvious wartime modification of an A-20H was a machine adapted to take a caterpillar track main landing gear for operating from mud, snow or sand. This experiment was not developed but, like all the other thirty or so uses to which the DB-7 series was put, including strafing, low-level bombing, skip-dombing, night fighting, torpedo-bombing, observation, reconnaissance and smoke-screen laying, to mention only a few, it proved the inherent adaptability of the design.

In Europe, A.A.F. A-20s flew a total of 39,492 sorties in which 28,443 tons (31,856 U.S. tons) of bombs were dropped. They destroyed eleven enemy aircraft in the air during these raids, and lost 265 of their number. The loss rate per sortie of 0.7 per cent was the same as for the B-26 Marauder in Europe, and 0.1 per cent more than that for the B.25 Mitchell. Adaptable, dependable, tractable, and potent, the DB-7 was perhaps overshadowed in its career by the more spectacular exploits which fell to the lot of other bombers, but it ranked high among the most brilliant combat aircraft designs evolved by the U.S. aircraft industry.

Douglas A-20G-20 to -45-DO Havoc

Dimensions:	Span, 61 ft. 4 in.; length, 48 ft. 0 in.; height, 17 ft. 7 in.; wing area, 465 sq. ft.
Armament:	Six 0.5-in. Colt-Browning machine guns in fixed nose positions with 350 r.p.g.; two 0.5-in. machine guns with 400 r.p.g. in Martin power-operated dorsal turret, and one 0.5-in. machine gun with 400 rounds in ventral tunnel. Maximum internal bomb load, 2,000 lb.; maximum external bomb load, 2,000 lb.
Power Plants:	Two Wright R-2600-23 Double Cyclone fourteen-cylinder radial air-cooled engines with two-speed superchargers and driving 11 ft. 3 in. diam. three-blade Hamilton Standard Hydromatic airscrews. Each rated at 1,600 h.p. for take-off (1,675 h.p. war emergency), 1,400 h.p. at 10,000 ft., and 1,275 h.p. continuous at 11,500 ft.
Weights:	Basic, 17,200 lb.; combat, 24,000 lb.; maximum flight manoeuvre, 27,000 lb.; war maximum (ferry purposes only), 30,000 lb.
Performance:	Maximum speed, 317 m.p.h. at 10,000 ft.; maximum continuous speed, 308 m.p.h. at 10,000 ft.; typical cruising speed, 230 m.p.h.; initial climb rate, 1,300 ft./min.; service ceiling, 25,000 ft.; range (with 2,000-lb. bomb load and 604 Imp.gal., fuel), 1,025 mls. at max. cruise power at 238 m.p.h.; take-off to clear 50 ft. obstacle, 1,417 yds.; landing distance from 50 ft., 1,250 yds.

The last production variant of the Havoc was the A-20K (below), 413 examples of which had been delivered when production of the aircraft was terminated in September 1944.

The first Mitsubishi Ki.21-Ia Type 97 Model 1a bombers reached the J.A.A.F. early in 1938, and were immediately assigned to units operating over China. Operational experience dictated an increase in defensive armament, the result being the Ki.21-Ib, a formation of which bombers is illustrated above over the Chinese mainland.

THE MITSUBISHI Ki.21 TYPE 97

The Mitsubishi Type 97 Heavy Bomber was, in its heyday, the backbone of the strongest air arm in the Far East: the Japanese Army Air Force. Entering service in 1937, it was a formidable bomber by any standard. It fought the Russians at Changkufeng and Nomonhan; it was in action throughout the "Chinese Incident", and at the commencement of the Pacific War it was the mainstay of the J.A.A.F. heavy bomber force. By the time the Pacific War reached the Japanese home islands, the Type 97 was totally obsolete, but it had remained a standard first-line type until late in 1943, and had earned the distinction of serving operationally with the J.A.A.F. longer than any other Japanese combat aircraft.

The Ki.21-Ib (below) enjoyed relatively clean lines. It was used as a tactical bomber over Mongolia but was withdrawn soon after the beginning of the Pacific War.

The last operational task of this venerable bomber, which for several years had served as a symbol of Japanese aerial domination in Asia and the Orient, was typical of the desperation with which Japan greeted the Pacific War's twelfth hour. The American invasion of Okinawa in April 1945 had placed B-29 Superfortress bombers a mere few hundred miles from Japan's principal cities, presaging final victory for the Allies. In a daring but hopeless attempt to destroy the American installations and aircraft on Okinawa, nine Type 97 bombers, converted for use as assault transports, were assembled on an airfield in Southern Kyushu. On May 24, 1945, loaded with specially-trained demolition troops, the aircraft took-off for Okinawa. Flying low over the water, seven of the aircraft succeeded in reaching the target area where they encountered American interceptors which destroyed all but one of the intruders. The surviving machine crash-landed on the American-held Yontan Airfield, and the twelve Japanese troops that it carried immediately set about their appointed task. Before they were overwhelmed by American marines, the Japanese destroyed seven aircraft, damaged two others, burned 2,600 drums of fuel and blew up a vast quantity of ammunition, putting the American base out of commission for ten hours. But this suicidal effort gave Japanese cities only a few hours' respite, and a few weeks later when the Mitsubishi Type 97 was again encountered by the Allies it was painted white overall and carried green surrender crosses.

The Type 97, eventually to become known to the Allies as *Sally*, was the result of an Army specification

Numerically the most important J.A.A.F. bomber when the Pacific War began, the Ki.21-IIa 97 Type Model 2a was essentially similar to the Ki.21-Ib but employed 1,490 h.p. Mitsubishi Ha 101 engines in place of the original Nakajima Ha.5-Kai Zuisei radials with a consequent improvement in overall performance.

issued in February 1936. The Japanese High Command was dedicated to the "theoretical enemy" concept, and the specification called for a bomber suitable for long-range overland operations, Russian installations north and west of Japan's Manchurian hinterland being its potential target areas. Russian ambitions in the Far East, being directly opposed to those of Japan, rendered the Soviet Union the principal potential enemy. With the continued growth of Russian power, Japan's expanding area of military responsibility on the Asiatic mainland, and the J.A.A.F.'s obvious inability to retain control in the air and maintain an air offensive against pressure from the north, a programme of J.A.A.F. revitalization was called for, and the new bomber specification was an integral part of this programme.

For an aircraft industry that had produced few aircraft of modern configuration by international standards appertaining at the time, the requirements of the specification were stiff, demanding as they did a modern twin-engined monoplane with a retractable undercarriage, capable of a maximum speed in excess of 250 m.p.h. at 10,000 feet, and the ability to carry a 1,650-lb. bomb load for five hours at 190 m.p.h. The specification also stipulated the use of either the Nakajima Zuisei Ha.5 or Mitsubishi Kinsei Ha.6 power plant, both newly-designed fourteen-cylinder two-row radial air-cooled engines at that time in the experimental stage; a crew of four; a loaded weight of less than 14,000 lb.; a take-off run of less than 330 yards; and the ability to attain an altitude of 10,000 feet in eight minutes.

Only two manufacturers entered the competition, both having enjoyed some measure of success in the multi-engined aircraft field. The Nakajima company,

armed with a background of experience provided by the licence manufacture of the Douglas DC-2, the development of the small AT-2 transport, as well as the DC-2-inspired 9-*Shi* LB-2 experimental Naval bomber, entered a mid-wing monoplane powered by two 950 h.p. Nakajima Ha.5 engines and designated Ki.19. The Mitsubishi company's design team of Nakata and Ozawa developed an aircraft entirely different to any previously evolved by the firm and bearing no relationship to the successful G3M1 9-*Shi* Naval bomber which was also a twin-engined all-metal monoplane with a retractable undercarriage. The design team was an experienced one. Nakata was well-known for his 1931 adaptation of the Junkers K-51—a bomber variant of the massive G-38

The cowlings of the Ha.101 engines employed by the Ki.21-IIa were very much cleaner than those of the Ha.5-Kai engines of the Ki.21-Ib illustrated on the opposite page.

The early production Ki.21-Ia illustrated above carried a crew of seven and a defensive armament of three 7.7-mm. machine guns. The first two prototypes of the Ki.21 (left) featured angular nose contours and a "stepped" rear fuselage for the ventral gun.

transport—as the Ki.20 Type 92 heavy bomber for the J.A.A.F., and both Nakata and Ozawa had assisted in the design of Mitsubishi's Ki.2 Type 93 Light Bomber based on the Junkers K-37. Their project was assigned the designation Ki.21, and work was initiated on four Ki.19 and five Ki.21 prototypes for exhaustive comparative tests and evaluation trials.

The first two prototypes of the Ki.21 were completed at Mitsubishi's 5th Airframe Works in November and December 1936. They were large, blunt-nosed mid-wing monoplanes with nose armament, a dorsal turret, and a stepped rear fuselage providing a ventral gun position. Power was provided by the Mitsubishi Kinsei Ha.6 of 850 h.p., and although performance more than met the demands of the specification, it was patently obvious that the defensive armament was ineffective. The nose-mounted 7.7-mm. machine gun could be moved on a vertical axis only; the traverse of the dorsal turret was strictly limited, and the ventral gun was virtually useless. Three further prototypes were therefore completed, each differing in defensive armament. Dorsal gun positions of semi-exposed, spherical, cylindrical, oval and flush type were tested, and the contours of the fuselage were revised and improved. The ventral step was removed from the rear fuselage, a hand-held 7.7-mm. gun being mounted above a flush sliding panel, and the lines of the nose were refined, terminating in a hemispherical glazed nose

cap containing a 7.7-mm. gun on a ball-and-socket mount. Lateral gun positions were proposed and rejected, and the fifth prototype embodied an innovation in the form of a remotely-controlled 7.7-mm. gun in the extreme tail, a device to be employed by later production models of the Ki.21.

The five Ki.21 prototypes were extensively tested against the four Nakajima Ki.19 prototypes throughout the spring and summer of 1937, with ultimate J.A.A.F. selection of the Ki.21 with the proviso that the Mitsubishi bomber utilize the Nakajima Ha.5 power plant. The production model was allocated the designation Ki.21-Ia Type 97 Heavy Bomber Model 1a, and as deliveries of the new bomber began to reach the J.A.A.F. early in 1938, Japanese military stature grew considerably in importance. The rapid spread of fighting in China necessitated a rapid build-up of production, and Mitsubishi's 5th Airframe Works soon reached saturation point. Production orders for the Type 97 were, therefore, also assigned to Nakajima who began deliveries in August 1938.

Mitsubishi had completed three production aircraft by the end of 1937, and had delivered a further 163 machines by the end of 1938, subsequent production reaching an average of more than fifteen aircraft per month. In its original form, the Ki-21-Ia carried a crew of seven and defensive armament consisted of three 7.7-mm. machine guns. The dorsal gun position was covered by a long "greenhouse" enclosure, the hand-held machine gun being mounted at its rear end. Power was provided by two Zuisei Ha.5-Kai radials, production versions of the original Ha.5 and rated at 850 h.p. With its 1,650-lb. bomb load and 269 m.p.h. maximum speed the Ki.21-Ia bomber did much to change the balance of air power in the Far East.

Operational experience dictated numerous changes

The Ki.21 IIa (above) carried a defensive armament of five or six 7.7-mm. machine guns, one of which was mounted as a remotely-controlled "stinger" in the extreme tail. This "stinger" gun is shown in close-up on the right.

as production gained momentum. The bomb-bays were enlarged, the landing flaps were increased in area, the fuel tanks were provided with partial leak protection by rubber laminated covering, light armour protection was fitted for the crew, and defensive armament was increased to five and, on some machines, six 7.7-mm. machine guns. One of these was mounted as a remotely-controlled "stinger" in the extreme tail, this having been tested on the fifth prototype. The modified aircraft was known as the Ki.21-Ib Type 97 Model 1b, this becoming numerically the most important Army bomber in service over the Chinese mainland, and it soon appeared over Chungking and Lanchow, far inland. It also served as a tactical bomber over Outer Mongolia in the Khalkhiin Gol fighting, and during the opening days of the Pacific War bombers of this type raided Hong Kong, the Philippines and Burma.

In addition to the bomber models, the Ki.21-I was produced in several versions for the training and transport roles, the first transport model being a modified Ki-21-Ia with armament removed and the bomb-bays covered over. This was employed by the J.A.A.F., but a number were also built as civil freighters for use by the Japan Air Transport Company under the designation MC-21-I. The first of these commercial models, which served on domestic and overseas routes from the early 'forties throughout the war years, was J-BFOA *Hiei* which pioneered routes for a civil passenger transport derived from the Ki.21 series. This aircraft utilized the standard engines and nacelles, wings and tail surfaces of the Ki.21-Ia, these being married to an entirely new fuselage which accommodated four crew members and eleven passengers. The prototype was completed in the summer of 1940 as the Mitsubishi MC-20, and immediately began route-proving trials with J.A.T. Sales of the MC-20 were solicited in several Asian

and South American countries, and the type was subsequently used widely by J.A.T., also being accepted for service with the J.A.A.F. as the Ki.57-I Type 100 Transport Model 1, and the J.N.A.F. as the Type O Transport.

Increased opposition over China revealed certain defensive and performance deficiencies in the Ki.21-I, and in November 1939 work was initiated on an improved model, the Ki.21-II. The modified bomber used the basic Ki.21-I airframe but switched to 1,490 h.p. Mitsubishi Ha.101 fourteen-cylinder two-row radials which were housed in aerodynamically cleaner cowlings. The overall span of the tailplane was increased by four feet and, as the Ki.21-IIa Type 97 Model 2a, it was numerically the most important J.A.A.F. bomber when the Pacific War began. In spite of the improvements incorporated in the Ki.21-IIa, the bomber proved an easy target for the Hawker Hurricane fighters by which it found itself opposed over Burma and India, and the J.A.A.F. bomber squadrons suffered heavy casualties when unprotected by escort fighters. One of the chief disadvantages was the limited traverse of the dorsal gun, and the long "glasshouse" enclosure was, therefore, removed and replaced by a large conical turret containing a single 12.7-mm. machine gun. This turret was a marvel of inconvenience for it was operated by

The final major production version of the Type 97 heavy bomber was the Ki.21-IIb illustrated above. This featured increased armour protection for the crew and a large conical dorsal turret housing a single 12.7-mm. machine gun.

bicycle pedals with a chain drive for gun traverse. Some 16-mm. armour plate was mounted aft of the dorsal turret to protect the gunner, 12.5-mm. armour was mounted fore and aft of the pilot, and all fuel tanks were protected. To provide additional range, an auxiliary fuel tank could be installed in the bomb-bay, having a capacity of 110 Imp.gal., and when

carried, four 110-lb. bombs were usually mounted externally.

With the dorsal turret fitted, the bomber was designated Ki.21-IIb Type 97 Model 2b, but when first encountered by the Allies it was thought to be a new type and was initially given the identification name of *Gwen*. With the introduction of the Ki.21-IIb, the remaining Ki.21-Is and many Ki. 21-IIa bombers were relegated to training duties, the primary assignment being to the Hamamatsu Advanced Heavy Bomber Train-

The late production Ki.21-IIb bombers (illustrated below) carried four 100-lb. bombs externally when an auxiliary tank was fitted in the bomb-bay.

FINISH AND INSIGNIA: *Mitsubishi Type 97 bombers were frequently camouflaged to conform with the terrain over which they were operating and, in consequence, a variety of different schemes was employed. The aircraft illustrated on the opposite page is a Ki.21-IIb operated by the 14th Heavy Bombing Squadron in the South-West Pacific. The light jungle green "zebra stripes" were applied directly to the natural metal over all upper surfaces, and the under surfaces were left natural metal. The standard white "combat stripe" for I.F.F. identification was applied to the rear fuselage, and the circular red national insignia, or Hinomaru, was outlined in white on the fuselage sides, but appeared as a plain red disc on the wing surfaces.*

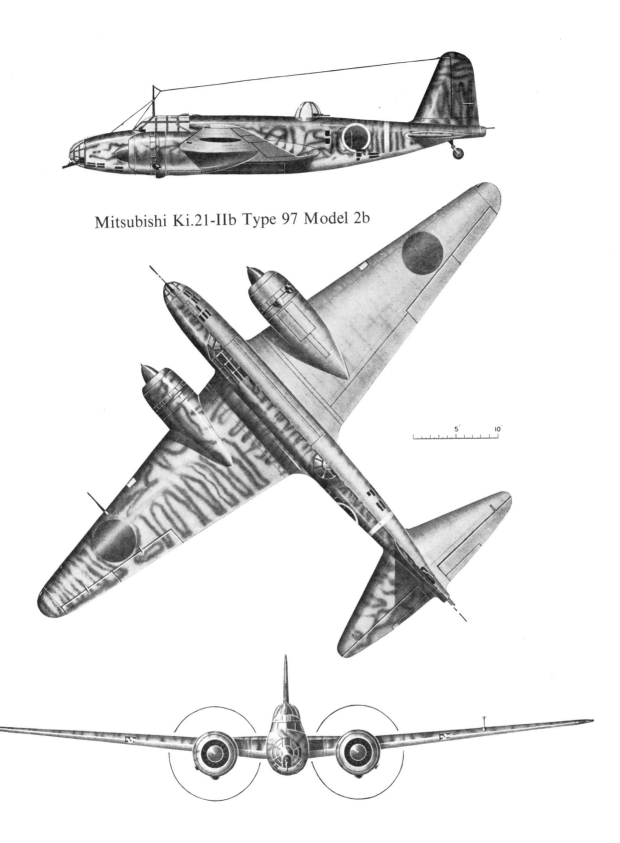

Mitsubishi Ki.21-IIb Type 97 Model 2b

Shown clearly in this photograph, the dorsal turret of the Ki.21-IIb was operated by bicycle pedals with a chain drive for gun traverse. It replaced the long "glasshouse" enclosure of the Ki.21-IIa and earlier models.

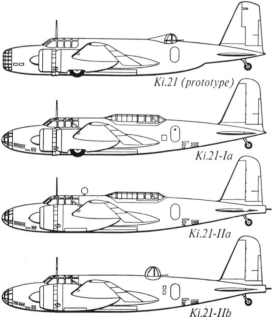

Ki.21 (prototype)

Ki.21-Ia

Ki.21-IIa

Ki.21-IIb

ing School. The Ki.21-IIb, despite its obsolescence, remained in service as a standard first-line bomber in company with the later Nakajima Ki.49-II Donryu until ultimately replaced by the Ki.67 Hiryu late in 1944. A parallel transport model was evolved as the MC-21-II, and limited production was undertaken for both civil and military use. The MC-20 transport series was also re-engined, receiving the 1,050 h.p. Mitsubishi Ha.102 Type 1 radial as the MC-20-II. One camouflaged MC-20-II was to be awarded the task of carrying the Japanese surrender delegation to Chirkiang airfield in China to arrange for the surrender of all Japanese forces in that country. The military version of the MC-20-II was built by

both Mitsubishi and Kokusai as the Ki.57-II Type 100 Transport Model 2.

The last projected version of the Type 97 bomber was the Ki.21-III which was abandoned in favour of the Ki.67 Hiryu, and production of the aircraft finally terminated at Mitsubishi's 5th Airframe Works in September 1944. The basic aircraft had been in continuous production for no less than eight years, and with the delivery of the last machine more than 1,800 aeroplanes of this type had been manufactured, 315 of these having been built by Nakajima who completed production in February 1941. Hopelessly outclassed during the last two years of the war, it had, nevertheless, served long and well on every Japanese battlefront, and can probably lay claim to the title of the most famous Japanese bomber of the Second World War.

Mitsubishi Ki.21-IIb Type 97 Model 2b

Dimensions: Span, 72 ft. 9¾ in.; length, 52 ft. 6 in.; height, 15 ft. 11 in.; wing area, 749.167 sq. ft.

Armament: One 12.7-mm. Type 1 (Browning) machine gun with 600 rounds in dorsal turret, and five 7.7-mm. Type 89 machine guns with 600 r.p.g. in hand-held nose, lateral and ventral positions, and remotely-controlled tail position. Maximum bomb load, 2,200 lb. Alternative loads: Sixteen 110-lb. bombs; nine 220-lb. bombs, four 550-lb. bombs, or two 1,100-lb. bombs.

Power Plants: Two Mitsubishi Ha.101 Type 100 fourteen-cylinder radial air-cooled engines rated at 1,490 h.p. at 2,450 r.p.m. for take-off, 1,445 h.p. at 2,350 r.p.m. at 8,550 ft., and 1,360 h.p. at 2,350 r.p.m. at 15,100 ft.

Weights: Empty, 13,382 lb.; normal loaded, 21,407 lb.

Performance: Maximum speed, 297 m.p.h. at 13,120 ft.; cruising speed, 236 m.p.h. at 16,400 ft.; initial climb rate, 1,660 ft./min.; time to 10,000 ft., 6.5 min., to 19,685 ft., 13.15 min.; service ceiling, 32,800 ft.; endurance, 7 hrs.; range (with maximum bomb load), 1,350 mls. at 176 m.p.h. at 1,500 ft., (with 440-lb. bomb load and auxiliary bomb-bay tank), 1,595 mls.

The Whitley, frequently referred to as the "Grand Old Lady of Bomber Command", dropped the first bombs on German soil and undertook the first attacks on Italy, being finally retired from Bomber Command in the spring of 1942.

THE ARMSTRONG WHITWORTH WHITLEY

The angularly ugly Armstrong Whitworth Whitley—the "Flying Barn Door"—heading into the gathering dusk *en route* to a nocturnal rendezvous over enemy territory was a familiar sight to dwellers on Britain's east coast during the early war years. With its characteristic nose-down flying attitude and unmistakable, rather irritating note variation of its twin Merlin engines which could rarely be synchronized for more than a few seconds at a time, the Whitley was the prop and mainstay of the Royal Air Force's night offensive during those first two years of war in which the seeds of strategic night bombing's future pattern were being sown. To this grand old lady of Bomber Command went the distinction of being the first British bomber to appear in the skies of Berlin; the first to drop bombs on German soil, and the first to attack targets in Italy—"firsts" which succeeded others of equal importance in the field of technical development.

With its ponderous, slab-sided fuselage, and thick, broad wings, the Whitley was aesthetically the least appealing of the bombers with which the R.A.F. went to war. Its wings and fuselage gave the impression that they were travelling along different paths, and in flight its attitude was disconcertingly nose down, but it was as sturdy as a rock; a docile, matronly aeroplane which enjoyed the affection of its crews, although, as one pilot put it, "The Whitley, like the old lady she was, never did quite what she was told to do, but the things that she did were for the most part reasonable and comfortable."

The Whitley represented an important landmark in the history of the R.A.F.'s offensive capability. Prior to its service début, the heavy-bombing squadrons were equipped for the most part with the Handley Page Heyford biplane, and the Whitley, which was then still classified as a "heavy" and the R.A.F.'s first bomber to feature turreted defensive armament and a retractable undercarriage, offered tremendous advances over its predecessor in both performance and load-carrying ability. Whereas the Hampden and the Wellington, the compatriots with

(Above and below) The first prototype Whitley (K4586) was flown for the first time at Baginton on March 17, 1936, by which time a contract for eighty machines had already been placed.

(Left) The first production Whitley I (K7183) was completed in March 1937. Together with the first few production aeroplanes, this did not feature the dihedral on the outboard wing panels introduced to improve lateral stability. The ninth production Whitley I (K7191) is illustrated above.

which it was to share the early phases of Bomber Command's offensive, were designed to meet the requirements of specifications issued in 1932, the specification which gave birth to the Whitley was not prepared until two years later, but by emphasizing produceability, and reducing the structure to as few component parts as possible, Armstrong Whitworth's bomber reached the squadrons before either the Handley Page or Vickers bomber. In fact, it progressed from initial design study to prototype trials within a mere eighteen months, and the first squadron deliveries were made within twenty months of the receipt of the initial production contract.

The A.W.38 Whitley was the outcome of Air Ministry Specification B.3/34, which called for a night bomber/troop transport. Work on the aircraft was initiated during the late months of 1934 by a team headed by Mr. J. Lloyd, Armstrong Whitworth's chief designer. The Whitley, named after the Coventry district in which the company's main factory was situated, bore a close family resemblance to its immediate predecessor, the experimental

A.W.23 bomber-transport, but all similarity was purely external. Whereas the fuselage of the A.W.23 featured a tubular high-tensile steel structure with fabric covering, a method of construction in which Sir W. G. Armstrong Whitworth Aircraft had undertaken much early research, the bomber's fuselage offered a noteworthy advance in structural techniques by employing a stressed-skin light alloy monocoque. At the time, information on the strengths of such structures was extremely limited, but the strength and reliability of the Whitley's fuselage were to be proven in no uncertain fashion during the war years when Whitley bombers were to return to their bases with sizeable areas of their fuselages shot away by anti-aircraft fire.

In order to simplify production, component parts were reduced to the smallest possible number and all were of standardized sections. Manufacture was further simplified and some structural weight was saved by the elimination of all curves—a straight line being the shortest distance between two points forming one of the guiding principles behind the Whitley's design. The rectangular, low aspect-ratio wing, with its very thick, high-lift section, was built up around a single, enormously strong box-spar of corrugated light alloy sheet externally stiffened by a series of bracing ribs. The wing leading edge and box-spar were covered with flush-riveted smooth metal sheet, and the trailing edge was fabric. The considerable physical depth of the wing enabled the leading edges to house the main fuel tanks outboard of the engines, each wing housing 185 Imp.gal., while the leading edge between the engines and fuselage was occupied by an oil tank. Aft of the oil tank were fourteen small bomb cells which supplemented the fuselage bomb-bays.

At the time the Whitley's design was initiated, flaps had not made their universal appearance, and in order to provide the optimum ground angle to reduce the landing float and run, the wing was given an 8.5° angle of incidence with the result that the engines were canted markedly upwards in relation to the centre line of the fuselage. This explained the Whitley's characteristic nose-down "sit" in normal flight. Before prototype construction was completed, however, hydraulically-operated split flaps had joined the Frise-type ailerons on the wing trailing edges.

The depth of the fuselage, which was built in three sections, was determined primarily by the size of the Armstrong Whitworth manually-operated turrets installed in the nose and tail plus the additional height demanded by the pilot's windscreen, and its structure consisted of a flat-sided metal monocoque covered with smooth Alclad sheet riveted to longitudinal stringers which were supported by open-section hoops. A 154 Imp.gal. fuel tank was installed in the fuselage above the spar, and the two separate bomb-bays had wooden-framed, metal-covered doors which were opened by the weight of the bombs and were closed by elastic ropes. Provision was made for

The Whitley II (below) differed from the Whitley I in having 920 h.p. Tiger VIIIs in place of the Tiger IXs. The first squadron to operate the Whitley was No. 10 at Dishforth, and one of this unit's Whitley Is (the sixth production aircraft) is illustrated on the right.

a crew of five comprising the pilot, co-pilot/navigator, wireless operator, forward gunner/bombardier, and tail gunner.

The first prototype Whitley (K4586), powered by two 795 h.p. Armstrong Siddeley Tiger IX moderately supercharged fourteen-cylinder two-row radial air-cooled engines, was flown for the first time from Baginton on March 17, 1936, with Armstrong Whitworth's chief test pilot, A. C. Campbell Orde, at the controls. The prototype Whitley, which was the first aircraft to be fitted with de Havilland three-bladed two-position variable-pitch airscrews, attained maximum speeds of 192 m.p.h. at 7,000 feet and 186 m.p.h. at 15,000 feet. At sixty-six per cent power it cruised at 160 m.p.h. at 15,000 feet, and its maximum range was 1,250 miles. Service ceiling was 19,200 feet, and an altitude of 15,000 feet was attained in 27.4 minutes.

Meanwhile the Air Ministry had decided to adopt the Whitley for the re-equipment of the heavy bomber squadrons, and in August 1935, some seven months before the prototype's initial flight, had placed a contract for eighty production machines, the first of these (K7183) leaving the assembly line in March 1937. A second prototype (K4587) preceded the first production Whitley I, and this was delivered to the Royal Aircraft Establishment for trials. The Whitley I immediately began to replace the Heyfords

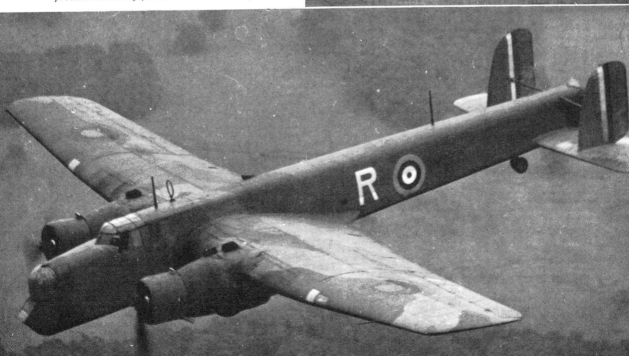

THE ARMSTRONG WHITWORTH WHITLEY

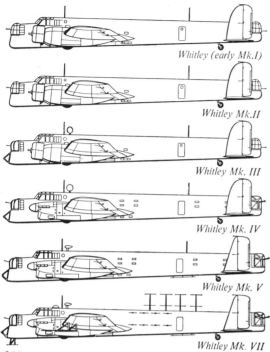

Whitley (early Mk.I)

Whitley Mk.II

Whitley Mk. III

Whitley Mk. IV

Whitley Mk. V

Whitley Mk. VII

of No. 10 Squadron, based at Dishforth, Yorks, and three months later this squadron was to come under the command of No. 4 Bomber Group which, ultimately equipped entirely with Whitleys and commanded by Air Commodore A. T. Harris (later Air Marshal Sir Arthur "Bomber" Harris and Commander-in-Chief of R.A.F. Bomber Command), was to become the only specialist night-bombing group possessed by any air arm at the outbreak of the Second World War.

The Whitley I differed little from the prototypes. It possessed an empty weight of 14,275 lb., and normal and maximum loaded weights of 21,660 lb. and 23,500 lb. respectively. Defensive armament comprised a single 0.303-in. Vickers machine gun in each of the manually-operated Armstrong Whitworth nose and tail turrets, and a total bomb load of 3,365 lb. could be carried. At an early stage in the bomber's production life it was found desirable to introduce dihedral on the outboard wing panels to improve overall stability, and this modification was applied on the production line after the completion of the first few machines, these being retroactively modified. The twenty-sixth production Whitley I (K7208) was modified to permit it to operate at an all-up weight of 33,500 lb.—10,000 lb. above the normal maximum loaded weight—with which it had a maximum range of 1,940 miles. This aircraft, together with the

twenty-seventh Whitley I (K7209), was eventually converted as a prototype of the Merlin-engined Whitley IV, while the twenty-ninth Whitley I (K7211) was successively modified as a prototype Mk.III and then as a prototype Mk.IV.

Only thirty-four Whitley I bombers were completed before production gave place to the Whitley II which entered squadron service in January 1938. The Whitley II, around which specification B.21/35 was framed, differed from the initial production model in having 920 h.p. Tiger VIII engines equipped with two-speed superchargers which markedly improved the bomber's performance. Maximum speed at 15,000 feet was raised to 215 m.p.h., and cruising speed at the same altitude was 177 m.p.h. Maximum range was 1,315 miles, service ceiling was boosted to 23,000 feet, and an altitude of 15,000 feet was reached in 23.5 minutes.

While development of the Whitley was proceeding, Armstrong Whitworth's design team was also engaged in work on the A.W.39, a proposed heavy bomber to specification B.1/35. Derived from the Whitley, the A.W.39 was to have had two 1,185 h.p. Armstrong Siddeley Deerhound twenty-one cylinder three-row radial air-cooled engines with two-stage superchargers buried in its wings, and although no development contract for this bomber was received by the company, a pair of Deerhounds were eventually installed for air tests in the twenty-seventh production Whitley II (K7243). In the event, the Deerhound was abandoned owing to difficulties associated with the adequate cooling of the rear row of cylinders, but the Deerhound-Whitley test-bed was eventually flown on several occasions by Eric Greenwood during 1940, but nearly every flight terminated in an emergency landing as a result of the engines over-heating.

With the delivery of the forty-sixth Whitley II (K7262) in the summer of 1938, thus completing the initial production order, work commenced on the improved Whitley III under a second contract for eighty aircraft placed with the company in 1936. The twenty-ninth Whitley I (K7211) served as a prototype for the Mk.III around which specification B.20/36 was prepared. The most important innovation in the Whitley III from the defensive viewpoint was the replacement of the manually-operated Armstrong Whitworth nose turret with its single Vickers gun by a similarly armed Nash and Thompson powered turret. The old Armstrong Whitworth manually-operated tail turret was retained, but to afford some measure of protection from attacks outside the traverse of its gun, a ventral "dustbin", retractable and rotatable through a full 360° and mounting twin

FINISH AND INSIGNIA: *The Armstrong Whitworth Whitley Mk.V (Z6635) illustrated on the opposite page was operated by No. 51 (York) Squadron and was finished matt black overall. However, part of the black finish had worn away along the top of the fuselage, the original dark green and dark earth camouflage showing through. The B.T.R. de-icers on wing, tailplane and tail fin leading edges were* *putty-chrome yellow in colour. The squadron code letters ("MH") and individual aircraft letter ("O") were painted in grey, as was also the serial number. Slightly modified "A.2" type roundels appeared on the fuselage sides, the yellow outline being thicker than the outer blue circle, and the white circle being darkened, and standard "B" type blue-red roundels appeared on the upper surface of the wings.*

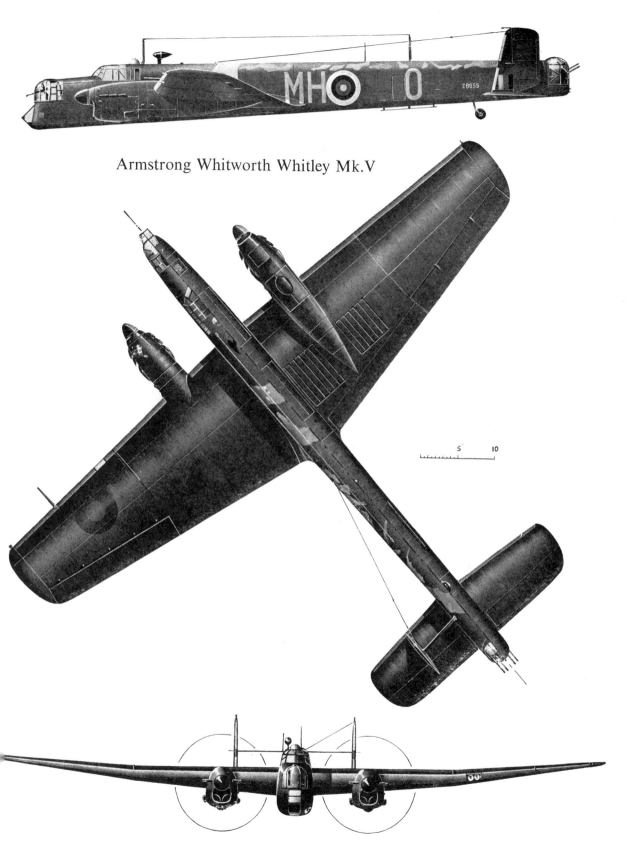

Armstrong Whitworth Whitley Mk.V

The Whitley V was powered by two Merlin X engines, and deliveries commenced early in 1939 with N1345 (illustrated above). The first Whitley Vs reached the squadrons of No. 4 Group a month before the Second World War began.

0.303-in. Browning machine guns, was installed in the aft fuselage. Since this "dustbin" weighed half a ton and, when lowered, drastically reduced speed at a critical time during combat, it was never used, although its "well" was subsequently to prove useful as a dropping hatch for paratroops.

In addition to the modified defensive armament, the Whitley III had new bomb racks to accommodate bombs of larger calibre, and increased dihedral on the wing outer panels, and the first bombers of this type were delivered in August 1938. Such had been the pace of combat aircraft development in the previous three years, however, that the Whitley III was already bordering on the obsolescent. Nevertheless, to the Whitley III went the honour of undertaking Bomber Command's first operation over Germany on the first night of the War, ten Whitley IIIs from Nos. 51 and 58 Squadrons operating from Leconfield dropping thirteen tons of leaflets on Bremen, Hamburg and the Ruhr. This was the first of many similar "bumph raids", as the Whitley crews dubbed these sorties, which characterized the so-called "phoney war", but not so many months later the Whitleys of No. 4 Group were to be carrying far less innocuous cargoes on their nocturnal visits to enemy territory.

By the time the eightieth and last Whitley III (K9015) had been delivered late in 1938, the bomber had taken on a new lease of life with the substitution of twelve-cylinder, liquid-cooled Merlin engines for the air-cooled Tigers. Three Whitley Is (K7208, K7209, and K7211) had been re-engined to serve as prototypes for the production Whitley IV which received Rolls-Royce Merlin IV engines each rated at 1,030 h.p. for take-off and 990 h.p. at 12,250 feet, and driving Rotol constant-speed airscrews. Forty Whitley IVs (K9016 to K9055) had been ordered in 1936, and the first of these reached the squadrons in May 1939. Apart from the liquid-cooled engines, the Whitley IV differed from its predecessors in several respects. From the viewpoint of defence, the most important innovation was the provision of a new power-operated Nash and Thompson tail turret mounting what was, for its time, the phenomenal armament of four 0.303-in. Browning machine guns.

These provided the Whitley IV with the most vicious tail sting of any bomber extant. A few early Whitley IVs did, however, retain the old manually-operated Armstrong Whitworth tail turret.

Fuel capacity was supplemented by the installation of two 93 Imp.gal. tanks in the wings, increasing the standard tankage to 705 Imp.gal., and another change was the fitting of a Plexiglas "chin" extension for the bombardier. This replaced the flush-fitting panel of earlier marks. With the substantial increase in power afforded by the Merlins, the Whitley IV possessed a markedly improved all-round performance. Maximum speed was 245 m.p.h. at 16,250 feet, and maximum cruising speed was 215 m.p.h. at 15,000 ft., this altitude being attained in sixteen minutes. Normal cruising range was 1,250 miles, but this could be extended to 1,800 miles with auxiliary fuel tanks in the fuselage, and empty and normal loaded weights were 17,520 lb. and 25,900 lb. respectively. The Merlin-engined Whitley retained the docility of the Tiger-engined machines in the air, although it could be something of a handful on take-off owing to a marked swing to port which could not be held satisfactorily on the rudders. This could be corrected by combinations of throttle and rudder, but the Whitley often took to the air in a crabwise fashion.

With the availability of the Merlin X engine rated at 1,075 h.p. for take-off and 1,130 h.p. at 5,250 feet, this power plant was installed in seven Whitley IV airframes which then became known as Mk.IVAs. Three Whitley IVs of No. 10 Squadron claimed the distinction of being the first British bombers to visit Berlin when they made a "bumphlet raid" on the German capital on October 1, 1939.

The largest pre-war production contract for the Whitley was placed in 1938, this calling for 302 examples of what was to prove the most important variant of the basic design, the Mk.V. Like the Whitley IVA, the Mk.V was powered by a pair of Merlin X engines, and deliveries (commencing with N1345) began early in 1939, the first bombers of this type reaching the squadrons of No. 4 Group a month before hostilities commenced. Externally, the Whitley V differed little from the Mk.IVA. In order to improve the field of fire of the tail turret, an extra section was installed aft of the rearmost fuselage frame, increasing overall length by fifteen inches, the tail fins and rudders were redesigned, and rubber de-icing boots were fitted along the wing leading edges. In general, performance differed little from that of the Mk.IVA, but normal loaded weight was increased to 28,200 lb., while maximum loaded weight rose to 33,500 lb.

When war was declared on September 3, 1939, six squadrons of Whitleys were ready for operations with Bomber Command's No. 4 Group, and, apart from No. 77 Squadron which had received the first Whitley Vs, these were equipped with Whitley IIIs and IVs. The Whitley's first wartime tasks were leaflet-dropping and security patrols over the German mine-laying seaplane bases at Borkum, Nordeney and Sylt, and it was not until the night of March 19-20, 1940, that Whitleys dropped the first bombs on German soil when thirty Whitley Vs drawn from Nos. 10, 51, 77 and 102 Squadrons, accompanied by a force of twenty Hampdens from No. 5 Group, attacked the seaplane base at Hornum. Seven weeks later, with the termination of the "phoney war" by the German offensive on the Western Front, Whitleys again joined forces with Hampdens for an attack on the railway junction at München Gladbach, dropping the first bombs on the German mainland. Soon Whitleys were visiting nearly all the important targets in Germany, and performing many noteworthy long-range missions, such as that on June 11, 1940, when Whitleys from Nos. 10, 51, 58, 77 and 102 Squadrons flew across the Alps to Turin and Genoa, becoming the first British bombers to raid targets in Italy. Whitleys penetrated deep into Austria and Czechoslovakia, and on some occasions even over Polish territory.

On May 15, 1940, representatives of the new Ministry of Aircraft Production, which had been established under Lord Beaverbrook, agreed with members of the Air Staff that complete production priority should be given to five selected warplanes, and one of these was the Whitley. An order for a further 150 Whitley Vs had been placed in 1939, but no fewer than 1,170 additional machines were now ordered, and production tempo rose rapidly, reaching a peak of twelve machines a week in 1942. Plans were prepared for the production of the Whitley VI with Merlin XX "power eggs", but, in the event, this version did not materialise.

Meanwhile, the Whitley's substantial endurance had commended it for the task of maritime reconnaissance, and in the autumn of 1940 when this bomber supplanted the Ansons of No. 502 Squadron based at Aldergrove, it embarked upon a new career with R.A.F. Coastal Command, a career which had been initiated when No. 58 Squadron was temporarily loaned to Coastal Command at the end of September 1939. No. 502 Squadron initially used the standard bomber version of the Whitley, and was

joined by the Whitleys of No. 612 Squadron in March 1941, the latter unit operating anti-submarine patrols from Reykjavik, Iceland. The success of the Whitley in the maritime reconnaissance role led to the appearance, by the end of 1941, of a modified version of the Whitley V intended specifically for Coastal Command use. Designated Whitley VII, this variant was first issued to No. 502 Squadron and was the first aircraft to carry the long-range A.S.V. Mk.II air-to-surface-vessel radar. The prototype (P4949) was a converted Mk.V.

The Whitley VII, which carried six crew members, undertook long and often hazardous patrols over hundreds of miles of ocean, and was frequently engaged by Arado Ar 196 floatplanes and Junkers Ju 88 fighters over the Bay of Biscay. Empty weight had risen to 19,605 lb., and its loaded weight of 33,950 lb., combined with the wealth of "Christmas trees" of its A.S.V. radar, reduced its minimum speed to 215 m.p.h. at 16,400 ft., its cruising speed to 195 m.p.h. at 15,000 ft., and its ability to remain aloft on one engine. Fuel capacity was increased to 969 Imp.gal. (normal) and 1,101 Imp.gal. (maximum), resulting in a maximum range of 2,300 miles. The first definite victim of the Whitley VII was U-206 which was sunk in the Bay of Biscay on November 30, 1941, by an aircraft of No. 502 Squadron, this being Coastal Command's first A.S.V. "kill".

Whitley Vs were finally retired from Bomber Command in the spring of 1942, performing their last operation on April 29th of that year with an attack on Ostend, and a few months later the last Whitley VIIs were retired from operational service with Coastal Command. During the Whitley's distinguished career many of the R.A.F.'s leading bomber aces had flown this type on their first operations. Surprisingly, the Whitley was still being employed as late as the Spring of 1943 in the role with which it initiated its operational career—that of leaflet dropping. It also made notable contributions in the roles of paratroop-trainer and glider-tug with the Airborne Forces. All marks of Whitley, apart from the Mk.VII, saw service at No. 1 Parachute Training School at Ringway, Manchester, and Whitleys carried paratroops operationally during *Operation Colossus* which took place on February 10, 1941, when a raiding party destroyed an aqueduct at Tragino in Italy. A year later, on February 27-28, 1942, the Whitleys of No. 51 Squadron carried paratroops on the famous Bruneval raid in which airborne troops captured a complete *Wurzburg* radar installation. With their tail turrets removed and fitted with a metal towing yoke Whitley Vs served as tugs for Horsa gliders at No. 21 Heavy Glider Conversion Unit at Brize Norton, and in mid-1942 fifteen Whitley Vs were converted for use as freighters by the British Overseas Airways Corporation, among their activities being the carriage of essential freight into beleaguered Malta. Three Whitleys were used by the Royal Aircraft Establishment for trials with

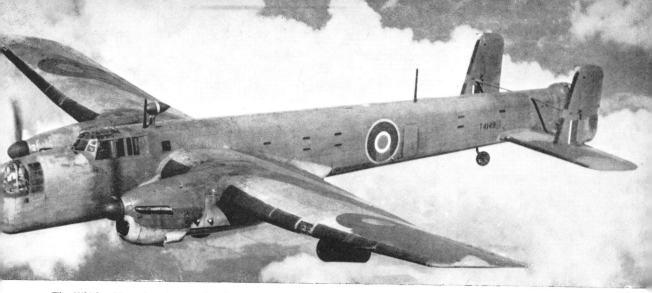

The Whitley V numbered among its duties those of leaflet, supply and agent dropping, and the machine illustrated (T4149) has supply containers mounted underwing.

braking parachutes, and another tested Rocket-Assisted-Take-Off packs.

The 1,824th and last Whitley (1,476 of which were Mk.Vs and 146 being Mk.VIIs) left the Baginton assembly line on July 12, 1943, this aircraft remaining at the factory as a test-bed, the last machine for the R.A.F. having been delivered on June 6, 1943. During its career, it had been operated by Nos. 7, 10, 51, 58, 76, 77, 78, 97, 102, 103 and 166 Squadrons with Bomber Command, by Nos. 77, 502 and 612 Squadrons with Coastal Command, by Nos. 295, 296 and 299 Squadrons in the transport role, and on special duties by Nos. 138 and 161 Squadrons. It had accumulated a long line of technical and operational

The Whitley VII was used extensively for maritime reconnaissance by Coastal Command. This aircraft was the first to carry the long-range A.S.V. Mk.II air-to-surface-vessel radar. Whitley VII (LA794) is illustrated below.

"firsts", and although the "Flying Barn Door" never enjoyed the popular acclaim that was to be the lot of its successors, its appearance in service was the equal in significance to that of any bomber destined to join R.A.F. Bomber Command during the years of the Second World War.

Armstrong Whitworth Whitley Mk.V

Dimensions: Span, 84 ft. 0 in.; length, 72 ft. 6 in.; height, 15 ft. 0 in.; wing area, 1,138 sq. ft.

Armament: One 0.303-in. machine gun in power-operated Frazer-Nash nose turret and four 0.303-in. machine guns in Frazer-Nash tail turret. Maximum bomb load, 7,000 lb.

Power Plants: Two Rolls-Royce Merlin X twelve-cylinder 60° Vee liquid-cooled engines each rated at 1,075 h.p. at 3,000 r.p.m. for take-off and 1,130 h.p. at 3,000 r.p.m. at 5,250 ft.

Weights: Empty, 19,350 lb.; normal loaded, 28,200 lb.; maximum overload, 33,500 lb.

Performance: Maximum speed, 228 m.p.h. at 17,750 ft.; maximum cruising speed, 210 m.p.h. at 15,000 ft.; economical cruising speed, 185 m.p.h.; normal cruising range (at economical cruising speed) at 12,000 ft., 1,500 mls.; maximum range (with auxiliary fuel tanks), 2,400 mls. at 12,000 ft.; range with 3,000-lb. bomb load, 1,650 mls., with 7,000-lb. bomb load, 470 mls.; initial climb rate, 800 ft./min.; time to 15,000 ft., 16 min.; normal service ceiling, 17,600 ft.; maximum ceiling, 24,000 ft.

The XB-24 (39-680) was flown for the first time on December 29, 1939, only nine months after the U.S.A.A.C. awarded a development contract for a prototype bomber. In 1940 this aircraft was fitted with self-sealing fuel tanks, armour and other modifications, and the mechanically supercharged R-1830-33 engines were replaced by turbo-supercharged R-1830-41 engines. It was then redesignated XB-24B (right).

THE CONSOLIDATED LIBERATOR

Although each type had its staunch adherents, the Consolidated Liberator was somewhat overshadowed in fame, if not in achievement, by the Boeing Fortress during the Second World War. This was despite the fact that, not only was the Liberator built in considerably larger numbers than the Fortress, it was produced in greater quantities than any other American aircraft. Such a unique production record is all the more remarkable for such a large, four-engined aircraft, and the Liberator operated over more operational fronts for a considerably longer period, and was produced in a greater variety of versions than any other Allied or enemy bomber.

By comparison with the Fortress, the Liberator was indeed an ugly duckling, with its deep, slab-sided fuselage and immense barndoor-like vertical tail surfaces, features hardly indicative of speed and agility, but one of the prime virtues of the Liberator, and one which invariably hallmarks a great warplane, was its versatility. In addition to strategic bombing, it was used with equal facility for maritime reconnaissance and anti-submarine operations, passenger and freight transportation, as a flying tanker, and for photographic-reconnaissance, as well as for many other duties. It was this quality, in fact, which largely accounted for the extraordinary total of 18,188 Liberators and Liberator variants constructed for the U.S.A.A.F. between delivery of the first production aircraft in June 1941, and the closing down of the last assembly line on May 31, 1945. The peak inventory of Liberators in the U.S.A.A.F. of 6,043 machines in September 1944, was, however,

only 1,500 or so more than the equivalent figure for the Fortress, but this was due to the fact that many Liberators had been diverted from the A.A.F. to the U.S. Navy, while the type also served with the R.A.F., the R.A.A.F., the S.A.A.F., and units of many other Allied nations.

While generally bracketed in historical perspective with the Fortress, the Liberator represented a later era of design which began with the intervention of President Roosevelt on behalf of American air power following the Munich Crisis of 1938. The Consolidated Aircraft Company had earlier commenced the study of multi-engined bomber designs, and when realistic finances for such aircraft appeared to be forthcoming, project work was intensified. The U.S. aircraft industry received much information on the development of large military aircraft from the original "Project A" programme, embracing the Boeing XB-15, B-17 Fortress and Douglas XB-19, and several companies, including Consolidated, had prepared detailed studies for future exploitation.

In January 1939 the Consolidated company was invited by General Arnold to prepare a design study for a bomber with a superior performance to that of the B-17 Fortress. The specification demanded a maximum speed exceeding 300 m.p.h., a range of some

The last of seven YB-24s (40-702) for service evaluation, later redesignated RB-24.

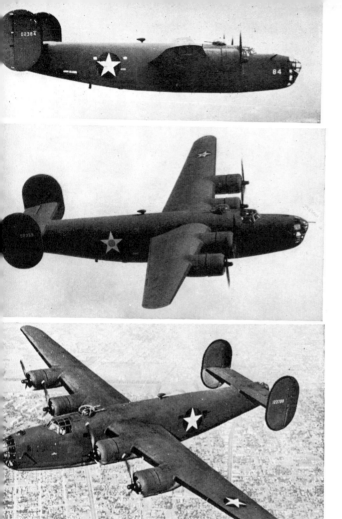

stowage of the main undercarriage members in the mainplanes, the wheels being faired by small underwing blisters when retracted. Following the example of the large Douglas XB-19, the Model 32 employed a nosewheel undercarriage, the short front unit retracting forward into the fuselage, and the long mainwheel legs folding outwards into their open wing stowage. After some deliberation, twin fin-and-rudder assemblies were selected for the tail unit of the Model 32, and these were basically similar in design to those evolved for the commercial Model 31 flying boat.

With the high-mounted wing arrangement, the twin vertical tail surfaces of the Model 32 gave adequate stability for precision bombing, although the control qualities of this arrangement were not entirely satisfactory. For good low-speed characteristics, the bomber was fitted with Fowler area-increasing flaps, and with fixed "letter-box" slots on the outer leading edges, although the latter were subsequently found to be unnecessary. The central bomb-bay had provision for up to 8,000 lb. of bombs, and was divided into front and rear compartments for bombs to be stowed vertically. The two sections of the bomb-bay were further divided by a central catwalk, which was also the fuselage keel beam, and a unique type of bomb door was fitted. This comprised two roller-type segments retracting upwards into the fuselage from the keel beam, and offering little additional drag when opened.

Contrasting with those of many contemporary bombers, the fuselage of the Model 32 was extremely commodious, which was one of the main reasons for the Liberator's subsequent adaptability. At that stage of design, however, there was not a great deal of equipment in the fuselage, which had provision for only a few hand-held 0.3-in. machine guns. One of these was mounted in the large transparent nose, which accommodated the navigator and also had an optical panel for a Norden bomb-sight. Removable hatches above, below, and on each side of the fuselage gave access to 0.3-in. Browning gun mountings, and there was a "cupola" for a further gun in the extreme tail of the fuselage.

Because of the advanced lofting practice employed in the Consolidated design department, the XB-24 was ready for its first test flight one day under the nine months stipulated by the contract, and became airborne for the first time on December 29, 1939, at San Diego. By that time, when the threat of war in Europe had become a reality, orders had already been placed by the Air Corps for an initial batch of seven service test YB-24s, and an evaluation quantity of thirty-six B-24As. The French government had committed itself even further on the totally unproven multi-engined bomber, having ordered no less than 120 machines, while in 1940 the British Purchasing Commission added 164 to these contracts.

Flight tests of the XB-24 (Serial No. 39–680), which

3,000 miles, and a ceiling of 35,000 ft. Preliminary engineering data was soon forthcoming from the company, and on the basis of this a contract for a prototype of the proposed bomber was awarded by the Air Corps on March 30, 1939, the aircraft, which was allocated the designation XB-24, to be completed before the end of the year.

Range was the primary aim of the Consolidated design team, led by I. M. Laddon, in producing the Model 32, as the design was labelled by the company. The bomber was designed around a high aspect ratio wing employing the Davis high-lift aerofoil. This aerofoil was claimed to offer twenty-five per cent less profile drag at low speeds, and 10 per cent less at high speeds than conventional sections. In the Model 32, the Davis aerofoil's characteristic reflex curve on the undersurface of the section was located aft of the rear spar, enabling heavy box-spars to be used, together with high aspect ratio and wing loading. The resultant wing structure was stiff, and yet offered the maximum accommodation for fuel. The wing was shoulder-mounted for maximum bomb stowage and easy loading, and although the rest of the design was relatively conventional, an unusual feature was the

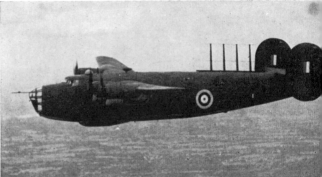

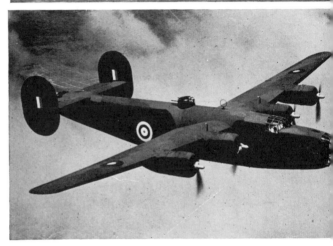

(Right) The last of a batch of twenty Liberator Is (AM929) purchased for the R.A.F., and prior to conversion for Coastal Command; (right, centre) the first Liberator I with A.S.V. radar array and ventral gun pack, and (bottom, right) a Liberator II which had no U.S.A.A.F. counterpart.

was powered by four 1,200 h.p. Pratt and Whitney Twin Wasp R-1830-33 (S3C4-G) fourteen-cylinder radial engines, and had an initial gross weight of approximately 41,000 lb., were successful, but further development of the design was required by the Air Corps. The XB-24 proved to have a maximum speed of 273 m.p.h., which was rather less than contemporary Fortresses, but the range potential of Consolidated's prototype was considerable. During 1940, when the seven YB-24s were delivered, these differing from the XB-24 only in having de-icing boots on wings and tail, an increased gross weight of 46,400 lb., no wing slots, and, initially, airscrew spinners, the collapse of France was followed by the transfer of the French aircraft orders to the British government.

Thus it was that the first bombers to come off the San Diego production lines were Model 32s for the R.A.F., ordered and paid for in hard cash prior to the commencement of Lend-Lease, and delivered under the designation LB-30A (Liberator built to British specifications), with no corresponding Air Corps equivalent. The first R.A.F. Model 32 (AM258), bearing the newly bestowed British name "Liberator" which was later to be adopted by the U.S.A.A.F., made its initial flight on January 17, 1941, and was similar in nearly all respects to the YB-24. This LB-30A was followed by five others (AM259-AM263) which, from March 1941 onwards, were used on the newly instituted Trans-Atlantic Return Ferry Service in the unarmed transport role. Owing to their range, and endurance at 10,000 ft. of 19.25 hours at 193 m.p.h., they were the only aircraft capable of flying non-stop the 2,994-mile route between Prestwick and Montreal. This capacity made possible the opening of a new era in long-range air transport, and operated with civil registrations by B.O.A.C. (AM258: G-AGDR; AM259: G-AGCD; AM262: G-AGHG, and AM263: G-AGDS), the LB-30As continued these vital, although non-operational duties for some considerable time.

The next batch of twenty production aircraft were accepted by the R.A.F. in mid-1941 as Liberator Is (AM910-AM929), and were the first of the type to see operational service. Their long range, light armament but reasonably heavy offensive warload rendered them a natural choice for R.A.F. Coastal Command, for which service they were extensively modified in the United Kingdom. The myriad aerials of an early mark of A.S.V. radar were fitted to the fuselage and wings, and the aircraft's offensive power was considerably enhanced by the addition of a gun pack housing four 20-mm. Hispano cannon which was fitted under the cockpit section of the nose. The standard bomber armament of two 0.3-in. guns in the tail, one under each beam hatch and one in the

ventral tunnel, all in hand-held positions, was retained, together with the operating crew of seven.

Liberator Is first equipped No. 120 Squadron of Coastal Command at Nutt's Corner, Belfast, in June 1941, and with their operating range of some 2,400 miles, almost doubled the reach of Britain's maritime reconnaissance force. They were classified as V.L.R. (Very Long-Range) aircraft, and were the first machines with the ability to close the Atlantic Gap, previously out of reach of Allied air power from Britain or the U.S.A. Apart from its armament and operational equipment, the Liberator I was unchanged in design or performance from the earlier development models, although its operating gross weight was restricted by the R.A.F. to 44,950 lb.

In June 1941 the U.S.A.A.F. took delivery of its first B-24A. Although thirty-eight examples of this model had been ordered, only nine were actually delivered, the remainder being converted on the assembly line to later variants. The B-24A was generally similar to the R.A.F.'s Liberator I, except for its armament of six 0.5-in. machine guns plus twin 0.3-in. guns in the tail, and was similarly powered by R-1830-33 engines. The U.S. military authorities were apparently prepared

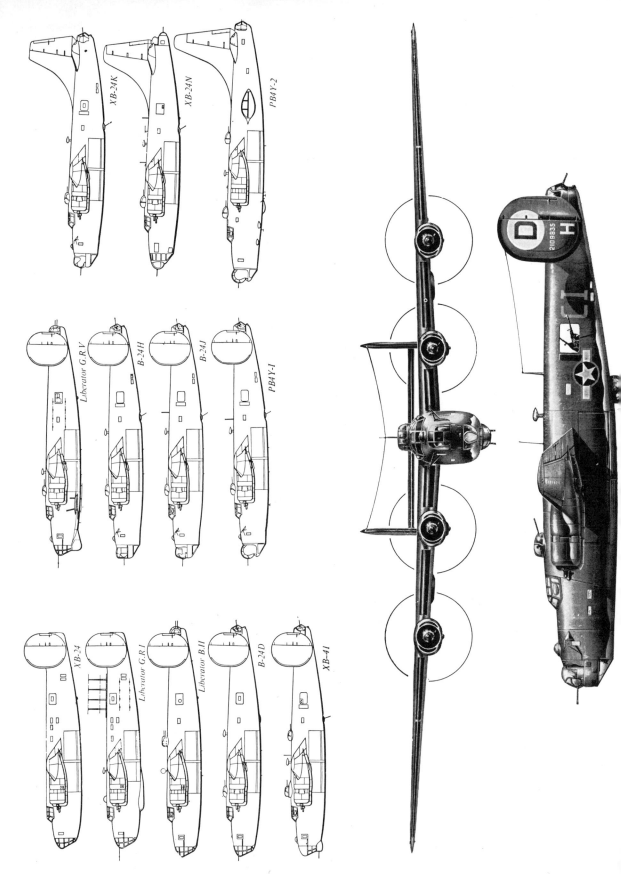

XB-24K

XB-24N

PB4Y-2

Liberator G.R V

B-24H

B-24J

PB4Y-1

XB-24

Liberator G.R I

Liberator B.II

B-24D

XB-41

FINISH AND INSIGNIA: The B-24J-105-CO illustrated belonged to the 392nd Bombardment Group of the Second Air Division's 14th Combat Wing, and had olive drab upper surfaces and dark sea grey under-surfaces. The national insignia (comprising a white five-pointed star on a dark blue circular field superimposed on a white bar, the whole outlined in red) appeared on the port upper and starboard lower wings and fuselage sides. It should be noted that from September 1943 blue supplanted the red

outline of the national insignia. The Bombardment Group's code-letter (i.e., D) appeared in black on a white circular field on the vertical tail surfaces. The serial number appeared in white beneath this symbol, and beneath this serial number appeared the individual aircraft letter (i.e., H), also in white. The squadron letters (i.e., CI) appeared in grey on the fuselage sides. Other B-24J Liberators employed natural metal finish overall.

CONSOLIDATED

B-24J-105-CO LIBERATOR

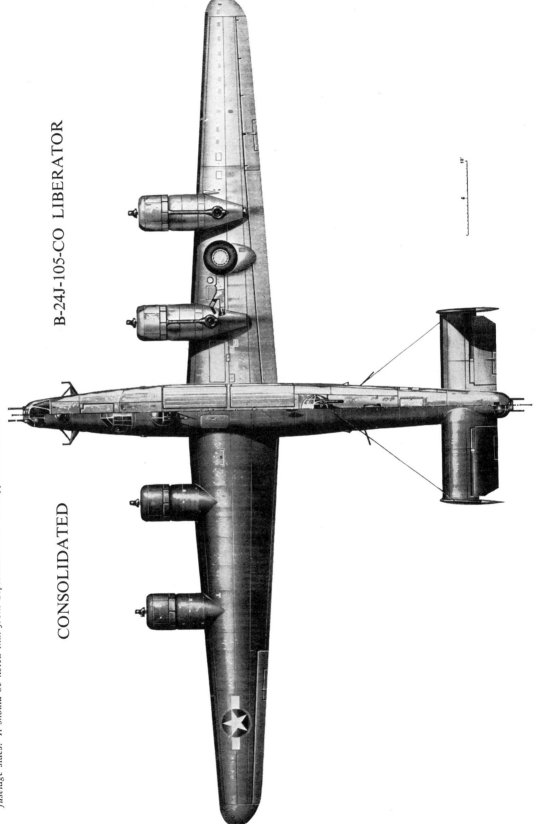

169

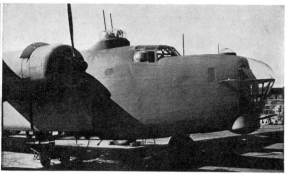

An early B-24D (41-11822) was modified as an experimental long-range escort fighter under the designation XB-41. It carried fourteen 0.5-in. guns but did not achieve operational service.

to operate their B-24As up to a maximum gross weight of some 53,000 lb., which was extremely useful for the transport role immediately embarked upon by these aircraft.

The B-24 seemed destined for a non-operational role for much of its early career, but its transport capabilities were as vital as its offensive power, since no other Allied aircraft could compete with its performance for the strategic carriage of passengers or freight. The pioneer transport service of the newly created Air Corps Ferrying Command was initiated on July 1, 1941, when Lt.-Col. Caleb V. Haynes took off in a B-24A from Bolling Field, Washington, for a North Atlantic schedule, and in September two more of these aircraft carried part of the Harriman Mission to Moscow, via the United Kingdom. The last leg of the flight to Moscow involved a non-stop distance of 3,150 miles, and from Moscow one of the B-24As continued for a complete global flight, with calls at Middle Eastern airfields, India, Singapore, Darwin, Port Moresby, Wake Island, Hawaii and Washington. The other B-24A returned to the U.S.A. through Cairo, Central Africa, the South Atlantic, and up through Brazil, so that both aircraft established invaluable information on ferry routes to be used after the U.S.A. had entered the war, in December 1941.

Just before America's entry into the Second World War, it was arranged for sixteen Liberators to be diverted from scheduled delivery to the R.A.F. in the United Kingdom to the Middle East. American Ferrying Command crews were to be used for this operation, and the first aircraft of the batch left Bolling Field on November 20th. This machine was wrecked on arrival, but four others arrived in Cairo before America's entry into the war froze the remainder for transfer to the Pacific Theatre. A few months later, however, deliveries of an improved Liberator model to the R.A.F. in the Middle East commenced. This, the Liberator II, equipped Nos. 159 and 160 Squadrons which became the first bomber units to operate this type of aircraft.

The Liberator II had no U.S.A.A.F. counterpart, but differed from the first mark of the British-specified aircraft only in having increased armament, and some revised internal equipment. Its main features were the insertion of an additional section in the fuselage nose ahead of the cockpit, increasing the overall length by 2 ft. 7 in. to 66 ft. 4 in., and the replacement of some of the hand-held gun positions in the fuselage by two Boulton Paul power-operated turrets, each housing four 0.303-in. Browning machine guns. One turret was installed in the extreme rear fuselage, while the other was installed in the mid-upper position. Additional armament comprised two 0.303-in. guns in the beam positions, and a forward-firing gun of similar calibre in the nose. The bomb load was increased slightly, and the gross weight was raised to 46,250 lb. The Hamilton Hydromatic airscrews of the Liberator I were replaced by airscrews of Curtiss Electric type, with their blade pitch-change motors in longer hub fairings, and the maximum speed was reduced to 263 m.p.h. owing to the additional drag offered by the turrets. The service ceiling was, however, raised from 21,200 ft. to 24,000 ft., and the maximum crew was increased to ten members.

In all, 139 Liberator IIs (AL503-AL641) were purchased by Britain, and equipped Coastal Command's No. 120 Squadron, and later Nos. 59 and 86 Squadrons of this arm, in addition to the previously-mentioned squadrons in the Middle East. In fact, the Liberator II can be looked upon as the first operationally effective bomber variant of the basic design, although some aircraft of this series were delivered without armament, under the designation LB-30, for use on transport duties with the Return Ferry Service and B.O.A.C., and, later in the war, by Qantas. The most famous LB-30 was AL504, named "Commando", which became the personal transport of the British Prime Minister, Winston Churchill, who made many epoch-marking journeys in this aircraft during the war. It is a little-known fact that fifteen LB-30s were commandeered by the U.S.A.A.F. at around the time of the Pearl Harbour attack and, still retaining their R.A.F. serial numbers, were hurriedly flown by the 7th Bombardment Group from McDill Field, Florida, to the Pacific Theatre in late 1941. In April 1942 two LB-30s were assigned to the South-West Pacific ferry route for the return of ferry crews from Australia and other bases to the U.S.A.

One of the handful of early series B-24s in service

with the U.S.A.A.F. had reached Hawaii by December 5, 1941, where its task was the photographic reconnaissance—*before* the entry of the U.S.A. into the war—of Japanese military installations in the Marshall and Caroline islands. Two of these aircraft, specially equipped for high-altitude photography, had been scheduled, in mid-November, to depart for the Philippines for this task, with instructions to avoid Japanese aircraft while using every possible means of self-preservation if attacked. Only one had arrived, however, by the time the Japanese attacked Pearl Harbour, and it was held at Hawaii to await the arrival of satisfactory armament until after the outbreak of hostilities with Japan.

Development of the original XB-24 prototype resulted, in 1940, in the flight trials of the XB-24B. Apart from the installation of self-sealing fuel tanks, armour and other internal modifications, the main difference from previous Model 32s was the replacement of the mechanically-supercharged R-1830-33 (S3C4-G) engines by turbo-supercharged R-1830-41 (S4C4-G) units. The turbo-superchargers were accommodated on the lower surface of each engine nacelle, which, because of the relocation of the oil coolers in the flanks of the front cowlings, took on the elliptical shape which was to become one of the Liberator's characteristic features. With turbo-superchargers fitted, the original take-off power of 1,200 h.p. could be maintained to well above 20,000 ft., resulting in an increase in maximum speed from the 273 m.p.h. of the XB-24 to 310 m.p.h. From the XB-24B stemmed a small production batch of nine B-24Cs, which reverted to Hamilton Hydromatic airscrews, and had additional armament in the form of a Martin dorsal turret and a Consolidated tail turret, each mounting two 0.5-in. machine guns.

Many Liberators served with R.A.F. Coastal Command, and B-24Ds retaining their original defensive armament, with the exception of the "ball"-type ventral turret which was replaced by a retractable radome, were designated Liberator IIIAs (below). This Liberator V (FL927/C), modified from a B-24D, featured an experimental rocket projectile installation on stub wings (right).

Unlike the dorsal turret installation on British Liberator IIs, the B-24C and subsequent variants had the electrically-operated Martin turret mounted above the forward fuselage, just aft of the cockpit. The B-24C retained the original hand-operated armament in nose and beam positions.

Immediately evolved from the B-24C was the first large-scale production variant of the Model 32, the B-24D, which was also the first variant to enter operational service with U.S.A.A.F. bombing units. Apart from minor changes attendant to the installation of 1,200 h.p. R-1830-43 engines, the B-24D was placed in production to a standard similar to that of its predecessor, and among several factories opened with government assistance to meet the required target of 2,000 heavy bombers per month. From 1941 onwards, 2,425 B-24Ds were built by Consolidated at San Diego (CO), 303 by Consolidated at Fort Worth (CF), and ten by Douglas at Tulsa (DT). The Ford Motor Company was also requested, in 1941, to aid the B-24 production programme with an enormous new plant at Willow Run, where it was initially planned to build one hundred sets of components per month for assembly elsewhere. As with the other companies in the B-24 "pool", this programme was later greatly expanded, and the Ford plant at Willow Run was committed to producing no fewer than two hundred complete B-24s each month, plus a further 150 in the form of "knock-down" assemblies.

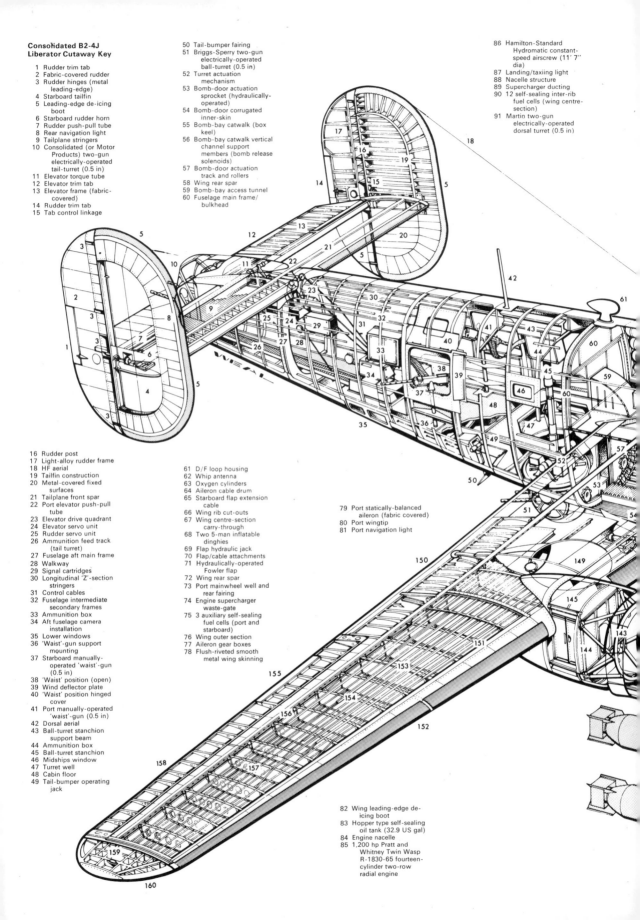

**Consolidated B2-4J
Liberator Cutaway Key**

1 Rudder trim tab
2 Fabric-covered rudder
3 Rudder hinges (metal leading-edge)
4 Starboard tailfin
5 Leading-edge de-icing boot
6 Starboard rudder horn
7 Rudder push-pull tube
8 Rear navigation light
9 Tailplane stringers
10 Consolidated (or Motor Products) two-gun electrically-operated tail-turret (0.5 in)
11 Elevator torque tube
12 Elevator trim tab
13 Elevator frame (fabric-covered)
14 Rudder trim tab
15 Tab control linkage

16 Rudder post
17 Light-alloy rudder frame
18 HF aerial
19 Tailfin construction
20 Metal-covered fixed surfaces
21 Tailplane front spar
22 Port elevator push-pull tube
23 Elevator drive quadrant
24 Elevator servo unit
25 Rudder servo unit
26 Ammunition feed track (tail turret)
27 Fuselage aft main frame
28 Walkway
29 Signal cartridges
30 Longitudinal 'Z'-section stringers
31 Control cables
32 Fuselage intermediate secondary frames
33 Ammunition box
34 Aft fuselage camera installation
35 Lower windows
36 'Waist'-gun support mounting
37 Starboard manually-operated 'waist'-gun (0.5 in)
38 'Waist' position (open)
39 Wind deflector plate
40 'Waist' position hinged cover
41 Port manually-operated 'waist'-gun (0.5 in)
42 Dorsal aerial
43 Ball-turret stanchion support beam
44 Ammunition box
45 Ball-turret stanchion
46 Midships window
47 Turret well
48 Cabin floor
49 Tail-bumper operating jack

50 Tail-bumper fairing
51 Briggs-Sperry two-gun electrically-operated ball-turret (0.5 in)
52 Turret actuation mechanism
53 Bomb-door actuation sprocket (hydraulically-operated)
54 Bomb-door corrugated inner-skin
55 Bomb-bay catwalk (box keel)
56 Bomb-bay catwalk vertical channel support members (bomb release solenoids)
57 Bomb-door actuation track and rollers
58 Wing rear spar
59 Bomb-bay access tunnel
60 Fuselage main frame/bulkhead

61 D/F loop housing
62 Whip antenna
63 Oxygen cylinders
64 Aileron cable drum
65 Starboard flap extension cable
66 Wing rib cut-outs
67 Wing centre-section carry-through
68 Two 5-man inflatable dinghies
69 Flap hydraulic jack
70 Flap/cable attachments
71 Hydraulically-operated Fowler flap
72 Wing rear spar
73 Port mainwheel well and rear fairing
74 Engine supercharger waste-gate
75 3 auxiliary self-sealing fuel cells (port and starboard)
76 Wing outer section
77 Aileron gear boxes
78 Flush-riveted smooth metal wing skinning

79 Port statically-balanced aileron (fabric covered)
80 Port wingtip
81 Port navigation light

82 Wing leading-edge de-icing boot
83 Hopper type self-sealing oil tank (32.9 US gal)
84 Engine nacelle
85 1,200 hp Pratt and Whitney Twin Wasp R-1830-65 fourteen-cylinder two-row radial engine

86 Hamilton-Standard Hydromatic constant-speed airscrew (11' 7" dia)
87 Landing/taxiing light
88 Nacelle structure
89 Supercharger ducting
90 12 self-sealing inter-rib fuel cells (wing centre-section)
91 Martin two-gun electrically-operated dorsal turret (0.5 in)

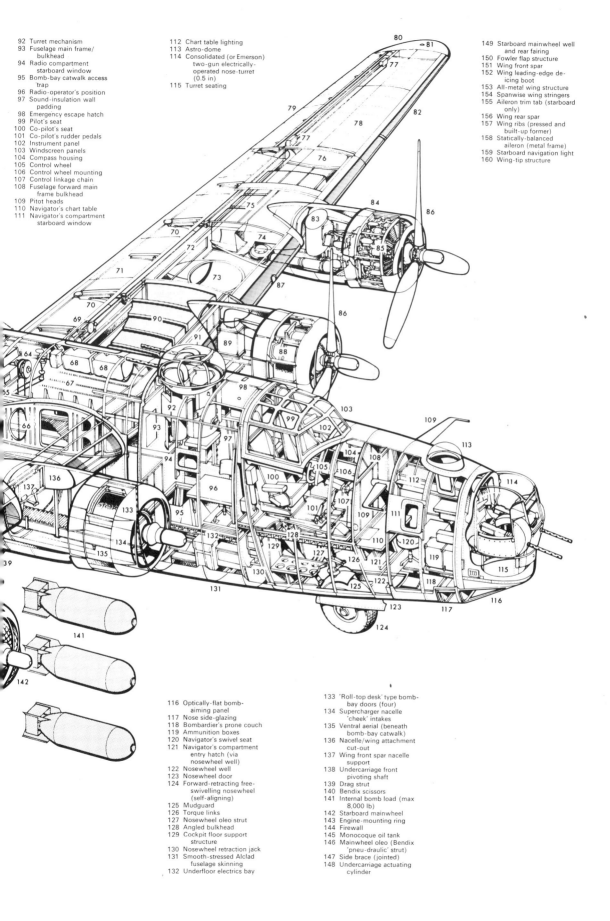

92 Turret mechanism
93 Fuselage main frame/bulkhead
94 Radio compartment starboard window
95 Bomb-bay catwalk access trap
96 Radio-operator's position
97 Sound-insulation wall padding
98 Emergency escape hatch
99 Pilot's seat
100 Co-pilot's seat
101 Co-pilot's rudder pedals
102 Instrument panel
103 Windscreen panels
104 Compass housing
105 Control wheel
106 Control wheel mounting
107 Control linkage chain
108 Fuselage forward main frame bulkhead
109 Pitot heads
110 Navigator's chart table
111 Navigator's compartment starboard window

112 Chart table lighting
113 Astro-dome
114 Consolidated (or Emerson) two-gun electrically-operated nose-turret (0.5 in)
115 Turret seating

149 Starboard mainwheel well and rear fairing
150 Fowler flap structure
151 Wing front spar
152 Wing leading-edge de-icing boot
153 All-metal wing structure
154 Spanwise wing stringers
155 Aileron trim tab (starboard only)
156 Wing rear spar
157 Wing ribs (pressed and built-up former)
158 Statically-balanced aileron (metal frame)
159 Starboard navigation light
160 Wing-tip structure

116 Optically-flat bomb-aiming panel
117 Nose side-glazing
118 Bombardier's prone couch
119 Ammunition boxes
120 Navigator's swivel seat
121 Navigator's compartment entry hatch (via nosewheel well)
122 Nosewheel well
123 Nosewheel door
124 Forward-retracting free-swivelling nosewheel (self-aligning)
125 Mudguard
126 Torque links
127 Nosewheel oleo strut
128 Angled bulkhead
129 Cockpit floor support structure
130 Nosewheel retraction jack
131 Smooth-stressed Alclad fuselage skinning
132 Underfloor electrics bay

133 'Roll-top desk' type bomb-bay doors (four)
134 Supercharger nacelle 'cheek' intakes
135 Ventral aerial (beneath bomb-bay catwalk)
136 Nacelle/wing attachment cut-out
137 Wing front spar nacelle support
138 Undercarriage front pivoting shaft
139 Drag strut
140 Bendix scissors
141 Internal bomb load (max 8,000 lb)
142 Starboard mainwheel
143 Engine-mounting ring
144 Firewall
145 Monocoque oil tank
146 Mainwheel oleo (Bendix 'pneu-draulic' strut)
147 Side brace (jointed)
148 Undercarriage actuating cylinder

A B-24J-145-CO (44-40052) belonging to the 389th Bombardment Group of the U.S. 8th Air Force's Second Air Division.

The first ninety-four B-24Ds produced by Consolidated (to B-24D-15-CO) had only a single 0.5-in. nose gun, with two hundred rounds, plus the two turrets, with four hundred r.p.g. for the dorsal turret, and six hundred r.p.g. for the tail turret. Maximum bomb load was 8,000 lb., made up of four 2,000-lb., eight 1,000-lb., twelve 500-lb., twelve 250-lb., or twenty 100-lb. bombs. The maximum fuel tankage was 1,978 Imp. gal. (2,364 U.S. gal). The aircraft between the B-24D-15 and -20-CO batches had the single hand-operated 0.5-in. gun in the ventral tunnel restored, with 100 rounds, and subsequent Liberators had the maximum fuel capacity increased to 3,009 Imp. gal. (3,614 U.S. gal.) with the addition of auxiliary self-sealing fuel cells in the outer wings, and provision for further tanks in the bomb-bay.

In the production batches between B-24D-25 and -140-CO, two additional 0.5-in. nose guns with 100 r.p.g. were added, plus two waist guns with 250 r.p.g., bringing the total armament to ten 0.5-in. Brownings, while B-10 shackles for eight 1,600-lb. A.P. bombs brought the maximum permissible bomb load to 12,800 lb. This resulted in the war maximum gross weight being increased to a formidable 67,800 lb. at which it was necessary to restrict all manoeuvres to a minimum. Fort Worth equivalents of these San Diego production aircraft were the B-24D-1 to -5-CF, prior to the increased bomb load, and B-24D-10 to -20-CF subsequently.

The next, and final batches of the D-model Liberator, the B-24D-140 to -170-CO, the B-24D-20-CF, and the few B-24D-1 to -5-DT, had slightly modified power plants—R-1830-65s—which still developed 1,200 h.p. at 26,500 ft. Maximum permissible weight had been increased, however, to 71,200 lb. An innovation on the last B-24Ds was the replacement of the hand-held tunnel gun by a retractable Briggs-Sperry electrically-operated "ball" turret containing two 0.5-in. guns with 508 r.p.g. aft of the bomb-bay. This turret was similar to that fitted to later model Fortresses, and appreciably improved the Liberator's defensive capabilities. Some B-24Ds and subsequent models also had an external rack fitted below each inner wing at modification centres for the carriage of two 4,000-lb. bombs on special missions.

Normal take-off weight for combat of the late B-24D series was 64,000 lb. with an 8,000-lb. bomb load, or 60,500 lb. with a 5,000-lb. bomb load. The maximum speed was 303 m.p.h. at 25,000 ft., and with 1,978 Imp. gal. of fuel in the main wing tanks, the range at maximum cruising power became 1,800 miles in seven-and-a-half hours elapsed time. Slight modifications were made to B-24Ds supplied to the R.A.F. in mid-1942, this air arm receiving batches of 249 (BZ711-BZ959) and eleven (LV336-LV346) as the Liberator III. These had the 0.5-in. guns of the B-24D replaced by a single forward-firing 0.303-in. Browning in the nose; two guns of similar calibre in the beam positions, and four more in the Boulton Paul tail turret. Many Liberator IIIs retained the U.S. Martin dorsal turret, with two 0.5-in. guns, while others incorporating American equipment and supplied under Lend-Lease were designated Liberator IIIAs.

Nearly all the Liberator IIIs and IIIAs entered service with R.A.F. Coastal Command in which they proved outstandingly successful, and eventually equipped some twelve squadrons. Other batches of B-24Ds, including thirty-two (FK214-FK-245) and ninety (FL906-FL995) aircraft, were extensively modified for use by Coastal Command, by which they were known as Liberator G.R.Vs. Fitted with extensive radar equipment, including chin and retractable ventral radomes, in addition to A.S.V. aerial arrays, they also had a Leigh Light for detecting surfaced submarines at night, installed under the starboard wing, while a few had eight rocket projectiles mounted four per side on stub wings projecting from the forward fuselage. The Liberator Vs were also distinguished by their increased fuel capacity, at the expense of armour and tank protection, while in most cases the defensive armament comprised one 0.303-in. or 0.5-in. gun in the nose; two 0.5-in. guns in the Martin dorsal turret; two 0.303-in. or one 0.5-in. gun in each beam position, and four 0.303-in. Brownings in the Boulton Paul tail turret. Like all B-24Cs and Ds, the fuselage length was 66 ft. 4 in., but the operational load of bombs or depth charges was reduced to 5,400 lb.

The U.S.A.A.F. also operated the B-24D on anti-submarine duties, initially from bases on the Atlantic seaboard of North America, where fifteen of Anti-Submarine Command's twenty-five squadrons in early 1943 were equipped with radar-carrying Liberators. Six of these squadrons were detached for anti-submarine duties to bases in Newfoundland, North Africa, and England, where they operated with success until the U.S. Navy won permission to take over all anti-submarine Liberators in August 1943. The U.S. Navy had begun to take over some B-24Ds from the A.A.F. deliveries in 1942, and to operate the aircraft on maritime reconnaissance as PB4Y-1s. When the Anti-Submarine Command was disbanded, on August 31, 1943, the A.A.F. exchanged its A.S.V.-equipped Liberators for an equal number of un-modified Liberators from the U.S. Navy, and a month or so later, the two A.A.F. anti-submarine squadrons with these aircraft attached to R.A.F. Coastal Command in the U.K., were replaced by three PB4Y-1 squadrons of the U.S. Navy.

The primary function of the Liberator had already emerged, however, as bombing, and American air combat in the Middle East began in June 1942, with the Halverson Detachment of twenty-three B-24Ds. Commanded by Colonel H. A. Halverson, this task force with picked crews was originally intended for bombing operations from Chinese bases against Japan. On reaching the Middle East, the force had been held, initially on a temporary basis, for a single strike against the Ploesti oilfields in Rumania, but the aircraft and their crews remained in the Middle East for eventual absorption by the U.S. 9th Air Force. The first Ploesti raid, by thirteen of the Halverson B-24Ds, on June 11–12, 1942, was also the first strategic attack of any significance to be executed in World War II by land-based aircraft of the U.S.A.A.F. Taking off from the R.A.F. base at Fayid, in the Egyptian Canal Zone, the Liberators flew all night across the Mediterranean, the Aegean, Greece, and Bulgaria, to Ploesti, meeting virtually no opposition owing to the improbability of the direction of attack,

and dropping their small bomb loads—about 4,000 lb. per aircraft—through cloud at 10,000 ft. Seven aircraft succeeded in reaching Habbaniya, in Iraq, which was the scheduled terminal base, two landing in Syria, and four more in Turkey, where they were interned and later taken over by the Turkish Air Force. This mission proved, without doubt, the long-range effectiveness of the Liberator, but it also alerted the Axis defence system to the possibilities of future attack across the southerly route.

The B-24D Liberators of the 98th and 376th Bombardment Groups, which were the first to operate from the Middle East with these aircraft, continued offensive missions against Axis ground targets in the Western Desert, and shipping in the Mediterranean, moving westwards to a succession of bases in company with the Allied advance. Further north, in Europe, other B-24Ds joined the B-17E Fortresses of the 8th Air Force in England, in the late summer of 1942, and made their operational début over Lille on October 9th. At first, the few Liberators operated in mixed formations with the larger number of Fortresses, and the abortive rate was high, but they continued attacks on U-boat pens, and two squadrons of 8th Air Force Liberators were sent to the south of England to operate on anti-submarine patrols with R.A.F. Coastal Command. In December, another three squadrons of 8th Air Force Liberators were detached to North Africa for three months, leaving only a handful of B-24Ds to operate alongside the British-based Fortresses. The single Liberator Wing in England, however, eventually grew to a complete Air Division of the 8th Air Force, with four combat wings, each of three groups of B-24s. The twelve

(*Immediately below*) *A remarkable wartime example of nasal surgery was this B-24J upon which was grafted the complete nose of a B-17G Fortress.* (*Bottom*) *One B-24E-15-FO was experimentally fitted with remotely-controlled gun barbettes in the fuselage sides.*

Liberator groups of the 2nd Air Division were out-numbered by the forty-one Fortress groups of the 1st and 3rd Air Divisions comprising the remainder of the "Eighth", by April 1945, but they completed some spectacular attacks against Axis targets. Of these, the the most sensational was the second strike against the Ploesti oilfields, on August 1, 1943.

For this mission, the 44th and 93rd Bombardment Groups of the then 2nd Bombardment Wing of the 8th Air Force were sent, in June 1943, after special low-level training, from England to Benghazi, Libya, where they joined two other Liberator groups of the 9th Air Force, the 98th and 376th Bombardment units, plus the new 389th Bombardment Group which had also arrived from the United Kingdom. After a con-siderable amount of further training, 177 Liberators from the five groups took off from their Benghazi bases on August 1st for the 2,700-mile round flight, each carrying 2,581 Imp. gal. (3,100 U.S. gal.) of fuel, and 5,000 lb. of delayed-action bombs and incendiaries. No fighter escort could possibly be provided, and the decision was therefore taken to attack at the lowest possible altitude. Additional armament was provided in the form of an extra nose gun for the lead aircraft, and the dorsal turrets were slightly modified to permit forward firing to quieten the defences on the ground. As an afterthought, the radio operator and flight engineer in each aircraft were given Thompson sub-machine guns to fire out of the waist position windows.

As is well known, the Ploesti raid turned out to be something of a catastrophe for the U.S.A.A.F., de-spite localised damage to certain parts of the vast oilfields, and of the 177 Liberators that set out, fifty-seven were lost, mostly to intense ground fire over the target area. Those which returned were scattered all over the Middle East, and it was some time before the survivors could be reassembled as an effective force.

Because of its extensive range, the Liberator really came into its own in the Pacific theatre, where it re-mained unchallenged from the arrival of the first six LB-30s in January 1942, in time to commence opera-tions as the Allies withdrew from Java, until it was supplemented by the bigger B-29 Superfortress in mid-1944. In addition to bombing attacks, the LB-30s proved useful in evacuating troops to Australia, carry-ing thirty-five passengers per aircraft, but these early Liberators proved vulnerable to Japanese fighter attack, and without superchargers did not perform satisfactorily above 20,000 ft. This situation was rectified late in 1942 with the arrival in the Pacific theatre of the first B-24Ds, and by 1943 Liberators had almost completely replaced Fortresses as the standard U.S.A.A.F. long-range heavy bomber in the area.

Other variants of the basic Model 32 design were by then rolling off the assembly lines in the U.S.A. Following the success of the early Liberators in the transport role, a modified version of the standard bomber was ordered from Consolidated by the A.A.F. for specialized logistics duties. Within the normal fuselage contours were installed a passenger or freight compartment in place of the bomb-bay and rear crew accommodation; the nose and tail gun positions were faired in, and a 6-ft. square door was provided in the port side for loading. Initially adapted from the B-24D, production of the C-87 Liberator Express began at Fort Worth in April 1942, and was subsequently transferred to San Diego in 1944. With accommoda-tion for a crew of five and twenty passengers, 276 C-87s were produced for the A.A.F. Twenty-four of these aircraft, which were distinguishable by a row of windows along the side of the centre fuselage, were also received by the R.A.F. (EW611-EW634) and operated by Transport Command as the Liberator C.VII. In 1943, five C-87s were diverted for flight engineer training, operating as AT-22s before being redesignated TB-24. The U.S. Navy also flew this ubiquitous transport as the RY-2, while a further six machines of a similar type, but powered by R-1830-45 instead of -43 engines, and equipped for the accom-modation of sixteen V.I.P. passengers, with sleeping facilities, were procured by the A.A.F. as the C-87A (U.S.N. RY-1).

The C-87B was an unfulfilled project for an armed transport version with two fixed nose guns, a dorsal turret and a ventral tunnel gun. Another transport variant of the Liberator, designated C-109, played a distinguished part in the Pacific campaign which has, hitherto, received little publicity. When, soon after the entry of the U.S.A. into the war, plans were being made for long-range bombing attacks against targets in Japan from bases, then unbuilt, in China, the problem arose of logistic support for the future B-29 Superfortress force. A particular difficulty was the supply of aviation gasoline to these forward bases, and the decision was made to use a fleet of transport aircraft, modified as flying tankers, to build up a reserve of fuel in advance of the Superfortress force.

The Liberator was selected for this task on the basis of its payload and range performance, and a Ford-built B-24E (generally similar to the B-24D) was modified, late in 1943, to take metal tanks in the nose, above the bomb-bay, and in the bomb-bay itself, with a total capacity of 2,415 Imp. gal. (2,900 U.S. gal.). This aircraft, which had a single hose union for loading and unloading in the side of the fuselage, and utilised a system of inert gas for flooding the tanks as they were emptied to avoid the possibility of an explosion, became the XC-109, and it was followed by several score more B-24Ds and Es modified as tankers. As C-109s, these were adapted by the Glenn Martin and other companies, and Mareng flexible bag tanks were installed to take the fuel. These aircraft were then flown on the hazardous run over the Hump, from India to China, for the initial Superfortress operations against Japan.

Yet another modification of the versatile Liberator, this time for photo-reconnaissance duties, resulted in the XF-7. This was adapted from a B-24D at the Northwest Airlines Modification Centre at St. Paul, Minnesota, in the autumn of 1943. The bomb racks

In 1943 a B-24D-40-CO (42-40234) was experimentally fitted with a single fin-and-rudder assembly as the XB-24K (right). A redesign of the XB-24K for production by Ford resulted in the XB-24N (44-48753). In addition to the XB-24N (above), seven YB-24Ns were completed before Liberator production terminated.

and other extraneous structure in the fuselage were removed, and extra fuel tanks installed in the front section of the bomb-bay. An upholstered cabin aft of the fuel tanks was provided with five windows for cameras. In all, eleven cameras were carried, and normal defensive armament was retained by this and subsequent photo-reconnaissance versions of the Liberator which were used operationally in the Pacific.

In the European theatre of operations, the heavy losses suffered by the American heavy bombers in daylight missions without fighter escort over Germany had resulted, late in 1942, in the proposal to equip both Liberators and Fortresses with extremely powerful armament, and employ them as "destroyers" which would accompany the bomber formations. A single B-24D (41-11822) was accordingly modified to take an additional dorsal turret mid-way along the fuselage, the original forward turret being raised in order to maintain its field of fire. Another twin-gun turret was mounted in the "chin" position on the modified nose, and duplicated mountings in the beam positions brought the total armament of the XB-41, as the escort Liberator was designated, to fourteen 0.5-in. machine guns. Unlike the "destroyer" Fortresses, the XB-41 did not achieve operational service, becoming redundant with the introduction of the American escort fighters.

In 1942, the Liberator lines at Consolidated (San Diego and Fort Worth) and Douglas (Tulsa) had been joined by the massive new Ford plant at Willow Run. This factory commenced operations by turning out 480 late-model "D" type Liberators with modified airscrews as B-24Es. Consolidated also built 144 B-24E Liberators which, with the 167 constructed on the Douglas line, and the Ford-built machines, brought the total of this variant of the Liberator constructed

to 791. Unlike the Ford- and Consolidated-built B-24Es, which had R-1830-65 engines, the Douglas-built aircraft retained the earlier -43 power plants. The R.A.F. reserved the designation "Liberator IV" for the B-24E, but there is no record that any of these aircraft were received in the United Kingdom. Another variant, but one which did not materialise in production form, was the XB-24F. This was a B-24D-CO modified by Consolidated to have a thermal de-icing system instead of the more normal pulsating rubber leading-edge boots.

Late in 1942, yet another Liberator production line came into operation, at the Dallas plant of North American Aviation, which started off by building a few "D" type aircraft with -43 engines and, initially, no ventral armament, as the B-24G-NT. In all, 430 B-24Gs were built, and the B-24G-1 to -5-NT batch were the first Liberators to introduce an upper turret in the nose, replacing the hand-held guns formerly fitted. American heavy bombers had proved vulnerable to head-on attacks by enemy fighters which adopted these tactics because of the excellent rear defensive firepower of the A.A.F. formations. To improve the forward-firing armament of the Liberator, an Emerson or Consolidated power-operated nose turret was introduced, with 600 rounds for each of its twin 0.5-in. calibre machine guns, and the lower part of the nose was also modified to retain optical bomb-aiming facilities. The length of this and subsequent versions was increased by ten inches to 67 ft. 2 in. In the B-24G-10 to -15-NT production batches, R-1830-65

The B-24L differed from the J-model in having a new tail position with two manually-operated guns, and the aircraft on the left is a B-24L-1-CO (44-41436). The last large-scale production model was the B-24M in which the hand-held tail guns were replaced by a lightweight powered turret. The photo above depicts a B-24M-45-CO (44-42691).

engines were introduced, and the offensive load was raised to 12,800 lb. of bombs.

As the B-24H, 738 examples of this Liberator variant were built by Consolidated at Fort Worth (B-24H-1 to -15-CF, and -20 to -30-CF with two 0.5-in. guns in the waist on K.6 mountings with 500 r.p.g.), these aircraft having electrically-operated Emerson nose turrets. Consolidated nose turrets utilising hydraulic power were fitted to the 1,780 and 582 B-24H Liberators built by Ford and Douglas respectively, the K.6 waist mountings being introduced on the final batches between -20 and -30-DT and -FO. All Douglas-built B-24Hs retained the -43 engines, but subsequent to the B-24H-5 production version on other assembly lines, the -65 engine was introduced.

Forty B-24H aircraft (BZ960-BZ999) were initially supplied to the R.A.F. under the designation Liberator VI, being used by both Coastal and Bomber Commands, while subsequent batches equipped fourteen British squadrons in the Far East. Others went to the Middle East where, in all, twelve R.A.F. squadrons operated with Liberators. In British service, the B-24H Liberators retained their Emerson, Martin and Sperry nose, dorsal and ventral turrets, but had the Consolidated tail turret replaced by the standard Boulton Paul unit mounting four 0.303-in. machine guns. The Liberator is probably the only bomber in the history of military aviation to have had four gun turrets each produced by a different company! In R.A.F. Coastal Command service, the "ball" turret was supplanted by retractable A.S.V. radar. One B-24H (42-7127 which commenced life as a B-24E-15-FO) of the A.A.F. was modified to have a unique system of barbettes on each side of the fuselage, controlled from adjacent observation blisters and mounting two 0.5-in. machine guns on each side.

As the version of the Liberator to be built in largest quantities, with 6,678 examples constructed by five contractors, the B-24J differed so little from its im-mediate predecessors that the B-24G-20-NT and the B-24H-DT, -CF, and -FO were redesignated "Js" when the C-1 autopilot and M-9 bomb-sight replaced the former A-5 and S-1 types, respectively. The production breakdown comprised 2,792 B-24J-CO (Blocks 1-210); 1,558 B-24J-CF (Blocks 1-105 and -401); 1,587 B-24J-FO (Blocks 1-20); 536 B-24J-NT (Blocks 1-5), and 205 B-24J-DT (Blocks 1-10). There were various minor differences in equipment between the production batches, but all were powered by the R-1830-65 engine. Those engines installed in later batches enjoyed the improved altitude performance bestowed by the new G.E. B-22 turbo-superchargers.

By September 1944, the U.S.A.A.F. had an operational strength of 6,043 B-24 Liberators, the peak figure for this type which, in the middle of the same year, equipped the record number of 45.5 groups of the U.S.A.A.F. overseas. In American service, the Liberators were concentrated mostly in the Mediterranean and the Pacific, operations in Northern Europe having shown it to be somewhat deficient in defensive armament and armour, as well as alarmingly prone to catching fire as the result of superficial strikes in air combat. The increased weight of the Liberator, which reached a maximum combat figure of 71,400 lb., did not improve its flying characteristics, and by January 1945 Lt.-Gen. J. H. Doolittle, Commander of the 8th Air Force, had expressed a clear preference for the Fortress.

In the Pacific, however, the Liberator reigned unchallenged until the operational début of the Superfortress, and four R.A.A.F. squadrons were formed with Liberators to aid the Allied offensive. The British and Commonwealth designation for the B-24J variant was Liberator B. and G.R.VIII, and something like 1,200 were received by the R.A.F. Many of these were converted for freight-carrying, with their turrets removed, becoming known as Liberators C.VI and C.VIII. Some were also employed for special duties missions, dropping agents and supplies by parachute over Europe and Far Eastern countries on very long-range sorties. Canada also joined Australia and South Africa in using the Liberator which was then operating in every theatre of war. In addition to the basic bomber or general reconnaissance versions, more Liberators were modified for photographic reconnaissance, including B-24Hs as F-7-FOs with eleven cameras; eighty-six B-24Js as F-7As with three cameras in the nose and three others in the bomb-bay, and other B-24Js became F-7Bs with six bomb-bay cameras.

The U.S. Navy's Liberators were designated PB4Y-1s, and with the earlier models the Navy also received some of the later versions, amounting to 977 aircraft in all, the same designation being applied to all variants. These were used for anti-submarine and reconnaissance patrols throughout the war and, modified to take cameras like the A.A.F.'s F-7s, many were destined to remain in U.S. naval service as PB4Y-1Ps until long after the cessation of hostilities. The U.S. Navy equivalents of the B-24J Liberator had modified nose contours resulting from the replacement of the standard Consolidated nose turret by a "bubble" type Aerco turret which also mounted twin 0.5-in. guns. The bomb-aiming panel of naval Liberators was shallower, and protruded slightly from beneath the turret. Perhaps the most remarkable nasal surgery performed on the B-24J, however, concerned a single aircraft on which was grafted the complete nose of a B-17G Fortress, from immediately forward of the cockpit! How, why and where this "shotgun wedding" was performed is not recorded, but the result was truly remarkable.

Wide-scale production continued with the B-24L at the Consolidated (San Diego) and Ford plants, this model being similar to the "J" except for a new tail position with two manually-operated 0.5-in. machine guns. With a wider field of fire, the manual tail position was designed by the Consolidated-Vultee Modification Centre at Tucson. It also saved some 200 lb. in weight. During 1944, 417 B-24Ls were built by Consolidated, and 1,250 by Ford. A few of these aircraft were modified to have the remotely-controlled turrets and sighting stations of the B-29 for training Superfortress gunners, and with their distinctive square-cut, "greenhouse" noses, and chin, dorsal, ventral and tail barbettes, were redesignated RB-24Ls. With additional radar equipment they became TB-24Ls.

The last large-scale production version of the Liberator for the U.S.A.A.F. was the B-24M, in which the hand-held tail guns were replaced by a lightweight power-operated twin-gun turret developed by Motor Products. Apart from the tail turret, this version differed little from the earlier versions, starting with the B-24G. Nine hundred and sixteen B-24Ms were built by Consolidated-Vultee (the Vultee Aircraft company having merged with the Consolidated Aircraft

The U.S. Navy equivalent of the B-24J was the PB4Y-1. The Consolidated nose turret was normally replaced by an Aerco turret.

Corporation in March 1943), including the 6,725th and last Liberator to be built at San Diego, and 1,677 were built by Ford. The remaining A.A.F. versions of the twin-tailed Liberator comprised the XB-24P-CO, modified from a "D" for experimental duties, and the XB-24Q-FO, developed from a B-24L to test a radar-controlled remote gun position in the tail.

It was slightly ironic that, although as early as 1942 the A.A.F. decided that the Liberator would have greater stability with a single fin-and-rudder assembly, it went through its entire operational career with the A.A.F. in its original twin-tailed configuration. In 1943, a B-24D (42-40234) was modified by Ford to have a large, square-cut, single vertical tail, together with more powerful R-1830-75 engines each developing 1,350 h.p. for take-off. The XB-24K, as this variant was designated, was also fitted with the power-operated nose turret of later Liberators, while retaining the standard Consolidated tail turret, and in extensive flight tests proved the A.A.F. contention of improved stability and control. With the single fin-and-rudder assembly and greater power, the XB-24K was 11 m.p.h. faster than previous Liberators, and possessed a greatly improved climb rate.

In April 1944, the decision was taken that all future Liberators would have a single vertical tail, and a redesign of the XB-24K for production by Ford resulted in the XB-24N. This differed only in having modified nose and tail gun positions, the rear turret becoming something like that on the Fortress, with 525 r.p.g., while a unique "ball" turret with the usual twin 0.5-in. guns was mounted in the nose. In addition to the prototype XB-24N (44-48753), seven YB-24Ns were built by Ford before Liberator production ceased on May 31, 1945. Orders for 5,168 B-24N-FO bombers were then cancelled, but the U.S. Navy received some 740 examples of an independently-developed single-fin Liberator. This was the PB4Y-2 Privateer, for which an original contract had been placed with Consolidated-Vultee by the U.S. Navy in May 1943.

Work on three prototypes began almost immediately,

Derived from the PB4Y-1, the PB4Y-2 Privateer (above and below, left) was extensively modified, but few reached the U.S. Navy before the end of the war.

and these made their initial flights on September 20th, October 30th, and December 15th, 1943, respectively. The PB4Y-2 was a rather more radical development of the Liberator than the A.A.F. single-fin variants, and although it retained the same Davis wing and standard undercarriage, the fuselage was extensively modified. The forward fuselage was lengthened by seven feet, increasing overall length to 74 ft. 7 in., and in addition to the normal Consolidated nose and Martin dorsal turrets, a further Martin turret was mounted in the mid-upper position. The Consolidated tail turret of earlier Liberators was augmented by two Erco blister-type waist gun positions, so that the total turret armament became twelve 0.5-in. machine guns. The bomb-bay remained similar to that of the Liberator.

The vertical tail was of much higher aspect ratio than that of the B-24N, the tailplane being given some dihedral to augment directional stability. Pratt and Whitney Twin Wasp R-1830-94 engines of 1,350 h.p. were fitted to the PB4Y-2 Privateer, but the oval cowlings were installed with their long axes vertical instead of horizontal as in the Liberator. A few PB4Y-2s reached operational squadrons of the U.S. Navy during the closing stages of the war, but most of the extensive global career of the Privateer was to be achieved after V-J Day. Versatile to the last, the PB4Y-2 was also produced in a transport version, becoming the RY-3 in the U.S. Navy, which service received forty-six, while the U.S.A.A.F. designation

for this variant was C-87C. The A.A.F. did not, in fact, receive any of these aircraft, but deliveries of twenty-seven RY-3s (JT973-999) began to R.A.F. Transport Command in February 1945, the type being designated Liberator C.IX. An interesting point is that Winston Churchill's veteran Liberator "Commando" (AL504), which was the second Liberator II to be ferried across the Atlantic, was modified by Consolidated-Vultee at San Diego early in 1944 almost up to RY-3 standards. The extended fuselage and single vertical tail modifications were completed, but the original 1,200 h.p. R-1830-33 type engines, with their mechanical superchargers, were retained. After a truly remarkable wartime career, and many historic flights, "Commando" was finally to be lost in the Atlantic, off the Azores, soon after the end of the war.

Apart from its unchallenged production record, the Liberator earned for itself a permanent place in aviation history for its remarkable record of achievement. Whether the material to be delivered happened to be bombs, depth charges, gasoline, freight, troops, or V.I.P.s, the Liberator established a reputation second to none for doing almost any job, anywhere.

Consolidated B-24J Liberator

Dimensions :	Span, 110 ft. 0 in. ; length, 67 ft. 2 in. ; height, 18 ft. 0 in. ; wing area, 1,048 sq. ft.
Armament :	Ten 0.5-in. Browning machine guns in nose, upper, ventral " ball ", and tail turrets, and in waist positions, with a total of 4,716 rounds. Maximum short-range bomb load, 12,800 lb. ; normal offensive load, 5,000 lb.
Power Plants :	Four Pratt and Whitney R-1830-65 fourteen-cylinder air-cooled radial engines with General Electric B-22 exhaust-driven turbo-superchargers, each developing 1,200 h.p. at 2,700 r.p.m. for take-off, and maintaining this power as a military rating up to 31,800 ft.
Weights :	Empty, 38,000 lb. ; combat, 56,000 lb. ; maximum overload, 71,200 lb.
Performance :	Maximum speed, 300 m.p.h. at 30,000 ft., 277 m.p.h. at 20,000 ft. ; maximum continuous speed, 278 m.p.h. at 25,000 ft. ; initial climb rate, 1,025 ft./min. ; service ceiling, 28,000 ft. ; range and endurance with a 5,000-lb. bomb load, 1,700 miles in 7.3 hrs. at 25,000 ft. (61,500 lb. a.u.w.) on 1,968 Imp. gal. (2,364 U.S. gal.) of fuel ; landing speed, 105 m.p.h.

The first Ju 88 prototype to employ Jumo 211A engines was the V3 (above) which flew for the first time on September 13, 1937

THE JUNKERS Ju 88 SERIES

No combat aircraft of the Second World War, either allied or enemy, was the subject of so much modification and extemporisation as was the Junkers Ju 88. Operating in its various forms throughout the entire period of the European war, and still in production when hostilities ceased, the Ju 88 was the true backbone of the Luftwaffe. Produced in greater numbers than all other German bombers combined —approximately 15,000 being built between 1939 and 1945, of which total more than 9,000 were bombers— the Ju 88 was continually adapted to perform roles other than that for which it had been conceived, and performed every task demanded of it with distinction. Like all combat aircraft, it possessed its share of shortcomings, but these were largely due to changes dictated by the needs of the overstrained and severely depleted German defences during the war's closing stages, and the ubiquitous Ju 88 was, without doubt, the finest German bomber to see extensive operational service.

The Junkers Ju 88 was conceived as a result of a meeting held early in 1935 between high-ranking officers of the fledgling Luftwaffe and chief designers of the leading German aircraft manufacturers at the Technical Office of the Reichsluftfahrtministerium in Berlin. General Erhard Milch informed the representatives of the industry that the Luftwaffe required a "schnellbomber"—a medium bomber with the speed of a fighter—and that the R.L.M. would welcome their proposals for such a machine. The leading German protagonists of bomber design, Dornier and Heinkel, were already fully committed with development and production programmes, but Focke-Wulf, Messerschmitt and Junkers submitted their proposals, and were each awarded development contracts.

The Focke-Wulf contender for production orders, the Fw 57, proved to be seriously overweight owing to the company's inexperience in all-metal construction —the wing structure alone was five times heavier than had been originally calculated—and after the loss of the first prototype, the second and third machines were scrapped. This left only two competitors:

The Ju 88 V1 which, first flown on December 21, 1936, became the progenitor of some 15,000 operational aircraft.

(Above) The Ju 88V5 specially modified for record-breaking purposes, and the Ju 88V6 (below) which featured a redesigned undercarriage, and served as the production prototype for the A-series.

within nine months. Design work was initiated on January 15, 1936, and in May the first metal was cut on the Ju 88V1. On December 21, 1936, the prototype was wheeled out of the experimental hangar, and, in great secrecy, flown for the first time by Junkers' chief test pilot, Flügkapitän Kindermann. The Ju 88V1 had taken 105,000 man-hours to complete, a record for the German aircraft industry at that time. Alfred Gassner, his work completed, had already returned to the U.S.A., via Sweden, before the prototype's maiden flight, and W. H. Evers was pushed into the background, receiving no official recognition for his work.

The Ju 88V1 differed appreciably externally from its numerous progeny; the cockpit was raised only slightly above the upper fuselage contours, the main undercarriage members were electrically-operated and, featuring twin oleo legs, retracted rearwards into the engine nacelles, and the two 900 h.p. Daimler-Benz DB 600 engines were housed in novel circular cowlings with segmented coolant and oil radiators grouped around the airscrew shaft. Only a limited amount of flight testing had been completed when the Ju 88V1 was destroyed, but on April 10, 1937, the Ju 88V2 made its début, being followed on September 13, 1937, by the Ju 88V3. The Ju 88V2 was generally similar to its predecessor, although, after initial trial flights, the additional radiators under the engine cowlings were removed, a modification which, together with some other slight changes, reduced drag to the extent that maximum speed was raised by some 10 m.p.h. to 289 m.p.h. Range was 1,242 miles, service ceiling was 19,680 ft., and with a 1,100-lb. bomb load, the loaded weight was 18,739 lb.

The third prototype, the Ju 88V3, was the first machine to receive the new Junkers Jumo 211A twelve-cylinder inverted-vee liquid-cooled engines with direct fuel injection and two-speed superchargers. Forerunner of the engines that were to power the majority of subsequent production models, the Jumo 211A was rated at 950 h.p. for take-off and 1,000 h.p. at 17,000 ft. The Ju 88V3 also embodied an extensively redesigned cockpit canopy with a raised roof, a small cupola intended to house a single 7.9-mm. MG 15 machine gun was offset to starboard under the nose, and a mounting was provided for a single fixed forward-firing 7.9-mm. MG 17 machine

Messerschmitt's entry, the Bf 162, and Junkers' entry, the Ju 88, but suddenly the R.L.M. decided that Messerschmitt should concentrate on fighters, and thus the Junkers Ju 88 was awarded a production contract.

It has not been revealed hitherto that the Ju 88 was not of pure German descent, owing much to design and construction techniques evolved by the U.S. aircraft industry. It owed nothing to any previous Junkers design, and although it was later credited to the Junkers chief designer, Dipl. Ing. Zindel, it was, in fact, designed by W. H. Evers and a citizen of the U.S.A., Alfred Gassner. Evers had spent some time working in the U.S. aircraft industry, and returned to Germany in 1935, accompanied by Gassner. The two engineers were employed by Junkers to design the new bomber demanded by the R.L.M., and they were informed that the first prototype must be ready gun. In the meantime, the R.I..M. had made various changes in its requirements, and when, on February 2, 1938, the Ju 88V4 was flown, it provided accommodation for four crew members, the earlier prototypes having been three-seaters. Overall length was increased from 45 ft. 5 in. to 47 ft. 1 in., loaded weight increased to 22,040 lb., and the "beetle's eye" of optically-flat panels made its appearance in the nose. Another innovation was the provision of a long ventral cupola which terminated in a position for a single 7.9-mm. rearward-firing gun.

At this time the German aircraft industry was intent on gaining international prestige, and, with the direct encouragement of Adolf Hitler, most German military prototypes were being adapted for record-breaking purposes. The Ju 88 was no exception, for what better way to reveal to the world the existence of the new German high-speed bomber than with a record-breaking flight. The fifth prototype, which had flown for the first time on April 13, 1938, was therefore modified for the proposed record flight. Fitted with a streamlined, pointed nose, and generally "cleaned-up", the Ju 88V5 first saw the limelight in March 1939, when, flown by Ernst Siebert and Kurt Heintz, it established a 1,000-km. closed-circuit record with a 2,000-kg. payload at an average speed of 321.25 m.p.h. Four months later, carrying the same load, the Ju 88V5 covered a distance of 1,242.7 miles at an average speed of 311 m.p.h.

While preparations for these record flights were being made, five additional prototypes had been completed, and plans had been laid for quantity production for the Luftwaffe. The sixth prototype, the Ju 88V6, was the production prototype for the A-series bomber, and featured redesigned main undercarriage members in which single hydraulically-operated legs were employed, the wheels turning through a ninety degree arc to lie flat in the engine

(Right) The Ju 88V4 was the first four-seat prototype, and the first machine to employ the "beetle's eye" of optically-flat panels for the fuselage nose. Ten pre-production Ju 88A-0 aircraft (below) were delivered for service evaluation, and some of these were used operationally at the beginning of the war.

nacelles. Like the record-breaking Ju 88V5, power was provided by a pair of Jumo 211B-1 engines rated at 1,200 h.p., loaded weight was increased to 22,590 lb., maximum speed was 301 m.p.h., range was 1,522 miles, and service ceiling was 22,300 ft. The Ju 88V7 was the first Zerstoerer, or heavy fighter prototype, a forward-firing armament of two 20-mm. MG FF cannon and two 7.9-mm. MG 17 machine guns being housed in a "solid nose". Serving as a prototype for the C-series, this machine was later converted as an eight-passenger V.I.P. transport for General Milch, replacing his obsolescent Heinkel He 111V16.

Plans for the quantity production of the Ju 88A had been prepared as early as the closing months of 1937, and tooling commenced early in 1938. The Junkers plant at Schoenebeck was primarily responsible for the tools and jigs, fuselage production commencing at Aschersleben, wings at Halberstadt, and tail assemblies at Leopoldshall, and preparations were made for the final assembly and flight testing to be undertaken at Bernburg. Contracts for the manufacture of complete aircraft or components were also awarded to the Volkswagenwerke, the Dornier factory at Wismar, the Heinkel plant at Oranienburg, the Arado plant at Brandenburg, and the Henschel factory at Schoenefeld.

A pre-production batch of ten Ju 88A-0 aircraft for service trials was completed early in 1939, by which time it was also envisaged as a dive-bomber,

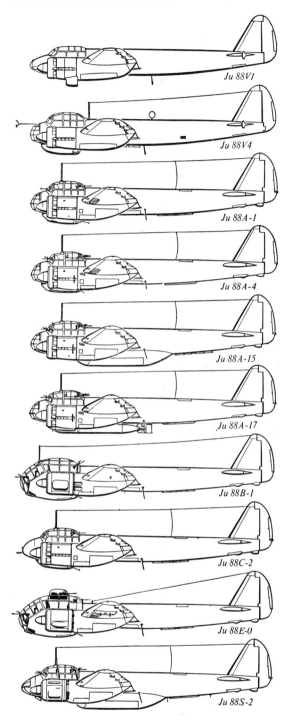

Ju 88 V1

Ju 88 V4

Ju 88 A-1

Ju 88 A-4

Ju 88 A-15

Ju 88 A-17

Ju 88 B-1

Ju 88 C-2

Ju 88 E-0

Ju 88 S-2

ten aircraft to be delivered by Arado's Brandenburg plant were all damaged on landing when their undercarriages collapsed. The slatted dive-brakes hinged beneath the front spar gave considerable trouble when extended, the fuselage already being highly stressed, and limitations had to be imposed upon high-speed manœuvres. All aerobatics were forbidden, and the crew's attention was drawn to the possibility of structural failure if the loading diagram was not strictly adhered to.

The crew of four was closely grouped in the fuselage nose, the pilot to port with the bombardier/gunner forward and to starboard, the radio-operator/gunner aft of the pilot, facing to the rear, and the mechanic/gunner who squeezed himself into the ventral gondola to operate the lower rear gun. Defensive armament soon proved inadequate, this comprising three, and later four, 7.9-mm. MG 15 machine guns, and the bomb load was normally 3,968 lb., the bulk of which was attached to four external carriers, two on each side of the fuselage, inboard of the engine nacelles. This could be increased to a maximum of 5,510 lb. The Ju 88A-1 had a maximum loaded weight of 27,500 lb., a maximum speed of 286 m.p.h., and a range of 1,553 miles. Power was provided by two Jumo 211B-1 engines each rated at 1,200 h.p. The Ju 88A-2 was generally similar but had special assisted-take-off fittings, and the Ju 88A-3 was a conversion trainer variant of the A-1 with dual controls, throttles and various instruments duplicated.

The "Battle of Britain" was the Ju 88A's first real test and, although it faired better than other German bombers participating in that epic action, some serious operational shortcomings revealed themselves, and the lengthy process of modification and improvisation which was to result in a remarkably complex development history commenced. By 1940 production had gained considerable momentum, a total of 1,816 bombers, 330 photo-reconnaissance aircraft, and sixty-two heavy fighters being delivered, and by the end of that year a version embodying the modifications dictated by experience gained during the "Battle of Britain", the Ju 88A-4, was on the assembly lines.

The most important structural change in the Ju 88A-4 was the six-foot increase in overall wing span which increased from 59 ft. $10\frac{3}{4}$ in. to 65 ft. $10\frac{1}{2}$ in. Defensive armament was substantially increased, a typical armament being a 13-mm. MG 131 and a 7.9-mm. MG 81 firing forward, two MG 81s or one MG 131 firing aft above the fuselage, and an MG 81 firing aft from the ventral gondola, and armour protection for the crew was increased, the gun mountings being armoured, the pilot being protected by a back plate, side pieces, a head plate and under-seat slats, the lower rear gunner having an armoured floor, and the radio operator having a folding plate which protected his chest. The undercarriage was strengthened, and provision was made for the attachment of rocket-assisted-take-off units with which the bomb load could be raised to a maximum of 6,614

slatted dive-brakes being fitted outboard of the engine nacelles. Production deliveries were slower than had originally been anticipated, and the test aircraft were pressed into operational service with the Luftwaffe, making their début, together with the initial production Ju 88A-1s, over the Firth of Forth in September 1939. Like most new combat aircraft, the Ju 88A-1 suffered some teething troubles, and the first

(Above) A Ju 88A-1 mounted on a compass base and (right) with 250-lb. bombs on racks between fuselage and engine nacelles.

pounds. Four external carriers carried either four 550-lb. or 1,100-lb. bombs. Alternatively, the inboard carriers under each wing root could carry one 2,200-lb. bomb each, and a 550-lb. or 1,100-lb. bomb could be carried by each of the outboard carriers.

Initially, the Ju 88A-4 retained the Jumo 211B-1 engines, but the Ju 88A-4/R which entered production in 1942 switched to Jumo 211Js which offered a maximum output of 1,410 h.p. at 820 ft. The installation of these engines was accompanied by a substantial increase in loaded weight (to 31,000 lb.) and, in consequence, maximum speed dropped by 20 m.p.h. to 273 m.p.h. The Ju 88A-4 was, incidentally, the first variant of the basic design to be supplied to Germany's allies, twenty being delivered to the Finnish Air Force, and others being supplied to Italy where they were assigned to the 9° Stormo Bombardamento Tuffo. The Ju 88A-4/Trop was a tropicalised variant for use in the Western Desert, carrying water containers, mattresses, sun blinds, and desert survival equipment.

Surprisingly, the Ju 88A-5 preceded the A-4 in production in 1940. Wing span and bomb load were identical to those of the A-4 but, in other respects, this type was similar to the A-1. Both Jumo 211B and 211D engines were employed, and balloon-cable cutters could be fitted. The Ju 88A-6 was generally similar to the A-5, but a balloon-cable fender and destroying gear were standard, the weight of these being compensated for by a 130-lb. trimming weight installed in the rear fuselage. The Ju 88A-6 with the balloon-cable fender proved extremely unwieldy, and was quickly withdrawn from service. The Ju 88A-6/U was a long-range overseas reconnaissance variant carrying three crew members and powered by Jumo 211H engines. The ventral gondola could be removed and search radar fitted. The Ju 88A-7 was a dual-control

(Above) A Ju 88A-4 with crew entry hatch open.

conversion trainer variant of the early production A-4; the Ju 88A-8 was fitted with the balloon-cable fender and destroying gear, differing from the A-6 in having an A-4 fuselage, and the Ju-88A-9, A-10 and A-11 were alternative designations for the Ju 88A-1/Trop, A-5/Trop and A-4/Trop.

The Ju 88A-12 was a dual-control trainer based on the A-4 airframe but with increased cockpit width and the ventral gondola removed, and the A-13 was a heavily armoured ground-attack version which could carry an attack armament of up to sixteen 7.9-mm.

A Ju 88A-4/R of the Finnish Air Force. Twenty aircraft of this type were supplied to Finland for operations against the Russians.

MG 17 machine guns, and special anti-personnel bomb containers under the wings which each housed seventy-two small bombs. No dive-brakes were fitted, and many machines had a special automatic pull-out device. The Ju 88A-14, which had electric balloon-cable cutters in the wing leading edges, was basically similar to the A-4 but served in the anti-shipping role; the A-15 featured a bulged bomb-bay; the A-16 was an improved A-12 dual-control conversion trainer, and the A-17 was a torpedo-bomber conversion of the A-4, the inboard carriers under the wings being adapted to each take one 2,200-lb. torpedo. Both the A-14 and A-17 employed the more powerful Jumo 211J engines introduced by the A-4/R, and were extremely active against Allied convoys in the Atlantic, Baltic and Mediterranean.

Like most other German wartime bombers, the Ju 88's ability to take alternative power plants was considered of some importance as it safeguarded against a production bottleneck arising from a shortage of a particular type of engine. Early in 1939, with the Ju 88A established in production, the Junkers design staff adapted the basic airframe to take a pair of the new Jumo 213A engines which, at that time running at 1,500 h.p., were eventually to be developed to give 1,776 h.p. In addition to the new engines, the

The Junkers Ju 88A-4 entered production in 1940, and differed from earlier models primarily in having increased wing span, heavier defensive armament, and improved armour protection.

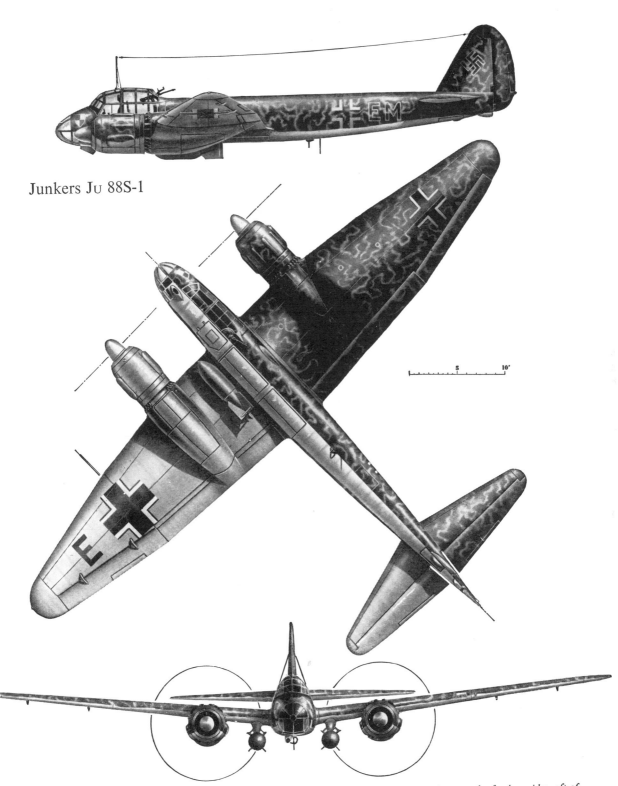

Junkers Ju 88S-1

FINISH AND INSIGNIA: *The Ju 88S-1 illustrated above employed a "wave-mirror" pattern of green and light blue over the upper surfaces of the wings and fuselage, the fuselage sides, and the vertical tail surfaces, and pale blue under-surfaces. The letters "EM" (indicating the individual aircraft, Gruppe and* Staffel) *appeared as white outlines on the fuselage sides, aft of the national insignia, and in black outboard of the national insignia on the wing under-surfaces, the "E" under the port wing and the "M" under the starboard wing. The national insignia on the fuselage sides and vertical fin appeared as a white outline.*

modified version, designated Ju 88B, also featured an entirely re-modelled and much cleaner forward fuselage, with more extensive glazing. The prototype Ju 88B, which flew early in 1940, had an overall fuselage length of 46 ft. 8½ in., but this was increased to 49 ft. 0½ in. on the pre-production Ju 88B-0, while development delays with the Jumo 213A engine necessitated the installation of two 1,600 h.p. BMW 801A air-cooled radials. Only a pre-production batch of ten Ju 88B-0 bombers was built, although B-1, B-2 and B-3 production variants were proposed. Armament comprised six 7.9-mm. MG 81 machine guns, the bomb load was 5,500 lb., and whereas the prototype had the same wing span as the Ju 88A-1, the pre-production B-0 had the extended wing span of the Ju 88A-4. The Ju 88B-0 had a maximum speed of 311 m.p.h., service ceiling was 30,840 ft., range was 1,555 miles, and loaded weight was 26,014 lb. One of the ten Ju 88B-0s was fitted with a power-operated dorsal turret containing one 13-mm. MG 131 machine gun, and, redesignated Ju 88E, this later served as a prototype for the Ju 188 series.

Development of the C-series of fighters paralleled development of the A-series of bombers, while the Ju 88D-1, which appeared in 1940, was a specialised strategic reconnaissance version of the Ju 88A-4. The aft bomb bay was converted to house three cameras with their heating installation, additional fuel could

be housed in the forward bomb-bay, and the range could be further stretched by the attachment of drop-tanks to the underwing carriers. The Ju 88D-2 was a conversion of the A-5 airframe, and the D-3 was a tropicalised version of the D-1. More than eighteen hundred Ju 88D reconnaissance aircraft had been delivered when production terminated in 1944. The Ju 88G series were specialised night fighters, while the Ju 88H, characterised by an elongated fuselage which resulted from the introduction of two additional bays, one forward and one aft of the wing mainspar, housing extra fuel tanks, was a long-range photo reconnaissance aircraft in its H-1 model, and a long-range heavy fighter in its H-2 form.

The demand for close-support aircraft on the Russian Front and in the Mediterranean led to the Ju 88Nbwe, a Jumo-powered machine converted from a standard Ju 88C-4 with a large ventral tray capable of housing either a flame-thrower or recoilless anti-tank weapons. Development of this version was abandoned in favour of the Ju 88P series, the first prototype of which, the Ju 88PV1, was converted from a standard Ju 88A-4 airframe, and was fitted with a single 75-mm. BK 7.5 long-barrel anti-tank gun in a large under-fuselage fairing. The relative success of firing trials with the Ju 88PV1 resulted in the conversion of further A-4 airframes at the Junkers Dessau plant, and a small number of Ju 88P-1 anti-tank aircraft were delivered in 1942-3. The P-1 featured an improved recoil brake, and the gun fairing, which was jettisonable, was of sufficient size to accommodate rearward-firing twin MG 81 machine guns in addition to the large, forward-firing cannon which was inclined downwards at a slight angle to

The Ju 88S-1 featured an entirely redesigned nose which was somewhat reminiscent of that employed by the first prototype.

the line of flight. Although designed for the anti-tank role, Ju 88P-1s made a few abortive attacks on U.S. day-bomber formations, but they proved too slow and unwieldy as interceptors, and were quickly transferred to the Russian Front for anti-tank duties. The BK 7.5, although an effective anti-tank weapon, had numerous shortcomings as an aircraft weapon. The exhaust gases from the gun were ejected sideways through special ducts, causing considerable interference in the plane of the airscrews, and this and other problems led to the replacement of the BK 7.5 by two 37-mm. BK 3.7 guns in the Ju 88P-2 and P-3 which were converted from A-4 airframes at Merseburg in small batches. The final P-series model was the Ju 88P-4 of 1944, this employing a single 50-mm. KWK 39 tank cannon, also known as the BK 5. Some thirty Ju 88P-4s were completed at Dessau, and abortive attempts were made to use these for both day and night fighting but, like the earlier P-1s, they were eventually relegated to close-support duties on the Russian Front.

By mid-1943 it was becoming increasingly obvious that the A-series bombers were now too slow for successful operation by day without fighter escort, and development was, therefore, commenced on the S-series. The Ju 88R-1 and R-2 were night fighters powered by BMW 801A and 801D radials respectively, and the pre-production Ju 88S-0, powered by the latter engines, differed from the A-series principally in having a smooth, hemispherical glazed nose—reverting to a shape very similar to that of the early prototypes—and the ventral gondola eliminated. The upper nose guns were removed, armament being reduced to three 7.9-mm. MG 81 machine guns and one 13-mm. MG 131 machine gun. Bomb load was reduced to 1,760 lb. The initial production model, the Ju 88S-1, had 1,700 h.p. BMW 801G engines with GM-1 power-boost, and defensive armament was further reduced to one rearward-firing 13-mm. MG 131 machine gun. The Ju 88S-2 differed from the S-1 in having an enlarged bomb-bay in which two rearward-firing MG 81 machine guns were fitted to supplement the single MG 131, and power was provided by two 1,810 h.p. BMW

801TJ engines with exhaust-driven turbo-superchargers. Loaded weight was 24,375 lb., and a maximum speed of 371 m.p.h. was attainable. The Ju

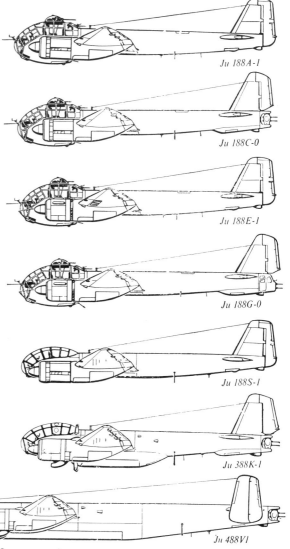

Ju 188A-1

Ju 188C-0

Ju 188E-1

Ju 188G-0

Ju 188S-1

Ju 388K-1

Ju 488V1

(*Above*) *Ju 188D-2 radar-equipped reconnaissance aircraft of a unit based in Norway, and* (*left*) *a Ju 188F-1 which differed in having BMW 801G-2 radials in place of the liquid-cooled Jumo 213As.*

88S-3 was generally similar to the S-1 but powered by 1,750 h.p. Jumo 213E-1 engines, while the Ju 88T-1 and T-3 were photo-reconnaissance versions of the S-1 and S-3 respectively. The Ju 88T-3 was originally scheduled for quantity production at Henschel's Schoenefeld factory in the autumn of 1944, but the order was cancelled in favour of Messerschmitt's Me 410A Hornisse.

A progressive development of the basic Ju 88 design, the Ju 188, was evolved from the Ju 88E mentioned earlier, but the first true prototype was the Ju 88V27 (D-AWLN) which was flown towards the end of 1940. As compared with the Ju 88, the Ju 188 had extended, pointed wingtips which increased the overall span to 72 ft. 2 in. The extensively re-designed forward fuselage was generally similar to that of the Ju 88B, and owing to delays in the deliveries of Jumo 213A engines, the first version to enter quantity production, in 1941, was the Ju 188E with 1,700 h.p. BMW 801G-2 radials. One hundred and twenty machines were delivered in 1942, including Ju 188E-0 and E-1 bombers, and Ju 188F-1 and F-2 reconnaissance aircraft, the last-mentioned types featuring GM 1 power-boost equipment. The Ju 188E-1 carried a maximum bomb load of 6,600 lb., and a 2,200-lb. torpedo could be carried inboard under each wing. Defensive armament normally comprised one 20-mm. MG 151 cannon in the nose, a similar gun in a dorsal turret, one hand-operated 13-mm MG 131 machine gun in a dorsal position below and aft of the turret, and one MG 131 or twin MG 81 machine guns in the lower rearward-firing

position. The Ju 188E-1 weighed 32,000 lb. loaded, and attained a maximum speed and range of 315 m.p.h. and 1,550 miles respectively. Incidentally, one of the pre-production Ju 188E-0 bombers was converted as a fast V.I.P. transport for General Milch to replace his Ju 88V7. Four seats were installed in the bomb-bays, and an armament of four MG 131 machine guns was carried.

With the completion of the BMW-powered Ju 188Es and Fs, and the availability of Jumo 213A engines, production at Bernburg continued with the Ju 188A-1 and, at Leipzig-Mockau, the Ju 188A-2. These were generally similar to the E-series bombers, apart from the installation of 1,776 h.p. Jumo 213A engines, and with a 3,000-lb. bomb load, these attained a maximum speed of 325 m.p.h. The Ju 188A-3 was a torpedo-bomber version carrying no internal bomb load, and the Ju 188C-0 was an experimental version of the A-model with a remotely-controlled tail turret housing two 13-mm. MG 131 machine guns. The rear fuselage was suitably reinforced, and the outer wing fuel tanks were deleted. The Ju 188D was a reconnaissance version of the A-model fitted with the same engines and armament. The camera installation was similar to that of the Ju 88D, and the Ju 188D-2 differed from the D-1 in having radar equipment.

The Ju 188G series was a development of the C-0 with a manually-operated twin MG 131 tail turret, and a large faired bomb-bay under the fuselage, although the latter feature did not appear on the pre-production Ju 188G-0. The proposed Ju 188G-2 production version, in which fuselage tankage was appreciably reduced, in order to provide the maximum possible internal bomb stowage, did not progress further than the experimental stage, and the Ju 188H-2 was a proposed photo-reconnaissance model of the G-2 which was abandoned. The Ju 188M-1 and M-2 were proposed long-range reconnaissance developments of the D-model, and the Ju 188R was a night-fighter modification, three prototypes of which were tested, one of these being flown to Sweden by its crew in 1944. The first two prototypes of the R-model had a fixed forward-firing armament of four 20-mm. MG 151 cannon, and were equipped with A.E.G. radar, but the third prototype had two forward-firing 30-mm. MK 103 cannon.

The Ju 188S-1 was a high-speed, high-altitude bomber development with a pressure cabin for its three crew members. Power was provided by a pair of 1,750 h.p. Jumo 213E-1 engines which gave the aircraft a maximum speed of 429 m.p.h. Service ceiling was 38,400 ft., and no defensive armament was fitted. The forward fuselage was completely redesigned, and a new, low-drag cockpit canopy introduced. The Ju 188S-1/U had additional armour protection for the crew, and was intended for close support and heavy fighter duties, with a single 50-mm. BK 5 cannon projecting from a ventral fairing, and the Ju 188T was a proposed photo-reconnaissance variant.

The Ju 188 series never attained large-scale production, only about a thousand machines being delivered, and towards the end of the war, development was overtaken by a further projection of the basic Ju 88 design, the Ju 388. In the meantime, Professor Hertel, formerly of the Ernst Heinkel company who had replaced Dipl. Ing. Zindel as Junkers' chief of technical development, was engaged in the development of the Ju 288 which had originally been intended to replace the Ju 88. Despite the numerical similarity of its type number, however, the Ju 288 was developed from neither the Ju 88 or Ju 188, and, in fact, bore no relationship to these machines. Thus, the Ju 388 formed the next stage in the evolution of the "eighty-eight" design.

With the approaching obsolescence of the basic Ju 88 bomber, and the demand for very much higher operational ceilings, speeds and load-carrying capabilities, the possibility of evolving very much more effective machines from the basic design with the minimum of disruption of existing design and production arrangements assumed considerable importance. The result was the Ju 388 based upon the final models of the Ju 188, the Ju 188S and T which had featured pressure cabins for high-altitude operations. The first prototype, the Ju 388V1, was converted from a Ju 188T-0 at Merseburg, this leading to the Ju 388L high-altitude photo-reconnaissance aircraft. The second prototype, the Ju 388V2, was the prototype for the Ju 388J Störtebeker high-altitude night fighter, and the third prototype, the Ju 388V3, led to the Ju 388K high-altitude bomber.

The first variant to enter service was the high-altitude photo-reconnaissance model which carried a crew of three and had three cameras. A pre-production batch of ten Ju 388L-0 aircraft was converted from Ju 188S airframes at Merseburg in 1944, and production continued with the Ju 388L-1 powered by two 1,810 h.p. BMW 801TJ radials, eighty-nine being produced before the war's end terminated the assembly line. The L-1a and L-1b models differed only in that the latter carried an additional 13-mm. MG 131 machine gun in the cockpit, increasing the defensive armament to four guns of this calibre.

Essentially similar to the Ju 388L, the Ju 388K high-altitude bomber was fitted with a large, wooden, bulged bomb-bay, and maximum bomb load was 6,610 lb. Defensive armament comprised an FDL 131Z remotely-controlled tail turret housing two 13-mm. MG 131 machine guns, although this installation was never made in the ten pre-production Ju 388K-0 bombers completed, these having two 7.9-mm. MG 81s in a fixed installation in the rear of the bomb-bay. The Ju 388K-0 and K-1 were similarly powered to the Ju 388L-1, but the proposed K-2 and K-3 variants were to have had Jumo 213E and Jumo 222E/F engines respectively. Only four production Ju 388K-1 bombers were completed, and the type was too late to see operational service. The projected Ju 388M was essentially similar to the K-model, apart from an increase in loaded weight and provision for an additional crew member. The performance of the Ju 388K-1 included a maximum speed of 378 m.p.h. at 38,000 ft., a range of 1,100 miles at 36,100 ft., and a service ceiling of 42,200 ft. Loaded weight was 31,400 lb., and overall dimensions included a span of 72 ft. 2 in., and a length of 49 ft. 0½ in.

Although the Ju 388 was the last development of the basic design to attain production status, a further development, the Ju 488, was under construction when

A Ju 188E-2 with special radar equipment and the upper turret removed. Aircraft of this type served at Bordeaux-Merignac in 1942.

the war ended. Like the Ju 388, the Ju 488 was intended to provide what was virtually a new aircraft without disturbing existing production arrangements. Intended for use as a high-altitude bomber-reconnaissance machine, the Ju 488 was derived from the Ju 188 by fitting a new centre wing section to carry two additional 1,810 h.p. BMW 801TJ radial engines, a lengthened fuselage, the modified tail of a Ju 288, and four main undercarriage members, a single wheel retracting into each engine nacelle.

The first two prototypes, the Ju 488V1 and V2, were under construction at Toulouse early in 1945, and the first of these was being readied for flight testing when both machines were destroyed in an Allied air attack. The Ju 488V3 and V4 were to have been generally similar to the first two prototypes, but fuel capacity was to have been increased from 900 Imp gal. to 1,250 Imp. gal., and the BMW radials were to have been replaced by 2,500 h.p. Jumo 222 engines, it being planned that the BMW-powered model should enter production as the Ju 488A-1 with the Jumo-powered model succeeding it as the Ju 488B-1 as soon as sufficient Jumo 222 power plants became available. Both versions were to have carried three crew members, and sole defensive armament was to have consisted of a remotely-controlled FDL 131Z mounting in the tail. The Ju 488A-1 was to have had a maximum continuous cruising speed of 385 m.p.h. at 42,600 ft., and a cruising range of 1,280 miles.

One of the last tasks of the Junkers Ju 88 was the ignominious one of pilotless missile. Numerous experiments with composite aircraft of various types had been conducted in Germany, and a number of Ju 88 airframes were adapted for use as the lower component of what was known as a *Mistel* combination. The upper component, or "control aircraft", was either the Fw 190 (in the case of BMW-powered Ju 88s) or the Bf 109 (in the case of Jumo-powered Ju 88s) and, except on training flights, all controls were operated by the pilot of the upper component. The Ju 88 airframe was modified to incorporate a large hollow-charge warhead, and the *Mistel* was intended primarily for attacking capital ships or heavily-protected land targets. The Ju 88 *Mistel* became operational during the Allied landings on the Continent, Ju 88A-4 airframes being employed. As some successes were recorded with these "flying bombs", seventy-five and then a further twenty-five Ju 88G-1s were rebuilt at Leipzig-Mockau for *Mistel* use.

The Ju 88 series might be considered to exemplify the German philosophy of using one good basic airframe for a multitude of tasks rather than evolving a variety of specialised machines and thus complicating production. It is true to say that, had the Ju 88 proved less amenable to the process of adaptation and modification to which it was submitted, the Luftwaffe would have found itself in serious difficulties at a very much earlier stage in the Second World War.

Junkers Ju 88A-4/R

Dimensions : Span, 65 ft. 10½ in. ; length, 47 ft. 1½ in. ; height, 15 ft. 11 in. ; wing area, 590 sq. ft.

Armament : One forward-firing 20-mm. MG FF cannon or two 7.9-mm. MG 81 machine guns (operated by the bombardier) and one 7.9-mm. MG 81 (operated by the pilot), one 7.9-mm. MG 81 or 13-mm. MG 131 in the upper rear firing position (operated by the radio-operator), and one MG 131 or two MG 81 in lower rear firing position (operated by flight mechanic). Internal bomb load, 1,100 lb. Normal external bomb load comprised four 550-lb. bombs, but alternatively, the inboard carriers under each wing root could carry one 2,200-lb. bomb or a torpedo, plus a 550-lb. or a 1,100-lb. bomb on each of the outboard carriers.

Power Plants : Two Junkers Jumo 211J-1 twelve-cylinder 60° inverted-vee liquid-cooled engines with direct fuel injection rated at 1,400 h.p. at 2,600 r.p.m. for take-off and emergency at sea level, and 1,350 h.p. at 2,600 r.p.m. at 820 ft.

Weights : Normal loaded, 26,700 lb. ; maximum permissible, 31,000 lb.

Performance : Maximum speed, 273 m.p.h. at 17,500 ft. ; range (with normal fuel), 1,553 miles, (with maximum fuel) 1,980 miles., (with maximum bomb load) 650 miles ; climb to 17,500 ft., 23 mins. ; service ceiling, 27,880 ft.

The Ju 388L-1b high-altitude photo-reconnaissance model (left) of the Ju 388K-1 bomber (below) which was too late to see operational service.

The first Martin B-26 (later RB-26) Marauder which was flown for the first time on November 25, 1940.

THE MARTIN MARAUDER

When the Martin B-26 Marauder was first introduced into U.S.A.A.F. service in 1941, the rather colourful title of "Flying Torpedo", earlier bestowed on the aircraft by the popular press as a result of its almost perfectly streamlined circular fuselage, rapidly gave place to such appellations as "Flying Prostitute", the "Widow Maker", and other less printable epithets coined by its pilots as a result of the somewhat lethal propensities which it manifested. On four occasions investigation boards met to decide whether or not development and production of the Marauder should continue, but, by 1944, the B-26s of the U.S. Ninth Air Force had the lowest loss rate on operational missions of any American aircraft in the European Theatre of Operations. This reached a point below one-half of one per cent in tactical operations against heavily defended French and German targets, and the Marauder had outlived the uncomplimentary names bestowed upon it during the early months of its service career.

Although the Marauder's combat career began in the Pacific, like the larger Fortress, it achieved its main successes in the European and North African theatres to which its operating characteristics were best suited. Its performance was framed by an Air Corps specification issued on January 25, 1939, for a fast and, by contemporary standards, heavily armed medium bomber. Speed was particularly stressed, with a maximum requirement for 350 m.p.h., while other features demanded were a maximum range well over 2,000 miles, a service ceiling exceeding 20,000 ft. a defensive armament comprising not less than four 0.3-in. machine guns, and a heavy bomb load. Apart from the range and load requirements, the size of the bomber was also governed by the specified crew of five.

Important omissions from the specification were take-off and landing speeds. This permitted the high performance to be attained by employing an unusually small wing area with a consequent high loading, and was used with advantage in a design by Peyton M. Magruder of the Glenn L. Martin company. His was the only one of several projects from within the

(Above) The third B-26 (40-1363) which was employed for trials by the 22nd Bombardment Group. This machine had no dorsal turret. (Below) One of the first B-26s with experimental vertical tail surfaces and a mock-up of the tail turret later employed by the B-26B.

The third Marauder I (FK111) of a batch of fifty-two supplied to the R.A.F. The Marauder I was similar to the B-26A of the U.S.A.A.F. (Left) A B-26A-I (41-17437) retrospectively fitted with the enlarged air intakes introduced with the B-26B-2 production model.

company to be approved by the veteran Glenn Martin. Apart from its small wing, resulting in the unprecedented loading of more than 50 lb./sq. ft., Magruder's design also featured a low-drag profile fuselage with a circular cross-section, offering a good aerodynamic form but substantial capacity for a heavy load of bombs, fuel and armament.

Detailed design was completed by June 1939, and on July 5th the Martin Model 179 was submitted to a Wright Field Board under Brig. Gen. J. Fickel. The exceptionally clean design was based on the use of two of the new Pratt and Whitney R-2800 Double Wasp eighteen-cylinder radial engines, each developing 1,850 h.p., and included in its specification was a guaranteed performance, plus a production schedule promising delivery in a remarkably short time. The latter was an extremely important factor in the critical days of late 1939, and doubtless assisted in the Model 179 gaining a margin of 140 points over its nearest rival in the design competition.

This victory was followed in that fateful September by a production contract not simply for a prototype or an evaluation quantity, but for no fewer than 1,100 aircraft! The technique of ordering "off the drawing board" was to become more commonplace in later years than prior to the Second World War, and in fact the Model 179 was the first American aircraft to be so ordered. Construction of the first aircraft took just about one year, and on November 25, 1940, the first B-26 (40-1361)—there being no prototype as such—made its initial flight in the hands of chief engineer and test pilot William K. Ebel.

Fortunately for the production schedules, flight testing of the first B-26 showed little need for modification, although slight rudder overbalance necessitated

reversing the direction of travel of the trim tabs. In its initial form the B-26 was practically the only aircraft able to qualify with virtual truth as having a "cigar-shaped" fuselage. In fact, aerodynamically, the fuselage approached perfection, the only excrescence marring its beautiful lines being the stepped windscreen. In the upper half of the symmetrical and frameless plastic nose was a ball mounting for a single 0.3-in. machine gun, while a similar hand-held gun was accommodated in the pointed tail cone. Defensive armament was completed by a low-profile electrically-operated Martin 250CE dorsal turret housing two 0.5-in. Browning machine guns—the first power-operated turret to be fitted to an American bomber. The shoulder-mounted wings were unusual in possessing no fillets, and the B-26 was equally in advance of its time in having such features as four-bladed airscrews with root cuffs to aid engine cooling, and a tailplane employing marked dihedral. In conformation with the rest of the design, the R-2800-5 engines were closely cowled and their housings were highly streamlined, and large spinners were fitted to the Curtiss electric airscrews. Two-speed mechanical superchargers were installed to maintain engine power up to medium altitudes, and ejector exhausts vented on each side of the nacelle.

Although possessing electric systems for turret power and propeller pitch actuation, the B-26 had hydraulically-operated bomb doors, flaps, cooling gills, and undercarriage. Like all its national contemporaries, it featured a tricycle undercarriage, with forward-retracting main members and an aft-retracting nosewheel. The bomb doors were unusual in being split in tandem, the forward pair folding in half when opened, and the aft set being hinged normally. The normal bomb capacity was 2,000 lb., with a maximum overload of 5,800 lb. The gross weight started off as 26,625 lb., but even then the wing loading resulted in extraordinarily high take-off and landing speeds.

The overall span of the B-26 was only 65 ft. for a fuselage length of 56 ft., but the maximum available power of 3,700 h.p. resulted in this variant being the fastest of the series, with a maximum speed of 315 m.p.h. Within precisely three months of the first flight of the first B-26, other machines began leaving the line at Baltimore, on February 25, 1941, and in all 201 examples of the initial production model were built. With 4,000 lb. of bombs and 387 Imp. gal. (465 U.S. gal.) of fuel, the B-26 had a gross weight of 28,340 lb., and soon began to encounter trouble as combat crews started training on the type. This process was accompanied by a number of accidents, several of which were serious, and the introduction into service of the B-26 was also delayed by difficulties with the four-bladed airscrews. An incidental disadvantage of the latter was the limited ground clearance that they offered, restricting the B-26 to smooth runways or airfield surfaces. Initially, the name "Martian" was considered by the U.S.A.A.F. for the B-26, but this was eventually displaced in favour of "Marauder".

As production continued in 1941, the first modifications were introduced in the design as a result of operating experience and combat reports from Europe. The single nose and tail guns were increased in calibre in some aircraft to 0.5-in. to match the turret armament, but additional changes resulted in the appearance of a new sub-type, the B-26A. This marked an increase in the power of the electrical system from twelve to twenty-four volts; the installation of two additional bomb-bay fuel tanks, enabling a total of four to be fitted as required, and the provision of shackles beneath the main fuselage beam for the carriage of a standard 22-in. torpedo.

Of the 139 B-26As built, the first few retained the original type powerplants, but 109 of the later models in the batch had R-2800-9 engines with slight modifications. The last B-26As were fitted with R-2800-39 engines, still of 1,850 h.p., but the gross weight of the aircraft had by now increased appreciably—to 32,200 lb. This naturally reduced the overall performance, and rendered the Marauder even more of a "hot ship", and by the time of Pearl Harbour, in December 1941, only one combat unit, the 22nd Bombardment Group, had equipped with the type. With its B-26As, this Group left Langley Field, Virginia, on December 8, 1941, for the Pacific, being originally based in Australia. At about the same time, three B-26As were ferried to Great Britain for evaluation by the Royal Air Force by whom they were designated Marauder Is. On the basis of their performance and defensive armament, they were considered suitable for tactical operations of the type then coming into prominence in the Western Desert, and subsequent deliveries were made direct to the Middle East. In all, fifty-two Marauder Is (FK109 to FK160) were received by the R.A.F. under Lend-Lease, No. 14 Squadron being the first to equip with this type, in July 1942. Four other R.A.F. squadrons were later to be equipped with the Marauder, but none became operational until early in 1943.

Before the Marauder entered combat service with the U.S.A.A.F. in the spring of 1942, the number of training accidents had occasioned so much concern that, in March, the Chief-of-Staff, General Arnold, appointed a special board, headed by Major General Spaatz, to investigate the design and decide if production of the type should be discontinued. The production of the Marauder was meanwhile suspended pending the outcome of the board's deliberations, but in the event the continuation of production was recommended, subject to a number of changes, including a substantial increase in wing area.

While these discussions were taking place, the B-26A had received its baptism of fire in the Pacific where, by April 1942, a total of forty-eight had reached North Australia. The first operational sorties were flown in the same month by the 22nd Bombardment Group against targets in New Guinea. For several weeks the B-26As flew regularly to bomb Rabaul, with intermediate landings at Port Moresby for fuel, with the assistance of a 208 Imp. gal. (250 U.S. gal.) bomb-bay tank. The aircraft carried four 500-lb. or twenty 100-lb. bombs which they dropped from 10,000 ft. on missions that should have been undertaken by heavy bombers. In June the B-26A made its début as a torpedo-strike aircraft, being used against Japanese warships in the Battle of Midway, and in the Aleutians, in both cases without scoring hits. In the latter campaign, the 73rd and 77th Bombardment Squadrons operated their Marauders from Alaska.

Production of the Marauder had been resumed in May 1942, after a number of modifications had been incorporated. These mostly resulted from combat experience rather than the decisions of the board of

(Immediately below) A B-26B (41-17704) which introduced the stepped tail gun position, and (bottom) an early production B-26B-2-MA (41-17876) delivered prior to the introduction of the enlarged air intakes.

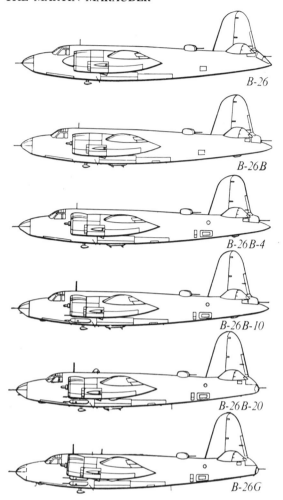

B-26

B-26B

B-26B-4

B-26B-10

B-26B-20

B-26G

substantial increase in the size of the two intakes on top of the engine cowling for the dual eight-port downdraught carburettors in order to accommodate sand filters for tropical operations. The oil cooler intake, at the bottom of the cowling, with its outlet flap just forward of the undercarriage bay, remained unaltered.

Apart from these powerplant changes, the most noticeable modification in the B-26B was the replacement of the single hand-held machine gun in the tail cone by a new stepped position accommodating two 0.5-in. guns (which increased the overall length to 58 ft. 3 in.) with 1,500 r.p.g. The 0.3-in. or 0.5-in. gun in the nose was retained, with 600 rounds, and a similar weapon with the same supply of ammunition was provided in a ventral "tunnel" for rear defence. The Martin 250CE electrically-powered turret, with its 360 degree traverse and 70 degree elevation, had 400 r.p.g., and completed the six-gun armament of the early B-26B, which had a gross weight of 36,500 lb. as a war maximum, and could carry up to 5,200 lb. of bombs, or other offensive weapons. This load could be made up of a 2,000-lb. torpedo and two 1,600-lb. bombs, the former having to be dropped first. More normal alternative loads comprised two 2,000-lb., four 1,000-lb., eight 500-lb., sixteen 250-lb., or thirty 100-lb. bombs. Fuel was carried in two 300 Imp. gal. (360 U.S. gal.) main, and two 100 Imp. gal. (121 U.S. gal.) auxiliary wing tanks, plus two 208 Imp. gal. (250 U.S. gal.) forward bomb-bay tanks, giving a maximum capacity of 1,216 Imp. gal. With this fuel load, a 1,500-lb. bomb load could be carried for nearly 2,000 miles in 9.7 hours, but a more representative load was 4,000 lb. with 801 Imp. gal. (962 U.S. gal.) of fuel, giving an operating range of 550 miles for a sortie time of two hours at maximum cruising speed.

In the B-26B-2-MA was fitted the R-2800-41 series engine, with a power increase from 1,850 to 1,920 h.p. for take-off, and a maximum of 1,490 h.p. at 14,300 ft., while the B-26B-3 and B-4 had the generally similar R-2800-43. The Marauder was unusual in having block numbers between the usual multiples of five allocated to it during manufacture instead of for field modifications, and the B-26B-4, which commenced with the 431st aircraft of the "B" series, incorporated several important changes. These included the provision of night and day drift signals, a life raft with automatic ejector gear, an inclinometer, astrograph and astro-compass, but the most significant concerned an attempt to improve take-off performance.

This was achieved by lengthening the nosewheel strut and rearranging the hydraulic equipment in the

enquiry. The next production version was the B-26B, and more Marauders of this series were built than of any other version, comprising a total of 1,883 machines. Although grouped under a common B-model designation, these had some widely varying characteristics, indicated by different production block numbers. The first B-26Bs retained the R-2800-5s of earlier Marauders, but featured extensively revised internal equipment. Crew armour disposition was improved, and the pilot's seat was reduced in height to provide easier access to the bombardier's compartment in the nose. The positions of oxygen and water bottles, together with fire extinguishers, were also changed. External changes included the removal of the airscrew spinners and, after the B-26B-2, a

FINISH AND INSIGNIA: *Two finishes were normally applied to Martin B-26 Marauders of the U.S.A.A.F., one (depicted by the drawing on the opposite page) being natural metal overall with an olive drab anti-glare panel ahead of the cockpit, and the other consisting of matt olive drab over all upper surfaces and neutral grey under surfaces, the two colours meeting in an irregular wavy line. Marauders of the Ninth Air Force had colourful Group markings on the vertical tail surfaces. The B-26B-55-MA (42-96165) illustrated was operated by the 397th Bombardment Group, and the diagonal tail marking was yellow edged with black. Three black and three white "invasion stripes" appeared on the upper and lower wing surfaces, and around the rear fuselage. The serial number was painted in black on the vertical tail surfaces of Marauders with natural metal finish, and in yellow on camouflaged machines. The squadron code letters (or letter and numeral, e.g., B6) and individual aircraft letter (e.g., T) appeared in black or (on camouflaged machines) in grey, and the national insignia appeared on the upper surface of the port wing, the lower surface of the starboard wing, and the fuselage sides. From September 1943, this comprised a five-pointed white star on a blue disc superimposed upon a white horizontal bar outlined in blue.*

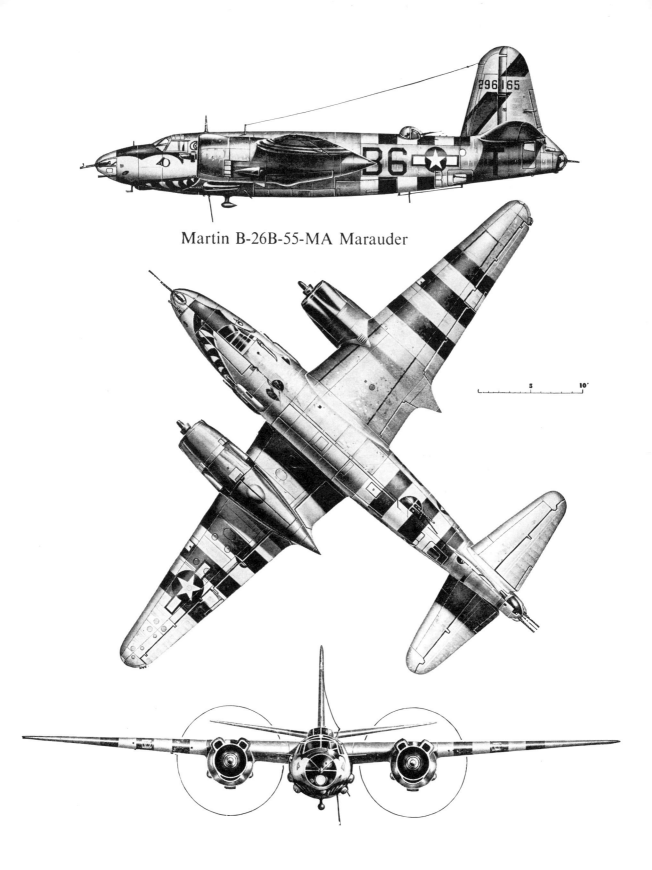

Martin B-26B-55-MA Marauder

Two Marauders of the 322nd Bombardment Group. The aircraft in the foreground is a B-26B-25-MA, and that in the background is a B-26C-5-MO.

A B-26B-4-MA (41-18176). Two hundred and eleven Marauders of this type were produced, being preceded by a batch of twenty-eight B-26B-3-MAs.

wheel well. The increased incidence of the wing resulted in an improved lift coefficient, but this was inevitably a makeshift solution. Another innovation in the B-26B-4 was the replacement of the ventral "tunnel" 0.3-in. gun by two 0.5-in. guns in the rear beam positions, firing through hatches on the flanks of the aft fuselage. These guns were mounted on extending arms swivelling from positions on the fuselage floor, and firing rearwards and downwards. Each was provided with some 240 r.p.g., and the beam guns were fitted to the last 141 B-26B-4s in addition to all subsequent models.

The B-26B-5-MA saw the introduction of slotted flaps and mechanically-operated main undercarriage doors, but with the B-26B-10-MA came a major redesign to cure the persistent troubles resulting from the excessively high wing loading of the Marauder. To all intents and purposes, the B-26B-10-MA was a completely new model. The wing was increased in span from 65 ft. to no less than 71 ft., with a corresponding increase in area from 602 sq. ft. to 659 sq. ft.,

resulting in a useful decrease in the wing loading. Inevitably, the U.S.A.A.F. did its best to offset the advantages resulting from this modification by approving an increased gross weight of 38,200 lb. for the B-10 variant, but at the former maximum of 36,000 lb., the take-off run was reduced from 3,150 to 2,850 ft. Maximum speed decreased from 298 to 282 m.p.h. at 15,000 ft., partly owing to the larger wing, but also as a result of the drag occasioned by the considerable extra armament fitted to this and subsequent variants.

With the introduction of the B-26B-10, the Marauder became another "Flying Fortress", with almost as heavy an armament as the heavy bomber, comprising some twelve 0.5-in. Colt-Brownings. The flexible nose mounting became standardised for a 0.5-in. gun with 270 rounds, and was augmented by a single fixed gun on the starboard front fuselage with 200 rounds. The forward-firing armament was further reinforced by two "package" guns mounted in individual blisters on each side of the fuselage, behind and below the cockpit, with 200–250 r.p.g., giving the Marauder as much fixed-gun punch as many fighters. The normal rear turret, beam and tail armament were retained, although on the B-26B-20-MA and later aircraft, the hand-held twin tail guns were replaced by a power-operated Martin-Bell turret, also accommodating two 0.5-in. guns with 400 r.p.g.

The blunt tail cone of this installation markedly altered the contours of the Marauder's rear fuselage, which had already been modified by the addition of a taller fin and rudder on the B-26B-10-MA to maintain stability with the bigger wing. The turret reduced the fuselage length to 56 ft. 1 in., but the new vertical surfaces increased overall height from 19 ft. 10 in. to 21 ft. 6 in. Other changes in the B-26B-20-MA included provision for two more 208 Imp. gal. (250 U.S. gal.) fuel tanks in the aft bomb-bay, bringing the total tankage to 1,634 Imp. gal.

The Glenn Martin production line at Baltimore, where, for some obscure reason, the B-26B-10-MA was known as the B-26B1 within the company, was augmented in 1942 by another Martin plant at Omaha, despite further U.S.A.A.F. doubts as to the combat capability of the Marauder. In July and in October 1942 enquiries had been conducted as to the bomber's future, but on the recommendation of Major General George C. Kenney, through his experience of B-26 operations in the South-West Pacific, further production was advised. At Omaha, the B-26B-10 to -20 were produced under the designations B-26C-5 to -25-MO, while the later series B-26B-25 to -55-MA had their equivalents in the B-26C-30 to -45-MO.

The later batches had the single fixed nose gun deleted, while all of these, except the first seventy-five B-26Cs, carried fewer bombs of the smaller weights because of the removal of the aft bomb-bay. The two additional bomb-bay tanks were removed, leaving stations for six 500-lb., ten 250-lb., or twenty 100-lb. bombs as an alternative to 4,000 lb. of larger weapons. Provision was still made for the carriage of an external torpedo in these variants, of which the B-26C was built to the tune of 1,235 aircraft.

Three U.S.A.A.F. units, the 17th, the 319th and the 320th Bombardment Groups, arrived in North Africa with B-26B and C Marauders at the end of 1942, after a considerable delay, and began tactical operations with slowly increasing success almost immediately. The R.A.F. was also operating nineteen B-26Bs (FK362 to FK380) as the Marauder IA, and with the South African Air Force received in addition 100 B-26Cs (FB418 to FB517), designated Marauder IIs. The U.S.A.A.F. Marauders were particularly prominent at the close of the Tunisian campaign, when their heavy armament, relatively high speed and long range enabled them to intercept the lumbering German Me 323 and Ju 52/3m transports far out over the

(*Top*) *The twenty-first Marauder III (HD422) for the R.A.F. Two hundred B-26Fs and 150 B-26Gs were supplied to the R.A.F. under this designation. (Immediately above) A Martin JM-1 target-tug of the U.S. Marine Corps.*

Mediterranean, and shoot them down in droves as they attempted to evacuate the beaten German forces.

But while the B-26 was proving itself as a long-range fighter over the Mediterranean, it was meeting less success elsewhere in its designed role. In the United Kingdom, as part of the medium bomber force of the Eighth Air Force, by May 1943 Marauders were attacking shallow penetration targets on the Continent at low level. On May 17th eleven Marauders attacked installations at Ijmuiden and Haarlem, in the Netherlands, but all except one aircraft, which aborted through mechanical failure, were shot down by flak and fighters. Once again, the future of the Marauder hung in the balance, but it was decided to transfer the type to VIII Air Support Command for employment on tactical operations in support of Allied ground forces during the forthcoming invasion of the Continent. In the meantime, the aircraft were to be used with different tactics in attacks against strategic

A B-26B-50-MA Marauder with the yellow and black diagonal stripes indicating that it was an aircraft of the 387th Bombardment Group.

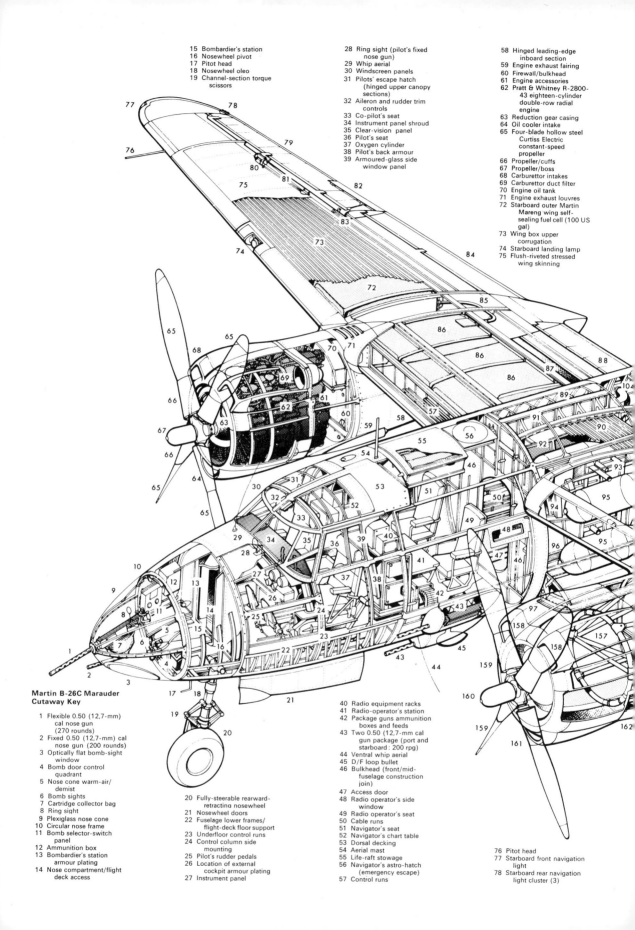

15 Bombardier's station
16 Nosewheel pivot
17 Pitot head
18 Nosewheel oleo
19 Channel-section torque
   scissors

28 Ring sight (pilot's fixed
   nose gun)
29 Whip aerial
30 Windscreen panels
31 Pilots' escape hatch
   (hinged upper canopy
   sections)
32 Aileron and rudder trim
   controls
33 Co-pilot's seat
34 Instrument panel shroud
35 Clear-vision panel
36 Pilot's seat
37 Oxygen cylinder
38 Pilot's back armour
39 Armoured-glass side
   window panel

58 Hinged leading-edge
   inboard section
59 Engine exhaust fairing
60 Firewall/bulkhead
61 Engine accessories
62 Pratt & Whitney R-2800-
   43 eighteen-cylinder
   double-row radial
   engine
63 Reduction gear casing
64 Oil cooler intake
65 Four-blade hollow steel
   Curtiss Electric
   constant-speed
   propeller
66 Propeller/cuffs
67 Propeller/boss
68 Carburettor intakes
69 Carburettor duct filter
70 Engine oil tank
71 Engine exhaust louvres
72 Starboard outer Martin
   Mareng wing self-
   sealing fuel cell (100 US
   gal)
73 Wing box upper
   corrugation
74 Starboard landing lamp
75 Flush-riveted stressed
   wing skinning

**Martin B-26C Marauder
Cutaway Key**

1 Flexible 0.50 (12,7-mm)
  cal nose gun
  (270 rounds)
2 Fixed 0.50 (12,7-mm) cal
  nose gun (200 rounds)
3 Optically flat bomb-sight
  window
4 Bomb door control
  quadrant
5 Nose cone warm-air/
  demist
6 Bomb sights
7 Cartridge collector bag
8 Ring sight
9 Plexiglass nose cone
10 Circular nose frame
11 Bomb selector-switch
   panel
12 Ammunition box
13 Bombardier's station
   armour plating
14 Nose compartment/flight
   deck access

20 Fully-steerable rearward-
   retracting nosewheel
21 Nosewheel doors
22 Fuselage lower frames/
   flight-deck floor support
23 Underfloor control runs
24 Control column side
   mounting
25 Pilot's rudder pedals
26 Location of external
   cockpit armour plating
27 Instrument panel

40 Radio equipment racks
41 Radio-operator's station
42 Package guns ammunition
   boxes and feeds
43 Two 0.50 (12,7-mm cal
   gun package (port and
   starboard : 200 rpg)
44 Ventral whip aerial
45 D/F loop bullet
46 Bulkhead (front/mid-
   fuselage construction
   join)
47 Access door
48 Radio operator's side
   window
49 Radio operator's seat
50 Cable runs
51 Navigator's seat
52 Navigator's chart table
53 Dorsal decking
54 Aerial mast
55 Life-raft stowage
56 Navigator's astro-hatch
   (emergency escape)
57 Control runs

76 Pitot head
77 Starboard front navigation
   light
78 Starboard rear navigation
   light cluster (3)

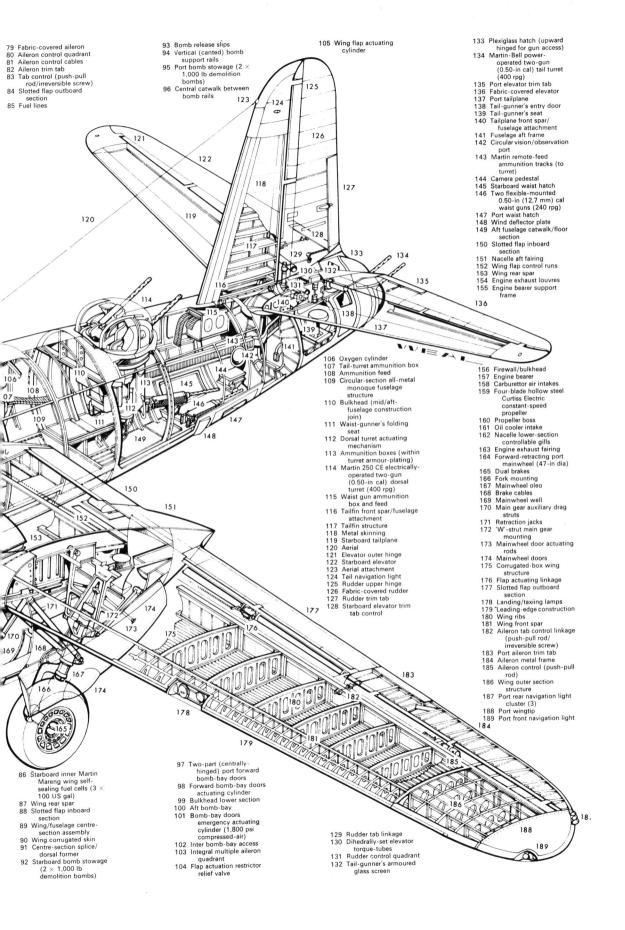

79 Fabric-covered aileron
80 Aileron control quadrant
81 Aileron control cables
82 Aileron trim tab
83 Tab control (push-pull rod/irreversible screw)
84 Slotted flap outboard section
85 Fuel lines

93 Bomb release slips
94 Vertical (canted) bomb support rails
95 Port bomb stowage (2 × 1,000 lb demolition bombs)
96 Central catwalk between bomb rails

105 Wing flap actuating cylinder

133 Plexiglass hatch (upward hinged for gun access)
134 Martin-Bell power-operated two-gun (0.50-in cal) tail turret (400 rpg)
135 Port elevator trim tab
136 Fabric-covered elevator
137 Port tailplane
138 Tail-gunner's entry door
139 Tail-gunner's seat
140 Tailplane front spar/fuselage attachment
141 Fuselage aft frame
142 Circular vision/observation port
143 Martin remote-feed ammunition tracks (to turret)
144 Camera pedestal
145 Starboard waist hatch
146 Two flexible-mounted 0.50-in (12,7 mm) cal waist guns (240 rpg)
147 Port waist hatch
148 Wind deflector plate
149 Aft fuselage catwalk/floor section
150 Slotted flap inboard section
151 Nacelle aft fairing
152 Wing flap control runs
153 Wing rear spar
154 Engine exhaust louvres
155 Engine bearer support frame

106 Oxygen cylinder
107 Tail-turret ammunition box
108 Ammunition feed
109 Circular-section all-metal monoque fuselage structure
110 Bulkhead (mid/aft-fuselage construction join)
111 Waist-gunner's folding seat
112 Dorsal turret actuating mechanism
113 Ammunition boxes (within turret armour-plating)
114 Martin 250 CE electrically-operated two-gun (0.50-in cal) dorsal turret (400 rpg)
115 Waist gun ammunition box and feed
116 Tailfin front spar/fuselage attachment
117 Tailfin structure
118 Metal skinning
119 Starboard tailplane
120 Aerial
121 Elevator outer hinge
122 Starboard elevator
123 Aerial attachment
124 Tail navigation light
125 Rudder upper hinge
126 Fabric-covered rudder
127 Rudder trim tab
128 Starboard elevator trim tab control

156 Firewall/bulkhead
157 Engine bearer
158 Carburettor air intakes
159 Four-blade hollow steel Curtiss Electric constant-speed propeller
160 Propeller boss
161 Oil cooler intake
162 Nacelle lower-section controllable gills
163 Engine exhaust fairing
164 Forward-retracting port mainwheel (47-in dia)
165 Dual brakes
166 Fork mounting
167 Mainwheel oleo
168 Brake cables
169 Mainwheel well
170 Main gear auxiliary drag struts
171 Retraction jacks
172 'W'-strut main gear mounting
173 Mainwheel door actuating rods
174 Mainwheel doors
175 Corrugated-box wing structure
176 Flap actuating cylinder
177 Slotted flap outboard section
178 Landing/taxiing lamps
179 Leading-edge construction
180 Wing ribs
181 Wing front spar
182 Aileron tab control linkage (push-pull rod/irreversible screw)
183 Port aileron trim tab
184 Aileron metal frame
185 Aileron control (push-pull rod)
186 Wing outer section structure
187 Port rear navigation light cluster (3)
188 Port wingtip
189 Port front navigation light

86 Starboard inner Martin Mareng wing self-sealing fuel cells (3 × 100 US gal)
87 Wing rear spar
88 Slotted flap inboard section
89 Wing/fuselage centre-section assembly
90 Wing corrugated skin
91 Centre-section splice/dorsal former
92 Starboard bomb stowage (2 × 1,000 lb demolition bombs)

97 Two-part (centrally-hinged) port forward bomb-bay doors
98 Forward bomb-bay doors actuating cylinder
99 Bulkhead lower section
100 Aft bomb-bay
101 Bomb-bay doors emergency actuating cylinder (1,800 psi compressed-air)
102 Inter bomb-bay access
103 Integral multiple aileron quadrant
104 Flap actuation restrictor relief valve

129 Rudder tab linkage
130 Dihedrally-set elevator torque-tubes
131 Rudder control quadrant
132 Tail-gunner's armoured glass screen

A B-26C-30-MO supplied to the R.A.F. as the Marauder II. This aircraft (FB482) was the sixty-fifth of a batch of one hundred machines.

targets from medium altitudes (10,000–14,000 ft.), with heavy fighter escort.

A slight repercussion from the Marauder's fling as a fighter came in July 1943, when, in the frantic search to find an escort "destroyer" for the heavy bombers of the Eighth Air Force, the A.A.F. Headquarters in the United States suggested the use of the B-26 in this role. The suggestion was not received with enthusiasm by the Eighth Air Force staff, since the Marauder not only had an entirely different performance envelope from the Fortress, but it had also just proved its own inability to survive without escort in the hostile European skies.

The development of suitable tactics for the A.A.F. Marauders, however, followed by their transfer in November 1943 to the Ninth Air Force for tactical sorties in support of the forthcoming invasion of Europe finally vindicated the turbulent career of the B-26. Just before D-Day, Marauders became the first A.A.F. aircraft in the European Theatre of Operations to operate at night, and gained a particularly impressive reputation for precision attacks on bridges and other transport targets in France in an intensive interdiction campaign. Marauders began operating from Continental airstrips as the Allied armies advanced, and in their first year of combat in Europe, the A.A.F. B-26s flew 29,000 sorties and dropped 46,430 tons of bombs for the extraordinarily low loss of 139 aircraft. In addition to American units, Marauders were flown by the First French Air Corps in Europe, and eventually Australian, South African, Canadian and Greek crews were added to the British and other personnel who had flown the B-26 in combat in the three main theatres of operations.

The use of the Marauder was further extended to the U.S. Navy by the adaptation of some of the earlier production series for target towing under the designation JM-1. One version, equipped for photographic-reconnaissance, became the JM-1P, while similarly stripped B-26As, Bs and Cs were used for training and general duties by the A.A.F. Initially, 208 B-26B and some 350 B-26C Marauders were converted as AT-23As and Bs respectively, but all training and target-towing versions subsequently became known as TB-26s. Lesser known variants of the basic type included a single XB-26D which was modified from an early B-26 in about 1942 to assess the value of hot-air de-icing on the mainplanes. Another "one-off" modification was the B-26E which was a lightened B-26B, weighing about 32,000 lb., and distinguishable mainly by the relocation of the Martin dorsal turret forward to the roof of the navigator's compartment.

One final change of some magnitude was to be made to production Marauders in the course of their career, and almost inevitably it was concerned mainly with the take-off performance. From late 1942 onwards, the wing incidence was increased by 3.5 degrees, which also gave slightly more airscrew clearance and a more level cruising attitude. The power plants remained unchanged as R-2800-43s, but the B-26F, as this version was designated, had a slightly modified fuel system, with a total capacity of 1,249 Imp. gal. (1,500 U.S. gal.). As in the later B-26Bs and Cs, the fixed nose gun was deleted, but there was a slight increase in the ammunition carried for the remaining eleven 0.5-in. guns. Torpedo provision was finally deleted, and the maximum offensive load became 4,000 lb.

In most respects, therefore, the B-26F was similar to previous models in performance, and other modifications, such as the introduction of mechanical gear for emergency lowering of the undercarriage, were not apparent externally. In all, 300 B-26Fs of block-numbers -1, -2, and -6 were built by Martin-Baltimore, and of these, 200 (HD402 to HD601) were supplied to the R.A.F. and S.A.A.F. as the Marauder III. Production then changed to the ultimate Marauder

A B-26F-1-MA of the 387th Bombardment Group. The F and G models introduced an increase in wing incidence which gave a more level cruising altitude.

variant to see combat, the B-26G. This was also built at Baltimore, 893 aircraft being completed by the time production ceased on March 30, 1945, and differing from the B-26F only in having universal AN (Army-Navy) instead of AC (Air Corps) type equipment; a larger life raft compartment in the top section of the forward fuselage, and mechanical emergency extension gear on the nosewheel. Both the B-26F and G, together with some earlier variants, were sometimes fitted with a tail bumper fairing beneath the aft turret.

One hundred and fifty B-26Gs were supplied to the R.A.F. under Lend-Lease (HD602 to HD751), and like the B-26Fs, these were known as Marauder IIIs. In the final reckoning, Marauders served with Nos. 14, 39, 326, 327, and 454 Squadrons of the R.A.F. during the war, and also with Nos. 12, 21, 24, 25 and 30 Squadrons of the S.A.A.F.

The final production version of the Marauder was the TB-26G, only fifty-seven of which were completed, for training and target-towing duties. A few of these were taken over by the U.S. Navy as the JM-2. This version did not quite end the development story of the Marauder, as a single additional and final variant was the XB-26H. Known colloquially as the "Middle River Stump Jumper", this was a TB-26G-25-MA modified to have tandem main-wheels retracting into the fuselage, and outrigger legs housed in place of the normal main members in the engine nacelles. The fuselage was externally stiffened to take the landing loads of this tandem or "bicycle" undercarriage. This was purely a research installation for the Boeing B-47 Stratojet then on the drawing boards.

In all, 5,157 examples of the Marauder left the production lines, and the type made its mark in every theatre in which it fought.

Despite its landing speed of 130 m.p.h., which remained virtually unchanged despite all the modifications made to reduce it, the Marauder had no really vicious flying characteristics, and in fact its single-engine performance was commendably good. It did demand, however, a high standard of training from its pilots, but in return offered a level of operational immunity unapproached by most other aircraft of its class.

Martin B-26G Marauder

Dimensions :	Span, 71 ft. ; length, 56 ft. 1 in. ; height, 20 ft. 4 in. ; wing area, 658 sq. ft.
Armament :	Eleven 0.5-in. Colt-Browning machine guns in fixed forward-firing, manual nose and waist, and power-operated dorsal and tail positions, with a total ammunition supply of 4,400 rounds. Maximum bomb load, 4,000 lb.
Power Plants :	Two Pratt and Whitney R-2800-43 eighteen-cylinder air-cooled radial engines with two-speed superchargers, each developing 1,920 h.p. for take-off and 1,490 h.p. at 14,300 ft.
Weights :	Empty, 25,300 lb. ; combat, 37,000 lb. ; maximum permissible, 38,200 lb.
Performance :	(At maximum weight) Maximum speed, 283 m.p.h. at 5,000 ft., 274 m.p.h. at 15,000 ft. ; initial climb rate, 1,000 ft./min. ; service ceiling, 19,800 ft. ; range (at maximum cruising power), 1,100 miles. ; endurance, 5.1 hours. ; take-off distance to 50 ft., 6,100 ft. ; landing distance from 50 ft., 2,400 ft.

This photograph of a B-26G-5-MA (43-34396) shows clearly the canted engines resulting from the 3.5° increase in wing incidence.

The first prototype Lancaster (BT308) was originally known as the Manchester III, and flew for the first time on January 9, 1941. It retained the central fin of the Manchester I.

THE AVRO LANCASTER

Many aeroplanes employed by the combatants of the Second World War became famous; few were truly great. Greatness is a quality which cannot be instilled in an aircraft on the drawing board or the assembly line. A great aircraft must have that touch of genius which transcends the good, and it must have luck—the luck to be in the right place at the right time. It must have flying qualities above the average; reliability, ruggedness and fighting ability, and, in the final analysis, it needs the skilled touch of crews to which it has endeared itself. All these things the Lancaster had in good measure.

Despite its power-operated turrets, those anathemas which plagued the wartime bomber designer striving for cleanliness of line, the Lancaster embodied a measure of grace which made it pleasing on the eye, and its neat aerodynamic shape contributed materially towards its excellent all-round performance. But like so many good aeroplanes, the essence of its design was its simplicity, its robust structure being ideally suited for mass production, and this was undoubtedly

one of the main factors in its success. It was also remarkably adaptable and a superlative bomber on every count, and of all the great aeroplanes which fought out the war, there are many who would insist that this was the greatest.

Most great aeroplanes result from inspired, far-sighted original designs, yet the Avro Lancaster was born in a somewhat devious fashion. Its true beginnings stretched back to 1936, for it was in that year that the Air Ministry outlined its requirements for a new generation of medium and heavy bombers. At that time, the Handley Page Heyford, a twin-engined biplane, was still standard R.A.F. night bombing equipment, together with a single squadron of Fairey Hendon monoplanes. The twin-engined Vickers Wellingtons and Handley Page Hampdens were coming along, but the Air Ministry now wanted something better.

Two specifications were drawn up in 1936; one called for a four-engined heavy bomber, and the other for a twin-engined medium bomber, although the latter was to be considerably heavier and larger than the Wellington which was then looked upon as a "heavy". After the various design studies had been evaluated, two designs for each requirement were adopted, and two prototypes of each were ordered. The B.12/36 contracts went to Short Brothers and to the Supermarine Aviation Works (Vickers) Limited. Short's design was eventually to emerge as the Stirling, but the prototypes of the Supermarine bomber, which was being built to the designs of R. J. Mitchell, were to be destroyed while still under construction when the Woolson factory was bombed in 1940. The medium bomber contracts, to P.13/36, were awarded to A. V. Roe for their Type 679, and to Handley Page for the H.P.56. The latter was destined never to materialise

(Immediately below) The first prototype Manchester (L7246), and (bottom) the second prototype Manchester (L7247) with central tail fin.

The second prototype Lancaster (DG595) was a "productionized" machine which flew for the first time on May 13, 1941. Like the first prototype, it started life on the assembly line as a Manchester.

in twin-engined form, being evolved into the four-engined H.P.57, the prototype of the Halifax, during construction.

Specification P.13/36 embodied very far-reaching requirements, and A. V. Roe's design team, headed by Roy Chadwick, was faced with the design and construction of an aeroplane weighing more than twenty tons, and carrying an extremely heavy bomb load at extremely high speeds considering the size of the machine. It was also faced with the task of installing elaborate hydraulic and electrical systems, and the latest technical equipment then evolved, and the Type 679 could therefore be considered as one of the major steps forward in bomber design. Furthermore, with the outbreak of war imminent, the normal period of development had to be compressed, and preparations made for quantity production before prototypes could be flown. Thus, by the middle of 1938, plans had been laid for a large production programme, with construction being undertaken at several shadow factories.

The specified power plant was the new and unorthodox twenty-four cylinder X-type Rolls-Royce Vulture, and with two of these, the first prototype (L7246) made its initial flight on July 25, 1939, with Avro's test pilot, Captain H. A. Brown, at the controls. One of the features of the P.13/36 specification had been a demand that the aircraft should be stressed for catapult launching—the term "frictionless take-off" was frequently used—and after some modification to the original tail assembly to improve the aircraft's stability (a central fin being added), the aircraft was used at the Royal Aircraft Establishment for catapult take-off and arrested landing trials. Perhaps fortunately, this idea was not pursued further. The machine ultimately crashed at Boscombe Down. The second prototype (L7247), which

followed on May 26, 1940, was flown from the outset with a central fin added to the original twin-finned tail assembly. Unlike its predecessor, the second prototype carried a full complement of power-operated turrets—nose, ventral and tail—each mounting two 0.303-in. Browning machine guns. The ventral Frazer-Nash FN.21A gun turret ultimately gave place to a dorsal turret, and other changes made on this prototype included the fitting of horn-balanced fabric-covered elevators and ailerons in place of the original metal-covered surfaces, and the extension of the wing span from 80 ft. 2 in. to 90 ft. 1 in.

In the meantime, production of the new bomber, which had been named Manchester, had reached an advanced stage, and the first Manchester Is to specification 19/37 started coming off the line in the middle of 1940, the first deliveries being made to No. 207 Squadron at Waddington before the end of the year. The initial production machines (commencing with L7276) had triple fins and a 22 ft.-span

(Immediately below) The Manchester IA with enlarged fins, and (bottom) the Manchester I with the central fin.

A standard production Lancaster I (ED413). The first squadron of R.A.F. Bomber Command to equip with the Lancaster I was No. 44 Squadron early in 1942.

tailplane, but with the Mk.IA the central fin was deleted, the size of the remaining fins was increased, and the span of the tailplane was increased to 33 ft. In the Manchester IA, the Vulture engines had been boosted from 1,760 h.p. to 1,845 h.p. for take-off, loaded weight had risen to 56,000 lb., compared with 45,000 lb. for the first prototype, and armament had been standardised on twin 0.303-in. Brownings in nose and dorsal turrets, and four 0.303-in. guns in the tail turret. The Manchester IA normally carried a crew of seven, and its maximum bomb load was 10,350 lb. with which range was 1,200 miles. With a 8,100 lb. bomb load range was increased to 1,630 miles, and fully loaded, maximum speed was 265 m.p.h. at 17,000 ft.

The Manchester made its operational début with an attack on Brest on the night of February 24–25, 1941, but its service life was destined to be extremely brief. Indeed, the Manchester might be considered as one of the R.A.F.'s major disappointments of the Second World War, but its failure was in no way due to its design. Rolls-Royce, who had extremely heavy commitments in other directions, had been unable to eliminate the teething troubles suffered by the large and complex Vulture engine by which the Manchester was powered. The Vulture proved totally unreliable

in service, and the Manchester suffered frequent engine failures owing to the big end bearings giving way, and other troubles. Many Manchesters which failed to return from operations are likely to have been lost as a result of such failures. Nevertheless, the Manchester remained in service with R.A.F. Bomber Command until June 1942, making its last operational sortie a raid on Bremen on the night of the 25th-26th of that month.

Owing to doubts as to the possibility of eliminating the Vulture's faults, a search for alternative power plants had been conducted before production of the Manchester had got under way. Two alternative installations were designed for the proposed Manchester II which would have had either two Bristol Centaurus or two Napier Sabre engines. Although some installational work was carried out, in the event neither type of engine was installed; as an alternative proposal, the Manchester III appeared more attractive. This proposal was to use four Rolls-Royce Merlin X engines in lieu of the two Vultures, and it was this suggestion that was to give birth to the Lancaster. A. V. Roe built only 159 Manchesters, including the prototypes, and Metropolitan-Vickers, responsible for the shadow production of the type, built a further forty-three after losing the first thirteen in various

One of the specially-modified Lancaster Is (ED817) issued to No. 617 Squadron for the attacks on the Moehne, Eder and Sorpe dams.

A Lancaster I (W4963) fitted with H2S radar bombing equipment.

stages of completion when their works were bombed on December 23, 1940.

The use of the Manchester airframe made possible the rapid construction of a prototype Manchester III (BT308) which, renamed Lancaster I, flew for the first time on January 9, 1941. Apart from the new wing centre section to take the four Merlins, it was almost standard Manchester throughout, right down to the central fin then still in use on the Manchester I with the 22 ft.-span tailplane. This was later changed to conform to the Manchester IA's tail assembly, and as time passed the Lancaster was progressively modified and refined until little of the original Manchester structure remained.

At this juncture, it is of interest to note that a parallel design, using the same wings, power plants, tail assembly and undercarriage, was initiated by Roy Chadwick's team, which foresaw the eventual need for an easily-produced aircraft with a good range and payload capable of taking care of the future transport requirements of the fighting services. A rectangular fuselage of generous cross-section was provided, and the aircraft was designated Type 685. However, owing to the pressing need to concentrate all production capacity on the Lancaster bomber, it was to be more than two years before the prototype transport was to emerge as the York, by which time specification C.1/42 had been drawn up around the design. Thus, contrary to popular belief, the York transport was not developed *from* the Lancaster bomber, both machines being contemporary in parallel developments, and both based on the Manchester. In view of the considerable strain on the capacity of Avro's design office in transforming the Manchester into the Lancaster, the parallel design of a transport for which there was no *official* requirement was very much a "hole-and-corner" occupation. By the time the load had eased, and the Lancaster had attained quantity production, an agreement had been reached whereby the British aircraft industry concentrated on the development and production of combat aircraft, leaving the supply of transports to the U.S. aircraft industry. Thus, when development of the York was resumed, no labour of any description could be made *officially* available for the work, and the first unit to be fully equipped with Yorks, No. 511 Squadron at Lyneham, did not appear until 1945.

Early flight trials with the Lancaster prototype, which commenced at Boscombe Down on January 27, 1941, were eminently successful, and there was no hesitation on the part of the Air Staff in ordering the Lancaster into immediate production, a step which was influenced as much by the wish to abandon production of the troublesome Vulture engine (thus leaving Rolls-

The Lancaster II prototype (DT810). A second prototype (DT812) was built and subsequent production was entrusted to Sir W. G. Armstrong Whitworth Aircraft.

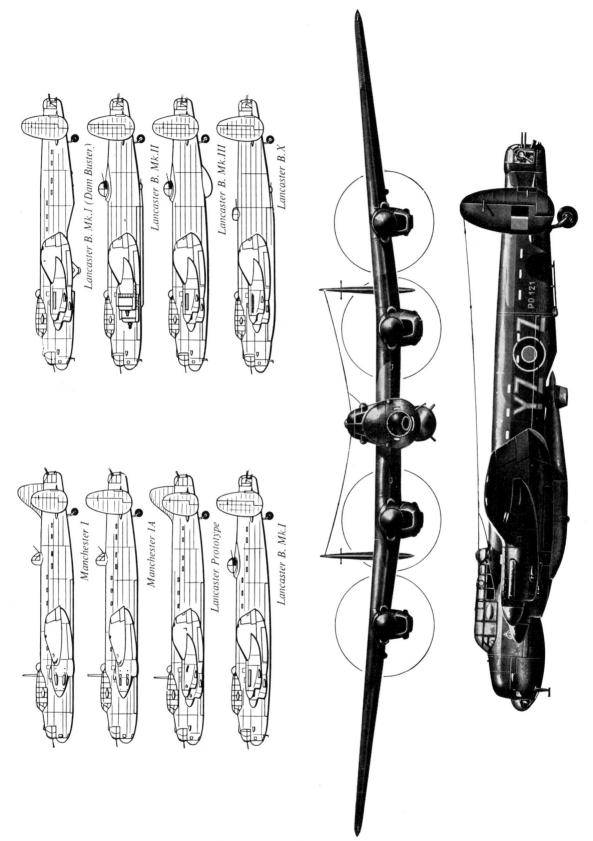

Lancaster B. Mk.I (Dam Buster)

Lancaster B. Mk.II

Lancaster B. Mk.III

Lancaster B.X

Manchester I

Manchester IA

Lancaster Prototype

Lancaster B. Mk.I

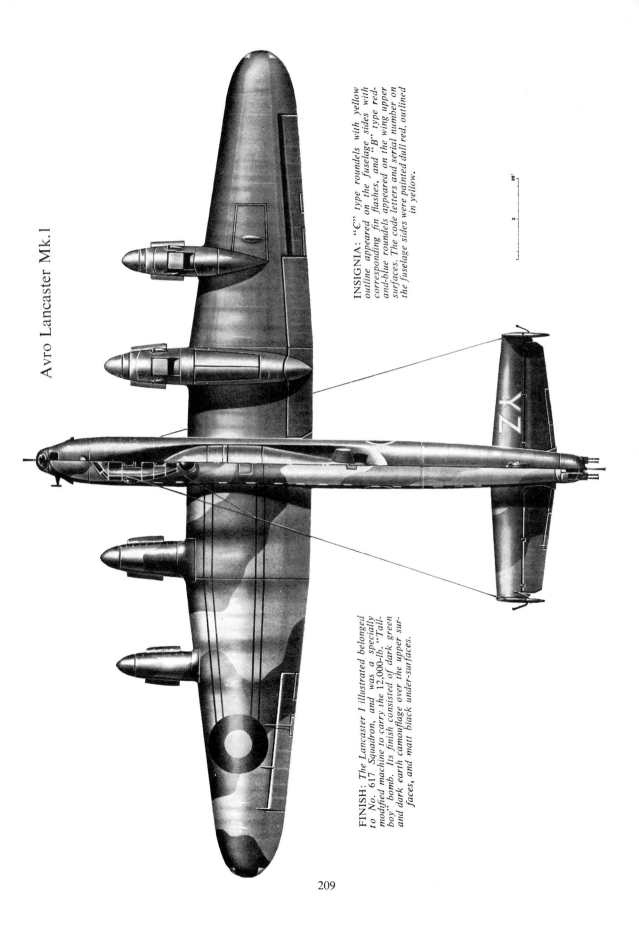

Avro Lancaster Mk.1

INSIGNIA: "C" type roundels with yellow outline appeared on the fuselage sides with corresponding fin flashes, and "B" type red-and-blue roundels appeared on the wing upper surfaces. The code letters and serial number on the fuselage sides were painted dull red, outlined in yellow.

FINISH: The Lancaster 1 illustrated belonged to No. 617 Squadron, and was a specially modified machine to carry the 12,000-lb. "Tall-boy" bomb. Its finish consisted of dark green and dark earth camouflage over the upper sur-faces, and matt black under-surfaces.

An Armstrong Whitworth-built Lancaster II (DS771). Three hundred production machines of this type were delivered.

Royce free to concentrate on the Merlin) as by the results of flight trials. A second "productionized" Lancaster prototype (DG585) flew on May 13, 1941, by which time all production contracts for the Manchester had been amended in favour of the Type 683 Lancaster. Thus, the first production Lancaster (L7527)—which flew from Avro's Woodford airfield on October 31, 1941—had, in fact, started life on the assembly line as a Manchester, and, in all, 243 Lancasters built by A. V. Roe, and fifty-seven built by Metropolitan-Vickers, had originally been the subjects of Manchester production contracts.

Whereas the prototype Lancasters had been powered by 1,130 h.p. Merlin X engines, production Lancaster Is had the later Merlin XXs developing 1,280 h.p. for take-off and delivering a maximum power of 1,480 h.p. at 6,000 ft. As production progressed, Merlin 22s of similar power were installed, and, eventually Merlin 24s offering 1,620 h.p. for take-off, and 1,640 h.p. at 2,000 ft. Provision was made for both dorsal and ventral turrets, although the latter were seldom used and soon discarded, and the Lancaster I's defensive armament stabilised on eight 0.303-in. Browning machine guns in three hydraulic-ally-operated Frazer-Nash turrets, two in each of the nose and dorsal turrets, and four in the tail turret. From the Manchester, the Lancaster inherited a capacious bomb-bay which was, in fact, designed to carry 4,000 lb. of bombs, but as the war continued it was to be progressively modified to take larger and larger bombs, culminating in the fantastic 22,000-lb. "Grand Slam", the heaviest bomb carried by any war-time bomber. Between these extremes, the Lancaster carried 8,000 and 12,000 pounders for which some bomb-bay changes had to be made. An armoured bulkhead was fitted across the centre section portion of the fuselage, being so arranged that it could be opened for passage along the fuselage on either side of the centre-line. The back of the pilot's seat was armour-plated; there was armour protection for his head, and certain vulnerable parts of the structure and turrets were armoured. Provision was made for a crew of seven.

Unlike many aircraft which achieved considerable operational fame, the Lancaster was an outstanding production design. The fuselage was an oval all-metal structure built in five separately-assembled main sections, its backbone being formed by pairs of extruded longerons located halfway down the cross-section of the three middle sections, cross beams between these longerons supporting the floor and forming the roof of the bomb-bay. The wing was also built in five sections, comprising a centre section of parallel chord and thickness, two tapering outer sections, and two semi-circular wingtips. The wing structure comprised two spars each consisting of a top and bottom extruded boom bolted to a single heavy-gauge web plate, the whole being covered by a flush-riveted aluminium-alloy skin. The undercarriage comprised hydraulically-retractable mainwheels and a fixed tail-wheel—the saving in drag that would have resulted from a fully-retractable tailwheel not being worth the weight and complication of the hydraulics. The Lancaster I began life at a gross weight of 60,000 lb., and its performance included a maximum speed of 287 m.p.h. at 11,500 ft., and a service ceiling of 24,500 ft. With a 14,000-lb. bomb load, it could cruise at 210 m.p.h. over a range of 1,660 miles.

Despite the relative simplicity of the Lancaster's structure, production in the quantities demanded called for facilities on the largest scale, and drastic developments in production techniques. A Lancaster manufacturing group was organised, involving the A. V. Roe factories at Manchester and, later, Yeadon; Metropolitan-Vickers at Trafford Park; Austin Motors at Longbridge; Vickers-Armstrongs at Castle Bromwich and Chester, and Armstrong Whitworth at Baginton. These companies were assisted by more than 600 direct subcontractors gradually brought into the programme. While these plants were tooling up, the first Lancaster prototype was sent to Waddington, where it arrived in September 1941 for service trails with the Hampden-equipped No. 44 Squadron, this unit gaining the distinction of becoming the first squadron in R.A.F. Bomber Command to be wholly equipped with the Lancaster a few months later.

No. 44 Squadron was closely followed by No. 97 Squadron at Woodhall Spa, but to "forty-four" went the distinction of being the first unit to employ the Lancaster operationally, with a mine-laying sortie in the Heligoland Bight on March 3, 1942. Bombs were first dropped "in anger" by the Lancaster on the night of March 10–11, 1942, when two aircraft from No. 44 Squadron went to Essen, yet the existence of the Lancaster was not publicly revealed after a nocturnal sortie, but after a long, unescorted, daylight raid on the Maschinenfabrik Augsburg-Nuremburg at Augsburg, Bavaria, on April 17th. Twelve Lancasters from Nos. 44 and 97 Squadrons set out to attack the factory which was engaged in the production of diesel engines for U-boats, and it was a target that Bomber Command believed could only be attacked by day if sufficiently heavy damage was to be inflicted. The Lancasters flew at low altitude throughout the mission in order to take maximum advantage of the element of surprise, but the formation suffered heavy losses, only five returning to base. However, the target was seriously damaged, and it was generally conceded that no other type of bomber then in service in Europe could have pressed home the attack. Of the leaders of the attack, Squadron Leader Sherwood was posted missing and Squadron Leader Nettleton was awarded the Victoria Cross, and this highest award for valour was later to be awarded to nine other Lancaster aircrew members.

Development of the Lancaster airframe from its original Mk.I form was dictated almost solely by operational requirements, and it speaks volumes for the basic soundness of the bomber's design that few modifications were required for technical reasons, and that little could be done to further improve the aircraft's aerodynamics. In order to guarantee a continuous flow of Lancasters to the squadrons in the event of an interruption in supplies of Merlins, an alternative Lancaster variant, the Mk.II, had been planned concurrently with Mk.I production, this version being powered by four Bristol Hercules VI or XVI air-cooled radials rated at 1,735 h.p. at 500 ft.,

and 1,725 h.p. for take-off. After A. V. Roe had built two prototypes with these engines (DT810 and DT 812), production of the Lancaster II was entrusted to Sir W. G. Armstrong Whitworth Aircraft at Baginton, but only 300 examples of this version were built, for supplies of the Merlin had been assured—thanks largely to the availability of Packard-built Merlins after the U.S.A. entered the war. The Lancaster II attained a maximum speed of 270 m.p.h., and carried a 12,000-lb. bomb load over a range of 1,000 miles.

Although the Packard-built Merlin closely resembled its British progenitor, it was built to American standards and measures, and Lancasters fitted with the American-built engines were designated Mk.III. The prototype Lancaster III was modified from an Avro-built Mk.I (W4114), and Packard-built (V-1650-1) Merlin 28s of 1,300 h.p., Merlin 38s of 1,390 h.p., and Merlin 224s of 1,620 h.p. were installed in production machines which also incorporated a few other differences, such as a modified nose to improve the view of the bombardier. Both Lancaster Is and IIIs continued in production side by side. For the most part, A. V. Roe concentrated on the Mk.III, building 2,774 of these as compared with only 896 Mk.Is. All Vickers-Armstrongs' Lancasters—300 at Castle Bromwich and 235 at Chester—were Mk.Is, as were 150 by Austin Motors, 944 by Metropolitan-Vickers, and 919 by Armstrong Whitworth. Metropolitan-Vickers also built 136 Lancaster IIIs, and Armstrong Whitworth built 110 examples of this version.

Early in 1942, the Lancaster was selected for production in Canada by Victory Aircraft Limited, a company wholly owned by the Crown and responsible to the Canadian Minister of Munitions and Supply. This provided an additional source of aircraft for the R.A.F. and for R.C.A.F. squadrons serving in the United Kingdom. The version selected for Canadian production was basically the Lancaster III, and the Victory-built aircraft was designated Lancaster X. In this connection, it is of interest to recall that the

The prototype Lancaster III (W4114) with Packard-built Merlin engines. This aircraft was originally an Avro-built Mk.I.

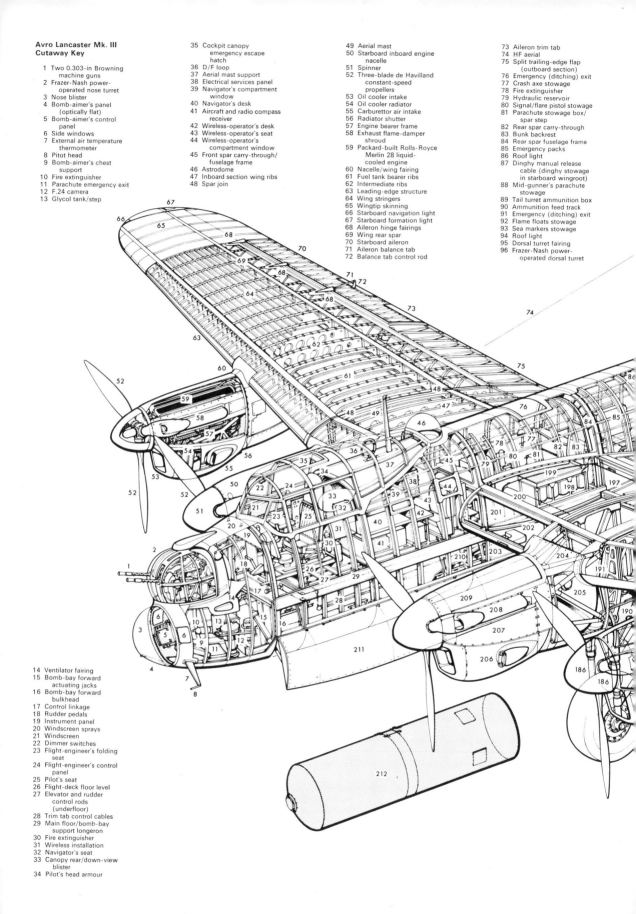

**Avro Lancaster Mk. III
Cutaway Key**

1 Two 0.303-in Browning machine guns
2 Frazer-Nash power-operated nose turret
3 Nose blister
4 Bomb-aimer's panel (optically flat)
5 Bomb-aimer's control panel
6 Side windows
7 External air temperature thermometer
8 Pitot head
9 Bomb-aimer's chest support
10 Fire extinguisher
11 Parachute emergency exit
12 F.24 camera
13 Glycol tank/step

35 Cockpit canopy emergency escape hatch
36 D/F loop
37 Aerial mast support
38 Electrical services panel
39 Navigator's compartment window
40 Navigator's desk
41 Aircraft and radio compass receiver
42 Wireless-operator's desk
43 Wireless-operator's seat
44 Wireless-operator's compartment window
45 Front spar carry-through/fuselage frame
46 Astrodome
47 Inboard section wing ribs
48 Spar join

49 Aerial mast
50 Starboard inboard engine nacelle
51 Spinner
52 Three-blade de Havilland constant-speed propellers
53 Oil cooler intake
54 Oil cooler radiator
55 Carburettor air intake
56 Radiator shutter
57 Engine bearer frame
58 Exhaust flame-damper shroud
59 Packard-built Rolls-Royce Merlin 28 liquid-cooled engine
60 Nacelle/wing fairing
61 Fuel tank bearer ribs
62 Intermediate ribs
63 Leading-edge structure
64 Wing stringers
65 Wingtip skinning
66 Starboard navigation light
67 Starboard formation light
68 Aileron hinge fairings
69 Wing rear spar
70 Starboard aileron
71 Aileron balance tab
72 Balance tab control rod

73 Aileron trim tab
74 HF aerial
75 Split trailing-edge flap (outboard section)
76 Emergency (ditching) exit
77 Crash axe stowage
78 Fire extinguisher
79 Hydraulic reservoir
80 Signal/flare pistol stowage
81 Parachute stowage box/spar step
82 Rear spar carry-through
83 Bunk backrest
84 Rear spar fuselage frame
85 Emergency packs
86 Roof light
87 Dinghy manual release cable (dinghy stowage in starboard wingroot)
88 Mid-gunner's parachute stowage
89 Tail turret ammunition box
90 Ammunition feed track
91 Emergency (ditching) exit
92 Flame floats stowage
93 Sea markers stowage
94 Roof light
95 Dorsal turret fairing
96 Frazer-Nash power-operated dorsal turret

14 Ventilator fairing
15 Bomb-bay forward actuating jacks
16 Bomb-bay forward bulkhead
17 Control linkage
18 Rudder pedals
19 Instrument panel
20 Windscreen sprays
21 Windscreen
22 Dimmer switches
23 Flight-engineer's folding seat
24 Flight-engineer's control panel
25 Pilot's seat
26 Flight-deck floor level
27 Elevator and rudder control rods (underfloor)
28 Trim tab control cables
29 Main floor/bomb-bay support longeron
30 Fire extinguisher
31 Wireless installation
32 Navigator's seat
33 Canopy rear/down-view blister
34 Pilot's head armour

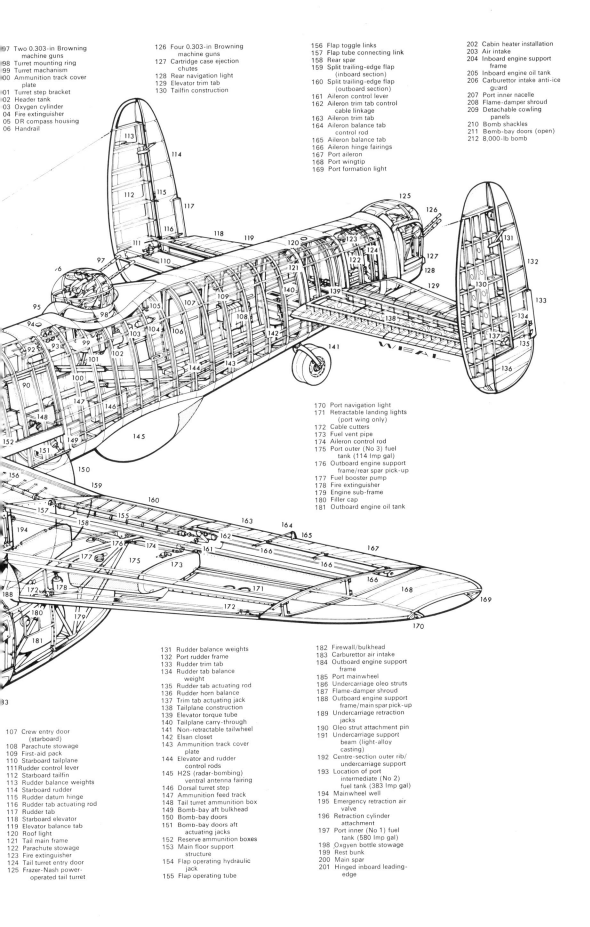

97 Two 0.303-in Browning machine guns
98 Turret mounting ring
99 Turret mechanism
00 Ammunition track cover plate
01 Turret step bracket
02 Header tank
03 Oxygen cylinder
04 Fire extinguisher
05 DR compass housing
06 Handrail

126 Four 0.303-in Browning machine guns
127 Cartridge case ejection chutes
128 Rear navigation light
129 Elevator trim tab
130 Tailfin construction

156 Flap toggle links
157 Flap tube connecting link
158 Rear spar
159 Split trailing-edge flap (inboard section)
160 Split trailing-edge flap (outboard section)
161 Aileron control lever
162 Aileron trim tab control cable linkage
163 Aileron trim tab
164 Aileron balance tab control rod
165 Aileron balance tab
166 Aileron hinge fairings
167 Port aileron
168 Port wingtip
169 Port formation light

202 Cabin heater installation
203 Air intake
204 Inboard engine support frame
205 Inboard engine oil tank
206 Carburettor intake anti-ice guard
207 Port inner nacelle
208 Flame-damper shroud
209 Detachable cowling panels
210 Bomb shackles
211 Bomb-bay doors (open)
212 8,000-lb bomb

170 Port navigation light
171 Retractable landing lights (port wing only)
172 Cable cutters
173 Fuel vent pipe
174 Aileron control rod
175 Port outer (No 3) fuel tank (114 Imp gal)
176 Outboard engine support frame/rear spar pick-up
177 Fuel booster pump
178 Fire extinguisher
179 Engine sub-frame
180 Filler cap
181 Outboard engine oil tank

131 Rudder balance weights
132 Port rudder frame
133 Rudder trim tab
134 Rudder tab balance weight
135 Rudder tab actuating rod
136 Rudder horn balance
137 Trim tab actuating jack
138 Tailplane construction
139 Elevator torque tube
140 Tailplane carry-through
141 Non-retractable tailwheel
142 Elsan closet
143 Ammunition track cover plate
144 Elevator and rudder control rods
145 H2S (radar-bombing) ventral antenna fairing
146 Dorsal turret step
147 Ammunition feed track
148 Tail turret ammunition box
149 Bomb-bay aft bulkhead
150 Bomb-bay doors
151 Bomb-bay doors aft actuating jacks
152 Reserve ammunition boxes
153 Main floor support structure
154 Flap operating hydraulic jack
155 Flap operating tube

182 Firewall/bulkhead
183 Carburettor air intake
184 Outboard engine support frame
185 Port mainwheel
186 Undercarriage oleo struts
187 Flame-damper shroud
188 Outboard engine support frame/main spar pick-up
189 Undercarriage retraction jacks
190 Oleo strut attachment pin
191 Undercarriage support beam (light-alloy casting)
192 Centre-section outer rib/undercarriage support
193 Location of port intermediate (No 2) fuel tank (383 Imp gal)
194 Mainwheel well
195 Emergency retraction air valve
196 Retraction cylinder attachment
197 Port inner (No 1) fuel tank (580 Imp gal)
198 Oxgyen bottle stowage
199 Rest bunk
200 Main spar
201 Hinged inboard leading-edge

107 Crew entry door (starboard)
108 Parachute stowage
109 First-aid pack
110 Starboard tailplane
111 Rudder control lever
112 Starboard tailfin
113 Rudder balance weights
114 Starboard rudder
115 Rudder datum hinge
116 Rudder tab actuating rod
117 Rudder tab
118 Starboard elevator
119 Elevator balance tab
120 Roof light
121 Tail main frame
122 Parachute stowage
123 Fire extinguisher
124 Tail turret entry door
125 Frazer-Nash power-operated tail turret

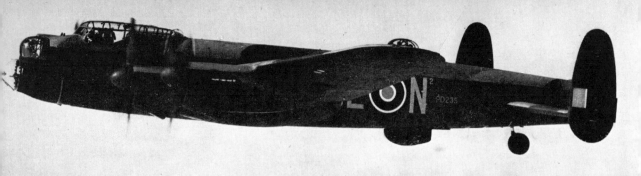

(Above) A production Lancaster III (PD235) and (below) a Lancaster III (PB995) carrying a 12,000-lb. "Tallboy" bomb.

first Atlantic crossing by the Lancaster was from East to West when, on August 25, 1942, a Lancaster I was flown to Montreal for demonstration purposes. One wing of this aircraft was damaged during tests in Canada, and it is an interesting example of inter-changeability achieved between Canadian- and British-built Lancasters to note that the wing of the British trans-Atlantic machine was replaced by one

One of two Lancasters (LL780 G) experimentally fitted with remotely-controlled dorsal and ventral cannon barbettes.

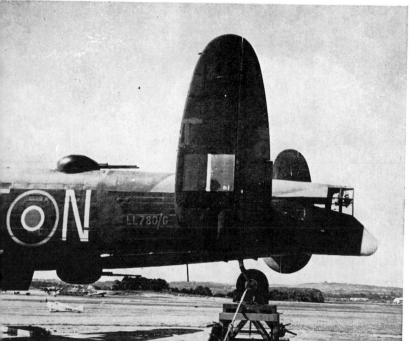

of the first Canadian-built mainplanes. In view of the fact that the Canadian aircraft industry had practically been created by war requirements, the building of the Lancaster in Canada was a notable achievement. The first Lancaster X built by Victory Aircraft (KB700), christened "Ruhr Express" by Mrs. C. G. Power, wife of the Canadian Minister of National Defence for Air, was handed over to the R.C.A.F. on August 6, 1943, and subsequently flown to Britain. Lancaster Xs, which were mostly powered by Packard-built Merlin 28s, were flown across the Atlantic without their gun turrets, which were produced and installed in the United Kingdom. Four hundred and thirty Lancaster Xs were built by Victory Aircraft.

Further power plant changes produced the Lancaster VI, a proposed production variant with either Merlin 85s of 1,635 h.p. or Merlin 87s of similar power housed in new cylindrical cowlings. Two Mk.I airframes and seven Mk.IIIs were converted as Lancaster VIs by Rolls-Royce Limited, and one or two were employed operationally by No. 635 Squadron in the Pathfinder Force. For this purpose, they had nose and dorsal turrets removed, improved H2S radar bombing aid and special radar-jamming devices—

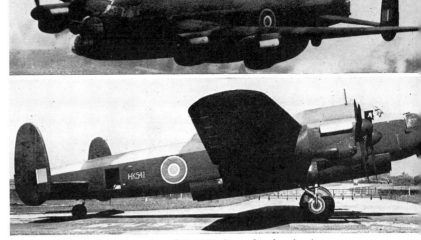

Two Lancasters, SW244 (top) and HK541 (immediately above), were experimentally fitted with long-range "saddle" tanks for operations in the Far East.

some of the first electronic counter-measures equipment. Performance of the Lancaster VIa was appreciably better than that of the Mk.III, but no production was undertaken and few operations were completed by this type. The intervening mark numbers had been allocated to progressive developments of the basic design to meet the requirements of specification B.14/43. The Lancaster IV and V embodied wings of very much higher aspect ratio, a lengthened fuselage and Rolls-Royce Merlin 85 engines. So different were the Lancaster IV and V to their predecessors that, before the first prototype (PW925) flew on June 9, 1944, they had been renamed Lincoln I and II.

At first using 4,000-lb. bombs and smaller weapons, the Lancaster carried the war into the heart of Germany, rapidly becoming the major offensive weapon of the R.A.F. In April 1942, the Lancaster had carried the 8,000-lb. bomb operationally for the first time, and by September 1943 it had progressed to the 12,000-lb. bomb. In the early days of Lancaster operations, navigation was largely of the dead-reckoning kind, and bomb-aiming was entirely visual. Gradually, radar navigational aids, such as Rebecca, Gee, Gee H, and Oboe became available, and the H2S radar bombing equipment, with its distinctive, semi-opaque Perspex "blister" beneath the rear fuselage, became a standard fitting.

The most remarkable offensive weapon to be used by the Lancaster was, perhaps, the spinning bomb or mine, which was to be used on one of the most spectacular and daring of the Lancaster's operations. This weapon, developed in the fertile brain of Dr. Barnes Wallis who had previously evolved the geodetic system of construction employed by the Wellington, was essentially a sphere which rotated as it dropped, and was intended to skid or skip across the surface of a lake or reservoir until it reached a dam, whereupon it would sink beneath the surface and explode at some depth. From the time of its conception, the weapon was intended for use against the strategically significant Moehne, Eder and Sorpe dams in the Ruhr. The Moehne and Eder dams between them held 346 million tons of water, and were major sources of hydro-electric power for the heavy industry of the Ruhr valley.

The evolution of the weapon was a long and, at times, painful process, sometimes pursued in the face of official apathy and even opposition. By the beginning of 1943, however, sufficient progress had been made for success to appear likely, and in March of that year a new Lancaster squadron, No. 617, was formed under the command of Wing Commander Guy Gibson, at Scampton. The Squadron spent two months on intensive low-level night-flying training. To function

correctly, the Wallis weapon had to be dropped from an altitude of 60 ft. above the surface of the water, and maintaining this constant height on the run-in was difficult enough in itself, without the hazards of enemy gunfire, barrage balloons and fighters. For the attack itself, specially modified Lancasters were issued to the squadron. To accommodate the bomb, with its 7-ft. girth, the bomb doors were removed; to lighten the aircraft the dorsal turrets were removed, and to assist in the bombing run, each aircraft was fitted with two spotlights so arranged that the beams they threw on the surface of the water converged into a figure eight when the aircraft was at the exact altitude of 60 ft.

After weeks of detailed planning, the attack was launched on the night of May 17, 1943. Nine aircraft were detailed to attack the Moehne and Eder dams, five others went to the Sorpe, and five more Lancasters flew as a reserve force. The success which attended the attacks, which released millions of tons of water and caused great dislocation in German industry, became a highlight in the Lancaster's scintillating operational history. Eight Lancasters were lost out of the force of nineteen despatched.

Another highlight in the Lancaster's career was provided by the long and difficult operations against the *Tirpitz*. On the night of September 11, 1944, Lancasters took off from Britain, each carrying a 12,000-lb. "Tallboy" deep-penetration bomb—another invention of Dr. Barnes Wallis—and flew the 1,750 miles to Archangel, in Northern Russia, in eleven hours, the longest flight made by any aeroplane carrying such a bomb load at that time. They were delayed for several days by weather, but on September 15th they bombed the *Tirpitz* in the Norwegian fjord of Kaa, making their attack in daylight. The attack was unsuccessful in sinking the *Tirpitz*, but on November 12, 1944, the Lancaster finally triumphed over the 45,000-ton German battleship, when eighteen aircraft from No. 617 Squadron and thirteen from No. 9 Squadron, each carrying a 12,000-lb. "Tallboy", finally sank the *Tirpitz* in Tromso Fjord.

THE AVRO LANCASTER

The ultimate in bomb sizes was reached with the supersonic deep-penetration 22,000-lb. "Grand Slam", an awe-inspiring weapon for which the bomb-bay doors of the Lancaster had to be removed, and the bomb-bay extended fore and aft. Thus modified, the aircraft was designated Lancaster Mk.I (Special), and the first "Grand Slam" was dropped by a Lancaster of No. 617 Squadron on March 14, 1945, during an attack on the Bielefeld Viaduct, many of the spans of which were completely destroyed.

Throughout its operations in Europe, the defensive armament of the Lancaster remained fairly constant, but during 1945 some Lancaster IIIs carried two 0.5-in. guns in the tail turret in place of the four 0.303-in. guns previously installed, and this armament was also used by the Lancaster VII which differed from all other Lancasters in having an American Martin dorsal turret with two 0.5-in. guns. This turret was located further forward than the Frazer-Nash turret on other marks. Austin Motors built 180 Lancaster VIIs after A. V. Roe had converted a Mk.III (NN801) to serve as the prototype. Armament experiments with Lancasters included the testing of a Bristol B.17 dorsal turret with two 20-mm. Hispano cannon on JB456 in May 1944, and two Lancasters (LL780 and RF268) were fitted experimentally with remotely-controlled dorsal and ventral barbettes, each containing two 20-mm. cannon, with a sighting position in the extreme tail.

When the war in Europe terminated, the Lancaster's contribution to R.A.F. Bomber Command's war of attrition against Germany was almost exactly two-thirds of the total tonnage of bombs dropped by the R.A.F. from the beginning of 1942, the actual figure being 608,612 tons. No fewer than 156,000 sorties had been flown by the Lancaster, during which more than 228 million gallons of fuel had been consumed, and, in addition to their loads of high explosives, Lancasters delivered 51,513,106 incendiary bombs. In all, at least fifty-nine squadrons of R.A.F. Bomber Command operated the Lancaster during this period. These were Nos. 7, 9, 12, 15, 35, 44, 49, 50, 57, 61, 75, 83, 90, 97, 100, 101, 103, 106, 115, 149, 150, 153, 156, 166, 170, 186, 189, 195, 207, 218, 227, 300, 405, 408, 419, 420, 424, 426, 427, 428, 429, 431, 432, 433, 434, 460, 463, 467, 514, 550, 576, 582, 617, 619, 622, 625, 626, 630, and 635 squadrons.

With the final defeat of Germany, the Lancaster was prepared for a new task, the assault on Japan in the Pacific theatre. Special modifications were required to render the Lancaster suitable for Far East operations, the modified aircraft being designated Lancaster I (F.E.), and distinguishable externally by a new finish comprising white upper surfaces and black undersides. Some Lancaster VIIs were also detailed for "Tiger Force", as the R.A.F.'s strategic bomber force in the Pacific was to be known, but in the event, Japan surrendered before this force joined operations.

One of the problems of using Lancasters in the Far East was that of sufficient range to enable the aircraft to be ferried out from this country and operated in the area subsequently. One early solution aimed at in-creasing the range of the Lancaster was the provision of a 1,200 Imp. gal. "saddle" tank along the top of the fuselage, aft of the cockpit. Two aircraft (SW244 and HK541) were converted by A.V.Roe to take this tank, but their take-off performances proved to be so poor when the tank was fully loaded, and handling characteristics left so much to be desired that alternative methods of obtaining the required range were investigated, including in-flight refuelling. The latter solution was eventually adopted, and it was proposed to operate substantial numbers of Lancasters from Burmese bases, refuelling them by converted tanker aircraft en route to targets in the Japanese homeland. A great deal of the in-flight refuelling equipment had been manufactured, and some Lancasters had been converted for trailing-line-type refuelling when the Japanese war ended and further development was abandoned.

The last Lancaster to be built was a Mk.I (TW910) which was delivered on February 2, 1946, by Armstrong Whitworth, bringing the grand total of all marks of this bomber to be produced to 7,374, including prototypes. Peak production was reached in August 1944, in which month 293 were built, apart from the appropriate quota of spare components.

Like old soldiers, good aeroplanes never die, and the Lancaster was destined to serve with many air arms for long after the war. It was a peculiar quirk of fate that the Lancaster, which came into being as a direct result of the failure of its twin-engined predecessor, should become, in the words of Marshal of the R.A.F. Sir Arthur Harris, wartime commander of Bomber Command, ". . . the finest bomber of the war!" Sir Arthur added, "Its efficiency was almost incredible, both in performance and in the way it could be saddled with ever-increasing loads without breaking the 'camel's back'. The Lancaster far surpassed all the other types of heavy bomber. Not only could it take heavier bomb loads; not only was it easier to handle, and not only were there fewer accidents with this than with other types, the casualty rate was also consistently below those of other types."

Avro Lancaster III

Dimensions :	Span, 102 ft. 0 in. ; length, 68 ft. 11 in. ; height, 19 ft. 6 in. ; wing area, 1,297 sq. ft.
Power Plants :	Four Packard-built Rolls-Royce Merlin 28 or 38 twelve-cylinder 60° Vee liquid-cooled engines rated at 1,390 h.p. at 3,000 r.p.m. for take-off, and 1,120 h.p. at 18,250 ft.
Armament :	Two 0.303-in. Browning machine guns in Frazer-Nash nose turret with 1,000 r.p.g. ; two 0.303-in. Brownings in Frazer-Nash dorsal turret with 1,000 r.p.g., and four 0.303-in. Brownings in Frazer-Nash tail turret with 2,500 r.p.g. Normal maximum bomb load, 14,000 lb. With special modifications, one 22,000-lb. "Grand Slam" deep-penetration bomb could be carried externally.
Weights :	Tare, 41,000 lb. ; normal loaded, 53,000 lb. ; maximum overload, 65,000 lb. Maximum fuel capacity, 3,540 Imp. gal.
Performance :	(At normal gross weight) Maximum speed, 270 m.p.h. at 19,000 ft. ; cruising speed, 210 m.p.h. ; rate of climb, 580 ft./min. at 2,000 ft. ; time to 11,000 ft., 19.3 min., to 20,000 ft., 43.5 min. ; service ceiling, 21,500 ft. ; range, 1,160 miles at 210 m.p.h. with 1,440 Imp. gal. and 14,000-lb. bomb load, 2,230 miles at 210 m.p.h. with 2,580 Imp. gal. and 7,000-lb. bomb load.

The He 177V1 (above) flew for the first time on November 19, 1939, and the engine overheating that was to plague the bomber throughout its career first manifested itself on this flight.

THE HEINKEL He 177 GREIF

"*Bomben auf Engeland.*" So read the title of a stirring martial song which blared out of loudspeakers all over Germany and the occupied territories in those fateful autumn months of 1940. With a background of roaring aero engines and accompanied by the beating of drums, it was an impressive battle hymn; but whatever its psychological effect on the German populace, it was hardly destined to raise the morale of the personnel of the Luftwaffe's Kampfgeschwader. They were aware that their bombers did not possess the range to attack effectively more than a small area of the British Isles. They knew that the Luftwaffe's lack of a long-range strategic bomber enabled the R.A.F. to concentrate virtually the whole of its defensive strength within the limited area to which the Kampfgeschwader were forced to confine their attentions; they saw their operational strength being sapped disastrously.

The Luftwaffe's complete lack of a long-range heavy bomber was the more surprising in view of the fact that this air arm's first Chief of Staff, Lieutenant General Wever, had for long championed such aircraft. Wever, believing rightly that the strategic bomber would prove a decisive factor in any future European conflict, demanded bombers capable of carrying a heavy load over distances sufficient to permit an assault on any part of the British Isles; aircraft which, in view of the weakness of the German Fleet, could also harass British shipping far out in the Atlantic. Prototypes of two four-engined heavy bombers, the Junkers Ju 89 and the Dornier Do 19, were built under his aegis, but with the death of this competent and far-sighted officer in an air crash the development of these aircraft was abandoned,

Wever's successors, Stumpff, Jeschonnek and Kesselring, favouring the smaller, medium-range, twin-engined bomber.

Lieutenant-General Wever did leave the Luftwaffe a legacy, however, in the Heinkel He 177 Greif long-range heavy bomber which was destined to provide the most dismal chapter in the wartime record of the German aircraft industry. Fires in the air, aerodynamic troubles and structural failures all contributed towards the unpopularity of this big bomber when it eventually reached the operational units. It encountered difficulties from its birth whose causes were recognised too late, and when they were recognised insufficient energy was devoted to eradicating them. Not that there was anything basically wrong with the design, which was sound and embodied as much ingenuity as any wartime German aircraft. Had effective measures been taken to solve the problems that it presented at a sufficiently early stage in its career, the Luftwaffe might have found itself possessed of a heavy bomber comparable with, if not superior to, the best of Allied machines in this category.

The Allies first became aware of the existence of the He 177 on June 13, 1940, when a Luftwaffe prisoner-of-war provided a description of the bomber's essential features which subsequently proved to be very accurate indeed, and it was feared that the appearance of this new and advanced warplane over the British Isles would not be long delayed. Had the He 177 appeared in operational service during 1940-41, it could have radically altered the picture of aerial warfare over the British Isles, but nearly four years were to elapse before, at 21.31 hours on January 21,

1944, an aircraft of this type was shot down near Hindhead, Surrey, during the bomber's operational début over the United Kingdom.

The reasons for the He 177's prolonged gestatory period were many and varied. Only partly to blame was the German aircraft industry's failure to remove certain shortcomings, including a proclivity towards catching fire in mid-air which earned for the bomber the uncomplimentary epithet of "*Luftwaffenfeuerzeug*" (Luftwaffe's Petrol Lighter). Major contributory factors were vacillation on the part of the Reichsluftfahrtministerium, or R.L.M. (German Air Ministry), conflicting military and political policies, and petty jealousies and commercial rivalry within the aircraft industry itself. These all conspired to prevent the co-operation and effort with which the bomber's defects could have been removed.

The He 177 was conceived early in 1938 when the R.L.M. prepared a specification resulting from Lieutenant-General Wever's energetic demands for a combined heavy strategic bomber and anti-shipping aircraft. The specification called for an aircraft capable of carrying a bomb load of at least 2,000 pounds over a range of 4,160 miles. It had to possess a maximum speed of not less than 335 m.p.h. and have the structural strength to launch its attack from a medium-angle dive.

The specification was issued solely to the Ernst Heinkel Flugzeugwerke at Rostock-Marienehe, on the Baltic Coast. At that time, the Heinkel concern was engaged in the production of the He 111 medium bomber, the He 114 reconnaissance float sesquiplane, the He 115 twin-engined torpedo-bomber floatplane, and a small batch of He 112 fighters for export. In addition to variants of these established aircraft, the drawing boards were occupied by the He 100 fighter, the He 116 long-range mailplane, and the He 119 high-speed bomber, as well as the purely experimental He 176 and He 178 rocket- and turbojet-propelled aircraft. The R.L.M. felt, with some justification, that the company was disseminating its design activities too widely and, in view of the success of the He 111, brought pressure to bear in order to force Heinkel to concentrate on bomber development. It was for this reason that the heavy bomber specification was issued only to Heinkel and not, as had been previously the practice, to several companies simultaneously.

When the Heinkel company received the specification from the R.L.M., Dipl. Ing. Heinrich Hertel had been Technical Director and Chief of Development for some four years, and the task of producing a design study to meet its requirements was entrusted to one of the most talented members of his team, Siegfried Gunter. The project, which was designated He P.1041, was submitted to the R.L.M. a few months later, and a development contract was awarded, Dipl. Ing. Hertel supervising the design, Gunter being responsible for detail design, and Ing. Schwarzler being placed in charge of construction.

The P.1041, now allocated the designation He 177 by the R.L.M., embodied many advanced and, in some respects, revolutionary features as originally conceived. These included coupled power plants (two engines paired in one nacelle and driving a common airscrew) with surface evaporation cooling. The estimated loaded weight of the bomber was 59,520 lb., and it was anticipated that its performance range would include a maximum speed of no less than 342 m.p.h. at 18,000 feet—a speed substantially greater than that attained by most contemporary single-seat fighters! Many of the bomber's features were unproven, and as work on the design progressed even Siegfried Gunter began to have second thoughts as to the wisdom of embodying so many innovations. Hertel believed, however, that all problems presented by these radical features would be successfully overcome by the time that the first prototype could be ready for testing.

The most noteworthy feature of the projected aeroplane was the use of coupled power plants—two liquid-cooled engines mounted side-by-side with a single gear casing connecting the two crankcases, the two crankshaft pinions driving a single airscrew shaft gear. The use of two engines of very large output in a heavy bomber was undoubtedly sounder aerodynamically than that of four separate engines of smaller capacity, resulting in a substantial reduction in drag and a considerable increase in manœuvrability. The coupled engine principle also avoided the uncertainty and delay attendant upon the development of a radically new high-powered engine, and simplified production since the same basic units could serve both in orthodox single engine installations and for the coupled power plants. Gunter, always engrossed with the idea of obtaining the best possible aerodynamic form, was largely responsible for the coupled engine conception, seeing in it a means of offsetting the lack of power plants in the 2,000 h.p. category.

At the time of the He 177's conception, Gunter was already working on the designs for an extremely fast bomber, the He 119, which utilised the coupled power plant arrangement. The He 119 was powered by a Daimler-Benz DB 606 coupled engine offering 2,350 h.p. for take-off, this comprising two DB 601 twelve-cylinder liquid-cooled engines mounted side-by-side and inclined so that the inner banks of cylinders were disposed almost vertically. Installed in the fuselage near to the aircraft's centre of gravity, the DB 606 drove the airscrew by means of a long extension shaft which, housed in a tube, passed through the cockpit. The He 119 was certainly one of the fastest aircraft of its time, eventually attaining 432 m.p.h., but the overheating of the coupled engine was never entirely eradicated.

In the He 177, the DB 606 coupled engine was combined with a system of surface evaporation cooling to augment the orthodox radiators. Surface evaporation cooling was first employed on the experimental He 100 single-seat fighter, the eighth prototype of which was to capture the world's absolute speed record on March 30, 1939, by attaining 463.92 m.p.h. An immense amount of research on surface evaporation cooling had been conducted, but by the spring of 1939 the Heinkel engineers were forced to admit that it was impracticable for a service aircraft, and the first major change in the original He 177 conception was rendered necessary. The adoption of orthodox radiators of greater area naturally added to airframe drag, reducing both speed and range, and in order to maintain the latter figure as originally specified, it was found necessary to make provision for additional fuel cells in the wings. This, in turn, necessitated some increase in wing strength and, consequently, structural weight, thus further reducing the estimated speed performance of the bomber.

Another design innovation featured by the He 177 as originally conceived was the use of remotely-controlled defensive gun barbettes which offered appreciably less drag than manned turrets. Work on remotely-controlled aircraft defensive systems had reached a relatively advanced stage in Germany in the late 'thirties, but progress in this field failed to keep pace with the He 177, and the design had once more to be modified; this time to accommodate manned turrets resulting in a further increment of drag.

An even more serious problem was posed by the R.L.M. who, having demanded the ability to undertake medium-angle dives in the original specification, now insisted that the heavy bomber be capable of performing 60° diving attacks such as those for which the very much smaller and lighter Junkers Ju 88 had been designed! In order to withstand the tremendous stresses that would be imposed during the pull-out from such a dive with an aircraft of the He 177's size and weight, further structural strengthening was dictated. By now the design gross weight of the bomber had increased so alarmingly that the provision of an undercarriage of sufficient strength became a serious problem. Neither the engine nacelles nor the wings, which featured a low thickness/chord ratio, provided much stowage space for the main undercarriage members, and after several extremely complex arrangements had been contemplated, a rather novel system was adopted. Two massive single-wheel oleo legs were attached to the main spar at each engine nacelle, the outboard legs with their single wheels retracting upward and outward into shallow wing wells, and the inboard units swinging upward and inward, all units being completely enclosed by flush-fitting doors.

Aerodynamically, the He 177 was a large, well-proportioned, mid-wing monoplane which, from the structural viewpoint, offered few novelties. Conventional metal stressed skin construction was employed, the wing being built up on a single main spar.

After the death of Lieutenant-General Wever, the R.L.M. interest in the long-range bomber cooled

The He 177V5 was employed for early armament trials but both power plants burst into flame during a simulated low-level attack early in 1941.

rapidly. Germany's leaders still envisaged a limited war confined to the European continent, and Major-General Hans Jeschonnek, who succeeded Stumpff as Chief of Air Staff, was adamant in his belief that if Germany built sufficient quantities of medium bombers, Britain and France would be so impressed that Germany would be left a free hand with Poland. It was decided, therefore, virtually to abandon the further development of the heavy bomber: a gamble based on Britain staying out of the future war and one of the greatest single mistakes made by the German High Command. Construction of the prototypes of the He 177 for experimental purposes was continued, however, in view of the German Admiralty's continual representations for such an aircraft for co-operation with submarines and long-range offensive reconnaissance out over the Atlantic.

By the summer of 1939—it now becoming increasingly obvious to German leaders that Britain and France would go to the aid of Poland in the event of an attack on that country—renewed interest was being shown in the He 177, and the Heinkel company was urged to speed prototype construction. During the previous March, however, Dipl. Ing. Hertel had left Heinkel, and this did not augur well for the future of the bomber. Finally, on November 19, 1939, the first prototype, the He 177V1, was flown for the first time with Dipl. Ing. Francke at the controls. Francke was the Chief of the Rechlin Experimental Establishment's E-2 flight test section, and his initial flight was terminated after only twelve minutes as the engine temperatures began to rise alarmingly. While Francke referred favourably to the take-off, general handling and landing characteristics of the bomber, he complained of some vibration in the airscrew shafts, the inadequacy of the tail surfaces under certain conditions, and some flutter which accompanied any vigorous movement of the elevators.

The He 177V1 had an empty equipped weight of 30,247 lb., and loaded weight was 52,734 lb. Overall dimensions included a span of 103 ft. 0¼ in., and overall length of 67 ft. 6¼ in., a height of 21 ft. 10½ in., and a wing area of 1,076.39 sq. ft. Although provision was made for a single 12.7-mm. NG 131 machine gun above and immediately aft of the flight deck, a similar gun in the ventral gondola and a third in the extreme tail, no armament was fitted, and only the aft bomb-bay installed. This bomb-bay projected

The He 177V7 featured a revised nose section and, together with the V6, underwent operational trials in the late autumn of 1941 with Kampfgeschwader 40.

slightly below the lower fuselage line as a result of an increase in bomb calibres during the aircraft's construction.

The He 177V2 completed shortly afterwards was essentially similar to its predecessor and was also flown on its maiden flight by Francke. The first prototype received several modifications dictated by the initial flight tests, including a twenty per cent increase in the tail surface area, and the machine was flown to Rechlin for further testing by Francke. The second prototype, the tail surfaces of which had not been modified, was tested by another Rechlin pilot, Rickert, who performed the first diving test with the new bomber. Serious control surface flutter immediately developed and the machine disintegrated. After this incident, the tail surfaces of the third, fourth and fifth prototypes, nearing completion at Rostock-Marienehe, were modified in a similar fashion to that of the He 177V1.

The torsional vibration in the airscrew drive shafts which had manifested itself on the bomber's first flight was relatively simple of solution by comparison with the problem of engine overheating. This resulted in a notorious inflammability eventually to earn the bomber its nickname of "*Luftwaffenfeuerzeug*". The third prototype, the He 177V3 which bore the civil registration D-AGIG and had its loaded weight increased to 60,198 lb., was allocated to the task of power plant development, and was flown to Rechlin in mid-February 1940. Engine tests were, unfortunately, awarded relatively low priority, for the bomber was suffering even more serious aerodynamic troubles.

The He 177V4 was retained at Heinkel's test field where another Rechlin pilot, Ursinus, undertook stability tests. While flying over the Baltic during the course of one of these trials, this prototype failed to recover from a shallow dive, crashing into the sea near Ribnitz. Attempts to salvage the wreckage in

order to determine the cause of the crash met with only partial success but it was discovered that the accident had resulted from the malfunctioning of the airscrew pitch gear.

Among the He 177's noteworthy features were its Fowler-type extensible trailing-edge flaps, which occupied the entire wing trailing edges, including those portions covered by the ailerons. Each aileron comprised upper and lower portions, the latter arranged to slide rearwards with flap extension while the upper part retained its function of providing lateral control for take-off and landing. The original wing design did not take into full account the stresses caused by the Fowler flaps, however, and as a result more internal strengthening proved necessary.

The first four He 177 prototypes were essentially similar, apart from the twin bomb-bays installed in the second machine and the increased internal fuel tankage of the fourth, but the fifth machine, the He 177V5 and last of the initial prototype batch, incorporated a number of changes which were principally concerned with armament installations for trials at Rechlin. Triple bomb-bays were fitted, and hand-operated 7.9-mm. MG 15 machine guns were installed in the extreme nose, in a turret immediately aft of the flight deck, in the nose of the ventral gondola, and in the extreme tail. Early in 1941, during a simulated low-level attack, both power plants burst into flames and the He 177V5 hit the ground and exploded.

The tendency on the part of the coupled engines to ignite became increasingly serious as the test programme progressed. There were several reasons for the inflammability of the DB 606 power plants. There was a common exhaust manifold on the two inner cylinder blocks which became excessively hot and caused the usual accumulation of oil and grease in the bottom of the engine cowling to catch fire. When throttling back there was a tendency for the injection pump to deliver more fuel than the reduced requirement of the engine, and the injection pump connections leaked. In order to save weight there was no firewall, and the coupled engines were fitted so close to the wing mainspar that there was insufficient space for the fuel and oil pipelines, electrical leads, etc. This "sardine can" arrangement, as it was dubbed at Rechlin, was frequently saturated in fuel and oil from leaking connections. In addition, at altitude the oil tended to foam, partly due to the fact that the return pump was too large, and in this condition it circulated in the engines, its lubricative qualities being virtually nil. The lack of adequate lubrication resulted in the disintegration of the connecting rod bearings which burst through the engine crankcase, puncturing the oil tanks which poured their contents on to the red-hot exhaust pipe collector.

The He 177V6, like the V5, had production-type DB 606 power plants in which the maximum power for take-off was increased from 2,600 h.p. to 2,700 h.p., maximum continuous output being 2,360 h.p., and maximum cruising power being 2,080 h.p. at 18,050 ft. The empty and loaded weights of the sixth prototype increased to 37,038 lb. and 61,883 lb. respectively, and performance included a maximum speed of 289 m.p.h., a cruising speed of 263 m.p.h., a service ceiling of 22,966 ft., and a range of 3,417 mls. The He 177V6 and the similar V7 featured a revised nose section which, while following the contours of the nose section employed by earlier prototypes, was considerably reinforced and had fewer glazed panels. Whereas the V6 had 13-mm. MG 131 machine guns in the forward part of the ventral gondola, a dorsal turret aft of the flight deck, and the extreme tail, the V7 had an MG 131 machine gun in the nose, a 20-mm. MG FF cannon in the gondola and a similar cannon in the dorsal turret. From the earliest months of the War, Kampfgeschwader 40 Wurm had been designated the first unit to re-equip with the new

bomber, and in the late autumn months of 1941, IV/K.G.40 based at Bordeaux-Merignac received the He 177V6 and V7 for operational trials in the anti-shipping role. The two machines soon became the bane of all concerned. They were the subject of interminable modifications to both airframes and engines, and were considered totally unsuited for operational use.

In September 1941, the He 177V8, the last of the aircraft built as prototypes from the outset, all sixteen additional prototypes being conversions of pre-production or production airframes, was made available for engine tests at Rechlin, but owing to the urgency of other development work it was returned to Heinkel after only forty days, and it was not possible to resume engine tests in the air until February 1942 when the second pre-production machine, the He 177A-02, was delivered. The first He 177A-0 (Werk-Nr. 00016) of a batch of fifteen pre-production machines laid down at Rostock-Marienehe had been flown in November 1941, the second pre-production machine flying in the following month. Owing to the limited capacity of the Rostock-Marienehe plant, an additional fifteen He 177A-0 pre-production aircraft had been laid down simultaneously at Heinkel's Oranienburg factory, and Arado's Warnemunde factory initiated licence production of the bomber with a further five He 177A-0 aircraft.

The He 177A-0 had a maximum loaded weight of 66,140 lb., maximum speed was 298 m.p.h., and service ceiling was 32,800 feet. Maximum bomb load was 5,290 lb., and defensive armament comprised one 7.9-mm. MG 81 machine gun in the glazed nose, one 20-mm. MG FF cannon in the nose of the ventral gondola, twin MG 81 machine guns in the rear of the ventral gondola, a 13-mm. MG 131 machine gun in the forward dorsal turret, and a similar gun in the

The He 177A-02, the second pre-production aircraft built at Rostock-Marienehe, first flew in November 1941.

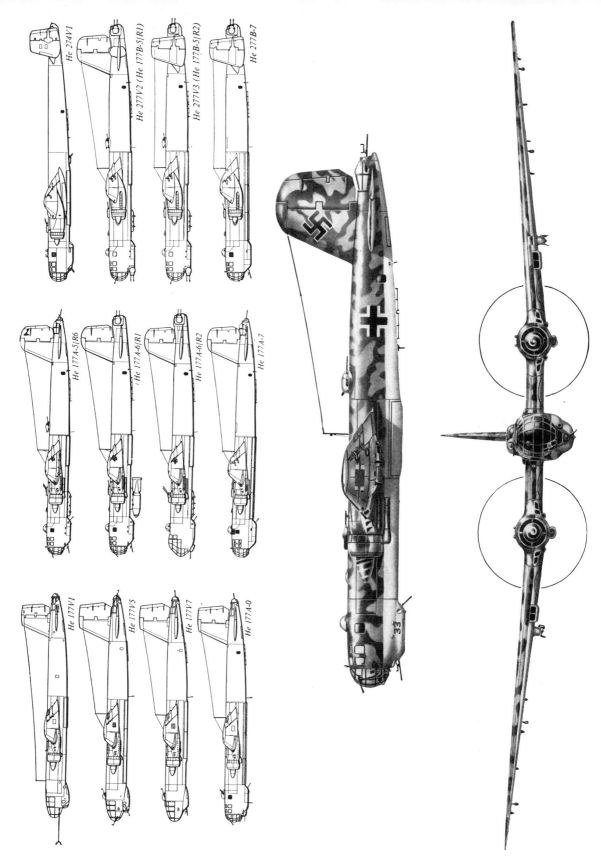

He 274 V1

He 277 V2 (He 177B-5/R1)

He 277 V3 (He 177B-5/R2)

He 277 B-7

He 177 A-5/R6

He 177 A-6/R1

He 177 A-6/R2

He 177 A-7

He 177 V1

He 177 V5

He 177 V7

He 177 A-0

Heinkel He 177A-5 Greif

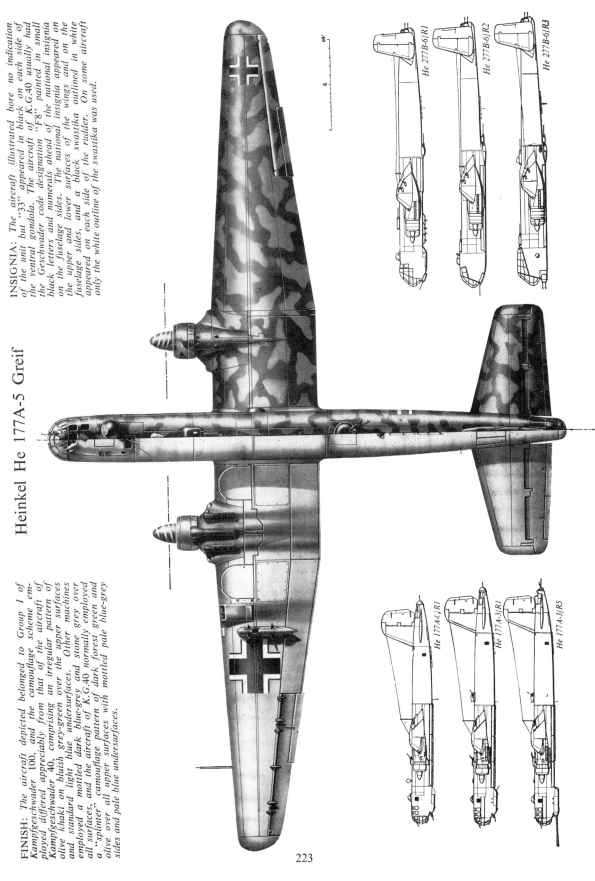

FINISH: The aircraft depicted belonged to Group 1 of Kampfgeschwader 100, and the camouflage scheme employed differed appreciably from that of the aircraft of Kampfgeschwader 40, comprising an irregular pattern of olive khaki on bluish grey-green over the upper surfaces and standard light blue undersurfaces. Other machines employed a mottled dark blue-grey and stone grey over all surfaces, and the aircraft of K.G.40 normally employed a "splinter" camouflage pattern of dark forest green and olive over all upper surfaces with mottled pale blue-grey sides and pale blue undersurfaces.

INSIGNIA: The aircraft illustrated bore no indication of the unit but "33" appeared in black on each side of the ventral gondola. The aircraft of K.G.40 usually had the Geschwader code designation "F8" painted in small black letters and numerals ahead of the national insignia on the fuselage sides. The national insignia appeared on the upper and lower surfaces of the wings and on the fuselage sides, and a black swastika outlined in white appeared on each side of the rudder. On some aircraft only the white outline of the swastika was used.

He 277B-6/R1

He 277B-6/R2

He 277B-6/R3

He 177A-1/R1

He 177A-3/R1

He 177A-3/R5

223

tail. The first He 177A-0 was intended primarily for armament tests, but initial trials indicated that the defensive system was unsatisfactory, and before modifications could be made the aircraft was destroyed when the engines caught fire during take-off. The second pre-production machine began engine flight trials on February 8, 1942, but a few weeks later, in May, both power plants ignited, necessitating a crash landing from which the crew escaped seconds before the plane exploded.

Tests with the He 177A-02 completed prior to its destruction had enabled the engine specialists to reach certain conclusions, however, and they recommended that the engine mounts be lengthened by some eight inches; the fuel and oil pipelines be relocated; a firewall be fitted, the oil tank be transferred to a less dangerous position, and the complete redesign of the exhaust system be undertaken. By this time the first production He 177A-1 had left Arado's Warnemunde plant, and the R.L.M. was demanding the service introduction of the bomber at the earliest possible date. Thus, only the recommendation that the oil tank be shifted was adopted as this change was thought unlikely to delay production. At a later stage, however, when service units began demanding exhaust flame dampers for night operations, the opportunity was taken to redesign the exhaust system, and with the introduction of the He 177A-3 the engine mounts were lengthened by the recommended amount.

The thirty-five He 177A-0 pre-production machines were employed for a wide variety of trials and, although the bomber was still considered to be "dangerous" because of the frequent engine fires, most experienced bomber pilots expressed favourable opinions concerning its handling qualities and general performance. Some expressed the view that the He 177 was fully as manoeuvrable as the very much smaller Ju 88, and one pilot claimed that it performed tighter turns than a Ju 88 fighter when the two machines were flown together in mock combat. However, during take-off the He 177 tended to swing badly, resulting in several accidents, and the vertical tail surfaces were therefore enlarged and the tail-wheel was modified. These changes only partially corrected the fault, and it was necessary to hold the tail down as long as possible during the take-off run. Heinkel had proposed the use of a nose-wheel undercarriage, but this suggestion was turned down by the R.L.M.

The He 177-05, -06 and -07 became the He 177V9, V10 and V11 respectively, and the He 177A-012 served for trials in the "destroyer" role. The first of the five He 177A-0 aircraft produced by the Warnemunde plant was used for shallow dive tests at Ludwigslust during which a speed of 443 m.p.h. was attained. This was the last aircraft to be fitted with the barred-gate type dive brakes, for, apart from the fact that the bomber had proven incapable of withstanding the stresses imposed by a pull-out from even a medium-angle dive, Allied anti-aircraft gunners had evolved effective means of combating the dive bombers. The removal of the brakes also made room for external bomb carriers.

The first Arado-built He 177A-1 was available for testing in March 1942. Although the bomber's teething troubles remained largely unresolved, Hermann Goring was persistently demanding the quantity delivery of the He 177 to enable his Luftwaffe to "Blow the British Fleet out of the water." In these demands he was echoed by Premier-Admiral Donitz who felt that Heinkel's bomber could do a far better job against British coastal shipping than his U-boats which were encountering increasingly serious opposition around Britain's coastline. But the continual modifications dictated by trials with the prototypes and pre-production aircraft, and the substantial number of these lost in accidents, necessitated the allocation of the first production batch for test purposes.

A total of 130 He 177A-1 Greif (Griffin) bombers was manufactured, all of these being produced by Arado at Warnemunde, the series being completed on June 28, 1943, and after initial attempts to employ the He 177A-1 operationally, all aircraft of this type were relegated to test, training, and special duty roles. Many of the A-1s were employed as conversion trainers at Fassberg, Lechfeld, Erfurt, Brandenburg-Briest and Ludwigslust; one was transferred to Deutsche Lufthansa (Werk-Nr. 15271) for transport duties; six were based at Fassberg for Henschel Hs 293 radio-controlled rocket-propelled missile dropping and control trials; one was transferred to the Junkers plant at Dessau for testing the DB 610 power plants to be installed in the Ju 288, and three were used by Rowehl's Kampfgeschwader 200 for special long-range duties. The last-mentioned aircraft were based at the Erfurt repair depot, and after each sortie the He 177A-1s were returned to their repair shops for complete overhauls!

The He 177A-1 carried 1,619 Imp.gal. of fuel for short-range operations, 1,914 Imp.gal. for medium-range operations, and 2,164 Imp.gal. for long-range operations. The fully glazed nose consisted of a series of optically flat panels and was bulged to form a ventral gondola which housed a forward-firing 20-mm. MG FF cannon with 300 rounds and an aft-firing pair of 7.9-mm. MG 81 guns (He 177A-1/R1) or a 13-mm. MG 131 (He 177A-1/R4). Additional defensive armament was provided by a hand-held MG 81 on a small spherical mounting in the glazed nose; an electrically-operated dorsal barbette containing an MG 131 machine gun and controlled remotely by a gunner from a sighting station in the roof aft of the pilot; and a single gimbal-mounted MG 131 machine gun immediately aft of the rudder with a rather restricted field of fire. The He 177A-1/R2 and R3 also featured a remotely-controlled ventral barbette housing one MG 131, while the He 177A-1/R4 had a manned aft dorsal turret with one MG 131. Maximum internal bomb load was 4,850 lb.

The forward fuselage provided accommodation for four crew members—the pilot, co-pilot/bombardier, navigator/radio-operator and gunner—all stationed in the extreme nose, the tail section housing a gunner. Empty weight was 35,494 lb., maximum loaded weight was 66,139 lb., and maximum landing weight was 50,706 lb. Maximum speed was 317 m.p.h., cruising speed was 267 m.p.h., service ceiling was 22,966 ft., and range varied from 746 mls. with short-range tankage to 3,480 mls. with long-range tankage.

While production of the He 177A-1 was being undertaken by Arado, the Heinkel factories had introduced an improved variant, the He 177A-3, on to the assembly lines. This differed from the initial production model principally in having the power plants mounted some eight inches farther ahead of the wing mainspar and an additional 5 ft. 3 in. fuselage section inserted aft of the bomb-bays to maintain the c.g. position. An additional dorsal turret was mounted midway between the trailing edge of the mainplane and the leading edge of the tail-plane, this being electrically-rotated and hand-elevated and containing two 13-mm. MG 131 machine guns with 1,500 rounds. The first prototype for the He 177A-3 was the He 177V15, although this aircraft did not feature the lengthened fuselage and, unlike the initial production variants of the He 177A-3 which retained the DB 606 engines, it had the more powerful DB 610 engines which had first been tested on the He 177V11. The DB 610 consisted of a pair of DB 605 engines and gave a maximum output of 2,950 h.p. for take-off and 3,100 h.p. at 6,890 ft. The second prototype for the A-3 series was the He 177V16 which was also powered by the DB 610, but the initial production model, the He 177A-3/R1, had the DB 606, and by the end of 1942 only a few had actually been delivered to the Luftwaffe, these being ferried to the Truppen-Erprobungskommando at Brandenburg-Briest for service testing.

A production rate of no less than seventy aircraft per month had been demanded but, because of the continual modifications called for, deliveries had fallen to five per month. All service reports still bitterly complained of the bomber's numerous short-comings, and the official minutes of a General-luftzeugmeister discussion held on October 15, 1942, read as follows: "He (Heinkel) is aware of the difficulties (experienced with the He 177). He has also recognised that the most important fault lies in the fact that his Technical Bureau has not carried out sufficient fundamental work to take up and carry out necessary modifications." Thus, in November 1942, Dipl. Ing. Hertel returned to Rostock-Marienehe as an R.L.M. Deputy with full powers to reorganise the development of the He 177.

In the autumn of 1942, Gruppe I of Kampfge-schwader 4, formerly flying He 111s on the Russian Front, had been withdrawn to Lechfeld where its 3rd

The He 177A-3/R3 (above) was the first version of the Greif to carry the Henschel Hs 293 missile.

Staffel commenced converting to the He 177. Train-ing began on seven He 177A-1s but progress was extremely slow because of an acute shortage of aircraft. It was not until the early months of 1943, by which time a 1st and 2nd Staffel had been formed, that the first He 177A-3s arrived. In the meantime, the Greif had received its baptism of fire, although hardly in the way its manufacturers might have envisaged.

Kampfgeschwader 50 at Brandenburg-Briest had received twenty He 177A-1s for conversion training, and Gruppe I was hurriedly trained on the He 177A-3/R1, and redesignated Fern-Kampfgeschwader 2, before being rushed to Zaporozhe on the Russian Front where it employed its aircraft as *transports* flying supplies to the beleaguered German garrison in Stalingrad. F.K.G.2 suffered an average of one loss per day in landing crashes, and the strength of the unit dwindled so rapidly that, in February 1943, after a few weeks of operations, the survivors were with-drawn to Fassberg. During the He 177's operations in the vicinity of Stalingrad, a forward maintenance unit modified several machines by installing a 50-mm. BK 5 anti-tank gun in the ventral gondola, the ammunition for the gun being housed in the forward bomb-bay. The modified aircraft were used with some success for ground attack in between transport sorties.

In April 1943 an improved variant, the He 177A-3/R2, was introduced. This featured an im-proved electrical system, a modified gun position in the nose of the ventral gondola, the MG FF cannon being replaced by an MG 151 of similar calibre, and a redesigned tail gun position. Prior to the introduc-tion of the He 177A-3/R2, the tail gunner lay prone

The He 177A-5/R6 (above) was one of the principal production models of the Greif, and carried its primary offensive load externally.

in the tail, but the new position enabled the gunner to be seated and the 13-mm. MG 131 machine gun was supplanted by a 20-mm. MG 151 cannon. The He 177A-3/R3 was the first Hs 293 missile carrier, two of these weapons being mounted under the wings and one under the fuselage, and the He 177A-3/R4 had the ventral gondola lengthened by 3 ft. 11 in. to house the Kehl III control equipment for the Hs 293. The first tests with the Hs 293 had been made in 1941 with an He 177A-0 at Karlshagen. A number of difficulties had been encountered, and it was not until the summer of 1942 that the first successful dropping tests with the Hs 293 took place. The He 177A-3/R3 was used primarily for the training of crews with the Hs 293 from May 1943.

The installation of a heavy cannon in the ventral gondola of some machines during the Stalingrad fighting resulted in yet a further variant, the He 177A-3/R5, or *Stalingradtyp*, in which a 75-mm. BK 7.5 cannon was installed in the gondola. The He 177A-3/R5 switched from the DB 606 to the more powerful DB 610 power plants, but only five machines of this type were completed as the firing of the cannon resulted in severe vibration and its installation affected the flying characteristics of the Greif adversely.

Allied advances in anti-submarine warfare rendered the operation of U-boats in British coastal waters increasingly suicidal, and Donitz was particularly insistent that the He 177 be supplied as a torpedo-bomber. Thus, the He 177A-3/R7 was evolved specifically for the torpedo-bombing role and was used for trials by the Lowengeschwader K.G.26. Initially, the Italian L 5 torpedo, standard with Luftwaffe torpedo-bombing units, was used, but these, with their jettisonable stabilizing extensions, could not be stowed within the bomb-bays. Initially, two L 5 torpedoes were carried beneath the fuselage, but it was soon found preferable to carry the torpedoes beneath the wings. Unlike its predecessors, the He 177A-3/R7 had no Fowler-type flaps along the ailerons, the outer wings being similar to those of the

He 177A-5 which was being produced in parallel at Oranienburg, but only three examples of the A-3/R7 were produced, this variant being abandoned in favour of the A-5. The He 177A-3/R7 was also used for trials with the new electrically-driven LT 50 torpedo which approached the target vessel at considerable depth without revealing its track, and was exploded by magnetic force beneath the ship. The LT 50 could be dropped by parachute from an altitude of some 800 feet a considerable distance from its target.

The first He 177A-5s left the assembly lines at Oranienburg in February 1943, and, together with deliveries from Arado's Warnemunde factory, the initial delivery tempo of six machines per month had been doubled by July and stepped up to forty-two aircraft per month by the end of the year, a total of 415 machines being delivered during 1943, of which 154 were He 177A-3s. At the end of that year, however, the R.L.M., prompted presumably by the high loss rate, issued instructions that all existing He 177 bombers were to be scrapped! The engine test section had modified one machine at Rechlin to conform with recommendations resulting from the findings of the special investigation into the possible sources of engine fires ordered by Dipl. Ing. Hertel in January 1943. This investigation had revealed *fifty-six* possible causes of fire, and the machine modified at Rechlin functioned perfectly, the engines giving no trouble whatsoever over a protracted test period. The R.L.M. Technical Office was finally convinced that the solution to the He 177's engine troubles had at last been found, but the order to modify all aircraft on the assembly lines in a similar fashion came too late as it would have seriously disrupted production deliveries, while the order to scrap existing machines was tacitly ignored.

The He 177A-5 was intended primarily to carry external loads, such as the LT 50 torpedo, the FX 1400 Fritz unpowered radio-controlled armour-piercing bomb, and the Hs 293 and 294 missiles. It featured a strengthened wing, shortened under-

He 177A-5 bombers of Kampfgeschwader 40 at Bordeaux-Merignac in June 1944. K.G.40 was trained from the outset for the anti-shipping role.

carriage oleo legs, and the Fowler flaps along the outboard wing sections were removed. The defensive armament stemmed from that of the He 177A-3/R2, and thus the standard production model was designated He 177A-5/R2. The triple bomb-bay was installed but the forward bay was blanked off and an under-fuselage weapon rack was fitted. Power was provided by the DB 610 engine.

Whereas Kampfgeschwader 4 had been trained primarily as a strategic bombing unit at Lechfeld, the three Staffeln of I/K.G.50 which had operated at Stalingrad had received training with the Henschel Hs 293 and, redesignated as the 4th, 5th and 6th Staffeln of K.G.40, had been transferred to Bordeaux-Merignac on October 25, 1943 for anti-shipping duties. Gruppe I of K.G.40, the 1st Staffel of which had begun converting to the He 177A at Fassberg early in December 1942, was trained from the outset for the anti-shipping role, although training had been erratic because of a shortage of aircraft and continuous troubles with what aircraft were available. The 1st Staffel of I/K.G.40 was fully trained on the He 177A-5 by the middle of December 1943 when it was temporarily transferred to Chateaudun to join I/K.G.100 for Operation *Steinbock*.

The first major operation of II/K.G.40 (formerly I/K.G.50) took place on November 21, 1943. This unit came under the control of the Fliegerfuhrer Atlantik who co-operated closely with the Fuhrer der U-Boote. Twenty He 177A-5s carrying Hs 293 radio-controlled missiles attacked a convoy in the Atlantic, but the action was regarded as a total failure because of unfavourable conditions. Five days later, the unit again went into action with fourteen aircraft carrying Hs 293s. An Allied convoy was attacked off Bougie but four of the bombers were lost in action and three more were written off after forced landings. Fifty per cent of the attacking force was, therefore, lost as a result of this one action, and the Gruppe was left with only seven serviceable aircraft. Among the casualties was Major Mons, the Gruppenkommandeur, who had previously con-

ceived a plan for attacking the water reservoirs in Scotland and Northern Ireland, an idea which was later toyed with by his successor, Major Rieder, but eventually abandoned.

The Hs 293 and FX 1400 were introduced operationally by the He 177 at the same time, but successes attained were of a fairly low order, and it proved difficult to guide the bombs with a high degree of accuracy. On occasions they behaved erratically, and if damaged the Hs 293 could be as much a danger to its parent as to its intended target. An example of this was given during an attack on H.M.S. *Winchelsea* and H.M.S. *Watchman* by a lone He 177A-5. The bomber released one Hs 293 at a range of 4,000 yards but this was hit by Oerlikon fire and dived into the sea. A second Hs 293 was then released but this was also hit by Oerlikon fire almost immediately it left the bomber. It then became extremely erratic, and appeared to be trying to nuzzle its parent craft, the pilot of the bomber having to resort to aerobatics in order to discourage this dangerous demonstration of affection. The Hs 293 then took station about thirty feet above the nose of the bomber which, by this time, had turned for home. For a few minutes the pair flew in this fashion, and the thoughts of the startled crew of the He 177 can well be imagined, and then the bomb dived steeply into the sea.

The heavy losses sustained by II/K.G.40 showed that daylight attacks with the Greif against convoys were impracticable, and it was decided that attacks on shipping would have to be carried out at night, either with the aid of bright moonlight or flares. New tactics were evolved, one Kette of aircraft dropping special 110-lb. flares on the beam of the convoy while another Kette attacked from the dark side, seeing their target silhouetted against the light of the flares. As the He 177s were less vulnerable to anti-aircraft fire in the darkness, they released their Hs 293s from a range of six to nine miles while flying directly towards their target, thus greatly simplifying the problem of aiming.

On October 1, 1943, I/K.G.4, which was training

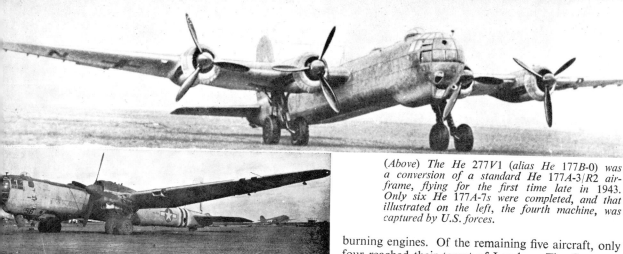

as a strategic bombing unit at Lechfeld, was redesignated as Gruppe I of K.G.100, and on December 18, 1943, the 3rd Staffel moved to Chateaudun where it was joined by the 1st Staffel of I/K.G.40 to participate in Operation *Steinbock* which was to mark the début of the Greif over the British Isles. Operation *Steinbock* had been conceived at the direct orders of Adolf Hitler as a reprisal against London. The Luftwaffe Supreme Command was forced to comb every operational unit in Italy and Russia for bombers to participate in *Steinbock*, and apart from the He 177s which were to form the core of the attack, some eighty He 111s, Do 217s, Ju 88s and Ju 188s were rounded up for the task.

The attack on London commenced on January 21, 1944, the Staffeln of I/K.G.40 and I/K.G.100 operating as a single unit from both Chateaudun and Rheine. After two attacks on London, I/K.G.40 was withdrawn to Germany, its place being taken by the 2nd Staffel of K.G.100 two weeks later, this unit having, in the meantime, become operational. While, as an operation, *Steinbock* could be regarded as a failure, the defences of London decimating the attacking medium bombers, the He 177s achieved some success. The more experienced crews carried maximum bomb loads and, climbing to 23,000 feet while still over German territory, approached their target in a shallow dive, attaining speeds approaching 435 m.p.h., at which night fighters could not intercept them and anti-aircraft fire could not follow them. In this way, only four He 177s were lost through enemy action, but, nevertheless, a very low degree of concentration was attained, and serviceability was invariably low because of last-minute mishaps before operations. Evidence of this was provided Major-General Pelz, appointed "Assault Leader against England" by Goring, on the night of February 13, 1944, when he witnessed the take-off and landing of the aircraft of the 2nd and 3rd Staffeln of K.G.100.

It was a cold night and the "cold start" procedure was employed. Thirteen aircraft took off—one having come to grief with a burst tyre—but eight of these returned to base suffering from over-heated or burning engines. Of the remaining five aircraft, only four reached their target of London. The Gruppenkommandeur, finding himself over Norwich, had turned back, dumping his bombs in the Zuyder Zee. Of the four aircraft which reached London, one was shot down by night fighters. Operation *Steinbock* was called off at the beginning of March.

Several sub-types of the He 177A-5 were produced: the He 177A-5/R5 had an additional remotely-controlled gun barbette mounted aft of the bomb-bays but only one example of this type was completed; the He 177A-5/R6 was similar to the A-5/R2 apart from the deletion of the two forward bomb-bays; the He 177A-5/R7 had a pressurized cabin which increased its operational ceiling to 49,870 feet, and the He 177A-5/R8, only one example of which was built, was equipped with remotely-controlled "chin" and tail barbettes, but was abandoned owing to difficulties with the control system. During 1944 a total of 565 He 177A-5s was completed, although the whole production programme virtually ground to a halt during October in favour of the "emergency fighter programme."

While production of the He 177A-5 had proceeded several improved versions of the Greif were evolved, including the He 177A-6. Work on this extensively revised model began early in 1944, and preparations were made to switch production from the A-5 to the A-6 immediately. The constant flow of modifications resulting from the complaints of frontline units delayed plans, however, and instead of fifteen He 177A-6s ready for delivery by the end of May 1944, only six were actually completed and their assembly was possible only by utilising ninety-eight per cent A-5 components. The first six He 177A-6/R1 long-range heavy bombers were conversions of standard He 177A-5/R6 aircraft and featured pressure cabins. The rear dorsal turret was deleted as an electrically-powered Rheinmetall-Borsig turret housing four 7.9-mm. MG 81 machine guns was installed in the tail, and this was considered to provide adequate rear defence. The two forward bomb-bays were deleted and the rear bay could accommodate a 1,100-lb. load, but the principal offensive load (5,500 lb.) was carried beneath the fuselage. Range was 3,600 miles, and the fuel cells were heavily armoured.

The seventh He 177A-6 was designated He 177V22 and intended as a prototype for the He 177A-6/R2 which differed from the A-6/R1 principally in having an entirely redesigned nose of improved aerodynamic form. Defensive armament comprised twin 13-mm. MG 131 machine guns in a "chin" barbette, twin 20-mm. MG 151 cannon in the remotely-controlled forward dorsal barbette, and one 13-mm. MG 131 machine gun in the rear of the central nose bulge in addition to the HDL/81V tail turret. Alternative offensive loads comprised one 5,500-lb. SC 2500 general-purpose bomb and one 1,100-lb. SC 500 general-purpose bomb; one 4,410-lb. SC 2000 bomb and one 2,200-lb. SC 1000 bomb; two Fritz-X guided bombs and one 1,100-lb. SC 500 bomb, or one Hs 293D missile and one 1,100-lb. SC 500 bomb. The whole He 177A-6 programme was abandoned after completion of the He 177V22 in favour of the He 277 (alias He 177B) programme.

The He 177A-7 was planned as a high altitude bomber making use of the additional power available from the DB 613 coupled engine which, comprising two DB 603G engines, provided 3,600 h.p. for take-off and 3,150 h.p. for climb and combat. To simplify and accelerate construction of the bomber, however, standard A-5 airframes and DB 610 power plants were employed by the six He 177A-7 bombers completed, the principal change being an increase in overall wing span to 118 ft. $1\frac{1}{3}$ in. Empty and loaded weights were increased to 39,913 lb. and 76,280 lb. respectively, and maximum speed was increased to 335 m.p.h. at 20,000 feet.

The Japanese Navy had evinced an interest in the He 177 from an early stage in its development, and work had actually commenced on a new Hitachi factory at Chiba specifically for the quantity production of this bomber. In view of the difficulties being encountered with the coupled power plants, Professor Heinkel himself had advised the Japanese Naval Air Mission visiting Rostock-Marienehe to employ four separate engines rather than coupled units and, following his advice, the proposed Japanese production variant was to have four separate air-cooled radials. Sample tools had been delivered to Japan by submarine, and an He 177A-7 was offered to Japan for service evaluation. The third He 177A-7, completed in May 1944, was prepared for the long-distance flight, much of its armour being stripped and additional fuel cells being installed in both the wings and bomb-bays. In the late summer of 1944, the machine was readied for its non-stop flight which was to be made at extreme altitude via Siberia. However, the Japanese insisted that the aircraft be flown via Persia and India, basing their refusal to permit the aircraft to be flown over the shorter route on their neutrality pact with Russia, and maintaining this attitude even after Russia had renounced the non-aggression pact. Consequently, the He 177A-7 remained in Germany and, together with the other five He 177A-7s completed, was to have been used to attack American targets.

An interesting experiment in aerial defence was conducted with the He 177 in the summer of 1944 by the Versuchs Jagdgruppe 10. Three He 177s were delivered to Pardubitz in June 1944, and modified for use as bomber "destroyers". Their bomb-bays were removed together with the fuel tanks immediately aft of the cockpit, and a battery of thirty-three rocket tubes was installed. The tubes were inclined to fire upwards at an angle of 60° to the horizontal axis of the aircraft and slightly to starboard. The upper section of the fuselage in which the tubes were installed was fitted with a cover containing thirty-three circular holes. For firing control purposes the battery was divided into two groups of eighteen and twenty-five rockets, and a selector switch allowed for the firing of the whole battery in groups or as single projectiles.

After flight trials, the three He 177s were flown from Pardubitz to Rechlin for firing and operational trials by V.J.G.10. It was proposed that the "destroyer" He 177s would follow an enemy bomber formation, pass below and to port of the intruders, and maintain a difference of altitude of 6,000 feet at the time of the attack from below. Some experimental daylight operations were flown by the He 177s, but no contact was made with Allied bomber formations, and as American escort fighters were becoming increasingly numerous the whole scheme was abandoned.

One of the simplest means of solving the power plant difficulties suffered by the He 177 would have been the adoption of four independent engines during the bomber's early development as was done with the Lancaster. Such a proposal was, in fact, made by Heinkel as early as 1940, and the projected variant with independent engines was designated He 177A-4. The application of cabin pressurization had already been considered, the nose section of the He 177A-1 having been redesigned to facilitate this modification, and the He 177A-4 was envisaged as a pressurized high-altitude bomber. The estimated performance of the He 177A-4 included a maximum speed of 350 m.p.h. at 21,650 feet, a maximum cruising speed of 317 m.p.h. at the same altitude, a service ceiling of 30,840 feet, and a maximum range of 2,270 miles at 258 m.p.h. There were numerous delays before the R.L.M. accepted these proposals, and then it was decided to transfer the design to the German-controlled Société Aéronautique des Avions Farman of Suresnes, near Paris, the type being redesignated He 274A.

Apart from the design study of the He 274, Heinkel's project office at Vienna-Schwechat produced a parallel study for a variant of the basic He 177 design powered by four independent engines, the He 277. Unlike the He 274, the He 277 was intended to retain the standard He 177 airframe which would enable the bulk of the existing tooling to be utilised in the event of a sudden switch to the new machine. However, the He 277 project was turned down firmly and, indeed, pressure on the part of Professor Heinkel for the development of this bomber in favour of the existing He 177A resulted in Goring expressly forbidding any further mention of the He 277!

Despite this official opposition, Heinkel secretly continued the development of the He 277, and in all official correspondence its continued existence was disguised under the designation "He 177B". In actual fact, all drawings, calculations and works memoranda referred to the bomber as the He 277!

Until 1943, the R.L.M. remained adamant in its refusal to permit any major redesign of the basic He 177A bomber, but, on May 23, 1943, Adolf Hitler summoned a meeting at Obersalzberg of leading members of the aircraft industry, during the course of which the Fuhrer demanded a dual-purpose bomber capable of attacking London by day and night from altitudes at which interceptors would be powerless to intervene, and also suitable for attacking Allied convoys far out in the Atlantic. Heinkel claimed that the "He 177B" could fulfil these demands, and received instructions to proceed immediately with development.

A standard He 177A-3/R2 airframe was promptly modified to take four independent Daimler-Benz DB 603A engines with annular nose radiators as the He 277V1. Flight tests commenced at Vienna-Schwechat late in 1943 and, to delude Goring and the R.L.M., the machine was referred to as the He 177B-0. The second prototype, the He 277V2, referred to in correspondence between Heinkel and the R.L.M. as the He 177B-5/R1, was a conversion of a standard He 177A-5/R8 airframe and was flown for the first time on February 28, 1944, at Vienna-Schwechat. The second prototype was used for stability trials and some directional instability already experienced with the He 277V1 had resulted in the addition of small auxiliary fins to the tailplane.

In April 1944, the He 277V2 was flown to Rechlin for extensive trials where the official test pilots reported that, although the machine suffered some directional instability, the prototype handled exceptionally well. The He 277V2's armament comprised a new remotely-controlled Rheinmetall-Borsig "chin" barbette containing four 7.9-mm. MG 81 machine guns, one 7.9-mm. MG 81 machine gun in the nose, twin 13-mm. MG 131 guns in the remotely-controlled forward dorsal barbette, one MG 131 in the rear dorsal turret, and four MG 81 machine guns in the tail turret. The He 277V3 was similar to the V2 but, after the initial flight tests, a new tail assembly with twin fins and rudders was fitted with highly satisfactory results. After a conference held on May 25, 1944, Goring, declaiming that the heavy bomber "remained the kernel of aerial armament", ordered the immediate initiation of quantity production of the new bomber, the aim being a delivery rate of 200 machines per month!

The initial production model was the He 277B-5/R2 (alias He 177B-5/R2) intended for operation as a heavy bomber over medium and long ranges. It was powered by four 1,750 h.p. DB 603A engines with which it attained a maximum speed of 354 m.p.h. and a cruising speed of 286 m.p.h. Service ceiling was 49,200 feet, range was 3,728 miles, and empty and loaded weights were 48,061 lb. and 98,105 lb. respectively. The internal bomb load was 1,100 pounds and externally under the fuselage a 5,500-lb. bomb, a Hs 293 missile or two Fritz-X guided bombs could be carried. Defensive armament comprised a 7.9-mm. MG 81 machine gun in the extreme nose which was interchangeable with a 15-mm. or 20-mm. MG 151 cannon, four MG 81s in the "chin" barbette, twin MG 131s in the forward dorsal barbette, one MG 131 in the rear dorsal turret, and four MG 81s in the tail. As a result of Goring's order, which, at that stage of the war, was unrealistic in the extreme, quantity production of the He 277B-5/R2 started immediately, but, on July 3, 1944, the whole bomber programme was abandoned in favour of the "emergency fighter programme", and only eight production He 277s were completed and only two or three of these actually test flown.

Prior to the termination of all bomber development, work had started on two further variants, the He 277B-6 and B-7. The He 277B-6 had a wing span of 131 ft. 2¾ in. and four 2,060 h.p. Junkers Jumo 213F engines, and the dihedral angle of the tailplane was increased and the fins and rudders enlarged. The fuselage length was 73 ft. 2½ in. The He 277B-6/R1 was to have employed the Rheinmetall-Borsig HL/131V hydraulically-operated tail turret containing four 13-mm. MG 131 machine guns. This turret was heavily armoured but, in view of some of its features, it was fortunate for Luftwaffe air gunners that it never saw operational service. In the event of the hydraulic elevation drive failing, the top of the gunner's control stick had to be unscrewed and removed before the handle for emergency operation could be turned; the emergency firing switch had to be operated by the gunner's left knee, and the turret door was hinged at the bottom, and after locking, could only be opened in level flight, an attitude unlikely to be adopted by the bomber at the moment the gunner wanted to bale out! Other armament comprised twin 20-mm. MG 151 cannon in the remotely-controlled "chin" barbette and a pair of similar weapons in dorsal and ventral barbettes.

The He 277B-6/R2 had the width of its fuselage reduced to 4 ft. 11 in. and its length increased to 74 ft. 7¾ in., and the nose redesigned to eliminate the ventral bulge, and the He 277B-6/R3 had a deeper fuselage and manned dorsal and ventral gun positions. The He 277B-7 was a projected long-range reconnaissance aircraft derived from the He 177A-7. Featuring the same wing span, it was to be powered by the Jumo 213A, 213E or 222 engines, but only one He 277B-7 was completed, and this with DB 603A

THE HEINKEL He 177 GREIF

its failure; a failure which prevented the Luftwaffe from maintaining any large-scale strategic bombing such as that so successfully initiated by the Allies. The Greif's chief claim to fame was the fact that it was the *only* German heavy bomber to attain quantity production during the war years. It was, in fact, one of the very few entirely new German combat aircraft designed to progress from prototype to operational service during the conflict. It was of ambitious conception, embodying as much ingenuity as any warplane to see combat, but the advances that it offered were nullified by the German aircraft industry's inability to devote sufficient effort towards its perfection.

Derived from the basic He 177 and built in France, the He 274V1 was almost ready to commence flight tests when the Germans were forced to withdraw from the Paris area.

engines. This aircraft was destroyed, together with the eight He 277B-5s, just before the arrival of Russian troops.

In the meantime, work had been progressing on two prototypes of the He 274A at Farman's Suresnes plant. The fuselage was very similar to that of the He 177A and the tail assembly closely followed that finally selected for the He 277B-5. Like the latter bomber, power was provided by four independent DB 603A engines, although DB 603Gs were proposed for production machines. Although design had been initiated at Vienna-Schwechat in 1940, actual construction at Suresnes did not commence until late in 1943, by which time two prototypes, the He 274V1 and V2, and four He 274A-0 pre-production machines had been ordered.

The pressurized fuselage nose of the He 274 provided accommodation for four crew members, and immediately aft of the flight deck and divided by a catwalk was the main bomb-bay with a maximum capacity of 8,800 lb. The estimated performance included maximum speeds of 267 m.p.h. at sea level, 310 m.p.h. at 18,700 ft., and 373 m.p.h. at 36,000 ft., and range was estimated at 2,500 miles at 285 m.p.h. The He 274V1 was almost ready to fly when the Germans were forced to withdraw from Paris, and although the retreating forces took most of the design data with them, they failed to destroy the airframe which was eventually completed by French technicians and flown several months after the end of the war.

It has been said that the He 177A Greif was deadlier to the crews that flew it than to their enemies. This was, of course, an exaggeration, but the bomber undeniably suffered more development troubles than any of its contemporaries, and these led to

Heinkel He 177A-5/R2 Greif

Dimensions: Span, 103 ft. 1¾ in.; length, 66 ft. 11⅛ in.; height, 20 ft. 11⅞ in.; wing area, 1,097.918 sq. ft.

Armament: One 7.9-mm. MG 81 machine gun with 2,000 rounds in the nose; one 20-mm. MG 151 cannon with 300 rounds in forward ventral gondola position; two 7.9-mm. MG 81 machine guns with 2,000 r.p.g. in rear ventral gondola position; two 13-mm. MG 131 machine guns with 750 r.p.g. in remotely-controlled dorsal barbette; one 13-mm. MG 131 machine gun with 750 rounds in rear dorsal turret, and one 20-mm. MG 151 cannon with 300 rounds in tail position. Offensive load: (Internally) Sixteen 110-lb., four 550-lb., or two 1,100-lb. bombs. (Externally) Two FX 1400 Fritz radio-directed armour-piercing bombs, two Henschel Hs 293A-D radio-controlled rocket-propelled missiles, two LMA III parachute sea mines, or two LT 50 torpedoes. Maximum bomb load, 13,200 lb.

Power Plants: Two Daimler-Benz DB 610A-1/B-1 (A-1 port and B-1 starboard) twenty-four cylinder liquid-cooled engines each rated at 2,950 h.p. at 2,800 r.p.m. for take-off, 3,100 h.p. at 2,800 r.p.m. at 6,890 ft. for emergency, and 2,750 h.p. at 2,600 r.p.m. at 6,800 ft. maximum continuous.

Weights: Empty (equipped), 37,038 lb.; normal loaded, 59,966 lb.; maximum loaded, 68,343 lb.

Performance: Maximum speed (normal loaded weight), 303 m.p.h. at 20,000 ft., 248.5 m.p.h. at sea level, (maximum loaded weight), 273 m.p.h. at 20,000 ft.; maximum cruising speed, 258 m.p.h. at 20,000 ft., economical cruising speed, 210 m.p.h. at 20,000 ft.; range (with two Hs 293 missiles), 3,417 mls., (with two FX 1400 bombs), 3,100 mls.; initial climb rate, 620 ft./min.; time to 10,000 ft., 10 min., to 20,000 ft., 39 min.; service ceiling, 26,250 ft.

The Ki.67-Ib Type 4 Model 1B Hiryu illustrated above was the standard production model of what was undoubtedly the finest Japanese Army Air Force bomber encountered in combat. Originally flush-mounted lateral gun positions were used but these were replaced by blister-type positions as shown in the photograph on the left.

THE MITSUBISHI Ki.67 TYPE 4 HIRYU

The job of intelligence officer is no simple task. An intimate knowledge of aviation is necessary in order to correctly evaluate combat reports, and it is inevitable that, at times, mistakes are made; errors which may not be corrected for many months and which may well prove costly in terms of lives and material. Such a mistake was made with the first identification of the Mitsubishi Hiryu (Flying Dragon), the finest Japanese Army Air Force bomber to be encountered in combat. When torpedo-carrying Hiryu bombers made their début in October 1944, during the second battle of the Philippine Sea, with an attack on the American Fleet, the type was promptly recorded as "a new Naval attack bomber". The conclusion was logical enough, for the new aircraft was indeed acting as a naval bomber in co-operation with Japanese Naval Air Force units operating from Formosa, and it was not until the Hiryu was met over China, far beyond the operating range of the nearest naval air units, and the wreckage of crashed Hiryu bombers had been analysed in the Philippines, that the truth was discovered.

The discovery was alarming. For three years the Allies had been at war with Japan and, although Japanese capabilities in the design of combat aircraft had been seriously underrated, it had been discovered that the Japanese Army bombers were exceptionally vulnerable to fighter attack. The appearance of the Hiryu signified an end to this vulnerability, and the rapid replacement of the obsolete Mitsubishi Ki.21-II

and Nakajima Ki.49-II bombers was ominous. The J.A.A.F. bomber force, hopelessly outclassed and believed largely impotent, was being revitalised with an aircraft far superior to any it had previously possessed.

The events leading up to the initial use of the Hiryu off Formosa created a paradox of genealogy and operational demand. Originally evolved as a high-performance bomber to meet an Army specification, the Hiryu owed much to the standard G4M naval bomber, and was superficially similar in configuration. Adopted as a standard J.A.A.F. bomber type in 1944, and produced exclusively for the Army, the urgent need for attack bombers for use against the American Fleet off the Philippines led to the Hiryu's baptism of fire as a naval attack aircraft flown by J.A.A.F. crews in consort with J.N.A.F. units. Following this operational initiation, the Hiryu was assigned to its basic Army mission, only to be returned to naval co-operation later in the war when, once again, the J.N.A.F. had insufficient attack bombers to handle the situation that had developed.

The most advanced Japanese Army bomber of the war to see operational service, the Hiryu was designed by the Mitsubishi Jukogyo K.K. in response to an Army heavy bomber specification issued in February 1941. In spite of the limited design personnel available, a situation that became progressively worse after Japan embarked upon the Pacific War, the Mitsubishi staff undertook the design and development of the new

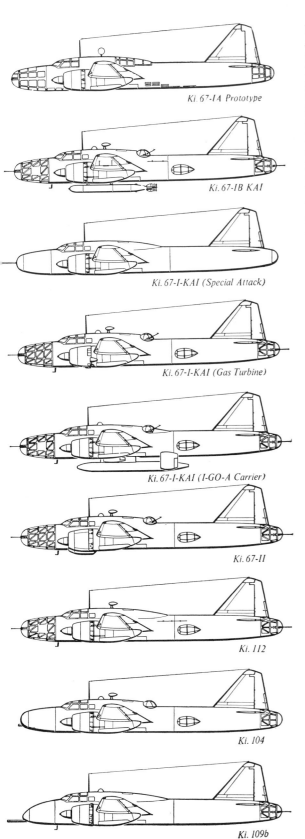

Ki.67-1A Prototype

Ki.67-1B KAI

Ki.67-1-KAI (Special Attack)

Ki.67-1-KAI (Gas Turbine)

Ki.67-1-KAI (I-GO-A Carrier)

Ki.67-II

Ki.112

Ki.104

Ki.109b

bomber with enthusiasm. The new aircraft presented a challenge, for it provided Mitsubishi with the opportunity to create a replacement for their earlier K.21-II Type 97 heavy bomber, as well as regain the profitable position of the leading J.A.A.F. heavy bomber designers and manufacturers, a position which was being threatened by the Nakajima Hikoki K.K. with their Ki.49 Donryu Type 100 bomber series. The J.A.A.F. specification called for a bomber that could carry a bomb load appreciably farther, faster and higher than the standard Ki.21 and Ki.49 bombers. It was to represent a major step forward in J.A.A.F. bomber equipment, providing equality with the bombers of the western nations, and offering an effective weapon for use against Russia in the event of an open conflict with that country. The specification called for an operational altitude of up to 23,000 ft., a tactical radius of 620 miles with a 1,100-lb. bomb load, and a maximum speed of at least 310 m.p.h. in order to bring J.A.A.F. equipment into line with Naval bomber projects then under development. The specification recommended the use of the most dependable power plants available, such as the Mitsubishi Ha.101 Type 100 air-cooled radial of 1,450 h.p., then being employed by the Ki.21-II bomber; the successful Nakajima Ha.109 radial of similar power, later adopted as the Type 2 and used in the Ki.49-II bomber, or, if development progressed favourably, the unproven Nakajima Ha.103 radial engine of 1,800 h.p. The new bomber was to carry nine or ten crew members and an effective defensive armament comprising six 7.92-mm. machine guns in nose, dorsal, ventral, waist and tail positions.

With Mitsubishi's acceptance of the specification, and the J.A.A.F. assignment of the experimental Ki.67 project designation to the bomber, work began in earnest late in 1941 at Mitsubishi's Nagoya plant, Kumishiko Kono, General Manager of the Nagoya Works and Chief of the Engineering Department, being appointed Chief Project Engineer. Kono's position and acclaimed success with the Ki.15, Ki.30 and Ki.51 series of J.A.A.F. light bombers gave considerable stature to the Ki.67 project, and he was assisted by Chief Engineer Ozawa Kyunosuke, well-known in Japan for his work on the standard Ki.21 bomber, and earlier work on the Ki.2 Type 93 light bomber, a type based on the Junkers K-37. Early in 1942 the design team was augmented by the addition of Yoshio Tsubota, a young engineer who had received his degree from the California Institute of Technology, and possessed a background of practical training in the U.S.A. Free rein was given to the Ki.67 design team in order to encourage new ideas, and, as a result, the bomber project became a showpiece of advanced thinking on the part of Japanese engineers, incorporating an advantageous blend of combat-tested innovations and contemporary Western ideas as a result of American-oriented training and the analysis of captured Allied aircraft obtained during the opening months of the war. Crew safety was

The Mitsubishi Ki.67-Ib Hiryu was used by the Japanese Navy as a torpedo bomber in a desperate bid to stem the Allied invasion of the Philippines. External torpedo racks were fitted as seen in the photograph.

awarded higher priority than previously, with ⅜-in. three-ply rubber protection for most fuel and oil tanks, and armour protection for the crew members. Other advanced ideas incorporated in the design included fully-feathering airscrews, radio altimeter, etc.

The first prototype Ki.67 was completed at Mitsubishi's 1st Airframe Works at Nagoya in December 1942. An unusually slim and clean mid-wing monoplane, the Ki.49 was beautifully proportioned, and when the prototype entered its flight test programme at Mitsubishi's Kagamigahara airfield in Gifu soon after the first of the year, it was soon discovered that the aesthetic qualities of the Ki.67 did not belie its performance, and despite the size of the aircraft, it was found to be highly manœuvrable, and could effect loops and vertical turns with ease. The J.A.A.F. was highly enthusiastic regarding the test results, and made immediate preparations for the mass production of the new bomber, anticipating that the first deliveries would be made in little more than a year's time.

The Ki.67's excellent performance was no accident, for the design team had quietly side-stepped the original specification in order to provide the aircraft with as much power as possible. Coincident with the design of the Ki.67, Mitsubishi were also engaged in a programme of boosting the power ratings of existing engines. The most promising Army engine in the programme was the new Ha.42/11, designed by Diploma Engineer M. Shomura, and based on the successful Kasei series of radials. Experimental work had commenced in 1942 at Mitsubishi's 2nd Engine Works, part of the Nagoya factory complex, and the designation Ha.104 was applied to the developed engine. An eighteen-cylinder twin-row radial incorporating such innovations as a two-speed supercharger and fan-assisted cooling, and rated at 1,900

h.p. for take-off, the Ha.104 was incorporated into the Ki.67's design, the bomber becoming the first service type to use the new engine. Development work progressed rapidly, and the Ha.104 was placed in production in 1943 at many Mitsubishi factories.

Completed as a six- to eight-seat bomber with a defensive armament of four 12.7-mm. machine guns and one 20-mm. cannon, the Ki.67 experimental heavy bomber underwent an intensive test programme under J.A.A.F. direction, a second prototype being completed in March 1943, a third in May, and one or two additional aircraft were completed each month throughout the remainder of the year, and absorbed by the test programme, fifteen machines being completed by the end of 1943. In its original form as the Ki.67-Ia, or Model 1A, the bomber had flush-mounted gun positions in the waist of the fuselage. During the test programme these were replaced by blister-type positions; the nose and tail gun positions were modified; the engine cowlings were improved, and changes were made in the equipment and instrumentation. Although the numerous revisions improved the performance and operational capability of the bomber, the seemingly endless series of changes called for by the J.A.A.F. seriously delayed the Ki.67 programme, and by April 1944 only twenty-one machines had been completed, including the prototypes. The urgent demand for such bombers as the Ki.67 at the front owing to the worsening war situation dictated an immediate agreement on a basic production model if the J.A.A.F.'s production programme was to be realised, and, caught between the desire to incorporate the latest developments in the bomber and the need to finalise the design for production, the J.A.A.F. finally gave its approval for quantity manufacture of the type early in 1944 as the Mitsubishi

FINISH AND INSIGNIA: *The Mitsubishi Ki.67-I Hiryu illustrated on the opposite page employed, like virtually all Hiryu aircraft that entered J.A.A.F. service, dark olive green upper surfaces with medium sea grey under surfaces. In view of the haste with which the Hiryu bombers were introduced into operational service, many standard service markings, such as "combat stripes" and colourful squadron insignia, were ignored. The sole identifying markings carried by the Hiryu illustrated comprised a Japanese Kana character identifying the Buntai (Squadron) followed by the individual aircraft number (i.e., "148") which appeared in white across the vertical fin. Other aircraft of the same unit included "346", "135" and "146".*

The circular red national insignia, or Hinomaru, appeared on the upper and lower surfaces of both wings, and on the fuselage sides. On some aircraft this insignia was outlined in white, but most Hiryu bombers did not have the national markings outlined.

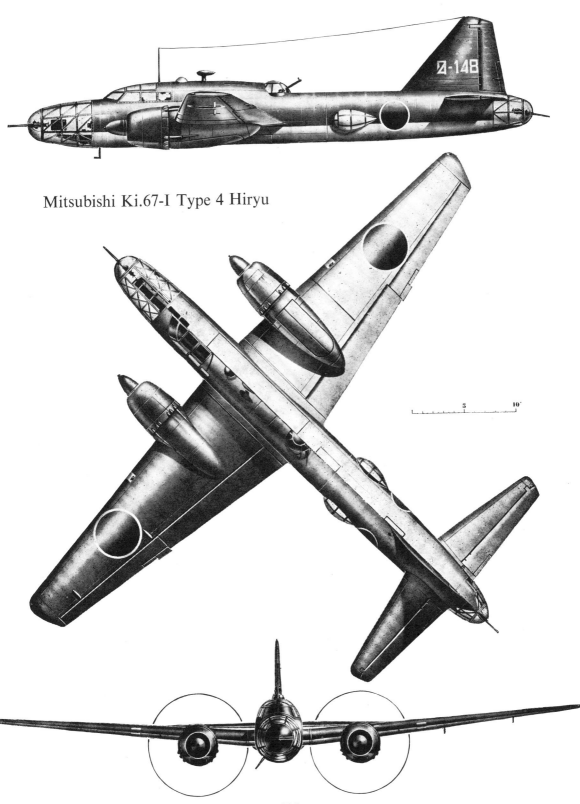

Mitsubishi Ki.67-I Type 4 Hiryu

During the closing stages of the Pacific War, the Hiryu was adopted for suicide attack. The modification of the Ki.67-Ib for this role was undertaken at Tachikawa where the type was designated Rikugun Type 4 Special Attack Aircraft. A long rod projected from the nose to serve as an impact trigger for the explosive charges, and the gun positions were faired over. The accompanying photographs show a suicide crew boarding their aircraft and (left) taking off on their mission.

Ki.67 Type 4 Heavy Bomber, and the name "Hiryu", or Flying Dragon, was adopted.

After a short production run of Model 1A aircraft, the basic wartime model was stabilised in production as the Ki.67-Ib, or Model 1B, and this version was to remain on the assembly lines throughout the remainder of the war. In spite of this standardisation, the J.A.A.F. continued to demand modifications, and these changes were incorporated on the production line, although the basic airframe remained unaltered and its designation unchanged. With the placing in production of the Ki.67-Ib Hiryu at two Mitsubishi plants—the No. 5 Airframe Works at Oe-Machi, near Nagoya, and the No. 9 Airframe Works at Kumamoto, on the island of Kyushu—deliveries increased rapidly, both factories completing their first Hiryu bombers in April 1944. The No. 5 Airframe Works had succeeded in producing 251 Hiryus by the end of 1944, and in spite of the ever-increasing American air attacks, completed a further 223 aircraft in 1945. The main plant at Oe-Machi was ultimately destroyed by Superfortresses combined with the destructive earthquake which rocked Japan in December 1944, and production of the Hiryu was transferred to the Chita factory where it remained until the end of the war, the completed aircraft being tested on the spot at Chita airfield before being turned over to the J.A.A.F. Work at the No. 9 Airframe Works proceeded more slowly due to the limited amount of industry and trained subcontractors on Kyushu, and the Kumamoto plant was forced to remain dependent on the Oe-Machi factory for many components. Although production deliveries

had commenced in April 1944, the Kumamoto factory succeeded in completing only forty-six Hiryu bombers by the end of the war.

The production at both Hiryu factories was complicated by the intensive plant-dispersal programme initiated after the fall of Saipan in the summer of 1944, both factories being forced to establish an extensive network of sub-assembly shops within their area, utilising former spinning mills, military barracks, caves and underground plants. Transportation and housing facilities for the personnel were virtually non-existent, and the main plants had to rely largely on ox-carts and hand-drawn wagons for the delivery of components. In addition to the Mitsubishi factories, the construction of the Ki.67-Ib was also assigned to the Kawasaki Kokuki Kogyo K.K., the Nippon Kokusai Koku Kogyu K.K., and the Dai-ichi Rikugun Kokusho. Of these companies, only Kawasaki succeeded in getting the bomber into production, although far below the delivery rate demanded by the J.A.A.F. Production lines were established at the firm's Kagamigahara Works, and plans were laid to produce 447 Hiryu bombers between December 1944 and August 1945, but Superfortress raids and plant dispersal severely hampered the production schedule. The initial batch of fifteen aircraft was completed with fuselages provided by Mitsubishi's No. 5 Airframe Works, and throughout the final months of the war Kawasaki remained dependent on Mitsubishi for many components. Production of the Hiryu by Kawasaki was further complicated by the decision to build the bomber in the dispersed underground Mizunami

The Ki.109a was an interceptor version of the Hiryu which, employing a standard Ki.67-Ib airframe, carried a 75-mm. cannon in the nose.

plant. In view of all the difficulties, the production of ninety-one Hiryu aircraft by August 1945 represented a creditable performance. Mitsubishi supplied twenty-nine fuselages and a smaller number of wing assemblies to Kokusai, but the company never achieved full Hiryu production, and severe air attacks and plant dispersal slowed down the Rikugun programme so much that this company had completed only one Hiryu by the end of the war.

Another factor in slowing down the Hiryu production programme was the serious shortage of Ha.104 engines, a situation due to the same problems that confronted the airframe industry. When final approval of the Ha.104 had been given in 1944, Mitsubishi had assigned production to their No. 4 Engine Works at Nagoya, and the No. 16 Engine Works at Ogaki. Both plants placed the engine in mass production, and the growing demand for this reliable engine for such new developments as the Ki.74, the Ki.92 and the Ki.119, threatened to further restrict supplies for the Hiryu, but in the event this anticipated crisis failed to materialise owing to the termination of fighting.

In the early summer of 1944 the Ki.67-Ib Type 4 Hiryu heavy bomber began reaching J.A.A.F. squadrons in increasing numbers, with deliveries to both home-based bomber groups and newly reorganised overseas squadrons, and by the autumn the Hiryu was one of the few modern bomber types available to the Japanese forces in some numbers. This resulted in the J.N.A.F.'s request for the use of the type in the Philippines in a desperate bid to stem the Allied invasion of the islands. External torpedo racks were fitted, and crude radar equipment was mounted on the Army bombers, and for this brief period of naval service the Hiryu was the fastest, most heavily armed torpedo-bomber available to the Japanese Navy, participating in the decisive battles off Formosa and the Philippines. As the situation deteriorated, the Hiryu, planned as a high-speed land bomber, was soon allocated the task of long over-water flights for strikes against advanced American bases. Hamamatsu-based Hiryu bombers attacked Superfortress bases in the Marianas in an attempt to hold back the growing might of the American bombing forces. The Hiryu was also active along the massive land front in China and, in April 1945, was attacking Allied forces in the Okinawas.

Continued Japanese reverses led to the introduction of the Hiryu in a new guise, for, with the adoption of *Kamikaze* (Divine Wind) or suicide attack, the Type 4 was found to be one of the few aircraft capable of carrying a heavy bomb load internally at speeds sufficient to render fighter interception difficult. The Hiryu suicide bomber was a specialised development built specially for attacks against Allied shipping. The modification of standard Ki.67-Ib bombers for this role was undertaken by the Army Air Arsenal at Tachikawa, where the type was designated the Rikugun Type 4 Special Attack Aircraft. It carried a crew of three and a 1,760-lb. bomb load internally plus, for certain targets, a similar weight of bombs externally. A long rod projected from the nose, serving as an impact trigger for the explosive charges, and the nose, waist blister and tail gun positions were faired over with plywood. On later conversions the dorsal turret was also removed in order to save drag, resulting in an extremely clean fuselage. These suicide aircraft were supplied to both the J.A.A.F. and the J.N.A.F. during the closing months of the war, and proved to be the most destructive *Kamikaze* type to see operational service. The J.N.A.F.'s *Yasukuni* or "Nation's Security and Peace" squadron, equipped with the Type 4 suicide attack aircraft, became famous throughout Japan for its remarkable attacks on the Allied surface fleets, and the popularity of the squadron was such that it was soon identified with all navalised Type 4 suicide attack aircraft.

Work continued on a never-ending series of projects, many of which represented attempts to increase the range and bomb load of the Hiryu. Scheme after scheme was initiated, with slight increases achieved through drastic reduction in armament and crew members, and the Hiryu was eventually selected as the parent aircraft for the experimental Mitsubishi I-Go-1A guided missile, a short-span flying bomb with a 1,760-lb. warhead which was launched in the air and guided to its target by radio control. First built in 1944, tests with the new weapon were conducted with a modified Hiryu serving as the carrier, with successful launchings conducted as far away as six miles from the target. The war ended before the I-Go-1A became operational, and only ten prototypes were completed.

Great efforts were also made to increase the Hiryu's power, first by the modification of the existing power plants, and eventually by the installation of new engines. In February 1944 a standard Ki.67-Ib was modified to take a turbo-supercharged model of the Ha.104, known as the Ha.104ru. In a series of test flights between February and October, the modified Hiryu attained 345 m.p.h. at 20,000 ft., and 305 m.p.h. at 27,800 ft. Continued work on the supercharged Ha.104 led to the introduction of the 2,500 h.p. Mitsubishi Ha.214, an advanced turbo-supercharged development of the earlier power plant. With the decision to produce the new Ha.214, a companion airframe was developed as the Ki.67-II in late 1944 at the new assembly and testing facilities of Mitsubishi's No. 1 Works located in the city of Matsumoto, in the Nagano Prefecture. Constant delays in the development of both engine and airframe hampered the original plan to complete the first proto-type by June 1945. Additional delays in redesign in order to increase the Ki.67-II's operating range and improve the turbine of the Ha.214 held produc-tion back, and the first Ki.67-II prototype was only half finished when the war ended in August 1945.

The Hiryu's excellent performance led to the parallel development of the aircraft as a fighter, with initial design work commencing in the summer of 1942. Although the Hiryu appeared to hold great promise in this role, three years of spasmodic development did not succeed in producing an effective "destroyer". The first Hiryu fighter design was initiated as a dual project with the design of the original bomber as the Ki.69 Army experimental bomber escort. With con-centration on the Ki.67 project, the proposed escort fighter was shelved, but work was resumed again over a year later as the Ki.112 experimental multi-seat fighter. This project was also abandoned without the construction of a prototype, and the first concrete steps towards producing an operational Hiryu fighter were taken in 1944, following a design discussion regarding the merits of mounting large-bore cannon in the nose of the Type 4 in order to use the aircraft as a Superfortress interceptor, the American bomber being expected to make its début over Japan at any time.

Two standard Ki.67-Ib bombers were turned over to the Army Air Arsenal at Tachikawa for modifica-tion and testing. The first conversion, known as the Ki.104 experimental interceptor, was essentially a Ki.67-Ib with a new nose section mounting an Army 75-mm. cannon just slightly smaller than a standard field piece. Initial firing trials, although providing frightening experiences for the crew, indicated that, providing a suitable mounting could be developed, the aircraft would be able to fire the weapon in the air with an acceptable degree of accuracy. Work began immediately on a second model intended as a proto-type for a production version to be built by Mitsubishi. The new prototype had a completely redesigned cannon mounting and nose section, but retained the basic Ki.67-Ib airframe. While testing proceeded with the second Ki.104, the Ki.109 experimental interceptor designation was assigned to Mitsubishi in January 1944 for the development of a turbo-super-charged version of the fighter which would be capable of engaging the Superfortress at its own altitude.

Design work on the Ki.109 was simplified by the basic groundwork already undertaken by the Army Air Arsenal, and standard Ki.67-Ib airframes were ready for modification and merely awaited delivery of the advanced Ha.104ru engines. With the arrival of the Superfortress over Japan, in June 1944, the Ki.109 development programme was given urgent priority, only to be held up by Mitsubishi's complete inability to deliver any of the supercharged power plants. With the demand for Superfortress inter-ceptors at fever pitch, it was agreed to turn out the initial batch of Ki.109 fighters with standard Hiryu engines, and in August 1944 the first of the new interceptors was completed, followed by a second in October, and an additional twenty in the next few months. This first model, known as the Ki.109a, was an interim fighter, still retaining the original dorsal, waist and tail guns, although the crew was reduced to four members. Use of the 75-mm. cannon was limited as the aircraft carried only fifteen shells, each of which had to be laboriously loaded by the co-pilot.

Completion of the twenty-second Ki.109a fighter ended reliance on existing Hiryu fuselages, and pro-duction continued as the Ki.109b, the new version having an extensively modified fuselage built from the ground up as a fighter. The standard Hiryu wing and tail assemblies and engines were retained, but the fuselage was appreciably cleaner, the dorsal and waist guns being deleted. Armament was restricted to the 75-mm. nose cannon and a single 12.7-mm. machine gun in the tail position, and twenty-two Ki.109b fighters were built. Although designated as experi-mental aircraft, the dire need for operational inter-ceptors led to the limited assignment of the Ki.109s to squadrons, one of these units operating against the Superfortresses from the Micaharra airfield, Kuma-gaya. Their combat début proved a dismal failure, for, without the turbo-superchargers originally specified, the Ki.109s were incapable of engaging the high-flying Superfortresses.

The Hiryu was an exceptional bomber from several viewpoints. Its performance was good and it was remarkably manœuvrable for its size; it was structu-rally simple and easy to build and maintain, and it was extremely versatile. The type earned the respect of its antagonists as the finest bomber to be introduced by the J.A.A.F., and a tough opponent, comparing favourably with the best Allied warplanes in its cate-gory. Dubbed "Peggy" under the Allied system of naming Japanese warplanes, there was nothing effeminate about the Hiryu, which was an outstand-ing example of the extremely high standards in design, workmanship and performance that the Japanese aircraft industry was capable of attaining.

Mitsubishi Ki.67-Ib Type 4 Hiryu

Dimensions: Span, 73 ft. 9¾ in.; length, 61 ft. 4¼ in.; height, 15 ft. 9 in.; wing area, 741.094 sq. ft.

Armament: One 12.7-mm. Type 1 (Browning) machine gun in each of nose, tail and two waist positions, and one 20-mm. Type Ho 5 (Browning) cannon in dorsal turret. Maximum bomb load, 1,760 lb., or one standard 1,760-lb. naval torpedo.

Power Plants: Two Mitsubishi Ha.104 Type 4 eighteen-cylin-der two-row air-cooled radial engines rated at 2,000 h.p. for take-off and war emergency, 1,900 h.p. at 6,560 ft., and 1,750 h.p. at 20,050 ft.

Weights: Empty, 19,068 lb.; normal loaded, 30,346 lb.

Performance: Maximum speed, 334 m.p.h. at 19,980 ft.; cruising speed, 248 m.p.h.; normal range, 1,740 miles; maximum range, 2,360 miles; time to 19,685 ft., 14 min. 30 sec.; service ceiling, 31,070 ft.

The Handley Page H.P.52 prototype (K4240) was flown for the first time on June 21, 1936. On one flight an airscrew and part of an engine came adrift, striking the fuselage just aft of the cockpit. Six weeks later the first flight production orders were placed.

THE HANDLEY PAGE HAMPDEN

All military aeroplanes are to a greater or lesser extent compromises between conflicting requirements, and the Handley Page Hampden was no exception. It reflected the indecision of the Air Staff who were wavering between the desire to carry a moderate offensive load quickly and a larger load at more sedate speeds over considerable distances. The Hampden represented the middle path. It lay roughly between its contemporaries, the Wellington and Whitley and the Blenheim, in load-carrying ability and operational range, yet its performance compared closely with that of the last-mentioned bomber. Named appropriately enough after the 17th-century opponent of tyranny, John Hampden, the bomber was unique in several respects, not least of which being its distinctive appearance. Its fine aerodynamic form, characterized by sharply tapered, slotted and flapped wings, and a deep, slab-sided fuselage to which was appended a slim boom carrying the tail surfaces, inspired a variety of affectionate epithets during its operational career, ranging from that of

"The Frying Pan" to "The Flying Tadpole".

The Hampden was one of the world's most advanced warplanes at the time of its début, and it came of a distinguished line, tracing its ancestry from the O/100 of 1915 which, together with its successors, the O/400 and the V/1500, established the name of Handley Page in the forefront of the world's bomber manufacturers. The Hampden was the Handley Page company's first bomber monoplane, and it was fortunate in retaining many of the characteristics which had popularized its predecessors in Royal Air Force service. It was a forgiving aeroplane from the pilot's viewpoint, and its ease of control rendered it an extremely pleasant aeroplane to fly. It was small enough to be highly manœuvrable; its cockpit offered an excellent "fighter-like" field of vision, and it possessed a remarkable speed range.

Although the Hampden's operational exploits were to be overshadowed by those of its larger successor and stablemate, the Halifax, it was one of the quartet of British twin-engined bombers which bore the brunt

The second prototype H.P.52 (L7271) was converted after initial flight trials to take Dagger XIII engines as the prototype H.P.53. It was flown with Daggers for the first time on July 1, 1937, and, with these engines, was produced as the Hereford.

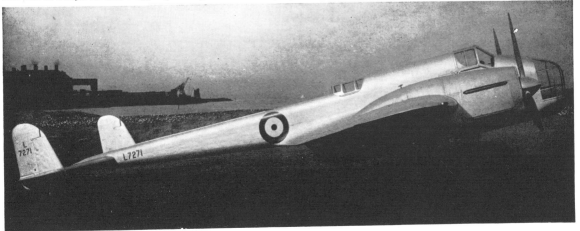

This Hampden I (AE257) was one of three hundred ordered on July 6, 1940, and was operated by No. 44 (Rhodesia) Squadron. The twin Vickers K guns in the dorsal position can just be discerned. These were introduced as part of an attempt to reduce the Hampden's vulnerability early in 1940.

of the R.A.F.'s early offensive sorties, and some ten Hampden-equipped squadrons were almost continuously in action over the Continent during the first two years of the war, apart from a brief period after the near calamitous use of the type on daylight operations. Undeniably, the Hampden possessed its share of operational shortcomings, and these came to light at a very early stage in the air war. Its original defensive armament of a fixed forward-firing Browning and a trio of hand-held Vickers K guns with limited traverse proved woefully inadequate, leaving blind spots which were immediately ferreted out by opposing interceptors, and after early setbacks on daylight sorties, the Hampdens were fitted with heavier defensive armament and confined largely to nocturnal activities. Another shortcoming of the Hampden, one resulting from the choice of an extremely narrow fuselage to reduce drag, was the near-impossibility of removing a badly wounded pilot

from his seat so that another crew member could take over the controls. Later, when the Hampden was used for mine-laying operations and a relief pilot was carried, changing seats called for a display of extreme dexterity.

In the middle of 1932, the Air Ministry issued specification B.9/32 which called for a twin-engined day bomber offering an appreciably higher performance than any such machine previously envisaged. The Handley Page design team headed by Mr. G. R. Volkert began work on what was for that time an extremely radical machine, but it was not until mid-1934 that the Air Ministry relaxed the strict limit imposed by B.9/32 on the bomber's tare weight that an official prototype contract was awarded for Handley Page's bomber which now bore the designation H.P.52. The H.P.52 could not have been more unlike its immediate predecessor, the wire-braced Heyford biplane that had just entered service with the

The first production Hampden I (L4032), illustrated below, was flown for the first time in May 1938, and three months later the first aircraft of this type (the third production machine—L4034) was delivered to the R.A.F.

This English Electric-built Hampden I was operated by No. 16 Operational Training Unit. The first English Electric-built Hampden flew on February 22, 1940, and the company manufactured 770 aircraft of this type.

R.A.F. It featured a highly tapered, low-drag wing incorporating the most advanced slot equipment. This was to enable the bomber to achieve a phenomenally high maximum speed without sacrifice of low speed qualities. Another outstanding feature was its exceptionally slim, compact fuselage—the maximum width of which was only 3 ft.—which carried the tail surfaces on a long boom-like extension, permitting the provision of dorsal and ventral defensive armament without incurring any serious penalty from drag.

Various power plants had been considered for the H.P.52 during its progress across the drawing boards, including the steam-cooled Rolls-Royce Goshawk highly favoured by the Air Ministry at one period, but when the first prototype (K4240) made its appearance in 1936, it was powered by two Bristol Pegasus P.E.5S(a) nine-cylinder radial air-cooled engines with single-stage blowers and driving three-bladed de Havilland controllable-pitch airscrews. This prototype was flown for the first time at Radlett on June 21, 1936, with Major J. L. H. B. Cordes, the company's chief test pilot, at the controls. The initial success of flight trials was such that, in August 1936, within some six weeks of the prototype first taking to the air, an initial production order for 180 machines to specification 30/36 was placed by the Air Ministry, and, simultaneously, one hundred machines powered by the 24-cylinder H-type Napier Dagger air-cooled engine were ordered, the responsibility for their production being allocated to Short and Harland's Belfast factory.

The flight testing of the first prototype H.P.52 did not proceed entirely without untoward incidents. On one occasion an airscrew and part of one of the engines detached themselves in mid-air, striking the fuselage just aft of the pilot's cockpit, and on another occasion a wheels-up landing resulted from a fault in the indicator circuit which displayed a green light despite the fact that the wheels were still retracted. The observer on this flight was Mr. R. S. Stafford, who was later to succeed G. R. Volkert as the company's technical director. Seated in the extensively glazed nose, the wheels-up landing elicited from

The first production H.P.53 Hereford (L6002), illustrated below, flew for the first time late in 1939. It was powered by two Dagger VIII engines but these proved extremely temperamental, and their teething troubles were never entirely eradicated.

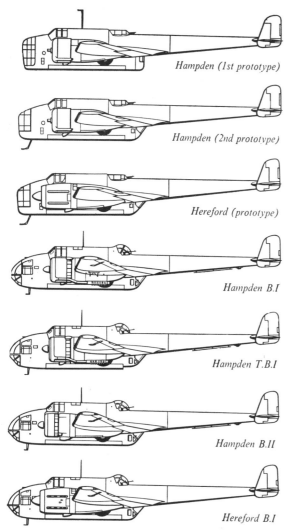

Hampden (1st prototype)

Hampden (2nd prototype)

Hereford (prototype)

Hampden B.I

Hampden T.B.I

Hampden B.II

Hereford B.I

superchargers supplanted the early P.E.5S(a) radials, the birdcage-like forward gun position was replaced by a curved perspex moulding which, incorporating an optically-flat bomb-aiming panel, was more in keeping with the Hampden's clean lines, and the angular dorsal and ventral gun positions were revised, the former having a semi-circular cupola which could be pushed back over the gunner's head.

As unconventional as its configuration were the methods employed in the Hampden's construction. While development of the H.P.52 had been proceeding, the Air Ministry had ordered the H.P.54 Harrow heavy bomber into production as an interim type due to the pressing requirements of the R.A.F. Expansion Scheme. A split-assembly method of construction had been evolved by Handley Page for Harrow production, and this technique was adapted for the Hampden. For example, the fuselage was built in two halves, just like a split lobster, and all pipelines, control runs, etc., were installed before the two halves were mated, greatly simplifying manufacture, and enabling Hampdens to flow from the assembly lines in record time. The fuselage of the Hampden was a flush-riveted stressed-skin all-metal monocoque built in three sections, the nose portion, the centre section and the tailboom, the two latter being split longitudinally for ease of manufacture. The all-metal flush-riveted stressed-skin wing was built in three sections, and was fitted with leading-edge slots and hydraulically-operated trailing-edge flaps. All fuel was housed in six tanks in the wing centre section, these having a total capacity of 654 Imp.gal. Four crew members were carried, and armament comprised one fixed forward-firing 0.303-in. Browning machine gun and three hand-held Vickers K guns of similar calibre.

The first Hampden was delivered to the R.A.F. on August 8, 1938, this aircraft (L4034) going to the Central Flying School at Upavon. Manufacture proceeded rapidly, and by the end of November, No. 49 Squadron based at Scampton, one of the squadrons of the newly-formed No. 5 Group which was eventually to be equipped throughout with Hampdens, had received its full complement of machines. By the end of the year, Nos. 50 and 83 Squadrons were also re-equipping, and the R.A.F. had taken thirty-six Hampdens on strength. In the meantime, arrangements had been made for the Hampden to be built under sub-contract by the English Electric Company's Preston plant, this company being awarded its initial contract for seventy-five aircraft on August 6, 1938, while in Canada several prominent organisations had banded together to form Canadian

Stafford the impassive remark "There's a lot of grass in here!" During the spring of 1937, a second prototype H.P.52 (L7271) joined the test programme. Initially, this machine was similarly powered to its predecessor, but it was subsequently converted by Handley Page to take two Dagger XIII H-type engines and, as the H.P.53, flew with these for the first time on July 1, 1937.

The production prototype H.P.52 (L4032) flew for the first time in May 1938, and on June 24th was christened by Viscountess Hampden at an official ceremony at Radlett. The production bomber differed from the prototype in several respects. Two 1,000 h.p. Pegasus XVIII engines with two-speed

FINISH AND INSIGNIA: *The aircraft illustrated on the opposite page is a Canadian-built Hampden T.B.I. (AN127) of No. 489 (New Zealand) Squadron. This aircraft employed the temperate sea scheme of dark slate grey and dark sea grey camouflage on the upper surfaces and so-called sky-grey on the under surfaces. The squadron letters ("XA") and individual aircraft letter ("Y") which appeared in white on the fuselage sides read XA-Y on the starboard side and Y-XA on the port side. The serial number appeared in black. No national insignia appeared on the under surfaces of the wings, Type B blue and red roundels appeared on the wing upper surfaces, Type C red, white and blue roundels appeared on the fuselage sides, together with the appropriate fin flashes. No. 489's Hampden T.B.Is operated from Wick in 1942.*

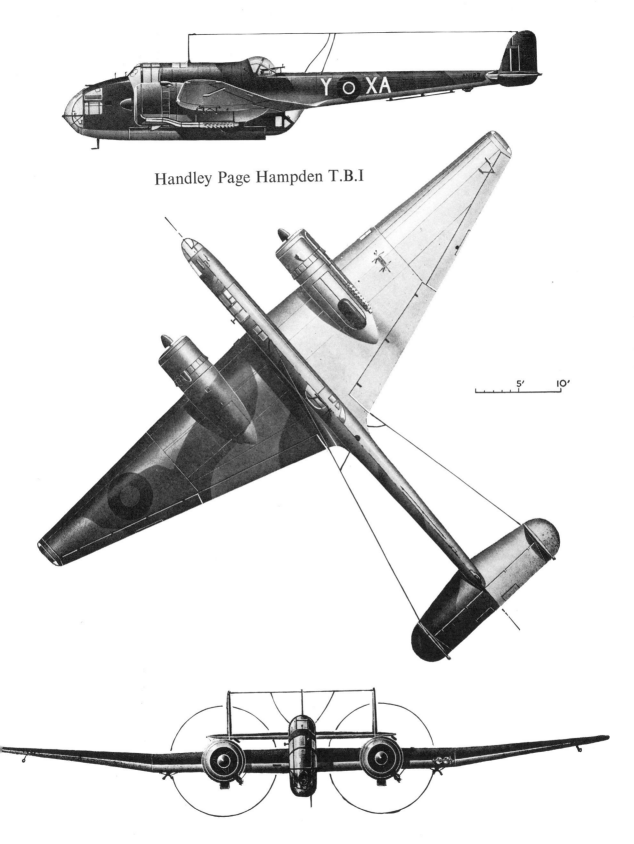

Handley Page Hampden T.B.I

5'   10'

THE HANDLEY PAGE HAMPDEN

Associated Aircraft Limited, receiving an order for eighty Hampdens for the R.A.F. During this period, one Hampden powered by 1,010 h.p. Pegasus XXIV engines was supplied to the Royal Swedish Air Force, being flown to Sweden in September 1938. At one time it was proposed to manufacture the Hampden in Sweden under licence, but this scheme was abandoned.

On September 3, 1939, there were eight Hampden squadrons in the R.A.F.'s line of battle, and on the following day Hampdens of No. 83 Squadron made a sortie against German warships in the Schillig Roads. Unfortunately, their first operation was abortive as they were unable to find their target owing to bad visibility. It was during an attack on two destroyers off Heligoland by eleven Hampdens from Nos. 61 and 144 Squadrons on September 29th that it became apparent that the bomber's defensive armament was inadequate to fend off any determined fighter attack, five of the Hampdens being lost. Shortly afterwards, Bomber Command tacitly abandoned the belief that medium bombers could successfully operate in small formations by day in the face of German fighter opposition, and after December 18, 1939, the Hampden ceased to undertake daylight sorties. The Hampdens were hastily withdrawn from service to undergo a programme of modification designed to reduce their vulnerability. Armour protection for the crew was fitted, twin Vickers K guns were mounted in the dorsal and ventral positions, and flame-damping exhaust pipes were fitted for night operations.

During the early months of 1940, the Hampden was awarded its full share of "bumphlet" sorties—dropping propaganda leaflets, and during the German invasion of Norway, in the spring of 1940, the bomber embarked upon a new career—that of aerial minelaying. Many long and hazardous minelaying sorties were flown during the Norwegian campaign, the Hampden being the first Bomber Command aircraft to engage in these activities. The squadrons became particularly skilled in planting their mines

under the noses of German defence units, but the Hampden was to find its true forte in night bombing and, despite its frail appearance, prove itself capable of absorbing a surprising amount of battle damage. On the night of March 19-20, 1940, Hampdens had dropped their first bombs on German soil with an attack on the seaplane hangars and slipways at Hornum, and on the night of May 11-12th, Hampdens, in concert with a force of Whitleys, dropped the first bombs on the German mainland.

In the late summer of 1940, Hampdens played a leading part in the attacks on the German barges concentrated at Antwerp and other occupied ports in preparation for the invasion of the British Isles. It was during one of these attacks on Antwerp, on the night of September 15-16th, that a member of a Hampden crew performed the deed for which he was to be awarded the Victoria Cross. During the attack, Hampden P1355 of No. 83 Squadron received a direct hit. Fuel tanks in both wings were holed, and fire rapidly enveloped the navigator's and rear gunner's cockpits, forcing the rear gunner to bale out. The whole of the bomb-bay, the flames fanned by the inrush of air through holes blown in the fuselage, was such an inferno that the aluminium floor of the gunner's cockpit melted in the heat. Sergeant John Hannah, the wireless operator/air gunner, forced his way aft and, despite severe burns, extinguished the flames, after which, crawling forward, he discovered that the navigator had also baled out. Despite his serious condition he assisted the pilot to bring the crippled bomber safely back to its base.

This was not the first Victoria Cross to be awarded to a member of a Hampden crew, however, for the first of these very signal honours bestowed so sparingly to be gained by a Bomber Command pilot was that won by Flt. Lieut. R. A. B. Learoyd of No. 49 Squadron. On the night of August 12-13, 1940, five Hampdens drawn from Nos. 49 and 83 Squadrons attacked an aqueduct forming part of the Dortmund-Ems Canal. Heavy anti-

The second production Hereford (L6003) is illustrated below. A total of 150 Herefords was ordered but many were converted to Hampden configuration either before or after leaving the production line at Belfast.

The Hampden T.B.I (above) differed from the standard Hampden bomber in having a slightly deeper bomb-bay to accommodate an 18-in. torpedo. Hampden T.B.Is continued to operate until December 1943.

aircraft defences were disposed so as to form a lane down which attacking aircraft were forced to fly to reach their target. At intervals of two minutes the Hampdens went in from the North, and two of the first four aircraft were shot down and the other two seriously damaged. The fifth Hampden, P4403 piloted by Flt. Lieut. Learoyd, dived to 150 feet, despite the fact that the anti-aircraft guns were firing at point blank range, pressed home an attack and successfully blocked the canal. Many holes were shot in the Hampden's wings and the hydraulic system was put out of action, but the pilot nursed the seriously damaged bomber back to base, waited for the dawn and landed, despite lack of flaps or undercarriage, without injury to his crew.

The parent company completed its 500th and last Hampden in July 1940, and of the initial production order for 180 machines, four (L4208-4211) had been sent to Canada to serve as prototype aircraft for Canadian Associated Aircraft's Hampden production, and another, L4207, was delivered to the English Electric Company at Preston for the same purpose. One machine, P4285, was used for experiments with balloon cable cutters, and P4290 was employed on overload tests. Prior to the completion of the last Handley Page-built Hampden, deliveries from English Electric's assembly line had commenced, the first of these, P2062, flying on February 22, 1940. By this time, the initial production order placed with English Electric for seventy-five machines had been supplemented on April 21st and December 20, 1939, by orders for 150 and 125 machines respectively, and by January 31, 1941, no fewer than 300 Hampdens had been delivered from Preston, the grand total of English Electric-built Hampdens reaching 770 by the time the last aircraft (AE439) left the line on March 15, 1942.

The first Canadian-built Hampden (P5298) flew on August 9, 1940, a delivery rate of fifteen aircraft per month being attained by Canadian Associated Aircraft by the following October. These aircraft were ferried over to the United Kingdom, the total

Hampden production in Canada reaching 160 machines when the last was delivered at the end of 1941. At one time it was envisaged that Canadian Hampdens would be fitted with 1,100 h.p. Wright Cyclone GR1820-G105A radials, but this proposal did not see fruition. However, two Hampdens were fitted with Cyclones for test purposes, these being known as the H.P.62 Hampden II. One Cyclone-powered Hampden II (X3115) actually served with No. 415 (Canadian) Squadron from 1940 until the end of 1943.

The version of the Hampden fitted with Dagger engines built by Short and Harland at Belfast had been designated H.P.53 by the parent company and named Hereford. Built to specification 44/36, the first production Hereford (L6002) flew late in 1939, powered by twenty-four-cylinder Napier Dagger VIII engines each offering 955 h.p. at 4,200 r.p.m. at sea level and 1,000 h.p. at 4,200 r.p.m. at 8,750 ft. The Hereford weighed 11,700 lb. tare and 17,800 lb. loaded. Performance was slightly higher than that of the Hampden, maximum speed being 265 m.p.h. at 15,500 ft., and cruising speed being 172 m.p.h. The astonishingly noisy Dagger engines with their remarkably high revs proved, to say the least, temperamental, and their teething troubles were never satisfactorily eradicated. The original production order for one hundred Herefords had been increased to 150 machines, but only one machine of this type is known to have reached operational service—with No. 185 Squadron which was to have operated a Hereford flight alongside two Hampden flights. Many of the Herefords were converted to Hampden configuration either before or after leaving the assembly line, and others were employed as crew trainers by No. 16 Operational Training Unit at Upper Heyford, as well as other training units, the first Hereford being delivered to No. 16 O.T.U. on May 7, 1940.

As Bomber Command's night offensive increased in tempo, Hampdens attacked all parts of Germany. Twelve Hampdens of Nos. 61 and 144 Squadrons

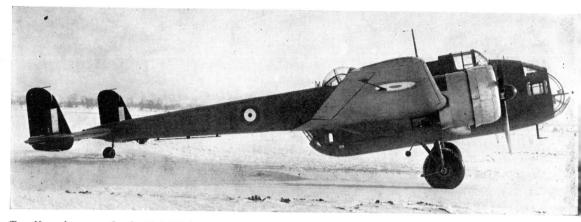

Two Hampdens were fitted with 1,100 h.p. Wright Cyclone GR1820-G105A radials, these being known by the designation H.P.62 Hampden II, and one of these (X3115) is illustrated here.

took part in the R.A.F.'s first bombing raid on Berlin on the night of August 25-26, 1940, and on the night of May 30-31, 1942, a small force of Hampdens was present on the occasion of Bomber Command's first 1,000-bomber raid which was made against Cologne. But by this time, the Hampden's days as an operational night bomber were numbered, and on the night of September 14-15, 1942, they operated with Bomber Command for the last time. During its years of service with that Command, the Hampden had operated with Nos. 7, 44, 49, 50, 61, 76, 83, 97, 106, 144, 185, 207 and 408 Squadrons.

Although no longer operated by Bomber Command, the Hampden was still to continue in action, for, during the previous summer, it had gained a new lease of life as a torpedo-bomber with R.A.F. Coastal Command, and following experiments with six Hampdens at the Torpedo Development Unit at Gosport, three Hampden squadrons were detached from No. 5 Group for anti-shipping duties with Coastal Command. The torpedo-bombing variant was designated Hampden T.B.I, different from the standard Hampden B.I in having a slightly deeper bomb-bay to accommodate an 18-in. torpedo internally, and racks under the wings for two 500-lb. bombs.

Two of the Hampden torpedo-bombing squadrons, Nos. 144 and 455, flew to Russian bases to attack German supply ships off the Norwegian coast north of Bergen and in the Barents Sea. The outward journey proved extremely hazardous, and one of the Hampdens was shot down by a Russian fighter while coming in over a prohibited area. As one of the Hampden pilots subsequently put it, they reached Russia "without wireless, in very bad weather, with very poor maps, and having as our only means of identification the undercarriage which we put down as a friendly gesture when the quick-fingered Russians started to shoot." The Hampdens forced the Germans to provide both escort vessels and air cover for their convoys, and after completing their operations,

the two squadrons handed over the fourteen remaining serviceable Hampdens to the Russians. What use the Russians made of these is unknown. No. 144 Squadron re-equipped with Beaufighters at the end of 1942, and No. 408 Squadron re-equipped with Halifaxes and returned to Bomber Command, but not before the two squadrons had given a good account of themselves with their torpedo-carrying Hampdens. No. 455 Squadron retained its Hampden T.B.Is until December 1943 when the operational career of Handley Page's first bomber monoplane finally drew to a close.

A grand total of 1,580 Hampdens (including a few Herefords) during the six years in which the bomber was in production played no small part in what were for the Allies the most difficult years of the war. It may be said that the Hampden did not entirely live up to its designer's more sanguine expectations in the stern test of war, but whatever its operational shortcomings, it played an important role in raising Allied air power to the pre-eminent position which it was eventually to enjoy.

Handley Page H.P.52 Hampden B.I.

Dimensions: Span, 69 ft. 2 in.; length, 53 ft. 7 in.; height, 14 ft. 11 in.; wing area, 668 sq. ft.

Armament: One fixed and one movable 0.303-in. machine gun in the nose and twin 0.303-in. machine guns in dorsal and ventral positions. Maximum internal bomb load, 4,000 lb.

Power Plants: Two Bristol Pegasus XVIII nine-cylinder radial air-cooled engines each rated at 965 h.p. at 2,475 r.p.m. for take-off and 1,000 h.p. at 2,600 r.p.m. at 3,000 ft.

Weights: Empty, 11,780 lb.; normal loaded, 18,756 lb.; maximum permissible, 21,000 lb.

Performance: Maximum speed (at 18,756 lb.), 265 m.p.h. at 15,500 ft., 254 m.p.h. at 13,800 ft.; maximum cruising speed, 217 m.p.h. at 15,000 ft.; economical cruising speed, 167 m.p.h. at 15,000 ft.; initial climb rate, 980 ft./min.; time to 15,000 ft., 18.9 min.; service ceiling, 22,700 ft.; range (at 21,000 lb. with maximum bomb load of 4,000 lb.), 870 mls. at 172 m.p.h. at 15,000 ft.; maximum range (with 2,000-lb. bomb load), 1,900 mls.

Originally designed as a high-speed commercial aircraft, the Do 17V1 illustrated above, together with the V2 and V3, employed a single fin-and-rudder assembly.

THE DORNIER Do 17 SERIES

Throughout the 'twenties and the early 'thirties, the name Dornier was virtually synonymous with shapely flying boats. Manufactured under licence in Italy, Spain, Switzerland, the Netherlands and Japan, the waterborne aircraft stemming from the Dornier Metallbauten G.m.b.H., as the company was then known, made a remarkable name for themselves in the annals of aviation, blazing their way across the world, pioneering many lines of development, and establishing an enviable reputation. Yet, despite the fame attained by these flying boats, it was for its association with a landplane that the name Dornier became best known in the years immediately preceding and during the Second World War.

Dornier's interest in landplanes had been desultory until 1933, when the advent of Adolf Hitler and his National Socialist Party provided the political background for a radical expansion of the still secret Luftwaffe, and, in consequence, large-scale production orders for military aircraft. At that time, the Do 23, an angular, twin-engined bomber with a fixed spatted undercarriage, derived from the Do F which had masqueraded as a mail and freight transport, was under development, and was ordered into quantity production for the Luftwaffe which still, officially, did not exist. Little more was heard of Dornier's land-based bombers until 1937, when rumours of an exceptionally fast and efficient Schulterdecker Kampfflugzeuge were confirmed by the appearance of a graceful shoulder-wing bomber at the International Military Aircraft Competition at Zurich, where, to the consternation of other nations, the slim bomber displayed a clean pair of heels to the fighters of every country represented in the competition!

The slender contours of the Dornier Do 17, as the bomber was initially designated, in side elevation immediately earned it the popular appellation of "Flying Pencil", and its basic airframe was to change little during the course of its subsequent long career. The structure was re-stressed from time to time in order to take more powerful engines and greater loads; the fuselage was deepened to increase its internal capacity; the clean hemispherical nose surrendered to the dictates of defensive armament, and the aircraft underwent continual modification and adaptation necessitated for the multifarious roles that it was called upon to perform, but despite changes in designation which accompanied some of the more extensive alterations, the original design was still recognisable—if somewhat distorted in outline—until the war's end terminated its further development.

(Immediately below) The Do 17V9, production prototype for the E-series, and (bottom) the same aircraft after conversion for use as a high-speed liaison monoplane, in which capacity it served until 1944.

The Do 17P-1 was the last production model to retain the slender nose and hemispherical glazed cap. It was similar to the Do 17M apart from the BMW 132N engines.

The Do 17Ka was an export version of the Do 17M for Yugoslavia.

The Do 17MV1 was a special high-speed demonstration machine.

The Do 17MV2 (above) served as a prototype for the Do 17M-1, and the Do 17RV2 (below) served primarily as a test-bed for bomb-aiming devices.

The Dornier Do 17 initiated the German trend towards relatively small, highly-loaded and high-powered but versatile aircraft which was maintained until the end of the war. It was evolved at a time when, according to the theories of air strategy prevalent in the German High Command, the fighter was to play a secondary role in any future aerial conflict, the bomber having sufficient speed to elude interceptors. This theory, which was to prove so fallible several years later, was reinforced by the début of the Do 17, but the most remarkable feature of the bomber's development was the fact that, unlike the He 111, which was designed from the outset as a bomber and first revealed as a commercial transport, the Do 17 was designed solely as a commercial transport!

Germany's national airline, Deutsche Lufthansa, announced a requirement for a high-speed mailplane, capable of carrying six passengers, and suitable for use on European express services. To meet these requirements, Dornier began the construction of three prototypes, the first of which, the Do 17V1, was completed and flown for the first time in the autumn of 1934. It was powered by two 660 h.p. BMW VI twelve-cylinder Vee liquid-cooled engines, and its extremely slim fuselage contained two tiny cabins; one compartment accommodating two passengers being situated immediately aft of the two-seat flight deck, and the other, seating four passengers, being positioned aft of the wing. The second and third prototypes, the Do 17V2 and V3, were completed but, despite the exceptional performance offered by the design, Deutsche Lufthansa considered it impracticable for commercial purposes—the passengers had virtually to perform acrobatics to enter their diminutive compartments, and extreme dexterity was called for if they were to gain their seats!

The Dornier Do 17 transport was thus abandoned, and the three prototypes were placed in a hangar at Löwenthal where, in all probability, they would have ended their days had it not been for a well-known German pilot, Flugkapitän Untucht, a former employee of Dornier. Untucht who, after leaving Dornier, had become the Deutsche Lufthansa's star pilot, and who, between March 14 and April 28, 1933, had gained eight international records while flying the

A Do 17Z-2 photographed in May 1940. This variant, which entered service in the summer of 1939, was powered by Bramo 323P engines with two-speed superchargers.

Heinkel He 70V1 Blitz, had joined the staff of the Reichsluftfahrtministerium to supervise the department concerned with commercial transports. Finding the prototypes at Löwenthal, Untucht decided to flight test one of them. Praising its flying characteristics, he expressed his opinion that, with additional keel surface to provide a steady bombing platform, the type would make an excellent high-speed bomber. The R.L.M. thus ordered a further series of prototypes for evaluation in the bombing role, and the Do 17V4, which appeared in 1935, had the small single fin-and-rudder assembly replaced by endplate twin fins and rudders.

The Do17V4 was similarly powered to the transport prototypes, and carried no armament. The wing span remained constant at 59 ft. $0\frac{2}{3}$ in., but the overall length was reduced from 58 ft. $0\frac{7}{8}$ in. to 56 ft. $3\frac{1}{4}$ in. The slenderness of the fuselage, accentuated by the long, pointed nose cone, was only apparent in the side view, and the centre fuselage was, in fact, abnormally broad, the section commencing more or less oval, changing rapidly to what can best be described as an inverted triangle, about twice as wide at the top as at the bottom, and returning once more to an ellipse. The stepped cockpit provided accommodation for three crew members, and the fuselage structure comprised built-up frames and intermediate stiffeners with channel-section stringers, the whole being metal-covered. The shoulder-mounted wings were of two-spar design covered by metal and fabric, slotted flaps extending between the ailerons and the fuselage. Of low aspect ratio, they housed the fuel cells between the spars of the inboard sections. The main under-carriage members retracted rearwards into the engine nacelles, leaving sections of the wheels exposed, and the tailwheel was also retractable. The second bomber prototype, the Do 17V5, differed solely in having a pair of 770 h.p. Hispano-Suiza 12Y engines, and the V6 reverted to the BMW VI power plants.

These prototypes, together with the Do 17V7 which had provision for a single 7.9-mm. MG 15 in an enclosed mounting above the fuselage and corresponding roughly with the leading edge of the wing,

The Do 215V1 (D-AIIB), originally a Do 17Z-0, demonstrated in the Balkans.

(Above) A Do 17M employed to test the dive brakes of the Do 217, and (below) a Do 17Z-1 reconnaissance-bomber.

D

by the pilot, or operated as a free gun by one of the other crew members. This armament was sometimes augmented by a further MG 15 mounted in the floor of the fuselage to fire downward through a hatch, and during 1939–40 defensive armament was increased to five MG 15s by forward maintenance units. A hemispherical glazed nose was fitted, immediately aft of which was an optically-flat panel for the bombardier, and the bombs were carried horizontally in the bomb-bay which was situated aft of the plane of the front spar. Overall dimensions included a span of 59 ft. $0\frac{2}{3}$ in., a length of 53 ft. $3\frac{3}{4}$ in., and an overall height of 15 ft. 1 in. A parallel production model was the Do 17F-1 long-range reconnaissance aircraft which, delivered to the Luftwaffe simultaneously with the E-1, differed only in being fitted with two cameras in the floor of the centre fuselage.

The first squadrons to equip with the Do 17E-1 and F-1 became operational by mid-1937, and early in the following year a number of E-1 bombers were despatched to Spain to equip one of the staffeln of Kampfgruppe 88 of the Condor Legion. The Do 17E-1 proved fast enough to evade most of the interceptor fighters serving with the Republican forces, apparently vindicating the German High Command's theories formulated several years earlier, and the increasing importance of aerial reconnaissance resulted in the despatch of fifteen Do 17F-1s to Spain to equip a special unit.

The basic Do 17 design was by this time displaying remarkable adaptability, and was being fitted with both air-cooled and liquid-cooled engines with equal facility. This flexibility was later to prove of considerable worth in developing the basic aircraft. The Do 17V8, which was more usually known as the Do 17MV1, was a special high-speed version primarily for demonstration purposes, powered by two 950–1,000 h.p. Daimler-Benz DB 600A inverted Vee liquid-cooled engines driving three-bladed V.D.M. controllable-pitch airscrews, and featuring a longer, more angular nose than that adopted as standard by the

were extensively evaluated by Luftwaffe test pilots, and flown during air manœuvres to test their ability to evade existing German fighters. In the meantime, preparations for the quantity manufacture of the bomber were being made at Dornier plants at Allmansweiler, Löwenthal and Manzell in the vicinity of Friedrichshafen. The initial production model for the Luftwaffe, the Do 17E-1, appeared late in 1936, its immediate prototype being the Do 17V9 (D-AHAK). The V9, incidentally, was converted for high-speed liaison and communications duties in 1938, and served to transport officials of the R.L.M. until 1944. The Do 17E-1 was powered by two 750 h.p. BMW VI-7.3 engines which provided it with a maximum speed of 220 m.p.h., and a service ceiling of 18,050 ft. Range with a 1,760-lb. bomb load was 990 miles, and empty and loaded weights were 9,920 lb. and 15,520 lb. respectively.

The crew of three were grouped in the forward section of the fuselage—an example of the German belief in close-grouping the crew in order to provide mutual moral support and ensure fighting efficiency —and defensive armament normally comprised one hand-held MG 15 machine gun in the raised dorsal cupola and a second MG 15 mounted to fire through the starboard side of the cockpit windscreen. The latter weapon could be clamped in position for use

The Finnish Air Force received a small quantity of Do 17Z-2 bombers (above). The Do 17S (right) was the first variant to be fitted with the deepened forward fuselage.

Luftwaffe, with transparent panelling in the lower section. This special aircraft was demonstrated publicly at Dübendorf, Zurich, in July 1937, during the International Military Aircraft Competitions, where the remarkable performance evinced by the bomber had a profound effect. The Do 17MV1 proved 25 m.p.h. faster in a climbing flight than France's Dewoitine D.510 single-seat fighter monoplane—then considered the best production interceptor in Europe —and attained a speed of 284 m.p.h. It was not, of course, revealed that the machine was a specially stripped model with engines offering one-third more power than those installed in production aeroplanes.

This demonstration did much to raise German aviation prestige abroad, and the Yugoslav government decided to equip its air arm with a bomber basically similar to the Do 17MV1 but with 986 h.p. Gnôme-Rhône 14No fourteen-cylinder radial air-cooled engines which were being built under licence at Rakovica, near Belgrade. The designations applied to the export versions for Yugoslavia were Do17Ka-2, Ka-3, and Kb-1, according to the equipment installed, and the first machine was flown to Yugoslavia in October 1937. The Do 17Ka had a similar angular nose section to that of the Do 17MV1, and armament comprised two fixed forward-firing machine guns and one 20-mm. cannon, and two free-mounted machine guns, one in the floor forward of the bomb-bay and one in the dorsal cupola, and the normal bomb load was 2,200 lb. Performance included maximum speeds of 222 m.p.h. at sea level and 259 m.p.h. at 11,320 ft., and range was 1,490 miles. A manufacturing licence was acquired for the type by Yugoslavia, and the first Yugoslav-built Do 17Ka was delivered by the Državna Fabrika Aviona (State Aircraft Factory) at Kraljevo early in 1940. When German forces attacked Yugoslavia on April 6, 1941, the Yugoslav Air Force had seventy Do 17s which equipped the 3rd Bomber Wing. Many of these were destroyed during the initial assault—twenty-six being wiped out in one attack alone—but others attacked

Sofia and other targets in Bulgaria, and were used for low-level attacks on German tanks and troop concentrations, those that survived being handed to the Croat Air Force by the Germans after the formation of that air arm.

In the meantime, a considerable number of additional prototypes had been completed and tested. It was realised that, with the unsupercharged BMW VI engines, the Do 17 no longer possessed the edge in speed over contemporary fighters that it had once enjoyed, and the Do 17V11 and V12, known alternatively as the Do 17LV1 and LV2, were fitted with the Bramo 323A nine-cylinder air-cooled radial engine with two-speed supercharger which offered 900 h.p. for take-off and 1,000 h.p. at 10,200 ft. These carried an additional crew member and, apart from the engines, were basically similar to the Do 17E. Maximum speed and range were 301 m.p.h. and 1,758 miles, service ceiling was 22,640 ft., and empty and loaded weights were 11,376 lb. and 19,400 lb. respectively. No production of the Do 17L was undertaken, but the Do 17V13 and V14, alias Do 17MV2 and MV3, served as prototypes for the Bramo 323A-powered Do 17M-1 bomber which entered production in 1938. Essentially similar to the Do 17E-1, the Do 17M-1 carried three crew members, and

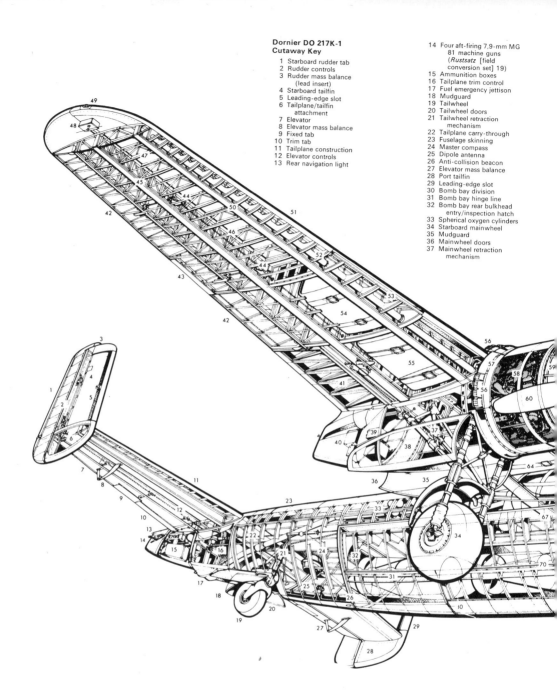

Dornier DO 217K-1
Cutaway Key

1 Starboard rudder tab
2 Rudder controls
3 Rudder mass balance
  (lead insert)
4 Starboard tailfin
5 Leading-edge slot
6 Tailplane/tailfin
  attachment
7 Elevator
8 Elevator mass balance
9 Fixed tab
10 Trim tab
11 Tailplane construction
12 Elevator controls
13 Rear navigation light

14 Four aft-firing 7,9-mm MG
   81 machine guns
   (*Rustsatz* [field
   conversion set] 19)
15 Ammunition boxes
16 Tailplane trim control
17 Fuel emergency jettison
18 Mudguard
19 Tailwheel
20 Tailwheel doors
21 Tailwheel retraction
   mechanism
22 Tailplane carry-through
23 Fuselage skinning
24 Master compass
25 Dipole antenna
26 Anti-collision beacon
27 Elevator mass balance
28 Port tailfin
29 Leading-edge slot
30 Bomb bay division
31 Bomb bay hinge line
32 Bomb bay rear bulkhead
   entry/inspection hatch
33 Spherical oxygen cylinders
34 Starboard mainwheel
35 Mudguard
36 Mainwheel doors
37 Mainwheel retraction
   mechanism

48 Mainwheel well
49 FuG 25 (A-A recognition)
40 FuG 101 radio altimeter
41 Outer section split flaps
42 Starboard aileron
43 Aileron tab
44 Control lines
45 Rear spar
46 Braced wing ribs
47 Intermediate ribs
48 EGS 101 antenna
49 Starboard navigation light
50 Front spar
51 Leading-edge hot-air
de-icing
52 Hot-air duct
53 Balloon-cable cutter in
leading-edge
54 Starboard outer fuel tank
(35 Imp gal/160 l
capacity)

55 Starboard oil tank (51.7
Imp gal/235 l capacity)
56 Flame-damping exhaust
pipes
57 Sliding-ring cooling air
exit
58 BMW 801D 14-cylinder
two-row radial engine
59 Annular oil cooler
60 VDM Three-blade metal
propeller of 12.79 ft
(3.90 m) diameter
61 Cooling fan
62 Cowling sliding nose-ring
63 Propeller boss
64 Starboard inner fuel tank
(175 Imp gal/795 l
capacity)
65 Fuselage main fuel tank
(231 Imp gal/1050 l
capacity)
66 Wing spar carry-through
67 Bomb bay top hinge line
68 Load-bearing beam
69 Bomb shackle
70 Bomb bay centre hinge line
71 Typical bomb load : two
2,205-lb (1000-kg)
SC 1000 bombs
72 Forward bomb doors
73 13-mm MG 131 machine
gun in ventral position
(1,000 rounds)
74 Ammunition ejection chute
75 Ventral gunner's station
76 Armoured bulkhead
77 Cartridge collector box
78 Batteries (two 24-Volt)
79 Radio equipment
80 Dorsal gunner's seat
support
81 Cabin hot-air
82 Dorsal gunner's station
83 Armoured turret ring
84 Aerial mast

85 Gun safety guard
86 Starboard beam-mounted
7,9-mm MG 81 machine
gun (750 rounds)
87 13-mm MG 131 machine
gun (500 rounds)
88 Electrically-operated
dorsal turret
89 Revi gunsight
90 Angled side windows
91 Jettisonable decking
92 Bomb-aimer's folding seat
93 Navigator's table
94 Pilot's contoured seat
95 Rear-view gunsight
96 Upper instrument panel
97 Nose glazing
98 Control horns
99 Engine controls
100 One 13-mm MG 131 in
strengthened nose
glazing (alternatively
twin 7,9-mm MG 81Z)
101 Balloon-cable cutter in
nose horizontal frame
102 Cartridge ejection chute
103 Ammunition feed
104 Lotfe 7D bombsight
105 Bomb aimer's flat panel
106 Control column
counterweight
107 Nose armour
108 Ventral gunner's quilt
109 Ammunition box (nose
MG 131)
110 Cartridge collector box
111 Entry hatch
112 Entry hatch (open)
113 Entry ladder
114 Port mainwheel doors
115 Mudguard
116 Port mainwheel
117 Mainwheel leg cross struts
118 Port engine cowling
119 Landing light (swivelling)
120 Control linkage
121 Pitot head
122 Port navigation light
123 Port aileron
124 Aileron trim tab

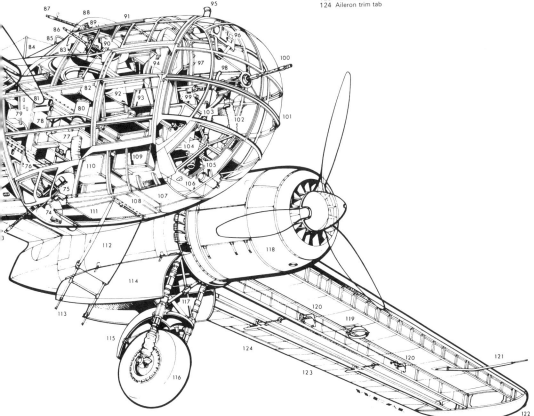

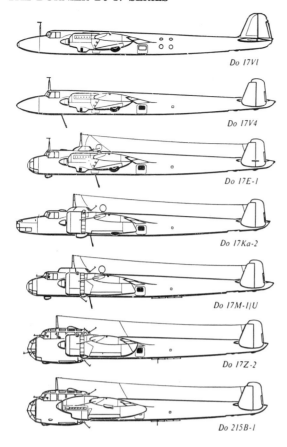

Do 17V1

Do 17V4

Do 17E-1

Do 17Ka-2

Do 17M-1/U

Do 17Z-2

Do 215B-1

cylinder radials affording 865 h.p. for take-off, and 960 h.p. at 9,850 feet.

Further experimental versions included the Do 17RV1 (D-AEEE) and RV2 (D-ATJU). The Do 17RV1 was first flown with BMW VI engines and later with DB 600Gs, and was used principally as a test-bed for new bomb-aiming devices, and the RV2, with DB 601A engines, served in a similar role. With the next experimental model, the Do 17S-0, changes were introduced which divested the bomber of one of its most characteristic features—its clean, slender nose and hemispherical glazed cap. During the operational testing of the Do 17E in Spain, it had become obvious that better protection would have to be afforded the bomber's belly. The downward-firing MG 15 machine gun which was poked through a hatch in the floor of the Do 17M's cockpit had too limited a field of fire to provide satisfactory protection. Thus, an entirely new forward fuselage was adopted, its design owing everything to the dictates of operational efficiency and nothing to aerodynamic refinement.

This new forward fuselage was first applied to the Do 17S-0 reconnaissance aircraft which made its appearance in 1938. The nose, containing the bombardier's station, was fully glazed with a series of small flat panels, or "facets", and the lower part was bulged and extended aft to a point just forward of the wing leading edge, terminating in a position for a rearward- and downward-firing MG 15 machine gun. To improve the pilot's view, the cockpit roof was raised and fully glazed, and the crew was increased to four members. Apart from the "swollen" forward fuselage, the airframe was identical to that of the Do 17M. Armament remained three 7.9-mm. machine guns—one on a pillar-type mounting at the rear of the cockpit, above the fuselage, a second protruding through the starboard panel of the windscreen, and the third in a hemispherical mounting firing below the fuselage. The overall length of the Do 17S-0 was 52 feet, and power was provided by either DB 600A or G liquid-cooled engines.

Only three examples of the Do 17S-0 were built, but the new forward fuselage was retained for the next variants of the design, the Do 17U and Do 17Z. Carrying a crew of five, which included two radio-operators, the Do 17U was intended to serve in the

the downward-firing MG 15 gun was adopted as standard. In comparison with the L-model, loaded weight was reduced, being 17,640 lb. The Do 17M-1/U1 (the suffix "U" indicating "modification") was fitted with an inflatable dinghy in a housing ahead of the dorsal gun cupola, and the Do 17M-1/Trop was a tropicalised version with dust filters and desert survival equipment. The Do 17V15, alternatively known as the Do 17PV1, served as the prototype for a reconnaissance version with a battery of cameras in the bomb-bay. This entered production as the Do 17P-1 and P-1/Trop, being identical to the M model apart from the engines which were BMW 132N nine-

NOTES ON FINISH AND INSIGNIA: *The finishes applied to Do 217K bombers varied considerably with their primary role. Night bombers had matt black under-surfaces, the black extending more than half-way up the fuselage sides. A number of different schemes were employed for the upper surfaces, but the most widely used were: (1) a "splinter" camouflage pattern of dark forest green and olive, and (2) mottled dark blue-grey and stone-grey. Many aircraft engaged on anti-shipping duties had a "wave-mirror" pattern of green and light blue over the under surfaces and fuselage sides which made them difficult to see when flying at wavetop height. Early production Do 217K bombers had dark forest green and light green "splinter" type camouflage—"woods and meadows"—over the upper surfaces and pale blue under-surfaces.*

The national insignia comprised the black "Balkenkreuz" outlined in white on the upper and lower surfaces of the wings, and the fuselage sides, and a black swastika outlined in white and positioned low on the tail fin. During the early service life of the Do 217K it was standard practice to apply a four-letter radio call-sign (e.g., KC + JA) for factory flight tests and delivery to a maintenance unit. In service these letters were replaced by a combination of three letters and a numeral, indicating the Geschwader, Gruppe and Staffel (e.g., U5 + EL). The first letter and numeral indicating the Geschwader (i.e., U5 indicated Kampfgeschwader 2), the second letter identifying the individual aircraft, and the last letter (i.e., "L") identifying the Gruppe and Staffel ("L" indicating the 1st Gruppe, 3rd Staffel). These letters were normally painted in grey on night bombers, but as the war progressed the Geschwader code letter and numeral (i.e., U5) was painted in small white letters on the fuselage sides (aft of the "EL") and, sometimes, at the base of the rudder. Later, all indication of the Geschwader was obliterated, and only the letter indicating the Gruppe and Staffel (i.e., "L") remained on the fuselage sides, a numeral being allocated to each individual aircraft, this appearing on the vertical tail surfaces in white. The Gruppe and Staffel letter was also painted on the under-surfaces of the wings, outboard of the national insignia.

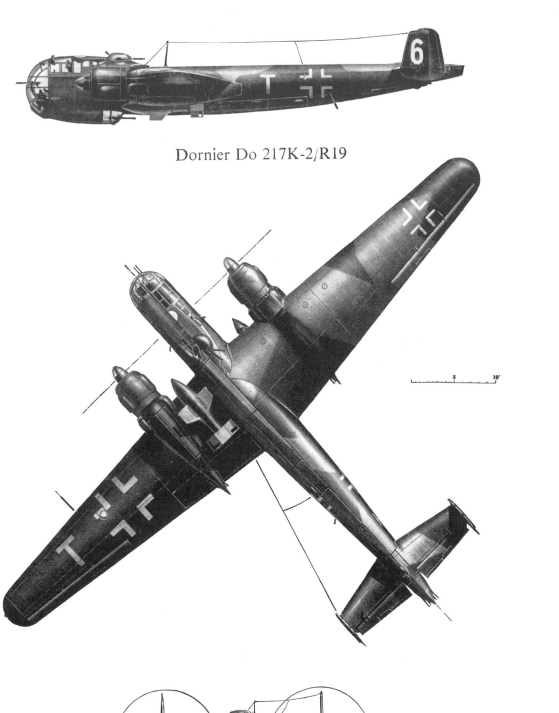

Dornier Do 217K-2/R19

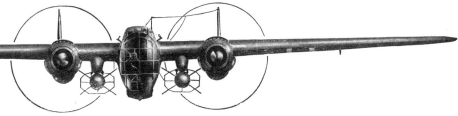

The Do 217E-4 (above) was identical to the E-2 apart from having BMW 801C engines in place of the BMW 801As.

(Above) The Do 217V7 (D-ACBF) did not possess the deepened fuselage which was introduced on the Do 217V9. (Below) The tail-mounted air brake of the Do 217V1 which was first flown in August 1938.

pathfinder role. Powered by DB 600A engines, fifteen Do 17U-0 and U-1 aircraft were built. The Do 17Z, the last aircraft in the series to retain the original type number, was essentially similar to the S- and U-models except for the power plants, inadequate supplies of Daimler-Benz engines, which were in considerable demand for Bf 109 and Bf 110 fighters, and He 111 bombers, necessitating the use of Bramo 323A radials. After the delivery of a pre-production batch of Do 17Z-0 bombers, the Do 17Z-1 was introduced onto the assembly lines but, by the beginning of 1939, this had been supplanted by the Do 17Z-2 with Bramo 323P engines fitted with two-speed superchargers and developing 1,000 h.p. for take-off and 940 h.p. at 13,120 ft.

The Do 17Z-2 normally carried four crew members, but an additional crew member could be accommodated for certain missions, and defensive armament was increased to six MG 15 guns—two firing forward, one firing aft above the fuselage, one firing aft below the fuselage, and two firing laterally from side windows. Internal bomb stowage arrangements for a maximum load of 2,200 lb. were similar to those of the Do 17M, the horizontally stowed bombs dropping through two sets of doors in the flattened bottom of the fuselage. Empty weight was 11,484 lb., and normal and maximum loaded weights were 18,832 lb. and 19,481 lb. respectively. Performance included a maximum speed of 263 m.p.h. at 16,400 ft., the maximum cruising speed was 236 m.p.h. at 14,200 ft., service ceiling was 26,740 ft., range with maximum bomb load was 745 miles, and maximum range was 1,860 miles. The Do 17Z-3 was a reconnaissance version with a battery of RB 20/30 cameras in the bomb-bay; the Z-4 was a dual-control trainer version, and the Z-5 was fitted with inflatable flotation bags and special rescue equipment, but was otherwise similar to the Z-2 bomber.

Considerable interest in the Do 17Z was displayed by several foreign air arms, and particularly that of Yugoslavia, and an export version, which, for some obscure reason, was designated Do 215A, was evolved. A Do 17Z-0 carrying the civil registration D-AIIB was used for demonstration purposes, and was redesignated Do 215V1. This resulted in some confusion initially, as it was assumed that all Dornier bombers fitted with the redesigned forward fuselage were designated Do 215 irrespective of their engines. In view of the fact that the Gnôme-Rhône 14No radial engine was manufactured under licence in Yugoslavia, a second Do 17Z-0 airframe was fitted with these power plants and designated Do 215V2. This did not offer a sufficient advance in performance over the Do 17Ka for the Yugoslav government, however, and early in 1939 an order was placed for a version powered by a pair of 1,075 h.p. Daimler-Benz DB 601A liquid-cooled engines which offered a marked improvement in overall performance, maximum speed being 292 m.p.h. at 16,400 ft. Maximum cruising

The Do 217E-1 (above) was fitted with an unusual four-ribbed "umbrella"-type tail brake, but this proved unsuccessful on operations, and was eventually removed.

speed was 257 m.p.h., service ceiling was 31,170 feet, initial climb rate was 1,195 ft./min., and normal range was 965 miles.

The Yugoslav order was followed by one from Sweden for eighteen machines, but, in the event, neither order was fulfilled as the aircraft were taken over for the Luftwaffe as the Do 215A-1. Some machines still on the production lines were modified to Luftwaffe standards as the Do 215B-0, and production continued with the Do 215B-1 reconnaissance-bomber, essentially similar to the A-1 apart from the equipment installed. It is of interest to note that the Do 215B-3 was an export version for Russia, two examples of which were delivered in the winter of 1939–40, and the Do 215B-4 was a reconnaissance-bomber generally similar to the B-1 apart from the types of cameras fitted. An RB 50/30 camera was mounted beneath the ventral gun position, and an RB 20/30 camera was installed in the crew entry hatch. In addition to the cameras, twenty 110-lb. bombs could be carried.

The Do 215B-5 was a night fighter and intruder conversion, a few of which were modified from standard B-0 and B-1 airframes. Previously, one Do 17Z had been experimentally converted for this role, being designated Do 17Z-6 Kauz I (Screech-Owl I), and this was fitted with a solid nose containing one 20-mm. MG FF cannon and three 7.9-mm. MG 17 machine guns. A similar nose was fitted to the Do 215B-5, and these were to be used for a brief period by Nachtjagdgeschwader 2 which was formed in June 1940 at Düsseldorf for the night-intruder role. Operating from Gilze Rijen in Holland, and attacking R.A.F. Bomber Command airfields in the Home Counties, East Anglia, Lincolnshire and Yorkshire, they were later joined by the Do 17Z-10 Kauz II which carried a very early Lichtenstein SN-2 radar array and a nose armament of four MG FF cannon and four MG 17 machine guns. Only nine Kauz II night fighters were delivered as their performance proved inadequate.

Only three Do 215B-1s were completed in 1939; ninety-two B-1s and B-4s were built in 1940, and production was completed in 1941 with six additional machines. A total of 475 Do 17Z-2 and Z-5 bombers, and twenty-two Z-3 reconnaissance aircraft was completed between 1939, when deliveries commenced, and the end of 1940, when the type was finally supplanted in production by the Do 217. On September 1, 1939, when German forces invaded Poland and thus started the Second World War, the Luftwaffe's first-line strength included twenty-one staffeln equipped with Do 17P reconnaissance aircraft, one reconnaissance staffel equipped with the obsolescent Do 17F, and eleven Kampfgruppen equipped with the Do 17M and Do 17Z bombers. Do 17-equipped units attached to Luftflotten 1 and 4 figured prominently in the Polish campaign, but when employed for daylight sorties against the British Isles in 1940, these aircraft fared badly, and owing to their inadequate defensive armament their formations were severely mauled by British fighters. Attempts were made to increase the defensive armament by adding two free-mounted machine guns, but losses remained so damagingly high that the Do 17s were withdrawn from daylight operations. Some Do 17Z-2 bombers were later delivered to the Croat and Finnish air forces for operations against the Russians.

The next stage in the development of the basic Do 17 design was the Do 217, the first prototype of which, the Do 217V1, had flown for the first time in August 1938. Very similar to the Do 215B and similarly powered, the Do 217V1 was stressed for bigger loads and had a much wider range of functions, being intended for precision bombing, dive bombing, torpedo dropping, mine laying and reconnaissance. The aircraft was slightly bigger than its predecessor, the wing span being increased from 59 ft. 0⅔ in. to 62 ft. 4 in., and overall length from 51 ft. 10 in. to 60 ft. 10⅓ in., 3 ft. 8½ in. of this additional length being accounted for by a novel form of air brake, previously tested on a Do 17M. This brake worked somewhat after the fashion of a parachute, or a four-ribbed umbrella, the "ribs" when closed forming the four sides of the tail extension. The brake was operated by a threaded collar and spindle, the movement of the collar pulling the "ribs" open against four short

The Do 217K-01 (above) was the first pre-production model of the K-series, distinguished by the redesigned nose.

hinged struts. The Do 217V1 carried no armament, although the trio of MG 15 machine guns standard at that time was proposed, and crashed in September 1938 after relatively few test flights. The Do 217V2 and V3 were essentially similar but powered by Junkers Jumo 211A twelve-cylinder 60° inverted Vee engines rated at 950 h.p. for take-off and 1,000 h.p. at 17,000 ft., and the similarly powered Do 217V4 (D-AMSD) was the proposed production prototype, but this was not accepted by the Luftwaffe.

The next prototype, for unexplained reasons, received the designation Do 217V1E, and featured slotted vertical tail surfaces, rendered necessary by some directional instability, and a revised control system, and the V5 and V6 were essentially similar, but the Do 217V7 (D-ACBF) abandoned the tail-mounted air brake which had proved singularly troublesome, and which, contrary to general belief, was rarely used subsequently by operational aircraft, although all Do 217E-2 aircraft were initially fitted with a similar brake. The V7 was also the first proto-type to be fitted with radial engines, having two 1,550 h.p. BMW 139s, predecessors of the widely-used BMW 801A which powered the Do 217V8 and V9, the prototypes for the E-series. The BMW 801A was

an appreciably heavier engine than its predecessor, although the overall dimensions differed little. It offered 1,600 h.p. for take-off and 1,380 h.p. at 15,100 ft. The Do 217V8 (D-AHJE) retained the slim fuselage which had characterised the whole series until that time, but the Do 217V9 had a considerably deeper fuselage which permitted a major increase in the size of the bomb-bay to take full advantage of the extra power now available. The main bomb-bay was 14 ft. 10 in. in length, and in this cell there was stowage space for a maximum load of 5,550 lb. A 5 ft. 8 in. extension was provided at the aft end of the bomb-bay to take the extra length of a torpedo, and the warload could be made up of one LT 950 torpedo, two mines or various combinations of bombs.

Prior to the flight testing of the Do 217V9, a small batch of eight Do 217A-0 reconnaissance aircraft had been ordered for evaluation, and these entered service with the Luftwaffe in 1940. The Do 217A-0 was powered by two DB 601A engines and, retaining the original slim fuselage, carried two cameras and a defensive armament of three MG 15 machine guns. The Do 217CV1 was an experimental bomber gener-ally similar to the A-0 but powered by Jumo 211A engines and subsequently used as an engine test-bed,

The Do 217K-2 featured an extended wing span to enable it to operate with a pair of FX 1400 radio-corrected armour-piercing bombs.

and the Do 217C-0 was a further experimental bomber with DB 601A engines and a heavier defensive armament comprising one 15-mm. MG 151 cannon and five 7.9-mm. MG 15 machine guns. The four Do 217C-0 aircraft completed served as test aircraft for bomb sights.

The Do 217PV1, high-altitude reconnaissance-bomber with pressure cabin, flown in 1943.

Deliveries of the initial production model really got under way in 1941, 277 pre-production Do 217E-0 and production E-1 aircraft being delivered in that year. Powered by two BMW 801A eighteen-cylinder double-row radial engines enclosed by low-drag cowlings, and intended for use primarily as an anti-shipping bomber, the Do 217E-1 carried a crew of four. Its most outstanding feature was its phenomenally high wing loading, the maximum loaded weight of 33,730 lb. and net wing area of 522 sq. ft. resulting in an effective wing loading of no less than 64.6 lb. per sq. ft. Both defensive armament and armour protection for the crew displayed major improvements over earlier Dornier bombers. One fixed 15-mm. MG 151 cannon was mounted in the lower port side of the nose, being operated by the pilot using a Revi 120 gunsight, two 7.9-mm. MG 15 guns were fired laterally through the rear upper side windows, two further MG 15s fired aft from dorsal and ventral positions, and a fifth MG 15 was fitted in the lower starboard side of the nose for use by the bombardier. The last-mentioned gun was sometimes replaced by a free-mounted 20-mm. MG FF cannon, and gymbal mountings were provided for two additional MG 15s which could be fired through upper side windows about midway along the cockpit. The pilot's seat was fitted with an 8.5-mm. thick armour shield, 5-mm. armour plate was fitted on top of the cockpit, and the other crew members enjoyed the protection of 5-mm. or 8.5-mm. armour. Up to 5,550 lb. of bombs could be stowed internally, and this could be made up of eight 550-lb., four 1,100-lb., two 2,200-lb. plus two 550-lb., one 3,086-lb., or one 3,970-lb. bomb. In addition, external racks were provided under the wing for two 550-lb. bombs.

The Do 217E-1, which had a maximum speed of 326 m.p.h. at 18,500 ft., a service ceiling of 29,850 ft., and a range of 1,500 miles at 255 m.p.h. at 19,100 ft., with maximum bomb load, was a formidable general-purpose bomber, but its high wing loading resulted in poor low-speed qualities, and considerable trouble was experienced during its early service life with the undercarriage. The Do 217E-1/R4 was used extensively for anti-shipping duties from French bases during 1941, by which time two further versions had reached the production lines, the Do 217E-2 and E-3. The latter actually preceded the Do 217E-2, and the principal change was the adoption of a free-mounted MG FF cannon as standard. Only about one hundred E-3s were built. The E-3/R1 had a rack for an SC 1800 bomb; the E-3/R3 had racks for sixteen SC 50X bombs; the E-3/R4 had a PVC 1006B rack for a torpedo; the E-3/R5 had one fixed 30-mm. MK 101

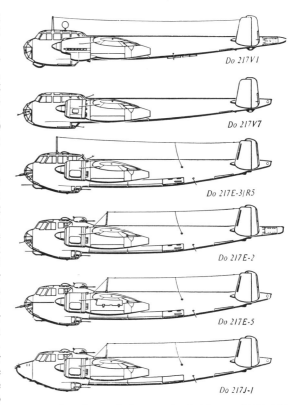

Do 217V1

Do 217V7

Do 217E-3/R5

Do 217E-2

Do 217E-5

Do 217J-1

cannon in place of the standard 15-mm. MG 151, only one machine being equipped with this gun; the E-3/R6 had cameras for the reconnaissance role; the E-3/R7 carried an inflatable dinghy above the fuselage, and the E-3/R8 and R9 were long-range anti-shipping bombers, the former having a 165 Imp. gal. fuel tank in the forward bomb-bay and the latter carrying a similar tank in the rear bomb-bay.

Produced simultaneously with the Do 217E-3, the Do 217E-2 was initially intended for the dive-bombing role, and differed primarily in having a single 13-mm. MG 131 machine gun in a power-operated dorsal turret, and an MG 131 in the ventral position. The offensive load comprised four 2,200-lb. PC 1000 bombs and, initially, the tail-mounted air brake was fitted. Owing to the inefficiency of this type of air brake, the thirty-sixth Do 217E-2 was employed as an air brake test-bed during the summer of 1941. Slotted plates turning through 90° were mounted between the fuselage and the engine nacelles, and a series of diving tests were carried out near Friedrichshafen. After one test, the pilot levelled out at about 2,500 ft., and retracted the air brakes, but the elevator tabs which

The Do 317V1 was a multi-purpose bomber prototype, but development of this type was abandoned.

should have returned to their normal flight position with the retraction of the brakes failed to function, and the aircraft crashed, both members of the test crew being killed. Shortly after this, further attempts to perfect the Do 217E as a dive bomber were abandoned, and all dive brakes were removed.

With a single 3,970-lb. SC 1800 bomb housed internally, the designation Do 217E-2/R1 had been applied, but with the removal of the air brakes and modification for the anti-shipping role, the aircraft were designated E-2/R2 with wing racks for two 550-lb. bombs and internal racks for two 3,086-lb. and two 550-lb. bombs, or E-2/R3 with internal stowage for sixteen SC 50X bombs. The Do 217E-2/R4 was a torpedo bomber; the E-2/R6 was a reconnaissance bomber; the E-2/R10 was a long-range anti-shipping bomber with tanks for 330 Imp. gal. of fuel in the bomb bay and racks outboard of the engine nacelles for two 4,410-lb. bombs; the E-2/R13 had a 165 Imp. gal. tank in the forward bomb-bay; the E-2/R14 had a 165 Imp. gal. tank in the rear bomb-bay; the E-2/R19 had four fixed rearward-firing 7.9-mm. MG 81 machine guns in a special tail cone, and the E-2/R21 carried two 66 Imp. gal. drop tanks under the outboard wing panels. The Do 217E-4 was identical to the E-2 apart from the installation of BMW 801C engines, and the E-4/R4, R6, etc., corresponded to the equivalent E-2 variants. The final production E-model, the Do 217E-5, was developed to carry the Henschel Hs 293 rocket-propelled radio-controlled glider bomb on carriers outboard of the engine nacelles. Special radio equipment for controlling the bombs was carried.

A serious shortage of night fighters and intruders resulted in the conversion of a number of Do 217E-2 bombers for these roles. Designated Do 217J-1, the initial variant had a redesigned nose containing four 20-mm. MG FF cannon and four 7.9-mm. MG 17 machine guns. The dorsal turret was retained, and a 13-mm. gun could be mounted in the ventral position. For intruder duties the aft bomb-bay was retained, and this normally carried eight SC 50X bombs. A second version, the Do 217J-2, had no bomb-bay and was usually fitted with FuG 202 (Lichtenstein) radar. A total of 157 Do 217J-1 and -2 aircraft was produced in 1942, together with 564 bomber variants.

The Do 217K was a further development of the Do 217E, the distinguishing feature of this version being a redesigned deeper and more rounded nose. Powered by two BMW 801D radials each rated at 1,700 h.p. for take-off, and 1,440 h.p. at 18,700 ft., the prototypes, the Do 217KV1 and KV2, were built primarily for use as night bombers, and the latter was first flown with a single fin and rudder for comparison purposes, but later switched back to the standard twin fin-and-rudder assembly. The pre-production Do 217K-0/R25 was intended primarily for anti-shipping duties, was equipped with a Perlon braking parachute in a special tail housing, and carried a defensive armament of two 13-mm. MG 131 and six 7.9-mm. MG 81 machine guns. The production Do 217K-1 had this defensive armament reduced by two MG 81 guns, and the K-1/R4, R6, R7, etc., corresponded to the equivalent E-2 and E-4 variants. The Do 217K-2 featured an extended wing (81 ft. 4⅓ in. span) to enable it to operate with two FX 1400 radio-corrected armour-piercing bombs for attacking armoured ships. The Do 217K-3 differed solely in that it could carry two FX 1400 bombs or two Hs 293 glider bombs.

During 1942, in order to safeguard against production delays resulting from shortages of BMW 801D radials, a further development of the bomber was evolved which was identical to the Do 217K-1 apart from its power plants which consisted of two liquid-cooled Daimler-Benz DB 603A engines each rated at 1,750 h.p. for take-off, and 1,620 h.p. at 18,700 ft. Designated Do 217M-1, this model entered service alongside the K sub-type, carrying the same offensive loads. Development resulted in the Do 217M-5 which could carry an Hs 293 glider bomb under the fuselage for long-range operations, and although this model did not enter service, it led directly to the Do 217M-11 which featured the extended wing of the Do 217K-2, and could carry either the Hs 293 or the FX 1400 under the fuselage. The K and M sub-types were the last bomber versions of the Do 217 to reach Luftwaffe squadrons before production of the series terminated at the end of 1943.

A substantial number of M sub-type airframes were modified on the assembly lines for the night-fighter role, these being designated Do 217N. Two basic versions were produced, both being equipped with FuG 202 Lichtenstein radar and having a fixed forward-firing armament of four 20-mm. MG 151 cannon and four 7.9-mm. MG 17 machine guns. The Do 217N-1 retained the standard power-operated dorsal turret containing one 13-mm. MG 131 gun, and had two

7.9-mm. MG 81 guns in the ventral position, but the latter was removed and covered by a wooden fairing on the Do 217N-2, and some examples of the latter version (Do 217N-2/R22) carried a battery of four MG 151 cannon which were fixed to fire upwards at an oblique angle. With the completion of Do 217 production, 1,366 bombers and 364 night fighters and intruders had been manufactured. The Do 217 bomber was operated exclusively by the Luftwaffe, but a few Do 217J night fighters were delivered to the Regia Aeronautica, being operated by the 2° and 59° Gruppi Intercettori.

The termination of production was not accompanied by any cessation of development of the basic Do 217 design, and several experimental versions were evolved. At one time a twin-float torpedo-bomber variant, initially known as the Do 217W, and subsequently, for a brief period, as the Do 216, was proposed but abandoned before actual construction commenced. In 1942 Dornier had commenced development of a high-altitude reconnaissance-bomber version, the prototype of which, the Do 217PV1, was flown for the first time during the following year. Prior to the completion of this prototype, which was radically modified from the Do 217M by the addition of a pressure cabin and an HZ Anlage supercharger installation in the fuselage, a Do 217K airframe had been modified for preliminary tests. This machine featured an extremely angular nose section. The Do 217PV1 had two DB 603A engines and a DB 605T engine housed in the fuselage which drove a two-stage compressor. Large intercooler radiators were slung between the fuselage and engine nacelles, and air intakes for the blower and DB 605T were located below the fuselage. Two further prototypes, the Do 217PV2 and PV3, were completed, together with three Do 217P-1 production machines, and these were employed operationally alongside the last two prototypes.

The wing span of the three prototypes was that of the standard Do 217, but the P-1 had a wing span increased to 80 ft. 4½ in. Wing area was 720 sq. ft., and overall length was 58 ft. 10½ in. Normal and maximum loaded weights were 31,600 lb. and 35,200 lb., and defensive armament comprised six MG 81 machine guns. A 2,200-lb. bomb load was carried, and performance (at 29,250 lb.) included a maximum speed of 388 m.p.h. at 46,000 ft., an initial climb rate of 955 ft./min., and a service ceiling of 53,000 ft.

Further development resulted in the Do 317V1 multi-purpose bomber prototype. Although this aircraft followed the general lines of the Do 217P, with the characteristic bulbous nose, equal taper wings with rounded tips, and twin fins and rudders, it embodied extensive redesign. The Do 317V1 was powered by two DB 603A engines and had a wing span of 67 ft. 8 in. The proposed production version was designated Do 317A and, essentially similar to the prototype, was to carry an armament of one fixed forward-firing 15-mm. MG 151, twin 7.9-mm. MG 81s and three 13-mm. MG 131s, and a 6,600-lb. bomb load.

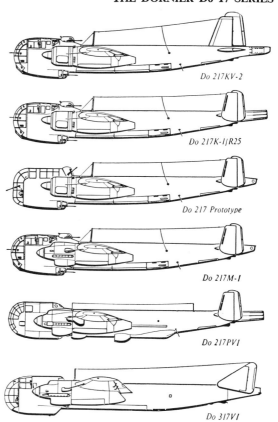

Do 217KV-2

Do 217K-1/R25

Do 217 Prototype

Do 217M-1

Do 217PV1

Do 317V1

Development of the Do 317A was abandoned in favour of the more advanced Do 317B.

No prototype of the Do 317B had been completed, however, when the end of the war terminated any further development.

Although not built in such quantities as the Heinkel He 111, the Do 17 series of bombers, which operated in a wide variety of forms throughout the entire period of the European war, were among the most important of the Luftwaffe's operational aircraft.

Dornier Do 217M-1

Dimensions : Span, 62 ft. 4 in. ; length, 55 ft. 9¼ in. (M-1/R25) 58 ft. 8 in. ; height (to tip of airscrew), 16 ft. 3⅜ in. ; wing area, (gross) 610 sq. ft., (net) 522 sq. ft.

Armament : One twin 7.9-mm. MG 81Z with 1,000 rounds in the nose ; two or four 7.9-mm. MG 81 machine guns with 750 r.p.g. in lateral positions; one 13-mm. MG 131 machine gun with 500 rounds in dorsal turret; and one 13-mm. MG 131 machine gun with 1,000 rounds in lower rear position. One 20-mm. MG 151 cannon could also be installed, firing forward, and the M-1/R19 had four fixed rearward-firing 7.9-mm. MG 81 in the tail cone. Two additional MG 81 guns were sometimes fitted in the rear of each engine nacelle. Maximum bomb load, 8,820 lb.

Power Plants : Two Daimler-Benz DB 603A twelve-cylinder inverted Vee liquid-cooled engines each rated at 1,750 h.p. at 2,700 r.p.m. for take-off, and 1,620 h.p. at 2,700 r.p.m. at 18,700 ft.

Weights : Empty, 19,985 lb. ; loaded, 36,817 lb.

Performance : Maximum speed, 348 m.p.h. at 18,700 ft., 294 m.p.h. at sea level ; range with maximum fuel, 1,550 miles ; maximum ceiling, 31,168 ft. ; service ceiling (fully loaded) 24,000 ft.

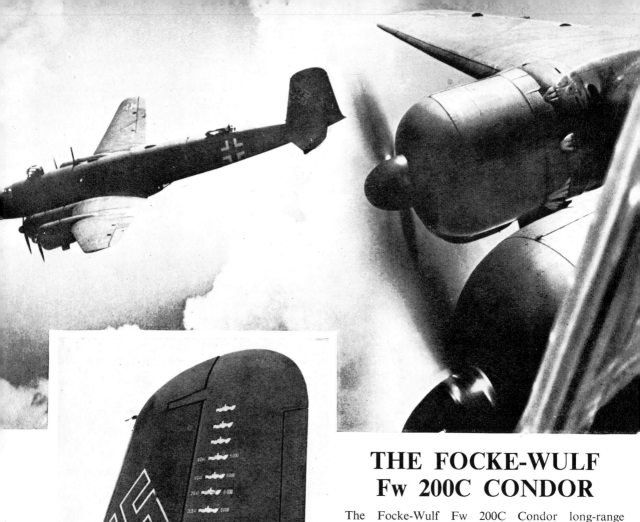

THE FOCKE-WULF
Fw 200C CONDOR

The Focke-Wulf Fw 200C Condor long-range reconnaissance bomber was purely an improvisation forced upon Germany by circumstances against which her leaders had gambled, but it was an amazingly successful improvisation. Little suited to its task, possessing a ponderous performance and extremely vulnerable to both anti-aircraft fire and aerial attack, the Condor had nothing more than a respectable endurance to commend it, yet, for some two years, it was regarded as the scourge of the Atlantic, sinking hundreds of thousands of tens of Allied shipping and giving Atlantic convoys a terrible mauling. For much of the Battle of the Atlantic, the Condor appeared ubiquitous, yet the actual number of Condors built was relatively small. Few though the Condors may have been, they demanded an inordinate effort on the part of the Allies before their menace was nullified.

The Condor was designed purely as a commercial transport, and its introduction as a combat aircraft was purely accidental. With Britain's declaration of war, the German High Command immediately realised the seriousness of its mistake in abandoning the long-range heavy bomber after the death of its leading German protagonist, the first Chief of Staff of the Luftwaffe, Lieutenant-General Wever. The need for an aircraft capable of harassing British shipping

The Fw 200C Condor, the notorious "Focke Wolf", as Winston Churchill referred to it, was the scourge of the Atlantic for a considerable period of the war, and responsible for the sinking of hundreds of thousands of tons of Allied shipping. The Condor demanded an inordinate effort from the Allies before its threat was nullified, and the first years of its operational career as a commerce raider were remarkably successful. Yet it was purely an improvisation forced upon the Luftwaffe by the lack of foresight of the German High Command.

far out in the Atlantic was obvious, and the only solution to their dilemma was to extemporize. The result was the adaptation of the Condor transport for long-range reconnaissance-bomber sorties.

The design of the Condor had been initiated by Prof. Dipl. Ing. Kurt Tank, the Technical Director of the Focke-Wulf Flugzeugbau, in the spring of 1936 as a 26-passenger commercial transport for the Deutsche Lufthansa (D.L.H.). Tank secured an official type number of his own choosing from the Reichsluft-fahrtministerium (R.L.M.), the transport being designated Fw 200. This was a considerably higher type number than those being allocated to new designs at the time of the Condor's conception, but one which Tank believed to be easily remembered and ideally suited for publicity purposes.

The first prototype Condor, the Fw 200V1, later registered D-ACON and named "Brandenburg", was flown for the first time in July 1937 with Kurt Tank himself at the controls. It had been completed within twelve months and eleven days of the date that D.L.H. placed the development contract. Apart from some redesign of the tail surfaces, only minor modifications were called for as a result of initial flight tests, and two further prototypes had been flown by the following summer when planning commenced on a series of long-distance publicity flights.

The first of these flights, from Berlin to Cairo, was made on June 27, 1938, by the Fw 200V2 (D-AERE "Saarland") with one intermediate stop at Salonica, and a further long-distance flight took place on

The first operational version of the Condor was the Fw 200C-1 (illustrated at the top of the page) which was delivered to Kampfgeschwader 40 during the late months of 1940. During 1941, the two Condor-equipped Gruppen of K.G.40 became almost as serious a menace to Allied shipping as the U-boat. Later in the Condor's career it was fitted with FuG 200 Hohentwiel radar which, used in conjunction with a blind bombing procedure, enabled it to attack through cloud. The Hohentwiel array is illustrated immediately above. Some machines also had Rostock which had a wider search angle.

"Friesland") were delivered to D.L.H. for route-proving trials and crew training, and two were delivered to the R.L.M. for evaluation at the official test centre and subsequent use as staff transports. The first of these, the Fw 200V3 (D-2600), subsequently named "Immelmann III", was eventually modified for use as the official *Führermaschine*, and the second was used to transport members of Adolf Hitler's staff. The Führer's personal pilot, Hans Baur, spent several weeks at Focke-Wulf's Bremen factory familiarizing himself with the special Condor, the interior appointments of which had been given considerable thought. The apartment normally occupied by Hitler featured a large, armour-plated seat placed over an escape hatch and incorporating a parachute pack.

By this time, work had been initiated on more powerful versions of the Condor, the first of which was the Fw 200B. The Fw 200B-1 was powered by four BMW 132Dc engines each rated at 850 h.p. at 8,200 feet, and empty and loaded weights were increased from 21,560 lb. to 24,860 lb., and from 32,120 lb. to 38,500 lb. respectively. The Fw 200B-2 differed in having BMW 132H engines rated at 830 h.p. at 3,600 ft., and loaded weight was reduced to 37,400 lb. Two Fw 200B Condors were ordered by the Brazilian Sindicato Condor Limitada, with which D.L.H. co-operated closely, and these were delivered in August 1939.

The Japanese, always interested in aeronautical developments abroad, evinced a marked interest in the Condor, and on November 28, 1938, the Fw 200V1 took-off for Tokyo, stopping at Basta,

August 10, 1938, when the Fw 200V1 took-off for a non-stop flight from Berlin to New York, covering the 4,075 miles against strong headwinds in 24 hrs. 55 min., at an average speed of 164 m.p.h. The return journey was made in 19 hrs. 47 min., at an average speed of 205 m.p.h. over a slightly more southerly route. This impressive demonstration flight received considerable publicity, and Danish Air Lines (D.D.L.) placed an order for two Condors. These (OY-DAM and OY-DEM) were of the initial Fw 200A production model which, like the first prototypes, was powered by four BMW 132G-1 nine-cylinder radial air-cooled engines each rated at 720 h.p. and driving two-bladed controllable-pitch airscrews. The Fw 200A attained a maximum speed of 233 m.p.h. at sea level, and its normal range with a 6,380-lb. payload was 775 miles.

Apart from the two Condors delivered to D.D.L. all the first nine Condors were of the A-series and bore *Versuchs* (Experimental) numbers. The Fw 200V2 and five additional machines (D-AETA "Westfalen", D-ACVH "Grenzmark", D-AMHC "Nordmark", D-AXFO "Pommern" and D-ARHW

The Fw 200C differed from the B-model in several respects. It was appreciably strengthened structurally, twin-wheel main undercarriage members were adopted, and the engine nacelles were redesigned. The photo depicts an early Fw 200C-1.

The Fw 200B (right) transports under construction for Japan and other countries were taken over by the Luftwaffe. Some Fw 200C-0 Condors were completed without the ventral tray or gondola, and operated as transports during the invasion of Norway (below right).

Karachi and Hanoi for refuelling, and arriving at the Japanese capital in slightly less than 48 hours, of which 42 hrs. 18 min. were flying time. On the return flight, however, a fuel shortage resulted in the aircraft being ditched in shallow water off Manila. Nevertheless, the Condor's visit to Japan was to prove fortunate so far as the Luftwaffe was concerned. Apart from placing an order for five Fw 200B transports—which, in the event, were never to be delivered because of the start of the Second World War—the Japanese, impressed by the Condor's long-range capabilities, were interested in an adaptation of the Condor for the long-range maritime reconnaissance role. This was the germ of the idea that was to give birth to the Luftwaffe's Fw 200C reconnaissance-bomber.

To meet Japanese requirements, the Focke-Wulf company began work on adapting the Fw 200B for maritime reconnaissance duties early in 1939, and the result was the Fw 200V10, destined to become the forerunner of the Fw 200C series of commerce raiders. Powered by four BMW 132H-1 engines, the Fw 200V10, which bore Werk-Nr. 0001, was essentially similar to the Fw 200B transport but had a single 7.9-mm. MG 15 machine gun in a dorsal turret mounted slightly forward of the wing trailing edge, and a short ventral gondola, offset to starboard under the forward fuselage and housing single hand-operated MG 15 machine guns firing fore and aft. Much of the fuselage was occupied by fuel tanks; two vertical cameras were attached to the floor of the centre fuselage with the camera operator seated aft.

With Britain's declaration of war and the immediate need for a long-range aircraft for anti-shipping duties, it was decided that the Condor's airframe was the only one available remotely suitable for adaptation as an interim reconnaissance-bomber until Heinkel's He 177 became available in quantity. Germany's only other multi-engined transport, the Junkers Ju 90, was seriously underpowered already, and could not be immediately adapted for the military role, and therefore Focke-Wulf were instructed to commence work immediately on a suitable conversion.

As a four-engined transport carrying four crew members and twenty-six passengers, the Condor employed a relatively light structure totally unsuited for the military role now envisaged. The Japanese had

The Fw 200C-3, built in larger numbers than any other version of the Condor, embodied further structural strengthening and more powerful engines. Defensive armament was improved by the addition of lateral guns and a power-operated turret.

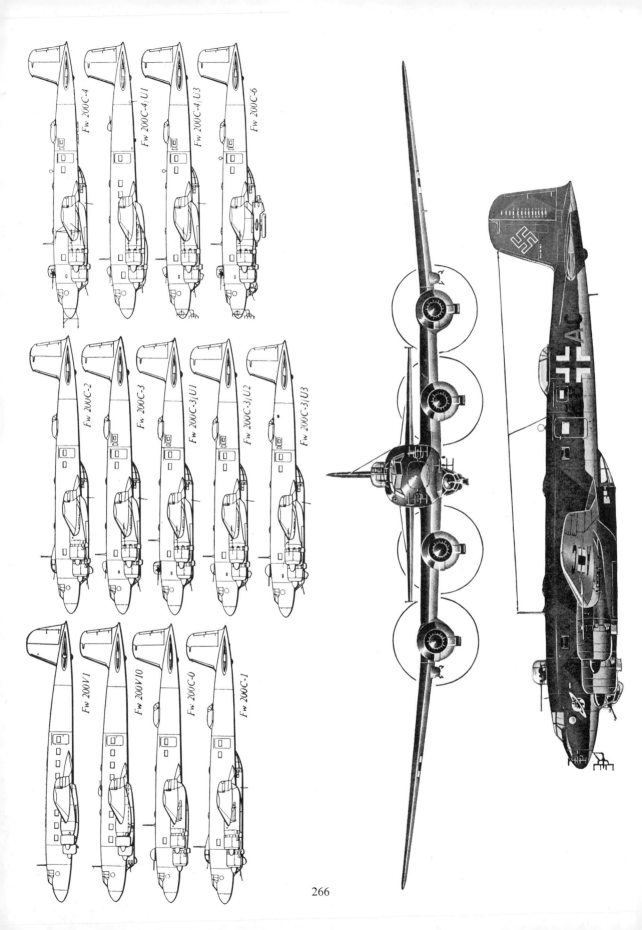

Fw 200C-4

Fw 200C-4/U1

Fw 200C-4/U3

Fw 200C-6

Fw 200C-2

Fw 200C-3

Fw 200C-3/U1

Fw 200C-3/U2

Fw 200C-3/U3

Fw 200V1

Fw 200V10

Fw 200C-0

Fw 200C-1

The Focke-Wulf Fw 200C-4 Condor

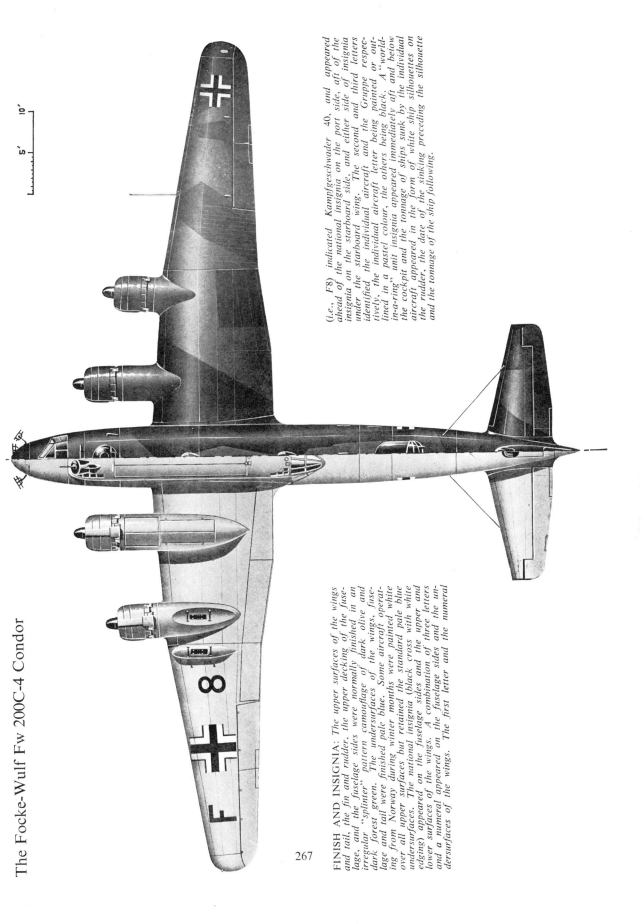

5' 10'

267

FINISH AND INSIGNIA: *The upper surfaces of the wings and tail, the fin and rudder, the upper decking of the fuselage, and the fuselage sides were normally finished in an irregular "splinter" pattern camouflage of dark olive and dark forest green. The undersurfaces of the wings, fuselage and tail were finished pale blue. Some aircraft operating from Norway during winter months were painted white over all upper surfaces but retained the standard pale blue undersurfaces. The national insignia (black cross with white edging) appeared on the fuselage sides and the upper and lower surfaces of the wings. A combination of three letters and a numeral appeared on the fuselage sides and the undersurfaces of the wings. The first letter and the numeral*

(i.e., F8) indicated Kampfgeschwader 40, and appeared ahead of the national insignia on the port side, aft of the insignia on the starboard side, and either side of insignia under the starboard wing. The second and third letters identified the individual aircraft and the Gruppe respectively, the individual aircraft letter being painted or outlined in a pastel colour, the others being black. A "world-in-a-ring" unit insignia appeared immediately aft and below the cockpit and the tonnage of ships sunk by the individual aircraft appeared in the form of white ship silhouettes on the rudder, the date of the sinking preceding the silhouette and the tonnage of the ship following.

The Fw 200C-3/U2 was fitted with the Lotfe 7D bomb-sight which projected beneath the ventral gondola. A 7.9-mm. MG 15 machine gun was fitted in the nose of the gondola in place of the 20-mm. MG 151 cannon, the breech of which interfered with the bomb-sight's stowage.

been willing to accept the Fw 200B's structure as they envisaged using the aircraft solely for long-range reconnaissance missions at medium altitudes, but the R.L.M. demanded a commerce raider, and the basic structure therefore had to be extensively restressed. The modified Condor received the designation Fw 200C, and the construction of a batch of ten Fw 200C-0 pre-production aeroplanes began almost immediately. Power was provided by four BMW 132H-1 radials, and defensive armament comprised a hand-held 7.9-mm. MG 15 machine gun in a raised position aft of the flight deck firing forward, and a second MG 15 firing aft from a dorsal position enclosed by a sliding hood. It was proposed to fit a long ventral gondola which, offset to starboard like that of the Fw 200V10, was to house a prone bombardier's position, bomb sight and a 550-lb. bomb, and to support the greatly increased loaded weight, the main undercarriage members were fitted with paired wheels in place of the single wheels of the commercial transport. However, the pending invasion of Norway and the consequent demand for transport aircraft necessitated the hurried completion of the Fw 200C-0 Condors to participate in this campaign, and when delivered in the late spring of 1940, the majority of aircraft had not been fitted with the ventral gondola, and some lacked all defensive armament. Together with the Fw 200B transports which had been on the production line at the beginning of the war and had been taken over by the Luftwaffe, and the former D.L.H. Condors, these served in the transport role in April-May 1940.

Meanwhile, a production line had been laid down at Cottbus for the Fw 200C-1, deliveries of which commenced in the summer months, some twenty-five machines having been completed by the end of 1940. The Fw 200C-1 featured a semi-monocoque fuselage with an all-metal, two-spar wing built in three sections, metal covered to the rear spar, and fabric covered aft. Two-piece ailerons extended along two-thirds of the outer section trailing edges, and split flaps were mounted inboard of the ailerons. The Fw 200C-1 normally carried a crew of five comprising pilot, co-pilot, navigator/radio-operator/gunner, engineer/gunner and rear dorsal gunner, and defensive armament comprised a 7.9-mm. MG 15 machine gun in the forward dorsal position, an MG 15 in the rear dorsal position, a 20-mm. MG FF (Oerlikon) cannon in the nose of the ventral gondola, and an MG 15 in the rear of the gondola. The outboard engine nacelles were extended and fitted with racks to carry either a 550-lb. bomb or a 66 Imp.gal. auxiliary tank, two racks outboard of the engine nacelles each carried a 550-lb. bomb, and the ventral gondola could carry either a 550-lb. bomb or an armoured auxiliary fuel tank.

The first deliveries of the Fw 200C-1 were made to Kampfgeschwader 40 during the late months of 1940, and, after a brief period of working-up, the Condor began its relatively brief but certainly spectacular career as a commerce raider. During the months that followed, the two Condor-equipped Gruppen of K.G. 40 began to take an increasingly serious toll of Allied shipping, the inadequate anti-aircraft armament of the merchant ships, insufficient escort vessels, and an almost complete lack of long-range aircraft and escort carriers rendering their task a relatively simple one. Gruppe III based at Bordeaux-Mérignac patrolled far out into the Atlantic, while Gruppe I, based at Trondheim-Vaernes, reconnoitred beyond the Faroes, over the Irish Sea and down to the English Channel, wreaking havoc among the convoys and co-operating with U-boats under the operational control of Fliegerführer Atlantik.

The Fw 200C-1 was followed on the production line during 1941 by the Fw 200C-2 which had modified outboard engine nacelles, new faired bomb racks, and several internal modifications resulting from operational experience, but despite its operational successes, the Condor was suffering its full share of troubles which stemmed from its commercial transport heritage. Despite the fact that the military Condor had undergone some structural strengthening, this soon proved inadequate to meet the strain of continuous operational flying at low altitudes for long periods, and the violent manœuvres that were sometimes called for when taking evasive action. There were numerous instances of the rear spar failing and the fuselage breaking its back immediately aft of the wing on landing. These failures resulted in the hasty introduction of the Fw 200C-3 during the summer of 1941, fifty-eight Condors being delivered during the course of that year. Despite the fact that the Fw 200C-3 embodied major structural strengthening of both the rear spar and the fuselage, the Condor continued to suffer structural failures, and the Focke-Wulf concern never succeeded in entirely solving the problem.

In order to maintain the performance of the Condor despite the increased structural weight, the Fw 200C-3 received four BMW-Bramo 323R-2 nine-cylinder radial air-cooled engines with methanol-water injection which offered 1,200 h.p. at 2,600 r.p.m. for take-off and emergency. Loaded weight had risen to 46,297 lb., an additional crew member was carried, and maximum bomb load was

Throughout its career the Fw 200C suffered from failures of the rear spar and rear fuselage, despite continual structural strengthening. The Fw 200C-3 in the upper photo has had a rear spar failure during take-off, and that in the photograph immediately above has broken its back.

increased to 4,620 lb. (one 1,100-lb. bomb under each outboard engine nacelle, one 550-lb. bomb on each of the two under-wing racks, and twelve 110-lb. bombs in the ventral gondola). A low-drag Fw 19 turret housing one 7.9-mm. MG 15 machine gun replaced the raised fairing immediately aft of the flight deck, and two MG 15 beam guns were mounted behind panels in the fuselage sides. As the Fw 200C-3 was intended primarily for low-altitude attack, its bombardier had to rely on a Revi sight for his bombing. The Fw 200C-3/U1 differed in having a 20-mm. MG 151 cannon in place of the old MG FF in the ventral gondola, and a large hydraulically-operated turret housing a 15-mm. MG 151 cannon in the forward dorsal position. This turret took some 20 m.p.h. off the Condor's maximum speed but the cannon was considered to be a very much more effective defensive weapon than the MG 15.

The Fw 200C-3/U2 reverted to the Fw 19 forward dorsal turret, and was fitted with the Lotfe 7D bomb-sight. This necessitated the installation of a 7.9-mm. MG 15 machine gun in the nose of the ventral gondola as the breech of the MG 151 cannon interfered with the Lotfe 7D's stowage. Increasingly effective

Allied anti-aircraft defence was rendering the low-level attacks of the Condor's heyday extremely hazardous, and the most satisfactory bombing altitude for the Lotfe 7D was 11,500-13,000 feet. The Fw 200C-3/U3 had an EDL 131 turret containing one 13-mm. MG 131 heavy machine gun in the forward dorsal, while the Fw 200C-3/U4 reverted to the Fw 19 forward dorsal turret but had MG 131 beam guns. The last-mentioned variant carried a crew of seven, had increased fuel capacity, and had a loaded weight of 50,045 lb.

Production of the Fw 200C-3 gave place to the C-4 early in 1942, this model being manufactured in greater quantities than any other version of the Condor. The C-3 and C-4 were basically the same aircraft, the principal differences being those associated with search radar and new radio equipment. Early production Fw 200C-4 Condors were fitted with FuG *Rostock* shipping search radar, but later machines standardised on FuG 200 *Hohentwiel* which was used in conjunction with a blind bombing procedure. Some machines were fitted with both *Rostock* and *Hohentwiel*, the double installation being necessitated by the fact that the former, although having a wider search angle and a greater range than

the latter, would not give readings at a range of less than three miles and was therefore unsuitable for blind bombing.

The 15-mm. MG 151 forward dorsal turret introduced by the Fw 200C-3/U1 was also fitted to the Fw 200C-4, and either a 20-mm. MG 151 cannon or a 13-mm. MG 131 machine gun was fitted in the nose of the ventral gondola according to the installation of the Lotfe bomb-sight. The rated altitude of the Fw 200C-4 was 15,750 feet, at which maximum speed was 205 m.p.h. as compared with 224 m.p.h. at the same altitude for the Fw 200C-3. At sea level, the average cruising speed was 150-168 m.p.h., with a maximum speed of 174 m.p.h. Service ceiling was 19,000 feet but at this altitude the airframe was subject to violent vibration. The basic tankage of 1,773 Imp.gal. gave a normal endurance of fourteen hours at economical cruising speed with normal safety reserves. An additional 220 Imp.gal. could be carried in an armoured tank in the ventral gondola, a 66 Imp.gal. auxiliary tank could be carried under each outboard engine nacelle, and sometimes two or three 66 Imp. gal. drums were carried to refill the fuselage tanks, thus extending the maximum endurance to some eighteen hours.

The Condor was extremely vulnerable to both anti-aircraft fire and aerial attack, and with the provision of more anti-aircraft armament on merchant ships and the introduction of CAM-ships (Catapult Aircraft Merchantmen) with their specially-strengthened Hurricane fighters, the Allies began to take the

measure of the Condor. Only the first pilot of the Condor enjoyed any armour protection and, all fuel connections to the engines being on the underside of the aircraft, it was extremely vulnerable to light anti-aircraft fire. The port outer engine drove the generator for the hydraulically-operated dorsal MG 151 turret and, in the event of hydraulic damage, it was extremely difficult to operate the turret by hand against a fast-moving opponent.

With the appearance of the very-long-range Liberators of R.A.F. Coastal Command, effectively closing the Atlantic Gap, Condor pilots received orders not to initiate any attack but to seek cloud cover when attacked, only offering fight if absolutely necessary. Furthermore, Condor crews had orders to return to base immediately in the event of the slightest damage rather than jeopardise the safety of a valuable aircraft, production of the Condor barely keeping pace with K.G. 40's demands. Only eighty-four Condors were produced in 1942, some of these aircraft being diverted for special transport purposes, and immediately an aircraft came off the line at Cottbus, a crew was sent specially from K.G. 40 to collect the new aircraft.

As the danger of interception by long-range patrolling Beaufighters and Mosquitoes increased, the most northerly point to which Biscay-based Condors flew was 40° N, there thus being no longer any link between the Biscay area and northern waters patrolled by the Norwegian-based Condors. There were two main areas of armed reconnaissance patrol operated by Condors flying from Bordeaux-Mérignac and Cognac; one, known as the Kleine Aufklärung, or small reconnaissance, and the other known as the Grosse Aufklärung, or large reconnaissance. The dividing line between the two reconnaissance areas was approximately 45°, the smaller extending to the limit already mentioned, and the larger to approximately 34° N. The westerly limit of both areas was normally 19° N, although, on special reconnaissances, Condors reached as far as 25° W. When approaching the northerly reconnaissance area, the Condors normally flew in formation at sea level for mutual protection, breaking up and proceeding singly on their shipping search at 11° W. Sometimes Condors *en route* for this area had to make a detour as far south as Cap Ortegal to avoid patrolling fighters. One method of shipping search frequently adopted was known as the *Facher* (Fan). A typical *Facher* search in a southerly direction starting from 15° W was to fly due West for 3°, due South for thirty miles, due East for 3°, due South for thirty miles, and so on until the allotted area had been covered.

During the early months of 1943, Condor activity fell sharply, for the 2nd Staffel of Gruppe I, based at Trondheim-Vaernes, was the only unit still operating over the Atlantic, the remainder of the staffeln of Gruppe I and those of Gruppe III being scattered on various urgent transport assignments. In January 1943, the 1st and 3rd Staffeln were sent to the Russian Front where, based at Stalino, they formed a special transport unit for ferrying supplies into Stalingrad. This unit was known as the Sonder-Unternehmung Stalingrad, and received the designation K.G.z.b.V. 200. Initially, the Condors were landing supplies on an airfield in the vicinity of Stalingrad, but as the German perimeter shrank they were forced to drop supplies by parachute, each aircraft having four supply containers attached to its bomb racks. On January 18th, the Condors were transferred to Zaparozhe from where they continued their supply-dropping activities for a month before it was decided that this transport undertaking was proving too costly. For five days the Condors then confined their activities to bombing railway communications in the Stalingrad area, after which they were recalled to Staaken.

At Staaken the survivors of K.G. 40's 1st and 3rd Staffeln were amalgamated into one staffel, their aircraft were fitted with the Lotfe 7D bomb-sight and the unit was transferred to Cognac to be absorbed by Gruppe III as the 8th Staffel, and resume activities over the Bay of Biscay. In the meantime, the 7th and 9th Staffeln of Gruppe III, which had been undertaking transport tasks in Italy, had also returned to France, and once again the Condor began to appear in numbers.

The Condors now discontinued their previous practice of flying routine reconnaissance in search of shipping targets, these duties being taken over by the Junkers Ju 290A-5s of F.A.G. 5 based at Mont de Marsan. The Condors of III/K.G. 40, together with the He 177As of II/K.G. 40, and the 1st and 3rd Staffeln of I/K.G. 40 (the 2nd Staffel based at Trondheim-Vaernes being the only component of Gruppe I still equipped with the Condor), were now solely concerned with shipping attack, being sent out only when a definite target had been sighted and its position reported by the aircraft of F.A.G. 5.

The departures of Allied convoys from Gibraltar were regularly reported from Spain, and as the time of arrival of the convoys in K.G. 40's sphere of opera-

tions could therefore be calculated, it only remained for the reconnaissance aircraft to establish their exact position as well as weather conditions before the Condors and He 177s took-off. The only exception to this new policy was when the total effort of all aircraft in the Biscay area was ordered by the Fliegerführer Atlantik, such as when German blockade runners were attempting to make port. On these occasions the Condors reverted to armed reconnaissance to report the presence of any Allied warships in the area. When Allied shipping was reported, a minimum of four Condors would take-off to attack, the aircraft usually flying at sea level in line abreast in close formation to a point such as Cap Ortegal where they would fan out and fly on parallel courses at intervals of twenty-five to thirty miles. Each aircraft would periodically climb to 1,500 feet in a wide circle while making a search with its *Hohentwiel*, after which the original course was resumed. The first Condor to sight the shipping would then make R/T contact with the other aircraft. Low-level attack in conditions of clear visibility was expressly forbidden, a minimum attacking altitude of 9,000 feet being prescribed.

Some Fw 200C-3s were modified to carry two Henschel Hs 293 radio-controlled rocket-propelled bombs under the outboard engine nacelles, the wing bomb rack being removed. Condors so modified were designated Fw 200C-6, and the Hs 293 was carried operationally for the first time on December 28, 1943, when one of four Condors flying on a *Facher* search for British naval units carried two of these missiles experimentally. The Hs 293-equipped Condor encountered a patrolling Sunderland before it could make contact with the British ships, however, and was forced to ditch with the missiles still on their racks. Most of the last production variant, the Fw 200C-8, were built as He 293 carriers, but this missile was not used on a large scale by the Condor, production of which had already begun to taper off in 1943 when only seventy-six new machines were delivered, and terminated completely at the beginning of 1944 with a further eight aircraft.

By mid-1943, the He 177A was beginning to take over the roles previously performed by the Condor which, not inappropriately, was being employed increasingly for the purpose for which it had been originally designed—that of transportation. Several Fw 200C-3s had been converted for use as the personal transports of Germany's leaders; machines of this type were used on several occasions by the notorious Gruppe I of Kampfgeschwader 200 for dropping agents and saboteurs, and one special all-black Fw 200C-3 was also used for this purpose by the 9th Staffel of K.G. 40. In 1942, two special transport variants of the Condor were produced. These were the 137th and 138th production machines and were designated Fw 200C-4/U1 and U2 respectively. To reduce drag, an Fw 19 turret containing a single MG 15 machine gun was fitted in the forward

The final production version of the Condor was the Fw 200C-8. The C-8 illustrated above (Werk-Nr. 256) was the standard model with Hohentwiel radar and turreted MG151 cannon. The aircraft illustrated below, an Fw 200-C8/U10 (Werk-Nr. 259), has the deeper outboard engine nacelles and extended ventral gondola of the Henschel Hs 293 carrier.

dorsal position, a generally similar Fw 20 turret also containing a single MG 15 was mounted in the aft dorsal position, and an abbreviated and re-designed ventral gondola mounted single MG 15s fore and aft. The Fw 200C-4/U1 and U2 differed solely in seating arrangements, the former providing accommodation for eleven passengers and the latter for fourteen, and they were appreciably faster than the standard Fw 200C-4 Condors.

The last known wartime flight of a Condor was made, perhaps surprisingly, by one of Deutsche Lufthansa's original machines. These had been handed back to D.L.H. by the Luftwaffe after the Norwegian campaign, and on the evening of April 21, 1945, one was hastily loaded with the luggage of the Berlin Headquarters Staff, the pilot, Flugkapitan Künstle, planning to fly to Barcelona via Munich. The Condor reached Munich and took-off again, heavily loaded, the pilot confident that he was un-likely to encounter Allied aircraft because of the prevailing bad weather. That was the last time the Condor was ever seen. Enquiries in Germany, Switzerland and Spain continued for years, but it was not until ten years after the end of the war that the mystery was solved when evidence was found near Munich that the plane had crashed and burned out with no survivors shortly after taking-off.

As a warplane the Condor was not a particularly brilliant aircraft, yet it established a formidable reputation. In view of the surprisingly small number of Condors built, this aircraft cost the Allies dear. For a time, co-operating with the U-boat packs, it posed one of the major threats to Britain's survival, and even though its threat had been largely nullified by the third year of the war, the Condor will always be remembered as the "Scourge of the Atlantic".

Focke-Wulf Fw 200C-3/U4 Condor

Dimensions: Span, 107 ft. 9½ in.; length, 76 ft. 11½ in.; height, 20 ft. 8 in.; wing area, 1,290 sq. ft.

Armament: One 7.9-mm. MG 15 machine gun in Fw 19 forward dorsal turret with 1,000 rounds; one hand-operated 13-mm. MG 131 machine gun with 500 rounds in aft dorsal position; two 13-mm. MG 131 machine guns with 300 r.p.g. under beam hatches; one 20-mm. MG 151 with 500 rounds in forward ventral position, and one 7.9-mm. MG 15 machine gun with 1,000 rounds in aft ventral position. Maximum bomb load, 4,620 lb. (comprising one 1,100-lb. bomb under each outboard engine nacelle, one 550-lb. bomb on each of the two underwing racks, and twelve 110-lb. bombs in the ventral gondola).

Power Plants: Four BMW-Bramo 323R-2 Fafnir nine-cylinder radial air-cooled engines rated at 1,200 h.p. at 2,600 r.p.m. for take-off and emergency with methanol-water injection, 1,000 h.p. at 2,500 r.p.m. at sea level, and 940 h.p. at 2,500 r.p.m. at 13,120 ft.

Weights: Maximum loaded weight, 50,045 lb.; landing weight, 38,800 lb.

Performance: Maximum speed, 224 m.p.h. at 15,750 ft., 190 m.p.h. at sea level; maximum cruising speed, 208 m.p.h. at 13,120 ft., 172 m.p.h. at sea level; economical cruising speed, 158 m.p.h.; service ceiling, 19,000 ft.; endurance (with 1,773 Imp.gal. of fuel) at economical cruising speed, 14 hrs., (with 2,190 Imp.gal. fuel), 17 hrs. 30 min.; normal range, 2,210 mls.

THE HANDLEY PAGE HALIFAX

"From Hull, Hell and Halifax, good Lord deliver us." This quotation from an old Yorkshire prayer was used by Lord Halifax in a speech before the christening ceremony for the second of Britain's war-time "heavies", the Handley Page Halifax, and Germany had ample reason to echo the latter part of that sentiment in the years that followed. No less than four out of every ten heavy bombers built in the United Kingdom during the Second World War were Halifaxes, and these shared with the Avro Lancaster the major night-bombing offensive, which, from small beginnings in 1941, built up to its tremendous crescendo in 1944. The latest in a continuous line of Handley Page bombers which had formed the back-bone of the Royal Air Force's striking power since the time of that service's inception, the Halifax was not as shapely an aircraft as its Avro contemporary, but its deeper, more capacious, slab-sided fuselage rendered it suitable for a wider variety of roles, and unlike the Lancaster which was used almost ex-clusively as a bomber during the war years, the Halifax achieved an enviable reputation as a freighter, personnel transport, ambulance, glider tug, and maritime reconnaissance aircraft.

Almost since the earliest days of flying the name of Handley Page had been associated with bombers. Indeed, one was almost synonymous with the other, and it was to be expected that when, in 1936, the Air Staff outlined its requirements for a new generation of R.A.F. bombers, Handley Page would be among the companies to receive development contracts. The beginnings of the Halifax reached back further than this, however, for its starting point was to be found in the H.P.55, a projected bomber to meet the requirements of specification B.1/35. The H.P.55 design was tendered with two Bristol Hercules H.E.1SM air-cooled radials, and alternative layouts were studied with Rolls-Royce Merlin and Rolls-Royce Vulture liquid-cooled power plants, but the contract was given to a Vickers-Armstrongs design which, developed in parallel with the Wellington, was eventually to emerge as the Warwick. A year later, a

Halifax Mk.I L9485 was employed for tests with dorsal and ventral turrets, the latter being adopted for the Halifax II.

new specification was issued, P.13/36, calling for a Vulture-powered medium bomber with a greater bomb load and range than had been specified for B.1/35, and from the H.P.55 Handley Page's design team, headed by G. R. Volkert, evolved the H.P.56.

Both Handley Page and A. V. Roe (for the Type 679 Manchester) were awarded contracts for two prototypes, and both types were to be powered by a pair of Rolls-Royce Vulture twenty-four cylinder X-type engines. The order was placed in April 1937, and construction of the two H.P.56 prototypes, which were allocated the serial numbers L7244 and L7245, was put in hand immediately. At this stage, the H.P.56 had a design gross weight of 26,300 lb. Within a few months of the initiation of design work, however, Handley Page learned that production of the Vulture, which was suffering rather more than its share of teething troubles, was likely to be curtailed, and such an event would mean, of course, that the H.P.56 would not be ordered in production quantities. With official encouragement, G. R. Volkert immediately set about redesigning his bomber to take four Rolls-Royce Merlins as none of the other big engines at that time under development seemed likely to be ready soon enough to replace the Vulture in a twin-engined layout. The redesign was, not unexpectedly, an extensive one, and although the

wing and fuselage contours remained relatively unchanged, the size of the aeroplane grew appreciably, and the weight increased to a basic 40,000 lb.

On September 3, 1937, an official contract was issued to cover the construction of two prototypes of the H.P.57, as the redesigned aircraft was known, this contract replacing that previously issued for the H.P.56. The bomber was still required to meet the demands of specification P.13/36, and the serial numbers originally allocated were retained for the two prototypes. Construction began at Handley Page's Cricklewood plant in January 1938, and the first prototype (L7244) was transported to R.A.F. Station, Bicester, in the autumn of 1939 for final assembly. At Bicester, it was flown for the first time on October 25, 1939, with the company's chief test pilot, Major J. L. B. H. Cordes, at the controls. As first flown, the aircraft was powered by four Merlin X engines each rated at 1,075 h.p. for take-off and 1,130 h.p. at 5,250 ft., and driving de Havilland three-blade metal airscrews. Although the design provided for power-driven nose and tail turrets, and beam gun stations, these were not fitted for the initial trials, their positions being covered by metal fairings. Like the earlier Hampden, the prototype was fitted with automatic leading-edge slots as well as slotted flaps, the combination giving a higher lift coefficient than

This early production Halifax I (L9515) was subsequently converted to serve as the prototype Halifax II Series IA. It tested the low-drag Boulton Paul four-gun turret, and at one stage in its career featured extended inboard engine nacelles.

The Halifax II tended to spin uncontrollably when fully loaded, and the dorsal turret introduced on this version contributed considerably to drag. The machine illustrated (W1245) belonged to No. 233 Squadron.

flaps alone, but an Air Ministry requirement for barrage balloon cable cutters in the wing leading edges necessitated the subsequent deletion of the slots. The design overload weight had now risen to 50,000 lb., and the second prototype (L7245) flew at this weight on August 17, 1940.

In the meantime, the bomber, which had already been allotted the name Halifax, had been ordered into production. Following the redesign of the original H.P.56, a production specification, 32/37, had been drawn up to cover the H.P.57, and Handley Page had been instructed to proceed with preparations for quantity manufacture, although the first contract—for one hundred aircraft—was not, in fact, formally confirmed until January 1939, despite the fact that in the previous October the Air Staff was already talking about having five hundred Halifaxes in service by April 1942—clearly somewhat optimistic but indicative of the importance already being attached to the new bomber at that early date.

The first production Halifax (L9485) flew on October 11, 1940. Powered by four Merlin X engines, it had a tare weight of 33,860 lb. and a maximum take-off weight of 55,000 lb. Boulton Paul power-operated turrets in the nose and tail housed two and four 0.303-in. Browning machine guns respectively, Rotol constant-speed compressed-wood airscrews replaced the metal de Havilland units of the prototypes, and, for simplicity, the retractable tailwheel was replaced by one of fixed type. Maximum speed was 265 m.p.h. at 17,500 ft., initial climb rate was 750 ft./min., service ceiling was 22,800 ft., normal range with 2,242 Imp.gal. of fuel and a 5,800-lb. bomb load was 1,860 mls. From the production viewpoint, one of the Halifax's most interesting features was the method of split assembly by which it was built, this possessing the virtues of making possible the employment of more personnel in each stage of the aircraft's construction, and dividing the bomber into pieces for transportation and repair.

The initial production batch were designated Halifax B.Mk.I Series I, followed by the Series II stressed to operate at weights up to 60,000 lb., and the Series III in which the normal fuel capacity was increased from 1,392 to 1,636 Imp.gal., and the maximum fuel capacity from 2,242 to 2,326 Imp.gal. Some early machines were fitted with beam guns, and some late Series III aircraft had Merlin XX engines which offered 1,280 h.p. for take-off and 1,480 h.p. at 6,800 ft.

The first result of the programme of divesting the bomber of its many drag-producing excrescences was the Halifax II Series I which had a "Z" fairing and, on some machines such as W7776 illustrated, the dorsal turret was removed.

All Halifax B.Mk.I production was handled by Handley Page at their Cricklewood and Radlett factories, but as part of the rearmament programme established shortly before the war, the Halifax was made the subject of a group production effort of a unique kind. Four separate assembly lines were established for the Halifax in addition to those laid down by the parent company. The first company involved in the Halifax group was English Electric, who had previously re-entered the aircraft industry to produce the Hampden. English Electric were asked to collaborate in Halifax production early in 1939, and on February 22 of that year received instructions to proceed with planning and the training of personnel for the production of one hundred Halifaxes, the first of which (V9976) was destined to fly on August 15, 1941. Next came the London Aircraft Production Group, made up of Chrysler Motors (making the rear fuselages): Duplex Bodies and Motors (forward fuselage shell and components); Express Motor and Body Works (inner wing sections); Park Royal Coachwork (outer wing sections), and the London Passenger Transport Board Works, the latter making a considerable amount of the equipment and fittings, and being responsible for the final erection and testing, at Leavesden. The first Halifax built by this group flew late in 1941. At a Stockport factory taken over for the purpose, Fairey Aviation also built Halifaxes, while Rootes Securities built others at Speke.

The R.A.F. gained its first acquaintance with the Halifax in November 1940, when the first prototype (L7244) was sent to No. 35 Squadron at Leeming for preliminary familiarisation—this machine, incidentally, ended its career in November 1941 in a crash at Boscombe Down. In December 1940, No. 35 Squadron moved to Linton-on-Ouse, and there received its operational aircraft—B.Mk.I Series Is. After a brief period of working-up, the squadron took its Halifaxes into operation for the first time on the night of March 10, 1941, when six of its aircraft (from the first twelve production machines) made a sortie against Le Havre, and two nights later these aircraft gained the distinction of being the first R.A.F. four-engined bombers to drop bombs on Germany with an attack on Hamburg. Some three months later, on June 30, 1941, Halifaxes operated for the first time by day, raiding Kiel, and in July they attacked the battlecruiser *Scharnhorst* at La Pallice.

Throughout the remainder of 1941, Halifaxes continued to operate by both day and night, frequently attacking the battlecruisers *Scharnhorst* and *Gneisenau* but, with its comparatively meagre armament, the Halifax was not entirely suited for daylight operations, from which increasing losses as German fighter defences were strengthened resulted in its withdrawal at the end of 1941. Steps were already being taken to improve the defensive armament of the Halifax, however, one rather dubious scheme (the H.P.58) being a four-cannon installation in the fuselage. This project did not proceed beyond the mock-up stage as operational experience had indicated the desirability of a power-operated dorsal turret. The opportunity provided by the introduction of a new version of the Halifax, the B.Mk.II, was taken to introduce a bulbous Boulton Paul twin-gun turret similar to that installed on the Lockheed Hudson. Like late production B.Mk.I Series III aircraft, the Halifax B.Mk.II Series I was powered by four Merlin XXs and, later, Merlin 22s. The gross weight was held at 60,000 lb., and the fuel capacity was increased—normal tankage being raised to 1,882 Imp.gal. and maximum tankage to 2,572 Imp.gal.

The prototype Halifax II (L9515) was a converted Mk.I, and was first flown on July 3, 1941. On September 12, Lady Halifax undertook the official naming ceremony at Radlett, the subject aircraft being the last production Mk.I (L9608). The first production Mk.II (L9609) flew in the same month, and this was the version built initially by all the other assembly lines in the Halifax production group. The development and service introduction of the Halifax had not been without its troubles, however, for the bomber had always been slightly underpowered, and the appreciable increases in loaded weight since the basic design was frozen began to tell. The higher weights combined with the drag of the new dorsal turret seriously affected performance. When fully loaded the aircraft developed a tendency to spin uncontrollably, and losses began to grow alarmingly. A programme of divesting the Halifax of many of its drag-producing excrescences was started, and in the process many of what had previously been characteristic features of the bomber were shed.

The programme was initiated by taking a standard Halifax II (R9534) and stripping it of all equipment, replacing only essentials. It had been found on operations that head-on attacks by fighters rarely occurred, rendering the power-operated nose turret a dispensable luxury, and this was therefore removed, being replaced by a streamlined Perspex fairing, the protruding bombardier's "chin" giving place to an optically flat panel in the symmetrical nose. A single hand-operated Vickers "K" gun on a gimbal mounting was fitted for the use of the bombardier, rather more as a gesture than a serious form of defence. A new Boulton Paul power-operated turret of shallower type was mounted snugly on top of the fuselage, housing four 0.303-in. Brownings and offering negligible drag as compared with the two-gun turret that it replaced, and much internal equipment was omitted altogether. The tailwheel was made semi-retractable; the radio mast was eliminated, the aerial being attached to the D/F loop, and with all these modifications the aircraft went into production as the Halifax B.Mk.II Series IA. Rolls-Royce Merlin 22 or 24 engines were standard, the former offering 1,280 h.p. for take-off, and 1,480 h.p. at 2,250 ft., and the latter giving 1,620 h.p. for take-off and 1,500 h.p. at 9,500 ft., and these were fitted with Morris block-

The Halifax II Series IA of No. 35 "Madras Presidency" Squadron illustrated above features the rectangular fins which were introduced to cure the rudder stalling experienced under certain conditions with the original triangular fin. The earlier fin is seen fitted to Halifax II Series IA HR679 (right).

type radiators, which permitted a reduction in the engine nacelle cross-section, in lieu of the Gallay circular-type radiators. Other changes included the provision of a shallower astro-drome, the removal of the underwing fuel jettison pipes and the cylindrical asbestos shrouds around the exhausts, and the sealing of the gap at the elevator spar and the fuselage at the rear bulkhead. The bomb-bay doors were modified to permit the carriage of larger bombs, and the overall length was increased from 70 ft. 1 in. to 71 ft. 7 in. The net gain resulting from these extensive changes was approximately ten per cent in both maximum and cruising speeds.

Before the Halifax B.Mk.II Series IA had reached the squadrons, an interim scheme had been introduced. Firstly, the nose turret was removed and replaced by what became known as a "Z" fairing on some squadron aircraft—a few new aircraft also left the factories with this nose fairing prior to the availability of the new Series IA moulded plastic nose —and these were known as B.Mk.II Series I (Special). The cumbersome two-gun dorsal turret was also removed from some aircraft to reduce drag, together with the exhaust shrouds, and the fuel jettison pipes which had projected from the trailing edge of each wing, and these aircraft joined operations with the four-gun Boulton Paul tail turret as their sole defensive armament. Later, some B.Mk.II Series I (Special) Halifaxes had the low-drag, four-gun Boulton Paul dorsal turret fitted.

At this period in the Halifax's development the bomber suffered a series of unexplained crashes in which the aircraft got into an inverted dive. Attempts on the part of Aircraft and Armament Experimental Establishment pilots to simulate the conditions under which the crashes had occurred failed to produce the desired effect. Finally, after a prolonged and worrying period of testing it was ascertained that the trouble was resulting from rudder stalling. Under certain conditions the triangular fin stalled and turbulent air passing through the gap between fin and rudder locked the latter hard over. New rectangular fins were designed to rectify this trouble, and these were introduced as a retrospective modification during 1943.

In service, the Halifax B.II had been performing valuable work throughout 1942, and recorded several notable "firsts". Halifax B.II V9977 was the first aircraft to be equipped with the H2S radar bombing aid with the ventral radome—which was to become such a familiar sight as the war progressed—flying with this on March 27, 1942. One Halifax (W7650) flew with a ventral turret, and another (V9985) was employed for dropping trials with dummy 4,000-lb. "Block Buster" bombs. One B.Mk.II Series IA aircraft was converted by Rolls-Royce to take Merlin 65s in low mountings as the B.Mk.II Series II (HR756). The engines were fitted with four-blade airscrews, and the aircraft was subsequently employed for Merlin development flying. The Series II aircraft was part of a development programme for the Halifax IV, this mark number having been reserved for an extensively modified variant, the H.P.60A. This stemmed from Handley Page's tender, in 1939, of a Halifax derivative to meet specification B.1/39. Features of this design included a new fuselage floor, enlarged bomb-bay, and Merlin 65 engines. This devleopment was eventually abandoned, as were plans to build a Pobjoy Niagara-powered flying scale model, but certain features of the Halifax IV design, including lengthened inner nacelles, were flown on a Halifax I (L9515) and two Halifax IIs (HR679 and HR756).

After the H2S radome had become a standard production line fitting, considerable shortages of H2S equipment manifested themselves, and, not infrequently, a 0.5-in. machine gun was mounted in the scanner fairing. Another production shortage— of British Messier undercarriages—produced the H.P.63 Halifax B.Mk.V which differed from the B.Mk.II only in having a Dowty levered suspension undercarriage. This was first flown on a Mk.I

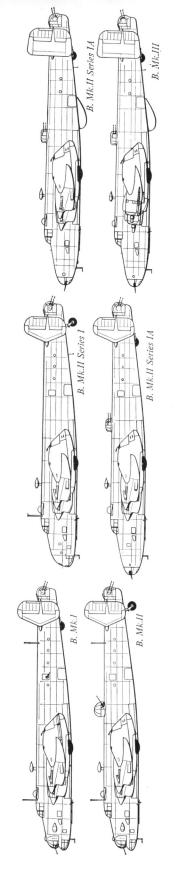

B. Mk.II Series 1A

B. Mk.III

B. Mk.II Series I

B. Mk.II Series 1A

B. Mk.I

B. Mk.II

Handley Page Halifax B.VI

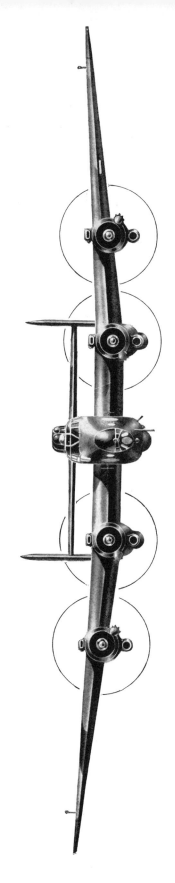

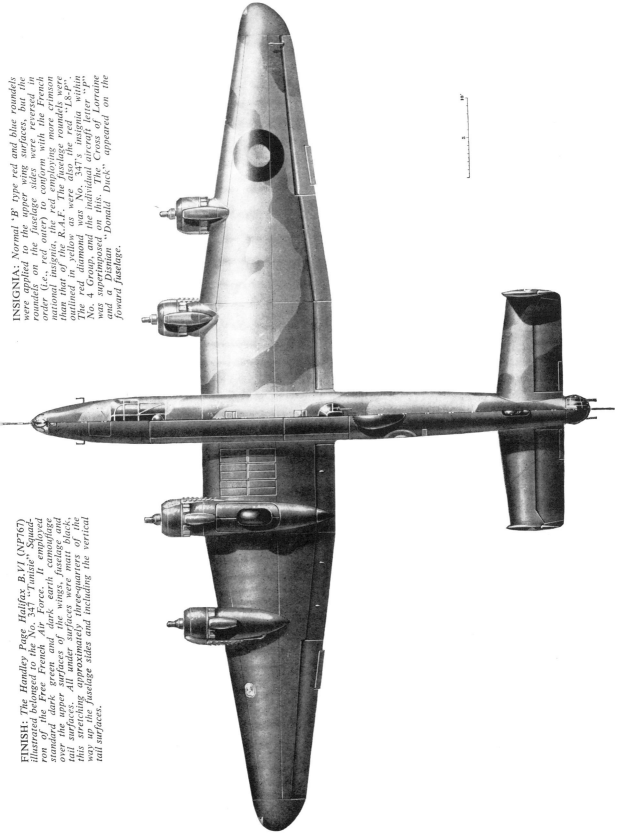

FINISH: The Handley Page Halifax B.VI (NP767) illustrated belonged to the No. 347 "Tunisie" Squadron of the Free French Air Force. It employed standard dark green and dark earth camouflage over the upper surfaces of the wings, fuselage and tail surfaces. All under surfaces were matt black, this stretching approximately three-quarters of the way up the fuselage sides and including the vertical tail surfaces.

INSIGNIA: Normal 'B' type red and blue roundels were applied to the upper wing surfaces, but the roundels on the fuselage sides were reversed in order (i.e., red outer) to conform with the French national insignia, the red employing more crimson than that of the R.A.F. The fuselage roundels were outlined in yellow as were also the red "L8-P". The red diamond was No. 347's insignia within No. 4 Group, and the individual aircraft letter "P" was superimposed on this. The Cross of Lorraine and a Disnian "Donald Duck", appeared on the foward fuselage.

(Above) The Halifax II Series IA prototype (L9515) with extended inboard engine nacelles.

Some Halifax IIs were fitted with four-blade airscrews as seen on this G.R.II Series IA (JD376).

Features for the proposed Halifax IV (H.P.60A), such as lower engine thrust lines and extended inner engine nacelles, were tested on this Mk.II Series IA (HR756).

(L9520), and production Mk.Vs were built by Rootes and Fairey. The B.Mk.V Series I (Special) and Series IA corresponded to the Mk.II variants. The majority of the Halifax Vs were supplied to the squadrons of No. 6 (R.C.A.F.) Group, No. 427 Squadron based at Middleton St. George being the first unit to re-equip with these (B.Mk.V Series I (Special) being delivered early in May 1943). In the Battle of the Ruhr, from March to July 1943, Halifax IIs of No. 4 Group made no less than 2,339 sorties for the loss of 138 machines.

In 1942, Handley Page's "hack" Halifax II (R9534) was fitted with 1,615 h.p. Bristol Hercules VI air-cooled radial engines, and the company designation H.P.61 and the official designation B.Mk.III were reserved for a possible production variant employing these engines. The extra power afforded by the Hercules power plants offered significant advantages to the Halifax, and the decision was taken to place the B.Mk.III variant in production. The first production Halifax III (HX227) made its first flight on August 29, 1943, and this and the next few production machines were used for development purposes at the A. and A.E.E. at Boscombe Down and elsewhere. The extra power afforded by the Hercules restored the Halifax's performance, and permitted a maximum all-up weight of 65,000 lb., although much of the additional weight was absorbed by the extra fuel required for the radials, total fuel capacity being boosted to 2,688 Imp.gal. Hercules VI or XVI engines driving de Havilland hydromatic airscrews were fitted, and during production the wing span was increased from 98 ft. 10 in. to 104 ft. 2 in., the increase in wing area improving the operational ceiling.

The service début of the Halifax III in February 1944 reinstated the Handley Page bomber as a fully-operational type, for five months previously the Halifax IIs had been relegated to less hazardous targets owing to a steep rise in the losses sustained, mostly as a result of enemy fighters which found the Halifaxes easy prey as they laboured along at moderate altitudes. The Halifax III played a prominent part in the attacks on the V-1 missile sites during 1944, and returned to daylight operations after the Allied landings in France on D-Day, attacking French marshalling yards, gun emplacements, strong points and troop concentrations. In June 1944, Halifaxes of a single Group—No. 4—set a Bomber Command record by shooting down thirty-three enemy fighters while operating over Europe. The Halifax III displayed an ability to absorb considerable battle damage, for a little earlier, in March 1944, Pilot Officer C. J. Barton of No. 578 Squadron had become the only Halifax captain to be awarded the Victoria Cross (posthumously) for his great gallantry in bringing home a crippled aircraft after a raid on Nuremberg, and there were many examples of Halifax IIIs sustaining apparently fatal punishment and yet returning to base, such as the machine which, in July 1944, returned to base with the port side of its tail assembly completely shot away by flak! In August 1944, by which time the Luftwaffe in France was putting up only token resistance, No. 4 Group's Halifaxes flew 3,629 sorties, and there were twenty-six Halifax squadrons in the line.

Closely related to the Halifax III, the B.Mk.VI was really the final bomber variant, employing Hercules 100 engines, rated at 1,630 b.h.p. at 20,000 ft. and 1,800 b.h.p. at 10,000 ft., but as airframe production outpaced the supply of the more powerful radials, some machines were completed with Hercules XVI engines as the B.Mk.VII. The Halifax VI attained a gross weight of 68,000 lb., and its prototype (NP715) was first flown on October 10, 1944. With a view to its eventual use in the Pacific theatre, it was fitted with special sand filters over the carburettor intakes, and a pressurized fuel system. The B.Mk.VI was the fastest version of the Halifax to attain operational service. Its maximum speed was 290 m.p.h. at 10,500 ft., and 312 m.p.h. at 22,000 ft. The most economical speed was 195 m.p.h. at 10,000 ft., at which range was 2,350 mls. with 2,190 Imp.gal. and 3,220 mls. with 2,880 Imp.gal. Service ceiling at 56,200 lb. was 24,000 ft., and at 68,000 lb. was 20,000 ft. Maximum bomb load was 14,500 lb., comprising two 2,000-lb. and six 1,000-lb. bombs in the fuselage, and six 750-lb. incendiary clusters in wing bays. The B.Mk.VI supplemented the B.Mk.III in service, but was too late to see widespread use. Both marks III and VI were employed by squadrons operating with No. 100 Group on radar countermeasures, and B.Mk.VIs were operated by Nos. 346 and 347 Squadrons of the

The introduction of Hercules engines in the Halifax III offered significant advantages, and the first production example of this variant, HX227 first flown on August 29, 1943, is illustrated above. The prototype Halifax III was R9534 (right).

Free French Air Force in No. 4 Group. The B.VII was used principally by Nos. 408, 420, 425 and 426 Squadrons R.C.A.F. in No. 6 Group.

By the end of the war in Europe, the Halifax II and V had passed out of service, but a lone Halifax III of No. 462 Squadron, R.A.A.F., shared with the Mosquito the distinction of being the last Bomber Command aircraft to operate against Germany—on May 2, 1945. No. 462 Squadron was one of several attached to No. 100 Group for radar jamming duties, but on this particular sortie (against Flensburg) bombs were carried. During the war, the Halifax had served with the following squadrons of R.A.F. Bomber Command: Nos. 10, 35, 51, 76, 77, 78, 102, 103, 158, 171, 190, 192, 199, 346, 347, 405, 408, 415, 419, 420, 424, 425, 426, 427, 428, 429, 431, 432, 433, 460, 462, 466, 578 and 640. The Halifax was also used on bombing operations in the Middle East, from 1942 onwards, and was the only British four-engined bomber operational in that theatre, being first used by No. 462 Squadron which was later joined by Nos. 148, 178, 227 and 614 Squadrons. Two flights of Halifax bombers, Nos. 1341 and 1577, were also operational in the Far East, and after the termination of the war in Europe several squadrons flew their Halifax VIs out to this theatre. These were modified to carry three 230 Imp.gal. long-range tanks in their bomb-bays, and carried special radar-detection equipment to pinpoint Japanese radar stations.

Apart from its primary role as a heavy bomber, the Halifax performed many other important tasks for which its commodious fuselage made it suitable. One of the least publicised of these was the task of dropping special agents and supplies by parachute into enemy territory, this job being undertaken by Nos. 138 and 161 (Special Duties) Squadrons. Nine squadrons of R.A.F. Coastal Command flew with the Halifax during the war, including five units— Nos. 517, 518, 519, 520, and 521—specialising in meteorological reconnaissance duties, and four— Nos. 58, 502, 546, and 547—flying anti-submarine and shipping patrols. Special equipment was carried by the Halifax for its maritime roles, the aircraft being converted from standard bombers by Cunliffe-Owen Aircraft at Eastleigh. After these modifications had been incorporated, the Halifaxes were re-designated G.R.Mk.II, G.R.Mk.V, and G.R.Mk.VI, the last-mentioned not attaining service status before the end of the war. One Halifax G.R.II, JD212, was flown experimentally with rocket projectiles mounted under the centre section, but this armament was not adopted operationally. The Halifax G.R.II first entered service towards the end of 1942.

Other specially modified versions of the Halifax served from 1942 onwards with the Airborne Forces, as paratroop- and supply-droppers, and for glider-towing. A Halifax II towed a General Aircraft Hamilcar glider into the air for the first time in February 1942, and Halifaxes first towed Airspeed Horsa gliders operationally on November 19, 1942, in an attack on the German heavy-water plant in South Norway. Variants of the Halifax separately designated for the Airborne Forces were the A.Mk.III, A.Mk.V, and A.Mk.VII, and these served extensively in the invasion of Sicily, the airborne operations over Normandy, during the ill-fated Arnhem operation, and in the final crossing of the Rhine. Developed from the Halifax A.Mk.VII to incorporate the operational experience gained during 1944-45, the H.P.71 Halifax A.Mk.IX did not reach the R.A.F. until after the war, and the A.Mk.X, which was similar to the A.Mk.IX but with Hercules 100s replacing the Hercules XVIs, was not built.

Another version of the Halifax was produced in 1944 to serve with R.A.F. Transport Command, carrying personnel, freight and casualty stretchers in the fuselage. Standard bombers were converted to operate in this role, with dorsal turrets and H2S scanner removed, and these were redesignated C.Mk.III, C.Mk.VI and C.Mk.VII. These aircraft could carry twenty-four troops, and were extensively employed during the closing days of the war and immediately afterwards to fly home released prisoners-of-war. One transport Halifax (LV838) was modified from a Mk.III to Mk.VI standard and was fitted with a pannier capable of carrying 8,000

Shortages of British Messier undercarriages resulted in the Halifax V which differed from the Mk.II solely in having a Dowty levered suspension undercarriage. A Halifax B.V Series IA (LK665) is illustrated above, and an early Mk.V (DG235) is illustrated on the left.

The final bomber variant of the Halifax was the B.VI with Hercules 100 engines illustrated above.

lb. of freight. This installation was not adopted as standard until the Halifax C.Mk.VIII came into production in 1945. This, the H.P.70, was the first transport version of the Halifax to be designed as such from the outset, and apart from the pannier, it featured fairings which replaced the nose and tail turrets. The first production C.Mk.VIII (PP225) flew in June 1945.

R.A.F. Transport Command squadrons which flew the various freighter and personnel transport versions of the Halifax up to the end of the war included Nos. 190, 295, 296, 297, 298, 620 and 644 Squadrons. No. 298 Squadron, with Halifax A.Mk.VIIs, went to South-East Asia Command in the spring of 1945, and remained there until after the end of the war against Japan.

The grand total of Halifaxes built, including those completed after the war, was 6,176 machines. Of these, the parent company built 1,590, English Electric built 2,145, the London Aircraft Production Group built 710, Fairey Aviation built 661, and Rootes built 1,070. No records are available to show a complete breakdown of production, but it is known that Handley Page built eighty-four Mk.Is, in addition to the two prototypes, and the five Halifax manufacturers built 1,966 Mk.IIs. Just over 2,000 Mk.IIIs were built—about half by English Electric—and production of the Mk.V totalled 916 from Rootes' and Fairey's factories. Most of the 480 Mk.VIs constructed were built by English Electric, whose production terminated with this variant, and the Mk. VIIs included 161 bombers

and 45 A.Mk.VIIs from Handley Page; 120 from Rootes and sixty-nine from Fairey. The balance of the total included about one hundred C.Mk.VIIIs and Mk.IXs, the last of which (RT938) was delivered from Cricklewood on November 20, 1946.

During the war years, the Halifax flew no less than 75,532 bombing sorties during which 227,610 tons of bombs were dropped. It had its vicissitudes, but by persistent improvement and judicious innovation, incorporated without disrupting the production lines, it maintained its position as one of the two principal British "heavies", and proved itself a worthy successor to that first heavy bomber of the R.A.F., the Handley Page O/400—the "Bloody Paralyser" of the First World War.

Handley Page Halifax B.Mk.III

Dimensions:	Span, 194 ft. 2 in.; length, 70 ft 1 in; height, 20 ft. 9 in.; wing area, 1,275 sq. ft.
Power Plants:	Four Bristol Hercules XVI fourteen-cylinder two-row sleeve-valve air-cooled radial engines rated at 1,615 h.p. at 2,900 r.p.m. for take-off, 1,675 h.p. (for five min.) at 4,500 ft., and 1,455 h.p. at 12,000 ft.
Armament:	One flexible 0.303-in. Browning machine gun with 300 rounds in the nose, four 0.303-in. Browning guns with 1,160 r.p.g. in Boulton Paul dorsal turret, and four 0.303-in. Browning guns with 1,700 r.p.g. in Boulton Paul tail turret. Maximum bomb load, 13,000 lb. Alternative fuselage bomb loads, six 1,000-lb. plus two 2,000-lb., one 8,000-lb., two 4,000-lb., four 2,000-lb., eight 1,000-lb., or nine 500-lb. bombs, plus six 500-lb. bombs in wing bays.
Weights:	Tare, 38,240 lb.; normal loaded, 54,400 lb.; maximum overload, 65,000 lb. Maximum fuel capacity, 2,688 Imp.gal.
Performance:	(At normal loaded weight) Maximum speed, 278 m.p.h. at 6,000 ft., 282 m.p.h. at 13,500 ft.; maximum weak mixture cruising speed, 228 m.p.h. at 20,000 ft.; economical cruising speed, 215 m.p.h. at 20,000 ft.; range (with 1,150 Imp.gal. and 13,000-lb. bomb load), 1,030 mls., (with 1,968 Imp.gal. and 7,000-lb. bomb load), 1,985 mls.; service ceiling (normal loaded), 24,000 ft., (maximum loaded), 20,000 ft.; initial climb rate, 960 ft./min.; time to 20,000 ft., 37.5 min., (maximum weight), 50 min.